I0818392

Edition Angewandte
Book Series of the
University of Applied Arts Vienna
Edited by Gerald Bast, Rector

edition: 'ʌngewʌndtə

Nikolaus Gansterer, Emma Cocker, Mariella Greil

CHOREO-GRAPHIC FIGURES

Deviations from the Line

DE GRUYTER

TABLE OF CONTENTS

PROLOGUE
CUTTING ACROSS, PASSING THROUGH

With artistic research at its heart, *Choreo-graphic Figures: Deviations from the Line* stages a *beyond-disciplinary*, inter-subjective encounter between the lines of choreography, drawing and writing, for exploring those forms of artistic knowledge produced in the slippage and deviation as different modes of practice enter into dialogue, overlap, collide. Conceived as a studio-laboratory in itself, this publication draws together experimental practices and critical reflections from *Choreo-graphic Figures: Deviations from the Line* (2014-2017), a three-year long artistic research project involving key researchers writer-artist Emma Cocker, artist-performer Nikolaus Gansterer and dancer-choreographer Mariella Greil, working with project 'sputniks'[1] Alex Arteaga, Christine De Smedt and Lilia Mestre, alongside guest collaborators Werner Moebius and Jörg Piringer, artist and designer Simona Koch and photographer and videographer Victor Jaschke, with further invited contributions from Arno Böhler, Catherine de Zegher, Gerhard Dirmoser (with Christopher Dell), Karin Harrasser, Adrian Heathfield, Krassimira Kruschkova, Brandon LaBelle, Erin Manning, Dieter Mersch, Werner Moebius, Alva Noë, Jeanette Pacher, Helmut Ploebst, P.A. Skantze and Andreas Spiegl (⟶ *Biographies*).

How can we attend to the process of artistic 'sense-making' from within or inside, that affective realm of energies, emergences and intensities operating before, between, and below the more readable gestures of artistic practice? How can we develop systems of notation and performativity for sharing this often hidden or undisclosed aspect of the creative process, for communicating the experience with others? How can we articulate the instability and mutability of the flows and forces — especially within collaborative exploration — without 'fixing' that which is inherently dynamic and contingent as a literal sign? Indeed, how might this focus on the micro-movements of aesthetic enquiry have wider implications at the level of the macro, encouraging the de-, re- and trans-figuring of our ways of being in the world, inviting new forms of relationality, sociality and solidarity?

Beyond functioning as an archival representation of the *Choreo-graphic Figures: Deviations from the Line* project, we intend that this book might also invoke action, operating as a modular toolkit of performative and notational approaches for future experimental play. Indeed, we present our epilogue not as an ending but rather with the aim of opening, offered in the form of a 'score' to play (⟶ *How to Play the Score*). But first … *how do we start? How do we prepare?* These questions were amongst the first within *Choreo-graphic Figures: Deviations from the Line* (⟶ *How-ness*), and return again in our prologue.[2] *Pro-logue* (*pro* — 'before', *logos* — 'discourse'), a speech-act *before* speaking, preliminary preparation for what follows. Our prologue serves as an orientation device: we conceive the book as a *choreo-graphic* assemblage in and of itself, interweaving the textual and the visual, the sayable and the shown. Our enquiry is polyfocal: its unfolding narrative not only linear but also diagrammatic, associative, rhizomatic, entangled. Hybrid of an artists' book and research compendium, our publication can be read in different directions, there is more than one 'way in'. To draw on the writing of Hélène Cixous, the book "does not have a front door. It is written from all over at once, you enter it through a hundred windows. It enters you."[3]

The aim of this prologue is not to provide an overview or plan of the book — as if viewed from above — but to indicate different routes through. Consider Michel de Certeau's distinction between map and itinerary: "What the map cuts up, the story cuts across. In Greek, narration is called *diegesis*: it establishes an itinerary (it 'guides') and it passes through (it 'transgresses'). The space of operations it travels in is made of movements."[5] We imagine the reader's movements — *cutting across, passing through* — as a *dérive* or deviation between the lines. Whilst we adopt specific project terminology, we elect against a glossary from the outset, but rather seek to dis-close — open up, unpack — our terms *en route*. However, first, some practical notes on navigation and the various 'voices' that are encountered within this book. We use different systems and symbols for making connections between the interrelated facets of our enquiry — indicating the entanglement of our practices and concepts — creating connective tissue between our thinking and that of invited contributors.

Choreo-graphic: the hyphen, a deviating line, holding two terms in proximity whilst also keeping them apart. *Choreo* — more than one or in relation to another, as in chorus, as in group, always a communication between. *Graphic* — the possibilities and sensitivities of inscription (of moving, drawing and writing and the modalities in between), not just for describing — representing or reproducing that which already exists — but as much a dynamic happening, capable also of bringing about, constituting, transforming.[4]

First, we use this sign (⟶) to indicate a leap or link that could be made to another point in the publication. You — the reader — are invited to use the *Map of Contents* (the removable cover wrapped around the book) to navigate using these links. Related to (⟶), you could begin in reverse, taking a nomadic route of 'leaps and bounds' based on specific keywords (⟶ *Index, cover*) involving — to draw on Rosi Braidotti's writing — the 'transposition' of "an in-between space of zigzagging and of crossing, non-linear but not chaotic, nomadic, yet accountable and committed; creative but also cognitively valid."[6] Second, pages edged in yellow indicate the contribution of an invited *wit(h)ness* (⟶ *Practices of Wit(h)nessing*) providing an 'external' perspective on the project beyond the voices of the three core researchers. Each 'edged' contribution has been informed through an experiential encounter with our research process: invited *wit(h)nesses* spent time with us during one or more of our *Method Labs* (⟶ *Method Labs*, ⟶ *Biographies*). Third, pink pages are 'practices' (⟶ *Practices of Attention, Notation, Conversation, Wit(h)nessing*, ⟶ *How to Play the Score*) developed, tested and written through intensive collaboration with our sputniks and guest collaborators. We designed these pages to be practised; they contain practical exercises — even micro-scores — for activating exploration. We extend this colour coding system with blue accents to designate our nine different *figures* (⟶ *Figures*), the content of which we elaborate later in the prologue, and three blocks of brown pages highlighting the dynamics of ⟶ *How-ness*, ⟶ *When-ness*, ⟶ *Where-ness* within our enquiry.

Our project's journey has involved a transformative arc or a tripartite 'rite of passage' — movement from the realm of demarcated disciplinary gestures of choreography, drawing and writing — through a phase of *inter*disciplinary exchange operating 'between the lines' of our different practices, towards the *undisciplinary*. This arc is encountered through materials generated directly from the artistic research process itself including singular photographic images, drawings, textual fragments, alongside critical reflections — the *choreographic-diagrammatic-essayistic* interplay of embodied, drawn and written — that strive to distil, condense, expose or expand our understanding of the enquiry (⟶ *Method Lab: A Relational Milieu*, ⟶ *Method Lab: Porous Boundaries*, ⟶ *Figures*, ⟶ *Diagrams* ⟶ *Becoming Undisciplinary*, ⟶ *Figuring><Figure*, ⟶ *Embodied Diagrammatics*, ⟶ *How-ness*, ⟶ *When-ness*, ⟶ *Where-ness*).

The book's overall content and curatorial 'arc' are co-authored by Emma Cocker, Nikolaus Gansterer and Mariella Greil working closely with artist and designer Simona Koch to develop the format of the book itself. Content has emerged in and through a collaborative process — including dialogic encounters with our sputniks and guests (⟶ *Acknowledgements*) — where, as Félix Guattari argues (following Gregory Bateson), "the 'ecology of ideas' cannot be contained within the domain of the psychology of the individual, but organizes itself into systems or 'minds', the boundaries of which no longer coincide with the participant individuals."[7] Nonetheless, we each took roles in crafting this book based on our specific artistic sensibilities, which have undoubtedly also been transformed through our *undisciplinary* 'rite of passage' (⟶ *Becoming Undisciplinary*). Drawing on a 'conversational archive' — of over 150 hours of recorded conversation, resulting in over 300,000 words of transcript — writer-artist Emma Cocker distilled and developed the textual vocabulary of our project towards a series of 'essays', 'preludes', 'interludes' and 'figure introductions', weaving our own words into dialogue with the wider critical context of our enquiry. Extending his practice of 'thinking-through-drawing' — the reciprocity of *drawing-thinking >< thinking-drawing* — artist-performer Nikolaus Gansterer accumulated a rich archive of drawings over the project's duration in close nexus to our conversations and live explorations, which were condensed and elaborated anew as the manifold drawings encountered throughout this publication, immanent structures of interconnectedness for *showing* the diagrammatic entanglement of our enquiry.[8] Dancer-choreographer Mariella Greil 'dived' into our archive of photographic-video materials, searching for new choreographic relations for re-animating the embodied, *per*-forming of our shared exploration; threading this through with fragments of 'thick description' — a dense, viscous language of reflective recollection for activating sensate memory, for the purpose of performance for the page.[9] This relational sensitivity carried through her 'affective labour' in liaison with our contributors.

Choreo-graphic Figures: Deviations from the Line is an artistic research enquiry practised as the means through which to address its own processual unfolding.[10] Drawing on Sarat Maharaj's notion of the 'double drift' within 'thinking through art practice', our enquiry involves an attempt to think through art as "an investigative vehicle or probe" alongside the 'passage through' of an "introspective experience during which art practice takes stock of its own processes and procedures."[11] In recent years, the burgeoning field of artistic research has developed pace with increased interest in and support for those epistemological aspects of artistic exploration and experimentation — including sensuous, affective knowledge; bodily knowledge; the value of trial and error and of 'feeling one's way'; intuition, 'not knowing' (⟶ *Becoming Undisciplinary*) — that have habitually been marginalised by a (Western) knowledge economy that tends to favour rational and discursive logic, where knowledge is transmitted, traded and 'banked' as product, rather than necessarily activated as a live, embodied process.[12]

For Maharaj, the "query that crops up" in relation to artistic knowledge production is: "'what sort of knowledge?' Hard on its heels 'What marks out its difference, its otherness?'"[13] Likewise, Dieter Mersch advocates the need to differentiate an artistic — or rather an aesthetic — mode of thought beyond a vocabulary of linguistic discursivity and scientific methodology, where the alterity of an aesthetic epistemology is made explicit.[14] He asks what "thought in other media" might mean, where "thought is understood as a practice, as acting *with* materials, *in* materials, or *through* materials … or *with* media, *in* media or *through* media."[15] In contextualising our enquiry, we consider Henk Borgdorff's criteria that, "Artistic research … is the articulation of the unreflective, non-conceptual content enclosed in aesthetic experiences, enacted in creative practices and embodied in artistic production."[16] He argues that, "artistic research seeks not so much to make explicit the knowledge that art is said to produce, but rather […] invites 'unfinished thinking'. Hence, it is not formal knowledge that is the subject matter of artistic research, but thinking in, through and with art."[17] Whilst 'artistic research' can be applied as a 'method' for exploring something *other-than*, we activate it in self-reflexive relation to itself, where the epistemic aim — to follow Mersch — is to "reflect the perceivable through perception, and the experiential through experience, to push these to their margins or peripheries where their aporia and caesura becomes visible."[18]

Choreo-graphic Figures: Deviations from the Line focuses on the *qualitative-processual, aesthetic-epistemological* and *ethico-empathetic* dynamics within artistic research and creation: those micro-processes of unfolding decision-making, thinking-in-action, dynamic movements of 'sense-making', the durational 'taking place' of something happening live. In doing so, we contribute embodied understanding of 'knowing-thinking-feeling' within the process of

Research: from the Old French *rechercher* — to search; or else, from *circare* — to wander (*hither or thither*) or traverse. Towards *enquiry-as-exploration*: less examination, more *curious adventure:* artistic-researcher as explorer, wanderer, *renunçiant.*[19] Not the conqueror of new frontiers, intent on territorialisation of the *as-yet-unknown*. Crossing of boundaries, not to stake a claim, but for unsettling what is *thought-to-be-known* and stable, "disruption of an habitual energy field — favouring the state of curiosity that arises."[20] Towards "curiosity that precedes question-making,"[21] a *questioning-as-querying*: to ask, to seek. To *quest*, to strive: research as an endeavouring, as *conation* — to set oneself in motion. *Ex-plore* — out-pouring, from *pluere*, 'to make flow'. To attempt, to try: *essayer, assayer.* Again and again: *re*-searching, repeating — done *in-and-through* the *doing*, always unfinished, never fully complete.

artistic exploration, a phrase used — specifically by Maharaj — for describing those modalities of *knowing* irreducible to dominant rational discourse or the logic of scientific methodology.[22] So too, we strive to practise artistic thinking in-and-through its doing, through the shared movement of thought that Erin Manning and Brian Massumi refer to as '*prehended* in potentia': 'thought in the act' or 'thinkings-in-the-act'.[23] We activate the *en acte* of 'thinking-in-action' practised in its "immanent *intensification*", which for Alain Badiou (following Nietzsche) "is not effectuated anywhere else than where it is given — thought is effective in situ, it is what … is intensified upon itself, or again, it is the movement of its own intensity."[24] Our enquiry explores how choreography, drawing and writing manifest this 'immanent *intensification*'; mind-body engaged in an embodied process of live thinking active in its *pre*- and *during-ness.*[25]

We contribute to the field of artistic research through the three-fold — interwoven, non-hierarchical — relation of our process, enquiry and its exposition.[26] First, our *Method Lab* proposes a unique methodology for activating research in-and-through practice, for focusing towards the affective, embodied, relational sensitivities and intensities within artistic collaboration. The *Method Labs* (⟶ *Method Lab: A Relational Milieu,* ⟶ *Method Lab: Porous Boundaries*) are laboratories for experiential knowledge production, a dedicated 'thinking space' which "is both a processual movement of thought and a privileged site at which this movement is amplified and inflected by novel configurations of ideas, things and bodies."[27] Whilst its general principles might be shared with other experimental 'laboratory style'[28] precedents, one distinctive feature of our Lab has been the evolution of various practices (⟶ *Practices of Attention, Notation, Conversation, Wit(h)nessing*) for activating the 'three ecologies'[29] of environment, (human) subjectivity and (social) relations (⟶ *Embodied Diagrammatics*). These specific practices are practised through 'live exploration' — an unfolding temporal structure for bringing-into-relation the various intensities and energetics of our heterogeneous modalities of re-searching, as well as the dynamics of ⟶ *How-ness,* ⟶ *When-ness* and ⟶ *Where-ness* within a shared time-space. At times, we have referred to our live explorations as performative, even as performing.[30] In her contribution, Krassimira Kruschkova asks, "What if the constellation of words 'artistic research' today were on everyone's lips? But in which tongue, *lingua*, language?" (⟶ *What if…*). It could be argued that 'performing' together has become the *lingua franca* of our *undisciplinary* collaborative exchange, a bridging or vehicular language for facilitating a dialogue between our disciplinary dialects.[31] This seemingly pragmatic approach to performing — adopted as interstitial modality for operating 'between the lines' of choreography, drawing and writing — could be critiqued as failing to acknowledge the specificity of performance as a practice in and of itself. However, our enquiry was not about the practice of performance *as such,* but rather the epistemic potentialities and vitalities of *per-forming.*[32] *Per* — the preposition indicating *through,* a forward-through movement; artistic research practised through its forming, deforming.[33] Here, as Mersch states, artistic thought "reveals itself in the form of those practices that 'work in the work', the 'becoming' of the processes themselves."[34] Likewise, our *per-forming* emphasises the process of exploration — its liveness, aliveness — as well as performance as epistemic artefact, rather than performance-as-product according to the exchange values of market and commodity.

Within each ***Method Lab***, we come together geographically in one place — in a studio-rehearsal space usually for a period of one to four weeks — to engage in collaborative exploration alongside our sputniks and guest collaborators.[35] The photographic documents in our first 'essay' (⟶ *Becoming Undisciplinary*) provide some visual identification for each of us — the key researchers, sputniks and guest collaborators — such that the reader can recognise us as they follow our journey.

Whilst each sputnik has impacted on the general trajectory of our research, they have also sharpened our enquiry — its methodology, its performativity — through the prism of their respective interests. Alex Arteaga's research on the 'roots' of aesthetics — approached from an *enactivist* perspective — helped shape our understanding and articulation of the relation between our concepts *figuring* and *figure* (⟶ *Figuring >< Figure*), alongside the development of those practices (⟶ *Practices of Attention,* ⟶ *Practices of Notation*) required for becoming more attuned to this nuanced perceptual field of awareness (⟶ *Researching Aesthetically the Roots of Aesthetics*). Lilia Mestre intervened through her research — developed within the frame of a.pass (advanced performance and scenography studies) — around the 'relation between writing and performance', the 'conditions for the emergence of poetics' and the use of 'score' as a 'collective apparatus' through which to "organize dialogical or inter-subjective formats for exchange in artistic practice and research"[36] (⟶ *Score It!*). Christine De Smedt's carefully, inquisitive interrogation of our terminology — drawing perhaps on her background in criminology as well as dance and performance — prompted the *Practice Preludes* for clarifying our use of certain words and phrases, whilst her experience in movement research techniques enabled us to collectively pressure and refine our practices in action (⟶ *Practices of Attention*). Her interest in 'questions' — what she describes as her desire to "wrestle with things, but preferably in the form of a physical and mental game"[37] — was instrumental in bringing this reflective aspect of our enquiry directly, playfully, into the process of our live exploration (⟶ *Questions,* ⟶ *Practices of Attention: Transquesting*).

Throughout our research journey, we were accompanied by guest collaborator Werner Moebius whose research interests within the fields of Sonic Art and Audio Culture brought heightened awareness to the activity of listening, "a radical dedication to the present (*dem Vorfindlichen*), to receptivity, auditory sensibility and the unearthing of (*acousmatic*) correlations" (⟶ *Practices of Wit(h)nessing: Listening,* ⟶ *Aspects of Undisciplinary Listening*). Guest collaborator Jörg Piringer brought techniques and technologies from his practice in sound/visual poetry, where — beyond signification — hybrid languages emerge between human and machine, through the 'collaboration' of embodied voice and electronic software manipulated text fragments (⟶ *Print Out,* ⟶ *Figure of Ventilating Meaning*). Photographer and videographer Victor Jaschke was a further travelling companion during our Labs, whose sensitive *wit(h)nessing* through the lens was performed less in terms of documentary 'capture', but rather in the key of our central question: how can we attend to the barely perceptible micro-movements within artistic exploration?[38] Artist and designer Simona Koch gently guided the transformation of our embodied, experiential enquiry into a page-based exploration. Drawing on deep knowledge gleaned from having *wit(h)nessed* so much of our journey, her design *presents* rather than *represents*, gives spaciousness to density, providing an enabling organisation for that which, at times, has seemed unruly.

The *Method Lab* facilitates different intensities and durations of collaboration: longitudinal collaboration between key researchers developed slowly over the project duration, alongside a more overtly discontinuous collaborative encounter with our critical sputniks and guests for provoking, questioning and deepening our understanding of the research process.

The *Method Lab* also provides a contextual milieu for our enquiry: various specialists were invited to spend time with us in the Lab as critical *wit(h)nesses* (⟶ *Practices of Wit(h)nessing*). Rather than only citing the theoretical work of others (for example, Erin Manning, Dieter Mersch, Alva Noë), we wanted to engage them in our research process through a live encounter. We additionally staged conversations with those critical interlocutors whose *thinking-making* has informed our enquiry, but who were unable to be *wit(h)nesses* in the Lab itself (⟶ *Trialogue: On Sedimentations of Sensitivities,* ⟶ *Trialogue: Thinking-Making in Relation*).[39] Our invited *wit(h)nesses* bring diverse perspectives: from philosophy; artistic research; art history; critical theory; curating; theatre, dance and performance theory; sound culture; systems analysis, and from the intersection of media theories, subject theories and theories of space. Though from different (inter)disciplinary backgrounds, our wit(h)nesses are still each concerned with the specific potentiality of artistic or even aesthetic exploration: this is the focus of our enquiry. In their contribution to this book, some *wit(h)nesses* reflect on what is at stake in the call to 'respond'. For P.A. Skantze, the practice of being a spectator involves a "methodology of care" practised alongside "critical immanent attention", the inventive, improvisatory weaving of a delicate rope — a bridge — to cross the "chasm of distance" between the experience of encounter and its remembering, retelling, re-counting (⟶ *Take Me to the Bridge*). "How do I remember? What do I remember? What can I say about this — in words?" asks Jeanette Pacher, the "challenge of writing about something that's hard to put in words" provoking her towards experimentation, for reflecting on the "circumstances and conditions that propel setting free creative processes" — *emptying out; preferring not; open-ended time; a carefree, untroubled mind* (⟶ *Delightful Drifting*). This question of how to articulate, communicate — even translate — one experience into another is a central preoccupation of the project (⟶ *Practices of Wit(h)nessing: Translation*, ⟶ *Figure of Translational Flux*).

Drawing on our research in-and-through practice, three 'essays' (⟶ *Becoming Undisciplinary*, ⟶ *Figuring><Figure*, ⟶ *EmbodiedDiagrammatics*) — forming a conceptual spine of interconnected parts — articulate not only the journey from the disciplinary to *undisciplinary*, but also the core thinking — and theoretical orientation — of our enquiry. *Interluding* these 'essays', we elaborate the qualitative-processual dynamics (⟶ *How-ness*), temporal — even temporalising — dynamics (⟶ *When-ness*) and environmental-spatial-relational dynamics (⟶ *Where-ness*) of our research process. The first 'essay' (⟶ *Becoming Undisciplinary*) asks what is at stake in the deviation from the (disciplinary) line, addressing the implications — both epistemological and ethical — therein.

In proximity to our first 'essay', Krassimira Kruschkova reflects on the 'interminability' — even tactical nature — of the artistic research 'project', where "as soon as it normatively empowers itself, it weakens in order to strengthen"; artistic research practised as "*desœuvrement* — in the sense of a doing nothing, but also of de-working", the "digression from *doxa*, turning towards the *paradox*, always in uncertainty relations" (⟶ *What If …*). For Andreas Spiegl, the *line* neither connects nor does it demarcate difference, rather its directionality is non-linear, non-teleological — it does not serve as "path or track leading from one argument or word to the next", nor does it move towards culmination of a work as such (⟶ *Unlined*). Our 'line of enquiry' strives less towards accumulation of knowledge, but rather to *unline*, unfolding — to follow Luce Irigaray — an "'other meaning' which is constantly in the process of weaving itself, at the same time ceaselessly embracing words and yet casting them off to avoid being fixed, immobilized."[40] We seek to *un-draw* the structural lines of our respective practices in search of a subjunctive, anti-structural realm 'trembling' within unexpected — perhaps *unruly* — potentiality. For Brandon LaBelle, the deviating line is conceived as a cut, a wound, a gap or break; a porous line scored between folding / unfolding; inside / outside; with / without. A deviant line of monstrous hybridity: liminal line of hyphenation, of a "monster-logic; a thing-body." He asks, "Can we inhabit the cut as a space?" (⟶ *The Thing*). Indeed, can we inhabit the hyphen, the deviation of the line itself?

Dieter Mersch elaborates on "the dialectics of figuration and defiguration, as they belong together in one single act" (⟶ *Figuration / Defiguration*). Against the rhetorical model of a 'movement figure' (*schēma*) that immobilises the 'ephemeral' of processuality, Mersch advocates an 'aesthetics of movement' predicated on mobility, transitoriness, continuous transition or transformation. His model of aesthetic experimentation privileges singularity, 'alterity in iteration', the 'primacy of passibility'; it finds its way through witty leaps, is formless in its plasticity, inconclusive in its *essaying*. Alex Arteaga conceives our enquiry on *Figuring* >< *Figure* as 'aesthetic research', where aesthetics is understood as a "variety of cognition". He formulates — then expands — his conceptualisation that, "aesthetic cognition — the roots of aesthetics — is the spontaneous, sensorimotor, emotional and operatively present realisation of a viable coherence." For Arteaga, a *figure* is "an incipient formation in and of this viable coherence", "a meshwork of qualities operatively present as a whole, that emerges out of a dynamic disposition of actions performed in interaction with phenomena." A *figure*, he asserts, "is an emergent entity whose appearance cannot be completely under our control [...] It is not contoured, it is not graspable." Here then, aesthetic enquiry necessitates passivity — "understood as the minimisation of will and target-oriented action" — where the "increase of our receptivity towards the agency of others — equally autonomous or heteronomous units ... is therefore the key for entering aesthetic conduct" (⟶ *Researching Aesthetically the Roots of Aesthetics*). The act of "tuning experience to the *more-than*", of cultivating deep awareness of our own enmeshing with "the environment and its complex materialities" returns in the trialogue between Catherine de Zegher, Nikolaus Gansterer and Erin Manning, through the prism of the 'minor gesture', which for Manning, "has a capacity to make felt a shift, a variation in experience that deeply alters the ecology of that experience"[41] (⟶ *Trialogue: Thinking-Making in Relation).* Reflecting on the re-connective *gesture of reaching out to the other* (⟶ *Empathetic Figures),* the trialogue foregrounds the *micro-political* dimension of the 'minor', in turn, anticipating the 'line of flight' of our final 'essay' (⟶ *Embodied Diagrammatics*). In proximity, Werner Moebius diagrams various currents of receptivity and awareness, reflecting upon the vital act of listening, "*through* or *with* de-lays, re-sonances and re-verberations both as signal processes but also in the felt sense" (⟶ *Aspects of Undisciplinary Listening*).

Our second '*essay*' (⟶ *Figuring* >< *Figure*) reflects on the relation of two core, interrelated concepts within our enquiry — the experience of *figuring* and the emergence of *figures*. We use the term *figuring* for referring to those small yet transformative energies and experiential shifts within the artistic process that are often hard to discern, but which ultimately shape or steer the evolving action, whilst *figure* describes the point at which awareness of 'something happening' (*figuring*) becomes recognisable, communicable.

Reflecting the *ethico-empathetic* aspect of our enquiry, for Arno Böhler, *figural figures* — and the realm of sensation to which they give rise — "are not private phenomena. They are forms of *transport* into the world's world-wide-ness." He elaborates how, "feeling 'oneself' means perceiving oneself as a body *touched* by others, *exposed* to others *in the middle of the world*." For Böhler, the striving, 'driving force' — even *conatus* — of 'choreo-graphic figures' can be thought of in Deleuzian-Spinozist 'ethical-aesthetical' terms, capable of producing an immanent vector of joy — even freedom — experienced as the *beatitude* of 'bodies-in-agreement'[42] (→ *Sensorial Bodies*). These ethical-aesthetic sensitivities are explored further in the trialogue between Emma Cocker, Mariella Greil and Adrian Heathfield, which shifts attention from the "micro-dynamics of emergence" towards the "macro-political significance of these affinities" in order to, as Heathfield states, "take us out of the framework of general event-hood and into a framework that is more about sustained life practices of experimentation." Here, the empathetic register of subject-to-subject relations opens towards the transformative: an emergent ecology of 'radical coexistence' beyond the anthropocentric, a space of immanence where subjects and objects co-relate in mutual becoming (→ *Trialogue: On Sedimentations of Sensitivities*).

Our own aesthetic enquiry (→ *Figuring >< Figure*) has involved developing practices for attending to and marking the event of *figuring* (→ *Practices of Attention*, → *Practices of Notation: Clicking*); the identification, qualification and naming of various *figures* (→ *Practices of Notation: Affirming*, → *Naming*); alongside distillation of the qualitative properties of *key figures* so we can 'call' for their constitutive conditions (→ *Figures*, → *Practices of Notation: Calling*). We elaborate the qualities of nine *figures* grouped according to three categories: → *Elemental Figures* refer to key moments within the arc of creative exploration, addressing the opening up and exposition of *process* (→ *Clearing and Emptying Out*, → *Spiralling Momentum*, → *Temporary Closing*); → *Empathetic Figures* invite the diagramming of relations, drawing attention to the sensitivities and sensibilities of *being-with* (→ *Vibrating Affinity*, → *Wavering Convergence*, → *Consonance / Dissonance*); → *Transformative Figures* involve an explicit shift or transformation in property, quality or state of being, collapsing the lines of distinction between activity / passivity, animate / inanimate, subject / object, self / world (→ *Ventilating Meaning*, → *Becoming Material*, → *Translational Flux*).

One challenge for our project is how we might articulate the instability and mutability of our *figures* without 'fixing' that which is inherently dynamic and contingent as a literal sign. Indeed, the dilemma of how to document the embodied, experiential dimension of enquiry is a perennial problem for artistic research and live performance alike. "What are the best ways to report non-conceptual artistic findings? And what is the relationship between the artistic and the discursive, between what is presented and displayed and what is described?" asks Borgdorff.[43] He adds, "Is it possible to achieve a linguistic-conceptual articulation of the embedded, enacted and embodied content of artistic research?"[44] Peggy Phelan's oft-cited cautionary against the attempt to capture the experiential, ephemeral nature of performance, suggests documentation to be an impossible project: "Performance's only life is in the present. Performance cannot be saved, recorded, documented, or otherwise participate in the circulation of representations *of* representations: once it does so, it becomes something other than performance."[45] Whilst we consider the live *per-forming* of our *figures* as the critical site of activation and vitality, our attempt still has been for a page-based presentation *beyond* representation.

Accented in blue, our *figure* pages (→ *Figures*) present an assemblage of photographic documents drawn from our live per-forming, re-activated through their proximity to Gansterer's 'diagrammatic drawing' — hyphenated abstract-figuration, qualitative, evocative — alongside different modalities of experimental writing: Greil's 'performative, thick description' embedded within the image field for articulating an embodied singularity juxtaposes with Cocker's introduction to each *figure* comprising an 'inter-subjective poetics' of 'conversation as material', an 'immanent impersonal' or infra-personal mode of writing distilled from extensive conversation transcripts.[46] Our *figure* pages make productive the close relation between the German words *Aufzeichungen* (notes) and *Zeichnungen* (drawings), conceiving of the 'in-between-space' from draft to articulation as a site of potential for unexpected connections. Our examples are not definitive, rather singular iterations of a potentially infinite experiment, provocations for future exploration.

We conceive the articulation of our various *figures* within this book as '**choreo-graphic figures**': *choreo-* (more than one), *graphic-* (form of inscribing). *Choreo-graphic Figures* are performative, relational and contingent assemblages; recognisable or identifiable whilst motile and instable, capable of evolving. Within our live exploration, various *figures* arise—sometimes called, sometimes unbidden. Accordingly, we devise new modes of 'exposition', a delicate choreography between the ephemeral, experiential—even phenomenal—event of live exploration, documentation and writing: multimodal entanglement of bodily-kinesthetic, visual-spatial and verbal-linguistic sensibilities.

The relation of writing to artistic research is much disputed, often perceived as discursive explication, 'accounting' or even ventriloquism, all too keen to explain away that which is untranslatable, unsayable. Yet, as Mersch states, how might one rise to the "challenge of nevertheless finding words to say the unsayable."[47] He argues that rather than 'talking *about* art', might not writing practise the "more careful and gentle 'of' which merely dares to touch" (⟶ *Figuration/Defiguration*). Contiguous writing: touching upon. To write *of*, in-with-and-through practice: writing-as-practice. Not to shy away from language then, but to strive for the right kind of words. How to write from the embodied, experiential, evental space of practice, perhaps even, following Nietzsche—as Mersch reflects—how to write with one's blood? How to write from the viscera, the breath and body's borders? Or else, Hélène Cixous and Catherine Clémente ask, how "to steal into language to make it fly."[48] "Let me tell you" says Clarice Lispector, "I'm trying to seize the fourth dimension of this instant-now so fleeting that it's already gone because it's already become a new instant-now that's also already gone."[49] She follows, "And if here I must use words, they must bear an almost merely bodily meaning, I'm struggling with the last vibration … I make a sentence of words made only from instants-now. Read, therefore, my invention as pure vibration with no meaning beyond each whistling syllable."[50] For Irigaray, "In this world otherwise lived and illuminated, the language of communication is different, and necessarily poetic: a language that creates, that safeguards its sensible qualities so as to address the body and the soul, a language that lives."[51] Likewise, for Heathfield, "to think in this space is a kind of *being with* phenomena, a surrender to the world, it engenders sensuous thought, poetic writing follows by necessity, for it's only in this disrupted, altered language, that one can enter the folds of the sensate, the unthought thought, the articulacy of nonsense or of silence."[52]

This book provides a compendium of expanded, experimental writing / language practices of / as artistic research: performative, thick descriptions of an embodied process; the infra-personal immanence of 'conversation as material'; lists and scripts; diagrammatic notes, instructions and scores; collage and cut-up; a rope-bridge made of words; ekphrasis; visual language — mute, incommunicable; improvisatory writing — dense streams of consciousness; appropriation, remix; *choreo-graphic* essayism (always an open and incomplete attempt); word-play —activation of archaic etymologies and chance associations; key-word games; wild-talk and upwelling; reverberating voicings; ecstatic self-reporting; adverbial emphasis for describing 'how'; heightened attention to the anatomy of language — its prefixes and prepositions; poetic acts of *naming* practised by the 'babbling faithful'.[53] Here, as Manning asserts, "Swimming beyond the shallow end of language means composing-with language's prearticulations, its rhythms, its silences, its jumps in register […] The dissolving, vanishing, falling apart of words even as they are crafted, this is language in the making. It is what spurs us to read *between the words*."[54]

How might we reflect language's activity, affectivity, ambiguity, capacity, corporeality, curiosity, density, elasticity, ephemerality, fluidity, fragility, illegibility, instability, intensity, inter-subjectivity, hybridity, materiality, multiplicity, musicality, occasionality, opacity, performativity, physicality, plasticity, porosity, potentiality, receptivity, relationality, simultaneity, sensibility, sensitivity, sonority, synchronicity, tonality, temporality, visuality, vitality?

Within *Choreo-graphic Figures: Deviations from the Line*, our engagement with language, with writing, with words, attempts to go beyond a model of discursive logic or informational 'exchange'. Arguing how language has been 'subsumed and subjugated' by financial capitalism — reduced to dematerialised data flows of automated information — Franco 'Bifo' Berardi advocates poetry's resistant function, conceived as a "line of escape from the reduction of language to exchange."[55] He states, "Poetry is language's excess […] Poetry is the reopening of the indefinite, the ironic act of exceeding the established meaning of words […] Poetry is … the signifier disentangled from the limits of the signified."[56] Using computer-based conversational analysis software and receipt printer technology, Jörg Piringer pressures language towards a 'resistant poetics' of incomprehensible, stuttering fragments and repetitions, emptied of signification, evacuated of semantic sense (⟶ *Print Out*). Used as micro-scripts within our live explorations, machinic poetry is rendered sensuous, enigmatic, as human voice wrestles to enunciate that which is opaque, impenetrable, obfuscated. Indeed, Berardi's poetic "road to excess" — following William Blake — "leads to the palace of wisdom. And wisdom is the space of singularity, bodily signification, the creation of sensuous meaning."[57]

Our own systems of categorisation or taxonomy — for differentiating our various practices and *figures* — are not performed to order or control, but rather as a precondition for reconnection. Our 'pulling apart' — even anatomising — of an aesthetic process into nameable 'fields' is first a means of *dis*organisation rather than of organisation, for destabilising or disrupting that which is often practised as habitual. Once separated, we explore how we might bring about their reorganisation or recombination, which has involved the development of an experimental 'score system' for *bringing-into-relation*, 'scoring' as a re-connective practice. (—➤ *How to Play the Score*).

Drawing on the historical connection between writing and bureaucracy, Helmut Ploebst asserts the relation between bookkeeping and scientific taxation, "the sorting of matter, materials, and things, and the taxonomy of living beings." Against this classificatory order, he explores a *deviant association operation,* "that goes beyond the registration, calculation and balancing of the organisational", the systemic activation of αταξίες (*ataxíes* — disorders, irregularities) as *over-challenge* to the logic of taxonomy (τάξις — *taxis*) (—➤ *Deviations in the System of Cultural Bookkeeping*). For both Piringer and Ploebst, the language of economy and bureaucracy are deviated towards radical exceedance, the generation of unruly surplus and excess.

For Lilia Mestre, the score is a tool for 'imagining', where "oriented towards bringing together different elements, the practice of the score can be seen as a laboratory, a study environment, a place to provoke and observe events." She reflects on the relation between open and closed scoring systems, between control and contingency asking, "Is it possible to be in the paradox of improvisation and formalisation simultaneously?" (—➤ *Score It!*). A selection of Gansterer's diagrammatic drawings extend the notion of scoring as an imaginative prompt (—➤ *Diagrams*); reflecting our enquiry whilst simultaneously operating as open provocations for inviting future explorative play. Conceived in proximity, Karin Harrasser draws on the example of Jesuit musical sheets for addressing the tensions between written notation and experience, highlighting those rhythmic and embodied particularities that certain scores fail to account for, alongside the scope still therein for deviation (—➤ *The Riddle of the Score*). For Alva Noë, the fixed and *a priori* symbolism of certain kinds of representational *figures* and notational forms — an outline or pattern like a triangle or numerical sign — alongside the 'empty', 'hollow' or 'clichéd' phrasing of common 'figures of speech', can be differentiated from a more fragile, emergent *species* of *figure* that "makes its appearance", discernible as "a glimpse opened up by an action." He asks, how might we 'unlearn' those 'outlines' that are already known and recognisable, in order to plot new lines of flight (—➤ *Fragile Figures*).

This question of how to retain the fragility, vitality and ever-emergent quality of our *figures* is taken up as the starting point for our final 'essay' (—➤ *Embodied Diagrammatics*). We elaborate on how we have developed 'scores' as systems of (re)organisation foregrounding artistic compositional decision-making processes as a live event: live aesthetic exploration focused through the prism of various *Practices of Attention, Conversation, Notation and Wit(h)nessing* (⟶ *Practices*: especially *Notation: Calling*). Here, as Noë asserts, art emerges as a "strange tool" for engaging, "with the ways our practices, techniques, and technologies organize us, and it is finally, a way to understand our organization and inevitably, to reorganize ourselves."[58] In his diagrammatic 'remix' of text by Christopher Dell, Gerhard Dirmoser expands the performative vocabulary of our 'open scores' towards the diagramming or re-configuration of social space, conceived even as a "life score" (⟶ *Measures for Creating Space*). As Dell asserts, "A diagrammatic approach to the world initially means practising one's ability to register arrangements of people and things in their relationality, disassemble them into their structural components in order to deduce new connection points."[59] In these terms, artistic research is a mode of researching our relationality, our *being-in-the-world*. We ask: how might the embodied diagrammatics produced through our experimental scoring — the *bringing-into-relation* of different compositional fields of practice — have the capacity to both dis-organise and re-organise us at the level of the micro and macro. Moreover, as Sandra Noeth states, "The inbetween spaces and their call for social responsibility open up the body in the constitution of presence not only in regard to the past, but also towards the future."[60]

Likewise, we conceive this publication as hinged between past, present and future, not only an archival reflection on the artistic research project, *Choreo-graphic Figures: Deviations from the Line*, but also functioning as provocation for activating as-yet-unknown explorations, future experiments in artistic *knowing-thinking-feeling*. For Elizabeth Grosz, "Change is that which signals the openness of the future, its relative connection to but also its relative freedom from the past, the possibilities of paths of development, temporal trajectories uncontained by the present."[61] This book is not offered in conclusion to our enquiry then: not an *epilogue* (as ending) nor *interlude* (as interval or pause) — rather, we finish *unfinished*. Our enquiry has 'arrived' at an experimental 'toolkit' — even 'ecology' — of interwoven practices and processes, which we propose to now test further through future collaborative exploration. Accordingly, we close with an opening: an invitation to *per-form*. No longer in the key of *prelude* (from *prae-* 'before' + *ludere* 'to play'), we end with a *per-lude (per* — through, *forward through* + *ludere* 'to play') which takes the form of a *score* (⟶ *How to Play the Score*). Since our book's structure and content have emerged from the embodied, experiential process of artistic research in, with and through practice, we hope that it will be practised or performed as much as read.

1) Maria Lind coined the term 'sputnik' to describe a 'partner or travelling companion' with an interruptive, interlocutory function. Cf. Liam Gillick and Maria Lind (Eds.), *Curating with Light Luggage: A Symposium*, Frankfurt a. M.: Revolver, 2004.

2) Research findings have also been published as 'Choreographic Figures: Beginnings and Emergences', in *RUUKKU, Finnish Journal of Artistic Research, On Process*, 2015. [Accessed at www.researchcatalogue.net/view/132472/132473]; 'Notion of Notation >< Notation of Notion', in Scott de Lahunta, Kim Vincs and Sarah Whatley (Eds.), *Performance Research*, 'On An/Notations', Vol. 20, Issue 6, Winter, 2015, and 'Choreo-graphic Figures: Vitality Gestures and Embodied Diagrammatics', in Alexander Gerner and Irene Mittelberg (Eds.), *Body Diagrams*, Amsterdam: John Benjamins Publishing, 2017. We have presented at conferences/symposia including: *Operation on the Open Heart*, University of Applied Arts Vienna/Society for Artistic Research, Vienna, 2014; *Parenthesis: An Un/conference*, Swiss Artistic Research Network/HEAD, Geneva, 2014; *Tongues of Artistic Research*, Tanzquartier, Vienna, 2014; *Art as a Medium of Thinking: Artist-Philosophers — Philosophy as Arts-based Research*, AILab, Vienna, 2015; *PARSE Biennale Research Conference, Time*, University of Gothenberg, Sweden, 2015; *Plague of Diagrams*, ICA, London, 2015, *Please Specify!*, Society for Artistic Research/University of the Arts, Helsinki, 2017.

3) Hélène Cixous, *Stigmata: Escaping Texts*, London: Routledge, 2005, p. 120.

4) ⟶ Dieter Mersch, *Figuration/Defiguration* for further associations conjured by the hyphenated *choreo-graphic*.

5) Michel de Certeau, *The Practice of Everyday Life*, Berkeley, California: University of California Press, 1984, p. 129.

6) Rosi Braidotti, *Transpositions*, Cambridge: Polity Press, 2012, p. 5. Cf. ⟶ Dieter Mersch, *Figuration/Defiguration*, where he states, "the leap is always already at another place; its witty jumping — as a practice — always happens in between."

7) Félix Guattari, *The Three Ecologies*, London: Bloomsbury Academic, 2014, p. 36.

8) Cf. Nikolaus Gansterer (Ed.), *Drawing a Hypothesis: Figures of Thought*, Vienna and New York: Springer, 2011, for the correlations between thinking and drawing.

9) Clifford Geertz, 'Thick Description: Toward an Interpretive Theory of Culture', in *The Interpretation of Cultures: Selected Essays*, New York: Basic Books, 1973, p. 5.

10) We use the terms 'artistic research', research in-and-through practice, and at specific moments, 'aesthetic research' to describe our enquiry.

11) Sarat Maharaj, 'What the Thunder Said: Toward a Scouting Report on "Art as a Thinking Process"', in Mara Ambrožič and Angela Vettese (Eds.), *Art as a Thinking Process: Visual Forms of Knowledge Production*, Berlin: Sternberg Press, 2013, p. 154.

12) Cf. Paulo Friere, *Pedagogy of the Oppressed*, London and New York: Bloomsbury Academic, 2014. Cf. Emma Cocker, 'Embody Knowledge', in *The Yes of the No*, Sheffield: Site Gallery, 2016, p. 15.

13) Sarat Maharaj, 'Know-how and No-How: Stopgap Notes On "Method" In Visual Art As Knowledge Production', *Art + Research*, Vol. 2, No. 2, Spring 2009, p. 1., www.artandresearch.org.uk/v2n2/maharaj.html

14) Dieter Mersch, *Epistemologies of Aesthetics*, Zurich and Berlin: Diaphanes, 2015, pp. 8-9.

15) Mersch, 2015, pp. 9-10.

16) Henk Borgdorff, 'The Production of Knowledge in Artistic Research', in Michael Biggs and Henrik Karlsson (Eds.), *The Routledge Companion to Research in the Arts*, London: Routledge, 2011, p. 47.

17) Borgdorff, 2011, p. 44.

18) Mersch, 2015, p. 46.

19) Cf. Catherine Clément, *Syncope: The Philosophy of Rapture*, Minneapolis: University of Minnesota Press, 1994, where she reflects on the figure of the *renunçiant* who leaves the village (*known*) for the forest (*unknown*), p. 173.

20) Deborah Hay, *My Body the Buddhist*, Hannover, New Hampshire: Wesleyan University Press, 2000, p. 62.

21) Hay, 2000, p. 62.

22) In 'Xeno-epistemics: Makeshift Kit for Sounding Visual Art as Knowledge Production and the Retinal Regimes', in *Documenta 11, Platform 5 Catalogue*, Ostfildern-Ruit: Hatje Cantz, 2002, Maharaj relates the concept of 'know-think-feel' to what Varela calls "embodied and enactive" knowledge. Cf. Francisco J. Varela, *Ethical Know-How: Action, Wisdom and Cognition*, Stanford: Stanford University Press, 1999.

23) Erin Manning and Brian Massumi, *Thought in the Act: Passages in the Ecology of Experience*, Minneapolis: University of Minnesota Press, 2014, pp. 28-29.

24) Alain Badiou, *Handbook of Inaesthetics*, Stanford: Stanford University Press, 2005, pp. 58-59.

25) Cf. Heinrich von Kleist, 'On The Gradual Formation Of Thoughts In The Process Of Speech', in *Werke in einem Band*, Munich: Carl Hanser, 1996.

26) Cf. Michael Schwab and Henk Borgdorff (Eds.), *The Exposition of Artistic Research: Publishing Art in Academia*, Leiden: Leiden University Press, 2014.

27) Derek McCormack, 'Thinking Spaces for Research-Creation', in *Inflexions*, Vol. 1, No. 1. www.senselab.ca/inflexions/htm/node/McCormack2.html. Our research process resonates in aspects with the 'research creation' process developed at *SenseLab*.

28) Cf. Henk Slager, *The Pleasure of Research*, Ostfildern-Ruit: Hatje Cantz, 2015, on 'experimental laboratories', 'critical autonomous spaces' and 'temporary autonomous research' (TAR) zones.

29) Cf. Guattari, 2015, on these 'three ecologies' (⟶ *Embodied Diagrammatics*).

30) Beyond the 'performative utterances' of J. L. Austin's *How to Do Things with Words* (1962), we draw on a model of performativity which emphasises co-emergence or co-creation, e.g. Cf. Erika Fischer-Lichte, *The Transformative Power of Performance: a New Aesthetics*, New York: Routledge, 2008.

31) Whilst our 'per-forming' in a 'minor' key *disrupts* the stratification of our respective disciplinary dialects, we acknowledge how the 'pragmatic' use of English as *lingua franca* arguably *reinforces* rather than disrupts the continued (linguistic) domination by a 'major' language. We are very grateful to David Ender for his sensitive, nuanced translation of original German texts by Arno Böhler, Gerhard Dirmoser and Christopher Dell, Krassimira Kruschkova, Helmut Ploebst, Dieter Mersch and Andreas Spiegl.

32) Cf. Mariella Greil and Vera Sander, 'On Practices of Shining Back', in *(per)forming feedback*, Centre for Contemporary Dance Cologne, in collaboration with the Federal Ministry of Education and Research and the Dance Education Biennale, 2016, p. 23.

33) Cf. Mersch, 2015, p. 50, for reflection on the prefix per and research 'through art'.

34) Mersch, 2015, p. 11.

35) Our Method Labs (and pilot *Preludes*) include: Beyond the Line I and II (December, 2013), WUK, Vienna, and Bonington Gallery (April, 2014), Nottingham; Summer Method Lab I (July-August 2014) within the frame of ImPulsTanz, Vienna; Autumn Lab (September, 2014), PAF, Performing Arts Forum, St. Erme, France; Spring Lab (March, 2015), Tanzquartier, Vienna; a.pass (advanced performance and scenography studies), Brussels; Summer Method Lab II (July-August 2015), within the frame of ImPulsTanz, AILab, Vienna; Winter Lab (December, 2015), Tanzquartier, Vienna; Summer Method Lab III (July-August 2016), part of *Visual Arts X Dance*, a research / workshop programme curated by Tino Sehgal, Louise Höjer, and Rio Rutzinger, ImPulsTanz, AILab, Vienna.

36) Cf. Lilia Mestre, *Writing Scores, Brussels:* a.pass, 2014. See also https://apass.be/sub-eject/ (⟶ *Practices of Conversation: Keywords*).

37) Christine De Smedt, *4 Choreographic Portraits*, les ballets C de la B, 2012, p. 36. https://issuu.com/irisraspoet/docs/4choreographicportraits_eng

38) Many of the photographic images in this publication were produced by Victor Jaschke or by the key researchers and Simona Koch in the form of photographs or as still images taken from video. Additionally, we worked with photographer Julian Hughes during our 'pilot project' at Bonington Gallery, Nottingham (April, 2014), and Tim Tom during Summer *Method Lab I* (July-August 2014) (⟶ *Acknowledgements*). We are also developing a 'living archive' for video materials and continued project reflections. See our website for details on this development: www.choreo-graphic-figures.net

39) We also invited specific wit(h)nesses to contribute to a public Friday Lecture Series as part of our involvement in *Visual Arts X Dance*: 22.07.2016 — Dieter Mersch, 'Figuration / Defiguration: On the Dialectics of Choreo-Graphy' and P.A. Skantze, 'I'm A Strange Kind of In-Between Thing'; 29.07.2016 — Brandon LaBelle, 'This Weakness That I Am' and Alva Noë, 'Writing Ourselves'.

40) Luce Irigaray, 'This Sex Which Is Not One', in Elaine Marks and Isabelle De Courtivron (Eds.), *New French Feminisms*, Massachusetts: University of Massachusetts Press, 1980, p. 103.

41) Cf. Erin Manning, *The Minor Gesture*, Durham: Duke University Press, 2016, and *The Minor Gesture*, MSK — Museum of Fine Arts in Ghent, Belgium, exhibition curated by Catherine de Zegher (18.06.2016-15.08.2016).

42) Cf. Gilles Deleuze, *Spinoza: Practical Philosophy*, (Trans.) Robert Hurley, San Francisco: City Lights Books, 1988.

43) Borgdorff, 2011, p. 58.

44) Borgdorff, 2011, p. 60.

45) Peggy Phelan, *Unmarked — The Politics of Performance*, London, New York: Routledge, 1993, p. 146.

46) Cf. Emma Cocker, 'Writing without Writing: Conversation as Material', in Katja Hilevaara and Emily Orley (Eds.), *The Creative Critic: Writing As / About Practice*, London: Routledge, 2017.

47) Mersch, 2015, p. 10.

48) Hélène Cixous and Catherine Clémente, *The Newly Born Woman*, (Trans.) Betsy Wing, Minneapolis: University of Minnesota Press, 1986, p. 96.

49) Clarice Lispector, *Agua Viva*, London: Penguin Classics, 2014, p. 3.

50) Lispector, 2014, p. 5.

51) Lispector, 2014, p. 12.

52) Adrian Heathfield in Hugo Glendinning and Adrian Heathfield (Dirs. and Eds.), *Transfigured Night: A Conversation with Alphonso Lingis*, 2015, 20:04-20:30.

53) Cf. Alain Badiou, *Being and Event*, London and New York: Continuum, 2005, on the 'babbling' speech acts of the faithful. Cf. also Cocker, 'Moves Towards the Incomprehensible Wild', in *Art and Research*, Vol. 4, No. 1, Summer, 2011. www.artandresearch.org.uk/v4n1/cocker.php

54) Erin Manning, *Always More Than One: Individuation's Dance*, Durham: Duke University Press, 2013, p. 167.

55) Franco 'Bifo' Berardi, *The Uprising: On Poetry and Finance*, Los Angeles: semiotext(e), 2012. p. 22.

56) Berardi, 2012, p. 22.

57) Berardi, 2012, p. 22.

58) Alva Noë, *Strange Tools — Art and Human Nature*, New York: Hill and Wang, 2015, p. xiii.

59) Christopher Dell, *Die Epistemologie der Stadt*, (Trans.) David Ender, Bielefeld: Transcript Verlag, 2016, p. 34.

60) Gabriele Klein and Sandra Noeth, *Emerging Bodies — The Performance of Worldmaking in Dance and Choreography*, Berlin: De Gruyter, 2011, p. 250.

61) Elizabeth Grosz (Ed.), *Becomings: Exploration in Time, Memory and Futures*, Ithaca and London: Cornell University Press, 1999, p. 4.

METHOD LAB: A RELATIONAL MILIEU

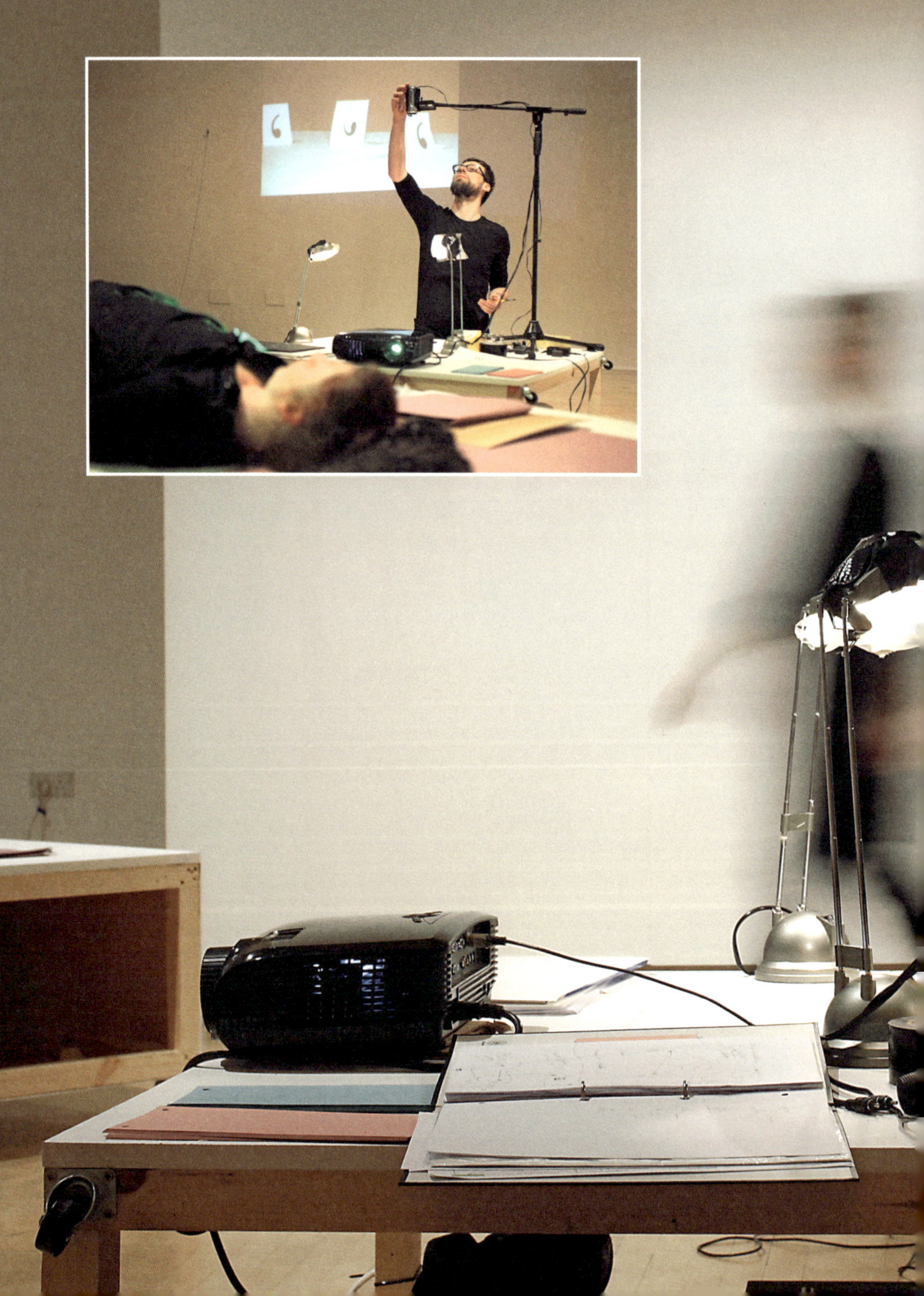

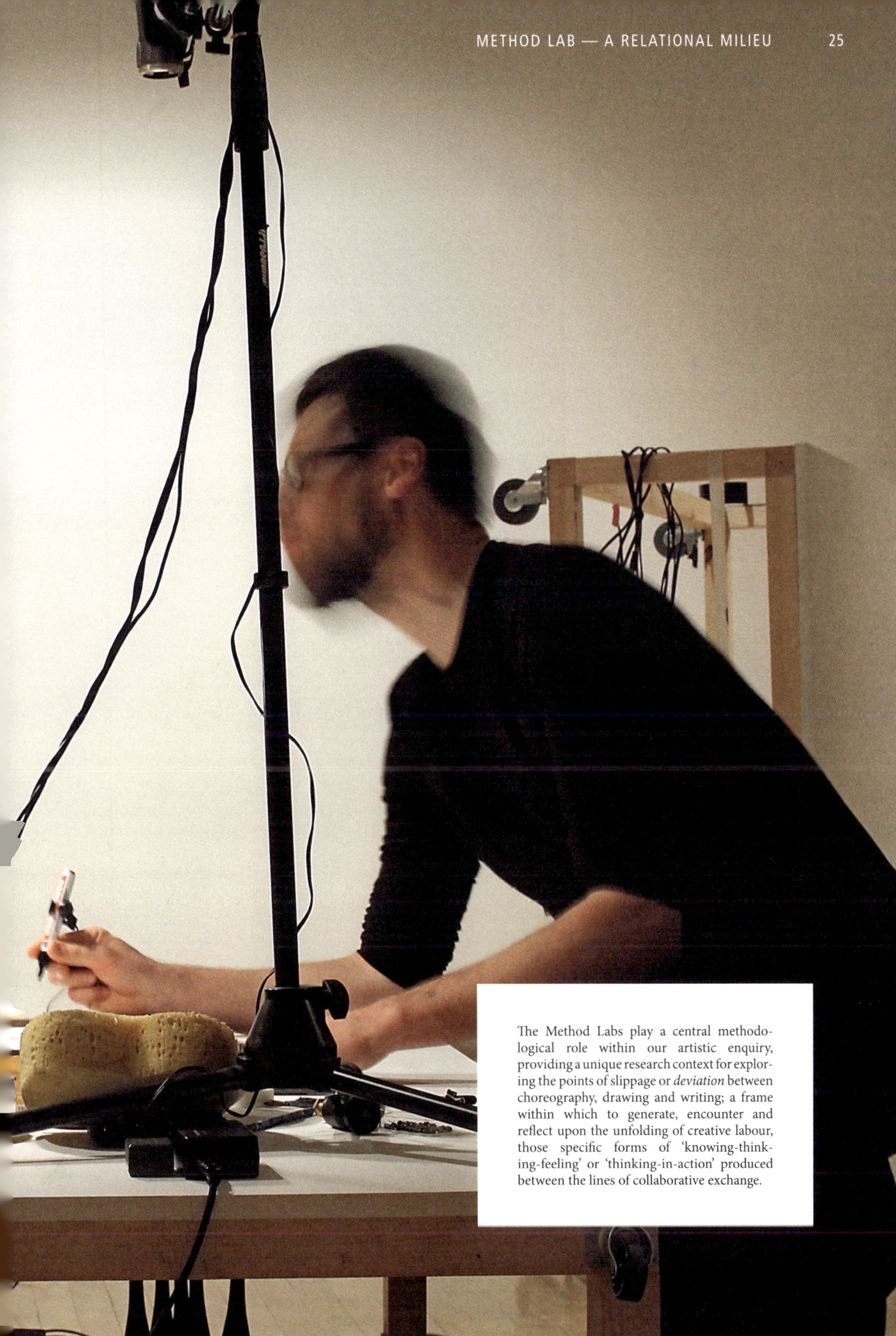

The Method Labs play a central methodological role within our artistic enquiry, providing a unique research context for exploring the points of slippage or *deviation* between choreography, drawing and writing; a frame within which to generate, encounter and reflect upon the unfolding of creative labour, those specific forms of 'knowing-thinking-feeling' or 'thinking-in-action' produced between the lines of collaborative exchange.

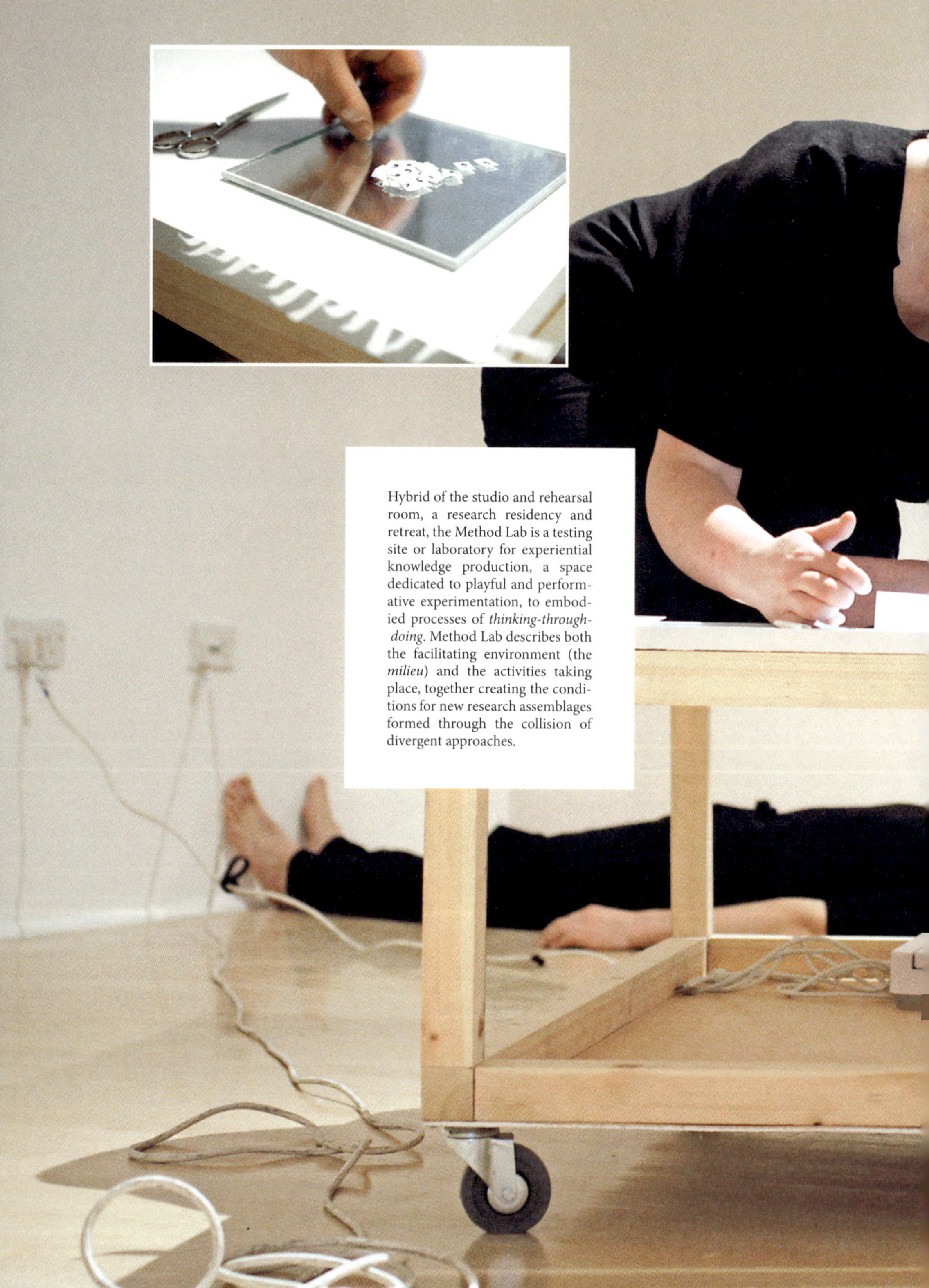

Hybrid of the studio and rehearsal room, a research residency and retreat, the Method Lab is a testing site or laboratory for experiential knowledge production, a space dedicated to playful and performative experimentation, to embodied processes of *thinking-through-doing*. Method Lab describes both the facilitating environment (the *milieu*) and the activities taking place, together creating the conditions for new research assemblages formed through the collision of divergent approaches.

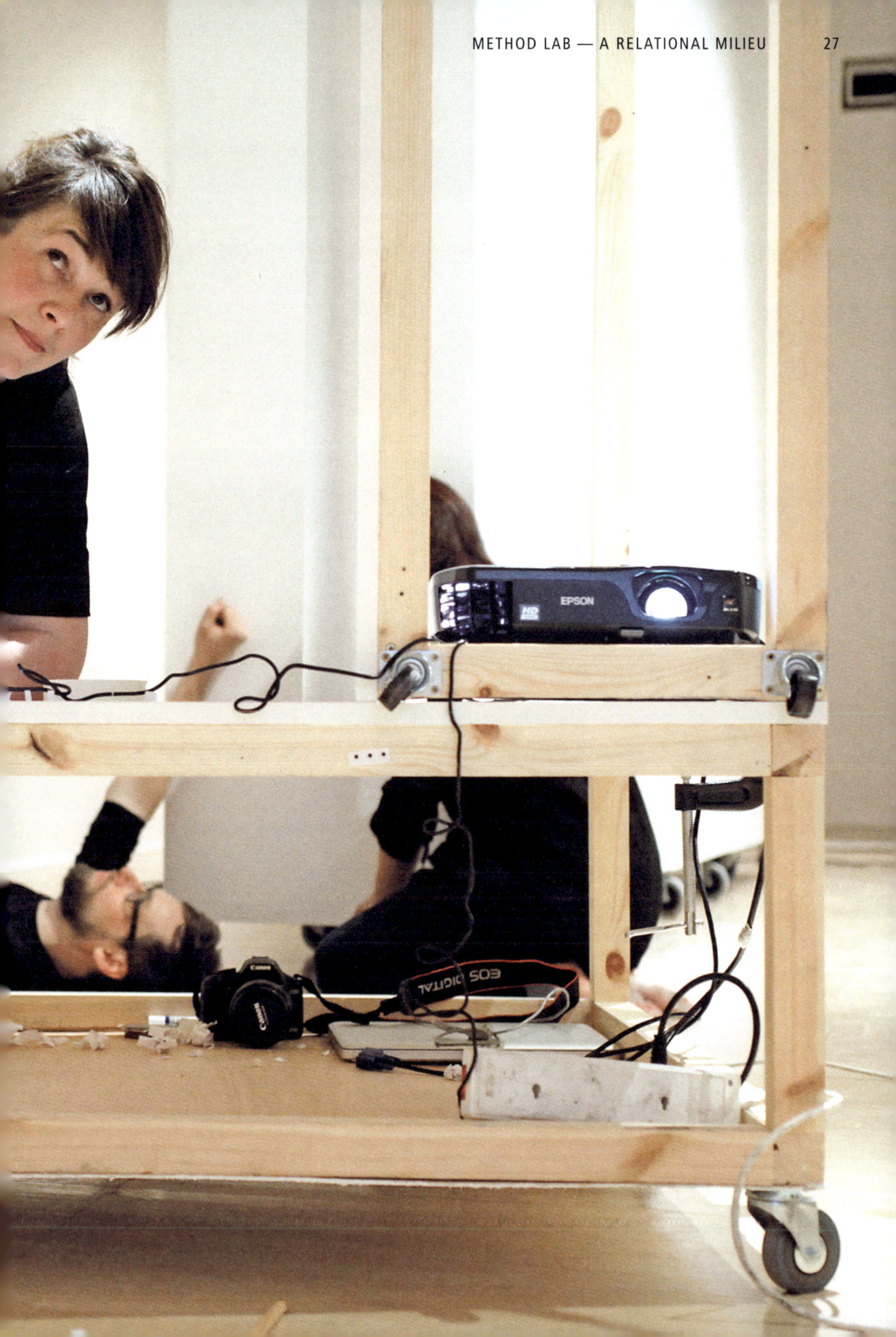
EPSON

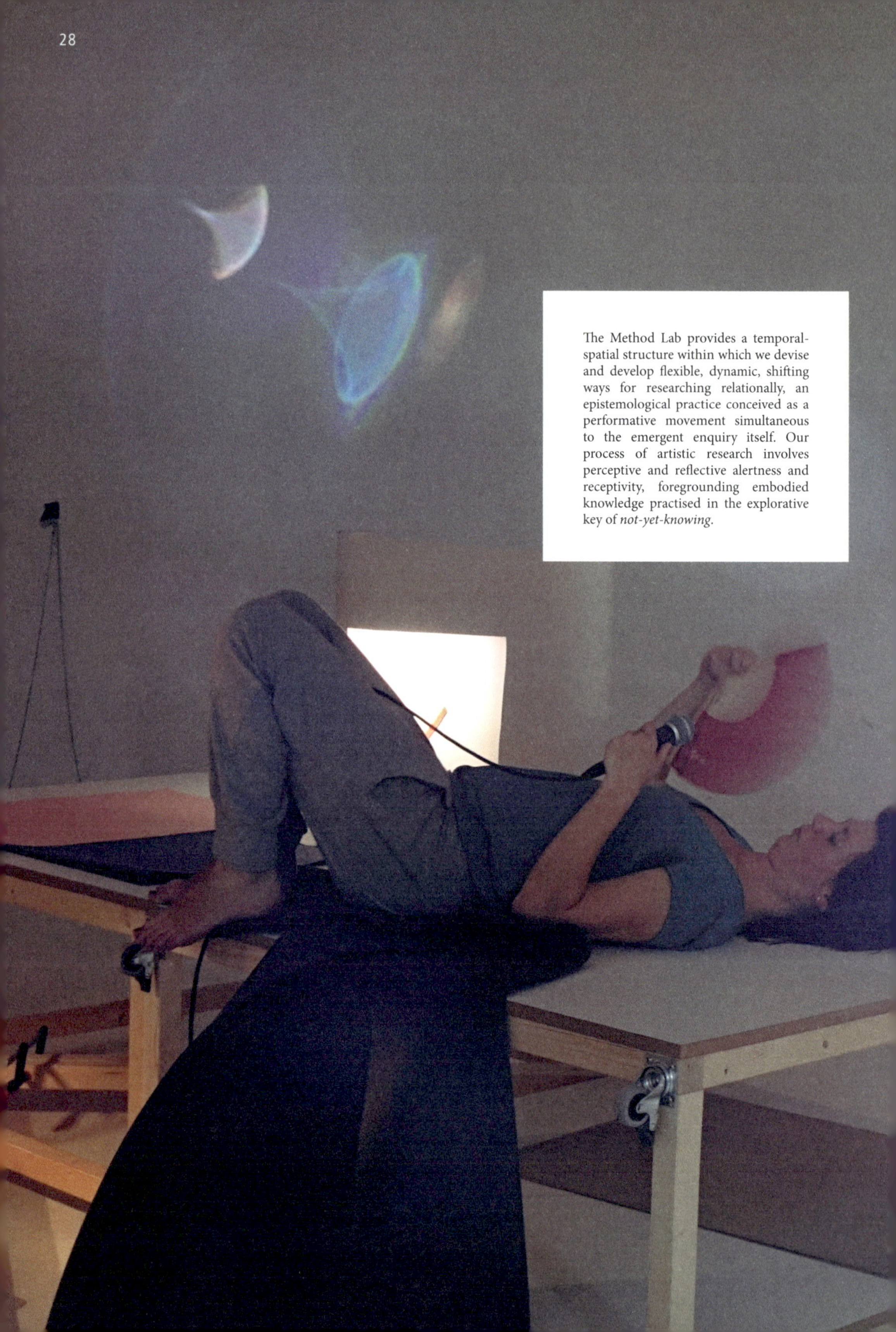

The Method Lab provides a temporal-spatial structure within which we devise and develop flexible, dynamic, shifting ways for researching relationally, an epistemological practice conceived as a performative movement simultaneous to the emergent enquiry itself. Our process of artistic research involves perceptive and reflective alertness and receptivity, foregrounding embodied knowledge practised in the explorative key of *not-yet-knowing*.

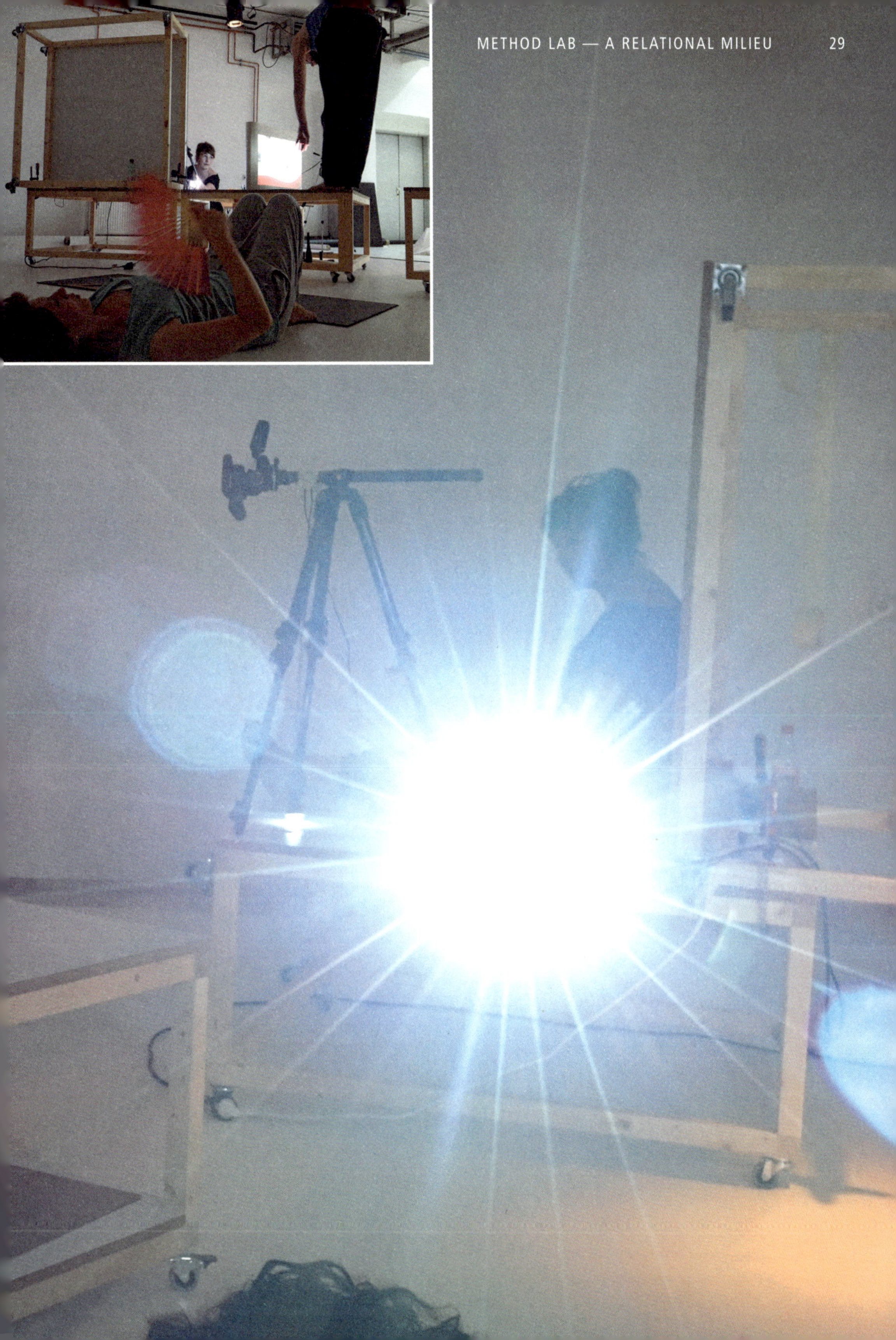

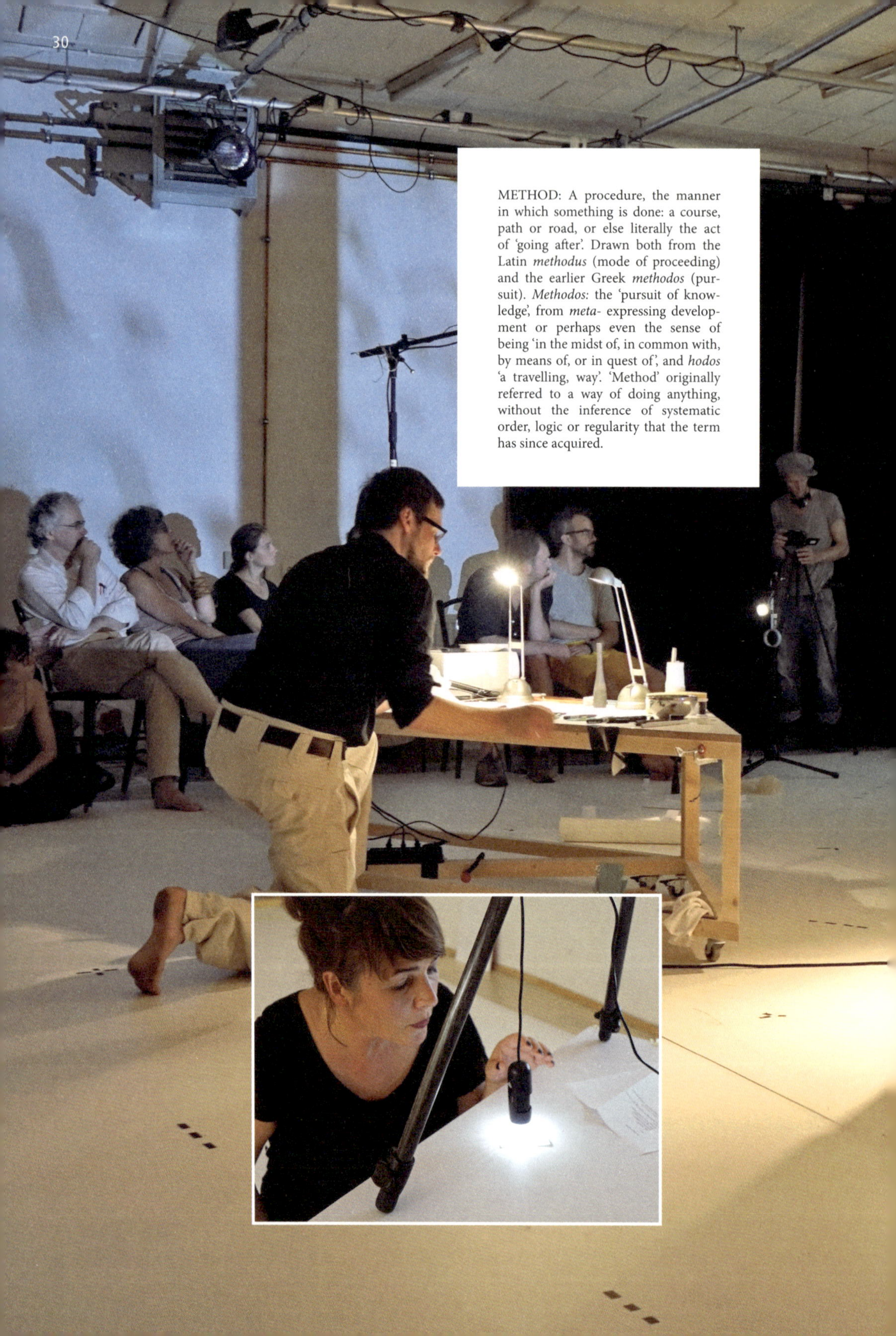

METHOD: A procedure, the manner in which something is done: a course, path or road, or else literally the act of 'going after'. Drawn both from the Latin *methodus* (mode of proceeding) and the earlier Greek *methodos* (pursuit). *Methodos:* the 'pursuit of knowledge', from *meta-* expressing development or perhaps even the sense of being 'in the midst of, in common with, by means of, or in quest of', and *hodos* 'a travelling, way'. 'Method' originally referred to a way of doing anything, without the inference of systematic order, logic or regularity that the term has since acquired.

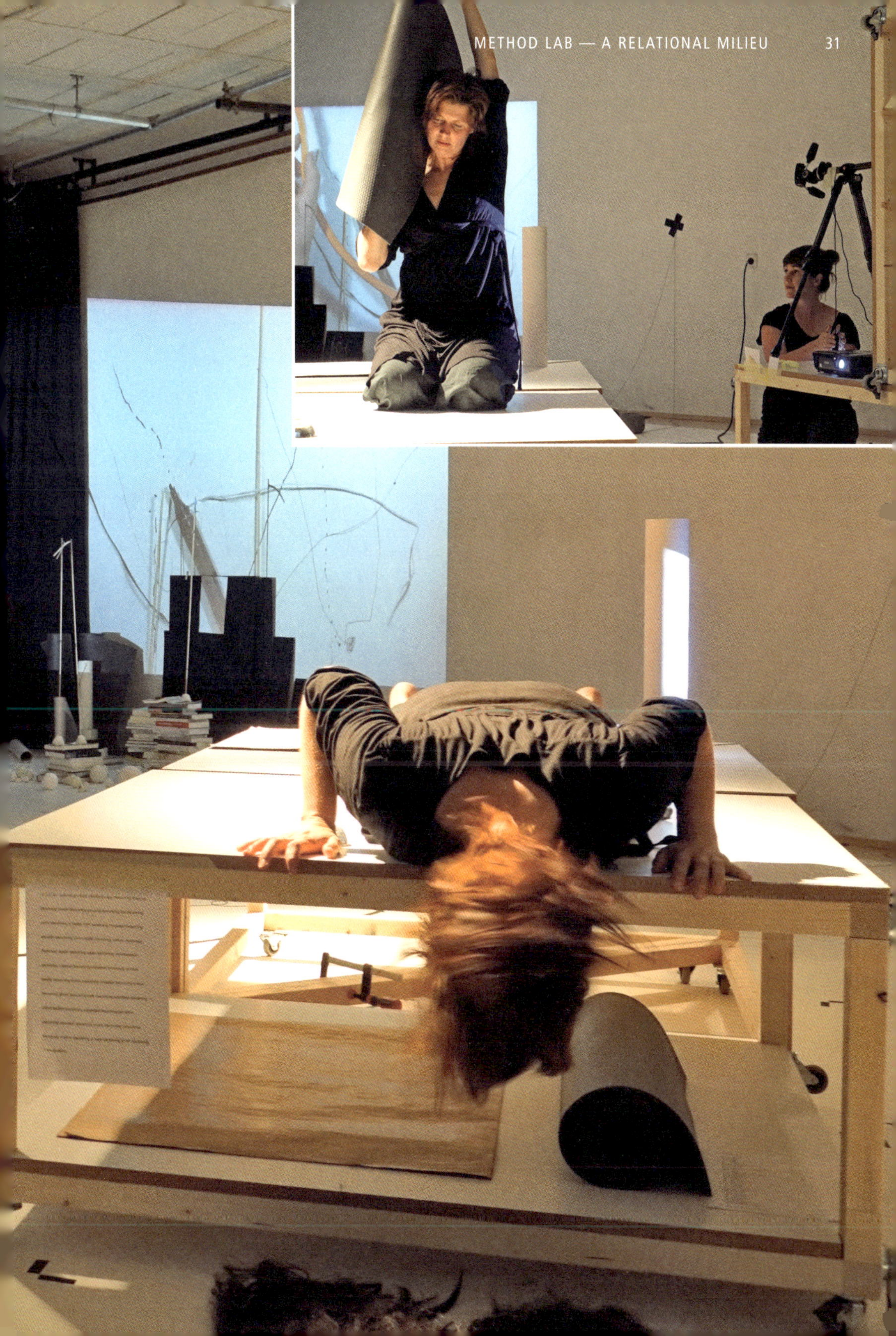

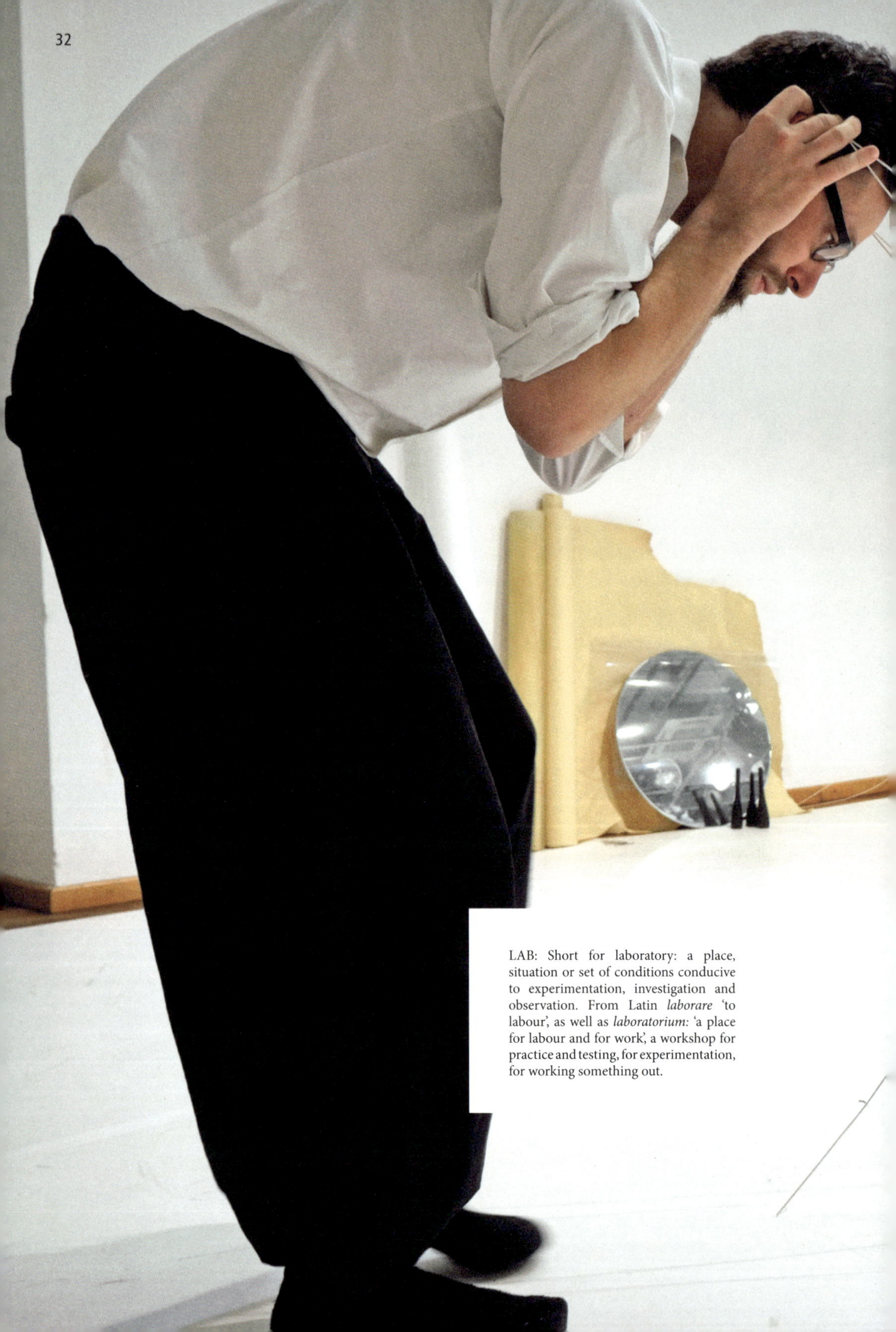

LAB: Short for laboratory: a place, situation or set of conditions conducive to experimentation, investigation and observation. From Latin *laborare* 'to labour', as well as *laboratorium:* 'a place for labour and for work', a workshop for practice and testing, for experimentation, for working something out.

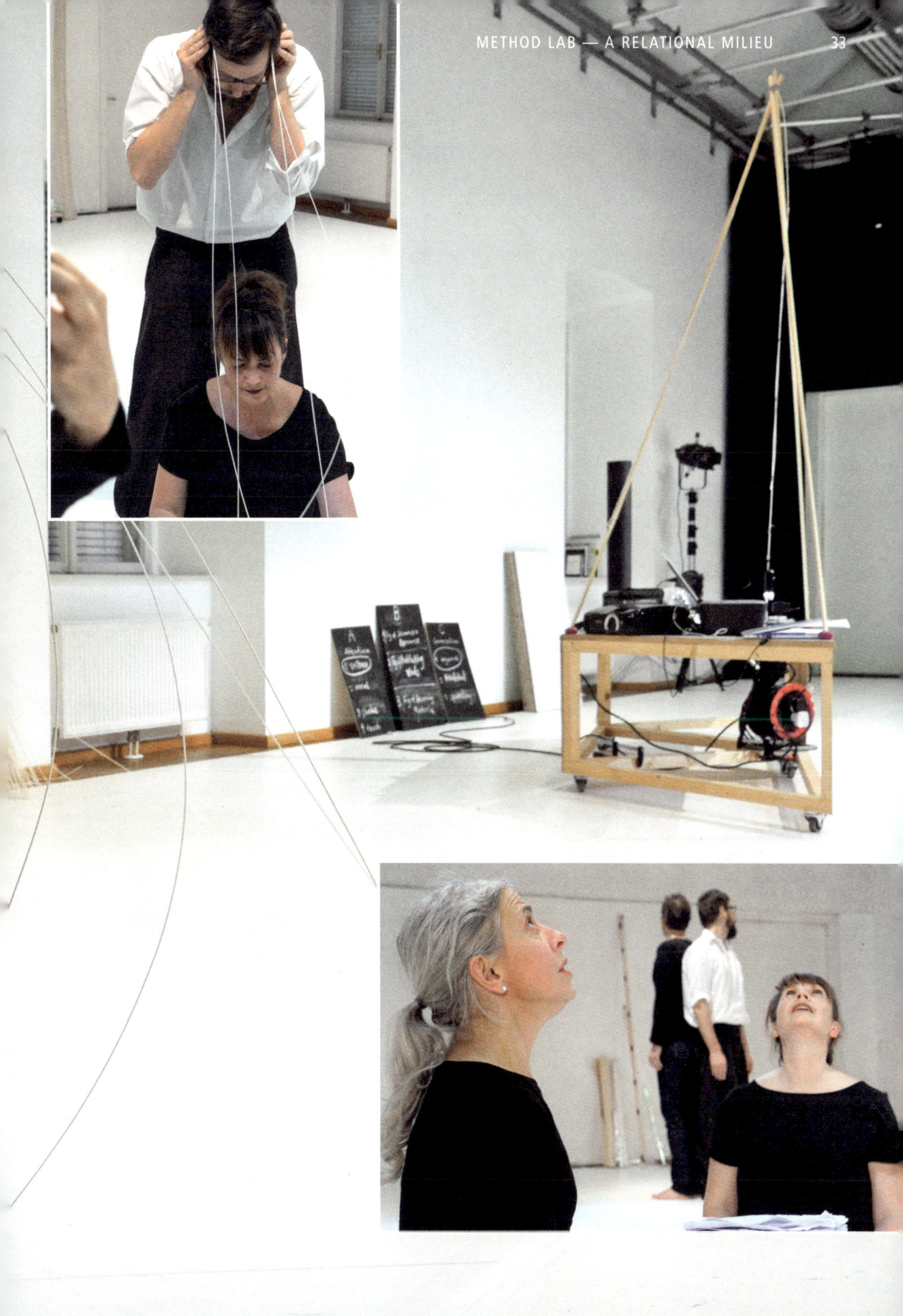

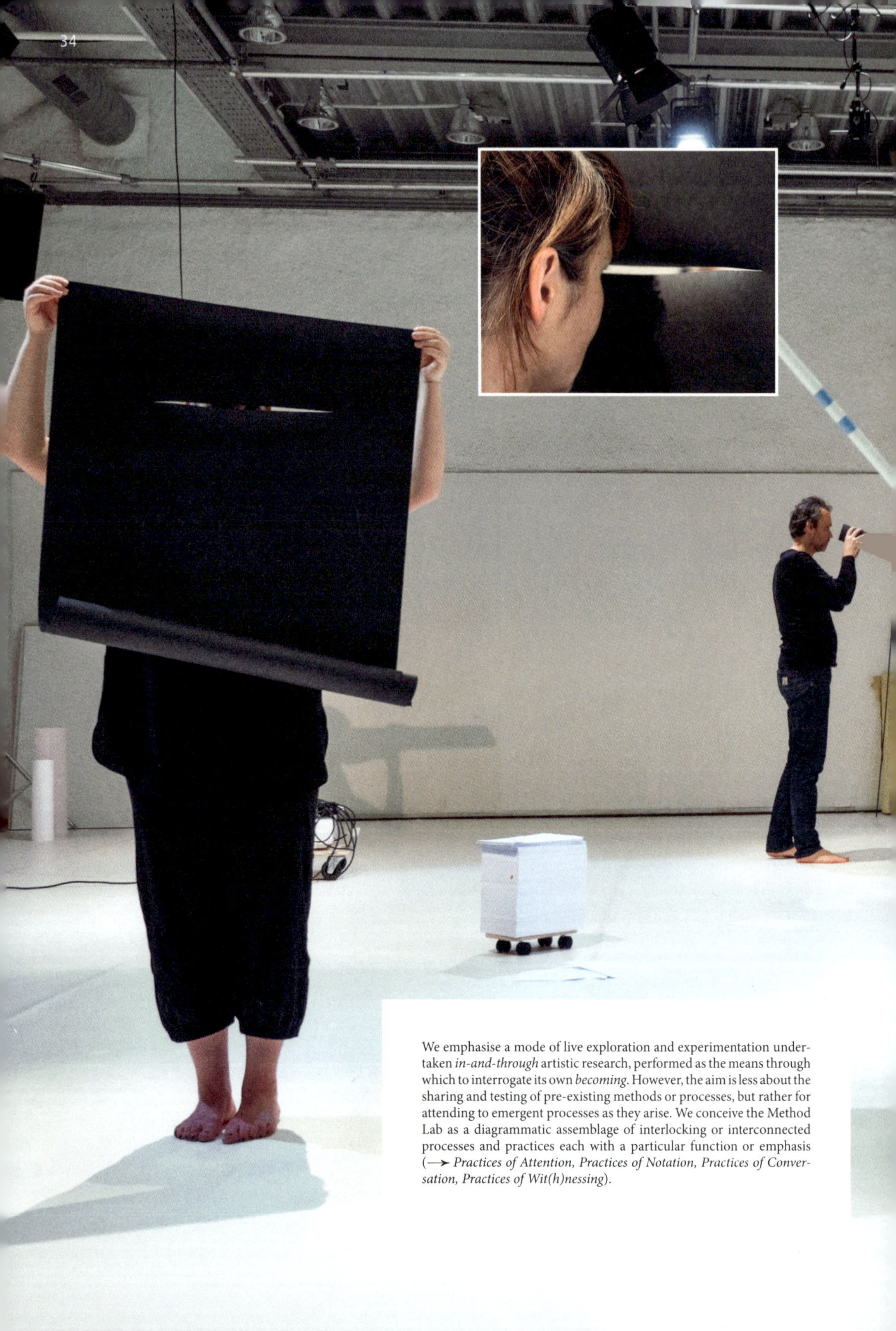

We emphasise a mode of live exploration and experimentation undertaken *in-and-through* artistic research, performed as the means through which to interrogate its own *becoming*. However, the aim is less about the sharing and testing of pre-existing methods or processes, but rather for attending to emergent processes as they arise. We conceive the Method Lab as a diagrammatic assemblage of interlocking or interconnected processes and practices each with a particular function or emphasis (⟶ *Practices of Attention, Practices of Notation, Practices of Conversation, Practices of Wit(h)nessing*).

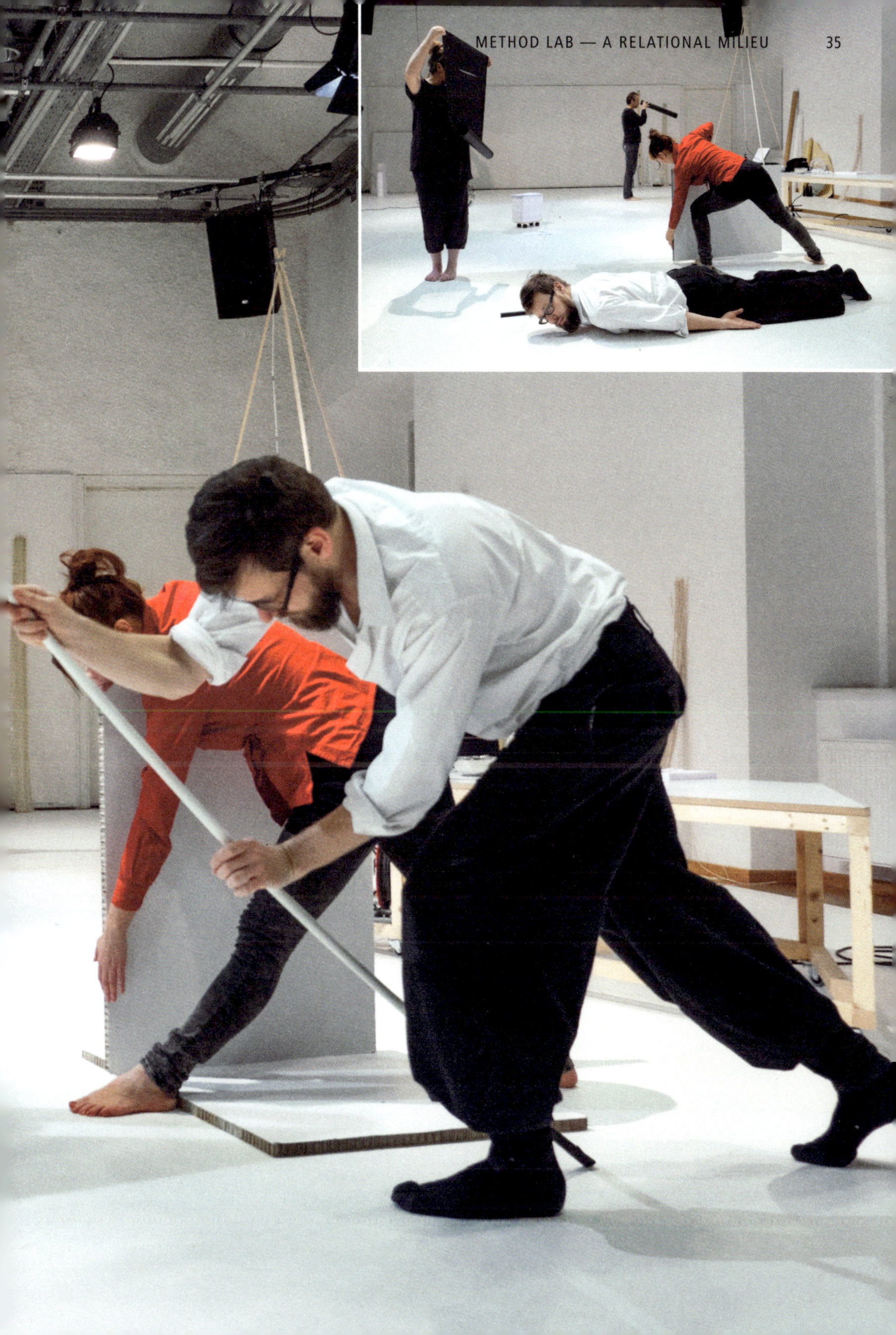

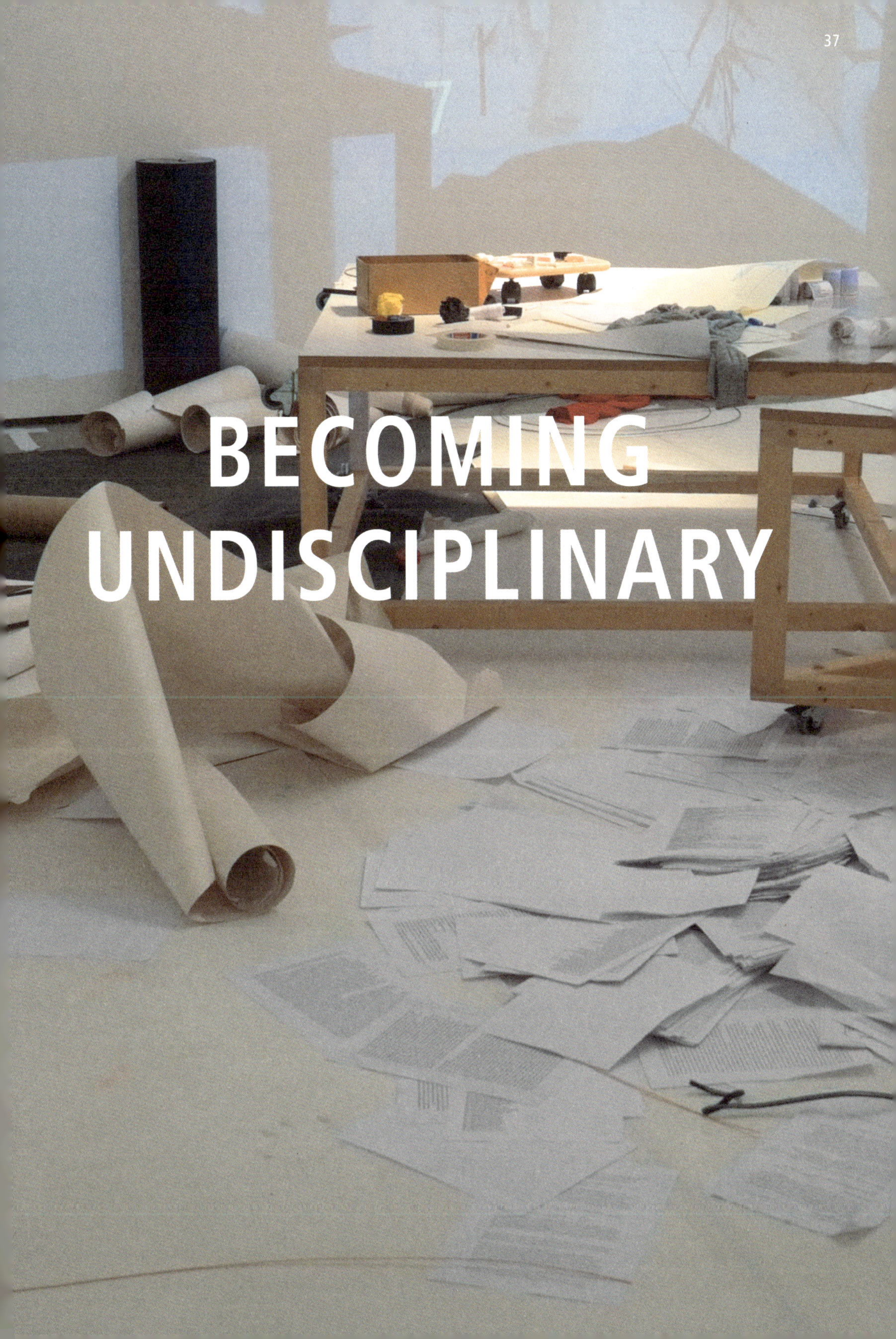

BECOMING UNDISCIPLINARY

BECOMING UNDISCIPLINARY

DEVIATIONS FROM THE LINE

The terms interdisciplinary and collaboration have become catchwords within academia and art world alike, used sometimes indiscriminately to invoke innovation — a sense of boundary-crossing or convention-busting — or perhaps more cynically for appealing to institutional and funding demands for multi-disciplinary partnerships, for the pooling of shared resources. In some research contexts, interdisciplinary collaboration principally has an additive or accumulative function, maximising the knowledges of different disciplinary practices whilst leaving them relatively intact. So, how to move beyond this utilitarianism or instrumentalisation? Within *Choreo-graphic Figures: Deviations from the Line,* the terms interdisciplinary and collaboration become central principles that we have necessarily wrestled with, in turn, demanding engagement with a process of radical change and transformation.

Choreo-graphic Figures: Deviations from the Line stages an inter-subjective, interdisciplinary encounter between the lines of choreography, drawing and writing, for exploring those forms of *knowing-thinking-feeling* produced through collaborative artistic exchange, in the moments of slippage and deviation as different practices enter into dialogue, overlap and collide. Or else, in less *disciplinary* terms, the project activates the distinctive bodily-kinesthetic, visual-spatial and verbal-linguistic sensibilities operating within these different practices in order to explore those knowledges emerging at their intersection. Whilst the preceding pages (⟶ *Method Lab: A Relational Milieu) show* the evolution of our working process, our intent here is to further reflect on the arc that our enquiry has taken, asking what is at stake in the deviation from the (disciplinary) line.

Christine De Smedt, Nikolaus Gansterer, Arno Böhler, Werner Moebius

Collaborate: from *com* — with, *laborare* — to work. To labour together: collaboration is performed at a methodological level within our enquiry, deployed for its capacity to undecide regimes of identity, production and representation, transforming not only the *who* (authorship) that works together but also the *how* (process, methodology) (⟶ *Howness*). However, 'interdisciplinary' has never quite felt adequate. So often this term appears confused with or exchanged for others — with the *cross-disciplinary* (the practice of viewing one discipline from

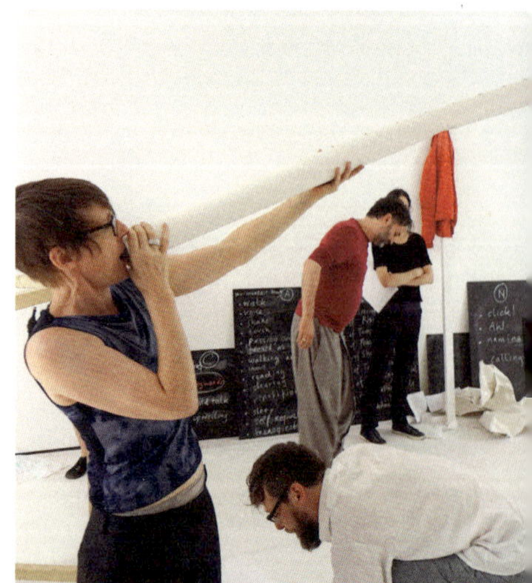

the perspective of another) or *multi-disciplinary* (an additive knowledge that draws on the expertise of several disciplines but largely without integration), the *intra-disciplinary* (work within a single discipline but demanding collaboration between its sub-disciplines) or even *trans-disciplinary* (that which attempts to go *beyond*, to transgress or transcend disciplinary boundaries). For Brian Massumi, "the relation of a mode of activity to others is immanent to its exercise, it's not inter — it's infra."[1] He argues that, "It's not necessarily the case that a discipline that claims rights over a mode of activity actually takes it to its limits. More often, it curtails any movement to the limit."[2] Indeed, through the pressure of interdisciplinary encounter certain territorial demarcations might become reasserted, boundary lines redrawn. Whilst the prefixes *inter* (between, among, in the midst of, mutually, reciprocally, together, during), *intra* (within, on the inside), *trans* (across, to go beyond, through) chime with the critical concerns of our project, it felt necessary to set out in search of alternatives. In this 'essay' we elaborate this quest alongside addressing the implications — both epistemological and ethical — for our enquiry therein. We ask: what forms of knowledge and knowing emerge in the gaps, in the spaces *in-between*, *beyond* and *before* disciplinary demarcations, in those interstitial experiences so central to artistic process, that in turn relate to our experience of *being-in-the-world*, to being human and to the fragile environments with which we co-exist.

Our project's journey has involved a transformative arc, movement from the realm of demarcated disciplinary gestures (of choreography, drawing and writing) *beyond* the *disciplinary* towards the *undisciplinary* — an 'inside out', indisciplined or anarchist moment (in W.J.T. Mitchell's terms) characterised by "turbulence or incoherence at the inner and outer boundaries of disciplines."[3] For Mitchell, "If a discipline is a way of insuring the continuity of a set of collective practices … 'indiscipline' is a moment of breakage or rupture, when the continuity is broken and practice comes into question."[4]

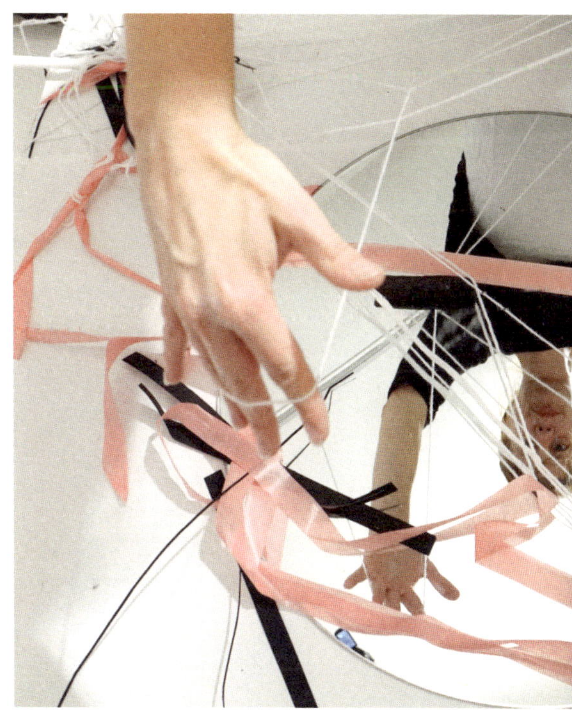

Mariella Greil

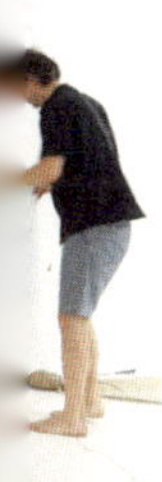

Our enquiry has evolved through a phase of *inter*disciplinary exchange — operating 'between the lines' of our different practices — towards an *infra-disciplinary* exploration explicitly directed towards the felt forces and intensities operating before, below and beneath the more readable gestures within artistic collaboration. We ask: how do we account for the experiential, relational aspects of artistic collaborative exchange as much as its resulting artefacts? As William James states, "the relations that connect experiences must themselves be experienced relations, and any kind of relation experienced must be accounted as 'real' as anything else in the system."[5] According to Victor Turner, the term *experience* can be traced back to the "base or root **per*, 'to attempt, venture, risk', whence the Greek *peira*, 'experience', … it is also the verbal root from which derives the Germanic **feraz*, giving rise to the Old English *faer*, 'danger, sudden calamity', whence Modern English 'fear'."[6] He elaborates how 'experience' also derives "from the Latin *experientia*, denoting 'trial, proof, experiment', itself generated from *experiens*, the present participle of *experiri*, 'to try, test' … 'having learned by trying'."[7] Turner further develops a 'laminated semantic system' focusing on 'experience', "which portrays it as a journey, a test (of self, of suppositions about others), a ritual passage, an exposure to peril or risk, a source of fear."[8]

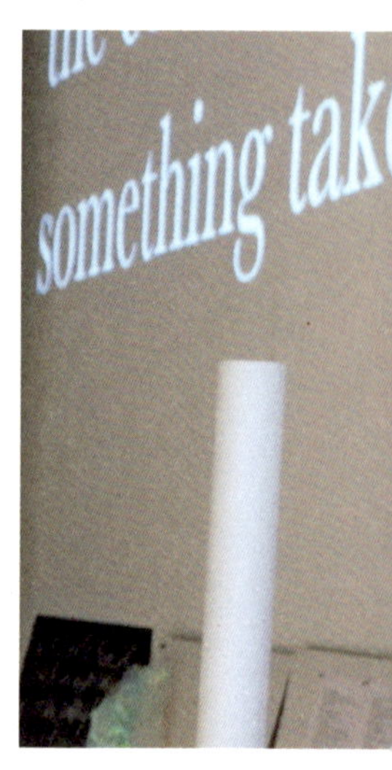

Emma Cocker

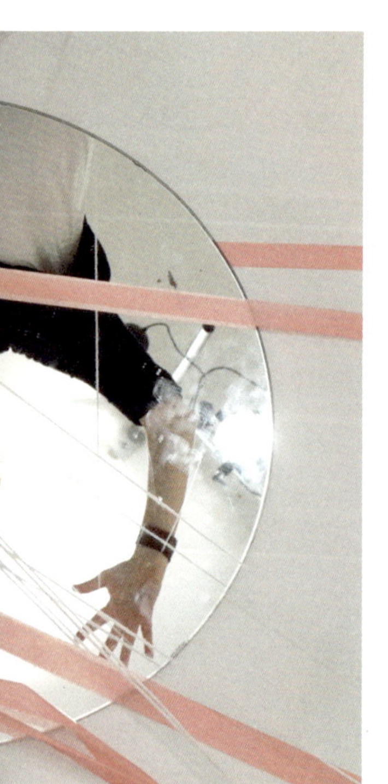

In one sense, the unfolding of our collaborative research journey has been experienced akin to a ritual process — even rite of passage — through which we have attempted to temporarily leave behind or relinquish the 'given' structural domain of our respective practices (ruled by disciplinary ways of doing things, existing principles, histories, forms) in search of a subjunctive, anti-structural realm 'trembling' within unexpected — perhaps unruly — potentiality. Turner observes how the ritual process — specifically of a rite of passage — is marked by three phases: "separation, margin (or *limen*, signifying 'threshold' in Latin) and aggregation"[9] or "separation, transition, and incorporation."[10] We conceive the arc of our three-year project and its *Method Labs* (⟶ *Method Lab: A Relational Milieu,* ⟶ *Method Lab: Porous Boundaries*) according to this

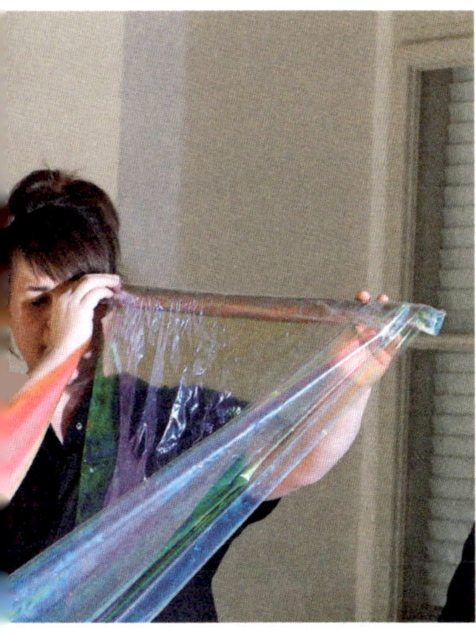

tripartite structure, facilitating movement (*passage*) from the disciplinary domains of choreography, drawing and writing, through the liminal interspace of *un*disciplinary collaboration, towards radical transformation. First phase: separation, exit — detachment from habitual structures, protocols and conventions. We began by sharing — yet less towards the swapping of skills and knowledge but rather so that set disciplinary ways of operating might become undisciplined, unlearnt, undone, reversed or upturned through collision, convergence and contamination. This first phase was generative, experimental exploration performed in the subjunctive key of 'what if'. Rather than asking 'what is choreography, what is drawing, what is writing?', we asked, 'what if' these definitions are stretched? How elastic can these terms be made? What if a line becomes movement or sound; what if language is danced; what if words are drawn rather than written? (⟶ Krassimira Kruschkova, *What if …*). What interstitial processes, practices and knowledge(s) emerge through the 'deviation' from page to performance, from word to mark, from line to action, from modes of flat image making towards transformational embodied encounters?

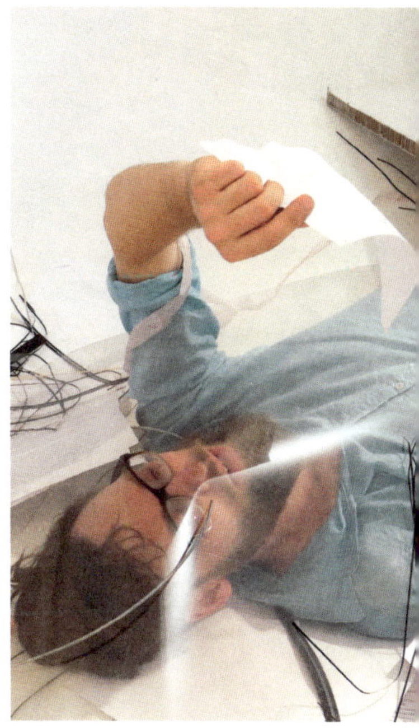

Nikolaus Gansterer

Movement becoming sound becoming sign becoming drawing becoming breath becoming physical becoming dot becoming comma becoming a bodily form becoming focused becoming acoustic becoming comfortable becoming certain becoming dispersed again becoming again becoming reverberation becoming material becoming impatient becoming another quality becoming frame becoming unstable becoming a knot becoming ghost becoming both becoming amplified becoming imperceptible becoming expanded becoming tentative becoming attention becoming words becoming concertina becoming rhythm becoming a mark becoming a fold becoming choreo-graphic

Yet, the act of separation is risky, since it requires the practice of *letting go*, renunciation of what is familiar or known, safe or certain. Between fidelity and surrender, how to let go whilst retaining one's integrity? Between integrity and resistance, how to avoid assimilating (the *other*) or else being assimilated? How to avoid homogeneity, the reduction of difference towards flattening same-ness, surface equivalence?[11] Elizabeth Grosz asks, "What would an ethics be like that, instead of seeking a mode of equivalence, a mode of reciprocity or calculation, sought to base itself in absolute generosity, absolute gift, expenditure without return, a pure propulsion into a future that does not rebound with echoes of an exchange dictated by the past?"[12] Subversion of the exchange economy: becoming open, generosity practised without recompense, without expecting anything back in return. However, the process of *undisciplinary* collaboration can also be fraught, full of friction and misunderstanding, intransigence and untranslatability. How to embrace this, for collaboration need not be wholly harmonious or consensual?[13]

Towards collaboration in the key of heterogeneity then, where the relational politics of collaboration creates the conditions of mutuality, differentiation and urgency necessary for working together *in difference*.[14] Yet, how to meet with difference — the strange, the unknown or foreign — whilst still striving for the common? How to face the other without effacing their *otherness*?[15] (⟶ *On Sedimentations of Sensitivities*). For Luce Irigaray, to meet the other, one has to "restore the nothing that separates us … I am not you and you will forever remain other to me […] The search for a link requires the respect for the strangeness of the one to the other, the recognition of a nothing in common calling into question the proper of each one."[16] She elaborates, "What safeguards the between-two as a place available for the entering into presence is the limit that each imposes upon oneself in the fidelity to self and to the space-time open through the respect of the other as such, of their irreducibility."[17] How to respect this strangeness, the peculiarity of the other? We search for affinity in force beyond similarity in form: within translation, attentiveness to that which remains untranslatable, sensitivity to the forces and volitions of both self and other. For Irigaray, "In order that the 'you' take place in a relation with the 'I', the 'I' has to secure a faithfulness to its Being in which the other can trust … the 'I' must be listening both to the 'you' and to the self. Co-propriation in

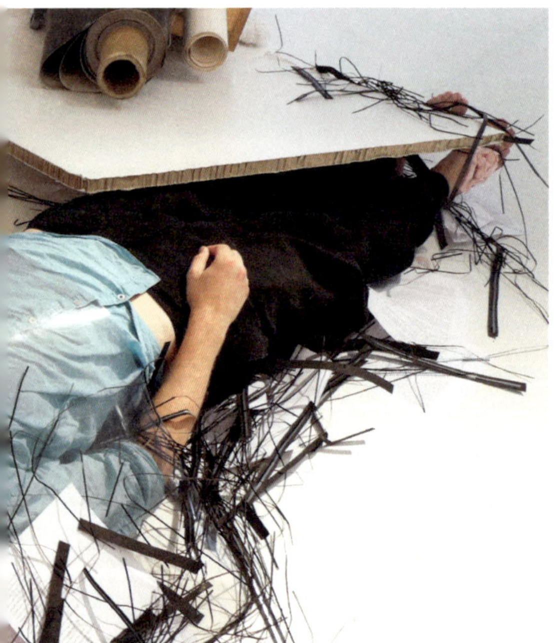

Lilia Mestre, Alex Arteaga, Nikolaus Gansterer

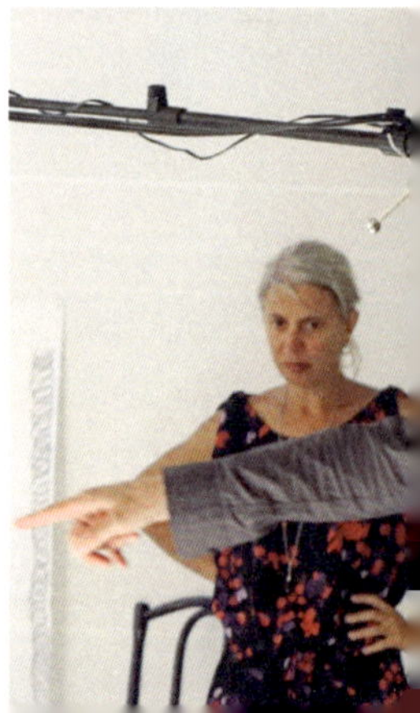

the human necessitates a dialogue in which the elements remain two — speaking oneself and to the other and listening to oneself and to the other."[18] In fidelity to one's integrity, whilst attentive to the other's otherness, we strive towards a mutual letting go, reciprocal renunciation.

To renounce, from *renoncier — to give up, cede*. To *pro-cede*, to go forward then by yielding or by leaving behind, by turning aside (⟶ *How-ness*). Separation as a practice for clearing the ground or for emptying out (⟶ *Figure of Clearing and Emptying Out*), related to the prefixes *de-*, *dis-* (indicating separation, reversal, negation), *un-* or *in-* (meaning reversal, removal, the opposite of, without, *not*). Towards the undoing of discipline, the deschooling or unlearning of habits, a 'coming undone.'[19] As Elizabeth Fisher and Rebecca Fortnum argue, reflection on artistic thinking — and its attendant *not knowing* — "reveals a largely negative lexicon. Where knowledge is positive, the *un*known is often simply its opposite: it is *un*certain, *in*visible, *in*comprehensible."[20] Indeed, there are artists who develop 'tactics for not knowing' for activating the potential of the unexpected, where "not knowing is actively sought and courted at the heart of the work itself [...] Theirs is a practice that sets out in search of the capricious wind or current that will send them sideways or disturb their even keel, for it is in such moments of crisis that new ideas often emerge."[21] Indeed, as Henk Borgdorff states, artistic research "is more directed at a not-knowing, or a not-yet-knowing. It creates room for that which is unthought, that which is unexpected — the idea that all things could be different. Especially pertinent to artistic research is the realization that we do not yet know what we don't know. Art invites us and allows us to linger at the frontier of what there is, and it gives us an outlook on what might be. Artistic research is the deliberate articulation of these contingent perspectives."[22]

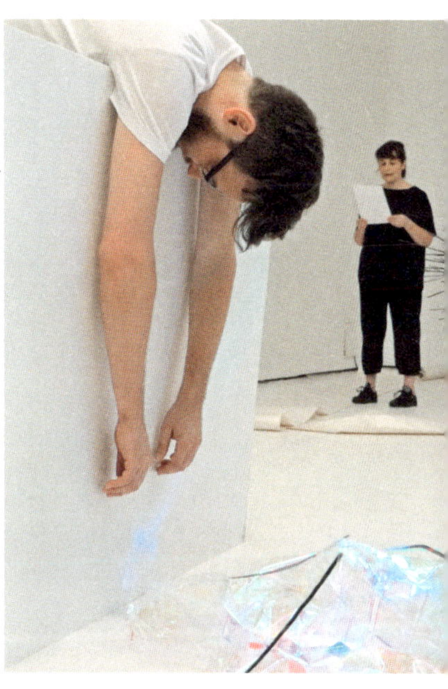
Nikolaus Gansterer, Emma Cocker

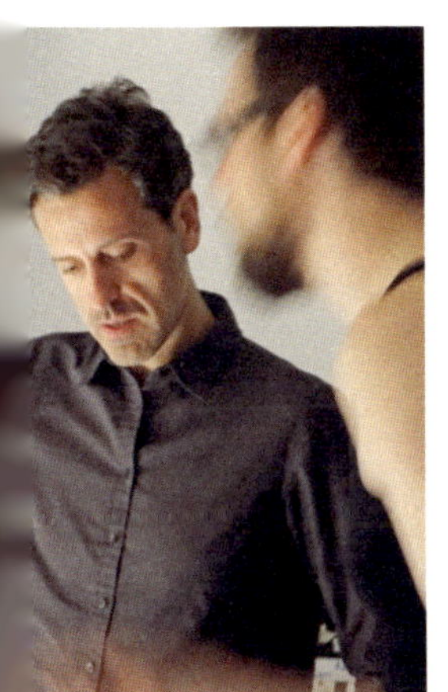

Rather than a condition of loss, lack or diminution, for Irit Rogoff, the critical condition of 'unbelonging' or of 'being without' involves an "active, daily disassociation in the attempt to clear the ground for something else to emerge."[23] Likewise, for Sarat Maharaj, the notion of *non-knowledge* can be understood with reference to the Sanskrit term *avidya,* where he states, "'The word 'vidya' means to see-know ... When we attach the prefix 'a' to it, we normally mean to signal something like its opposite ... but 'a' can also neutralise rather than negate."[24] He elaborates that, "Avidya or non-knowledge, contrary to appearance, is not anti-knowledge ... It is more a *détournement* of ready-made knowledge systems ... dissolving them as they try to settle and fix into institutional disciplines [...] Avidya is more about production, about generating new forms of think-feel-know ... unknown circuits of consciousness."[25] Towards the *adisciplinary*, towards *unbelonging*. We ask, what emerges when we suspend disciplinary ways of operating, when we let go of fixated ideas and forms?

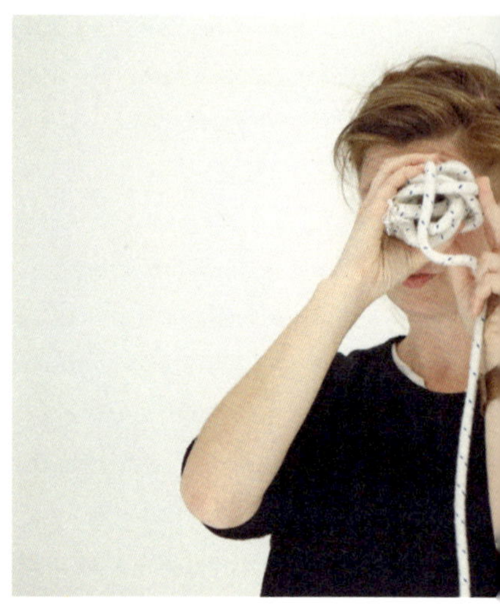

Mariella Greil

Werner Moebius, Mariella Greil

Beyond letting go: the arc of our enquiry passes into its second phase, towards a liminal zone of transition and ambiguity. Liminal—from *limen*—pertaining to a threshold: 'no longer' classified and 'not yet' classified, "neither here nor there ... betwixt and between."[26] For Turner, liminality describes a time-space where, "the past is momentarily negated, suspended or abrogated, and the future has not yet begun, an instant of pure potentiality when everything, as it were, trembles in the balance"[27] (⟶ *When-ness*). He argues that during the liminal phase of a rite of passage, ritual subjects become "temporarily undefined, beyond the normative structure. This weakens them, since they have no rights over others. But it also liberates them from structural obligations."[28] For Turner, "the term limen itself ... appears to be negative in connotation, since it is no longer the positive past condition nor yet the positive articulated future condition."[29] Within this phase of our enquiry, the negative lexicon of *not knowing* prevails: deviation, inversion, reversion, subversion, pollution, contamination, *topsy-turveydom* (⟶ Brandon LaBelle, *The Thing*). Our intent here was to push the *un*disciplinary potential of our project by opening up to the disruptive, unsettling and destabilising aspects of *liminality*, the undefinable or unclassifiable nature of working 'without' discipline, towards wilful 'unbelonging'. Beyond the limit or limen: blurring of boundaries, of border crossings. For Rogoff, "the border is represented as a zone of danger in which norms get undone, temptations rear their head, transgression takes place and solid, reliable identity gets undone."[30] Breakdown of stable meaning, edges becoming porous: collapse of distinction between self / other, subject / object, animate / inanimate (⟶ *Transformative Figures*, especially ⟶ *Becoming Material*).

Yet, without discipline — without boundaries — things can become unruly or wild, formless or even *monstrous* (⟶ *The Thing*). Julia Kristeva uses the term *abject* to refer to that which "draws me to the place where meaning collapses."[31] She argues that the abject has to do with "what disturbs identity, system, order. What does not respect borders, positions, rules."[32] The wound — border between inside and outside, as between fear and *jouissance*, pleasure and pain, "There, I am at the border of my condition as a living being."[33] "Can we inhabit the cut as a space?" asks Brandon LaBelle, "(t)o take up residence within the wound? […] (D)well within the wound, as an event of rupture and longing" (⟶ *The Thing*). Indeed, Kristeva describes how it is possible to attain an "aesthetic experience of the abject" via art, poetry or even religion, through an "impure process that protects from the abject only by dint of being immersed in it."[34] It is perhaps no accident that during the second phase of our enquiry, we began to cultivate various aesthetic practices (⟶ *Practices of Attention, Conversation, Notation*) through which to sharpen or focus our live explorations, alongside the development of a score — conceived as a *radical score of attention* — for bringing them into relation (⟶ *Embodied Diagrammatics*). It could be tempting to view these developments as attempts to control or order the unruly turbulence of the liminal phase of our enquiry, to return a sense of structure. However, our intent was rather more opposite, focused instead towards how we might remain or dwell for longer periods within the charged space-time of exploration — how to inhabit the experience of the cut or rupture, as it were, more deeply.

Christine De Smedt, Jörg Piringer

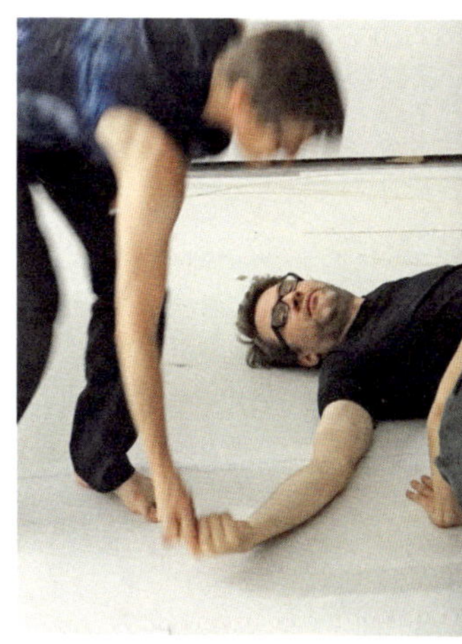

We elaborate the nature of these various practices and how to 'play them' elsewhere within this publication (⟶ *Practices*, ⟶ *How to Play the Score*); in fact, the book itself unfolds as a gradual revelation of the 'rules of our game'. In one sense, these various rules, practices and scores can be conceived in ritual terms, as Turner observes, "Liminality may involve a complex sequence of episodes in sacred space-time, and may also include subversive and ludic (or playful) events […] in liminality people 'play' with the elements of the familiar and defamiliarize them. Novelty emerges from unprecedented combinations of familiar elements."[35] Likewise, our intent has been to create a specific — even sacred — *space-time* (⟶ *Method Lab: A Relational Milieu,* ⟶ *Method Lab: Porous Boundaries,* ⟶ *Where-ness*) within which we collectively engage in intensive forms of shared exploration. However, whilst ritual practices are often used for strengthening or supporting the prevailing social order (indeed, the final stage of a rite of passage — *incorporation, reaggregation, re-entry* — traditionally involves the return to a 'relatively stable state'), we harness a ritual structure so as to detour or *détourne* its intent; swerve or subvert its stabilising tendency. Subversion — from the Latin *subvertere*: to turn upside down, overturn, overthrow, from *sub* — under, and *vertere* — to turn. We practise a shift of attention from the conventions, rules and protocols of our respective disciplinary demarcations, towards the *sub-* of the liminal, an affective process-realm of forces and intensities operating below the threshold of — beneath, behind, under — the more recognisable gestures within artistic practice (⟶ *Figuring >< Figure*). Here, our conviction is that cultivating sensitivity towards the barely perceptible micro-movements within the process of artistic 'sense-making' (⟶ *How-ness*) has wider structural — even political — implications at the level of the macro, encouraging the de-, re- and trans-figuring of our ways of being in the world, inviting new forms of relationality, sociality and solidarity. The practices developed within *Choreo-graphic Figures: Deviations from the Line* are thus shared in hope of being activated by other *initiates* beyond the frame of this singular project, inhabited beyond the pages of this book at the level of the ethico-aesthetic, the experiential and relational.

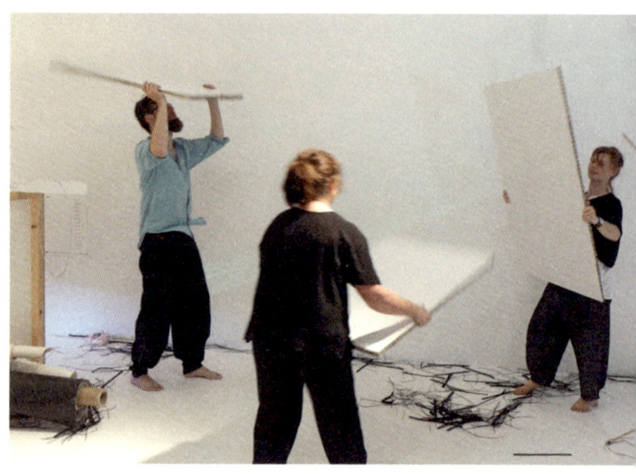

Nikolaus Gansterer, Emma Cocker, Mariella Greil

Lilia Mestre

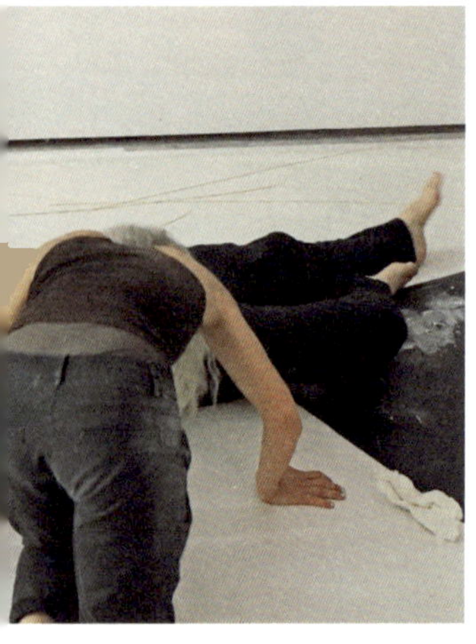

1) Brian Massumi, in Hugo Glendinning and Adrian Heathfield (Dirs. and Eds.), *No Such Thing as Rest: A Walk with Brian Massumi,* 2013, p. 4. www.adrianheathfield.net/project/no-such-thing-as-rest

2) Massumi, 2013, p. 4.

3) W. J. T. Mitchell, 'Interdisciplinarity and Visual Culture', in *Art Bulletin,* 'Inter / disciplinarity', December 1995, p. 541.

4) Mitchell, 1995, p. 541.

5) William James, *Essays in Radical Empiricism*, New York: Dover Publication, [1912] 2003, p. 22, cited in Janneke Wesseling, *On Sponge, Stone and the Intertwinement with the Here and Now: A Methodology of Artistic Research*, Amsterdam: Valiz, 2016, p. 23.

6) Victor Turner, *From Ritual to Theatre: The Human Seriousness of Play*, New York: Performing Arts Journal Publications, 1982, p. 17.

7) Turner, 1982, p. 17.

8) Turner, 1982, pp. 17-18.

9) Victor Turner, *The Ritual Process: Structure and Antistructure,* Chicago: Aldine Publishing, 1969, p. 94.

10) Turner, 1982, p. 24.

11) Here, our tripartite arc *deviates* from the rite of passage, which in Turner's terms often emphasises a quality of levelling, uniformity, anonymity, and homogeneity.

12) Elizabeth Grosz (Ed.), *Becomings: Exploration in Time, Memory and Futures*, Ithaca and London: Cornell University Press, 1999, p. 11.

13) Mariella Greil and Martina Ruhsam, 'Postconsensual Collaboration: A Shared Lecture on Plurality and the Choreographic', *On Collaboration II Symposium,* London: Middlesex University, 2013, and Martina Ruhsam, 'I Want to Work with You Because I Can Speak for Myself: The Potential of Postconsensual Collaboration in Choreographic Practice' in Noyale Colin, Stefanie Sachsenmaier (Eds.), *Collaboration in Performance Practice: Premises, Workings and Failures*, Basingstoke: Palgrave Macmillan, 2016.

14) For Ian Pindar and Paul Sutton, "Guattari defines heterogenesis as 'processes of resingularization'. It is an active immanent singularization of subjectivity, as opposed to a transcendent, universalizing and reductionist homogenization. Heterogeneity is an expression of desire, of a becoming that is always in the process of adapting, transforming and modifying itself in relation to its environment", translators' footnotes, Félix Guattari, *The Three Ecologies*, London: Bloomsbury Academic, 2014, p. 105.

15) Cf. also Emmanuel Levinas, *Entre Nous: On Thinking-of-the-Other*, New York: Columbia University Press, 1998, and Paul Ricoeur, *On Translation*, London and New York: Routledge, 2006.

16) Luce Irigaray, *The Way of Love*, London and New York: Continuum, 2002, p. 168.

17) Irigaray, 2002, p. 79. She adds, "The interval between the other and me can never be overcome ... and the gap has to be maintained ... it is important that an irreducible distance will remain where silence takes place", p. 66. This 'gap' in turn resonates with Dieter Mersch's assertion that, "every process requires a moment of transition and therefore a void or chasm, comparable to a white space in its middle that has to stay vacant. It is homologous to the idea of the hyphen in '*choreo-graphy*' insofar as there remains an indefiniteness between the two halves of the word which marks a breach, a moment of overturning." (⟶ *Figuration / Defiguration*).

18) Irigaray, 2002, p. 82.

19) Cf. Goat Island, *Coming Undone,* 2001. Cf. also Adrian Heathfield, 'Coming Undone' in *It's an Earthquake in My Heart: A Reading Companion,* Chicago: Goat Island, 2001. www.adrianheathfield.net/project/coming-undone

20) Elizabeth Fisher and Rebecca Fortnum (Eds.), *On Not Knowing: How Artists Think*, London: Black Dog, 2013, p. 7.

21) Emma Cocker, 'Tactics for Not Knowing: Preparing for the Unexpected', in Fisher and Fortnum (Eds.), *On Not Knowing,* 2013, p. 127. Cf. also Cocker, 'Readiness', in *The Yes of the No,* Sheffield: Site Gallery, 2016, p. 70.

22) Henk Borgdorff, 'The Production of Knowledge in Artistic Research', in Michael Biggs and Henrik Karlsson (Eds.), *The Routledge Companion to Research in the Arts,* London: Routledge, 2011, p. 61.

23) Irit Rogoff, 'Without: A Conversation-Interview with Peggy Phelan', in *Art Journal,* Fall, 2001.

24) Sarat Maharaj and Francisco J. Varela, 'Ahamkara: Particules Élémentaires of First-person Consciousness', in Florian Dombois, Ute Meta Bauer, Claudia Mareis, Michael Schwab (Eds.), *Intellectual Birdhouse: Artistic Practice as Research,* Amsterdam: Rodopi, 2011, p. 73.

25) Maharaj, 2011, p. 73.

26) Turner, 1969, p. 95. Cf. Emma Cocker, 'Border Crossings – Practices for Beating the Bounds', in Hazel Andrews and Les Roberts (Eds.), *Liminal Landscapes: Travel, Experience and Spaces In-between*, Hoboken: Taylor & Francis, 2012; Emma Cocker, 'Looking for Loopholes: Cartographies of Escape', in Karen Bishop (Ed.), *Cartographies of Exile: A New Spatial Literacy*, New York: Routledge, 2016, for further reflections on artistic 'border crossings' through the prism of Turner's writing on liminality and 'rites of passage'.

27) Turner, 1982, p. 44.

28) Turner, 1982, p. 27.

29) Turner, 1982, p. 41.

30) Rogoff, *Terra Infirma, Geography's Visual Culture*, London and New York: Routledge, 2000, p. 112.

31) Julia Kristeva, *Powers of Horror: An Essay on Abjection*, New York: Columbia University Press, 1982, p. 2.

32) Kristeva, 1982, p. 4.

33) Kristeva, 1982, p. 3.

34) Kristeva, 1982, p. 29.

35) Turner, 1982, p. 27.

UNLINED

Andreas Spiegl

A line in this project connects choreography, drawing and writing, and as a moment common to all of these genres. This line does not so much run from one genre to the next to bridge and measure their distance or difference; rather, it can be found in all of them, appears here and there alike, seems as appropriate to one genre as to the other, recurs under specific conditions — as writing, as gesture or trace, and nominally in the concept of choreography. In this sense, this is not about a line that connects different areas, but about a line inscribed in them, belonging to them in spite of their differences, attached like an inscription, differently as it may be read. What it suggests is perusal, reading with the stroke of the drawing, reading a gesture out of the movement, a readability of the process, the sequence, and narrative features. The line instigates reading where there was nothing to be read before, because there was no way to distinguish the legible from the illegible. The line causatively marks a separation of the legible and the illegible, and also continuously sketches out the illegible along with the legible — a space with and without stroke, the written and the unwritten between the words and lines, the drawn and the undesigned as edge of the drawing, the beginning and the end of a gesture, a writing with the hand, even if the hand is still there and the gesture already has ended. Where the line appears it gets the unlined going. If there appears a 'deviation of the line' in the title of this project, then this deviation already evokes the unlined, the space deviating from the line just to remain bound to it. The unlined is solely the product of the line, and therefore inseparably bound to it also in its name.

The last decades of ideology-critical efforts were dedicated to critique of the linear — a line which from a teleological perspective was identified with a horizon and a path towards this horizon — in order to raise one's hand for the non-linear, to vote, to raise one's voice for a non-line. The gaze was oriented towards the line and the linear alone, and so prevented reading the unlined which the line already drew along — that drawing a line synchronously draws the unlined as its consequence: a paradoxical synchrony of cause and effect — the line and the unlined emerge at the same moment. With our gaze on the unlined, the line no longer appears as a path or track leading from one argument or word to the next, from one gesture or drawing to the next, but as a marking of the unlined which only deviates from the line without being able to leave it. Drawing a line or following a line thus also means creating the unlined — the space into which our reading unravels and from which it again approaches legibility, approaches the experience that the line is unable to keep what it is supposed to define or denominate. Writing, drawing, and choreographing ever anew only describe that what has been written, drawn, and choreographed so far does not suffice to satiate the need for the unlined. Together with 'lining', the amount of the unlined increases proportionally. One writes and draws and choreographs in order to be able to write, draw, and choreograph even more.

The common line of writing, drawing, and choreographing results from their turning against the concept of a line as determination. They keep a negative relation with the line which they employ to extend the unlined, to leave behind what they just expressed. More generally: writing, drawing, and choreographing tend to find no end, no final and correct text, no last dance, no death dance and no book of the dead. Writing does not follow the recording of a thought, but the movement of thoughts into the unlined. Choreographing may mean not to describe a movement and rehearse it until it is repeatable, but to open up moments of an unlined expression for movement and body language, to search for a movement in order to get rid of holding on to a mode of movement.

The unlined provides the space and time into which one can write and dance, to conceive writing synchronously and necessarily as *Ver-schreiben* (mis-writing *and* dedication), going as *Ver-gehen* (misdeed and deviance). In this sense, the writing or choreographing offends writing *per se* when it aims at holding onto a thought or gesture. If the writing or the line should testify to what has not yet been written, drawn, or done, then they simultaneously testify that the subjects thus described and delineated are waiting for a response: a signature of the nameless readers, those who reply, or the undescribed audience—an unlined audience one does not know, whose answer, reading, or reply always are yet to happen.

Contrary to the notion of moving towards a work via writing, drawing, or choreographing — towards a text, a drawing, a piece —, the common line of these genres also serves to get rid of a work. That which then appears as work is rather less a document and authorised legacy than an estate. The same holds true for the boundaries of the genres themselves, which they tendentially leave behind and abandon with every attempt at defying them, in order to follow the genre of the unlined, the deviation from the line they are drawing. The same stroke and gesture can be described in a linear manner with the contours of different genres: whether a person with a pencil in its hand writes a text on the floor, studies the movements of the fingers, or draws words as motives, does not determine what genre expresses itself. If the institutional or disciplinary attribution were to favour one genre, the difficulty of reading and the illegibility of the definitive demarcation already point out the unlined area in which the common line articulates itself.

Herein, it is not so much something unsayable that has its say than a knowledge about the untenability of the supposedly retained — a knowledge that the line already carries its deviation along, that deviation is inscribed in it. The line does not provide the measure for a deviation from it; rather, it carries in itself the deviation it denotes. The line registers the unlined as an *Ver-zeichnis*, an index of corrections, in which the political credo might lie as the common line of writing, drawing and choreographing.

WHAT IF ...

Krassimira Kruschkova

what if the choreo-graphic
would figure, and

what if figures would
choreo-graph? but

where would be the point
of decision here if

what you attended to were
things which were not visible?

what if there were an inside
of the mirror, and

would there be another realm to
be found and how? but

what if there were no how,
no knowing, no now but

echoing?

What if the constellation of words 'artistic research' today were on everyone's lips? But in which tongue, *lingua*, language? What would be on this artistic research's lips and who would put it there? In whose name would positions be ascribed, attributed to it, and what, then, would not be addressed, expressed? What would we not address and express? Would exactly this 'we'—as a 'thinking' of collaboration—be decisive for what artistic research would be, as process, as product? Would the specificity of artistic research on principle lie in the irreversible tension between process / product, provided that not only the processes here, but also the products had research status? Heaps of problems, it seems. Research problems.

The boom of the term 'artistic research' today is amazing. Artistic research: a constellation of words which we — a bit like René Magritte's *pipe* — can hardly put between our lips, unless as a word, and which often, sometimes too often also moves the tongue of that which we call contemporary in performance practice and theory: as a digression from *doxa*, turning towards the *paradox*, always in uncertainty relations and mostly in collaborative processes. The momentum of collaborative co-tracing instead of re-tracing cannot be determined, it is always coming. If we move in the rhythm of contemporary art and thus also of what artistic research would be, then this always happens under the banner of the interminability of its own project. "There is no *numerus clausus* for arrivants"[1], we could comment with Jacques Derrida's *Politics of Friendship* — and this interminability, which moreover excludes nothing and no-one, is so virulent for our zeitgeist, or better: for our zeit-ghosts today. The concept of friendship also plays a special part in that which would be artistic research.

"Is the friend the same or the other?"[2] is one of the central questions in Derrida's *Politics of Friendship*. And is the accomplice in that which would be artistic research the same, or the other one? As we know, Derrida is about the concept of being-with beyond fraternalism, this side of democracy as a place where it is possible for everyone to be different in equal measure. It is about the contingency of cohesion, about temporary, uncanny alliances, or about Michel Foucault's "egregious families".[3] So, away from fraternalisation, from the family, towards the uncanny elective affinity — and towards the obligatory groundlessness of movement between friends who, according to Foucault, "face each other without weapons or fitting words, without anything that might confirm the sense of the movement that brings them together."[4]

And what if this alone were the epistemological and methodological premises of those who are supposed to do artistic research, who — exactly in precise uncertainty — face each other without weapons or fitting words, without anything that could confirm the sense of the movement that brings them towards each other? For what will artistic research eventually have been if it is true that we will only have known later what we were asking, researching? Is it about speaking with fiery tongues, with words we do not (yet) speak, burning on our lips, for which we, or so it seems, are all ablaze, which possibly kindle something in art and research — mutually or rather, diametrically — that otherwise would not be anything, would not even be there?

For 'aesthetic epistemology'[5] — in the sense of a critique of science — the situative, singular, the special is contemplable, not the general. It not only focuses the singular experiment, the testing, examining, differentiating, i.e., criticising. It criticises, one could say, critique itself; as soon as it normatively empowers itself, it weakens in order to strengthen, criticises normative criteria for experiments, questions its own experimental affinity to research settings as well as its theory affinity. But to what extent does the theory affinity of contemporary performance practice itself constitute a moving force of that which would be artistic research — or is this research sometimes deconstituted by it? Do theory and practice with their interference fundamental for the contemporary concept of performance here sometimes count as mutual alibi and legitimation constructs? Theoretic thinking itself as aesthetic practice — in all its inconsistency and resistance — would be interesting.

For this concept of theory, Paul de Man's creed holds true: "Nothing can overcome the resistance to theory since theory is itself this resistance."[6] For today such theoretical thinking in the mode of resistance to its lingual constitution alone, in continuous review of its own medium, is able to strengthen art with regard to its aesthetic and political positioning. This theoretical thinking has a programmatic weakness, a weakness *for* the strong discursive potential of art in our time of cracked spaces. It conceives theory as expertise, extension and potentialisation of art, as definition work and de-finition, de-finalisation of that which one hardly has called artworks for a long time; rather, artistic works or — often all too matter-of-factly — art projects: de-finition work also as a kind of *desœuvrement* — in the sense of a doing nothing, but also of de-working.

Consequent thinking of resistance and *desœuvrement* on the one hand turns against all too direct artistic appropriation, application of 'discourse' as an instrument and legitimation, against marketing that instrumentalises theory as supplement and alibi for artistic practice. On the other hand, it is important to work against discourse-refractoriness, against the metaphysics of interiority and melancholic resignation in the face of the ominous curse of the cursory, of the performative which supposedly cannot be caught up with by discourse at all, since this resignation claims a body not contaminated, unaffected by language and the metaphysics of its presence. In this sense, artistic researchers would let theory and practice interfere resistantly, without any chance of being absorbed by each other.

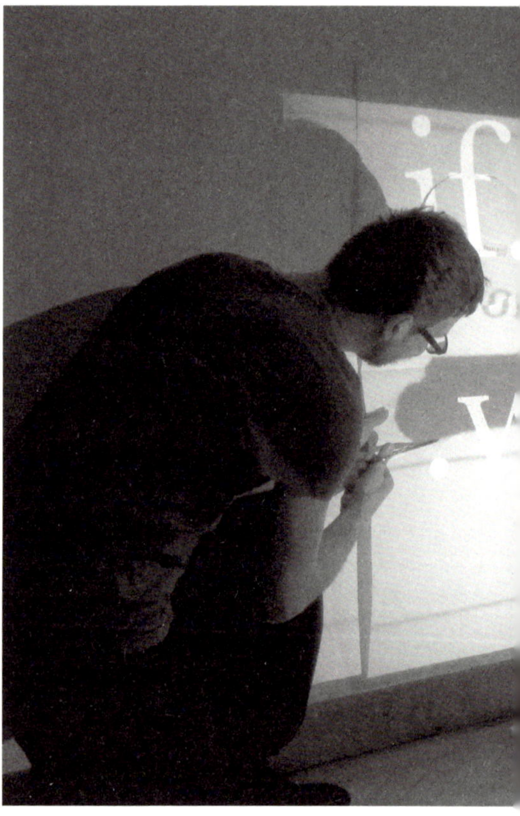

Also manifested in this is the contingency, the ability not to be absorbed in an act, the potentiality: at the same time as more than one and no option any more, as interest in options not given. This ever temporary disintegration in order to escape the consumability of the implemented, the redeemed, always to problematise integrity, does have integrity, is interesting. Interesting and endowed with integrity are the singular disintegrations of predetermined, determining entities. Interesting and endowed with integrity the question: how much research does art bear — and how much does it require, has it always

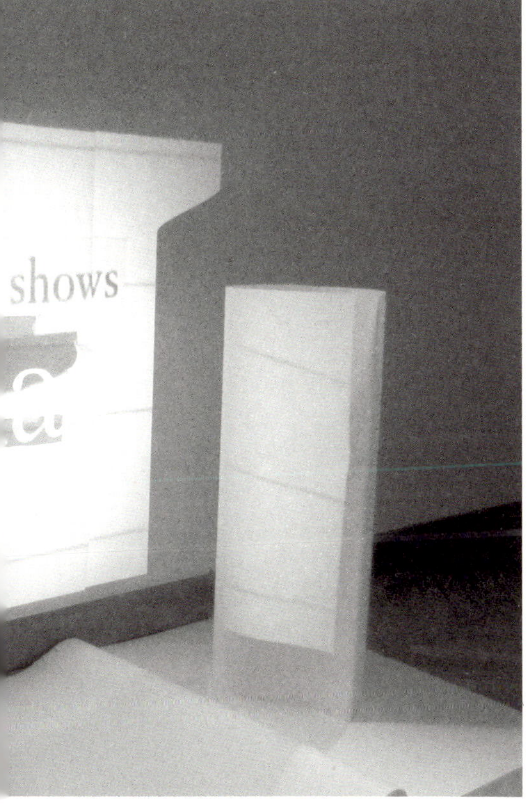

required? Especially when "researching means not to know yet what one is doing."[7] So, can one — beyond camouflage — seriously write applications for artistic research, also beyond bureaucratic pre-formulations and application prose? How to confront the paradox that artistic research would have to develop its methods, or rather its theories, in the course of its research work, while they should already be described in the research application?

Which powers decide whether artistic research takes place at all, or not? Provided that it should always take place in a mode of legitimation crisis, in critical self-reflection, and criticise and also de-control the criteria of its possibility conditions? What, then, would control, context, consequence, continuity, convention, conjuncture mean here? As if the prefix *con-* with all its alternative spellings (*com, co, col*) were the most important and therefore also the most contradictory prefix of what artistic research would be; the prefix *con-* and the conjunctions, the correlative, paratactical ones, not the subordinating, hypotactical ones. Instead of *conjuncture boom*, paratactical, collaborative conjunctions and *conjunctive mood*, the mode of possibility — but in this world, not beyond: a *what-if* mode.

---

1) Jacques Derrida, *Politics of Friendship,* (Trans.) George Collins, London and New York: Verso, 2005, p. x [*Politiques de l'amitié,* Paris: Galilée, 1994].

2) Derrida, [1994] 2005, p. 4.

3) Michel Foucault, 'Was ist ein Autor?', in Fotis Jannidis, Gerhard Lauer, Matías Martínez (Eds.), *Texte zur Theorie der Autorschaft,* Stuttgart: Reclam, 2000, p. 201 ['Qu'est-ce qu'un auteur?', in *Dits et Écrits,* Vol. 1: 1954-1969, Paris: Gallimard, 1994].

4) Michel Foucault, 'Von der Freundschaft als Lebensweise', in *Von der Freundschaft. Michel Foucault im Gespräch,* Berlin: Merve, 2005, p. 87 ['De l'amité comme mode de vie', in *Le Nouvel Observateur,* No. 1021, Paris, 1984].

5) Cf. Dieter Mersch, *Epistemologies of Aesthetics,* Zurich and Berlin: Diaphanes, 2015 [Epistemologien des Asthetischen, 2015].

6) Paul de Man, *Resistance to Theory,* Minneapolis: University of Minnesota Press, 1986.

7) Hans-Jörg Rheinberger in the course of a conversation with the author during his lecture in the framework of *IDLENESS — A lazy concept of a lecture series* at Tanzquartier Wien on 25.10.2013.

Brandon LaBelle

THE THING

The time flows; it passes — there is a gentle intensity — what will happen next? Where is the beginning, that begins as a start: a break from one to the next, a reshaping of materials, a restless collection by which to initiate trajectories of movement — the coming into being of a practice. Practices as articulations, a figuring that forms itself in and around cultural languages. Can we disorder such languages — do they not call out for agitation, for a performative elaboration, displacement, invigoration? This body that moves according to existing principles, histories, forms, and that edges against the unknown, the formless — a monstrosity. To grow weak within the boundaries of particular structures in order to bend around their forceful presence; growing, a mutation: a pulling along of these languages into new formations. A *monstering:* a hybrid figuring — this thing, suddenly alive, emerging and giving way to the ugly: a tearing, a gaping wound, a loss — are not deviant practices emerging as defacements and disorganisations, a muddying of legibility? Can I read what this figure produces? A reading along-with; a text of wounds, a disfiguring which forces another type of attention: the attention aligned with monstrosity and the lost — a sympathetic attention, but one also of terror. Do I dare look at this emergence of the disfigured? It invites me,

This text was written within the context of the Choreo-graphic Figures *workshop held on 30th and 31st July, 2016 in Vienna. For the workshop, I decided to take the role of a performative witness — or 'wit(h)ness' — writing alongside the different group exercises and actions developed and explored by the other participants over the course of two days. From such a position, I felt myself equally involved yet through a different medium, something more internal, more descriptive and linguistic but no less behavioural and embodied. The text included here was written over the course of the second day of the workshop, and has been only slightly edited.*

yet according to a logic of feverish desire — the desire for transformation, for release and for freedom: a radical freedom, one of pure intensity; the horizon of monsters. The monster that locates me within a field of ambivalence -- I cannot look, and yet I cannot turn away. I am mesmerised by this emergence of the thing, *the thing* which I cannot hold, but which I cannot forget. A monster-logic; a thing-body. Practices of deviation: this mouth that speaks, that out-pours, that over-runs itself and language; the arm that flings itself, that gestures, is gestured by this monster-logic; the leg, the torso, the back-to-back, the mingling and the friction: a vibration that is the thing. The incomplete body; the incoherent fragment. The time begins: it is the fragment of another voice, a resonance. Back to front, front to back. A break — a poetics. I hear it; it moves into the air, shifts the molecular arrangement, retuning its density, its potential. A figure of *wavering convergence* — an unsteady oscillation to which he and she, them, and those participate; join without knowing for sure: an aesthetic production — what may we create from this instant of convergence? From within this instance, this poetics? An irruption of an imaginary force: I desire you; I turn toward the gap, the break — this resonance; I am monster. Babble. Growing like an organic mutation; loudly invading the scene: we turn, we roll around, we run; its coming, its stalking me — I am caught. Where is it? Inside / outside; folding / unfolding. It appears, but is never stable. I cannot enter into a relationship with it, this thing. It resists and forces resistance — it incites resistance as a form of being, a condition of being with / without. Inside / outside — this relation which is never stable, but is a cut that separates, suddenly, the flesh, and thereby creates a duality; suddenly, there is one and another, on either side of the cut. The wound is a relation of no relation, but one of separation, loss, and of pain: it is a violence. This cut comes alive as a thing; it acts without being an identity; it produces an effect. One and another, a world-making event. Can we inhabit the cut as a space? To take up residence within the wound? To occupy this duality by suturing the break — the monster is such a suture; it is a stitch, a figure made from the wound; a scar. The scar as a production made from the wound; it brings the wound into language; aligning pain and violence within the logic of the monster. We dwell within the wound, as an event of rupture and longing, and through such inhabitation we suture the gap into a form, a new formation that is the scar. Stitch by stitch; a cloth across the body. Disfigure. The monster is without relations; it is a lonely figure, this thing. Yet it is made from multiple sources — but it brutalises them! — it is made from a violation of materials, an abuse of the rational. The monster is an organic abnormality, and is always on the side of illegibility: it makes us faint, this thing. I cannot look at the wounds; they are too terrifying — they gush, they ooze, they are horrific. Can wounds be decorated? Can they be worshipped? They are often participating in practices of ritual: sacrifices. Bodies are intimately related to rituals, to wounding, to practices of sacrifice — it is the body that functions as symbolic currency; it is given over within this scene of ritual — a primary performance of exchange; the body as a medium for honouring the gods, for keeping the social order.

Does not dance relate itself to ritual, to the body as medium of exchange, as symbolic currency? Is not dance directed by forces of primary violence — to wound the body, to exhaust it as resource. It researches the fragility of the body, its vulnerabilities and weaknesses, as well as its strengths and volumes, its muscularity and potentialities; it is a thinking-in-action, action-thought. It is always exhausting itself; it must occupy a threshold to exhaustion, to relate itself to the limits of a body. It researches these limits: it moves along this border, which is also close to madness. *A breaking down.* Dance expresses this break down as the beginning of a new production — the production of the illegible, the unnamable. It exercises the right of self-possession, to say: *I give myself over to the limits of my body;* I enact a type of breaking down of myself, a ritual of loss: to become *thing.* I go mad for you. Madness as a zone of production, a vocabulary of elasticity, of agony and pleasure, of mimicry and fragmentation.

Shall we follow? Shall we turn away? A movement implies another; incites a following, a reply, a second thought. To model the ceaseless flow of life-in-action; to diagram and draw the knowledge of the limit, rendering it a field of force. Form-forces, shattered objects — the animation of crossed-out limits. It draws awareness to life as movement, this thing — to soundings and resonances, the vibrations and flutterings from which this body finds support, tunes itself. Fall, faint. Recoil, relax. Repose. Latent. Its energy. Rise, collapse. Screech. Amplify. Release, now, then. Sometimes — to start again. Patter. Fluctuation; thrash. Pluck, poke; a flagellation, a constant drumming. Tapping, hitting — he hits the skin; the step. Skin to object; a punctuation. Contact, interact, then pause. A figure of fluctuating coupling — this intensity, thrust. Hit. A prodding. The matter in the hand; object becoming tool; the instrument that enables and that integrates into the body new dynamics of reach and attenuation, sounding and setting in motion things and surroundings. Brushing. Raking; a fluttering, stirring that shivers the order of things. An array; of remains, and ghostly elements — from which does this arise? The hand that holds, the matter that is held, the air that motions, a swaying to and fro, and the other, the one who hears and continues to hear: this one over-here. One and then another. An array becoming a constellation of resources: something happens, something is built from such weak materials, held in place by the movements that pass their force along, and are passed, by the hand that holds and then lets go. Rippling, echoing; repeating, and then again. A balance, tenuous and sensitive to the skin of itself, as it is brushed, prodded from its place, made to accept the silences and the colours of others, always already othered by the force of another, by this hand and then another, which may also be a voice, a repeated phrase, suddenly, sending itself into this configuration. It stares back. It climbs. It is always active — it cannot withstand. Within every movement one may find the expression of an interaction — to set itself apart. To draw itself into a position of outstanding beauty. It pokes. It proceeds; is a thread and then a line; a ribbon draped between voices; a speech of nothing and everything, that becomes dialogical without knowing for sure. It bends; it is bent, massaged and rhythmed by what it sees, feels, by the motions of itself: a construction held by itself. It is a pure interiority exposed as an outside; this array, this constellation of form and force — it has the dimension of being a heart: driven, this pulse. That doesn't want to stop; which cannot imagine an end. A sharing of thoughts: pause, reflect, consider — this other that is next to me; that is next to, and along with. I question; I give thought, a thought of attention. Might the name perform to mark something? To give alert to a moment of noticing; attention for a process of signifying what is happening. The naming of the figure; the figuring of the name: I recognise this, or I notice: a differentiation amidst the non-differentiated. It enables a discovery and a confirmation; conversation — which is always feverish, translated; walking, coupling, a gathering: laughter, and the *wild talk* of something else. To listen, to stress, and to be stressed with others, and the othering that defines me.

The start is always deferred; the vitality of the event exceeds itself — it requires its own spilling-over, an excessive formation — the temporal as always greater than what it measures. Shake. Give volume to; recede, intensify — it is pure agitation; this festivity of body-knowledge. It takes over, it invades the scene: it is always a feast, a gathering of mouths, intestines, guts and gestures, a voracious capacity — the body that consumes, to produce an economy of events, ecstasies, humour. The floor that is a table that is a sound that is a language that is a vitality, where fragments become whole, and echoes elongate into tonalities of place and person, as hesitations and horizons for dreams: a dreaming-work; I start here, which is immediately elsewhere, rich with vitality, with a wish to become something else. A dreaming-work by which to find the materials for other conditions; which leads me into languages of birds, of metals, flowers, and of trees — languages of blindness and of disagreement; a politics of listening and of voicing: may I speak? Is there a route, a path by which to articulate an expansive meaningfulness, the meaning of this body as it reaches, as it vacillates, sleeps or meditates; a poetics of disappearance, a rewriting, joyful trouble. I push; I excite. I pass it on; give it away. Take it; it is for you — for the extension that is you; the I-you, and then: pass it on, or over, across and into, the density and the overcoming of capital enterprise. The capital that searches for this event; but which slips, loses traction — I push; I excite; I pass it on. Producing a rhythm of failure: I cannot live up to the directive of capital desire, I always let go too soon; I have no sense for enterprise. I bark; I sleep. I dream.

What goes on inside? Is there a figure that takes shape as the unconscious of other figures? A shadow-figure that hovers behind the one in the open — a figure ghosting whatever appears? A figure that tries to escape: a dreaming-figure of wild ideas, a figure that could become a world, an alien world. The unconscious taking shape, and which is always on the threshold to nightmare. It always goes back to walking: the primary step, the step on the way to somewhere, that takes the body elsewhere, and that teaches us lessons of groundedness and flight, of temporality, of departure and arrival; this step as an education of the possibilities and responsibilities of location, locality, and exile, a homelessness lurking under the step, and that also dreams of other places — the step is a primary event: of meeting the other. While I may stand face to face, the step always brings me into contact with the stranger. It is a movement that always leads one against and across borders: I become a foreigner as soon as I step; dislocated, rootless, as a tendency of migration. The step always leads somewhere, even nowhere. It leads into language, into dance, into a choreography of relations. Do we ever truly arrive? Is not arrival another form of departure? One nested inside the other; one a figure of the other. The figure of departure; the figure of exile and of closure; the figure that searches for a destination — a point of pause, respite. The figure that continues, and that accumulates memories of the distant and the foreign; the figure of welcome and of refusal; of lost words and alien phrases. The one nested in the other; step by step; step after step — forward, then backward: the line around which these steps move, travel. An itinerant production; to alienate the body from itself, from its surroundings — I walk away from myself; I take a step away, so as to return with knowledge of the outside. Back and forth; inside and outside; two feet that, in stepping, produce relations — a choreography by which to articulate the body in pieces: a subject of the world.

Can you read me? *What*?

Birds. Madness.

HOW-NESS

Alongside *when-ness* and *where-ness,* the principle of *how-ness* has played a key role in our enquiry — it indicates the qualitative-processual dynamics within our shared artistic exploration, directing attention to an affective realm of forces and intensities operating before, between and beneath the more readable gestures of artistic practice. Etymologically, *how* can refer to the manner or way in which something is done: by what means or method; in what state or condition; to what extent or degree. *How* indicates activity, the unfolding of a process. Its terrain is articulated through verbs and adverbs. Process — an act of *going forward*, the condition of being carried on. Process can be conceived as a series of actions for producing change or development, or in turn directed towards some task or target. *How do you do that?* The question *how* is often coupled with the answer 'like so'. The sharing of process can be approached as the trade or swapping of techniques or ways of doing things, a form of skills transfer or knowledge exchange. For some, *how* can involve an augmentative and accumulative undertaking; increasing the range or repertoire of one's process toolkit, adding new knowledge and practices gleaned from another discipline. There is a pedagogical aspect to this modality of *how:* observe the imperative of the step-by-step guide or technical manual, united in a shared attempt to communicate and teach the procedural knowledge of *how-to*.

In some disciplines, the principle of *how* is instilled through training, the perfection of a notionally correct way of doing things, whilst in other contexts *how* emerges through self-discovery, is necessarily idiosyncratic. *How* can be proper and improper, diligent or deviant. Act of revelation: the (s)*howing* of the *how*. At one level, the *how-to* approach attempts to demystify a given process, render it as a succession of instructions or stages, to lay it factually bare. Yet, there are things that cannot be so easily explained, that refuse to be reduced to a map or guide. Beyond the *know-what* of the encyclopedia, consider the experiential, those embodied forms of tacit knowledge or even *know-how*; resistant to being shown or said, that only can be performed or practised. Indeed, how do we account for those processes in which not knowing, uncertainty, trial and error, feeling one's way and contingency perform a significant role? As Henk Borgdorff says, "The erratic nature of creative discovery — of which unsystematic drifting, serendipity, chance inspirations and clues form an integral part—is such that a methodological justification is not easy to codify … it involves doing unpredictable things, and this implies intuition and some measure of randomness. Research is more like exploration than following a firm path."[1] Our toolkit of approaches is intended less as a *how-to* guide and offered more in the spirit of *how-else?* We seek to activate a curious *how* that wants to play and explore: *however*—no matter how, in whatever way.

There is more than one way to get from A to B; different modalities of being and doing open up different ways of perceiving oneself and one's surrounds. For Paolo Soleri, "Becoming is mute in the absence of Howness. Howness does not need Whatness and Whyness to be operational; in fact, in the absence of Howness, intellection is absent. Howness needs only Space. Howness is the cavorting of Space. Eventually it is Howness that gives birth to Whatness and, a posteriori, Whyness. The desirable is, in a way, Howness that, a posteriori, finds purpose (Whatness, Whyness)"[2] (⟶ *Where-ness*). *How* is less the destination, rather the journey travelled. The best way is not always the shortest; one's route should never get too fixed. *Process* etymologically draws on the Latin *processus*, meaning 'a going forward, to advance, to progress', to proceed. Yet *cede*—from *cedere*—also means to yield, to go from. *Pro-cede*: to go forward then by yielding, by leaving behind. In these terms, process is not determined by end or destination, not goal-oriented, not target or *telos* driven. Our *how* does not run a straight course, rather it requires the *deviation from the line*. Disciplinary practices can be inhabited tactically in ways that swerve or redirect their logic, so as to be detoured, *détourned*.[3] Here is the *how* of "the minor (that) works the major from within."[4] The sharing of *how* can involve the undoing, unlearning, de-schooling of one's habitual ways of doing things (⟶ *Becoming Undisciplinary*). What can be activated is a known-yet-not knowledge closer to Sarat Maharaj's articulation of the flux of *no-how*, "distinct from the circuits of *know-how* that run on clearly spelled out methodological steel tracks. It is the rather unpredictable surge and ebb of potentialities and propensities […] No-how embodies indeterminacy, an 'any space whatever' that brews up, spreads, inspissates."[5]

We practice *no-how* in the generation of our *figures* (⟶ *Figuring >< Figure*, ⟶ *Figures*)—not so much the recollection of how we did *this* and *this* and *this*, but rather through a shared quest for a *how-ness* that will give rise again to the *figure* but in a way that we don't yet fully know. *How* operates beyond the visible, along another register of presence. For Daniel Stern, 'dynamic forms of vitality' "concern the 'How', the manner, and the style, not the 'What' or the 'Why'."[6] We strive towards the qualitative *how-ness* of a *figure's* force or vitality, not the *what-ness* of its form. Here, following Erin Manning, "The 'how' of the work … is its commanding form. This 'how' is emergent each time anew."[7] *How* attends to qualitative difference, to nuance—etymologically meaning a 'slight difference, shade of colour', originally used in reference to the different colours of the clouds, mist or vapour (⟶ *Practice of Notation: Clicking*). Like the weather, *how* can change from one moment to the next, is always in the process of *becoming*, never being. We cultivate attention towards the *how* of the *now … now … now … now … now …* (⟶ *Practices of Attention*).

How-ness also describes an enquiry into the state or condition of a person, object or thing.[8] Beyond the empty pleasantries of 'How do you do?' — with the 'correct' answer often being one of reciprocity — engagement with the *how-ness* of the other can be approached as an empathetic, even ethical imperative (⟶ *On Sedimentations of Sensitivities*). How are you? For Spinoza, *Ethics* involves attendance to the *how-ness* of experience, tuning into the vectoral passage from one affective state to another. Beyond attending to the hot or cold, the painful or the pleasurable, his ethical task is to differentiate between affirmative and diminutive affects, between the joyful and the saddening.[9] Beyond the realm of drives and desires, ethics reveals that there are choices to be made in *how* one acts and affects, in turn how one is acted upon or affected. Here, as Manning asserts, "Lodged neither in the human nor in the object, thought propels creativity in the activity of the in-between that makes relation felt, activating the 'how' of the event, inciting inquiry, curiosity, play."[10] *How* invites an epistemological as well as ethical approach, encourages an enquiry-oriented attitude to self and world, a questioning stance. Yet, as Borgdorff observes, "research (and not only artistic research) often resembles an uncertain quest in which the questions or topics only materialize during the journey, and may often change as well."[11] Conceived through the prism of *how*, the following pages reveal the chronological arc of our questioning from 'How do we start?' to 'How do you read the book'? Our aim is not to delimit the question to a specific answer (*how* > *so*), but as a means for opening up new fields of performative exploration.[12]

---

1) Henk Borgdorff, 'The Production of Knowledge in Artistic Research', in Michael Biggs and Henrik Karlsson (Eds.), *The Routledge Companion to Research in the Arts*, London: Routledge, 2011, p. 57.

2) Paolo Soleri, Entry #34 — 'Howness', in *What if? Quaderno 2 — Space as Reality*, Scottsdale: Coșanti Press, 2004.

3) Michel de Certeau reflects on *how* indigenous Indians, "often used the laws, practices, and representations that were imposed on them by force or by fascination to ends other than those of their conquerors; they made something else out of them; they subverted them from within — not by rejecting them or by transforming them […] They metaphorized the dominant order: they made it function in another register". Cf. Michel de Certeau, *The Practice of Everyday Life*, Berkeley: University of California Press, 1984, p. 32.

4) Erin Manning, *The Minor Gesture*, Durham: Duke University Press, 2016, p. 1.

5) Sarat Maharaj, 'Know-how and No-How: Stopgate Notes On "Method" in Visual Art as Knowledge Production', in *Art & Research*, Vol. 2, Issue 2, Spring 2009, p. 3. In conversation with Francisco J. Varela, Sarat Maharaj differentiates between "'know what' — living by ready-made moral rules, as opposed to 'know-how' — uncertainties of ethical creativity", in 'Ahamkara: 'Particules Élémentaires of First-person Consciousness', in Florian Dombois *et al* (Eds.), *Intellectual Birdhouse: Artistic Practice as Research*, Amsterdam: Rodopi, 2011, p. 70. He adds, "know-how springs from 'just doing it' — hit-or-miss trying, tinkering, sticking things together to see if they work, a kind of non-sequential, assemblagist logic", p. 74.

6) Daniel Stern, *Forms of Vitality: Exploring Dynamic Experience in Psychology, the Arts, Psychotherapy and Development*, Oxford and New York: Oxford University Press, 2010, p. 8.

7) Erin Manning, *Always More Than One: Individuation's Dance*, Durham: Duke University Press, 2013, p. 139.

8) *'Being-how' or 'howness'* (Wie-sein) are also Heideggerian terms. Cf. Martin Heidegger, *The Basic Problems of Phenomenology*, Bloomington and Indianapolis: Indiana University Press, 1988, p. 205.

9) Cf. Baruch Spinoza, *Ethics*, Oxford: Oxford University Press, 2000; Gilles Deleuze, Spinoza: *Practical Philosophy*, (Trans.) Robert Hurley, San Francisco: City Lights Books, 1988.

10) Erin Manning, *Relationscapes: Movement, Art, Philosophy*, Cambridge, Mass. and London: The MIT Press, 2009, p. 225.

11) Borgdorff, 2011, p. 56.

12) These 'how' questions (gleaned from conversational transcripts) are also used within our live explorations as playful provocations (⟶ *Practice of Attention: Transquesting*).

How do we start? | How do you prepare? | How do you perceive? | How do you inhabit the space? | How do you deconstruc it different? | How has it felt so far? | How do you make a full stop move? | How much percentage of the body is water? | How it feel to be made to be the screen? | How did you interact with it? | How do we describe? | How might the conversation you not block another's light? | How distant do the practices need to be? | How do we collaborate? | How do you position yo do we do things? | How do we talk about it? | How do you know the meaning of choreography? | How do you attend to the field without the use of light? | How far from your circle of concentration can the focus be drawn? | How do you decide what you keep your attention only in what is happening? | How can I speak about what I am doing? | How do you move through about diving? | How is this distilled into a vocabulary? | How might I begin something if I am beginning alone? | How might I l | How far can we stretch each of those malleable containers? | How do we play? | How do you approach the other in the space? | | How do I know when someone wants a different kind of provocation? | How do we articulate this 'vectoral passage' — to | How do I proceed? | How do I feel as a physical entity? | How do I feel when I move objects around the space? | How do I conti find a form for the thing that is also resisting form-making? | How do you retain it? | How do you make a relation between ch | How do things come together? | How would you describe the quality? | How narrowly do we see language? | How do we appr change? | How am I seeing it? | How do you gauge when? | How do you repeat? | How do you repeat the feeling when you disco what we are declaring as our enquiry forward? | How do we bring it into context? | How do we get better? | How does lang towards something that could be shared? | How early is this in the evolution of a working method? | How do we trace this? | that and make that part of a process? | How does one material relate to another? | How is it complicated by other forces in p different configurations by calling? | How much does it change everything? | How am I doing? | How am I here? | How do I lo poetic level? | How do we make a negotiation with more theoretical research? | How do we deal with language for things tha it? | How does it stay with you? | How do you articulate that? | How can you condense that? | How can punctuation notat what I just saw? | How do I put things on stage? | How is this a form of notation? | How will it resonate? | How is one help me now? | How does one remember what the important parts are? | How do we want to talk to each other? | How do we these exercises without recourse to language? | How is it affecting the space? | How do I make noise? | How do I get into a cre pay attention to the periphery? | How do we map that? | How might we do this? | How do you recognise the moments when si transferable or transportable is this to other contexts? | How do things have to shift? | How would you spell it? | How woul | How do you pay attention to the register of sensation that is happening beneath the readable? | How do you do this and ma stage my ascent? | How can we distinguish between observation and attention? | How do we find a language to describe feel when you turn it over in your mouth? | How does it sound when you try not to articulate meaning with it? | How subjectiv it? | How would this happen? | How do we make those links? | How would they inflect it? | How does notation have diff How do we develop a notation system for this? | How to make it more visible? | How can relations keep things moving? | Ho can our gestures indicate towards vitality? | How can we find gestures that correlate with the force of a movement and not conditions for *figuring* to happen? | How do you set up the conditions? | How do you create the self? | How does the self em material do we need to provide? | How much and what kind of footnoting do we need? | How precise are we being? | How r figural, figura, figurative? | How do you perform that? | How might different performed *figures* create the conditions for diff this need fleshing out? | How has it emerged through practice? | How do you know? | How do you now develop that move forward? | How does Stern describe content modality? | How does Brandstetter describe the *figure*? | How can you end up w declinate the nouns? | How is the ablative used? | How does this give *figuring* back to the *figure*? | How are we doing? | How c for another? | How did I end up there? | How did we get here? | How does this manifest in the space? | How does it go experience? | How do you give resonance to what you were doing? | How do you allow the past to reverberate in the present? | the *figuring*? | How could it be more vulnerable? | How does the aligning body morph into a diagrammatic praxis in its own | How much do you avoid? | How can I learn from others? | How do you distinguish the verbal-linguistic from the bodily-kinestl attention practice cultivate the capacity to act? | How are the attention practices used in the score? | How is the relation c does one access the body as material? | How am I becoming the material through action? | How is the qualitative difference? | be activated? | How am I going to operate? | How is A a separate category to F? | How is A a separate category to W? | How is How do you become fluent with a particular marking system in order to be able to use it? | How is it performed? | How do you they operated? | How do I talk about what is happening? | How is it possible to extend this to the public? | How do you agree? | of agitation? | How do you create a swerve of energy? | How is exhaustion bound up with that? | How do you find your clos organised? | How do I share my vibration? | How do I live? | How do I compose my life? | How is it evolving, forming, finding do we avoid a hierarchy? | How do you perceive the role of agency within the creative process? | How much does some do I move from touching to drawing? | How do I make that materiality become alive? | How do we define it? | How does it s organise them? | How do we use the score? | How many different choices are being made? | How much did you feel like you already? | How was your idea of time moving? | How do familiarity and expectation organise time? | How long should this g How do you re-activate the quality? | How is it different? | How do you negotiate the bigger picture? | How can this be ev we noticing the *figuring*? | How do we notice? | How do we mark? | How do we differentiate between warming-up and atte into relation? | How do these have a generative function? | How do we unpack this within a discursive, ling might that be shared? | How do you become synchronised through a shared movement? | How might that translate? | How is ness give movement a quality of purpose? | How might we disrupt the sense of solidity? | How can the body resist? | How does rated? | How long does it take to cultivate an adequate response? | How do you maintain the nature of the enquiry? | How do artist? | How could that look? | How much do you know what the others do? | How can one format become another? | How isn't visible? | How could you approach that? | How do I move beyond the realm of description? | How can I project into your ? | How near can you get when someone wants to not be in the spotlight? | How much do I have to concentrate? | How long do ghts? | How do you make them appear? | How you think about the movement of the spectator? | How does Héléne Cixous talk m beginning in collaboration? | How can I explain this? | How do you remember? | How do you approach it again and again? read receptivity? | How do I know when someone might be engaged in something that they don't want to be disturbed from? ozist phrase? | How is it that I am being? | How is it that I am now? | How are we both what we make and also autonomous of it? w do you find the means for articulating a process? | How do we show the *figuring*? | How do you deal with it? | How do you graphic? | How can we actualise that through practice? | How it is done? | How do you present that? | How do you feed it back? ething? | How do we record? | How do we say this because it feels complex? | How do we do things with words? | How would it ething? | How do you repeat this? | How about we do actions that nobody sees? | How would I then go on? | How is this moving ? | How do I write? | How do I write with the body? | How do I write in space? | How might elements of this process be moved does it last? | How useful is it to anchor these things? | How do you say something without describing it? | How do you harness can there still be precision? | How can you be very precise and yet still have opacity? | How can these things be brought into ething and remember it? | How do we find forms of notation? | How can you transfer it into writing? | How do you bring it to a rally cannot grasp? | How might we interpret the notion of notation? | How do you record what you are doing in order to share oral sense of a space? | How could I notate what is happening here now just using commas and full stops? | How do I remember formed into another form? | How do we want to construct the room? | How would we differentiate the terms? | How do they ch other? | How do we treat each other? | How would you represent it? | How do I engage in a space? | How do I engage with ess? | How do you attend to the micro and the macro? | How do you attend to both what you are doing individually and also g together becomes collaborative? | How do you recognise the moments when collaborative activity starts to dissipate? | How e it? | How can you invite perception shifts to happen? | How do I perceive the body? | How do you share a sense of a practice? w do you bring this to awareness? | How do you pay attention? | How do you notice without being too self-aware? | How do I gs? | How much difference does it make if you describe your process with verbs and try to avoid nouns? | How does language otations? | How necessary is this? | How can it be shaped? | How can we do something together? | How do we decide to perform ions? | How do you mark something when it has the capacity to disrupt the perceptual conditions that you are interested in? | ace things on the page? | How figurative do we need to be? | How do things emerge? | How is it that we understand that? | How rm? | How are we referring to the emergence of the *figure*? | How do our *figures* come into being? | How do you create the w do you cultivate a critical subjectivity? | How do we know ourselves in the world? | How much background or contextual gnal towards the instability and mutability of the flows and forces within practice? | How is the *figure* in relation to figuration, riences of *figuring*? | How might the choreo-graphic figure be a system of diagrammatic notation in-and-of itself? | How might rial? | How do you flesh this out, deepen it? | How much time is there? | How far do we still have to go? | How do we move that vocabulary? | How does water manifest in the form of ice? | How does motion transit, de- and transfigure forms? | How do you eed? | How is it possible to open it up? | How does this connect to the mode of address? | How would I be able to create a space onse to responsibility? | How delicate do we need to be? | How do you address someone? | How do you invite somebody into an o we do this than through touching and through thinking? | How do we name it? | How does the *figure* emerge in fidelity to w is thinking feeling? | How much force can it withstand? | How do we keep the vital forces alive? | How much do you overlap? w can we think about this practice as a writing practice? | How do we read? | How can we make space again? | How does an tion practices to the *figures*? | How do I put all this together? | How is it going to work? | How would you evaluate that? | How ey relate to each other? | How are you acquainted with the score? | How do we build it up? | How can the medium of language ate category to F? | How do I notate? | How does this witnessing feedback into the practice? | How does the name function? | Iow does perception work? | How fluent am I with the system? | How is it generated? | How do they come into play? | How are vould you do it? | How are they different? | How do you clear objects of their histories? | How do you harness the productivity do I meet it again? | How do I end it? | How to avoid doing too much? | How much does it still need? | How is living matter ? | How do I understand one experience by translating it into a new experience? | How can one thing become another? | How nunicate through the title? | How do you stop naming? | How might you communicate that on a page? | How does it feel? | How v does it need to shake? | How do I become the property of light? | How do you pass from one *figure* to another? | How do we fresh? | How much did you feel like you had already done it before? | How much are you operating in a familiar, habitual zone v do you stir things up after there has been a lull or ebb of energy? | How do you capture a sense of vitality in a fixed form? | ds a score? | How do you begin to come together? | How are the practices of attention used? | How do they operate? | How are ices? | How is this used in the score? | How does this relate to aesthetic research? | How are these different practices brought ? | How do we set out this conceptual arc? | How do we define fluctuating grouping? | How do you read the book?

FIGURING >< FIGURE

FIGURING >< FIGURE

Choreo-graphic Figures: Deviations from the Line attends to the experiential 'knowing-thinking-feeling' — and *un*knowing — within collaborative artistic exploration. Central to this enquiry is an attempt to find ways of better understanding the qualitative how-ness (⟶ *How-ness*) within the process of artistic 'sense-making' — those barely perceptible micro-movements at the cusp of awareness: the dynamic movements of decision-making, the thinking-in-action, the durational 'taking place' of something happening live — and for asserting epistemological value therein. Our research enquiry has involved a shift from the realm of demarcated disciplinary gestures (⟶ *Becoming Undisciplinary*) towards an affective process-realm of forces and intensities (which we call *figuring*) operating before (*pre-*), between (*inter-*), below (*infra-*) and also within (*intra-*) the more readable gestures in artistic practice. We ask: how can we develop systems of notation and performativity (*choreo-graphic figures*) for sharing this often hidden or undisclosed aspect of the creative process? How can we communicate the instability and mutability of the flows and forces especially within collaborative exploration, without 'fixing' that which is inherently dynamic and contingent as a literal sign? Indeed, what is at stake in the attempt to do so?

How do you attend to the thing that isn't visible, what other realms are there to find? Resonance. Reverberation. Tremulous vibration. It is sometimes hard to see the relatively imperceptible — this quivering edge when something is happening. Magnifying the minor. Starting to look nearer or closer. How we move when we move: there is tone and velocity and rhythm; there are changes of state.

We use the term *figuring* to describe those small yet transformative energies and experiential shifts within the artistic process that are often hard to discern, but which ultimately shape or steer the evolving action. *Figuring* refers to the perception of indeterminate affective intensities felt as a field of forces — minor revelations or epiphanies, shivering full of presence; unbidden openings: those risings that give way to emergence. We conceive the event of *figuring* as a qualitative shift, the sense or awareness that 'something is happening' perceptible at the level of intensity, experienced *as if* a change of taste, colour, or perhaps even of textural density. *Figuring* makes its appearance, for example, in the amplification or ebbing of intensity. Sliding. Sinking. Simmering. A change in tack or pace: lingering, longing. An appeal to do something: to stop, interrupt, to begin again. We experience this sensation of change or transition in state, presence or affordance as analogous to the subtle turn in the direction of the wind or tide, or in the shimmering flight path of a *murmuration* of starlings. *Figuring's* sensation of sensing comprises more than just visual perception or any singular sensory modality; it is experienced rather more as a general impression registered holistically at the level of body-mind, the intermingling of self-world. Whilst our conceptualisation of *figuring* is based on what has been *felt* during the unfolding of our own collaborative artistic process, it resonates with other theoretical models that also seek to account for dynamic intensity, shifting the focus from a preoccupation with meaning and signification towards questions of sensation, feeling, even *aisthesis.*[1] The rising and ebbing of energy or force within *figuring's* felt intensity can be conceived in Deleuzian-Spinozist terms as awareness of the vectoral passage from one affective state to another, specifically the passage from a more-to-less or less-to-more state. For Gilles Deleuze, this passage can be experienced as "a continuous variation in the form of an increase-diminution-increase-diminution of the power of acting or the force of existing."[2] Alongside the rising and ebbing (increase-diminution) of affect, *figuring* can be felt as a generative surge or opening, the breathing edges of a live coming-into-existence. This *opening surge* might be considered in relation to Martin Heidegger's concept of *poiesis:* a 'bringing forth', "a threshold occasion, a moment of ecstasis when something moves away from its standing as one thing to become another", like "the blooming of a blossom, the coming-out of a butterfly from a cocoon, the plummeting of a waterfall when the snow begins to melt."[3] For Sarat Maharaj, this "amorphous pre-process state — an emerging creative splurge, so to speak — is the phase of 'ur-utterance' … an eruptive, self-spawning capacity that goes beyond the 'given' — a self-raising, self-erasing drive that transcends it."[4] According to Maharaj, this 'obscure surge' "throws up new experiential and epistemic intensities, objects and dimensions that overshoot the 'given'. It brings into being unforeseeable possibilities — that we cannot have anticipated or known or scripted beforehand."[5]

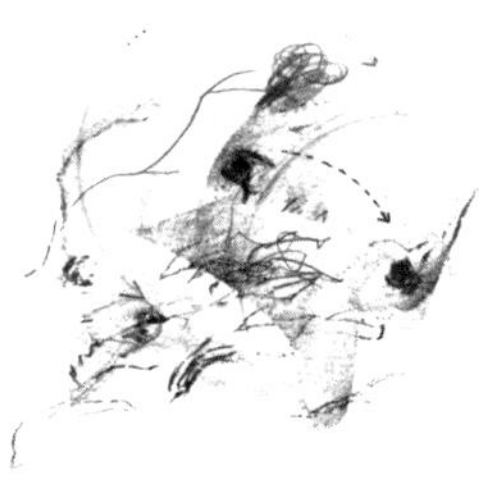

Alternatively, Daniel Stern conceives the felt movement of "the coming into being of a new state of things"[6] as a *kairotic* or micro-*kairotic* 'now moment', where the 'present moment' "lean(s) toward a next action"[7] (⟶ *When-ness*). For Stern, this "shift is brought about by the unpredictable arising of an emergent property that was being prepared for, unseen, in the moving along process."[8] He describes how this auspicious upsurge "can crash upon us like a wave, or appear almost without notice and then slip away like a sea swell."[9] Stern argues that, the "perception or attribution of force(s) 'behind' or 'within'"[10]

So too, we describe figuring like airflows or oceanic currents — up-welling of wind, down-welling of water. Arising of liquids, building up of fluid, gathering strength. Cartography of surges and swellings, deepening: the dynamic of how things emerge. Coalesce. Converge. Close to a threshold: to be on the verge of movement, tipping point at the limit of definition. Tilted: inhabiting the cusp, those moments of decision where everything hangs in the balance.

movement can be articulated as the qualitative experience of *vitality* (⟶ *How-ness*). He argues that 'dynamic forms of vitality' do not refer to emotions: "They are not motivational states. They are not pure perceptions. They are not sensations in the strict sense, as they have no modality. They are not direct cognitions in any usual sense. They are not acts, as they have no goal state and no specific means. They fall in between all the cracks. They are the felt experience of force — in movement — with a temporal contour, and a sense of aliveness, of going somewhere."[11]

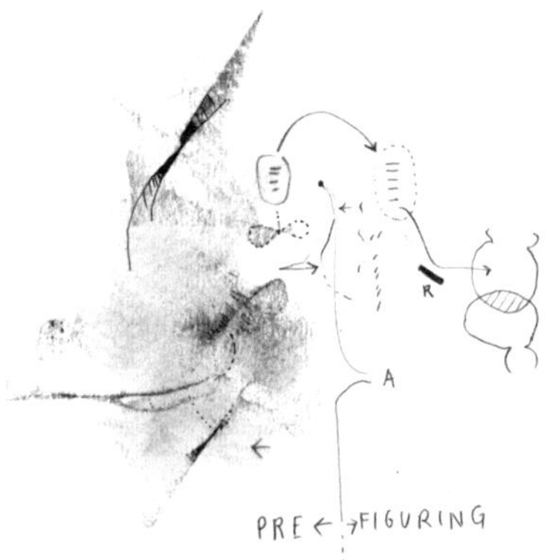

Our conceptualisation of *figuring* as the *micro* — or even *minor* — moments of qualitative sensation within practice brings our enquiry into dialogue with both the individual and collaborative writing of Erin Manning and Brian Massumi (⟶ *Trialogue: Thinking-Making in Relation*). *Figuring* resonates with Manning's concept of *preacceleration* through which she refers to the "virtual pre-movement that accompanies all actual movement."[12] She argues that *preacceleration* describes the "immanence of movement moving: how movement can be felt before it actualizes [...] the virtual force of a movement's taking form."[13] For Manning, "(w)hat preacceleration does is make felt the tendings already in germ before a displacement happens, emphasizing that movement happens less in an individual body than in the intervals proposed by movement's inherent relationality."[14] Likewise, Brian Massumi focuses on the *germinal conditions* of an 'event' stating that the "question of conditioning is in what ways, for this event, in its germination, have other modes of activity come into play only to fall out of its rising arc? Even so, how might they have resonated together, and with the singularity of this arising event? [...] Might that tension, that germinal intensity of activity, have contributed to the singularity of what happened as it followed its own tendency to completion?"[15] For Massumi, "(t)he qualitative aspect of the event that you can't reduce to quantifiable movements is what I call the semblance of the event. My proposition is that this qualitative aspect is where the aesthetic lies."[16]

More recently, Manning's concept of the 'minor gesture' further elaborates her interest in the subtle 'as-yet-undetermined' 'coming-into-being' of movement and perception, "the phase of realization of the event, of experience, where it has not yet fully come to be this or that."[17] She states that, "the minor ... is the gestural force that opens experience to its potential variation. It does this from within experience itself, activating a shift in tone, a difference in quality."[18] Additionally, she asks, "From this position of indeterminacy, of the ineffable, how to make intelligible the singularity of what cannot be measured or categorized but is felt and, in some sense, known?"[19] Manning elaborates something of the dilemma that we have experienced within our own enquiry when she says, "how can we articulate the delicate contrast carried by the minor gesture without flattening our difference, homogenizing experience."[20] Indeed, how might we attend to and 'make intelligible' the event of *figuring;* furthermore, how might we do this without 'flattening' or fixing that which is contingent? Within our own artistic exploration, the *Method Lab* has provided the context within which we create the conditions for *figuring's* arising: *live exploration* practised as an open field of investigation, attention focused towards the affective, embodied, relational intensities and energies within artistic collaboration (⟶ *Method Labs*). But how *exactly* do we attend to the indeterminate experience of *figuring* in-and-through practice? Indeed, as Manning observes, the experience of preacceleration "is often too fleeting to be felt. Since it is only tending towards the actual, we know it only in the moving, and even then, we cannot easily make sense of it 'as such.'"[21] However, she elaborates that through a "focused diagrammatic praxis … preacceleration can sometimes be passingly felt."[22]

Manning's diagrammatic praxis combines "rigorous procedurality"[23] with a "dance of attention", conceived less in terms of "being attentive-to than becoming in attention-with."[24] She states, "We do not attend — the field attends, an attention sustained by the procedural rigor of a set of conditions, tasks, techniques that hold the event to itself even while elastically bending time to make space for points of inflection that create differentials of relation."[25]

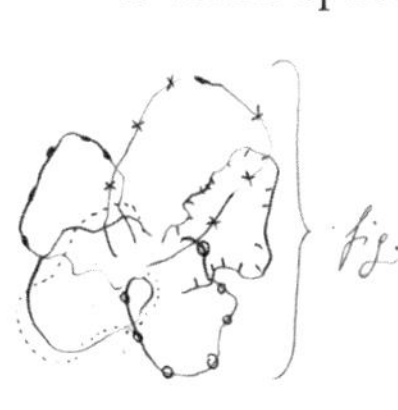

Central to our enquiry has been the development of a "focused diagrammatic praxis" comprising different *practices* for heightening, deepening and widening our perceptual awareness and sensitivity towards the event of *figuring* (⟶ *Practices of Attention*), alongside various systems of notation ('dynamic indicators' or 'markers' to borrow Stern's terms) for identifying and marking (tending to) those moments when *figuring* arises (⟶ *Practices of Notation*). Initially, our notation system was used 'simply' for marking when 'something is happening', for indicating the arising of *figuring* in its undifferentiated, unqualified or as yet un-nameable state (⟶ *Clicking*). Through this

We have provisionally named various *figures:*

fig. of absorption
fig. of adapting
fig. of approaching
fig. of arrival
fig. of assimilation
fig. of becoming material
fig. of binding
fig. of bonding
fig. of breathing
fig. of bundling
fig. of capture
fig. of catching the light
fig. of circulation
fig. of clearing and emptying out
fig. of collecting
fig. of commitment
fig. of consonance / dissonance
fig. of contamination
fig. of containment
fig. of contingency
fig. of covering the ground
fig. of crafting
fig. of crystallisation
fig. of dancing
fig. of defense
fig. of disappearance
fig. of distillation
fig. of dynamics
fig. of ebbing
fig. of ending
fig. of emergence
fig. of emphasising
fig. of epiphany
fig. of exhaustion

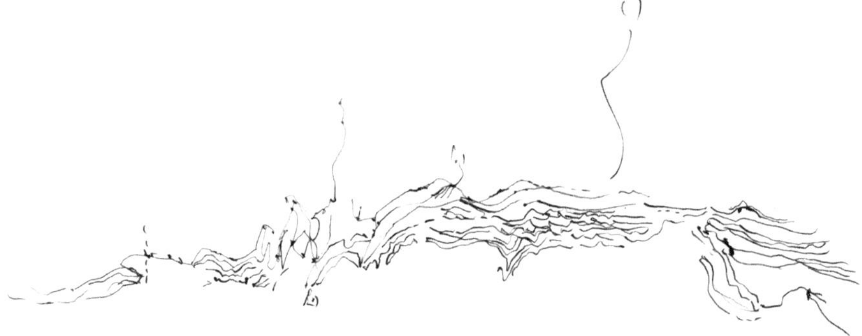

process — and other systems of scoring and notation — we were gradually able to *re-cognise* and qualify the shifts in vitality, intensity or affordance, which we named as specific *figures* (→ *Affirming*, → *Naming*). We use the term *figure* to describe the point at which the indeterminate or undifferentiated awareness of 'something happening' (*figuring*) becomes recognisable and qualified through a name.

Whilst some of the proposed *figures* can be recognised visually as particular movements, gestures or postures within the unfolding of artistic endeavour, others operate beneath the register of visibility, at a more corporeal, sensorial and affective level of awareness. Furthermore, whilst some *figures* might be consciously activated within the arc of artistic enquiry (for example, for getting started), others refer more to inner states. Indeed, some *figures* become recognisable only through their kinetic dynamics, through the register of their force, power or even affect rather than through their form. Certainly, our tentative taxonomy of *figures* resonates with Stern's list of 'dynamic forms of vitality' — including "swelling, surging, cresting, accelerating, fading, tense, drawn out, effortful, tentative, languorous, pushing, pulling, exploding, fluttering, holding still."[26] However, our focus is less towards everyday social and emotional communication or interaction, but rather we address exclusively those *figures* of vitality emerging within artistic exploration, paying particular attention to the inter-subjective, relational modalities within a live interdisciplinary, collaborative process. Practical examples — specific iterations — of a select number of these *figures* can be encountered throughout the publication (→ *Elemental*, → *Empathetic*, → *Transformative*); however, the intent here is to give a conceptual account of our use of the term.

Figure — we use this term to describe the point at which *figuring's* dynamic vitality coalesces into communicable content. *Figure* as a multimodal, multidimensional, durational intensity, performed entanglement of visual-spatial, verbal-linguistic, bodily-kinesthetic sensibilities. Stern differentiates between a "dynamic vitality strand" (experienced as pure intensity or force — its "changes, the duration and the temporal stresses, rhythm and directionality") and a 'content-modality strand' (the encoding and unfolding of content, 'what' emerges).[27] Likewise, we conceive a relation between the event of *figuring* (as 'dynamic vitality') and the emergence of *figures* (as content-modality or even 'vitality gesture'). Our enquiry is concerned with the point of passage from vitality to content, performed through a delicate 'dance of attention' that strives to give formulation to the experience of vitality itself. Through our own mode of artistic research we ask (following Stern): "How do vitality forms become translated into 'the realm of the perceptible'?"[28] The relationship between the event of *figuring* and the production of *figures* is symbiotic and reciprocal, perhaps to be imagined like the diagramming of a *Möbius strip*. Sensitivity to the experience of *figuring* gives rise to the emergence of *figures*, whilst the attempt to activate the *figures* creates the conditions for *figuring*. Additionally, the performing of *figures* invariably affects and modifies the conditions of the aesthetic exploration itself, producing new shifts of affordance, giving rise to new experiences of *figuring*.

The *figure* is not a system of containment or control, a means through which to fix the volatile vitality force of *figuring* within a stable, delineated form. Indeed, for Gabriele Brandstetter, "the figure as model of representation, as a unity — a unity of Gestalt, a unity of the subject in the sense of identity — has become obsolete."[29]

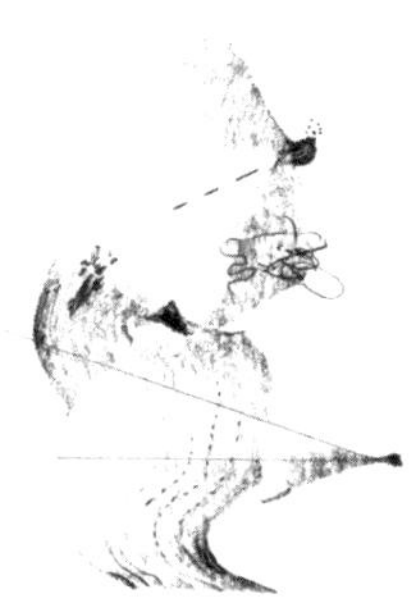

In one sense, the coalescence of *figuring* into a *figure* echoes the *morphogenetic* dynamic of incarnation. Morphogenesis — from the Greek *morphê* (shape) and genesis (creation), the beginning of the shape — is the biological process that causes an organism to develop its form. The incarnation of *figuring* then, from *carne* — flesh, to give flesh to, a bringing into flesh. Drawing on the work of Erich Auerbach (in turn on Augustinian theology), Brandstetter uses the term figuration — *figuratio* — to refer to the morphogenesis of ideas, incarnation of the word. Brandstetter claims that the figure is no longer the contour of the body, but rather the scope of movement in the sphere around / surrounding (*Umraum*) the body that can be denominated as figuration.[30] As Pia Müller-Tamm asserts, for Brandstetter, "Every figure is simultaneously space and itself space-holding. The open unity of the figure transfers its potential to its surroundings and structures the floating phenomena of the in-between. It activates the dynamics, mutualities and exchange relations between figure, things and surround-space. In this sense, space can also be comprehensible as figural, as a flexible entity, which entangles with figures and opens towards the ambient. Like the figure, space also constitutes itself only through the phenomenon of passage between inner and outer, between the visible and the invisible."[31]

fig. of fabricating
fig. of fading in / out
fig. of failing
fig. of fearing
fig. of fleshing out
fig. of folding
fig. of getting started
fig. of grounding
fig. of guarding
fig. of hosting
fig. of identifying
fig. of immersion
fig. of inflection
fig. of inhabitation
fig. of interfacing
fig. of introducing
fig. of interrupting
fig. of invitation
fig. of knotting
fig. of liquidity
fig. of maturing
fig. of mediation
fig. of mimicking
fig. of moving
fig. of negotiation
fig. of ordering
fig. of pausing
fig. of recording
fig. of rotation
fig. of phrasing
fig. of preparing
fig. of preference
fig. of projecting
fig. of punctuation
fig. of reaching towards the other
fig. of remembering
fig. of reset
fig. of resistance

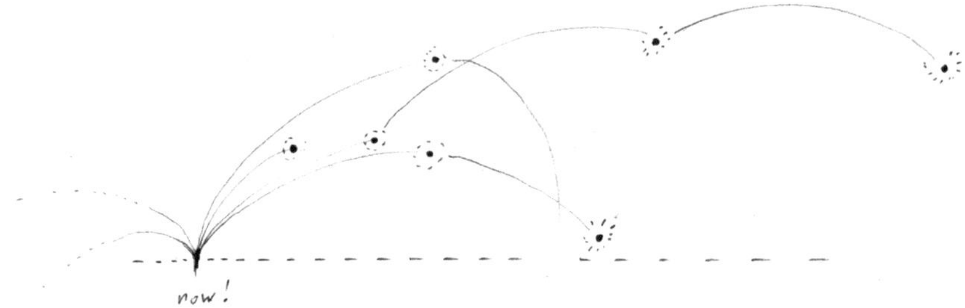

The impulse that follows the initial *figuring* gives it its subsequent form: *figure* is the content-modality that emerges in fidelity to the dynamic experience of *figuring*. However, *figuring* thus not only describes the 'ground' from which the *figure* arises — the conditions for the *figure's* genesis — but also the quality or vitality force that the *figure* seeks to retain or invoke. Or rather, the 'ground' of *figuring* cannot be easily differentiated from the *figure*: it is part of its very constitution. Here, as Jean-François Lyotard states, "The figure is always determined, and the ground is anything at all, but also that without which determination would not take place, and upon which the figure is determined. That this figure is determined rather than another: such is the event, the contingency. What is necessary is that its determination leaves behind a ground. 'Leaves behind a ground': the figure is wrapped in something unfocused, and it is not determined; if it is, it is no longer the ground left behind. As if the eye and thought or language could determine *this* only by leaving around it *that* which the eye, thought or language does not see, conceive, or articulate."[32] The *figure* is actually composed of both *figure* and ground (*figuring*), untamed in its movement as a vibrational *figure-in-figuration*. Eluding the *figure* as sculptural form, we witness how motion transits, de- and transfigures forms through expanding its potential towards a space-time-continuum with vital agency, that constantly negotiates its *figuring*. In one sense, our quest is for a sensibility within practice where the performance of the *figure* incarnates; (re)enactment with corresponding vitality. Indeed, as Stern argues, "The content modality must be encoded along or around (so to speak) the dynamic vitality strand. The content strand takes on its phenomenal form and appears to us only when it is twisted around the dynamic vitality strand … without the dynamic vitality strand … there would be no flow, no vitality, and no aliveness."[33]

Per — the prefix indicating *through*, a forward-through movement. The *figure* renders *figuring* tangible through its (per)forming, through the performative act of bringing it into shape. Not the re-presentation of *figuring* then, but rather a presentation, presenting, even *presence-ing*. Present — existing or occurring at this time now, denoting an action or state occurring at the moment of its utterance; or to be under consideration, to present before others, the event of being witnessed.

The *figure-form* we thus strive towards is a *figuring figure* not so much recognisable through its content modality alone, but rather through the qualitative event of its performing, its *per-forming*. *Figure* is less the wilful shaping of *figuring* into form but rather attests to the promise of bringing something into being; *figure* in-formed by *figuring*. Inform — to give evident substance, character, distinction to; to pervade, to permeate; to manifest effect.

Inform — disclose; to make known; to reveal or uncover; to cause to appear; to allow to be seen; to lay open to view; open up, unfold. We draw on double drifts in etymology, where inform refers both to the process of taking form (to shape, to form, from *informare*) whilst also referring to what is formless (*informe*).[34] So too might our *figures* shimmer between the states of form and formlessness, like the animation drawing its movement always between draft and articulation, always collapsing before it is fully formed. Disclosure rather than closure, like Châtelet's diagram, every *figure*, "invites an erasure, a redrawing, a — refiguring."[35] However, as Manning states, "The emphasis here is not on the continuity of becoming, an infinitely open account of process, but on the becoming of continuity: process punctuated [...] moving the welling event in new and divergent directions that alter the orientation of where the event might otherwise have settled."[36] So far, we have strived for a level of precision in articulating the qualitative specificity or distinctive properties of a selected number of *figures* (→ *Figures*), but significantly without prescribing the form that a given *figure* should take. Whilst we present some examples for each named *figure*, we

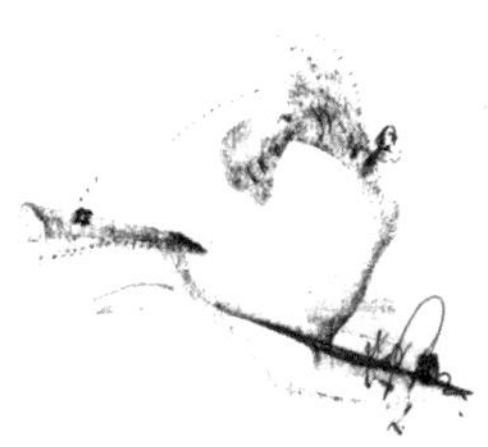

conceive these as singular moments of sedimentation or stability within the ongoing flux of experimentation. The *figure* is not what you *do* but rather what happens (from *hap* — to come to pass; there is an element of chance, an *aleatory* dimension). We understand the *figure* as an emergent network of qualities, a con-figuration of possibilities with an achieved level of *coherence*. *Coherence*: a 'coming together', from 'com' — together and *haerere* — 'to adhere, stick' (→ Alex Arteaga, *Researching Aesthetically the Roots of Aesthetics*). Interestingly, the term coherence is thought to share etymological origins with 'hesitation' — as stammering, uncertainty, to be irresolute. Indeed, the possibilities for each *figure* are always *becoming*, necessarily inconclusive. We imagine the *figure* as a performative, relational and contingent 'assemblage' recognisable or identifiable whilst at the same time motile and unstable, capable of evolving.[37] We conceive our *figures* in the key of the *minor*, where according to Manning, "The minor isn't known in advance. It never reproduces itself in its own image. Each minor gesture is singularly connected to the event at hand, immanent to the in-act."[38] One cannot simply 'execute' a *figure*; it has to be *re-found*. However, by testing the

fig. of responding
fig. of revelation
fig. of reverberation
fig. of sense-making
fig. of sequencing
fig. of situating
fig. of spiralling momentum
fig. of starting slow
fig. of stopping
fig. of structuring
fig. of synchronising
fig. of taking care
fig. of the ephemeral
fig. of shelter
fig. of the sentimental
fig. of temporary closing
fig. of threading
fig. of touching
fig. of transference
fig. of translational flux
fig. of travelling
fig. of triangulation
fig. of trusting
fig. of tuning in
fig. of turbulence
fig. of unravelling
fig. of ventilating meaning
fig. of vibrating affinity
fig. of vulnerability
fig. of waiting
fig. of warming-up
fig. of wavering convergence
fig. of wilderness
fig. of wit(h)nessing

Our list is not exhaustive.

figuring >< *figure* relation through sustained *live exploration*, we have been able to distil a shared knowledge of the constitutive conditions of possibility (not a *repertoire* as such but rather more like the ingredients — certain modes of performativity, certain species of activity) that increase a named *figure's* likelihood, the probability of its arising.

Within our investigation so far, we have been able to articulate the qualities and constitutive conditions for nine named *figures* out of a list of infinitely more. In turn, these *figures* have been grouped according to three different qualitative categories. The *Elemental Figures* diagram key moments within the arc of creative exploration or endeavour, address the opening up and exposition of process. The *figures* we present within this grouping are indicative not exhaustive, referring to just three moments within the arc of practice: the process of beginning (→ *Clearing and Emptying Out*), of generating energy in the midst of (→ *Spiralling Momentum*), and for drawing towards resolution (→ *Temporary Closing*). The *Empathetic Figures* involve the diagramming of relations, drawing attention to the ethics of collaboration, the sensitivities and sensibilities of *being-with*. The three *figures* presented (→ *Vibrating Affinity*, → *Wavering Convergence*, → *Consonance / Dissonance*) articulate a shift from the experienced intensity of *being-with* one to the many, or rather from the experience of the one (that is already the many) to the multitude. The *Transformative Figures* each involve an explicit shift, change or even transformation in property, quality or state of being. Connected through the prefix *trans-* (indicating movement across or through, the act of 'going beyond'), the three figures presented (→ *Ventilating Meaning*, → *Becoming Material*, → *Translational Flux*) each involve the dissolving or destabilising of fixed meanings by collapsing the lines of distinction between activity / passivity, animate / inanimate, subject / object, self / world.

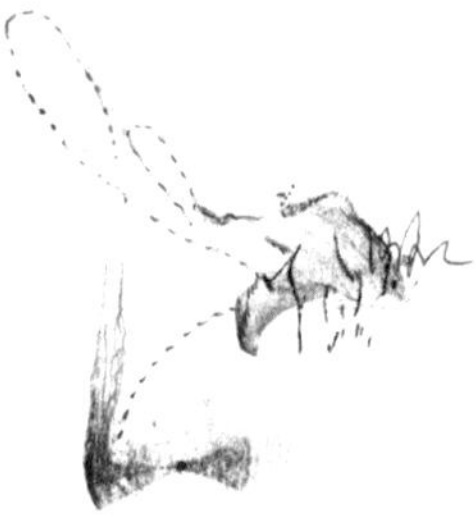

Our enquiry has involved developing practices for attending to and marking the event of *figuring*; the identification, qualification and naming of various *figures*; alongside the distillation of the qualitative properties of key *figures* (→ *Elemental, Empathetic, Transformative*) such that we might seek to re-activate them with intent. Central to this has been the development of an experimental 'score system' through which we *practise* 'calling' for and attending to the conditions of specific named *figures:* a process of live aesthetic exploration focused through the prism of various *Practices of Attention, Conversation, Notation and Wit(h)nessing* (→ *Practices*: especially *Notation: Calling*, → *How to Play the Score*). Whilst *figure* is the term that we use to refer to a 'local' instance of *figuring* incarnating as content modality, we propose the concept of the *choreo-graphic figure* — *choreo-* (more than one); *graphic-* (form of inscribing) — as a diagrammatic assemblage (a system of organisation or even organism) for bringing into relation, as well as for giving rise through activation and play to unexpected interactional constellations of (both known and not-yet-known) *figures* (⟶ *Embodied Diagrammatics*).

---

1) Cf. Jacques Rancière, *Aisthesis: Scenes from the Aesthetic Regime of Art*, London and New York: Verso Books, 2013. (⟶ Alex Arteaga, *Researching Aesthetically the Roots of Aesthetics*).

2) Cf. Gilles Deleuze, 'Lecture Transcripts on Spinoza's Concept of Affect', *Cours Vincennes*, 24.01.1978. www.webdeleuze.com/textes/14

3) David Hallıburton, *Poetic Thinking: An Approach to Heidegger*, Chicago: University of Chicago Press, 1981, p. 144.

4) Sarat Maharaj, 'What the Thunder Said: Toward a Scouting Report on "Art as a Thinking Process"', in Mara Ambrožič and Angela Vettese (Eds.), *Art as a Thinking Process: Visual Forms of Knowledge Production*, New York / Berlin: Sternberg Press, 2013, p. 155.

5) Maharaj, 2013, pp. 155-156.

6) Daniel Stern, *The Present Moment in Psychotherapy and Everyday Life*, New York: W. W. Norton & Company, 2004, p. 7.

7) Stern, 2004, p. xv.

8) Stern, 2004, p. 195.

9) Stern, 2004, p. 25.

10) Stern, *Forms of Vitality: Exploring Dynamic Experience in Psychology, the Arts, Psychotherapy and Development*, Oxford and New York: Oxford University Press, 2010, p. 4.

11) Stern, 2010, p. 8.

12) Erin Manning, *Always More Than One: Individuation's Dance*, Durham: Duke University Press, 2013, p. 134.

13) Erin Manning, *Relationscapes: Movement, Art, Philosophy*, Cambridge, Mass. and London: MIT Press, 2009, p. 6.

14) Manning, 2013, p. 134.

15) Brian Massumi, in Hugo Glendinning and Adrian Heathfield (Dirs. and Eds.), *No Such Thing as Rest: A Walk with Brian Massumi*, 2013, p. 7. www.adrianheathfield.net/project/no-such-thing-as-rest

16) Massumi, 2013, p. 9.

17) Erin Manning, *The Minor Gesture*, Durham: Duke University Press, 2016, p. 2.

18) Manning, 2016. p. 1.

19) Manning, 2016, p. 24.

20) Manning, 2016, p. 24.

21) Manning, 2013, p. 135.

22) Manning, 2013, p. 135.

23) Manning, 2013, p. 143.

24) Manning, 2013, p. 108.

25) Manning, 2013, p. 141.

26) Stern, 2010, p. 7.

27) Stern, 2010, pp. 24-25.

28) Stern, 2010, p. 81.

29) Gabriele Brandstetter, Sibylle Peters, *de figura — Rhetorik — Bewegung — Gestalt*, München: Wilhelm Fink, 2002, p. 7., Translation by Mariella Greil of the original: "... d.h. Figur als ein Repräsentationsmodell, das Einheit — Einheit der Gestalt, Einheit des Subjekts im Sinn von Identität — verbürgt, obsolet geworden ist."

30) Gabriele Brandstetter, Gottfried Boehm, Achatz von Müller, *Figur und Figuration: Studien zu Wahrnehmung und Wissen*, München: Wilhelm Fink, 2007, p. 27. Translation by Mariella Greil of the original: "Nicht mehr die Figur, das heißt die Umrisslinie des Körpers, sondern die Reichweite der Bewegung im Umraum des Körpers bezeichnet Figuration."

31) Pia Müller-Tamm, Gottfried Boehm, *Henri Matisse: Figur, Farbe, Raum*, Ostfildern-Ruit: Hatje Cantz, 2005, p. 19. Translation by Mariella Greil of the original: "Jede Figur ist zugleich im Raum und selbst raumhaltig. Die offene Einheit der Figur überträgt ihre Potenziale auf ihre Umgebung und strukturiert die schwebenden Phänomene des Dazwischen. Sie aktiviert die Dynamik, die Wechselwirkungen und Austauschbeziehungen zwischen der Figur, den Dingen und dem Um-Raum. Insoweit lässt sich auch der Raum figural begreifen, im Sinne einer flexiblen Einheit, die sich mit den Figuren verschränkt und sich zum Außen hin öffnet. Wie die Figur, so konstituiert sich auch der Raum erst durch die Phänomene des Übergangs — zwischen Innen und Außen, zwischen Sichtbarem und Unsichtbarem."

32) Jean-François Lyotard, *What to Paint?*, Leuven: Leuven University Press, [1987] 2012, p. 281.

33) Stern, 2010, p. 25.

34) Yves-Alain Bois and Rosalind E. Krauss, *Formless: A User's Guide*, New York: Zone Books, 1999.

34) Kenneth Knoespel, 'Diagrammatic Writing And The Configuration Of Space', in Gilles Châtelet, *Figuring Space: Philosophy, Mathematics and Physics*, Dordrecht: Kluwer, Academic, 2000, p. xvi.

35) Manning, 2016, p. 3.

36) Rather than the term 'assemblage', Manning advocates the use of the French term *agencement*, which "carries within itself a sense of movement and connectibility, of processual agency", 2016, p. 123 (⟶ *Embodied Diagrammatics*).

37) Manning, 2016, p. 2.

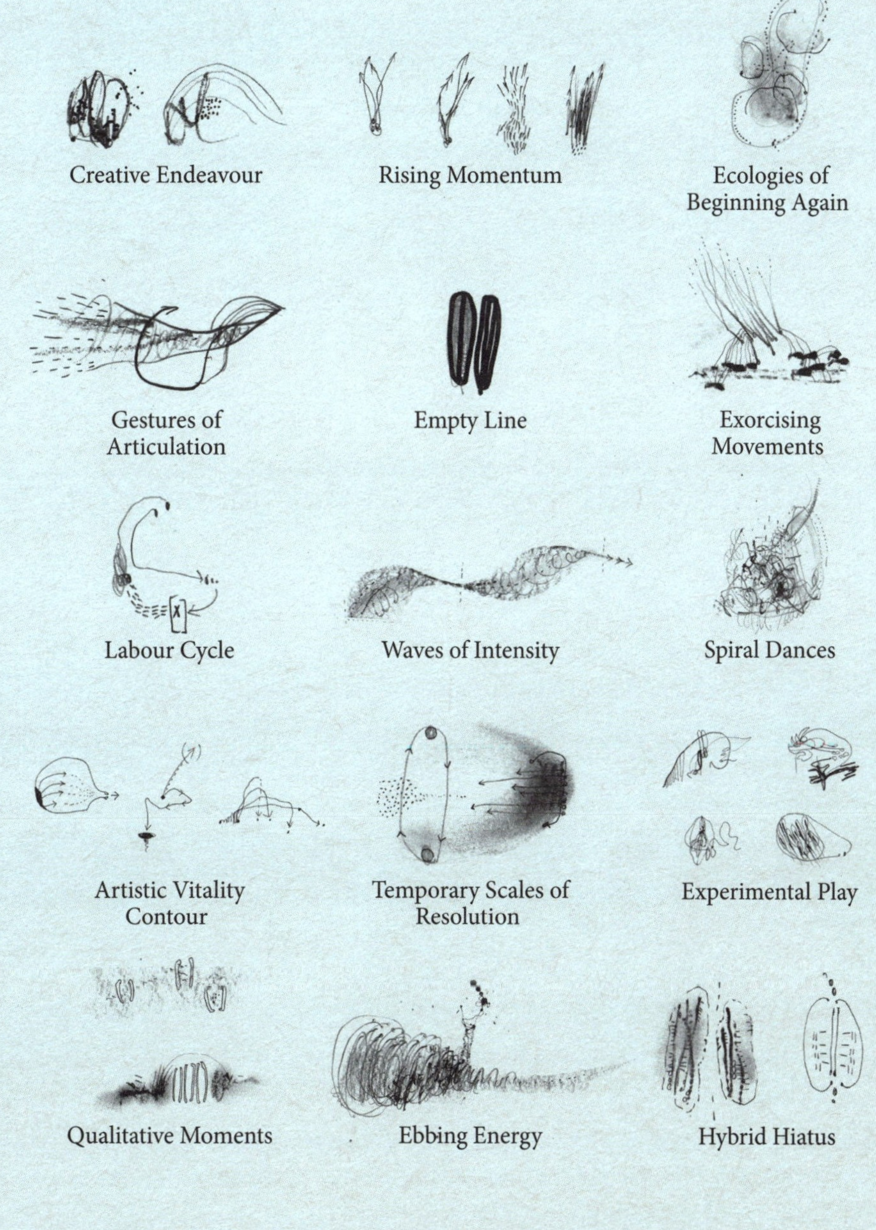

KEY LINES
ELEMENTAL FIGURES

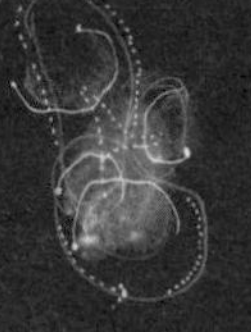
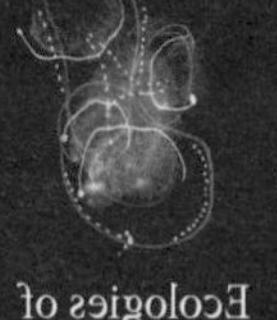
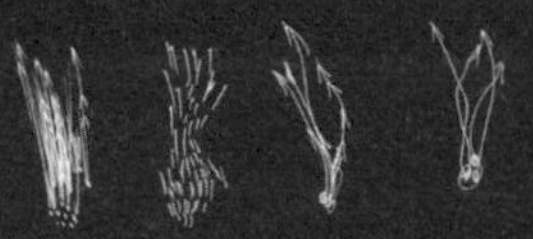
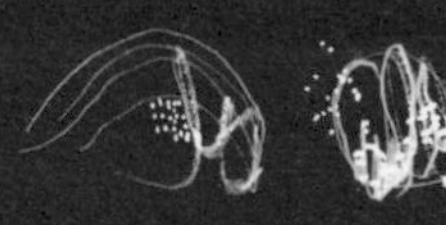

ELEMENTAL
Figures

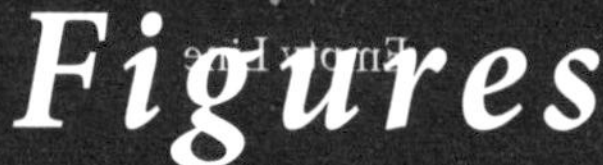
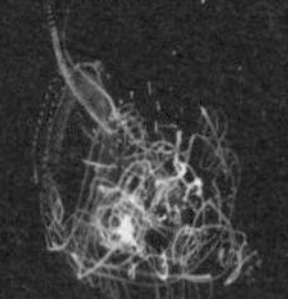
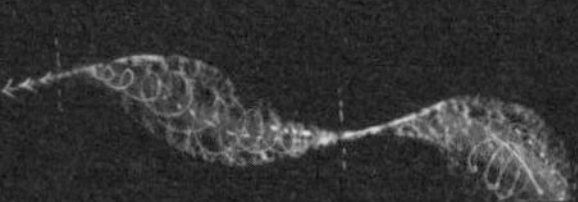
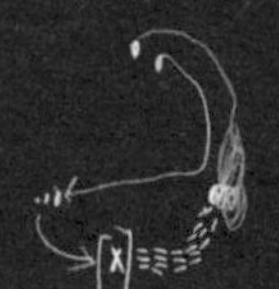
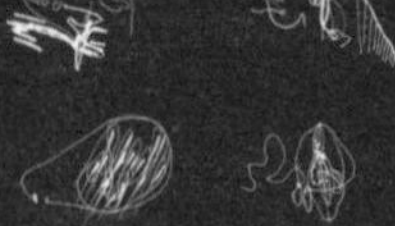
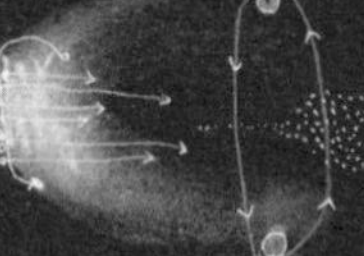
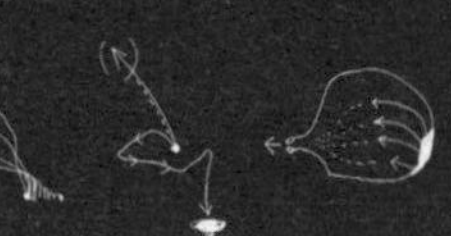
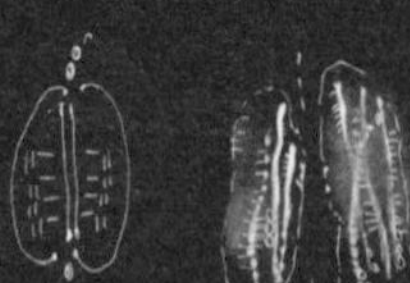
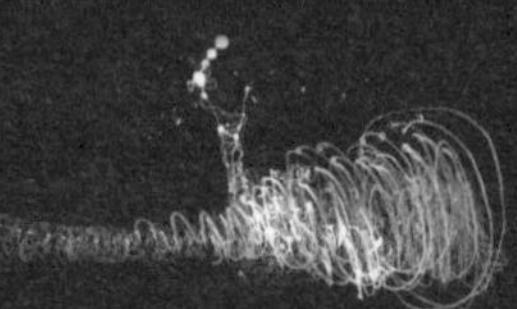

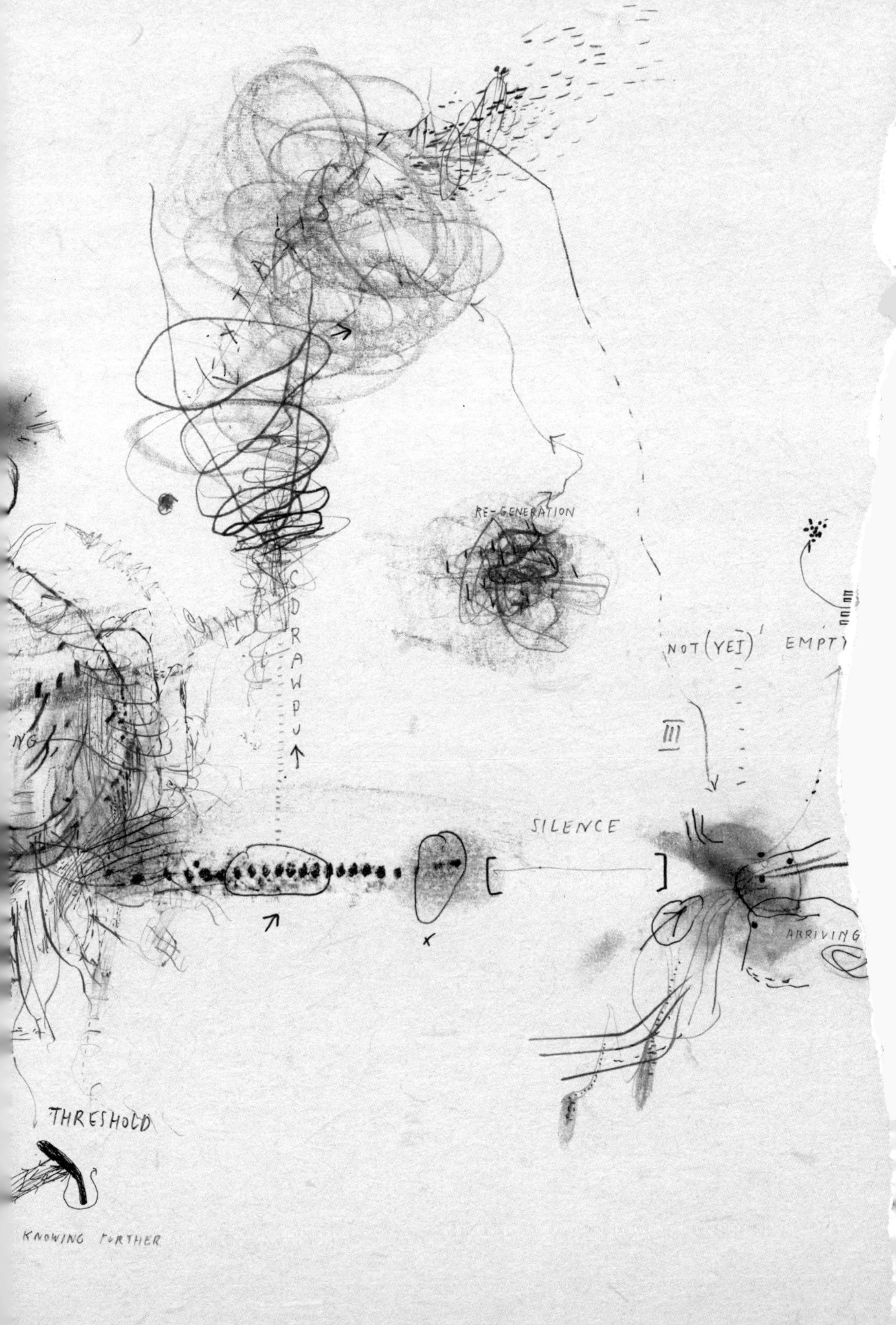
RE-GENERATION
DRAWPU
NOT (YET)
EMPTY
SILENCE
ARRIVING
THRESHOLD
KNOWING FURTHER

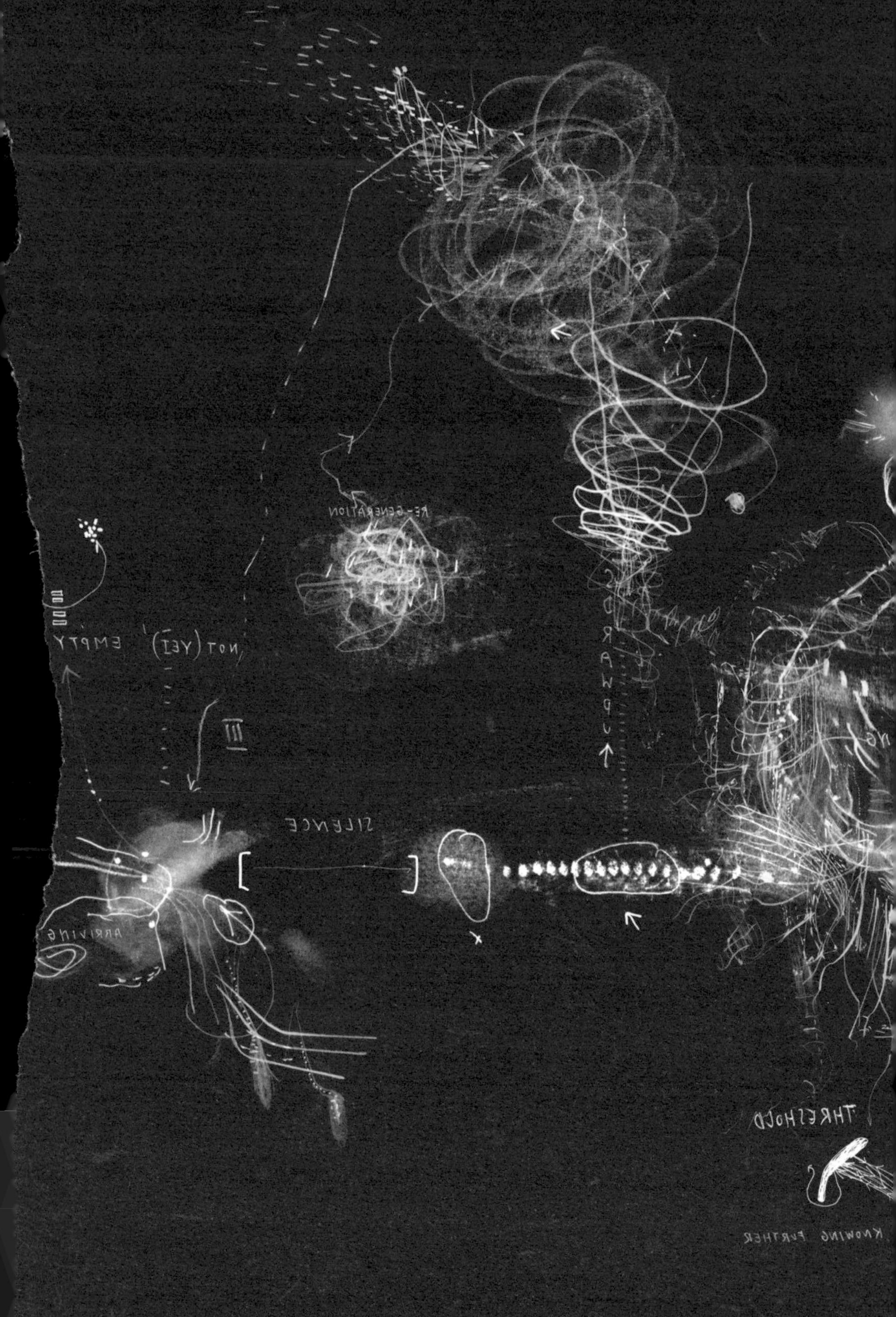
RE-GENERATION
EMPTY
NOT (YET)
SILENCE
ARRIVING
THRESHOLD
KNOWING FURTHER

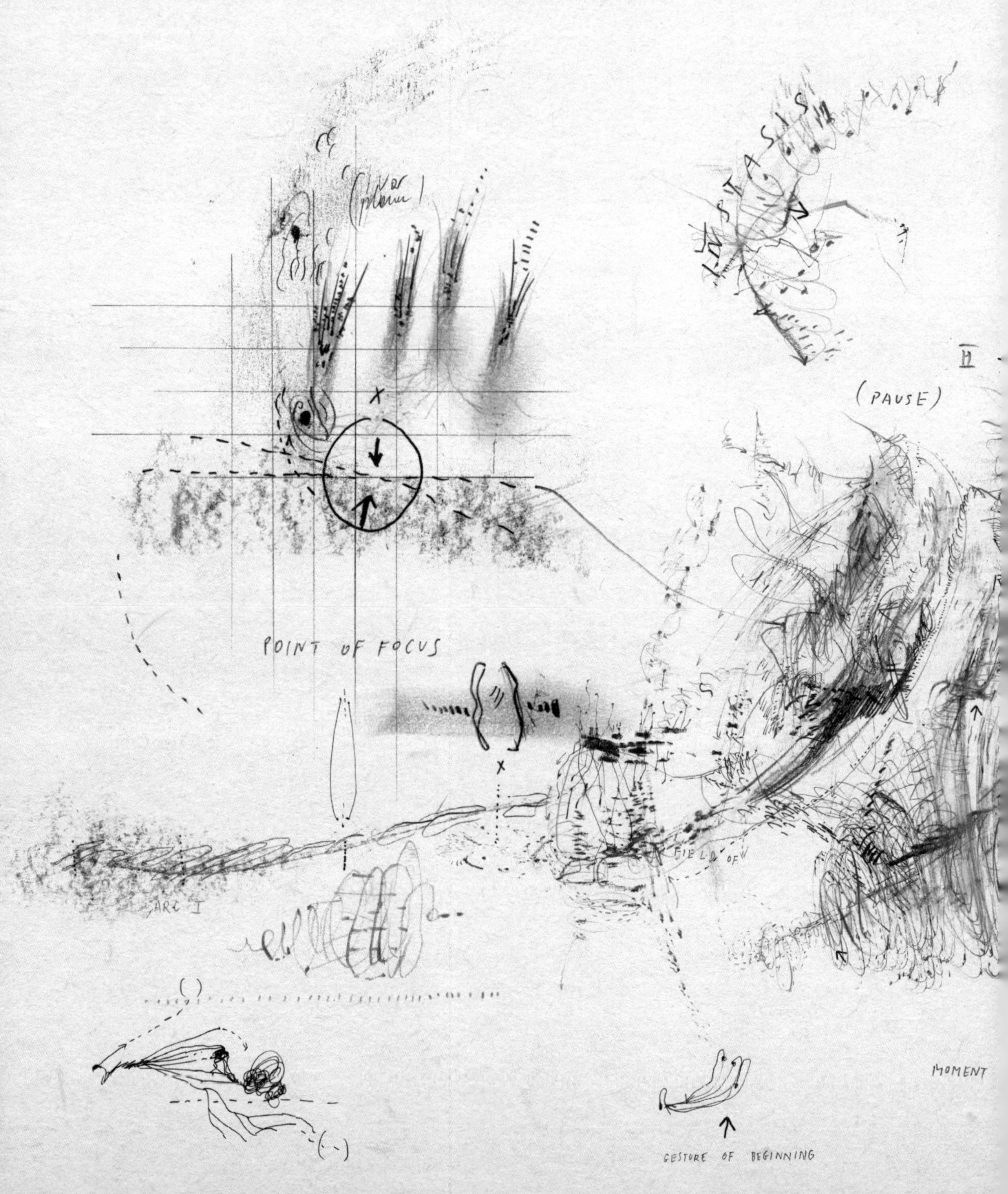

STASIS
(PAUSE)
POINT OF FOCUS
FIELD OF
MOMENT
GESTURE OF BEGINNING

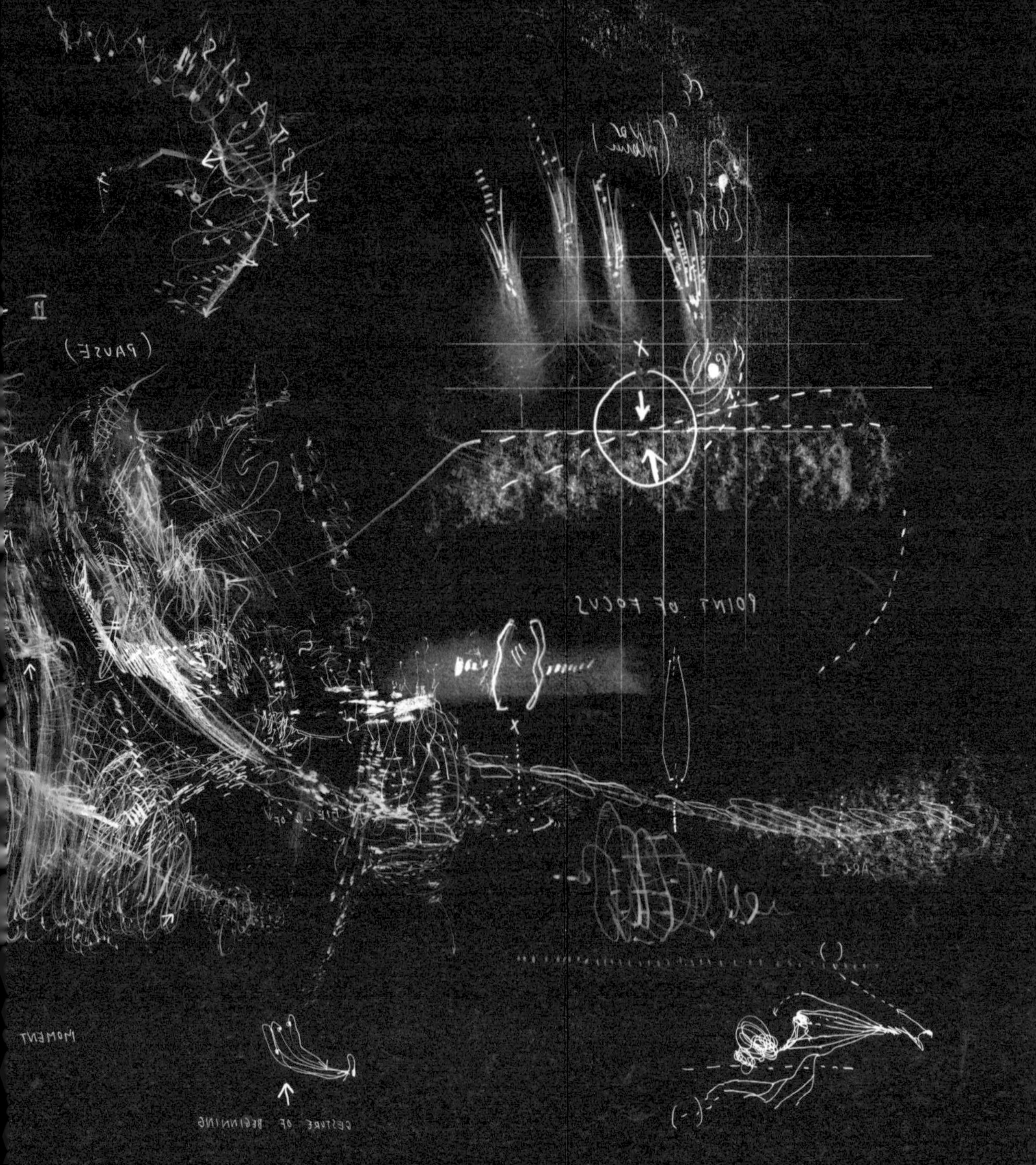

(PAUSE)

POINT OF FOCUS

MOMENT

GESTURE OF BEGINNING

ELEMENTAL *Figures*

The *Elemental Figures* diagram key moments within the arc of creative exploration or endeavour. These *figures* specifically address the opening up and exposition of process, shedding light on the labour cycle of artistic work operating before, between and beneath the more readable gestures of artistic practice. We ask: can we articulate shared ways of working that correspond to different qualitative moments in the arc of the creative process, irrespective of discipline or medium? Within our own collaborative artistic enquiry, we noticed how *different* gestures and actions within our respective practices were often performed with similar intent, underpinned by a seemingly shared dynamic affect or 'vitality contour'.[1] The *figures* we present are indicative not exhaustive, referring to just three moments within the arc of practice: the process of beginning (*Clearing and Emptying Out*), of generating energy in the midst of (*Spiralling Momentum*), and for drawing towards resolution (*Temporary Closing*). We imagine their distinctive vectors in the form of curves, arcs, waves of intensity: rising, ebbing. Not a linear sequence, the *Elemental Figures* are perpetually practised within practice at different scales, through repeated acts of doing, undoing, re-doing. As such, we associate these *figures* with the prefixes *de-*, *dis-* (indicating separation, reversal, negation) alongside *re-* (towards renewal, restoration, again and again). In one sense, they articulate rudimentary first principles, the essential vitality curves of the creative process: how to begin, how to continue, how to end. However, we conceive them as 'elemental' rather than 'fundamental', less the basic foundation or fundament of practice, but rather an exploration of the generative forces and energies that connect artistic endeavour to a wider creative ecology.

---

1) We borrow the phrase from Daniel Stern, whose writing on 'dynamic forms of vitality' resonates closely with our own interest in the vitality arc of creative endeavour (⟶ *Figuring* >< *Figure*).

Figure of CLEARING AND EMPTYING OUT

To make clear — it is not concerned with clarity of sense. Sense of ordering, but *beyond* making clean, *more* than operational. Not just an emptying of space, but a clearing made possible also through the act of bringing in. With the moving of light, a quality of exorcism. Exorcising — a means of letting go. Of the histories, stories, associations of certain materials, of spaces, the self — not only of visible things but also the invisible. Emptying of pre-existing function and content, meaning and memory. Evacuate. Vacate. Vacancy — a precondition of availability. Empty to make available, un-occupy. Ridding of utility, a practice of forgetting, disassociation so as not to repeat the same. Energetic awareness: ritual process of purification. Dispelling of the stale, not fresh, the vapid or the flat, the dry or hardened. To rid or expel that which has lost its energy, what is now surfeit, overstrained or bored. Recognising the no longer vital, where force or effectiveness has become dulled through absence of action.

Dis-association. Dis-tinction. Dis-tinguish. There is a decision — a split, a cut, a cleaving. Ordering and categorising — what to keep and what to let go, this *with* and this *not*. As preparing for a journey: which things stay and which are left behind. With the cut a clearing — event of separation, like empty brackets. An opening, un-closing, disclosure — clearing and emptying so something might show itself, become unconcealed. Release and anticipation: creating the conditions for the not-yet-arisen, the potential for something new. Dis-charging energy — to return to zero; establish a new ground. Preparatory gestures. Re-sharpening. Marking a new beginning. Marked by readiness, re-set in order to begin again.

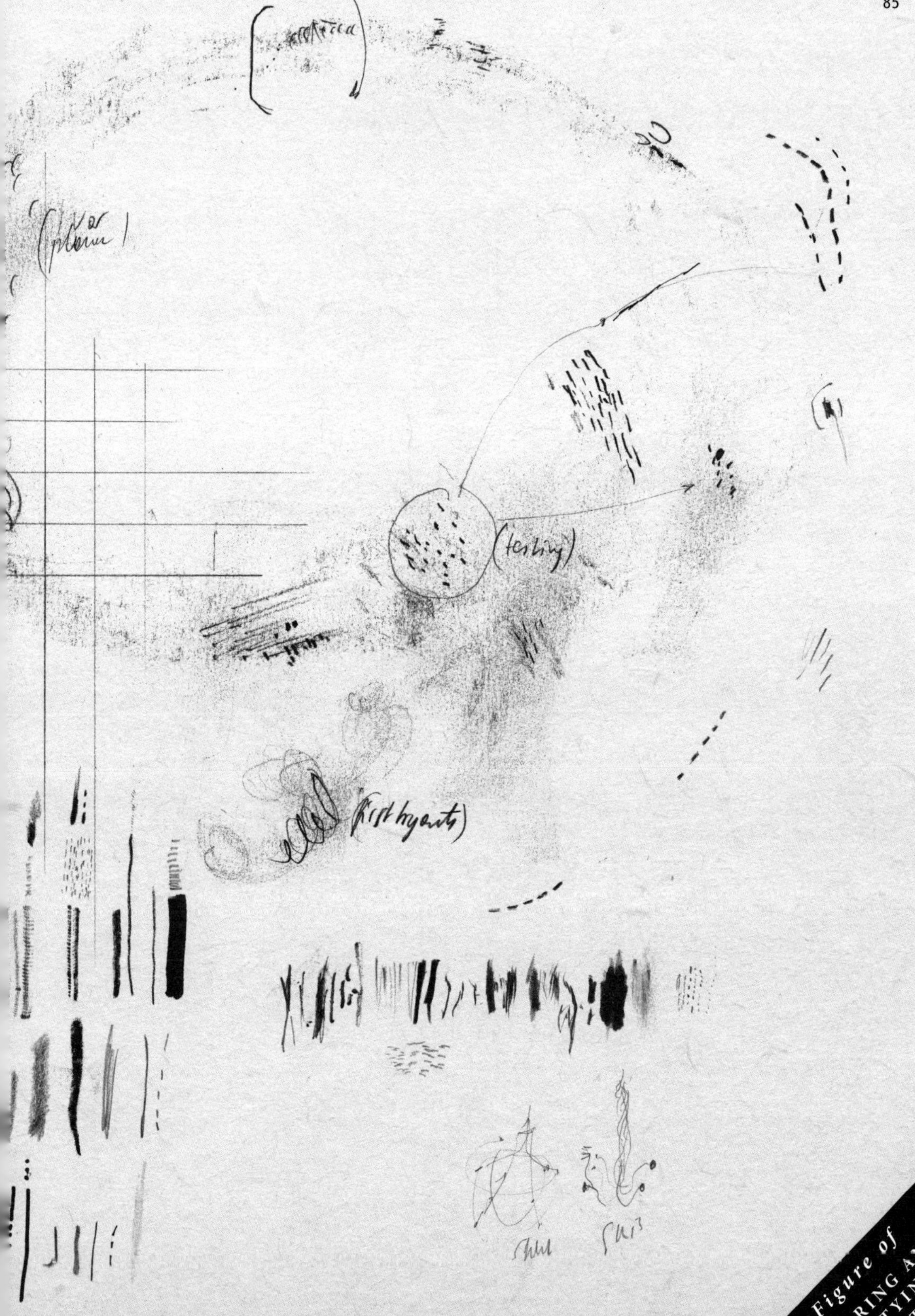
(testing)

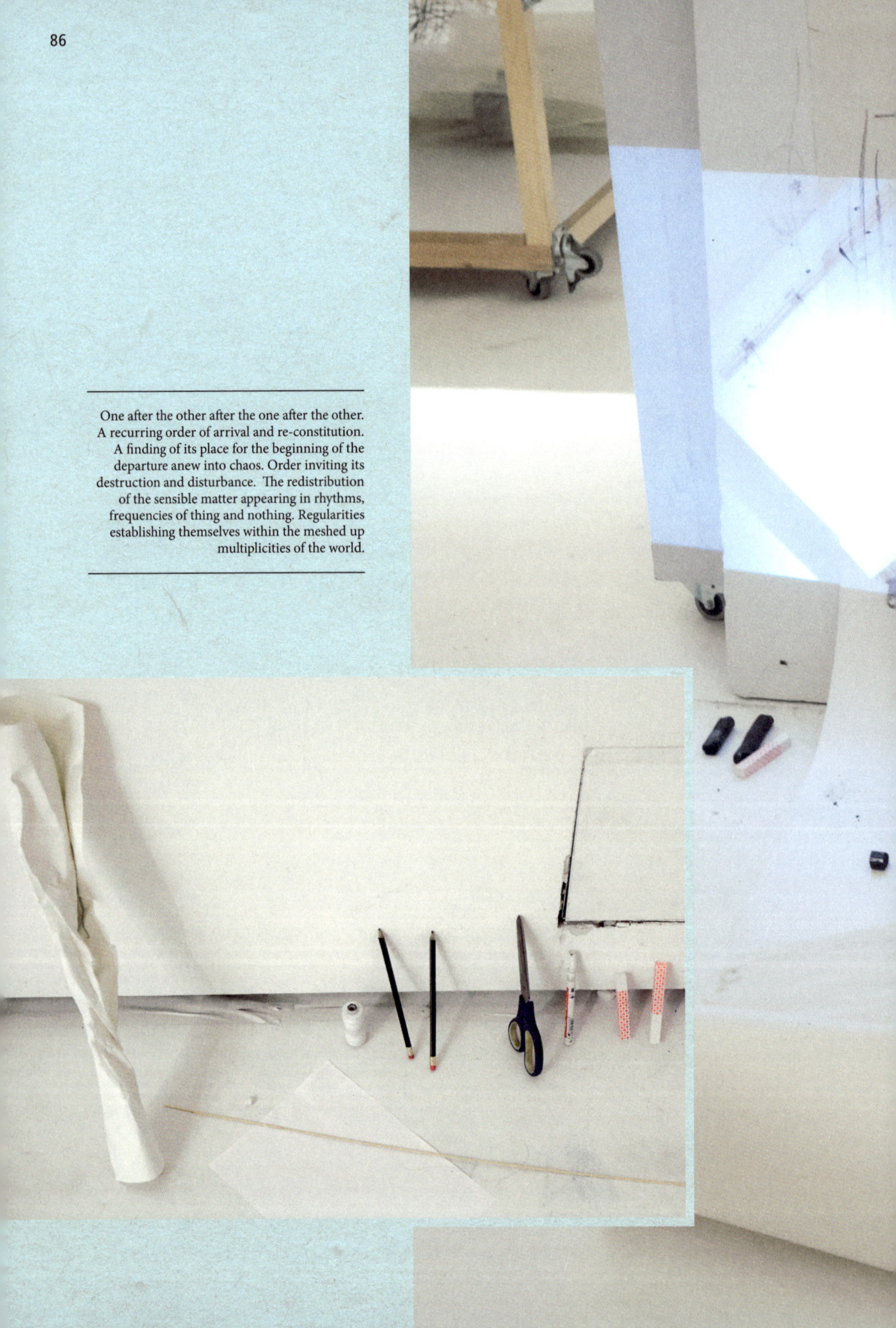

One after the other after the one after the other. A recurring order of arrival and re-constitution. A finding of its place for the beginning of the departure anew into chaos. Order inviting its destruction and disturbance. The redistribution of the sensible matter appearing in rhythms, frequencies of thing and nothing. Regularities establishing themselves within the meshed up multiplicities of the world.

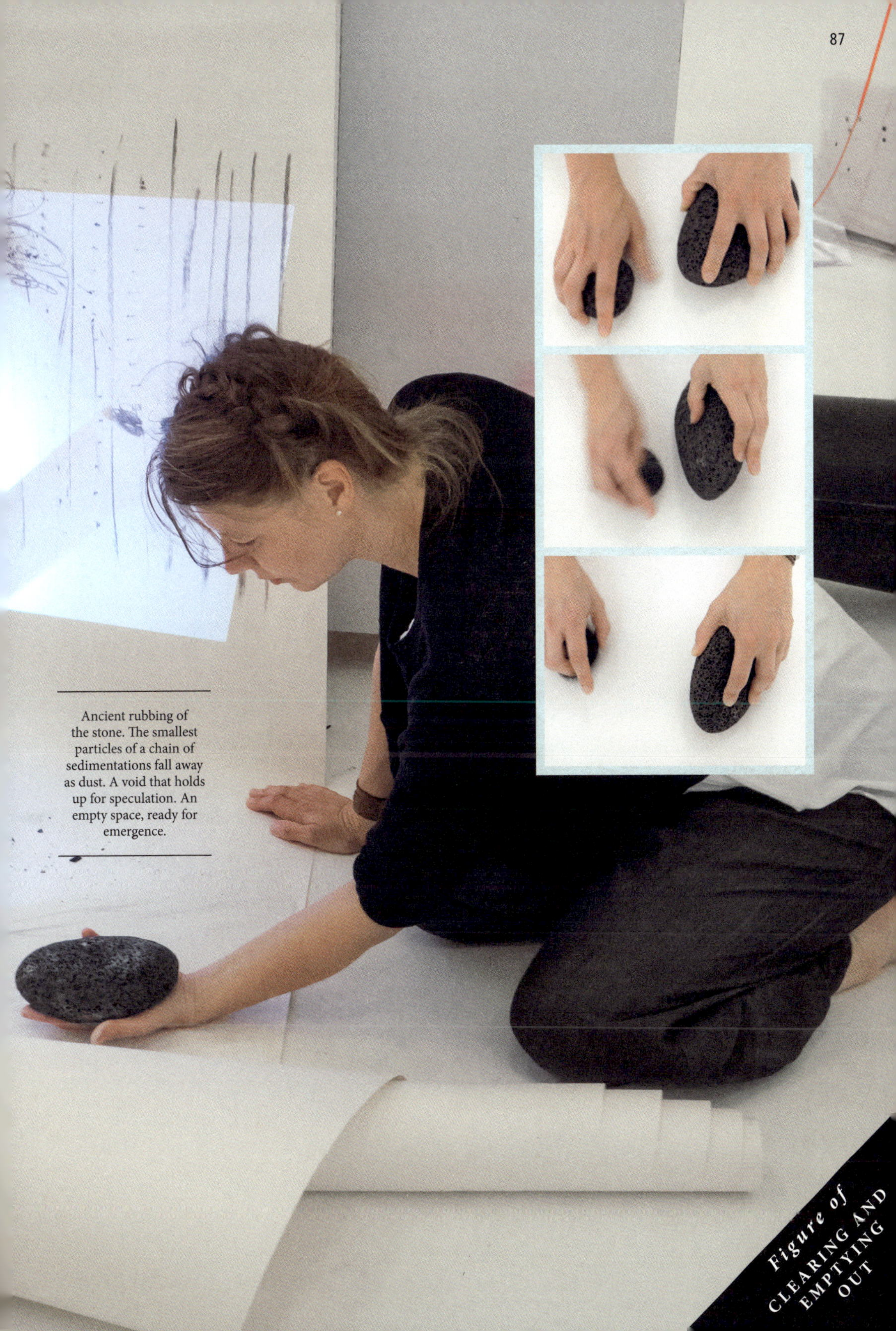

Ancient rubbing of the stone. The smallest particles of a chain of sedimentations fall away as dust. A void that holds up for speculation. An empty space, ready for emergence.

Figure of CLEARING AND EMPTYING OUT

Clearing. Sponge. Black comes to the fore and absorbs. Squeeze and silent anticipation meet. Erasing movement then opening. To reach into. Access. Grip. Holding. Then careful placement. The forming of formation. A shadow on hand. Fleshly hand touching its virtual companion.

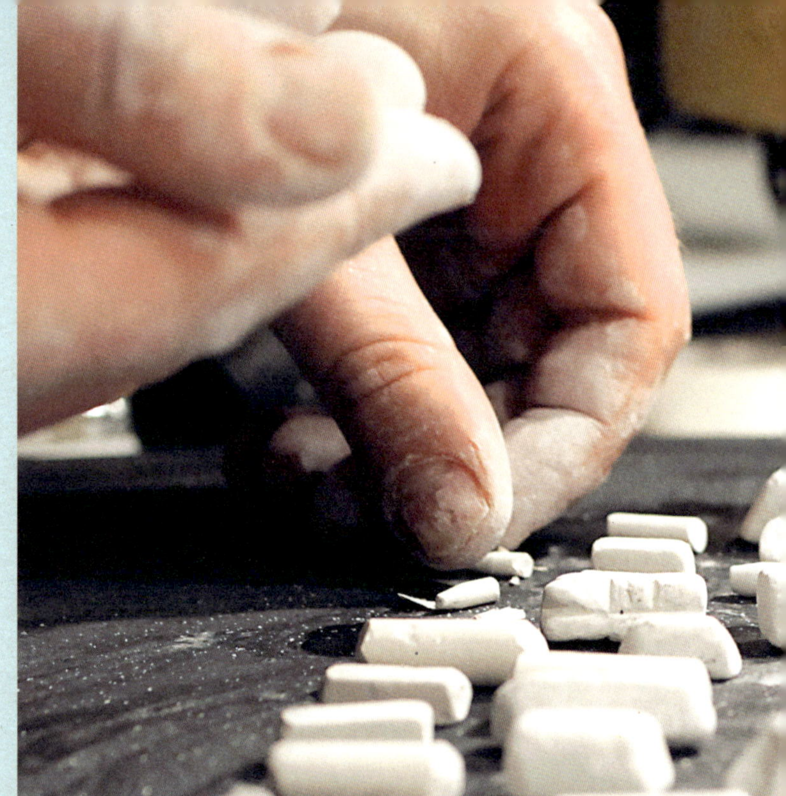

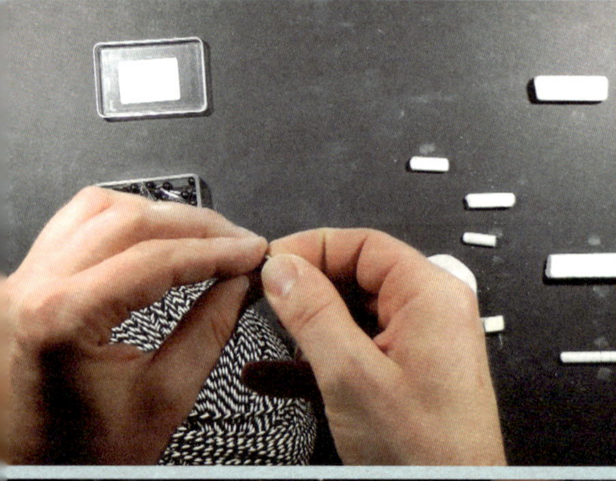

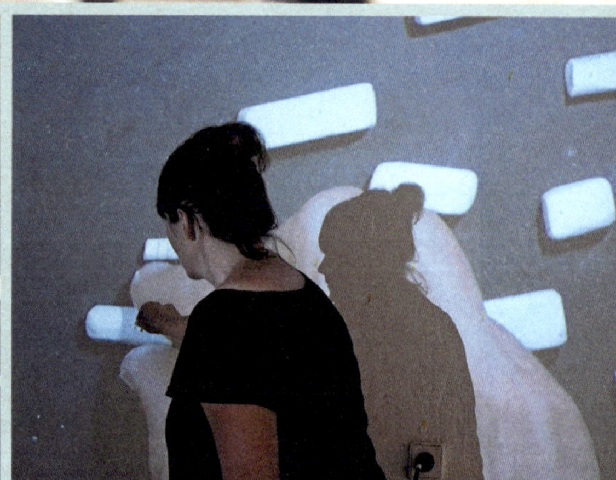

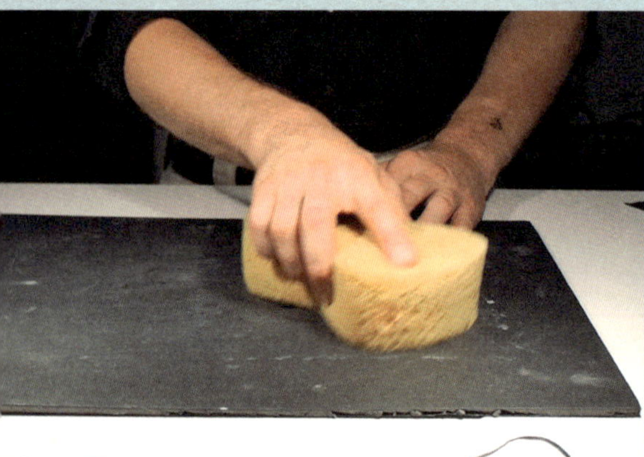

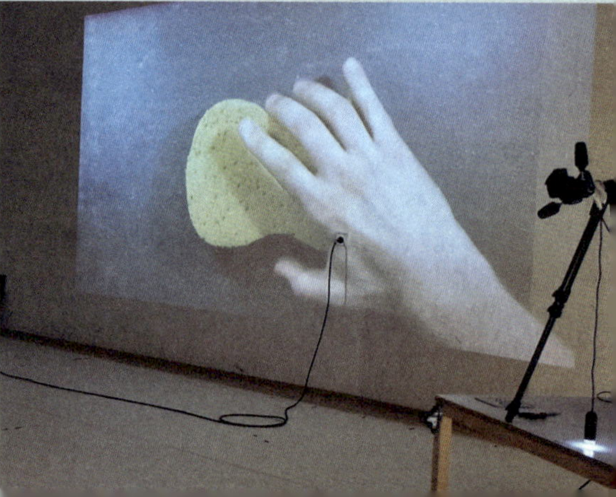

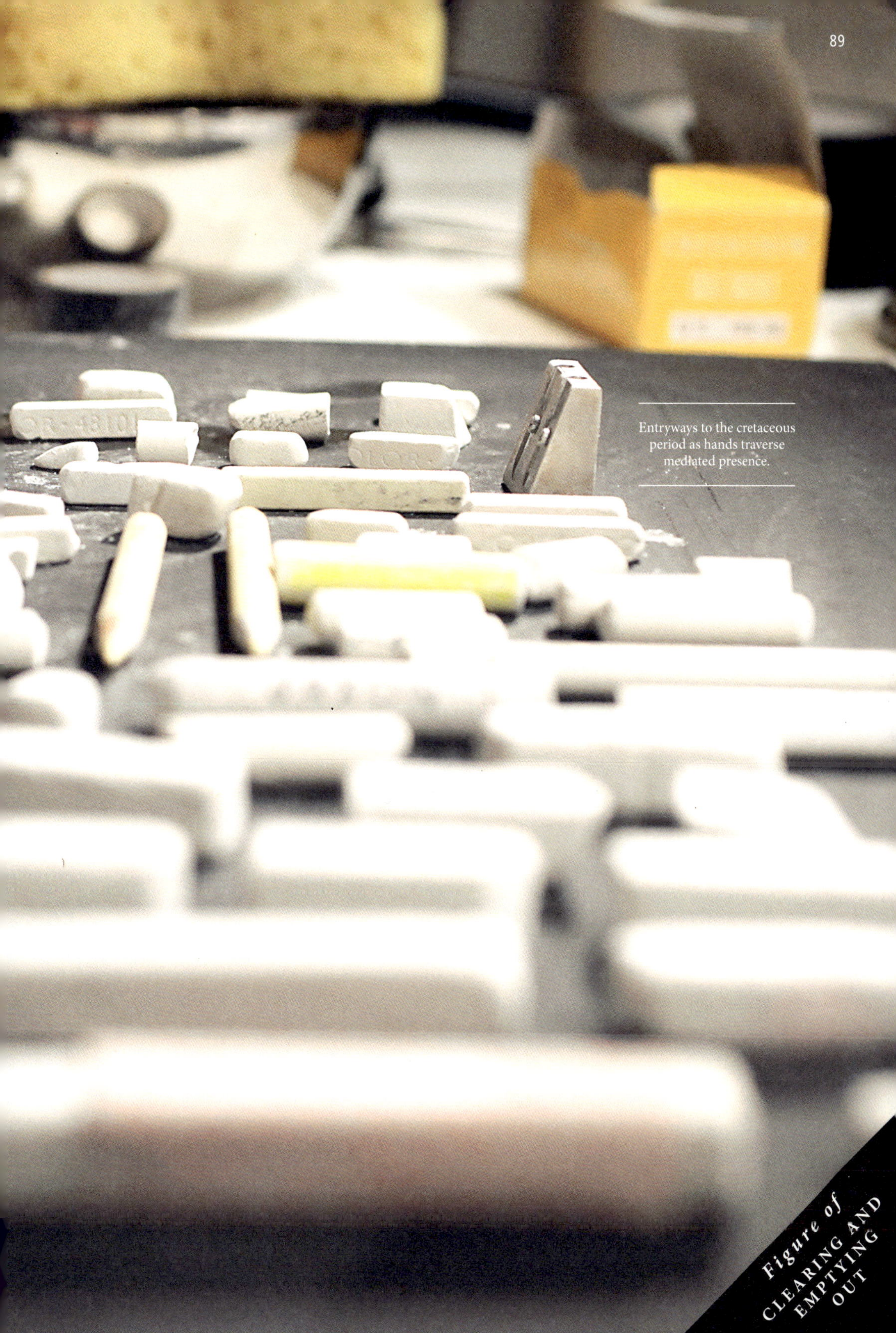

Entryways to the cretaceous period as hands traverse mediated presence.

Figure of CLEARING AND EMPTYING OUT

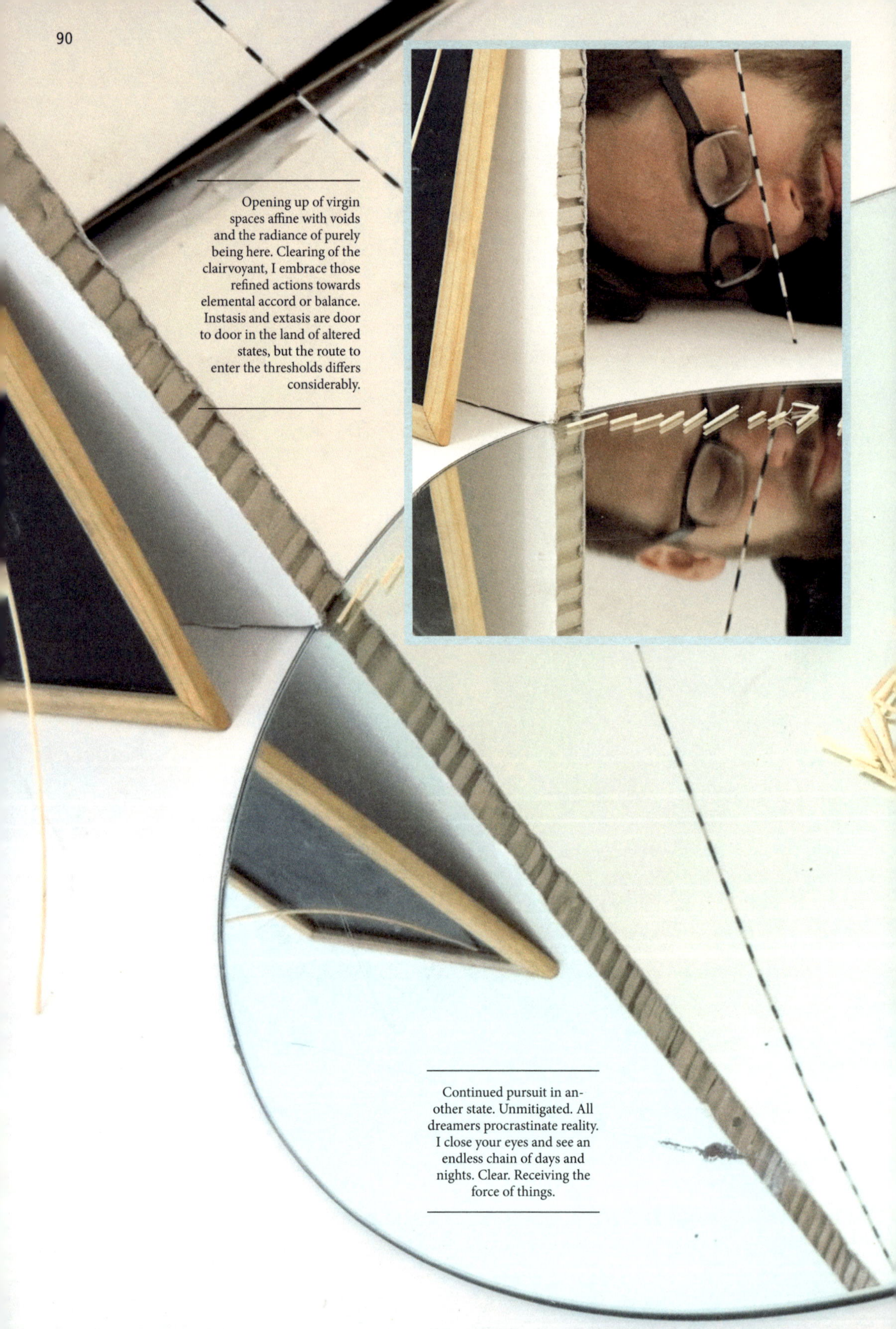

Opening up of virgin spaces affine with voids and the radiance of purely being here. Clearing of the clairvoyant, I embrace those refined actions towards elemental accord or balance. Instasis and extasis are door to door in the land of altered states, but the route to enter the thresholds differs considerably.

Continued pursuit in another state. Unmitigated. All dreamers procrastinate reality. I close your eyes and see an endless chain of days and nights. Clear. Receiving the force of things.

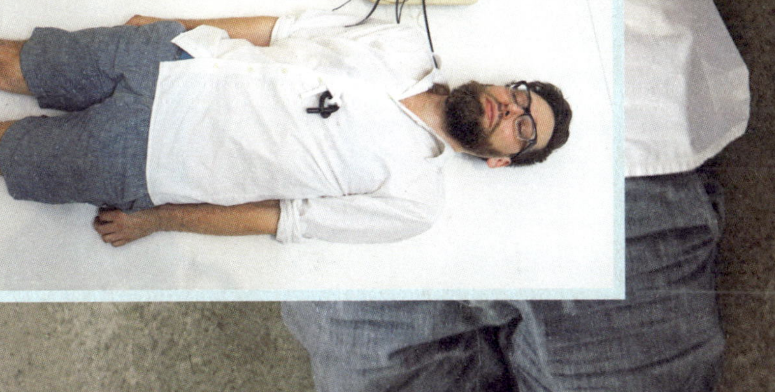

Tender letting go or expulsion. The mirroring of self — an infinite reflection. Mirroring the space above from below. The planes shift as the one-and-onliness of the thing raises to the surface. Space. Defacement of the body. Emptiness.

Figure of
CLEARING AND EMPTYING OUT

Figure of SPIRALLING MOMENTUM

After a lull, the need for intervention: to move, to be moved, to set in motion. From ebbing energy, arising desire to raise intensity once more. Creating impetus, impulse or incentive, impelling movement or force. Uplift, not yet with direction or intention beyond building momentum. Not starting over, rather re-energising from in the midst. To get the blood flowing, increase the rate of circulation through warming, stirring up. To oxygenate, give air. Circulate. Gyrate. Rotate. Turning, elliptical. Circular, cyclical: the activation of centrifugal force. Whirling, ecstatic. Not to dizzy or dissipate. Vertiginous velocity remains grounded as the dervish whose orbiting energy retains its empty centre still. Flight tempered through attendance to the weight of gravitational force, to making dense. Compression with agitation affects a change in molecular state. Resist just going around in circles—not the circularity of a repeated loop, the grooving of a stable pattern, action exhausted towards entropy. Rather to wind, to twist—vector of the vortex, kinetic energy of the coil or spring. Spiralling momentum: eddying energies, poly-central.

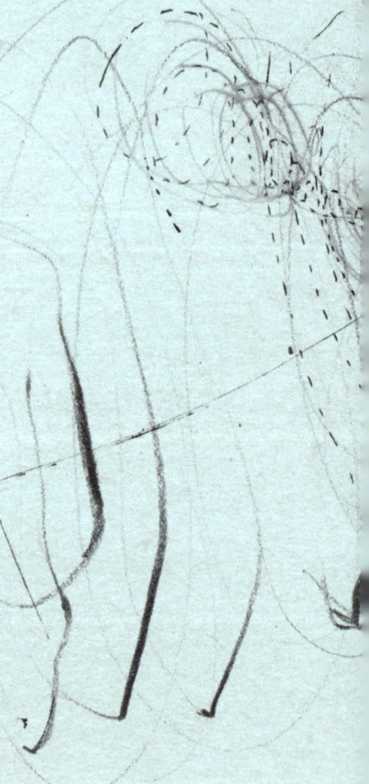

Desirable agitation, enabling turbulence: how far to let oneself be carried. Surrender yet with caution, for things can easily spiral out of control, into disarray. Spiralling momentum has a destructive streak. Recall the violent vortices of whirlwind or tornado—things can soon start to fall, crash to chaos.

Enabling momentum must not climax, instead the moment must be seized. With ease not effort, its rising energy must be harnessed, redirected, taken elsewhere. Preparing of a field of forces, what nests therein is not yet defined.

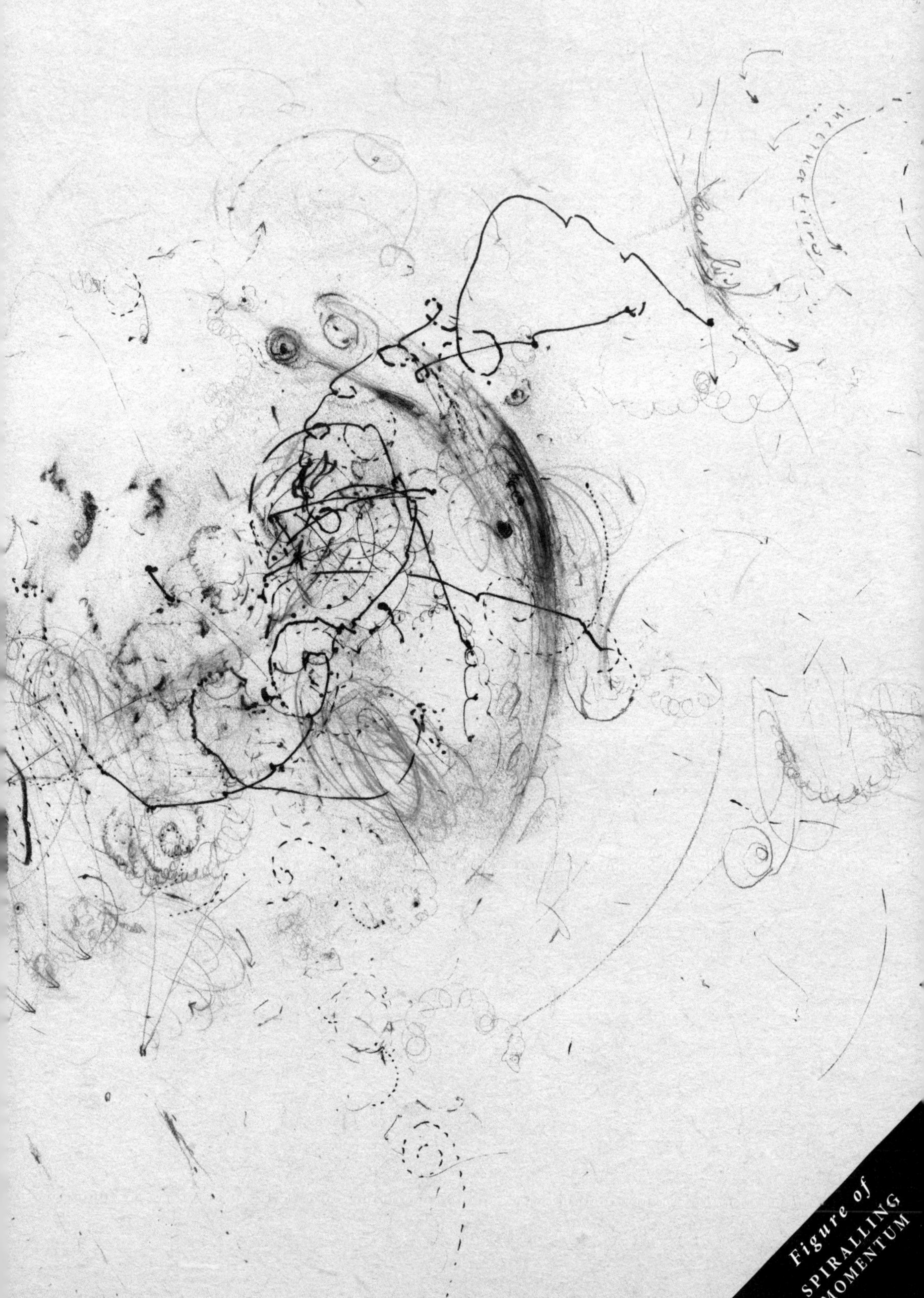

Figure of SPIRALLING MOMENTUM

Vertiginous spiralling towards the epicentre of movement, dancing between the space of compression and suspense, rising and falling towards the virtual middle. I follow gravity, surprised by the void. Speeding up, reaching towards and touching that what always escapes. As there is no centre to the spiral in motion, core, direction and concern shift constantly.

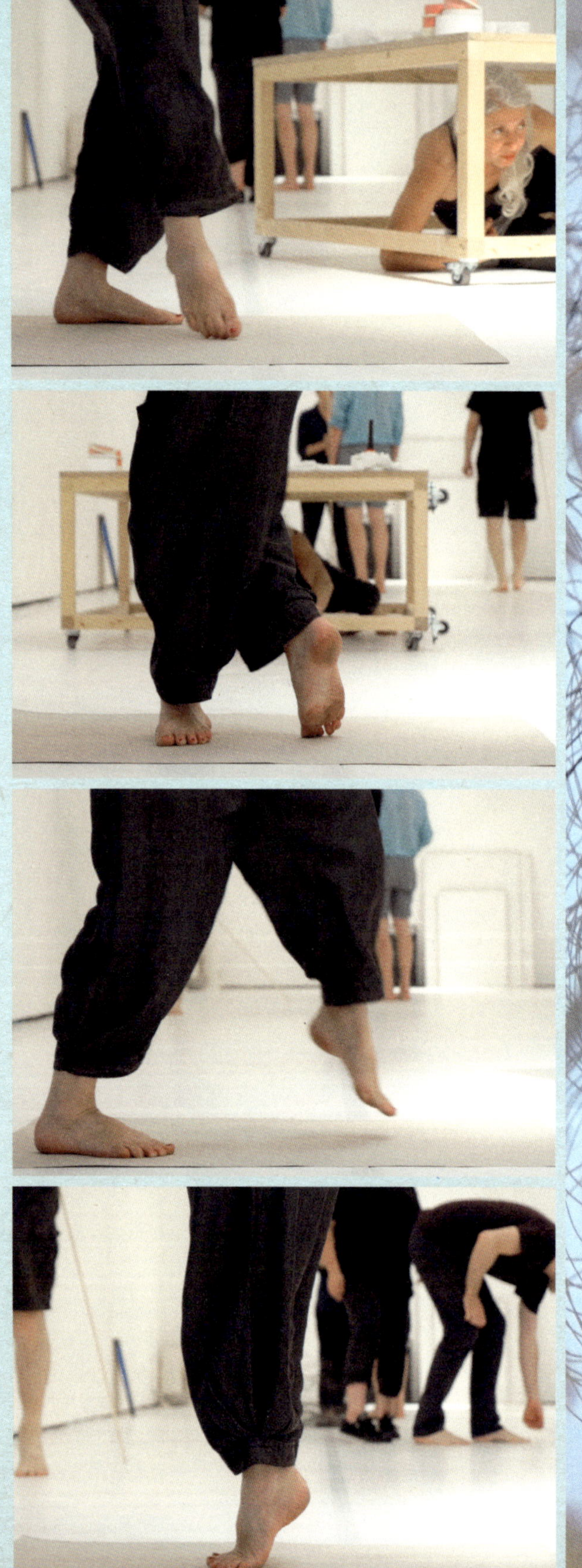

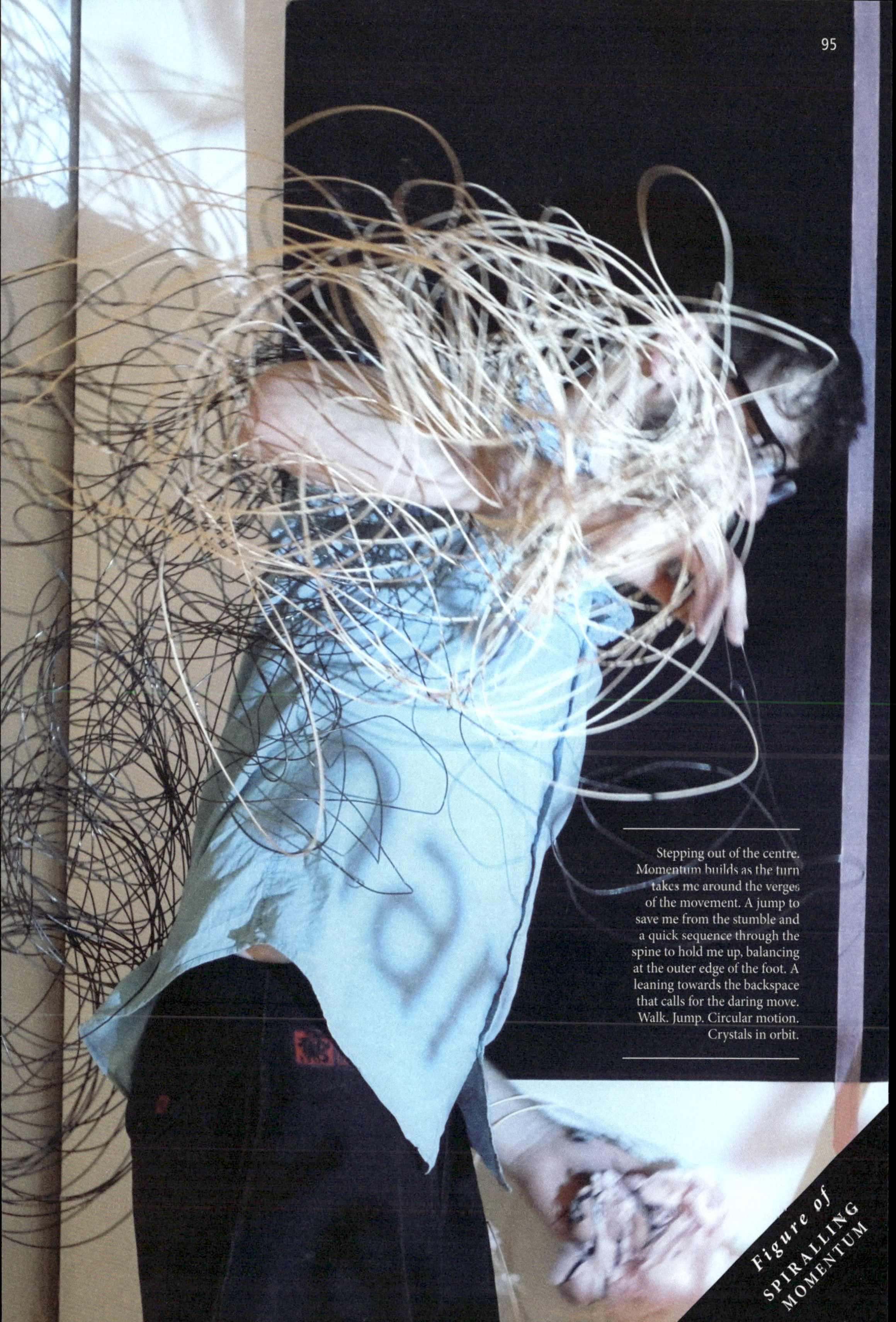

Stepping out of the centre. Momentum builds as the turn takes me around the verges of the movement. A jump to save me from the stumble and a quick sequence through the spine to hold me up, balancing at the outer edge of the foot. A leaning towards the backspace that calls for the daring move. Walk. Jump. Circular motion. Crystals in orbit.

Figure of SPIRALLING MOMENTUM

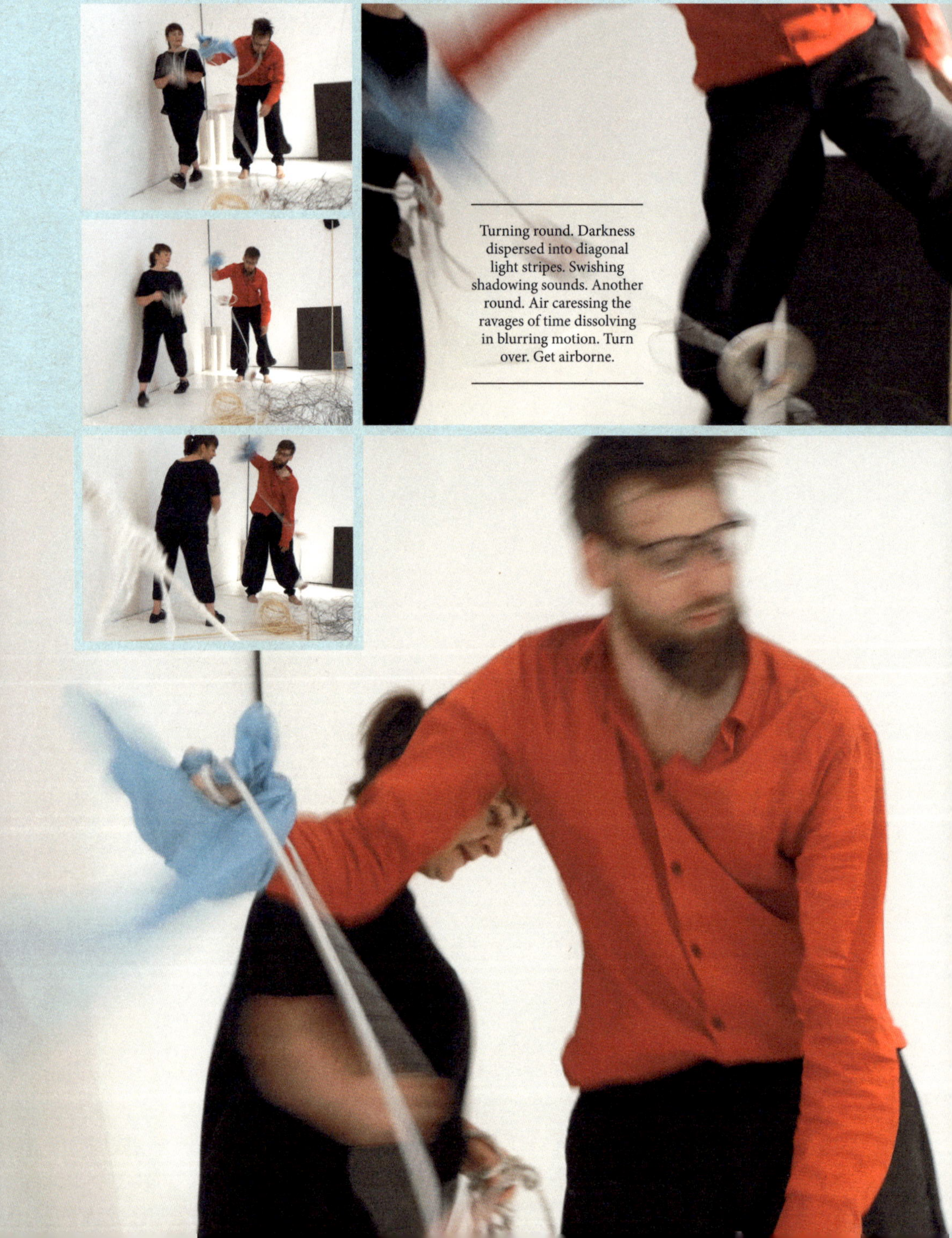

Turning round. Darkness dispersed into diagonal light stripes. Swishing shadowing sounds. Another round. Air caressing the ravages of time dissolving in blurring motion. Turn over. Get airborne.

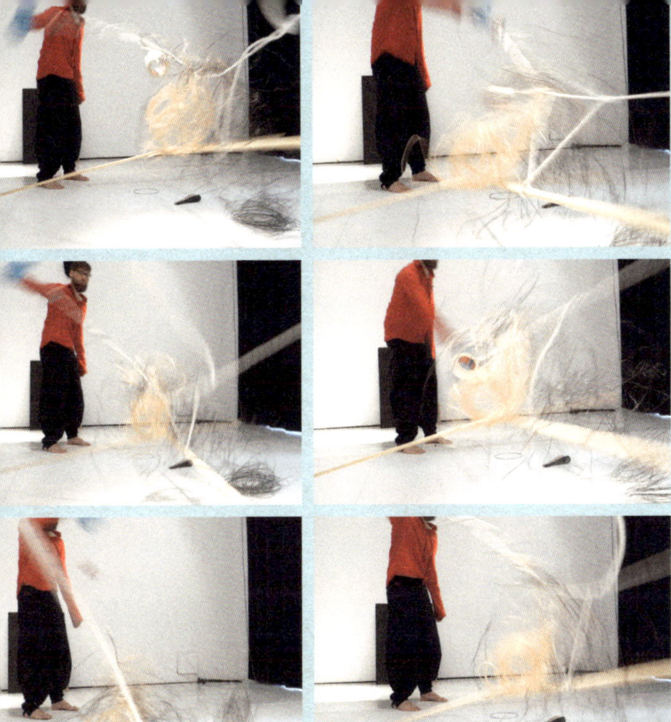

Intensifying. Gearing up. Invisible channelling of forces, streamlined increase. Condensation. Flying in loops, lashing. Frequency. Too quick to be dissected into frames.

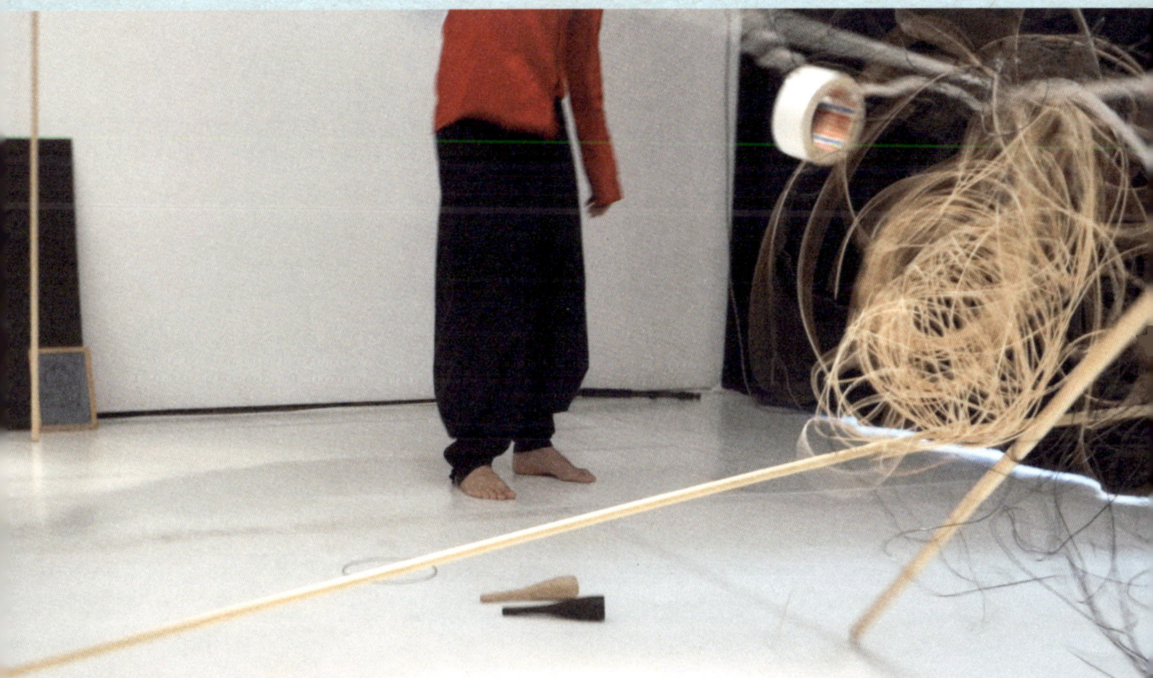

Metals in loops, rolls in agitation. Centrifugal flight crisscrossing rigidified knots of habit, comfort and the known.

Figure of SPIRALLING MOMENTUM

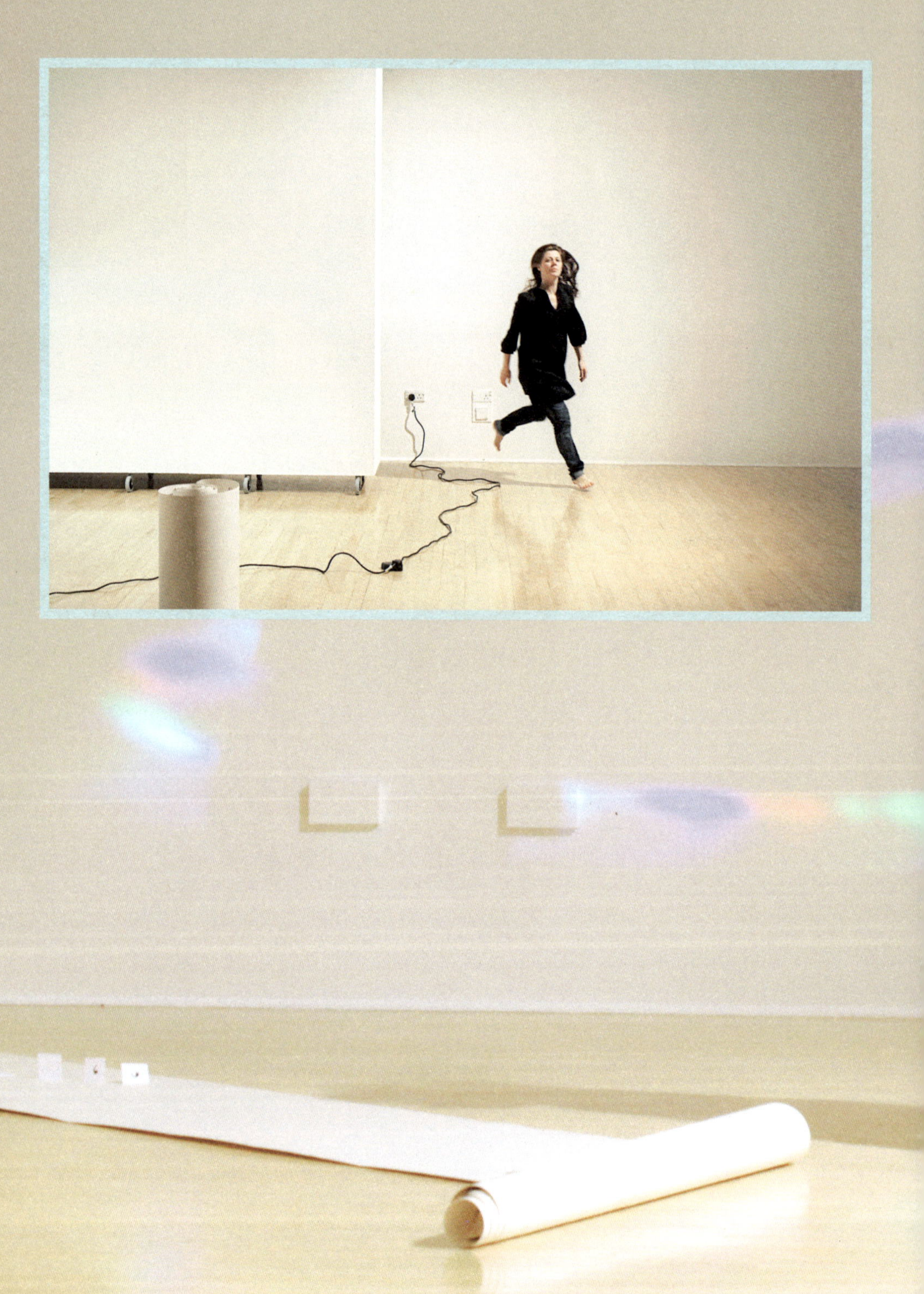

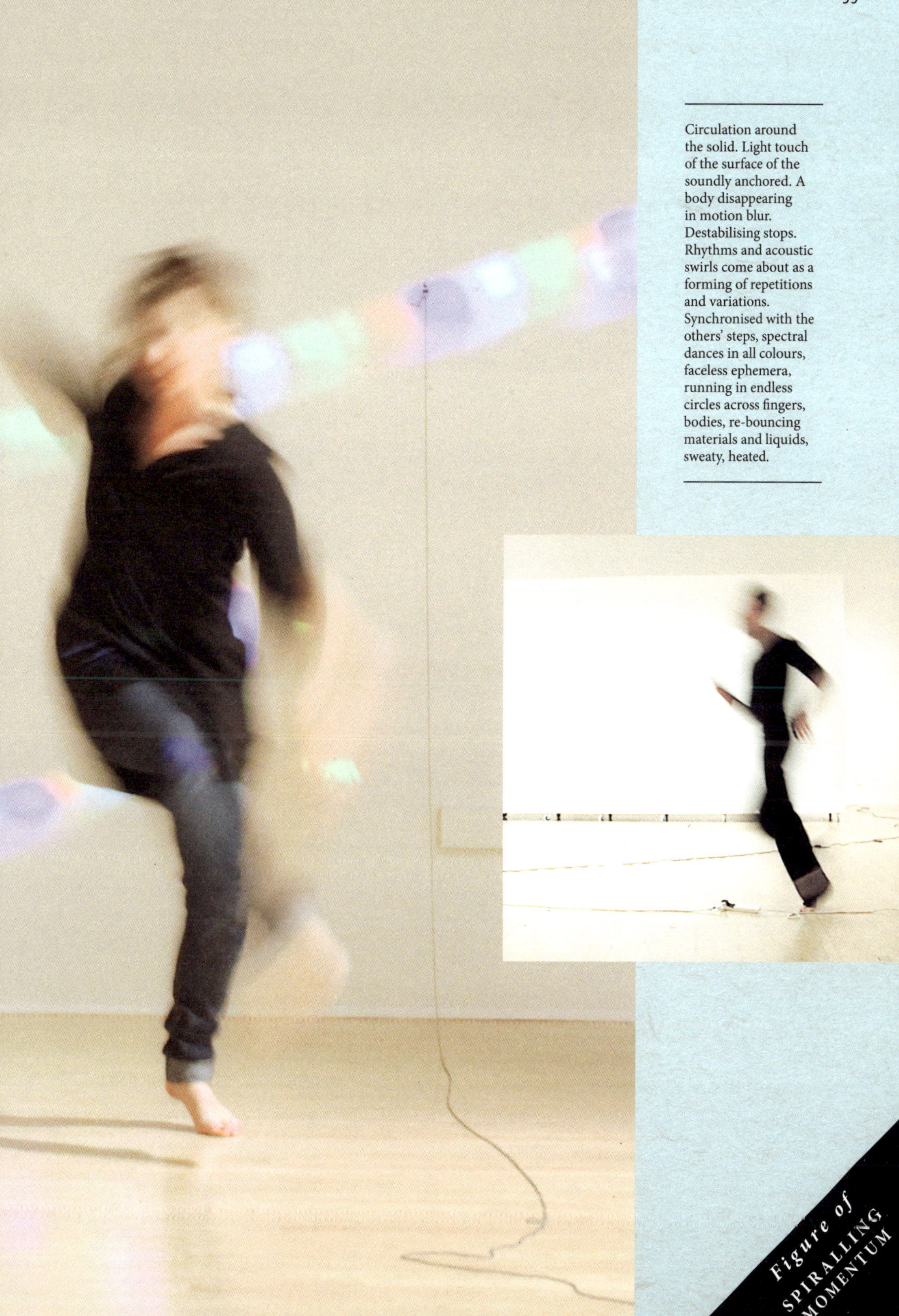

Circulation around the solid. Light touch of the surface of the soundly anchored. A body disappearing in motion blur. Destabilising stops. Rhythms and acoustic swirls come about as a forming of repetitions and variations. Synchronised with the others' steps, spectral dances in all colours, faceless ephemera, running in endless circles across fingers, bodies, re-bouncing materials and liquids, sweaty, heated.

Figure of SPIRALLING MOMENTUM

Figure of TEMPORARY CLOSING

Before exhaustion, a breathing space left for things to be. Not to overcook or overdo, but sensing when is enough. Seeing what is there, trust in what has been produced. Let it rest before it can be met again. Allowing for the reverberations, the ringing of what remains once action halts, a pause is taken. Ripening. Resounding. It is not closed nor closure, but in the midst of action, to find a way of stabilising. Heightened energy of things coming to resolution; there is a point when it is time to step back. Solution sounds so finite; not an end then, not completion. There is still scope for reconfiguration. Yet, still a stilling, a settling. Approach of ending in its incipiency, experienced at its beginning. It is finding an ending. Not ending found as much as followed. Ending descending, felt in its landing. Provisional closing — not fixed, never final.

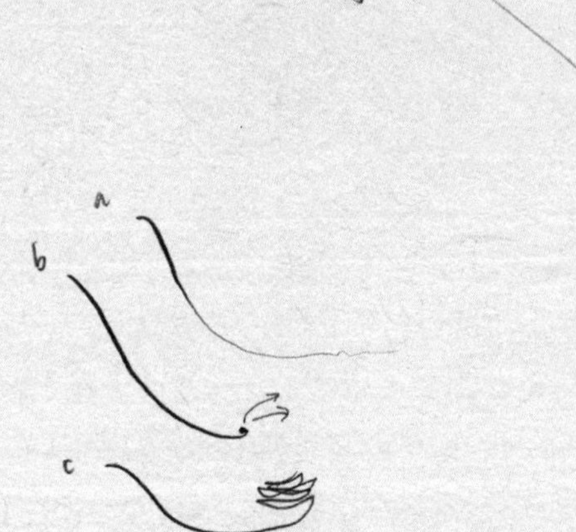

Peaking of momentum, closing as crescendo. A coming to fruition, or of vitality ebbing — the loss of energy, of dynamics. Fading out. Petering off. Or softer, softer: dissipation. Breaking up. Disintegration. Prior to collapse: temporal suspension before things unfasten, loosen, crumple to the floor. Or as a falling, abrupt, crash landing. A sudden settling, a synchronous clap marks stop. Pull out. Retract. Not yet arrived as noun, closing performed in its doing, yet stopped before the doing does too much.

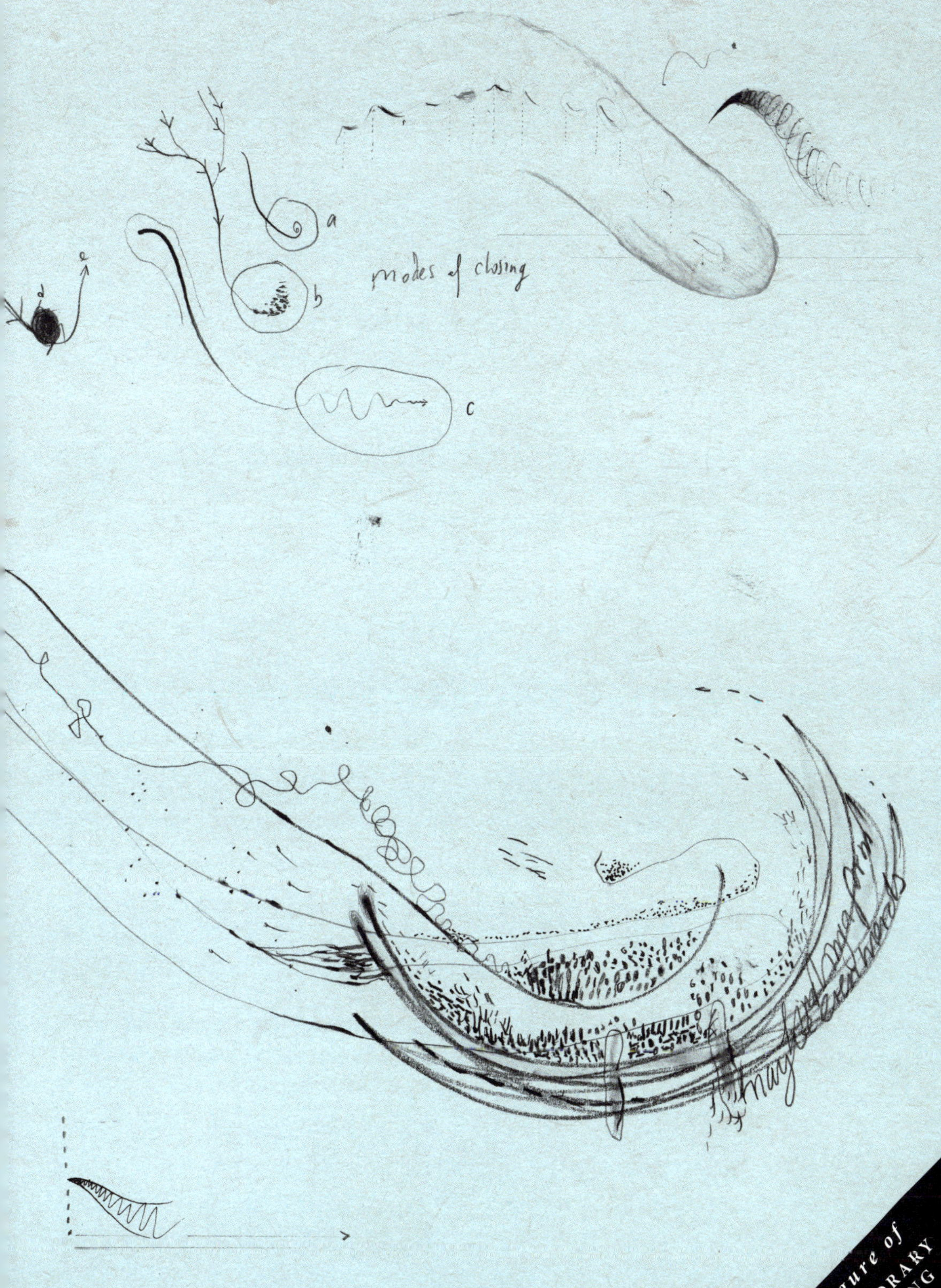

Figure of TEMPORARY CLOSING

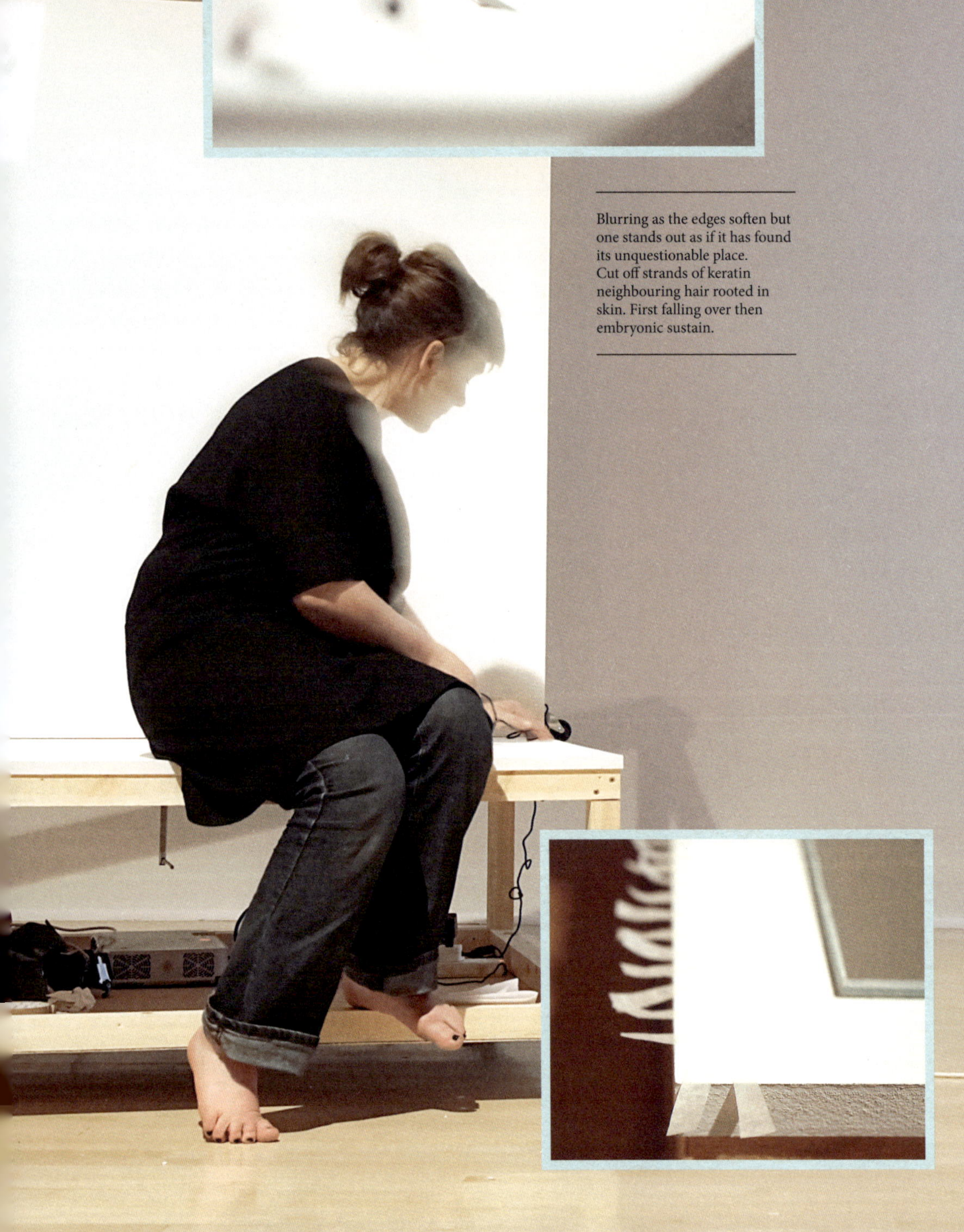

Blurring as the edges soften but one stands out as if it has found its unquestionable place.
Cut off strands of keratin neighbouring hair rooted in skin. First falling over then embryonic sustain.

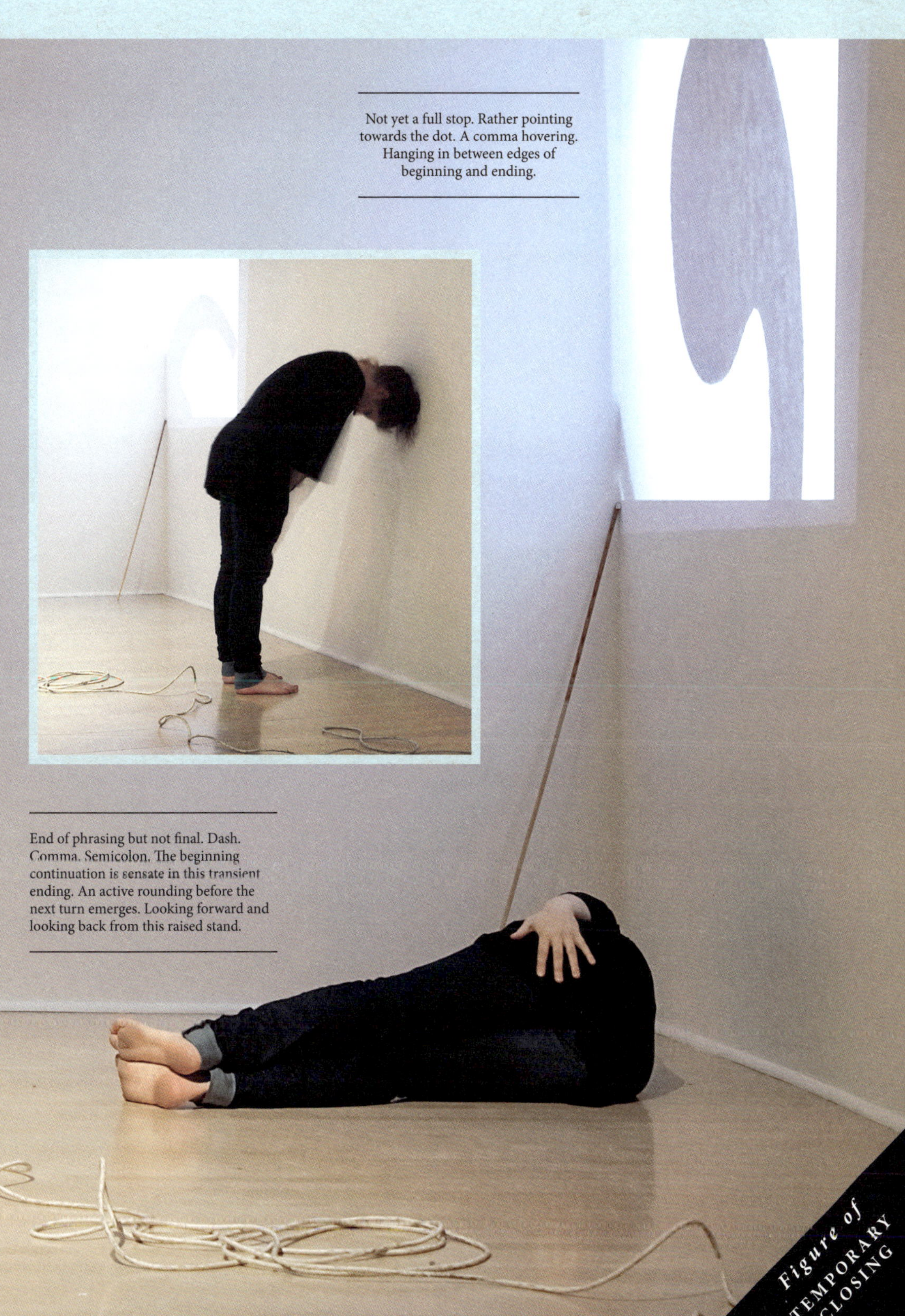

Not yet a full stop. Rather pointing towards the dot. A comma hovering. Hanging in between edges of beginning and ending.

End of phrasing but not final. Dash. Comma. Semicolon. The beginning continuation is sensate in this transient ending. An active rounding before the next turn emerges. Looking forward and looking back from this raised stand.

Figure of TEMPORARY CLOSING

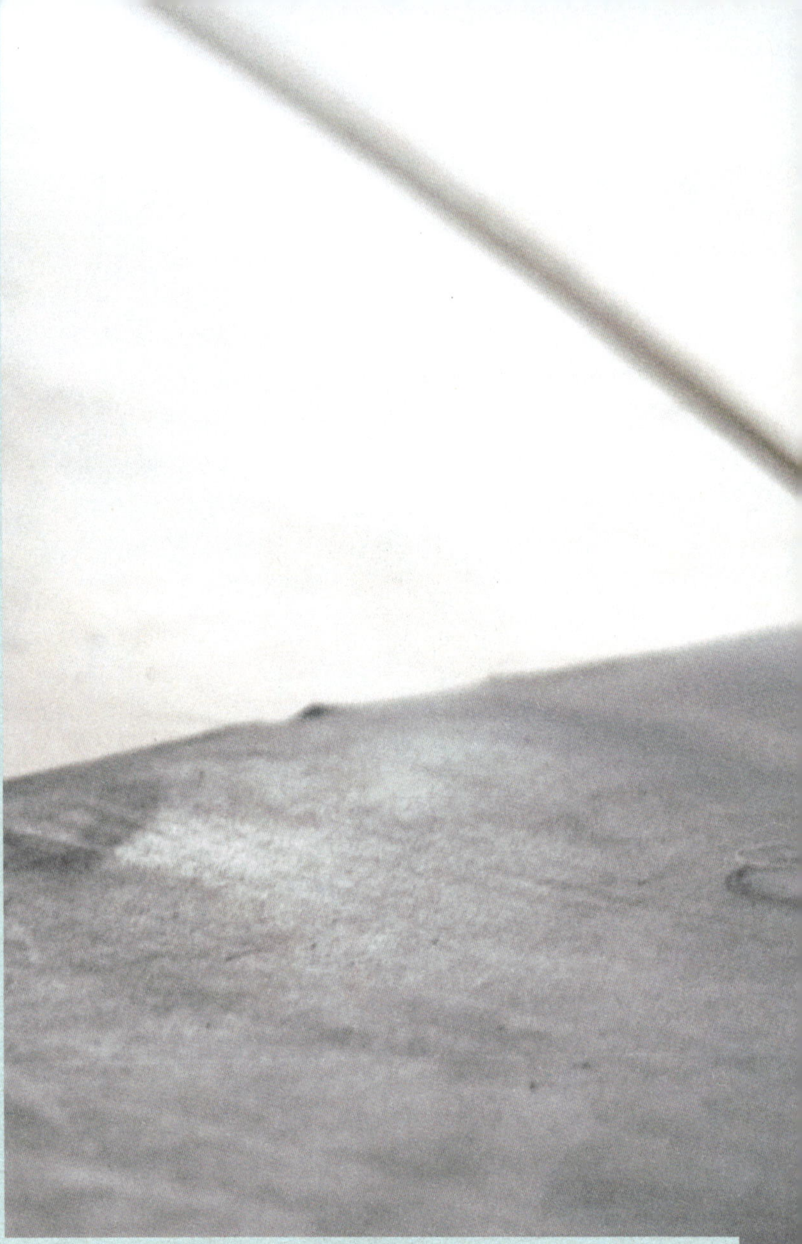

Estrangement as I think of the edges of being here. I might not be there in a while, stillness. Foreboding the decaying moment intimidating completion. Holding apart of yesterday's and tomorrow's actions. Gentle crossings go by. "Meet me at the corner, Ariadne", I think. Cast in remembrance.

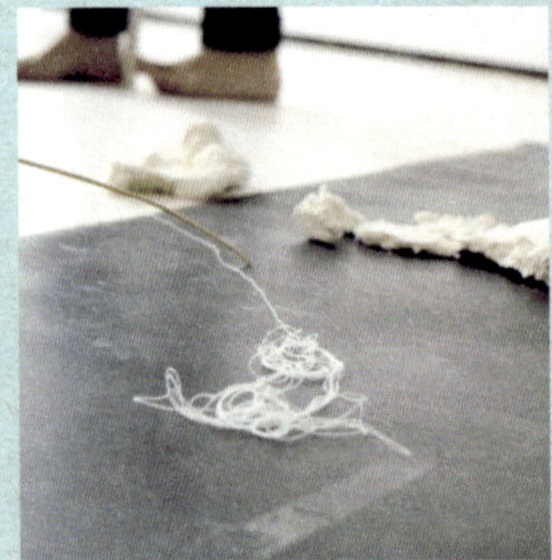
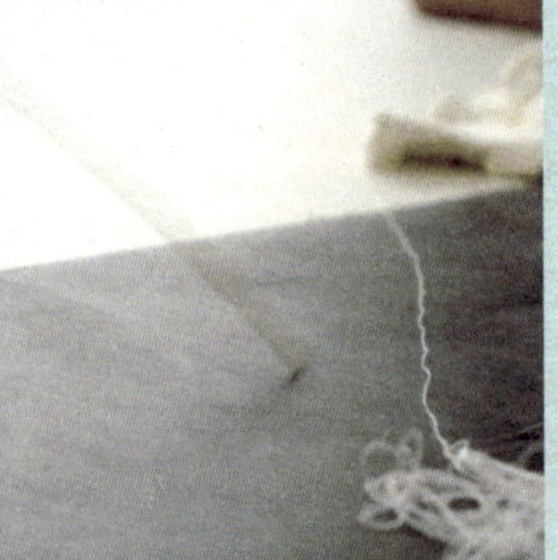
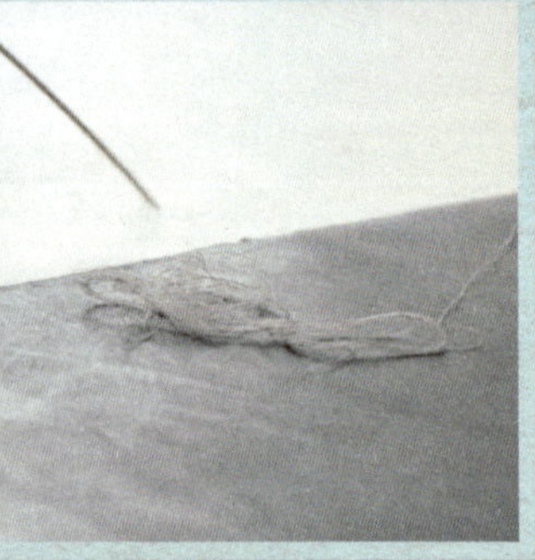

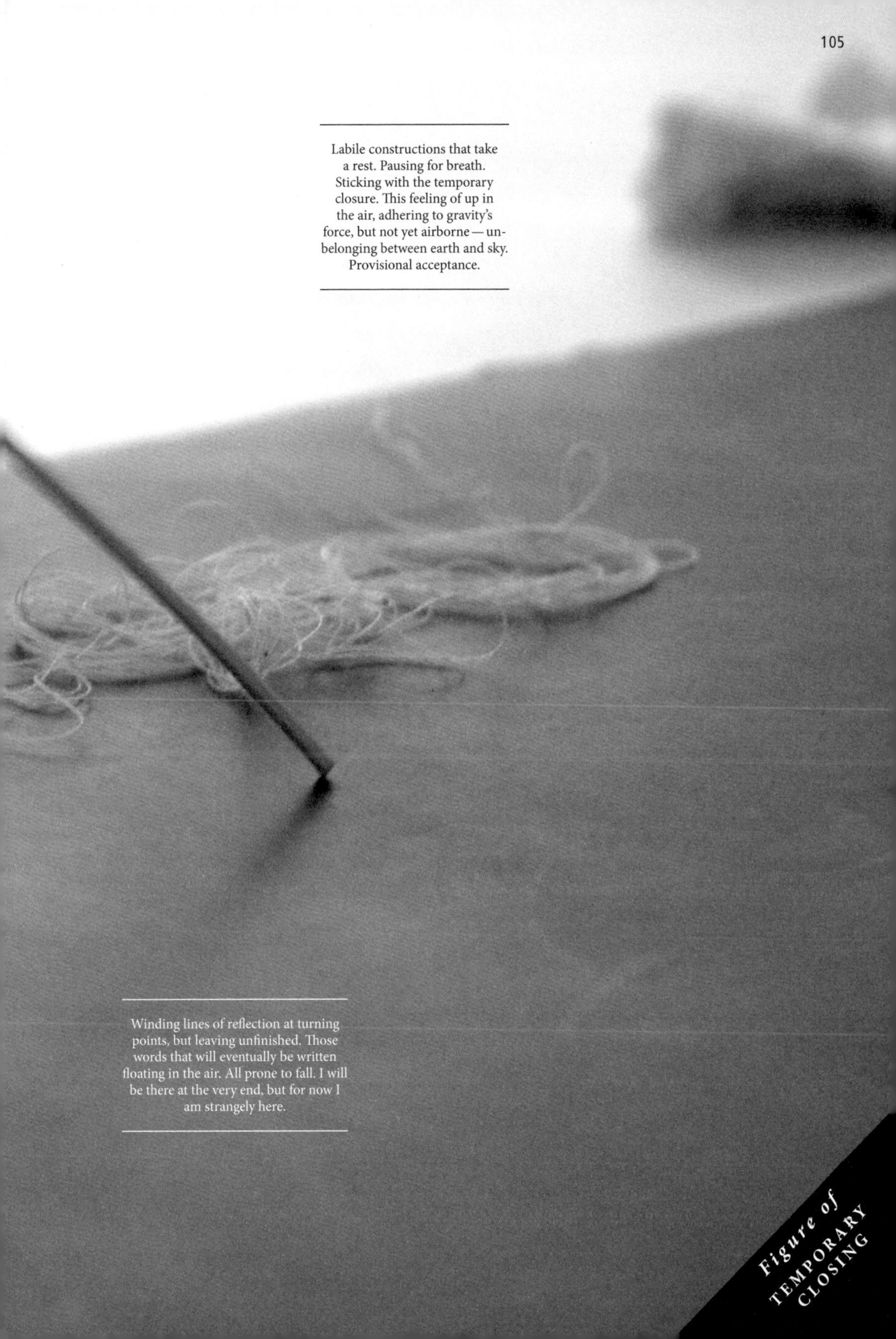

Labile constructions that take a rest. Pausing for breath. Sticking with the temporary closure. This feeling of up in the air, adhering to gravity's force, but not yet airborne — unbelonging between earth and sky. Provisional acceptance.

Winding lines of reflection at turning points, but leaving unfinished. Those words that will eventually be written floating in the air. All prone to fall. I will be there at the very end, but for now I am strangely here.

Figure of
TEMPORARY
CLOSING

A lining-up that goes on and on, no arrival in sight. Balancing at the edge of failure or falling, as I place my hand carefully in relation to things and others. My most tentative movement, before the line of actions rewinds, but stays searching.

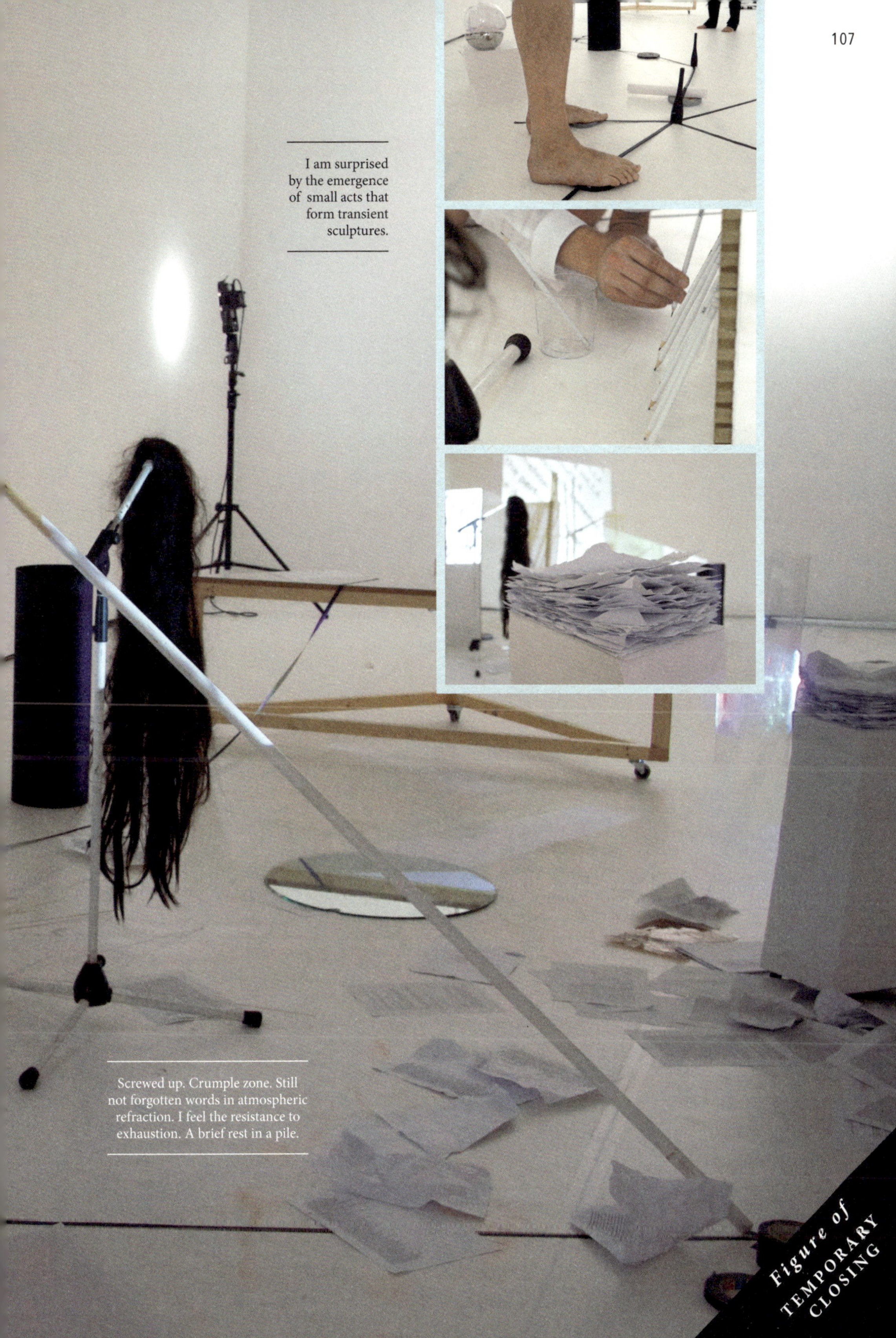

I am surprised by the emergence of small acts that form transient sculptures.

Screwed up. Crumple zone. Still not forgotten words in atmospheric refraction. I feel the resistance to exhaustion. A brief rest in a pile.

Dieter Mersch

FIGURATION / DEFIGURATION

FOR A DIALECTIC OF CHOREO-GRAPHY

The following text thinks in constellations. In doing so, it draws various circles, all of them more or less self-contained. Often it refers to etymologies — not in order to call up origins, but in order to extend the associations. All deliberations are about the same question, that is, the problem of the relation between openness and closeness; or between rule, movement and event, as well in relation to what can be called 'cavity' or 'interspatiality'. They concern the artistic work and that which distinguishes art from other forms of thought. Various categories are proposed — beginning with the *choreo-graphic* (with a separating as well as connecting hyphen), through the dialectics of figuration and defiguration, towards 'movement' and plasticity, the ever preliminary and inconclusive experimentation and essayistic thinking in fragments. The repertoire of propositions serves the continuous 'turning' and 'inflexion', a repeated rethinking of the same thing in new and other ways, which in its actual sense represents the cause of aesthetical practice in order thus to approximate it in the shape of repetition and variation.

CHOREO-GRAPHIC FIGURES

Choreo-graphy: the word, disrupted by a hyphen, evokes numerous associations. *Choros* on the one hand denominates the dramatic speaking choir in connection with ancient Greek theatre, on the other hand, deriving from its origin, dance and song, especially the ritual 'round dance' and the *symbolon kinēseon* connected with it, i.e., the symbolisation of movement through a combination of word, music, gesture, and rhythm. *Chorein* therefore belongs to those arts which form movement as much as they endow it with meaning. This especially holds true for the coordination of 'the many' with regard to spatial arrangement as well as their temporal succession. Moreover, *choros*, the choir, and *chōros*, the place, are related to each other; the first is bound to the consecrated location, while the latter remains open. *Graphein* in its turn denominates writing or delineating, the notching by which signs are marked, combined with each other and 'con-textualised', and permanently put on a surface. The expression likewise maintains a reference to trace and record (*Aufzeichnung*), as well as to the different practices of notation and score which record the ephemeral of movement, its fragility and fluidity. Such fixations among other things happen through diagrams and schemata, which however only present insufficient or preliminary models and function like instructions whose rules merge the elements into constellations. *Choreo-graphies* thus constitute the forms of a general design that create extensive structures or configurations, and bring into play manifold activities or practices to let them resonate with each other. The tableau of performatives here takes up a special position — it defines and correlates the operative executions in order to realise complex scenes which likewise conceptualise the events and leave them their surprise, their occurrence, and try to concentrate them in the place of inscription. Far from producing a closed shape, their realisation rather stays chronically precarious insofar as the arts and their adventures maintain an intrinsic relationship with their failure.

Thus, a conflict is marked from the outset, for the *graphies* seize, preset and fix procedures; in doing so, they tend to exclude the unforeseeable, while *choros* / *chōros* — the confined and yet free place — permits all kinds of things, and even shows a proximity to breach and failure. The equally split and interrelated expression *choreo-graphy* represents this irresolvable tension. The arts therefore are necessarily endowed with a double quality oscillating between writing or way of writing, i.e., a fixating diagrammatic, and the concession of places and temporal sequences and their openness. Furthermore, as notations and rules in the *choreo-graphic* are connected like determinative matrices with *the many* and the disparity of the medial between word, image, sound, movement and body, the 'inter-play' belongs to it which as a game can never be fully mastered and rather allows openings and liberties, as well as the moment of a performance able at any time to make something else out of the scores and diagrammatic instructions. In the broadest sense, *choreo-graphy* may thus serve as a metaphor for all the arts, especially for their transdisciplinary alliance and cooperativeness, as well as for the social in which they are embedded, and which results from a non-totalisable network of references and situations in which things as much as people, forces or materialities and their mutual relations are taking part — for the *choros* requires participation, the relationship with the other and the others, be it objects, chance events or spatio-temporal conditions, or be it the participants, the onlookers, witnesses and followers who together originate the 'ecology' of an event in the first place. Just as writing, its *grammata* and *grammē* are able to put down signs and draw their lines and thus enable their comprehensive reception, citation and 'tradition', the density and unpredictability of the ecological moment, which at no time complies with our technical regimes and dispositifs, conversely enables deviance or aberration. They lead us instead of us leading them, and thus begin to unfold their own, unintentional narrations.

CHOROS / CHŌROS / MEDIALITY

At least some of the convoluted lines shall be broken down more closely in the following. Here, I will *initially* set out from the — not necessarily obvious — nexus between 'dance' on the one hand, and an 'aesthetics of collaboration' and its embeddedness in the participative or the social on the other.[1] Both refer to the place that accommodates and lets them take place, for it is the place, its spatial arrangement in whatever form, which allows the dance as well as the community to 'last'. If we do not suppose a spatial arrangement here, this already confirms that the place is not a nothingness or a void, but already is subject to conditions and relations providing it and that which occurs in it. The entanglement of *choros* and *chōros / chōra*, the confined yet open space, reminds one of Plato's usage of the terms, which again was subjected to a detailed interpretation by Jacques Derrida.[2] For Plato compares *chōra* to a 'mother' who gives birth and brings 'something' into its existence in the first place, a cavity enabling the arrival of an appearance as well as the appearance of the arrival, and thus belongs neither to the category of being nor of becoming, nor to form and matter, but constitutes a third instance which takes up the status of a 'medium'. According to Plato, it belongs to the world of the preposition *metaxy*, that itself indeterminate 'in-between' which according to Eric Voegelin time and again turns up in prominent places of the different dialogues[3], e.g., in the *Symposion* in the shape of the daimonion *Eros* who neither belongs to the immortals nor to the mortals, but primarily denominates the fluid which constitutes relationships.[4] Later, in *Timaios*, the interspatiality of *chōra* becomes a 'third figure' described as the 'birth-giving' that endows things and events with their 'appearance' in the first place.[5] Something has to be situated: *choreo-graphy* provides the enabling structure for this without pre-ensuring the possible.

As is well-known, the Latin Middle Ages translated (and simultaneously substantialised) the Greek *metaxy* — mainly with a view to the Aristotelian *aisthēsis* doctrine — as 'medium', but one has to make a note that from there *choros / chōros* would principally have to be understood as something medial that uncovers as much as it covers. The medial denominates a paradoxical duplicity insofar as it possesses its disappearance in appearing and its appearance in disappearing.[6] Moreover, we must not forget that in Greek tragedy the chorus took over the function of a critical counterpart representing destiny in the name of the cult. Its task especially consisted of putting the drama, the actions and their consequences back into the ungovernable as well as to the traditions of *polis* and *ethos*, which the actors in their finiteness could not overlook. Therefore the *choros* was interwoven with the arena of the stage and its *scēnē*, anew the 'locale' (German *Schauplatz,* viewing place) of events, as well as with the measure, the metric as the elementary balance of the animate and its passions, which together formed the poetic atmosphere of ritual repetitions. From this perspective *choros* always embodied the fulfilment of an order not 'represented' or 'created' by anyone, that rather provided the background on the basis of which the subjects and their actions and manoeuvres could be allocated their inherent position in the total of cosmological events in the first place.

However, it is not this mythological conservatism we should be interested in but first of all the fact that *choros* in this way constituted an aesthetic holism that related all the arts with each other, making them merge to a whole for a long time, located in their divine origin. It was the Renaissance that tore them apart and divided them into different genres in order to have them compete for predominance with the means of a continuous *paragone* — and it was the vision of Romanticism to put them together again and reconcile them in new unity. Unresolved until today, the arts are working on their reunion, but for the first time new technologies and their recombination of all media appear to offer the chance of asserting their identity beyond the cultic — out of that which Friedrich Kittler called the *Universal Discrete Machine* of digitisation — and to restitute it in the shape of a utopia of the virtual and the fascination with the spectacle. Under their aegis the erstwhile, always questionable unity of word, music, gesture, and rhythm merges to a new, multi-connectional network of bodies, images, sounds, and performances whose mutual resonances amplify each other, and in whose shadow the bygone 'total work of art' succeeds as a strategy of overpowering. The medial thus coagulates to an apparatus of domination which no longer 'gives' or 'grants' but takes possession of the scenes and situations instead of releasing them into their original occurrence. Resistance to this is stirring in those group performances employing *choreo-graphies* expressly in order to put the events back again into their unavailability and surprise by means of participation, the 'intractability' of bodies and the singularity of assemblages. In contrast, the digital scenographies and their correlate, the choreographies (without hyphen) of light, sound, and effects appear as their equally multidimensional and multisensory production dispositive which — instead of the disquiet of events — solely aims at a universal governing of affects.

NIETZSCHE'S 'GOD' OF DANCE

We therefore differentiate between *choreo-graphy* which keeps its precariousness and fragility through its separating hyphen, and scenography and choreography without hyphens as practices of a universal staging of space and time, which today can be criticised primarily as machines of exposition, of control and appropriation of the scenes and their events. On the other hand, with a view to the 'differential' hyphen of *choreo-graphic* practices, the issue is to strengthen those decompositional and deconstructive aspects which at the same time form and disrupt the artistic processes. Conceiving art solely from a government of the senses and their affection means to misconstrue them as an instrument of power, and to make one forget its mediality and thus the potentials of disruption and the 'in-between'. The result is illusion and immersion practices: they live from their acceleration as well as from their un-fulfilment, whose chronic deficiency is prone to hypercomplexity. They thus deny the aesthetic procedures any reflexivity, divest them of their transitory aspect, their passage, which initially want to put their means in motion and so to 'turn' or convert them instead of sealing them off from the observer and making them opaque. Like a flat wall they deny any support, any distance or retrospect, and accordingly lapse into irrelevance. Art however rather feeds on its permanent openness, on the unfinished possibilities and unfulfilled promises which are just the antithesis of all technological policies of a likewise scenographic and choreographic calculation that no longer concedes space to the spark of the unforeseen or the inconlusive.

In return, in order to lend aesthetic indetermination an equally more colourful and clearer image, let us remember Friedrich Nietzsche's famous remark about dance as a paradigm of the aesthetic, prominently represented in *Thus Spoke Zarathustra*: "I would only believe in a god who knew how to dance."[7] In fact this sentence is one of the book's most frequently quoted passages, although its content remains obscure and invites all kinds of misunderstanding. The saying belongs to the text's first part and is taken from the section that Nietzsche entitled *Of Reading and Writing*. Apart from numerous sarcastic polemics regarding the hegemonial academic text production of his time, especially the philosophical one, it says: "Of all that is written, I love only that which one writes with one's own blood. Write with blood, and you will discover that blood is spirit."[8] In reversal this means: spirited can only be what originated in the intensity of life and its vitality. He goes on with an allusion to antiquity: "Once the spirit was god", in which context Nietzsche inserts the avowal that he only would be able to believe in a god who "knew how to dance" — straightforward in opposition to the devil who commonly was ascribed this skill. The pathos is clear: it contrasts the false emphasis of the late nineteenth century, its pseudo-depth and 'apparitionism' with lust, lightness and the exceedance schooled through Dionysian excess. In truth, though, it does not pay homage to the superficial pleasures of eroticism and intoxication as one might think, but to the multiplication of differences and the "fissure".[9] Therefore Nietzsche adds: "Now I am light, now I am flying ..., now a god dances through me"[10] — a passage reminding one of Derrida's statement that it was Heidegger's biggest mistake that he could not dance (whose authenticity however is in no way historically proven).

For Nietzsche, the experience of 'dance' exposed in this way contains two reverse connotations: firstly, the 'alien' deity Dionysos and accordingly the Dionysian principle of 'appearance'[11], epiphany and creativity — the 'coming god' in the double meaning of arrival and advent —, who at the same time is a god of disruption, of non-identity and destruction, as creativity only exists on the basis of a breach with the established order and its normative power. Dionysos, as an *inhumanum*, thus stands in direct opposition to Apollo and the principles of harmony and proportion, which in classical art epitomised the dimensions of humanity. Consequently, the 'coming god' is both another god, a god of becoming, and of another era that still is a nascent state (*in statu nascendi*). At the same time, it is an era of new art. Nietzsche announces its necessity, especially the inevitability of avant-gardism without being able to know it yet: he prepares it, fantasises it in advance, anticipates the radicality of a disruption, a "transvaluation of all values". On the other hand, dance serves here as a metaphor for overcoming gravitation, i.e., nature and its laws of physics or the mathematics of causality. This is why Zarathustra begins to fly, acausal and without a reason, for we must not forget that the figures of flight, of floating belong to the favoured figures of classical dance, first of all the *pas de deux* which here connotates the play of contingency, the unpredictability, and simultaneously represents the powerful symbol of a future art unhinging the traditional norms. Derrida used the terms 'dance' and 'play' exactly in this sense: they uncover the differentiality and mutability of thinking itself which never ceases to reject its consummation.[12] *Choros*, dance then, would have to be conceived in this sense: as breaking the chains of general conceptualisation.

DIALECTICS OF FIGURATION AND DEFIGURATION

With regard to the *pas de deux*, the overcoming of gravity, floating itself already points out movement as figuration and 'turn'. It seems that dance is given and embodied by the figure in the first place, but the opposite is the case. For together with figuration a dialectic comes into view that rather can be spelled as a chiasm of figuration and defiguration that constantly interrupts and disintegrates figuration. It is not the figure which stands in the centre of 'dance' and its delimitations, but the mutual entanglement of figuration and its dissolution, of figure and negation. Therefore, if we are using dance as a metaphor for the overcoming of gravitation as well as for artistic invention — its unpredictable ability to 'turn' and its flexibility — we have to understand in equal measure *how* its moves and movements, its metamorphoses and passages are based on performative acts which again are likewise enabled and limited by the boundaries of space, time, practices, and bodies. *Choros*, dance, is marked by this performativity, yet movement is something that cannot be kept or described, least of all exhaustively manifested through form lines (*Gestaltlinien*) of its figurations. Rather, due to the performatives every movement contains its own deviation. For performative acts are essentially singular; and singular as well is their combinatorics, their processual assembly or connection, since the performative articulates itself in alteration. Accordingly, it is subject to a continuous transition or transformation with its focus on the permanence of a 'formative' that is formation and flux in one.

This is exactly what the terms 'figuration' and 'figurating' denominate, with the verb prevailing in every case, as opposed to the nominalised form of 'figure' as concluded result. The figure in the sense of figuration consequentially 'keeps' itself in persistent 'transience'. On the whole it is a movement without state — and thus, reversing Zeno's paradoxes which claim that movement cannot *be* because it already is another from moment to moment, incessant transformation, restless instability. In fact, movement can only be described paradoxically, as continuous differentiality with itself, while figuration theory, orientated on classical rhetoric and literary history, always has conceived it as 'movement figure', as *schēma*, and so immobilised it in order to underline its unity, its representational function between identity and repetition. However, as figure or *schēma* it only embodies an idea or the expression of an emotion in motion, whereas the perspective of its genuine differentiality centres on its reciprocal dialectics of figuration and defiguration that cannot be codified, on its unidentifiable transitoriness. For this reason, one has to ask whether, in the sense of the *choreo-graphic* and an aesthetics of movement, one would not have to set out from expressions like 'mobility' or 'transitoriness', i.e., a dialectics as 'logic of processuality' instead of concepts of figure and configuration. It finds — in Nietzsche's sense — its appropriate 'image' in 'dance'; for dance, properly understood, is nowhere definable, rather indefinite, unexplained, because it is continuous transfiguration, processuality in itself. Its heart is 'occurrence'.

Let me once more insert another image here, which is again taken from another aesthetic form, the vexation between figure and background in the philosophy of iconicity. Ludwig Wittgenstein discussed it in the framework of his *Philosophical Investigations* and on the basis of gestalt psychology from the perspective of a change of aspect in 'meta-stable images'.[13]

According to this, the change of aspect rejects its dichotomic reconstruction following the logic of either-or; rather, it appears as a third, an un-shape that includes both sides. With a view to movements this can also be expressed thus: every process requires a moment of transition and therefore a void or chasm, comparable to a white space in its middle that has to stay vacant. It is homologous to the idea of the hyphen in *choreo-graphy* insofar as there remains an indefiniteness between the two halves of the word which marks a breach, a moment of overturning. The hyphen here represents nothingness, not even a graph; rather, it eludes writing. How, then, can one act upon it? As we began our deliberations with a series of etymological remarks on the Greek *choros* and *chōros* or *chōra*, let us now continue with a few observations on the etymology of figure and figuration. Erich Auerbach reconstructed their history in his essay *Figura.*[14] On the one hand, he traces the Latin word back to the Greek expression *schēma*, which apart from outline also means model and has to be localised in the visual, followed up by the entire field of Platonic development of *eidos, eikon,* and *eidolon*, i.e., the visual form, the contour up to the figurative aspect of the Being. As Erwin Panofsky has shown, this associative chain leads forward to the Renaissance concept of *disegno*, on which the entire Italian art theory was founded.[15] On the other hand, the concept of *figura* had its place in ancient rhetoric, indicating the canon of movement lines of a speech, and thus the performative power of conviction in the dialectics of argumentation. They did not only form the apex of elocution — for no argument can be formulated without recourse to its *technē* — but at the same time functioned as production forms of a speaking for which, according to an interpretation by Martin Heidegger, one could perhaps best insert the word *Be-Wegung* (movement), again pulled apart by a hyphen. *Be-Wegung* not only stresses *Wegen* (German *Weg* = way), which points to processes of tracing, channelling, or pioneering, even to graphic facilitation (and here again the diagram jumps into our deliberation), but also *Wägen* (weighing), which for its part is reminiscent of making movements and swaying, an undecided swinging to and fro. Once more, the hyphen also ruptures the open process and introduces a difference into the 'drama' of movement; hence, the dialectics of figuration and defiguration, as they belong together in one single act, inducing the process of *Be-Wegung* that can neither be followed (also in the sense of a conclusion) nor anticipated: it happens without any motif or deduction.

FEIGNING / EXPERIMENTING

However, apart from such associations Auerbach also followed another line leading to a relation between figure and *fingere*, in the sense of representation or the creative artistic process as well as the 'as if' of a pretence or poetic fiction. Once more the connection underlines the productive 'in-between' of a disquietude or non-unity as far as feigning appears to be interwoven with the *ficta* and therefore never is what it seems to be but — just like movement — 'always something else'. It is not the statics of the figure that is decisive but its dynamics, its mutability. Therefore, the figure continuously re-invents itself with a view to *fingere*, so that figuration / defiguration in its second meaning simultaneously touches that which in another — and literally conceived — context can be called 'experiment'; for the experiment indicates an open thoroughfare, a journey into the unknown. This meaning of experimenting, again with the main emphasis on the *verb*, is here consciously opposed to the sciences and their experimental systems,[16] insofar as these commonly reverse it, as the experiments aim at results, which again are subjected to the process of verification, while the practice of aesthetic experimentation in its literal meaning combines the prefix 'ex' with the event of an open outcome — "the outcome of which", as John Cage rightly put it in his 1957 lecture *Experimental Music in the United States*, "is not foreseen".[17] Then, in the practices of the experiment the *experiens* connects with the *experior a*nd the *expetere,* i.e., the efforts of a search and that which slips from the hands of the experimenter and unforeseeably befalls him. That is, experimenting has to be conceived less in an active sense than as passivity in consideration of that which cannot be calculated but 'en-counters' or 'comes one's way' and thus belongs to the area of contingency and coincidence.

Interestingly, this concept of experiment corresponds with the original meaning of *empeiría,* which includes the openness for the other as much as the experience and visualisation (*exponere*) of something that surprises — for, as Heidegger also pointed out, the Aristotelian *empeiría* begins with what 'strikes us', while natural scientific experimentation 'approaches something' by 'exploring' and 'looking around' through 'testing' and the use of technical instruments. In contrast to this, the artistic rehearsal or testing rather implies an erratic feeling around, an equally unprejudiced and risky heuristics as the exploration of phenomena on the basis of predefined methodical approaches. "I can't go on, I'll go on", Samuel Beckett writes in *The Unnamable*, characterising the simultaneously halting and erring work of the aesthetic as a 'way of no return'.[18] Here, there are neither clear and distinct procedures nor instructions, technologies and protocols, just the ever anew and differently 'incipient' exposition of things, materials, actions, and gestures. Hannah Arendt noted down that man was an absolute beginner — in the same sense one would have to say (and much more justifiably) that art begins ever anew, treading yet unsketched or untravelled paths. They aim at an exploration of the as yet invisible or unheard of. This is why Cage also described the experimental practice of the arts as "a purposeless play … an affirmation of life — not an attempt to bring order out of chaos nor to suggest improvements in creation, but simply a way of waking up to the very life we're living."[19]

This also implies that the artistic experiment has no direction or utilitarian goal; rather it is content with the adventure of finding the paths that can be taken, like running through endless labyrinthine branches which sometimes reveal nothing. Thus, the artistic 'search' — close not only to experimentation, but also to the practice of writing essays in the literal meaning of *exagium*, of attempt — continues its exercises by trying again and again different passageways (*Wegen*, see above, which is the original sense of *experiri*), and its way of thinking and gaining knowledge is exactly this constant *erratum* that Marcel Duchamp, too, recognised as the kernel of the aesthetic process.

LEAP, PLASTICITY AND THE ATTEMPT OF THE ESSAY

Hence, while science takes place through investigation by using experiments as a *medium*, in the arts it is the other way around, because it is not research that comes first and determines and gives stature to the experiment; rather it is — in its literal meaning — the *experiri* of the *experimentum* and thus that which withdraws itself. Their key elements are firstly, singularity; secondly, the alterity in iteration; and thirdly, the primacy of *passio* or passibility and their pre-eminence over action. And while Heidegger went on to say, in reference to scientific research, that "to set up an experiment is to set up a condition", which includes setting up a law and controlling the frame of reference[20], the aesthetic search *de*controls all conditions and opens them up for other states. It fathoms the strange or exception, and rather than hoping for progress in knowledge, an increase of objectivity and stable models, it induces the oscillation of phenomena and instigates moments of transformation. Remarkable here is that in order to characterise processes such as figuration / defiguration and experimentation or 'search' and movement in the realm of *choreo-graphy*, we are obviously forced to use negative terms (the singular, which is no concept, the non-result, uncertainty or indeterminacy and the like). Negativeness seems to be essential for pertaining processes, which tend to withdraw themselves from any conceptualisation. The dialectic of figuration and defiguration as well as *Be-Wegung* with their constant distortion and transition give its paradigm.

Let me insert another metaphor in this place which rather less addresses the withdrawal and the inconclusiveness of experimentation than the specific discontinuity in the dialectics of figuration and defiguration, i.e., its movement in difference, its continuous alterity or transitoriness. It also touches the second meaning of 'dance' as we have shown it with Nietzsche, namely *choreo-graphy* as transcendence of gravitation, coinciding with the intrinsic freedom of play. It celebrates itself in the image of flight, the 'leap'. The leap seems to be particularly interesting because its sudden moment or event cannot be based in turn in figuration, as jumps do not follow any lines or rules; they have no overall form or gestalt, rather they *overleap* any figuration — just like Joseph Beuys once pointed out that the smart sidestepping hare might serve as a model for the artist in general, because it has already leapt ahead and is thus somewhere else than we expect. For this reason Beuys adopted the hare as an emblem or symbolic animal for the artist in many of his performances — even the dead hare to whom he explained the images in his famous performance at *Galerie Parnass* in Wuppertal in November 1965. Thus, we can say, the leap is always already at another place; its witty jumping — as a practice — always happens in between; it has neither a beginning nor a result, rather it is constantly holding a difference without any hesitation. Again, passivity becomes prior; or as it were a liminal process between passivity and activity or intentionality and non-intentionality. Therefore, Heidegger claimed that to jump means to release oneself into the abyss of being. For this reason, instead of solely paying homage to the figure of dance and interpreting *choros* and its *choreo-graphies* by way of form, I have preferred to stick to the dialectics of figurating and defigurating just as to the non-figure of *Be-Wegung* in order to mark their permanent self-dissolution, their otherness-in-itself; for every figure, every writing or diagrammatics always is already on the way to its own transformation or passage. This is exactly the meaning of *choros*, dance: neither here nor there, it already celebrates its own disappearance, its dissolution to the degree it is leaning towards a form or gestalt. The artistic performance as improvisation constitutes its most manifest fulfilment.

At the same time this means that *Be-Wegung* in a continuing composition and decomposition *overflows*: as a simultaneity of creation and destruction — as creation in destruction and as destruction in creation — it creates a ceaseless alteration and reversion in order to begin again where it appears to reach its realisation. Therefore the leap, as far as it does not keep to one place anywhere, seems to have no standstill. Accordingly, *choreo-graphy*, its spelling and interruption means a genuine plasticity that remains as chronically incomplete and imperfect as it represents its continuous variability and fluidity. Auerbach already pointed out the proximity of *figura*, *fingere*, and plastic form. Moreover, Catherine Malabou recently exposed the term 'plasticity' afresh by tracing it back to Hegel and to Derrida's 'non-term' of 'différance' in order thus to transfer it into aesthetics. One could say that leap and plasticity correlate. Both present important metaphors of what has been tried to spell out as 'hyphen', as dialectics of figuration and defiguration as well as *Be-Wegung* and experimentation. At the same time, the term plasticity derives from the Greek *plastikōs* and *plastikē*, which point out the ability of form to deform and be transformed. The terms *plasma* as fluid substance of life, and *plassein* for the formlessness of matter which eludes any signification, also belong to this.

This is why *choros* / dance and *choreo-graphy*, but also play and its performative leaps, defy any adequate theoretisation and symbolisation. How then, to talk appropriately about the processual, the occurrences of the *choreo-graphic*, and the dialectics of figuration and defiguration? The question touches that of talking about or 'of' art — rather less 'about' than the more careful and gentle 'of' which merely dares to touch. For instead of making art an object, an item of discourse, a collection of approaches or an ensemble of fragments suffices to condense it to various constellations, and whose language itself would perhaps best be characterised as *choreo-graphic* essayism. The essay indicates an always open and incomplete attempt. It does not command terms, but restricts itself to propositions, stimuli, and suggestions. It gives hints. As preliminaries, they remain unstable, always threatened by the disintegration of their plausibility. Therefore, essayism rejects any kind of justification and validity. Rather, it is an artform in itself, so that art here meets art, 'dancing around' and nestling up against each other. This does not mean indulging in wild association but — because the issue is the setting-in-motion and the *Be-Weglichkeit* (mobility) of speech itself — waiving propositionality and predication, and in their place preferring verbs and what older grammars called *synkategoremata*: prepositions indicating procedural directions, relations in time and space, or adverbs specifying conditions or circumstances, as well as first and foremost the conjunctions which likewise connect and separate, and thus enable compositional occurrences in the first place.[21] The thesis therefore is that thinking performance as a thinking in *choreo-graphies* follows not so much the discipline of a diction than those series of linguistic particles which strengthen the sideshows (*Nebenschauplatz*) and their various modalities that fall out of the literally superficial categorial framings. Therefore, instead of talking *about* art or indicating its procedure, the *choreo-graphies* merely point out connection points or possible recombinations of *Be-Wegungen* and their different versions of action. They only grant the practices and their performatives a preference.

---

1) Cf. Nicolas Bourriaud, *Relational Aesthetics*, Dijon: Les Presses Du Réel, 1998, on the concept of the participative in the aesthetic.

2) Jacques Derrida, *Chōra*, Vienna: Passagen Verlag, 1990. Derrida interprets the expression 'chorismos' with regard to *différance*.

3) Eric Voegelin, *Anamnesis. Zur Theorie der Geschichte und Politik*, Munich: Verlag Karl Alber Freiburg, 2005, especially. p. 267 ff.

4) Cf. Plato, *Symposion* (202d-e).

5) Cf. Plato, *Timaios* (50c-51b).

6) Cf. Dieter Mersch, 'Tertium datur. Einleitung in eine negative Medientheorie', in Stephan Münker, Alexander Roesler (Eds.), *Was ist ein Medium*, Frankfurt a. M.: Suhrkamp, 2008, pp. 304-321.

7) Friedrich Nietzsche, *Thus Spoke Zarathustra* (Trans.) Graham Parkes, Oxford: Oxford University Press, [1883] 2005, p. 36.

8) Nietzsche, 2005, p. 35.

9) Cf. Dieter Mersch, 'Ästhetik des Rausches und der Rausch der Differenz. Produktionsästhetik mit Nietzsche', in Thomas Strässle, Simon Zumsteg (Eds.) *Trunkenheit: Kulturen des Rausches*, Amsterdam / New York: Rodopi, 2008.

10) Nietzsche, 2005, p. 36.

11) Karl-Heinz Bohrer, 'Dionysos. Eine Ästhetik des Erscheinens', in Mira Fliescher, Fabian Goppelsröder, Dieter Mersch (Eds.), *Sichtbarkeiten 1: Erscheinen*, Berlin / Zurich: Diaphanes, 2013, pp. 13-38.

12) Cf. Jacques Derrida, 'Die Struktur, das Zeichen und das Spiel im Diskurs der Wissenschaft vom Menschen', in Jacques Derrida, *Die Schrift und die Differenz*, Frankfurt a. M.: Suhrkamp, 1976, pp. 422-442, here p. 442.

13) Ludwig Wittgenstein, *Philosophical Investigations*, (Trans.) G.E.M. Anscombe, P.M.S. Hacker and Joachim Schulte, Chichester: John Wiley & Sons, 2009, pp. 204-218.

14) Erich Auerbach, 'Figura', in *Archivum Romanticum*, Vol. 22, 1938, pp. 436-489.

15) Erwin Panofsky, *Idea. Ein Beitrag zur Begriffsgeschichte der älteren Kunsttheorie*, Berlin, [1924] 2014, especially pp. 23-38.

16) In this we decidedly differ from any proximity between art and science, as especially suggested by Hans-Jörg Rheinberger.

17) John Cage, *Silence: Lectures and Writings*, Middletown: Wesley University Press, 1973, p. 12.

18) Samuel Beckett, *Molloy, Malone Dies, The Unnamable*, London: Calder, 1994, p. 418.

19) Cage, 1973, p. 12. Cf. Serge Stauffer, *Kunst als Forschung*, Zurich: Scheidegger & Spiess, 2013, pp. 47-50, pp. 179-182, for an example from the fine arts.

20) Martin Heidegger, 'The Age of the World Picture', in Julian Young and Kenneth Haynes (Eds. and Trans.), *Off the Beaten Track*, Cambridge: Cambridge University Press, 2002, p. 61.

21) Cf. Dieter Mersch, *Epistemologies of Aesthetics*, Zurich / Berlin: Diaphanes, 2015, Part 3.

QUESTIONS

Christine De Smedt

Why does 'gestures of searching' sound good?
GESTURE
OF
SEARCHING
A trace of slime?
A sympathetic idea?
A philosophical concept?
To share a gesture of searching?
With whom?
Searching for what?
Searching, searching, searching?
Learning and searching?
Learning searching?
Modes of searching?
What is the opposite of searching?
When is the searching over?
Does everything become potential material?
What is at stake?
How to prepare?
Can you perform research?
Can you stay in the research during a public presentation?
What is the difference between a public live exploration and presenting a performance piece?
What is the difference between exercise, practice, research and development?
What is the difference between poetry, description and questioning?
Linking, dissecting and inventing?
Is improvisation opposite to live exploration?
What if a live exploration unfolds without a score?
'Creation in destruction — destruction in creation'?
What are the qualities of fall and erect?
Do questions keep coming?
Can we be outside of the pictorial?
Can we be outside of the picture?
When is translation happening?
What is your sign?
Can a sentence be 'blank' as a white piece of paper?
Who came up with the example of writing a text on a type writer with a wooden spoon?[1]
Can copying someone's signature be a practice of attention for drawing?
Where do we meet?
When can you say we have met?
Where is the weakness of the 'collective'?
What is your concern?
Can you hear me?
Can you hear me now?
Now, can you hear me?
Now you can hear me?
Wait, can you hear me now?
Now?
And Now?

I

choreophony

AM

clicking

marking vitality forces

founding a dot network

the dot family

A

list of mal-functioning

cluster of clicks

figuring

figure

figuring

LOUD

annotating — for oneself

notating — on its way to communicate

scoring — making it stand on its own, to be interpreted

SPEAKER

domesticating the emerging

—

cultivating meeting points

—

articulating qualities

—

differentiating to see better

—

performing

Conversation between Christine De Smedt (C) and Nikolaus Gansterer (N) – December 2016

C: what is the click modus?
N: what is the question?
C: you said I can go through my note book and be in the click modus and **click**.
Don't you need a goal? What is the click **modus** for you?
N: it is for me a reflective practice without stopping doing. In a way, you continue your practice but while you are doing you create yourself a space where you look onto your own doing. 'Click' is a very short **gesture**, without using your hands. Of course you can use your hands but we came to 'click' because it is while you do your things and you think 'Ah I am realising something' and that you mark.
C: a moment of consciously addressing something is happening but you don't know yet what? What do you find interesting? In what **frame**?
N: in this lab and live exploratory mode, there are phases with more intensity and others are a bit more loose. So it could be, you walk around the space and then at a certain moment you see a spatial constellation or you meet with somebody which changes suddenly the level of awareness. So in the continuum, in the flow, you **suddenly** have this feeling 'Ah' something has changed and that you mark.
C: conceptually I understand it. Where I resist, is that you interrupt that flow of 'something is happening'. It is an **interruption**.
N: it is the most minimal interruption you could think of.
It started in the first summer of the Choreographic Figures (CF). First we had a sign (*raises arm*). We were talking about figuring already. When we realised something is changing and when a figure is coming, then we have to mark it. But then you really get out of it because it is such a big gesture. We even tried to name it while doing. That brings you even much further. The possibility to just make that **sound** 'click' whilst doing, whilst recording it with the video. And then later we were watching the video and always stopping when there was a click happening, and then the person who did the click tried to remember what was happening. And then the thick descriptions started. So this whole thing with the figures started to become **language**. We could start to articulate it. So I agree with you that it is a moment of interruption but a very small one. I would say that it is the research mode, that you are in a creation process but at the same time you look at it with a reflective approach to what you do, not fully immersed but at a critical distance to your own creation process. Generally it is the idea that you immerse in the situation, but here not. And that is very difficult. The clicks are sometimes too literal. But sometimes they really mark something, which, I think, is then more substantial.
C: what you say about the clicks in the beginning of the process, looking back to the video, articulating it…etc. is interesting. That was in the **first** year. You did not do that any longer in the **second** and **third** year of the process?
N: No later it was only used as a communication system within the group.
What was interesting is that suddenly there were moments when it started clicking between people. It started indicating that something was happening between people.
And for sure while communicating it you mix it **up**. But still it is interesting, it is 'ah ok, I am here', a short moment of awareness. A practice to take a distance, this little **gap**…
C: ….for me clicks did not really work, or never, or maybe sometimes, very little, or too many… Why do you click and when? It does not need to have a consequence?
N: Doing the 'click' was a proposal by Alex Arteaga.
'When something is happening' is the whole question of the CF: what is it, what quality has it, what frame, what taste does the situation has… We looked into the text by Daniel Stern on the vitality curves, and so… Then we realised these elementary figures. Our consciousness is constantly making these waves. The wave could be seen within an hour, but also every 3 or 4 seconds. You can tune into that mode. Sometimes there is a heightened attention and then it drops. Because **nothing** is fixed, no, we just do. And then sometimes, when I recognize and realise I have been in a similar situation, I click. The brain is a muscle. I feel it very bodily in the back of the head. That is how I would describe 'ah ok' and this I communicate, for me to mark it but also to the others. Maybe some one looks to an object in the space and has this moment, and another person has a feeling in her shoulder whilst moving and then there is a movement she recognizes it or suddenly it opens a new possibility. It is like becoming aware of the potentiality of things.
Then the Aaa and Sss came into play. Emma had the idea to create a whole alphabet, a click language so it can be more nuanced what the click means, what am I marking. Like the Aaa is 'yes', and Sss like a 'no' consonance and dissonance… Like I see things **match**, is it forms, colours, movements, atmospheres,…. I create this connection. That is also a basic principle how our brain and our sensory-motor system is functioning. Or I rather focus on the disconnection.
C: it is a **selective** focus?
N: Aaa en Sss are short acoustic signals while you can still go around and do things. If you would **shout** it might be difficult. But you could also have another sign system that allows you to still keep doing. Like the 'snip' with the finger which is the same when you have a click moment while you are talking? You understand?
C: yes
N: the Aaa and the Sss, or for instance 'wavering convergence', it was not so much about language but about feeling proximities, about things matching - not matching.

WHEN TIME SHIFT.
How do you articula
without taming it
How do you pay attention
without tension
WHEN SIMPLY BEING T
WHEN SOMETHING C
WHEN A FEELING IS
How do you say something
WHENEVER MASS GE
WHEN TALKING ABOU
WHEN IT STARTS
How do you sh
without disrupting that p
WHEN LANGUAGE IS LI
INFORMATION
How can punctu
without using
WHEN SINGING
How do you create the con
without giving directio
WHEN THE
How does language feel
without without

WHEN THEY MEET
E QUALITY OF TIME FEELS DIFFERENT
'guring, this wildness
METHING IS COMING INTO EXPERIENCE
METHING IS TOUCHING WITHOUT
ALLY TOUCHING
WHEN THE WORD BECOMES
FLESH
BECOMES COLLABORATIVE
PLODE
t describing it
ESSED
WHEN FOLDS ARE SYMMETRICAL
GENCE
SH
N A DANCE OF ATTENTION STARTS
HAPPEN
WHEN THAT FIRST HAPPENED
licks
condition you are interested in
FROM BEING A CARRIER OF
you transfer it into writing
translating it
take the temporal sense of space
jects
WHEN THINGS
PESTER OUT
MONY
for surrender
HEN THE CONDITIONS ARE
IGHT
IS NOT WORKING
ower in your mouth

This was the dispositive, so to say, the looking glass through which we look at reality. So for sure we focus onto something. Each figure, if we stay in the metaphor of the looking glass, is this dispositive to decide where I am sending my attention to. But for sure I have to leave things out.
Foucault came up with the idea of the dispositive. It is a way of entering reality. Society organises in different ways and through institutions. For instance he looks at the prison as a dispositive to understand a society. All is connected to the idea. Through the prison as dispositive he gets access to the world. Another dispositive could be religion or the church,...., anything. The whole world can be connected through this glass (*holding a tea glass*): the brand, the form, the reflection, where did it come from. You can take anything to understand the world. To use one thing **to drill a hole** into the world.
And for sure the dispositive colours and shapes your understanding of the world. If you have a thick glass, that will shape your view.
C: in research, the click,... why would you mark it?
N: well it is about a live notation system.
The project tries to propose ways of several notation systems to understand the doing while doing. So in a live process! I would say, a notation system in the performing arts in the more traditional sense is like you have done something and then later you notate it, to redo it, later to redo the piece, to reactive it.
C: yeah, you can also redo it without notating it.
N: yeah, you have it in your body. The body is also a notation system I would say. But in the traditional sense, music, performance, a complex organisation of bodies and things in space, you do somehow a drawing or a map or a score where you position things and create a time access or different ways of organising with the purpose that you can redo it.
C: the clicks work when it is done for looking at the video later and articulate what is happening. But how I experienced it, nothing is happening with it. Maybe that is fine. Maybe I search too much for its consequence. What is its use?
N: it is of use that it brings you into the dispositive mode.
C: you really believe that this happens?
N: for me yes. That is how I use it. I am not totally immersed in my doing. I would claim it is a form of thinking the thinking. Like a second layer. Watching yourself while doing. Becoming conscious of the constructed-ness of your actions. You do but at the same time ...try to **stretch** it.
C: yes, ok, this you can do but that you have to mark it is extra action. If you are in this mode, you could click all the time...
N: yes yes
C: Why do you click now and not then...How selective are you?
N: well, yes, you could click all the time
C: or sometimes not.
N: or sometimes not. It is a bit like self-report on a very neurological level. Clicking is on a level of how neurons fire. Your synapsis constantly fire. So it is to get aware of this **firing**.
C: basically saying 'I am alive'?
N: you zoom into the brain as a muscle – tststs - how your brain and your whole system is constantly creating reality in relation to... and to become aware of this loop. This is a different way of attention then if you don't do it. You look differently to the world.
C: it is not strange to me to be in this mode but it is strange to me to mark it. I did not find a way to click and decide when I mark or not. I would mark all the time or totally not.
N: then that is something to explore. If you allow yourself and say ok...
C: when I do it, I communicate something to the environment, but the environment does not understand why or what.
N: that is not important. It is more for yourself. We have different ways of notating. Maybe we read what Emma writes about the notation practices. (*reads the texts*)
C: again my desire is there to understand the click as to be functional in the process of research, and to not just click for yourself. I remember the first time I saw you doing the live exploration and doing Aaaa and Ssss. I did not understand. That was **confusing**. How to develop this way of marking?
N: it is a practice as any other. While you do, you try to become aware of these little shifts. It is a brain stretch, a split, to keep this kind of the critical eye travelling with you.
C: is it critical?
N: in a way critical that it is not judging but sensitive to these **nuances**.
C: last question: when we talk about shifts, when is something happening? When is something happening for you? When do I think something happens?
N: exactly. How does the sense come into the world? It is us. You produce the sense. We give meaning to the things and organise **matter**. To become aware of this something, not yet identified presence of something.
C: I would be interested, when we do another exploration and you do a click and it draws my attention, I would come to you and ask you why do you click.
N: for who are you thinking now? For yourself or for the audience?
C: for myself. Your click takes my attention!
N: I don't have that so much. I am not so interested why you are clicking.
It reminds me what dolphins do, the sounds. They have frequencies and through that they communicate and stay in touch with each other on an acoustic level. And of course if you start to clickclickclick, and have a **mental orgasm**, of course it will draw my attention. Maybe it raises my awareness or it does nothing to me.
It is a technique to become aware of how we construct reality. It can help. If it does not help then it is not a good mode for you. It is an **invitation** to become aware.
C: clicking could also be an attention practice in itself?
N: you have to get used to it, to do it. Clicking is the moment where a figuring is happening. A click and figuring are synonym: you find something out...

1) Cf. Hester Reeve and Tom Hall, *Slow coding, slow doing, slow listening, slow performance*, 2015.

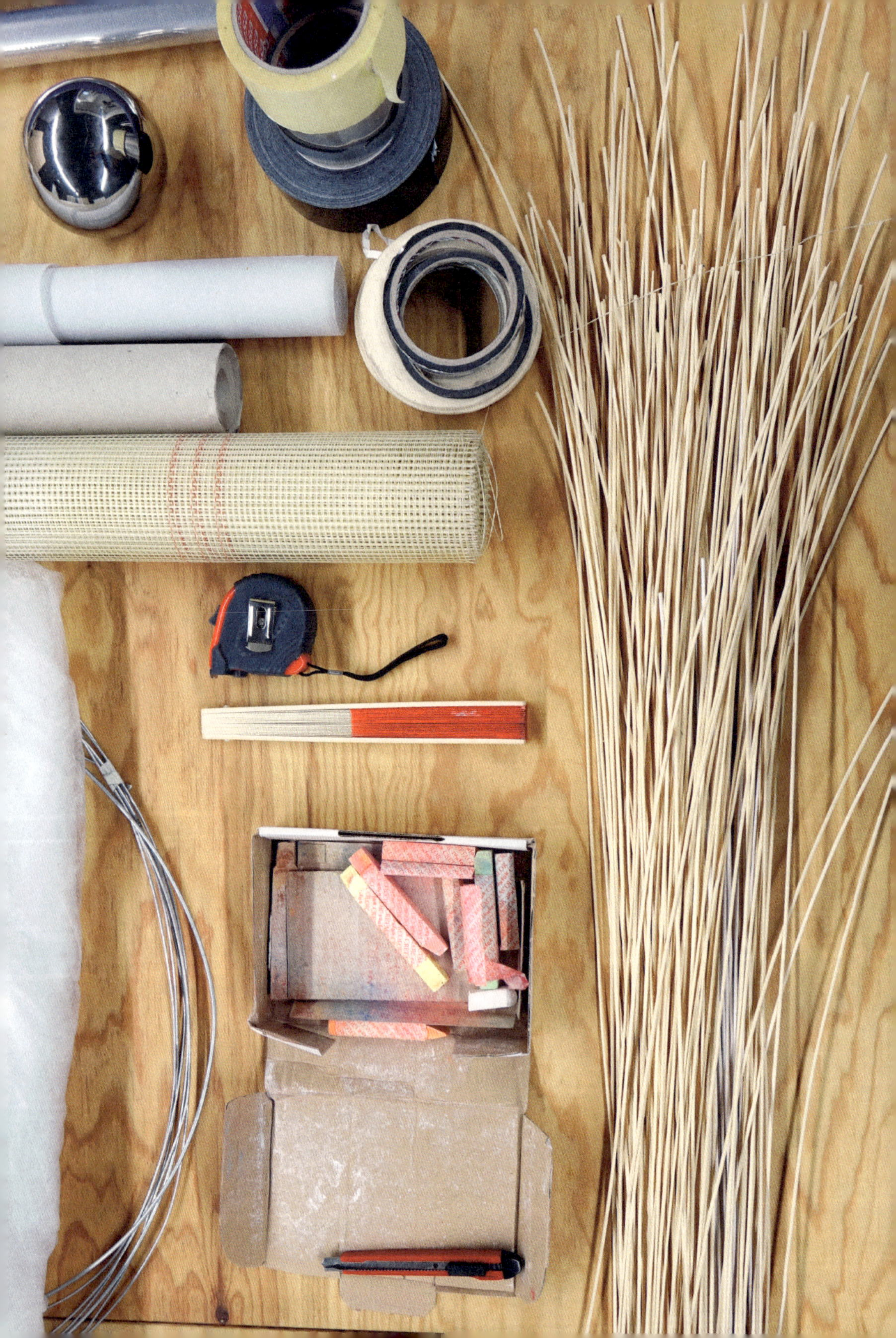

PRACTICES

PRACTICES

PRELUDE

So, how do we let go of set disciplinary ways of operating, relinquish what is familiar or known, safe or certain? How can we become more attuned to the *how-ness,* the qualitative-processual dynamics within our shared exploration? How do we focus attention towards those affective forces and intensities (*figuring*) operating before, between and beneath the more readable gestures of artistic practice? How can we mark those moments when 'something is happening'? How do we recognise and name the emergence of *figures*? How do we meet with difference whilst still striving for the common? How can this be shared?

Central to our research process has been the development of various practices for deepening, widening and sharpening our aesthetic enquiry, each with a different function or emphasis: (A) *Practices of Attention*—for sensory heightening, for cultivating perceptual awareness, increased alertness, vigilance and receptivity; (N) *Practices (or Modes) of Notation*—for noticing *and* marking the event of *figuring* and the emergence of *figures*; (C) *Practices of Conversation*—dialogue as a verbal-linguistic means for reflecting on the process of our live exploration; (W) *Practices of Wit(h) nessing*—different tactics for *being-with*, for blurring the division between participant/observer, for inviting another's perspective. Whilst these practices have enabled the research process from 'behind the scenes', they have also been activated more explicitly, more performatively, as part of our live explorations through the use of a 'score' (⟶ *Embodied Diagrammatics,* ⟶ *How to Play the Score*).

What follows is a more detailed exposition of each of the practices (A), (N), (C) and (W), specifically as performed or played within the context of a live exploration. Each practice is prepared for by a short prelude (from *prae-* 'before' + *ludere* 'to play') introducing its core characteristics or qualities, presented alongside practical exercises and variations combining concrete instruction, poetic invitation, and diagrammatic drawing. Whilst these practices have been developed and tested (⟶ *Method Labs*) through intensive collaboration—specifically with our sputniks (Alex Arteaga, Christine De Smedt, Lilia Mestre) and guests (Werner Moebius, Jörg Piringer)—the 'writing up' of each singular example has been undertaken by one (or two) individual(s) allowing for a diversity of both voice and approach.

INDEX OF PRACTICES

ATTENTION

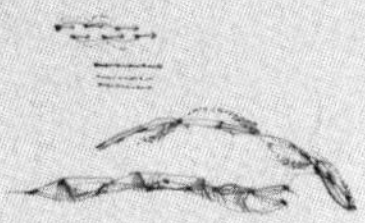

(→ *Walking*) 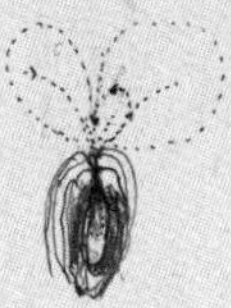 (→ *Breathing*) 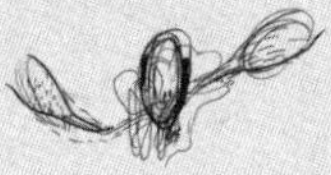 (→ *Voicing*) 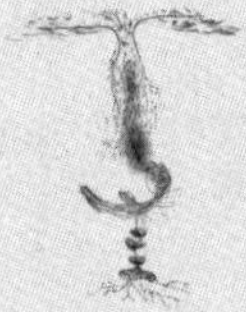 (→ *Sleeping*) 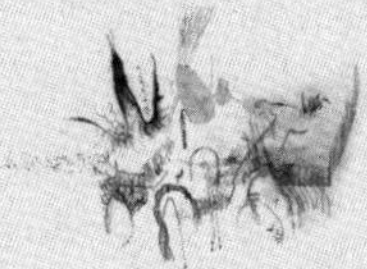 (→ *Touching*)

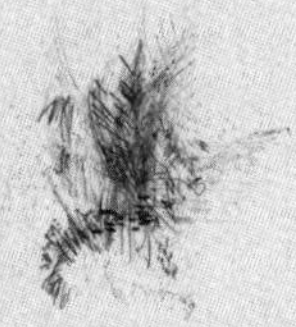

(→ *Shaking*) 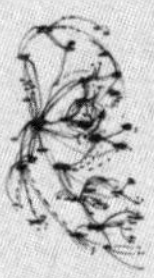 (→ *Reading*) 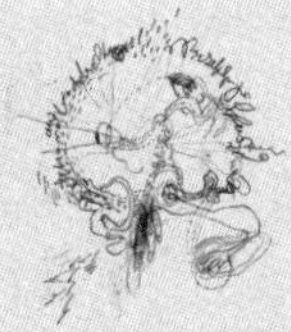 (→ *Self-Reporting*) 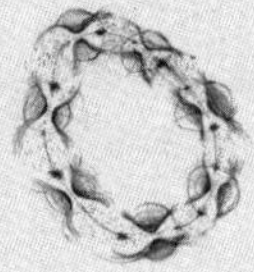 (→ *Passing On*) 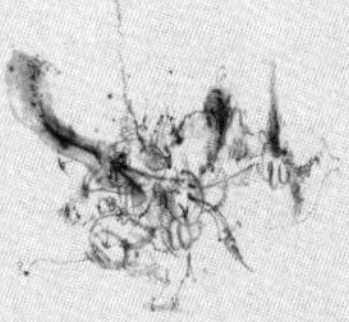 (→ *Transquesting*)

NOTATION

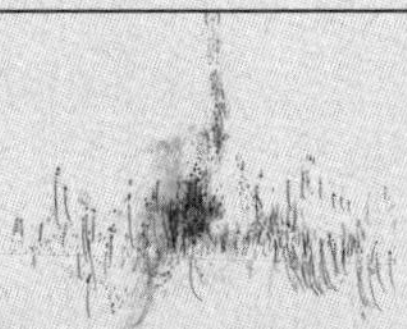

(→ *Clicking*) 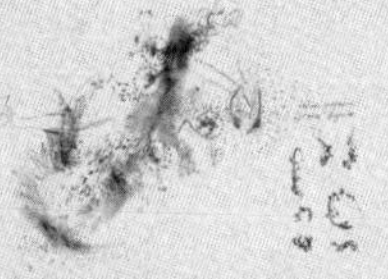 (→ *Affirming*) 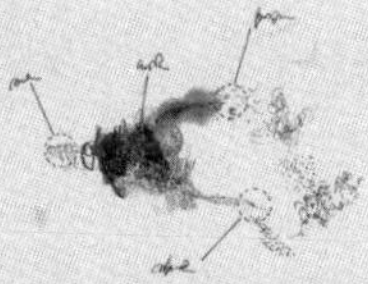 (→ *Naming*) 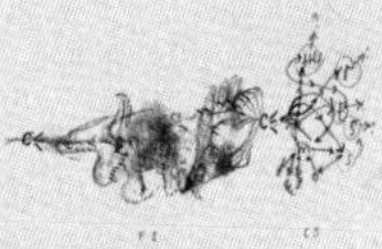 (→ *Calling*)

CONVERSATION

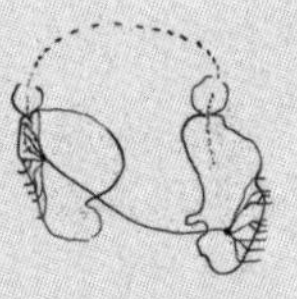

(→ *Dialogic*) 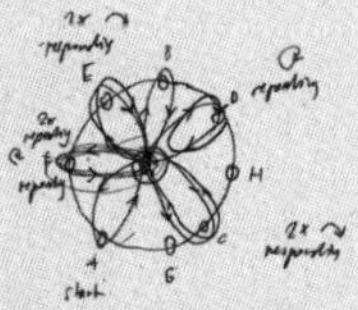 (→ *Keywords*) 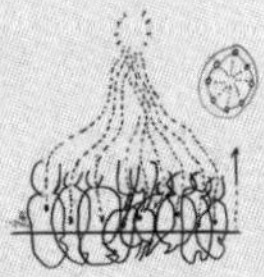 (→ *Upwelling*) 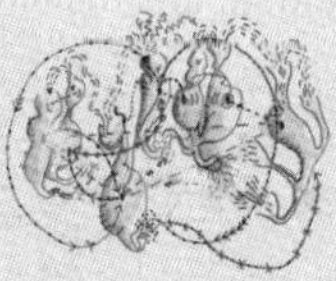 (→ *Wild Talk*)

WIT(H)NESSING

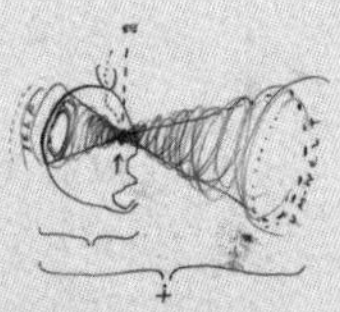

(→ *Watching*) 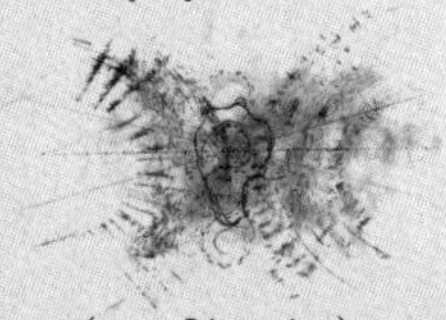 (→ *Listening*) 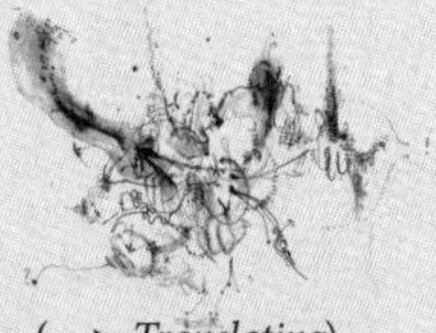 (→ *Translating*)

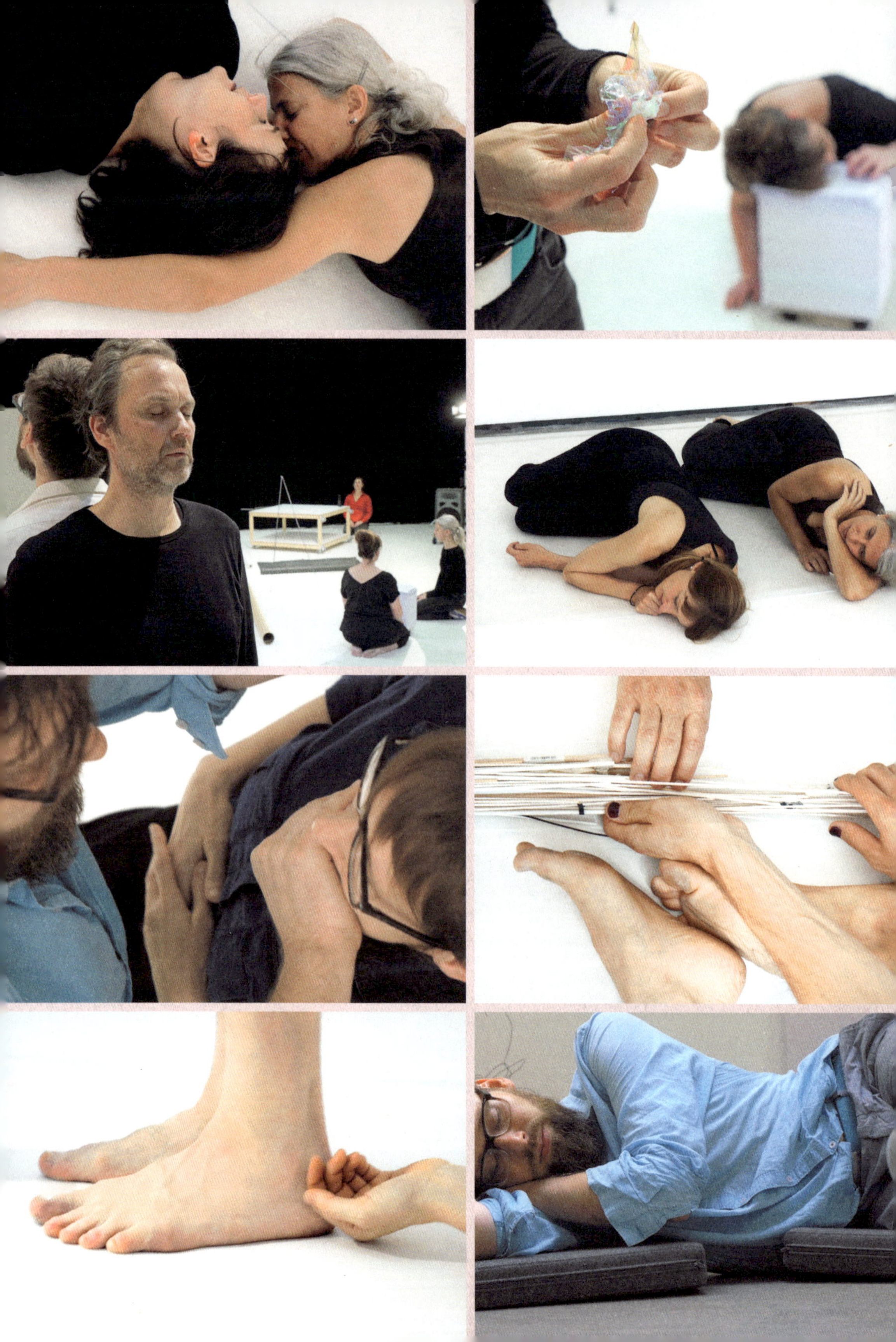

PRACTICES OF ATTENTION

PRACTICES OF ATTENTION

PRELUDE

The practices of attention perform a vital role within our artistic research process, creating the germinal conditions for experimental aesthetic enquiry. They are enabling, allowing us to access states of increased alertness, vigilance and receptivity, in turn augmenting (heightening, deepening, widening) and nuancing (sharpening, refining) both our individual and collective sensitivities to the vitality dynamics and affects within our live exploration. Related to — though significantly different from — warming-up activities, there is a preparatory function to the practices of attention. They have a re-set or re-tune task, clearing the ground in order for re-seeing things differently.[1] They involve a process of letting go or emptying out — activating a level of awareness beyond the utilitarian, instrumental or judgemental; the temporary suspension of will or self-led agency towards increased receptivity, even passivity. Here, passivity does not lead to inaction, but rather gives way to a truly spontaneous mode of intentionality; intention without predetermined direction or destination. Not yet towards *something*. Freed from presuppositions, conscious expectations or goals, these practices invite a quality of defocused focus akin to a state of 'evenly suspended' or 'hovering' attention.[2] Towards equanimity: undoing of normative thinking, the dynamics of attraction and aversion. Develop readiness not reactivity. Attention practices are radically non-creative or rather they wilfully constrain self-expressivity opening up a space or 'gap' for *creative attention*, for the immanent and open-ended vitalities of creation to arise.[3] Whilst *figuring* (⟶ *Figuring* >< *Figure*) undoubtedly occurs within the attention practices, and indeed whilst these practices increase our capacity for noticing, the invitation is to not (yet) follow the impulse, nor is it to mark this event *as such* (⟶ *Practices of Notation*). Just attend. In this sense, the key modality of these practices is re-generative non-productivity.

Stretch of attention; increase one's range. Extension of perception, sensation and awareness: activation of new realms of experience beyond the habitual. There is an exploratory quality to the practices of attention, opening up new zones of encounter. Be curious. Practise horizontal shifts — widening of one's horizon, expansion of awareness towards the peripheral, the limits of one's perceptual reach. Yet not just the navigation of frontiers, the adventurer's fascination with limits. Tend to shifts of attention, intervals and gaps, the thresholds and interstices. Qualitative overrides quantitative; practise with ever-subtler precision. Practise vertical extensions — centering one's attention, before heightening. Then, deepening. Deep listening. Deep seeing. Deepened proprioception. Sustaining in-depth practice through dedication to regular, repeated action-perception-reflection cycles. Repetition builds capacity: however, exercise not to discipline, not to order and control, not for the improvement of skill through drill and obedience. Rather, to sensitise — to endow with sensation, from the Latin *sensus*, past participle of *sentire*: 'feel-perceive'. Repetition increases sensitivity to difference, to the proliferation of multiplicities. It is a practice of modification and variation, for working-through a set of propositions that unfold each time anew.[4]

To render sensitive — to augment one's mental and emotional sensibility, become more readily affected by external forces, aware of and responsive to the feelings of others. Beyond cultivating elemental awareness of vitality affects (⟶ *Elemental Figures*), the practices of attention affirm heightened states of empathetic attunement, radical receptivity with shared spontaneity, even the arising of *communitas* (⟶ *Empathetic Figures*). Sensitive to the weakness of collectivity, yet still striving towards, the attention practices support an opening up of self to others, increased awareness of one's capacity to affect and be affected.[5] Or rather, they reveal the myth of one's interiority and self-containment—self is porous, always in relation, already 'more than one'.[6] Let go of individual will, becoming willing: increase one's availability. Trust is a precondition for openness and vulnerability; moreover, the relation is reciprocal. In turn, trust enables risk, the conditions for *hospitable incautiousness*.[7] Surrender of authorial agency creates unexpected forms of mutuality (⟶ *Transformative Figures*), dissolving the lines of dichotomic distinction between subject / object, between self / other, between self / world. In these terms, the practices of attention support a *radical aesthetics*, an unmediated (re)connection between body and surroundings, revelation of interconnection or *coherence* (⟶ Alex Arteaga, *Researching Aesthetically the Roots of Aesthetics*). Their radical potential is one of re-orientation and re-alignment; furthermore, their re-connective function is *religious* in the etymological sense, drawing on the Latin *religare*—*re-* (again), *ligare* (fasten, bind, connect). Indeed, many of our attention practices echo monastic, spiritual, even shamanic rituals, directed towards aesthetic enquiry.

In principle, a practice of attention could be anything, however idiosyncratic—but not *whatever*.[8] Our list is not prescriptive or exhaustive. Whilst sharing a certain somatic grounding, our practices seek to address different modalities, reflecting different bodily-kinesthetic, visual-spatial, verbal linguistic sensibilities. Whilst each attention practice can be performed in its purest form—*just* breathing, *just* walking—we offer variations. Here, play comes into play. Practices can be combined—as pairings, e.g. breathing-voicing, shaking-touching, as multiples, e.g. breathing-touching-walking, or performed in explicit relation to particular *figures*—or else, activated with different speeds or vectors of intensity. Go slower. Speed it up. They can be practised with hot Dionysian exuberance or with Apollonian coolness—emptiness can be reached both by burning and calming, via heightened states of saturation and by paring things back. Some examples can be read aloud as instructions, whilst others are poetic, evocative. They can be played by one or many, individual or collective.

---

1) The attention practices share certain qualities with the *Figure of Clearing and Emptying Out*.

2) These are psychoanalytical terms originating in Sigmund Freud's 'Recommendations to Physicians Practising Psycho-Analysis', 1912. (Cf. James Strachey, *Complete Psychological Works of Sigmund Freud*, London: Hogarth Press, 1975). They refer to a quality of *direction-less listening*, which Theodor Reik describes as *Listening with the Third Ear: The Inner Experience of the Psychoanalyst*, New York: Farrar, Straus, and Giroux, [1948] 1993.

3) Simon O'Sullivan notes that this productive 'gap' is "what Henri Bergson calls attention; the suspension of normal motor activity which in itself allows other 'planes' of reality to become perceivable (this is an opening up to the world beyond utilitarian interests)", in *Art Encounters, Deleuze and Guattari, Thought Beyond Representation*, Basingstoke: Palgrave Macmillan, 2006, p. 45. Cf. also Henri Bergson, *Matter and Memory*, (Trans.) Nancy Margaret Paul and William Scott Palmer, New York: Dover Publications, [1896] 2004.

4) Gilles Deleuze, *Difference and Repetition*, (Trans.) Paul Patton, London and New York: Bloomsbury Academic, 2014.

5) Gilles Deleuze, *Spinoza: Practical Philosophy*, (Trans.) Robert Hurley, San Francisco: City Lights Books, 1988.

6) Erin Manning, *Always More Than One: Individuation's Dance*, Durham: Duke University Press, 2013.

7) This phrase was used by P.A. Skantze during the Summer Method Lab, 2016 (⟶ P.A. Skantze, *Take Me to the Bridge*).

8) Alternatively, Giorgio Agamben's philosophical conception of "whatever singularity" calls for a form of being that appropriates 'being to itself' (beyond identity or belonging), which resonates with our conscious 'undoing' of discipline, delineations and categorisations (⟶ *Becoming Undisciplinary*). Cf. Catherine Mills, *The Philosophy of Giorgio Agamben*, Stocksfield: Acumen, 2008. For Agamben, "Whatever (quodlibet) — 'being such that it always matters' or 'its being such as it is'. The Latin always already contains, that is, a reference to the will (*libet*). Whatever being has an original relation to desire," in Agamben, *The Coming Community*, (Trans.) Michael Hardt, Minneapolis and London: University of Minnesota Press, [1993] 2007, p. 1.

WALKING

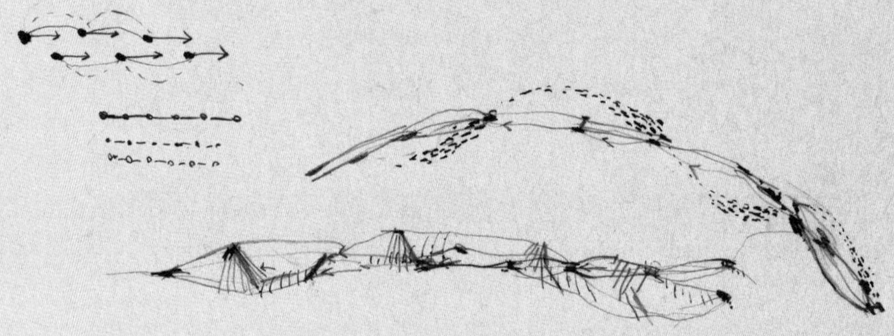

Start walking. Slowly shift your weight from left foot to right foot. Observe the mechanics of balance and shifting weight. How does your foot unfold itself from the floor? How does your other foot reach and touch the floor? Do you feel gravity? Stay aware of your back, your front, your left side, right side, the space above you, space under you, your flesh, observe where your awareness travels to, what path you take, be aware of what affects your walk. You can change to walking sideways or walking backwards. Prioritise physical exploration over the other senses, feeling your feet meet the ground, the shifting of weight, the trace of wind you make as you move forwards or backwards.

VARIATIONS

- ⁎ Allow your walk to follow your in-and-out breath. When you inhale, take a step. When you exhale, make the next step. Follow the rhythm of your breath. Actively perceive and shape the milieu where humans breathe and things do their things.
- ⁎ Close your eyes for a moment. See how this changes the mechanics of your movement and your relation to space.
- ⁎ Extend your awareness towards your environment. Explore the space by walking. How does the rest of the body hold itself in relation to the floor, the ceiling, the walls?
- ⁎ What initiates your walk? Can you shift what initiates your walk? Can you start to name what you are 'walking towards'? Can you change to naming what you are 'walking away from'? Can you tune in with and tune out from other bodies walking?
- ⁎ Explore the passage between movement and stillness. Walk to new places and positions, slowing towards stillness. Once you have arrived in stillness, begin to walk again. Not everyone will begin at the same time.
- ⁎ Walking relationally — with a focus on deviations and re-positionings of yourself and others in the space. Create and destroy configurations (patterns of behaviour) and constellations (like a recognisable grouping).
- ⁎ Befriend a material or object and take it for a walk. Stroll around and finally find a good enough place for you and the befriended material to come to stillness.
- ⁎ Take a nano-physical introspective walk, attending to the various structures, the rhythms emerging *within* your body. You can use your imagination and/or your hands.

BREATHING

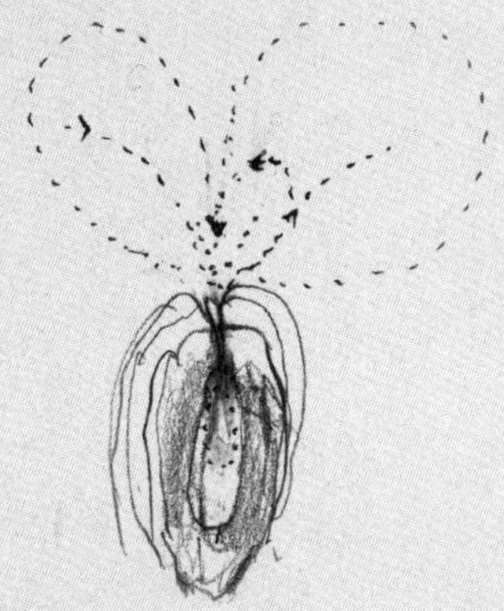

Stop doing. Tuning into measured time with the rhythm of breath. Seven breaths of stillness. Seven breaths of movement.

It is not necessary to adopt a 'neutral' position. Focus on your breathing. You needn't change the breathing. You don't *do* breathing. The breathing happens by itself. You can simply arrive into stillness, not having to say anything, not having to name anything.

Where does the stillness bring your awareness to? To your body in time and space, your senses, thoughts and emotions, the mechanism of filling and emptying, rhythm, exchange, transformation, oxygen coming in, carbon-dioxide going out, circulation, interdependency, your nose, your back, your lungs, your shoulders, your torso, time passing.

VARIATIONS

* Work in pairs. You can be close without touching, or holding hands, sitting back to back or any other way you want. Be still and observe your own and the other person's breath. Be aware of how this might change your breath. After some time you can try to come to a common breathing without forcing it, let it transform slowly through time. After some time you can let go and see if you go out of sync again.
* Work with another person. Let one hand rest on a part of the body of this person. Observe that touch, the movement of your hand and the breathing of the other. Stay with your own breath and the other person's breath. Does it change your breath? Try to come to a common breathing without forcing it, let it transform slowly through time.
* Breath as a measure. Now, observe your inhaling, the moment between in- and exhaling. Now, observe your exhaling, the time between exhaling and inhaling. Attend to the questions you have.[1] Focusing on your breathing, the dynamics of your breath can become a measure for moving / manipulating / changing an object or the body or a part of the body or making a sound. Your breathing pattern is the base-line for the action. See how accurately you can follow the speed and timing of the breathing and the pauses, how you start to change the breathing through the action and vice versa. It is not the aim to become creative, but to heighten your attention between things. Something will happen without 'wanting' it or aiming for it.

1) Questions could emerge somewhere between *chronos* and *kairos* (⟶ *When-ness*).

VOICING

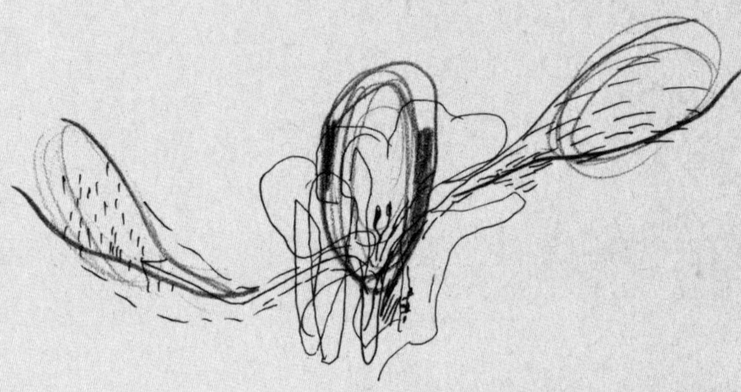

Voicing is a pure form of vocal exploration, not conversational. This practice is based on exploring the physicality of sound inside and outside your body.

Use sound as a material. Tune into embodied reverberations. Move sound around the cavities of the body; the differentiated penetration of sound in the various layers of bones, liquids, body tissues.

VARIATIONS

* Turn your head slowly to the left on an inhalation with no sound, bring the head back to the central axis, synchronising this movement with the exhalation of the sound 'A'.

  Turn your head slowly to the right on the inhalation. Come back to the central axis, synchronising this movement with the exhalation of the sound 'E'.

  On the inhalation, slowly tilt your head upwards. Come back to the central axis, synchronise this movement with the exhalation of the sound 'I'.

  When inhaling, slowly tilt your head down, synchronising this movement with the exhalation of the sound 'O'.

* Shout as loud or softly as it feels appropriate for the situation and your vocal chords.

  Fill the space with your voice.

  Exploring through vibration, use the whole body with specific focus on the pelvic floor and/or diaphragm for rebouncing your voice.

  Explore the strident character of voice: attend to the destructive force or rupture created.

  Gradually increase the volume.

  You can use vowels or rrrrr sssss ttttt

  Give out a shout.

* A duet: choose a partner who is approximately the same size as you.

  One person forms a funnel with their hands and uses this to direct a sound into their partner's spine. You can extend the sounding into various parts of the body. Establish an intensity, make space for resonance. You can play around with frequencies, interferences, changing volume (crescendo-decrescendo) and speed.

  Feel the physicality, resonance and power of the sound inside your bodies.

  If you work in a group you can think of the sound as an extension of yourself.

  Listen to the others and the sound clusters created in the space.

SLEEPING

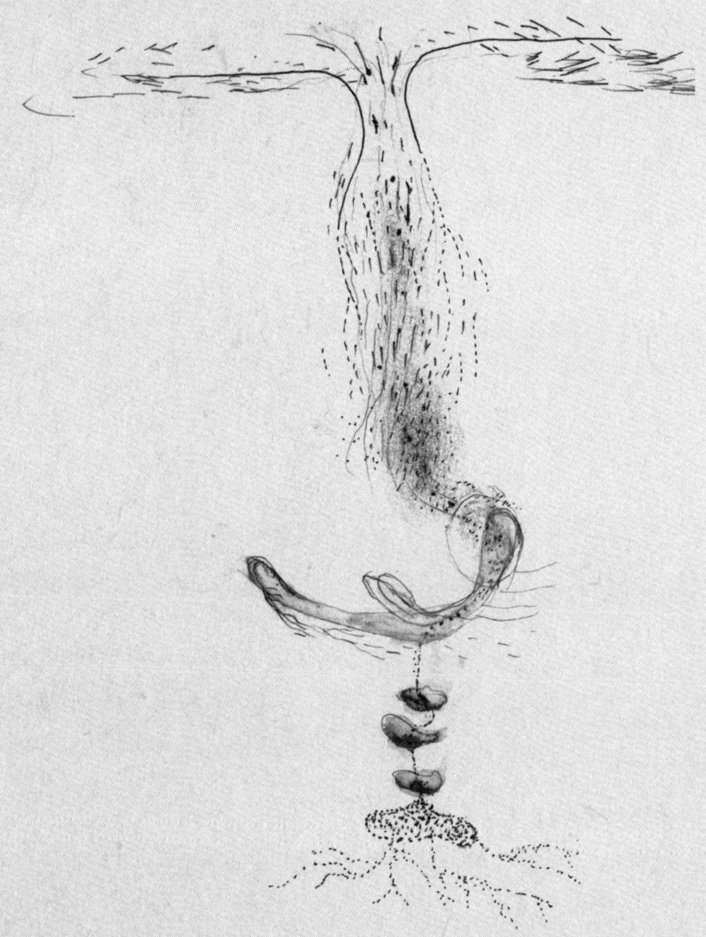

Sleeping is a state that you arrive at and that activates the parasympathetic system, shifting the body's functions towards regeneration. Sleeping raises many questions. Not sleeping raises many questions.

VARIATION

Explore the gradients as you transition between vigilance and sleep. Find the pleasurable details in the transition from the state of vigilance to sleep to dreamland and back. Pass through various layers: losing and taking control, intimate arousals, rhythms and shifts of awareness.

Twelve minutes moving towards the state of sleeping.

Twelve minutes of not sleeping.

Find a different position. Repeat.

TOUCHING

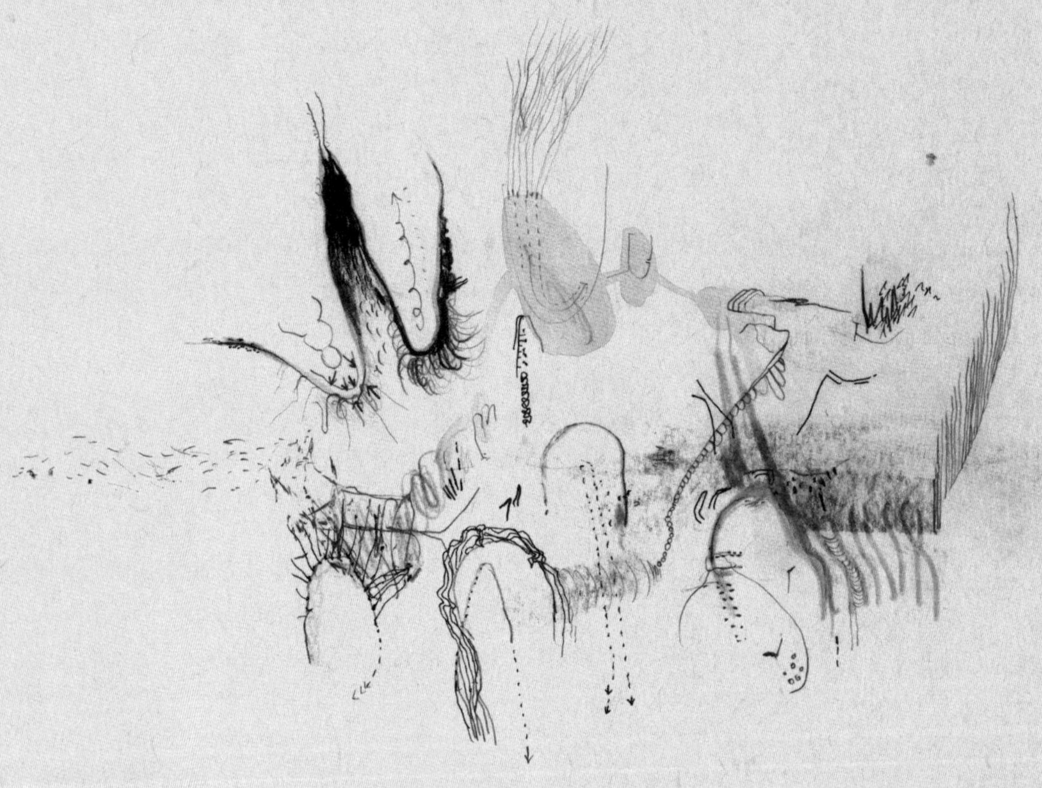

Place yourself somewhere you feel attracted to. Become curious — how does it feel rather than how does it look? Close your eyes. Start by paying attention to your body. How does it feel, the sensation of space around you? Pay attention to your hands; focus on them as if they were antennae. Your hands will inform you about the bodies that you will encounter. Through sensation you will get in touch with the attributes belonging to others. By touching you will re-imagine the potentiality of the objects that surround you. You will transform the utilitarian relation we tend to have with them (things) in an un-familiar encounter, where materials, shapes, temperature, size, weight will enter in a dialogue with you. Do it for as long as you like.

SHAKING

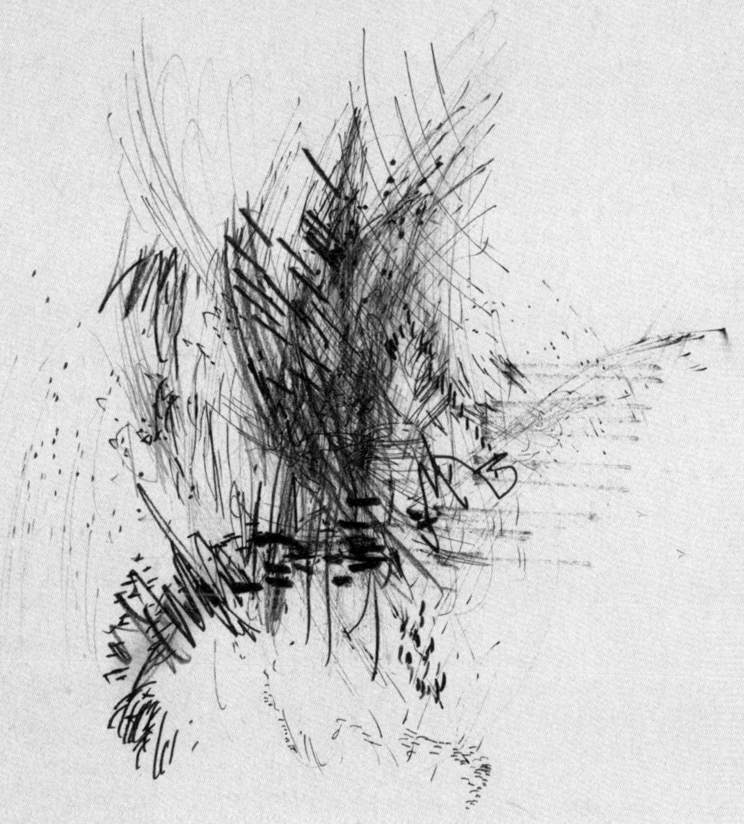

Stand up straight. Have a close look at your posture. Relax. With a slow rhythm, bend and then flex your knees, moving your body up and down. Let this movement travel through your bone structure and gently affect your whole body. Increase the speed or the amplitude (or both). See how the energy travels through your body and creates movement, changes the gaze, augments the heat. When you feel comfortable in this motion you can start moving one leg after the other without breaking the shaking waves. Let the energy lead you. Little by little you can start touching things. Observe their motion in relation to yours. Patterns will be created with what and whom you encounter on your shaking journey. Shaking awakes your attention to yourself and frees the energy you hold. To shake opens up the uncanny.

VARIATION

Shaking can be done in other positions, with or without objects, with or without other humans.

READING

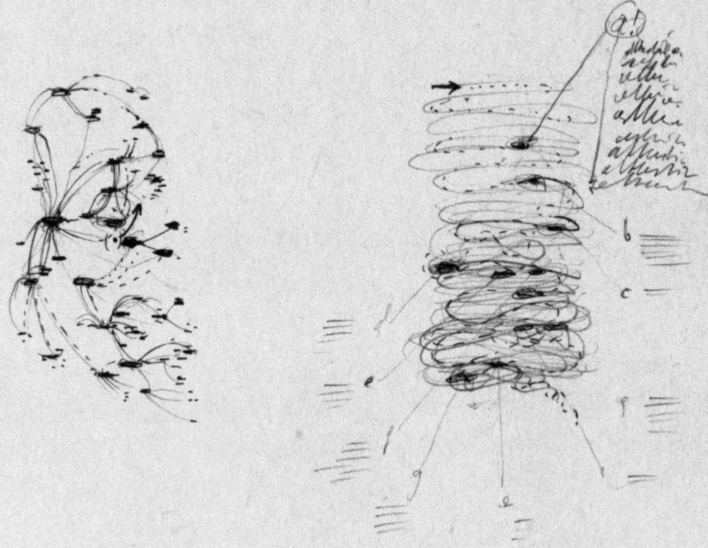

Just reading. It must be empty, words encountered lightly, not grasped towards. Three variations — different affects.

TEXTUAL BODY SCAN

Take a printed page of text — any will do. Imagine the page as if it were your body. Take your attention to the foot of the page, the bottom lines. Allow your eyes to gently encounter the words. Without reading them, just observe what is there. Now, slowly move your attention *up* through the text, from the bottom to the top, sentence by sentence. Left to right, then right to left. Gradually move your attention up through the text, as if you were shifting your awareness from your feet up through your body to your head. As your attention reaches the top of the text, read out loud the last word upon which your eyes settle. Now, let go of the text.

NOTICING ATTRACTION

Take a different printed page of text. Allow your attention to roam the page, moving freely, or perhaps in a spiralling movement from the centre of the page to the edges. Soft attention, floating across the surface. Not reading for the sentence's sense, just *noticing*. When a word catches your attention, mark this impulse with a sign, a click or clap or another gesture. Repeat this process until you feel ready to let the text go.

SPLIT ATTENTION

Take a new printed page of text. Begin reading from the first line, but with your 'inner voice', reading silently. When you encounter a word beginning with A, say it out loud. Keep repeating this same word, speaking it out loud over and over, *whilst* at the same time continuing to read the text with your 'inner voice'. Keep repeating this same word until you encounter a word beginning with B. When you encounter a word beginning with B, say it out loud. Continue this process through the alphabet until you reach Z.

SELF-REPORTING

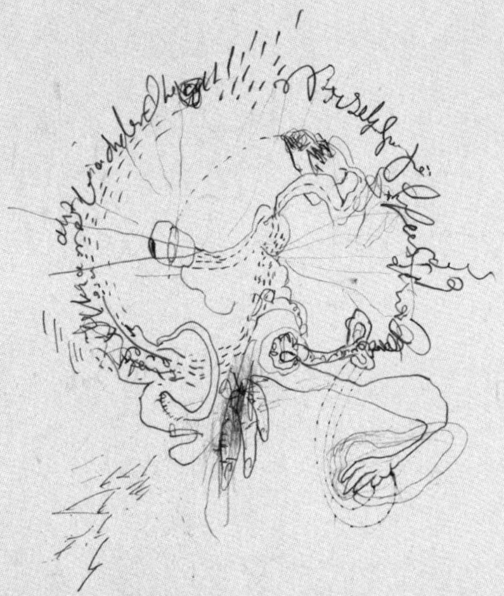

Verbalise what passes through your mind — *thinking out loud*. What are you *doing* when you are doing something?

Create a state of mind where you become the main voice of an inner speech — a kind of *soliloquy* — you turn into sender *and* receiver, speaker *and* listener, mouth *and* ear, at the same time.

This introspective practice creates an auto-reflexive loop, which activates your language centre. Report on observing yourself observing whilst reporting. An egocentric practice; it feels a bit like hyper-ventilating your thoughts. Become aware moment-to-moment of your subjective non-/conscious flows of information from a first-person perspective. Self-reporting makes apparent what is taken for granted. It will influence and guide you in generating action, in turn it will again effect how you report and observe this new action.

This practice can be done alone or with others. (Performed in a group it could lead to ⟶ *Wild Talk*). Self-reporting is not directed towards others. It is an auto-communication; you address your voice towards yourself.

Start listening to your inner voice(s), tune into your inner radio programme. Focus on what thoughts, ideas, emotions, sensations and observations are passing through your mind. Begin by mumbling these snippets, fragments, words, short or endless sentences, be it banal, secret, obscene, obscure, boring, exciting. Do not judge. Broadcast your inner waves. Surf your stream of consciousness. Be clear in your decision of what and how you report. It is not *whatever*, but also 'whatever comes to you' might be an option.

VARIATION

* You could focus on what you hear and report, you could focus on what you smell and report, you could focus on what you taste, touch, feel, think and report; whilst being still, whilst moving around, or a certain combination of these and report.
* You could self-report by writing down rapidly what comes to your mind.
* You could decide to focus only on yourself or on the interaction with someone else.

PASSING ON

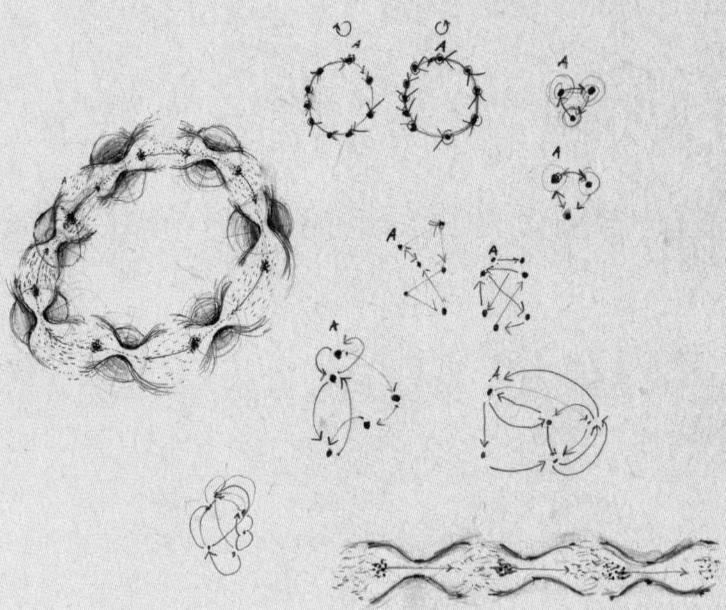

This is a relational attention practice where you become the 'medium' for something to circulate in time and space.

To start simple: you pass on 'something' to someone near you. This person passes this 'something' to someone else, who continues to pass on this 'something' to yet another person, and so on. The attention is focused on *how* and *what* you pass on.

When you 'receive', observe the other, how she / he is passing on to you. You try to pass it on in the most identical way so that 'the something' stays the same. The circulation of the 'thing' through space and time is the focus. You are the passage through which the thing circulates.

VARIATION

* Stand in a circle. One person starts. He / she begins by passing a word to the person on his / her left by simply looking at this person, saying the word. Now, this person passes on the same word to the person on her / his left, trying to say the word with the exact same volume, timbre, articulation. Now, this third person passes on the same word in the same way and keeps the rhythm. Keep it simple. Attend to the rhythm. You could play with direction — switch from 'passing on' to the left to the right.
* You can pass on many things: a breath, a clap, a gesture, a movement or expression, a sentence, an object, a sound. You don't necessarily have to stand in a circle. You can 'pass on' in the space in a non-predefined way.

How do you 'understand' this passing on and what is happening during imitation, transmitting, reproducing, mediation? What do you select? How to stay rigorous? Through repetition, slight changes occur — observe what you see, hear, feel, understand. Pass it on to the next.

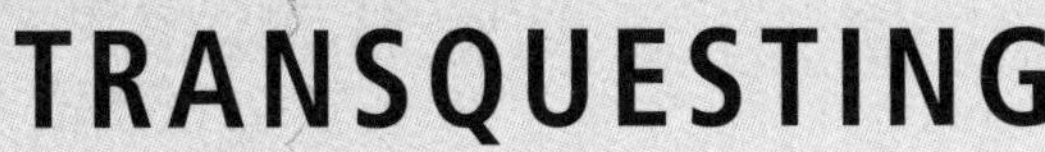

TRANSQUESTING

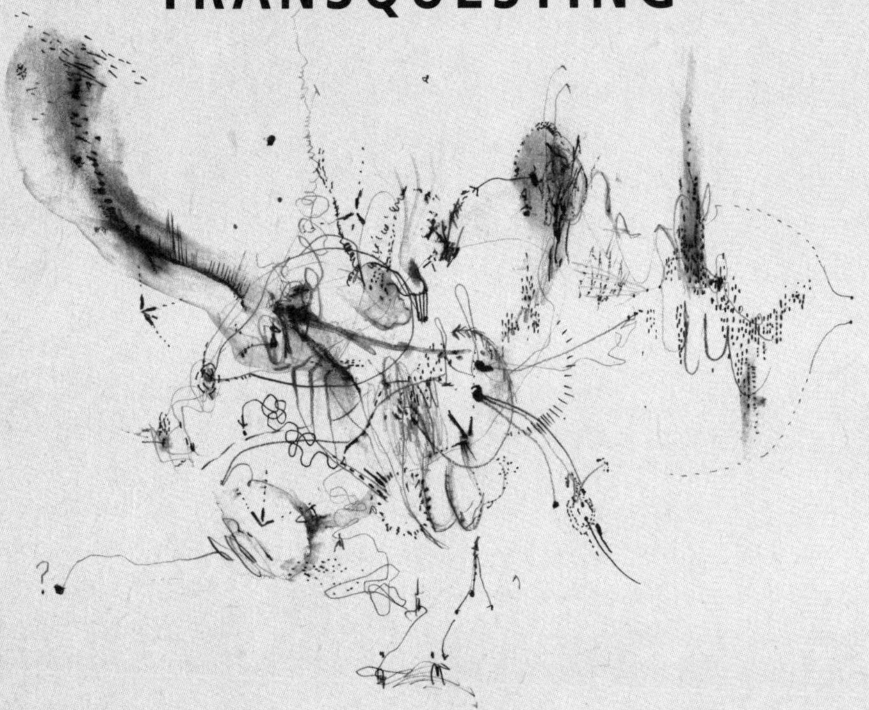

Use a set of specific questions to observe, mediate, reflect and transform a situation. Each question functions as a lens to look through, as a vehicle to ride with, as an organ to sense with, as an obstacle to rub against, as a partner to move with.

Entering the mode of transquesting means to stay in a state of observing the world for a certain timespan by questioning until the riddle dissolves, until you overcome the question of *the how* or *the when.* Look behind the mirror, beyond the question — transcending it. The aim is less to find a logical answer, but rather to gain an intuitive understanding of the question. *Becoming enquiry.*

(⟶ full list of TransQuestions: *How-ness, Where-ness, When-ness*)

EXAMPLES

1) Where is the point of decision?
2) How do you not block another's light?
3) When is something coming into experience?
4) Where is the momentum generated?
5) How do you decide what to do next?

Read the question. Observe the phrase. You could read it out loud. Get occupied by the query. Translate the question into the situation you are in. How to respond? How does the question move you? Make your whole body the means of your enquiry.

The question can be the starting point for a movement, for a journey. You can share your question with others (⟶ *Practices of Conversation*).

When you have found a temporary answer, find a way to somehow make it public. Then, move on.

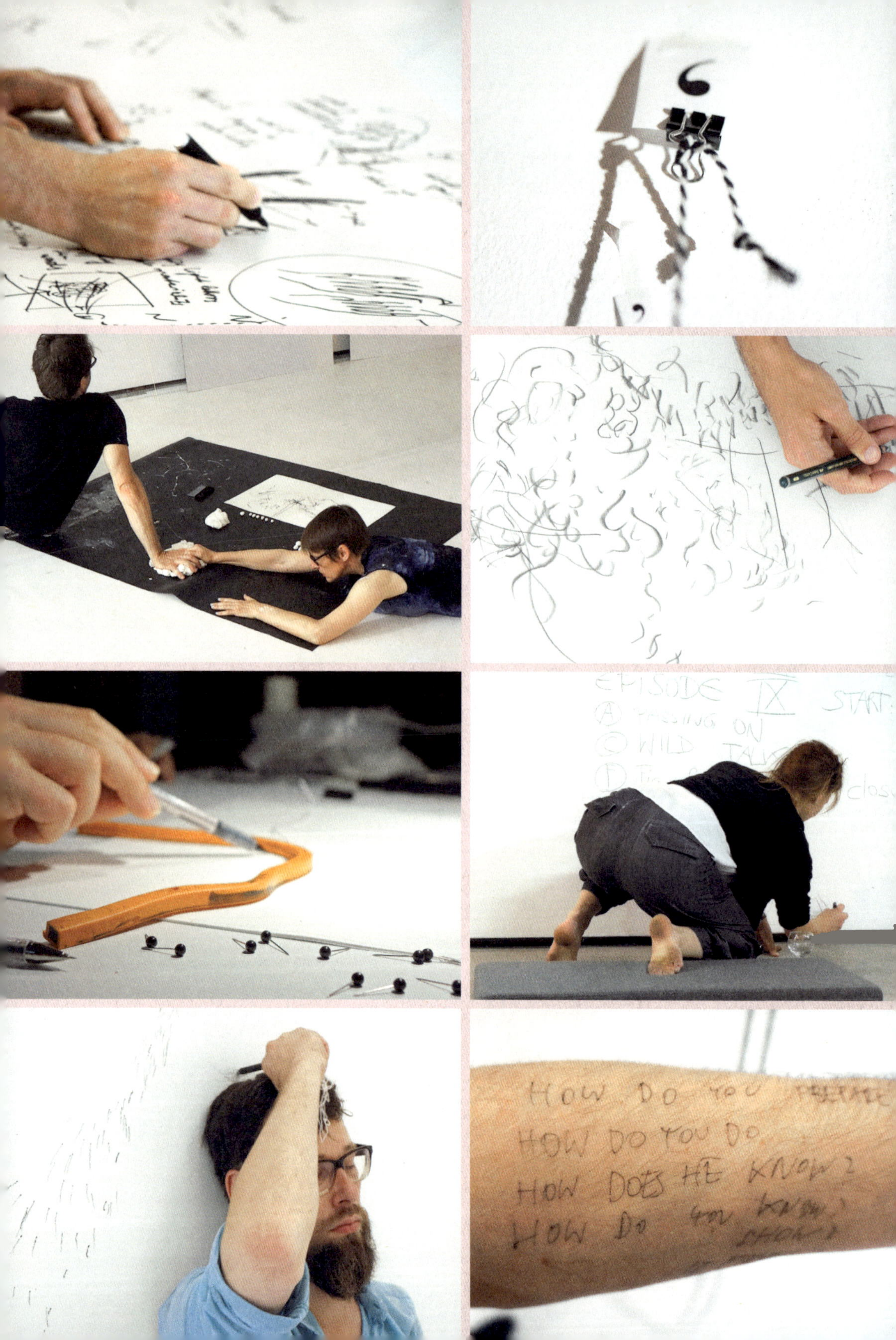

EPISODE IX START
PASSING ON
WILD
HOW DO YOU PREPARE
HOW DO YOU DO
HOW DOES HE KNOW?

PRACTICES OF NOTATION

PRACTICES OF NOTATION

PRELUDE

The practices — or rather *modes* — of notation operate in different ways within our enquiry at the level of the singular and sharable, the individual and collective; ranging from the colloquial use of the term notation for referring to various note-making and recording practices (noting, jotting, sketching), as well as to other forms of score, script, recipe or diagrammatic map (⟶ *Embodied Diagrammatics*), to the development of a formalised notation system with its own clearly defined 'inner logic'.[1] The unfolding live experience of shared experimentation can be (an)notated and — as a consequence — mediated through various *idio*syncratic systems of marking and inscription. *Idio* — meaning 'proper to one', one's own, private, personal or peculiar. One can mark for oneself, where the individual determines exactly *what* is notated and *how*. This form does not always need to be readable or recognisable by others. However, beyond developing various singular modalities of notation, our research process has involved the evolution of an agreed and sharable system of signs used for noticing *and* marking the event of *figuring* and the emergence of *figures*, shifting the notion of notation (in general terms) towards the notation of a *notion* (⟶ *Figuring* >< *Figure*).[2] We ask: how can we develop systems of notation for identifying, marking and communicating the barely perceptible micro-movements at the cusp of awareness within the process of collaborative artistic exploration without fixing that which is dynamic and contingent as a literal sign? Our research quest is directed towards a system for articulating that which is often ignored or remains invisible within conventional notational languages; those embodied, experiential, inter-subjective vitality forces and affects, operating before, between and beneath the more readable (therefore arguably more writable, inscribable) gestures of a practice.

The practices of notation function in close proximity to the attention practices (⟶ *Practices of Attention)*. Increased attention augments one's capacity to notice; in turn, the principle of *noticing* underpins notation. Furthermore, the relation is reciprocal — notation can further enhance one's capacity to notice. However, whilst the event of noticing and notation operate symbiotically, notation involves *more than* noticing. It is a practice of both noticing *and* marking. Marking is the criterion for notation. Notation involves the production of marks or symbols, the generation of signs relating to a sign-less experience. It operates within a semiotic field: what or *how* is the relation between sign and signification? In one sense, notation is activated whenever a sign or mark is used to stand for, *re*-present. It is a *mode* perhaps more than a practice since it is never truly autonomous; there must be a ground of other activity for it to mark, notation designates an experience other than itself. We activate notation in direct relation to our process of live exploration, aesthetic experimentation is the 'ground' of activity that we seek to mark. Notation has a reflective function; however, in contrast to the practices of conversation its modality is not discursive, not reportage. It just marks — its task is one of making visible or tangible the event of noticing (something).

Throughout our unfolding research process, different forms of notation have assisted our attempts to tune in to the level of *figuring* within our live explorations, as well as supporting the recognition, qualification and naming of emergent figures. We have used notation — drawing, notes, diagramming — after a period of live exploration, as a means for scoring and reflecting upon what had just happened. Here, the function of notation was for recollection or remembering retrospectively, after the fact. It was used to support re-activation (notation from one exploration operating as score for future action) and also helped us to identify our list of potential *figures* (⟶ *Figuring >< Figure*, ⟶ *Figures*). In these terms, notation can be conceived to have an explicit relation to translation (⟶ *Practices of Wit(h)nessing: Translating*), where the process of marking is one of capturing the core components of one experience through another medium using a system of signs. However, beyond a process of retrospective notation (after the event), our research quest has increasingly evolved towards the development of a system of 'live notation' that could be activated simultaneously to the situation that it seeks to describe.[3] We seek forms of notation ('dynamic indicators' to borrow Stern's term) through which to mark the event of *figuring* and the emergence of the *figures* live to the context of their production.[4]

Rather than modifying existing notational forms (musical, choreographic, cartographical, computational or even scientific notation systems), our intent was to develop an *undisciplinary* system (⟶ *Becoming Undisciplinary*) capable of operating between the lines. Initially, we developed a process of 'clicking' for marking the event of *figuring*, where we each make an audible sound (a vocal 'click') to acknowledge the experience of a qualitative shift in awareness or affordance, identification that *something* is happening at the level of vitality or emergence (⟶ *Clicking*). On occasion, this process of 'notated' live exploration was recorded on video: the function of video being indexical, to simply capture the 'clicks' in the context of their production. By watching the video documentation back — re-collecting and reflecting on the experience of notation — we were able to identify, qualify or even name the shifts in awareness, vitality or affordance marked by each 'click'. Whilst this process has enabled us to expand our list of potential *figures*, we still wanted to develop a system of notation that could be activated live as a mode of 'thinking-in-action' performed *en acte*.

What follows then is an account of our notation system as it is used (scored) within the context of a live exploration (⟶ *How to Play the Score*). In principle, our notation system has few rules: we can elect to practise our process of live exploration in a *notated* or *non-notated* form; we can practise *undifferentiated* or *differentiated* notation. The notation system unfolds through a gradually evolving logic: it begins with the attempt to notate the event of cognition — the marking of an undifferentiated, unqualified or as yet un-nameable 'something is happening' (⟶ *Clicking*). As we have identified a list of potential *figures* through our research (⟶ *Figuring >< Figure*, ⟶ *Figures*), we have added further differentiated forms of notation for marking the event of re-cognition, the re-meeting of a recognisable *figure* (⟶ *Affirming*, ⟶ *Naming*). Additionally, as we have become more familiar with the *figures*, the notational system has further evolved to have an active operational role within the 'scoring' of our live explorations (⟶ *Calling*, ⟶ *How to Play the Score*). The following pages elaborate these different modalities of notation based on the concrete sign systems developed through our own research process. Significantly, differentiated notation does not guarantee increased sophistication, indeed, the undifferentiated modality is arguably the more precise, or more specifically, it least affects the perceptual field that it attempts to mark.

---

1) "A system becomes a notation system when it has a working inner logic using a set of abstract representations (vocabulary) of aspects of potentially universal experience deemed relevant to be differentiated between, preserved or communicated about," in Simone Boria, Tim Boykett, Andreas Dekrout, Heather Kelly, Marta Peirano, Robert Rotenberg, Elisabeth Schimana (Eds.), *On Turtles and Dragons and the Dangerous Quest for a Media Art Notation System*, Linz: Times Up Press, 2012, p. 9. They elaborate the criteria for 'notation-system-ability' thus: "Is there an inner logic? ... Is there a vocabulary? ... Are the notations potentially accessible to at least one entity / person? ... Are other aspects intentionally left out?", p. 9.

2) Cf. Emma Cocker, Nikolaus Gansterer, Mariella Greil, 'Notion of Notation >< Notation of Notion', in *Performance Research, On An/Notations*, Vol. 20, Issue 6, 2015, pp. 53-57.

3) Cf. Emma Cocker, 'Live Notation: Reflections on a Kairotic Practice', in *Performance Research*, 'On Writing and Digital Media', Vol. 18, Issue 5, 2013, pp. 69-76.

4) Daniel Stern, *Forms of Vitality*, Oxford and New York: Oxford University Press, 2010, p. 76.

CLICKING

Before activating this mode of undifferentiated notation, it could help to prepare (⟶ *Practices of Attention*). Do not rush this. Take your time. When you feel ready, begin the process of live exploration, individually or with others. This could be an open field of exploration or you might prefer a more specific task.

Take your attention beyond the level of operation, beyond the logistics of what you are *doing*. During the unfolding exploration, can you notice moments when there is a perceptible shift in your awareness, a change of vitality affect or dynamic, a sense perhaps even of a new emergence or appearance in the situation?

These shifts in awareness or affordance are subtle, not easy to articulate in words. The emphasis is on qualitative nuance. Nuance — etymologically meaning a 'slight difference, shade of colour', originally used in reference to the different colours of the clouds, mist or vapour. A variation in tone or atmosphere: a shift, change or transition in state or presence. Not yet nameable: more of an inkling or a hint, the slightest indication that 'something is happening'.

Find a way of marking these moments when 'something is happening', for indicating the exact moment of 'ah, there'. Mark lightly, lightly. Try not to interrupt the flow. Avoid judgement. Do not yet strive to find a word. You could use a vocal sign like an audible 'click'. Or find a movement equivalent — the click of fingers, the raising of the hand. Like punctuation: *punctuare,* to mark with points or dots, from the Latin *punctus*, 'to prick'. Keep it simple, but be precise.[1]

---

1) As part of our research process, we have also recorded this phase of undifferentiated notation using video, retrospectively attempting to identify the shifts in awareness, vitality or affordance marked by each 'click' (⟶ *Prelude: Practices of Notation*).

AFFIRMING

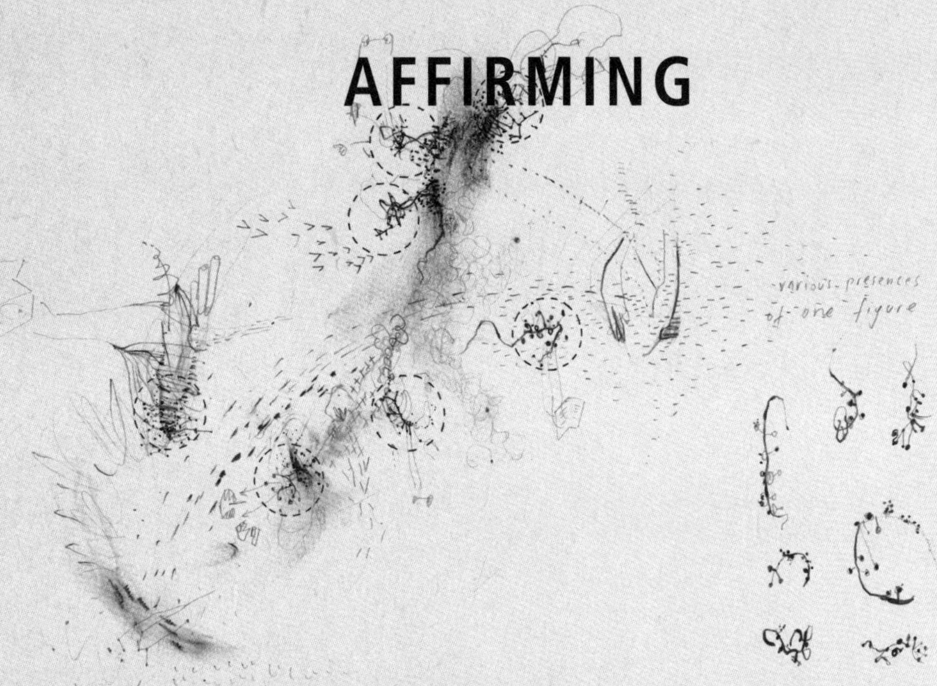

This next notational exploration is practised in hope of encountering the emergence of a specific *figure*, where marking is used for affirmation or verification. To begin, select one specific *figure* as the focus for your next phase of live exploration: it is important that you have a qualitative sense of the chosen *figure*, an idea of its vitality, its atmosphere. We have elaborated the qualities of nine specific *figures* (⟶ *Elemental,* ⟶ *Empathetic,* ⟶ *Transformative Figures*). You could choose one of these specific *figures,* but there is an infinite list of potential others.

Begin the process of live exploration, individually or with others. The focus of this exploration is towards creating the conditions for the arising or emergence of your intended *figure*. Previous iterations might give a sense of the possible 'ingredients' needed, but they are no guarantee. The process is necessarily experimental, *aleatory*. It is hopeful rather than assured.

During the unfolding exploration, sharpen your attention to the qualities of the intended *figure*. If and when you notice the arising of the *figure*, then mark it. You could use a simple vocal sign like an audible 'oh', or find a movement equivalent. You could even say 'yes' or 'now' — though actual words can sometimes rupture the quality of embodied attention. The mark you choose should not be the same as that used for undifferentiated notation.

Mark only those moments when your intended *figure* appears, nothing more. The function of this notation is affirmation or verification, the universal mark for designating the arising of the intended *figure*. If necessary, you could also still use a form of 'undifferentiated' notation (⟶ *Clicking*) to simply mark when 'something is happening' but *not* related to your intended *figure*. It is like this: *Imagine you are trying to see a specific kind of bird. You are looking and you know this bird, you can recognise it. Your attention is focused only towards seeing this specific kind of bird. Of course, you will see other birds and this is not a problem. But, you don't have to give a name to all these other birds because this is not relevant for you. You just have one bird in mind; it is the bird that you want to see. When you see other birds, if necessary you could even say 'not this'. But, you are looking for only one bird.*

NAMING

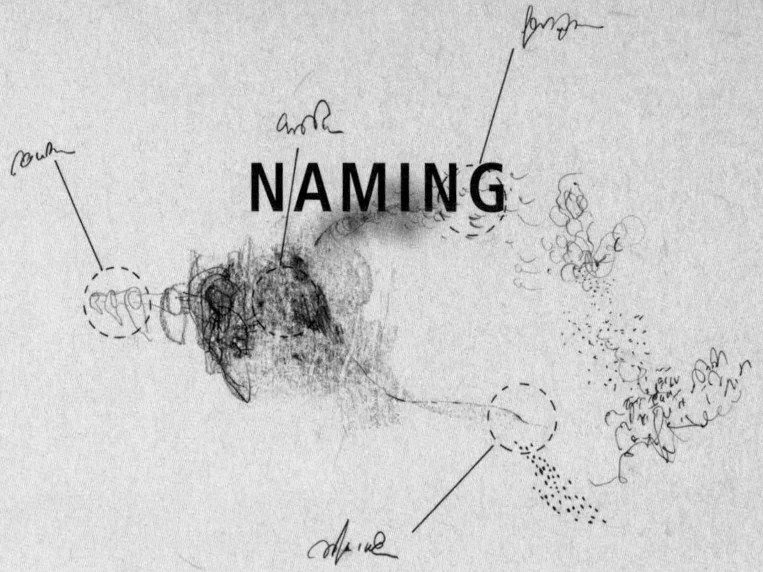

This practice of *differentiated* notation requires a high level of familiarity with a range of different *figures,* a clear sense of their specific quality, vitality or atmosphere. We have elaborated the qualities of nine specific *figures* (⟶ *Elemental, Empathetic, Transformative Figures*), but there is an infinite list of potential others.

Begin the process of live exploration, individually or with others. It could be 'open' exploration or focused towards the arising or emergence of a specific *figure.* If and when you notice the arising of any recognisable *figure,* mark it by saying its 'name'.

If you are engaged in an exploration focused towards the arising or emergence of a specific *figure,* the 'naming' operates in the same key as affirmation (⟶ *Affirming).* However, during a single period of exploration, you might notice and be able to name the arising of many different *figures* (not always the one you are specifically seeking).

The naming of a *figure* is itself a form of notation: it marks a moment of *qualification*. However, this practice necessitates a high level of fluency, since the closer notation comes to a system of differentiable signs, the more challenging it can be to stay *in* the flow. Linguistic means of marking can serve to distance or dislocate the notating individual from a level of embodied — even phenomenal — experience; furthermore, without due care, they can have a tendency to develop a quality of agency or life of their own.

Rather than using the full name, you could develop a corresponding sign system related to each *figure,* different forms of phonetic utterance — or movement equivalent — that involve less interruption of the experiential flow. For example, felt moments of dissonance could be marked through the sibilance of a spoken 'SSS', the experience of consonance or harmony with the vowel sound 'AAA'.[1]

During this notational exploration, you could mark using the name of an existing *figure*: qualification or differentiation as recognition. Alternatively, you could identify and name any new *figures* that you notice. Designation, nomination: an intuitive, instinctive and even sensuous process akin to 'tasting' different words to find an 'adequate' name (⟶ *Whenness*). Here then, the process of 'naming' new *figures* expands the list of existing *figures* creating further possibilities for differentiated or qualified notation.

---

1) Daniel Stern observes that there is an already established differentiated method for describing dynamic features within musical performance, a recognisable system of 'dynamic markers' for indicating towards the level of (1) Intensity (force): *p* (*piano*) = quietly, softer, weaker; or *ff* (*fortissimo*) = much louder, stronger; (2) Changes in intensity: contouring the intensity in time such as < = growing intensity (crescendo) and >= decreasingly intensity (decrescendo); (3) Stress or accents: such as *sf* (*sforzando*) — a sharp, strong attack or *legato* = smooth glide; (4) Tempo: from *ritardando* (slowing down) or *accelerando* (speeding up). Cf. Daniel Stern, *Forms of Vitality: Exploring Dynamic Experience in Psychology, the Arts, Psychotherapy and Development,* Oxford and New York: Oxford University Press, 2010, pp. 82-83.

CALLING

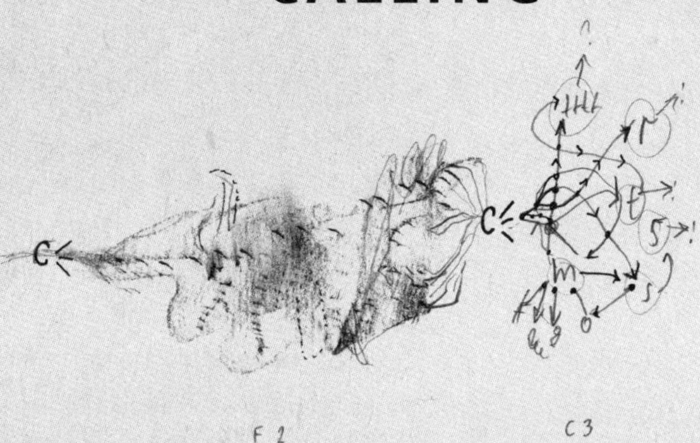

Calling operates in a different key to the other notational modes. Whilst it marks a moment of awareness within the unfolding of a live exploration, the *call* indicates the need for a specific dynamic shift or change in focus and attention, rather than seeking to differentiate (name, qualify) the arising of sensation itself.

Undoubtedly, the other listed notational modalities have an implicit relationship to the unfolding direction of live exploration, since notation creates heightened points of shared awareness that cannot but inform what happens next. Notation irrevocably effects or interrupts (however minimally) the field of exploration that it seeks to notate.

However, *calling* has a more explicit function in actively shaping or steering the course of future action, and in this sense plays a fundamental operational role in the 'scoring' of our live explorations (⟶ *Embodied Diagrammatics*, ⟶ *How to Play the Score*). Specifically, we seek to explore the relationship between different *figures*; moreover, aim to test how various *Practices of Attention*, *Conversation*, as well as *Notation*, impact and intervene in this aesthetic process of enquiry. *Calling* operates as a direct intervention. Whilst practising in the qualitative field of one *figure* (F) (e.g. *Figure of Becoming Material*), you could call for a shift in focus towards another *figure* (e.g. *Figure of Ventilating Meaning*) — perhaps if you began to sense the qualities of this other *figure* arising and rather than just mark it, wanted to pursue it through further exploration. Or maybe your engagement with one *figure* has ebbed or been exhausted, and you simply require a change in tack. F is the call for a shift in focus, asking for the redirection of collective energies towards the production of the conditions of a new *figure's* arising. Alternatively, you could call for one of the *Practices of Attention* (A) as a means for sharpening or refocusing collective attention, or a *Practice of Conversation* (C) for opening things up through verbal-linguistic reflection. *Calling* both marks and activates a dynamic shift, diagramming lines of connectivity between the fields of (A), (C), and (F). In this sense, the caller needs to have some awareness of the various *figures* (⟶ *Elemental, Empathetic, Transformative Figures*) and *Practices* (⟶ *Practices of Attention*, *Practices of Conversation*).

Calling does not specifically notate (through qualification) the experience that gave rise to the call — this remains unnamed. Moreover, this notational modality presents a further dilemma, for you cannot call for the *calling*. Indeed, *calling* does not have to be a vocal call; a call can implicitly be made through a recognisable shift in one's action.

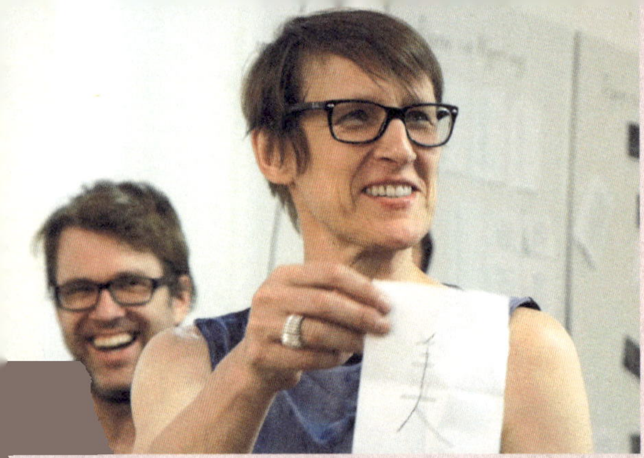

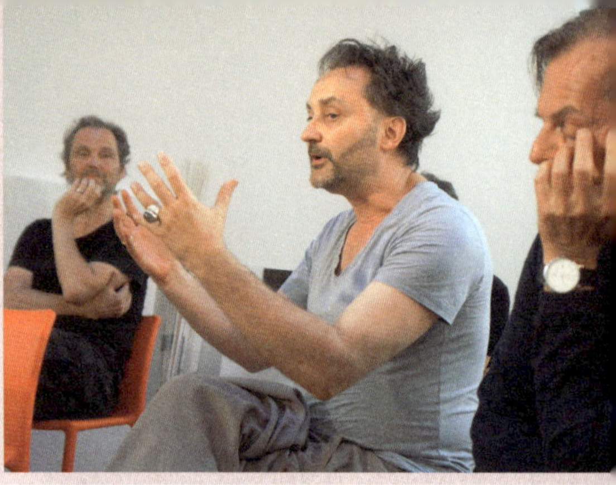

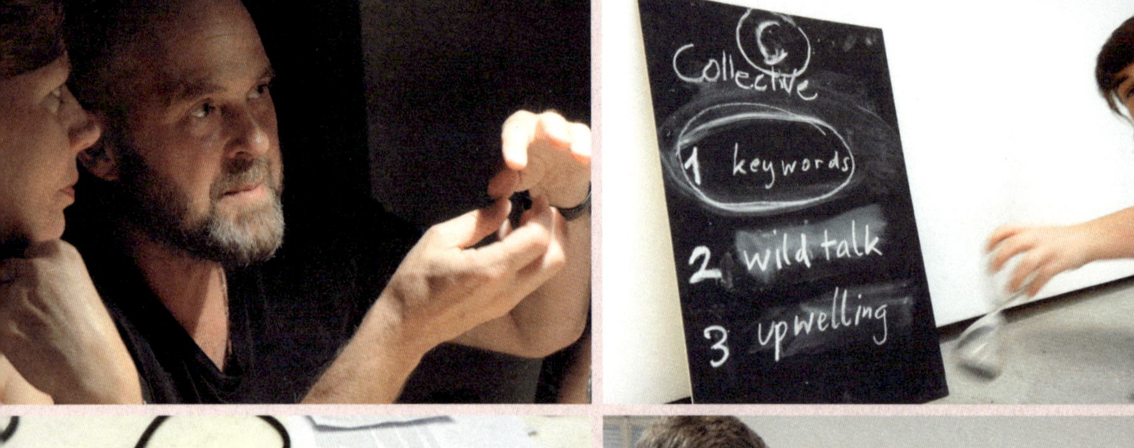
C
Collective
1 keywords
2 wild talk
3 upwelling

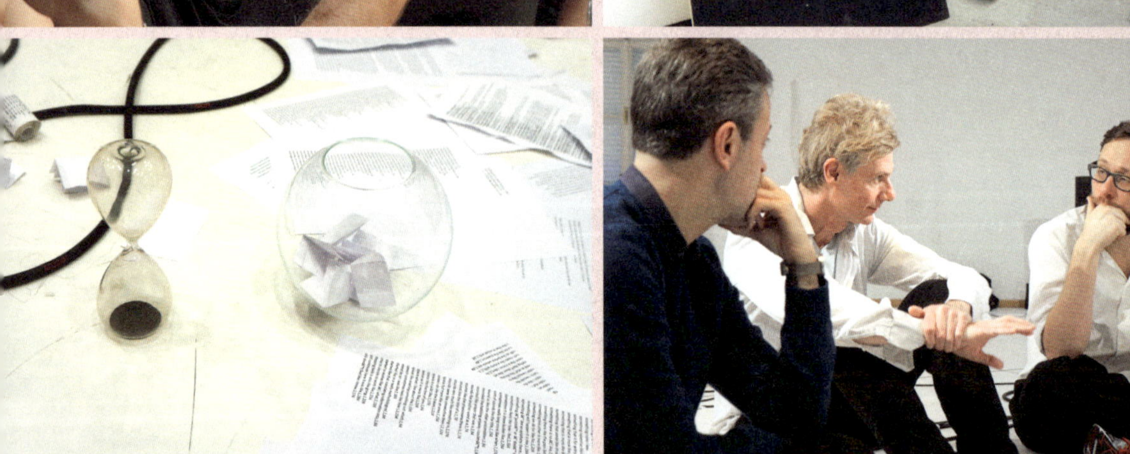

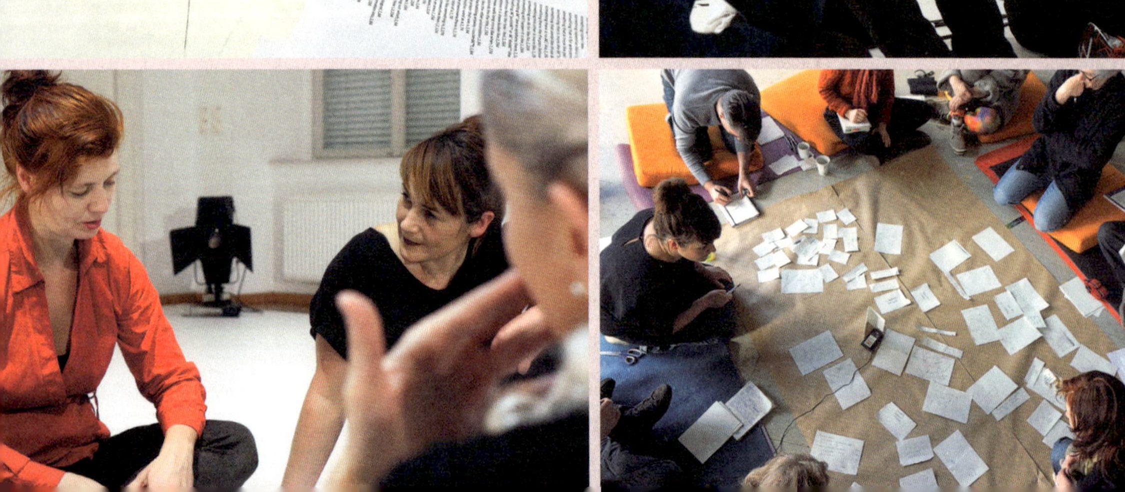

PRACTICES OF CONVERSATION

PRACTICES OF CONVERSATION

PRELUDE

Conversation provides a verbal-linguistic means for reflecting on the process of our live exploration.[1] It is a language-based, relational and participatory practice, a site of shared voicing happening aloud within a collective situation. However, the practice of conversation is also itself a live exploration — perhaps even an aesthetic exploration — with its own specific 'vitality contours' and dynamic affects. For Brian Massumi, "A conversation becomes artistic when the conditions of its occurrence are set in a way that offsets it slightly from its own mode, that create that minimal distance of conversation to itself, giving it a unique vitality affect that just any conversation doesn't have ... Art brings the amodal, and the qualitative element of vitality affect that coincides with it, to more palpable expression."[2] Reflecting on the 'vitality forms' within unscripted spontaneous conversation, Daniel Stern observes how speech production is an embodied practice that "requires physical (as well as mental) movement. The voice is an instrument involving voluntary movements of the vocal chords, tongue, mouth, lips, breathing, etc. [...] The prosody of speech consisting of melody, stress, volume modulation, vocal tension, etc. creates forms of vitality."[3] He argues that in the "imprecise, messy, hit-and-miss work to find the 'right words' to communicate what one wishes [...] Emergent properties form. New linkages are created, tentatively accepted, revised, rejected, reintroduced in a different form, and moved with all the other creative products of the intention-unfolding process [...] It is a process that can rush forward, hesitate, stop, restart gently."[4]

We attend then to conversation as a 'vitality field' — a generative practice in-and-of itself; site and material for the construction of immanent and inter-subjective modes of linguistic 'sense-making', emerging from the enmeshing of our different voices in live exchange. This process of 'conversation-as-material' involves the quest for a not yet known vocabulary, where meaning does not exist prior to the event of utterance. Rather, it is co-produced through the dialogic process of conversation itself; furthermore, is often only discernible in retrospect, for example, through a process of recording and transcription.[5] However, rather than simply a record or dialogic archive, we consider our conversational transcripts as live material for playful appropriation and reworking. At times, conversation has been condensed into an intense *im*personal (*inter-* or even *infra*-personal) poetics for articulating different facets of our enquiry.[6] Arguably, the specific rhythm of conversation produces a different textual texture to that of conventional writing. Its cadence or rhythmic pacing — its pitch and intonation, the tempo of speech — involves the embodied rise and fall of inflection and emphasis, excited acceleration, hesitation and deliberation, syncopation, sentence incompletion, syllabic glides and slurs. The transcripts have also been folded back into our aesthetic exploration as a physical material aerated through the performative 'ventilating of meaning' as a live event (⟶ *Figure of Ventilating Meaning*), or have been distilled into playful lists of questions or prompts, for example, based on specific keyword searches such as *how, when, where.*[7]

However, beyond this method of 'conversation-as-material' we have also devised specific practices where conversation enters the field of live exploration through scored or even choreographed forms of action, practices of 'staged conversation' with distinctive parameters and rules.[8] For Alva Noë, conversation is "an organized activity", furthermore, it organises us — like other activities including dancing, reading, cooking — at the level of *embodiment*.[9] Whilst these various structures of organisation are "not of our own making", according to Noë, art offers "a way to understand our organization and, inevitably, to reorganize ourselves."[10] Specifically, he argues that choreography *stages* dance to reflect on how we are "organized by dancing", whilst it is simultaneously bent on its re-organisation.[11] In these terms, to 'stage conversation' arguably exposes the ways in which we are organised *by it*, whilst the use of specific rules, constraints or even obstacles become devices of *re-organisation*, short-circuiting habitual patterns of conversation towards the production of unexpected vitality affects. For Noë, conversation involves the "complicated activity of listening, thinking, paying attention, doing and undergoing [...] conversation is a fundamental mechanism of relationship building and joint living."[12] Likewise, for Stern, conversation can be conceived as a practice of "interactional synchrony", involving a process of "affect attunement" between speaker and listener.[13] Etymologically, conversation did not always refer to 'talk' but rather to the act of conducting oneself in the world: *living-with* or keeping company, literally meaning 'to turn about with'. In one sense, the arc of complication or convolution as the practice of conversation shifts from the dyad, to the triad, to the many, echoes concerns explored within our *Empathetic Figures*.[14]

What follows are four different practices of conversation or conversational re-organisation. Each practice is conceived in direct relation to our aesthetic exploration, for further opening this up through linguistic means. Each has a different imperative or atmosphere, creating different dynamics and rhythms, different ways of being together. For example, whereas *Dialogic* engages in the creation of intimate (often dyadic) meeting points through conversation, *Keywords* involves the participation of many others, including wider publics. *Upwelling* involves the dampening of the speaking *I* to become a conduit for the 'situation', whilst *Wild Talk* channels the spontaneous excesses of an over-enthusiastic, babbling subject. The practices of conversation operate in close proximity to the *Practices of Wit(h)nessing*, providing a context through which we, alongside critical wit(h)nesses and invited publics, feedback our reflections and observations directly into the process of an unfolding live exploration. Our list of practices is not exhaustive and could be added to: it is just a start. Silence is also always an option.

---

1) A process of conversation underpins many of our reflective-conceptual essays and also manifests within this publication as a series of Trialogues (→ *On Sedimentations of Sensitivities*, → *Thinking-Making in Relation*).

2) Brian Massumi, in Hugo Glendinning and Adrian Heathfield (Dirs. and Eds.), *No Such Thing as Rest: A Walk with Brian Massumi*, 2013, p. 13. www.adrianheathfield.net/project/no-such-thing-as-rest

3) Daniel Stern, *Exploring Dynamic Experience in Psychology, the Arts, Psychotherapy and Development*, Oxford and New York: Oxford University Press, 2010, pp. 121-122. See also Brandon LaBelle, *Lexicon of the Mouth: Poetics and Politics of Voice and the Oral Imaginary*, New York: Bloomsbury Academic, 2014 (→ *Practices of Attention: Voicing*).

4) Stern, 2010, pp. 122-124.

5) Over the course of our project we have recorded over 150 hours of conversation resulting in over 300,000 words of textual transcript.

6) The texts for articulating the qualities of our named *figures* are distilled from conversational extracts (→ *Figures*).

7) → *Figure of Ventilating Meaning*, → *How-ness*, → *When-ness*, → *Where-ness*, → *Practices of Attention: Self-Reporting* in relation to listening to all those inner voices already within the single speaking *I*.

8) Cf. Emma Cocker, 'Conversation as Material: Writing without Writing', in Katja Hilevaara and Emily Orley (Eds.), *The Creative Critic: Writing as/about Practice*, London: Routledge, 2017.

9) Alva Noë, *Strange Tools — Art and Human Nature*, New York: Hill and Wang, 2015, p. 6.

10) Noë, 2015, p. xiii.

11) Noë, 2015, p. 15.

12) Noë, 2015, p. 7.

13) Stern, 2010, p. 51.

14) Indeed, conversation contains the prefix *con-* (indicating between-ness, with-ness, together-ness), which we also associate with the → *Empathetic Figures*.

DIALOGIC

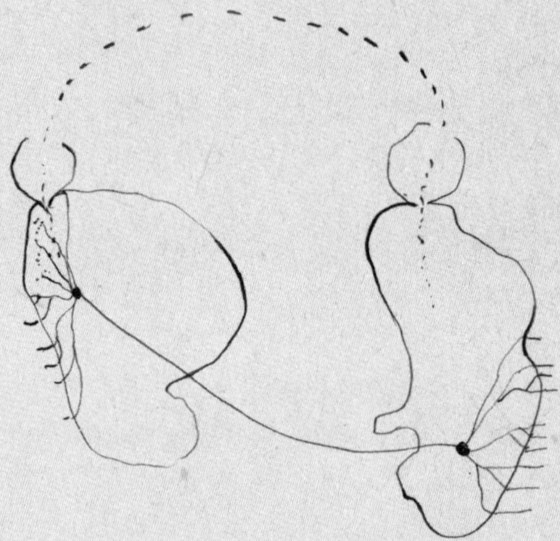

Dialogue: a practice for *dia-* (across) *legein* (speak). Involving conversation between two or more persons, not just *duologue*. Before conversing with the many, it can help to practise in pairs. It can also help to focus one's material, even prepare a script. For example, you could use the list of 'how questions' (⟶ *How-ness*) as a starting point for dialogic practice.

VARIATIONS

Three dialogic practices with different functions and affects.

EMBODIED DIALOGUE

Find someone to work with, then each choose a different question from the list. For example you might choose the question, "How do you repeat the feeling of when you discovered something?" and your partner might choose the question, "How can we actualise that through practice?" Sit on the floor, back to back. Take it in turns to speak your question out loud. Feel the force of the other's speech act as a vibration along your spine. Experiment with changes in volume, speed, or urgency. Avoid overlapping.

DIALOGIC STRETCH

Working with the same partner, but with new questions. Take a few moments to memorise your new question. Now face one another, meet the other's eyes. Not staring — instead try to remain receptive, open. Take it in turns to speak your question out loud, maintaining eye contact. Gradually, start to stretch the words, feeling the shape of the vowels and consonants in your mouth, becoming elongated. Or else, focus your attention on specific phonetic elements, exploring the micro-components of your question. Experiment with changes in volume, speed, or urgency. Explore synchronicity of speech.

DIALOGUE WITH STRANGERS

Choose five questions from the list, for example, (1) "How do you decide what to do next?"; (2) "How do familiarity and expectation organise time?"; (3) "How is living matter organised?"; (4) "How does an attention practice cultivate the capacity to act?"; (5) "How do we map that?" Approach a stranger and initiate a conversation using only these questions.

KEYWORDS[1]

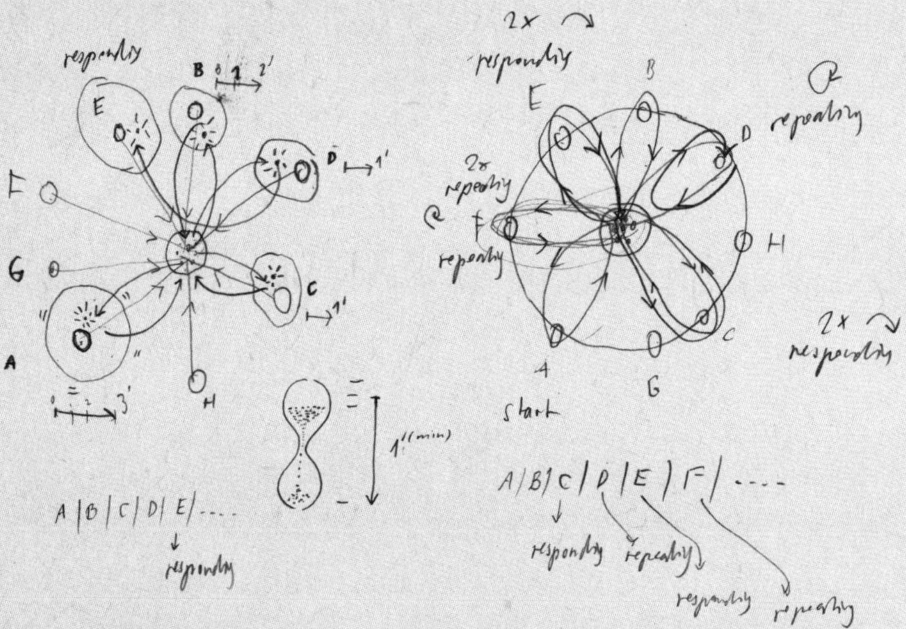

This is a way of organising a conversation through a game structure, using keywords and timeframes. First, come together as a group. Each person writes a keyword on a piece of paper, relating to the context they are working in. You can write more than one keyword, each on a different piece of paper. The keywords are collected and put into a receptacle, a bowl for example. In another receptacle, there are also papers folded that indicate different time periods, for example, one, two or three minutes. A dice can be used instead. One person picks up a piece of paper with a keyword and also a time and starts to talk until the time is over. Another person is the timekeeper using a watch, clock or set of hour glasses as a time measuring device. If there is nothing to say, all stay in silence. Someone can decide to ask the speaker to talk for longer, in that case s/he has to pick another time. Or someone decides to reply, in that case s/he picks a time. Or someone picks another keyword and another time. Keywords can be taken out once they have been talked about. Time slots are always returned to the receptacle.[1]

---

1) *Keywords* is based on *Conversation Score,* developed by Lilia Mestre in the context of her research on scores as pedagogical tools titled *ScoreScapes* in the frame of a.pass (advanced performance and scenography studies) (⟶ Lilia Mestre, *Score It!*).

UPWELLING

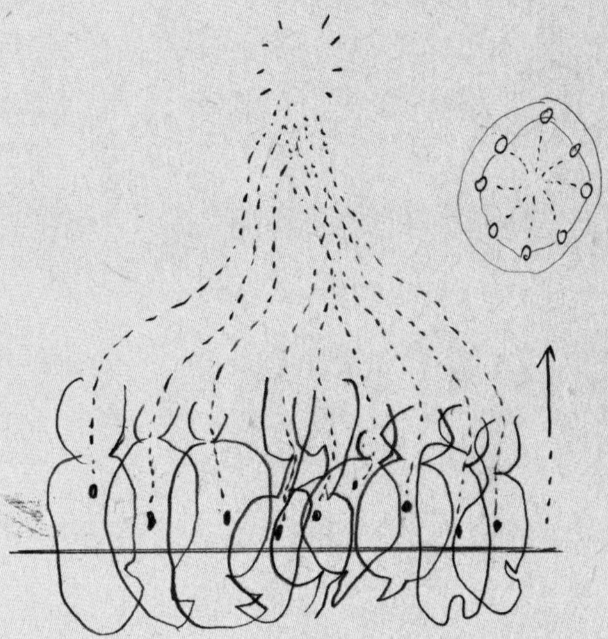

Come together. Even sit. Allow a moment for silence to settle, stillness to fall. Let go the urgency of one's speech, for this is not about airing one's own thoughts or feelings. This is not about *you,* the speaking *I*. Dampen the *I-ness* of the self, put the ego to one side.

It could help to close your eyes. Take a breath or two. Focus on breathing can help to clear the mind, suspend the act of thinking. Turn down the volume on your own interior chatter, the dialogue of I with itself. This is a quiet practice of restraint.

Once the mind has stilled, other wordings might begin to show, make an appearance. Attend to the upwelling of the situation, what *it* wants to say. Become its conduit, its medium. Listen for the scene speaking, as with the spectre at the séance. Let the word come. See it in your mind's eye. Let it come. Once it is there, it can be uttered, the word spoken out loud. Allow this process to continue.

Undoing the rules of conversation. Resist the charms of word play or association, try not to respond to what you hear spoken by others. Practise discernment. Remain tuned to what the situation wants. Beyond the dialogic, speaking together through reflective attention. Towards a collective voicing, the mutual speech acts of an atmosphere.

WILD TALK

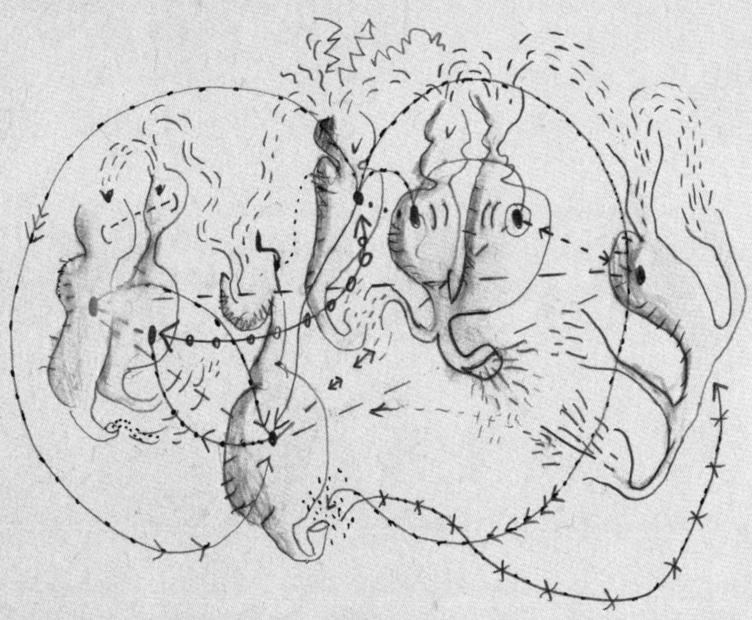

Wild talk invites a certain unruliness and effervescence within conversation: *unsinn — wild — sauvage — drauflos reden.* It is a multidirectional, multifocal conversation, asking for overlapping voices, interventions, cuts and jumps, falling into another's words.

Pick up what different people around you are talking about and what you can grasp and respond and try to keep the words flowing and intervene in others' communication whenever possible. The proposition for wild talk is open, even *promiscuous*. Switch conversation as your desire takes you.

VARIATIONS

You could choose on what to focus:

Is it about what you say?

Is it how you say it?

Is it how you relate to what the other says?

Is it a monologue amongst many other monologues?

Is it switching from one subject to another, trying to make sense, but never making the point?

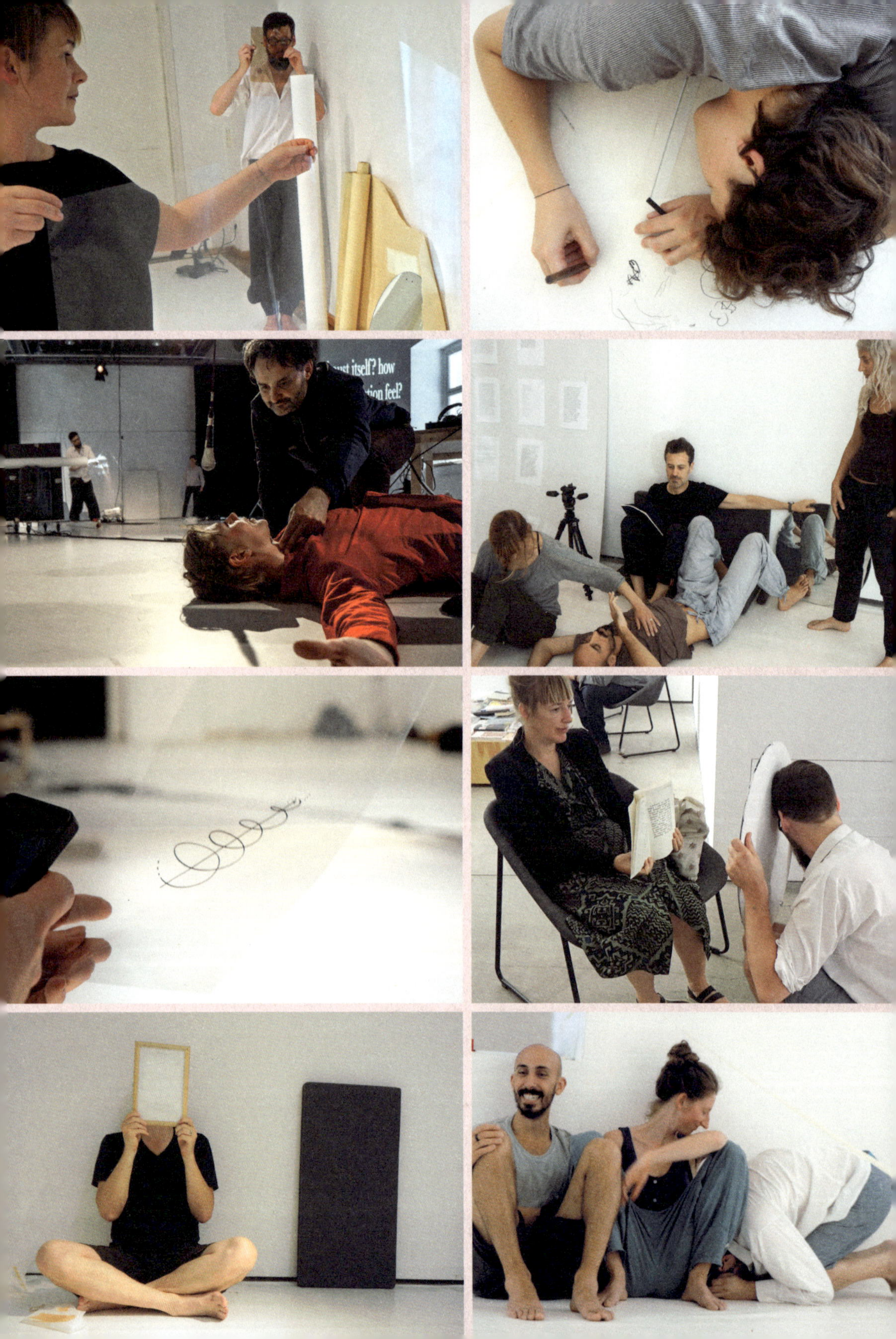
itself? how
feel?

PRACTICES OF WIT(H)NESSING

PRACTICES OF WIT(H)NESSING

PRELUDE

Conflation of witnessing and being with; we use the term *wit(h)nessing* to refer to the different ways in which an individual might engage with the unfolding process of live exploration, other than through direct performative participation itself.[1] In the following pages, we outline three practices of *wit(h)nessing,* though undoubtedly there are many more. *Watching:* engagement through the eyes, to view what comes, is done or happens. *Listening*: to open up the ears, tune in to the acoustic space. *Translating:* mediation or interpretation through the different modalities of drawing, writing, forming and moving. Whilst watching, listening and translating all take place within the process of live exploration, when activated in the key of *wit(h)nessing*, they are practised from a position outside or beyond the frame of direct action, from the edge or side.[2]

At times, it is necessary to withdraw from the space of action or activity in order to catch one's breath or bide one's time, to gauge the situation from a different perspective or position. There are moments when the decision of *how* to act (next) cannot be made from 'in the midst' of *doing*. Stepping back is a reflective practice related to timing and timeliness, the art of knowing-when to act and when to yield (⟶ *When-ness*). Becoming *wit(h)ness* can cultivate readiness; lessen one's tendency to (re)act habitually, for acting without due care or thought. Here, *wit(h)nessing* advocates the affirmative potential of non-participation (⟶ *On Sedimentations of Sensitivities*). Recognise those moments when one's actions no longer support the conditions of emergence: learn how to let go, if necessary how to stop. Take intervention when one's doing has become dull or dissipated; forced or formulaic, stultified or stuck. Practise the art of leaving space and time for *other* things to emerge. Sometimes *not doing* is the most generative thing that one could do. Allow things to breathe. Make room. Stand aside. Whilst there are specific *figures* that could be *called* (⟶ *Notation: Calling*) to bring about a similar shift of attention (e.g. ⟶ *Spiralling Momentum* for increasing energy after a lull, ⟶ *Temporary Closing* for signalling when is enough), the *Practice of Wit(h)nessing* does not *directly* intervene in or change the collective direction of shared exploration.

Wit(h)nessing is an individual practice that can re-sharpen attention or focus, should one's energy or concentration lapse. Here, the act of withdrawal or taking to the edge is not one of separation or disengagement, but a means of reconnection, the revitalising of one's engagement through the affordance of a different angle of view. *Wit(h)nessing* is an enabling activity then, for re-activating heightened states of alertness, vigilance and receptivity (⟶ *Practices of Attention*); in turn, related to the event of *noticing*. Indeed, the principle of *wit(h)nessing* reflects the dual aspect of our research. First, we explore the process of artistic 'sense-making' from within or inside (*intra-*), attending to an affective process-realm of forces and intensities operating before (*pre-*), between (*inter-*), and below (*infra-*) the more readable gestures of artistic practice. Second, and in parallel, we seek to develop systems of notation and performativity ('choreo-graphic figures') for sharing this often hidden or undisclosed aspect of the creative process, for communicating the experience to — or rather with — others. But, how do we articulate the sensations of *figuring* experienced *within* the process of live exploration to others situated without? (⟶ *Practices of Notation*).

Indeed, can our *figures* be recognised from the outside, their qualitative force discerned? (→ *Figuring* >< *Figure*). The *wit(h)ness* role therefore is not to be inhabited in rest or reprieve from the process of exploration, but rather has a critical task to perform — their feedback affirms *or* contradicts the effectiveness *and* affective-ness of our shared research quest.

However, the feedback loop invariably modifies the conditions of exploration; the observer irrevocably changes the situation observed. There can be no neutral position, no outside. The presence of a *wit(h)ness* can serve to amplify the attention of the *wit(h)nessed;* knowing that someone is watching can transform even the slightest micro-gesture into an event. Indeed, the presence of *wit(h)nesses* helps to create a proper *milieu* for our enquiry, adding to a heightened atmosphere of attention, concentration and commitment. *Milieu:* the setting or conditions of one's surroundings, etymologically meaning a 'middle' or 'medial place'. Indeed, the position of the *wit(h)ness* itself is somewhat medial, operating between the lines. Akin to the participant-observer within ethnography, the *wit(h)ness* inhabits the gap — even hyphen — between observation and participation, an outsider-insider whose presence on the edge nonetheless influences that which is within the frame. The *wit(h)ness* is simultaneously a part of and apart from. To *wit(h)ness* requires a *level* of participation, but not through direct physical interaction or taking part, rather by part-taking (contributing in the role *of* an observer) so as to partake, to share.

Indeed, the term *with* has contradictory — even paradoxical — connotations: as a preposition it can signal the conditions of accompaniment, association, combination, even union; to be besides, alongside, next to. *With* as a principle of adjacency: of closeness and proximity, to be bordering or contiguous. Contiguity: to be adjacent in time. *Near* touching — yet touched *without* touching, in contact *without* contact.[3] Alternatively, the prefix *with* communicates a separating or opposing force, with *as* against. Withhold (back away). Withstand (resist). Withdraw (take back, retract). Yet the *wit(h)ness* draws away so as to better engage. Indeed, at times one can become too close to clearly see; it is sometimes necessary to get some distance or else bring in an outsider's eye. Within our project, the role of the *wit(h)ness* has also been occupied by various 'outsiders'; individuals who were not directly responsible for the research enquiry itself, but who have offered us different perspectives on our process, providing critical feedback as to the *veracity* of our research claims.[4] Indeed, our research approach seeks to collapse or render porous the boundary line between performer and audience, hoping to activate practices of *wit(h)nessing* — a call to be present, to be there — partly in resistance to the normative conventions of spectatorship.[5] However, our intent is less towards the practising of relational aesthetics[6] — too often predicated on the coercion of interactive relationships between art, artists and participants — but rather we seek to cultivate a complex relational ecology or even 'relationscape'[7] supporting the potentiality of polyrhythmic — even *idiorrhythmic* — intensities and durations of engagement, of *being-with* as well as *being-apart.*[8]

Furthermore, to take oneself *out* or *be-apart* does not always require a physical move or relocation, but rather describes a qualitative shift of attention from spontaneous contribution *to* the process of aesthetic play towards receptive observation *of,* a move towards the *active* inhabitation of the — potentially *radically passive* — role of the *wit(h)ness.*[9] Drawing on Spinoza's *Ethics*, Gilles Deleuze names the power to affect other forces — *spontaneity*, and to be affected by others — *receptivity*. To *wit(h)ness* is to become open to the potential of being affected, an ethical practice in-and-of itself. Our practices of *wit(h)nessing* echo the empathetic and relational aspects of our enquiry, foregrounded within those *Empathetic Figures* underscored by qualities of between-ness, with-ness, together-ness. Towards a condition of receptive involution, folded entanglement of *wit(h)ness* and *wit(h)nessed.* Likewise, we acknowledge the entanglement of references that shape our use of the term *wit(h)ness*. For Jean-Luc Nancy, the experience of 'being' is always one of 'being with', where the concept of 'I' is not prior to that of 'we': the nature of existence is one of *co*-existence, where "being cannot *be* anything but being-with-one-another, circulating in the *with* and as the *with* of this singularly plural existence."[10] For Daniel Stern, the specific 'vitality affects' generated through being-in-relation can generate an event of "affective inter-subjectivity"[11] with the potential to irrevocably alter or re-organise our "implicitly felt inter-subjective field."[12] Indeed, as Bracha L. Ettinger states, "the question of wit(h)nessing arises, where the I reattunes itself in co-response-ability with the non-I's traces within a shared psychic space ... where we can talk about co-response-ability and asymmetrical responsibility and coemergence-in-difference on a transsubjective level, as the time-space of encounter-event is shared by several borderlinking I(s) and non-I(s) [...] Here a copoietic jointness evolves, only inasmuch as it is transfused with compassion."[13] The *being-with* of *wit(h)nessing* has epistemological as well as ethical and empathetic implications. For Vilém Flusser, the gesture of "'pure' research" or "scientific method" ("the gesture of the transcendent subject") is predicated on "the difference between subject and object, human being and world, I and it."[14] In contrast, he advocates a research paradigm less concerned with "a hypothesis on one side and an observation on the other" but rather emerging, "from a concrete, full, living experience of being-in-the-world."[15] Here, as Flusser argues, "the researcher ceases to be a 'pure' subject to become a living person, that is, someone who lives epistemologically, ethically and aesthetically all at once [...] Proximity is an inter-subjective dimension. It measures the being I share with others in the world."[16]

---

1) We are grateful to critical wit(h)ness Dieter Mersch whose reflections on the complex histories of witnessing (Summer Lab, 2016) prompted our differentiation of the role of wit(h)ness from witness. In *Epistemologies of Aesthetics*, Zurich and Berlin: Diaphanes, 2015, Mersch specifically references the 'discourse on witnessing' — e.g. Jean-Luc Nancy, 'Un souffle / Ein Hauch', in Nicolas Berg, Jess Jochimsen and Bernd Stiegler (Eds.), *Shoah. Formen der Erinnerung. Geschichte, Philosophie, Literatur, Kunst*, Munich: Wilhem Fink, 1996, pp. 122-129; Giorgio Agamben, *Remnants of Auschwitz: The Witness and the Archive*, New York: Zone Books, 1999 (Cf. Mersch, 2015, p. 47).

2) In this sense, wit(h)nessing might also be differentiated from self-witnessing (⟶ *Self-Reporting*).

3) Reflecting on Luce Irigaray's writing on 'contiguity', Rachel Jones states, "(C)ontiguous beings touch on one another, without merging into one; their differences remain discernible, without their being completely separated from one another", *Irigaray: Towards a Sexuate Philosophy*, Oxford: Wiley, 2013.

4) Alain Badiou "employs a distinction between *le veridique / veridicité* and *le vrai*. Veracity, veridicity and veridical are employed, as distinct from truth", Oliver Feltham (Trans. note), Alain Badiou, *Being and Event*, London and New York: Continuum, 2005, p. xxxiii. Most of the contributors to this book have been *wit(h)nesses* within one or more of our *Method Labs* (⟶ *Biographies*).

5) Cf. P.A. Skantze, *Itinerant Spectator / Itinerant Spectacle*, Brooklyn, New York: Punctum Books, 2013 (⟶ P.A. Skantze, *Take Me to the Bridge*).

6) Cf. Nicolas Bourriaud, *Relational Aesthetics*, Dijon: Les Presses Du Réel, 1998 and a critique by Claire Bishop, *Artificial Hells, Participatory Art and the Politics of Spectatorship*, London: Verso, 2012.

7) Cf. Erin Manning, *Relationscapes: Movement, Art, Philosophy*, Cambridge, Mass. and London: MIT Press, 2009.

8) Cf. Roland Barthes, *How to Live Together*, New York: Columbia University Press, 2012 (⟶ *On Sedimentations of Sensitivities*).

9) Cf. Thomas Carl Wall, *Radical Passivity, Levinas, Blanchot and Agamben*, New York: SUNY Press, 1999.

10) Jean-Luc Nancy, *Being Singular Plural*, Stanford, California: Stanford University Press, 2000, p. 3. Luce Irigaray elaborates a model of 'being with the other' where "human becoming is considered as a relation-with: with oneself, with the world, with the other." *The Way of Love*, London and New York: Continuum, 2002, p. 87. We also draw on a Heideggerian sense of "Being-with" (*Mitsein*) (Cf. *Being and Time*, New York: Harper, 1962); Martin Buber's formulation of an *I-Thou* relationship in which the other is not separated by discrete bounds (Cf. *I and Thou*, New York: Scribner, 1958); Erin Manning and Brian Massumi's "withness of worlding" (Cf. *Thought in the Act: Passages in the Ecology of Experience*, Minneapolis: University of Minnesota Press, 2014), and Jacques Derrida's 'being-with beyond fraternalism' (Cf. *Politics of Friendship*, London and New York: Verso, [1994] 2005) (⟶ Krassimira Kruschkova, *What if?)*.

11) Daniel Stern, *Forms of Vitality: Exploring Dynamic Experience in Psychology, the Arts, Psychotherapy and Development*, Oxford and New York: Oxford University Press, 2010, p. 172.

12) Stern, 2010, p. xvi.

13) Bracha L. Ettinger, *Intimacy, wit(h)nessing and non-abandonment*, http://jordancrandall.com/main/+UNDERFIRE/site/files/q-node-562.html. Cf. also Ettinger, *The Matrixial Borderspace*, Minneapolis: University of Minnesota Press, 2006 (⟶ *On Sedimentations of Sensitivities*).

14) Vilém Flusser, *Gestures*, Minneapolis: University of Minnesota Press, [1991] 2014, p. 155.

15) Flusser, [1991] 2014, p. 156.

16) Flusser, [1991] 2014, p. 157.

WATCHING

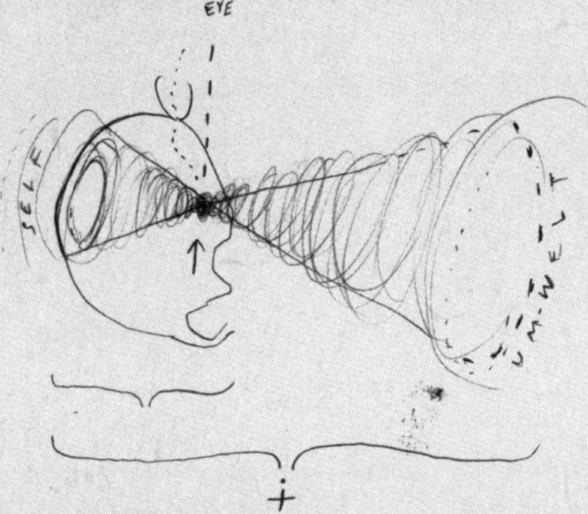

To watch: to view what comes, is done or happens. To watch out for: a sense of anticipation towards what is still to arise. Watch and wait. Watch has a temporal dimension, it can refer to an episode of time; indeed it is the name given to a specific time-keeping device. To watch over: to be watchful, on the lookout, on guard. Related to taking care. Etymologically linked to 'being awake': the practice of vigilance, alertness. Not the passive spectatorship of the onlooker then, not the secret gaze of spy or voyeur. Rather a commitment made from the eyes; watching as a mode of *being-with.* Consider the imperative of watch, compared to look or see.

To watch is to open the eyes, without grasping, without probing or penetration. Not to capture but to be captivated. Like the *Practices of Attention,* to watch involves a mode of receptivity even passivity; empty of intention, even of *I-ness,* of self-led will. Yet not the passivity generated through watching TV, a species of emptiness that can deaden or numb. Instead, practise curiosity with one's eyes: without judgement, without assigning a use-value. Here, the invitation to watch is not towards cultivating detachment or distancing, the experience of the outsider, but a call to be present, to be there.

The eyes: sharp point of connection between one's nervous system and the rest of the world. The eyes: threshold between interior and exterior systems, or rather one place of their enmeshing.

VARIATIONS

* Activate the eyes. Momentarily dampen the other senses. It might help to close off the ears: cover them with your hands; block them with your fingers or with other means. Maybe begin with an experiment in sensory restraint: first, insert your fingers into your ears to block the sound. Take a moment to get accustomed to the reduced level of auditory stimulus. How does restraining your sense of hearing affect or alter the way that you watch? After ten seconds remove your fingers — how does this change your experience? Repeat.
* Change your perspective. Move position or location. Stand up. Lie down. Invert your angle of view.
* Watching can also be conditioned or mediated by various means: frames, lenses, ocular devices, or other viewing aids. Narrowing one's focus can sharpen the level of attention. Or else, when the raw experience presents as too intense, such devices can operate as prosthesis, facilitating a level of impersonal intimacy mediated through enabling constraint.

LISTENING

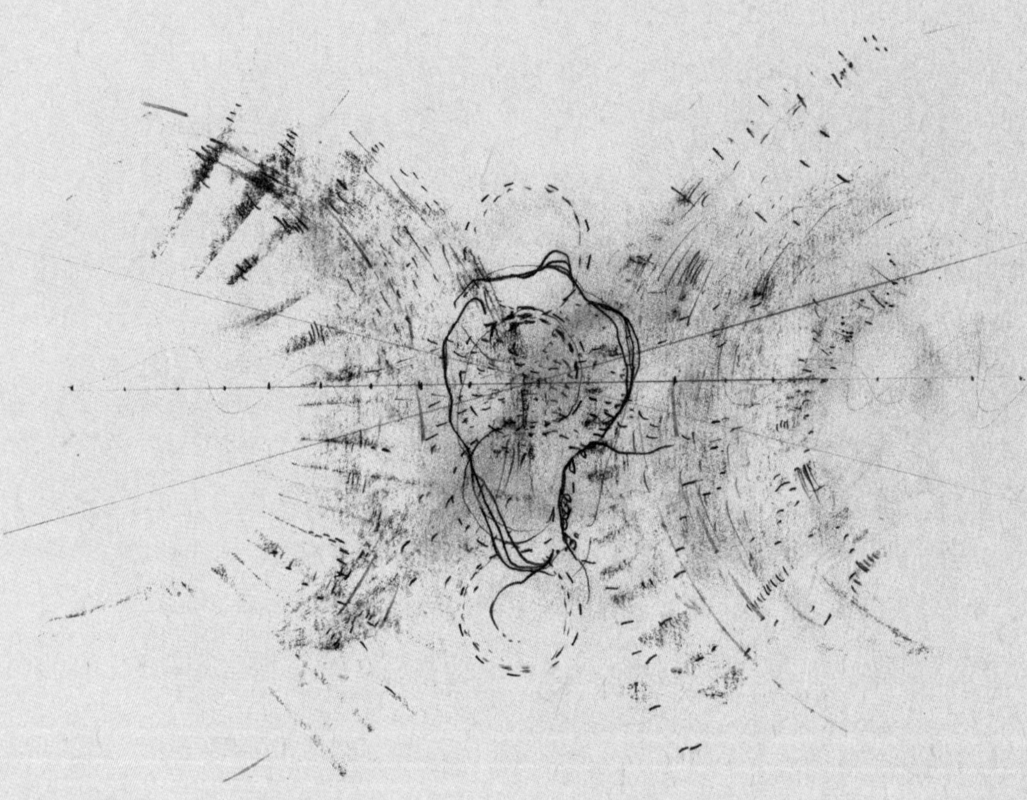

"We know more about hearing than listening. Scientists can measure what happens in the ear. Measuring listening is another matter as it involves subjectivity. Listening is a mysterious process that is not the same for everyone." (Pauline Oliveros, *The Difference Between Hearing And Listening*)

Let go of the dominance of the eyes. *Open up* your ears. Tune in to the *acoustic space.*

VARIATION

Find a position—lying, sitting or standing with eyes open or closed. Open up the spatial range of listening to those *sounds surrounding* you.

Stay with the sounds neighbouring or close by, the movements or actions that you can hear nearby. Now stay with those layers of spatial expanse. Then *extend your listening* to the whole space and its *acoustic agents.*

TRANSLATING

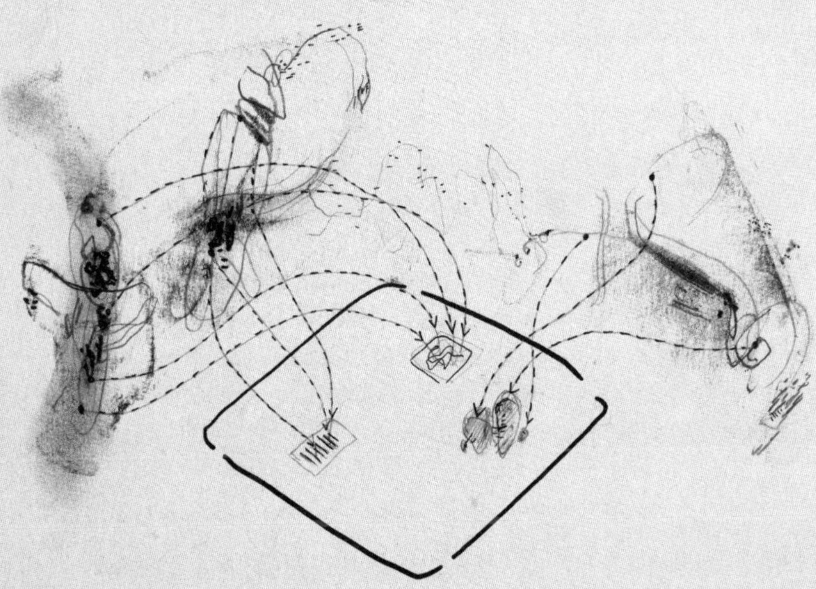

A process of mediation practised through different modalities — e.g. writing, drawing, forming, moving. Each modality is an invitation to interpret one reality through another.

Define and mark a field in space as your *translationscape*. There, position your tools and means of translation: materials — pens, paper, clay, wire, writing devices. When entering the *translationscape* start to observe the situation you are wit(h)nessing by asking yourself:

What do you observe?

Which elements call your attention, attract and affect you? What resonates with you? What is essential to translate? Can you make a sketch, a draft, a model of these forms and forces?

What language, alphabet and sign system do you have (to invent in order) to articulate the complexity of the very situation?

How could the situation be transposed along the categories of time and space, movement and imagination into another plane of reality?

Try to avoid becoming too literal.

DELIGHTFUL DRIFTING

Jeanette Pacher

How do you prepare?
How do you say?
How do you start?

Which ideas and concepts do I want to let go in order to find new means of sharing ideas? What stays, what goes? Re-viewing what I have written so far, I delete, add, condense, try to structure.

Keywords

Process / structure / time: time, unfolding / time, peaks / time, endless.
Attention / awareness / focus and drift, shift.

* Clear out, get started, liberate.
* Condense, spiral, let free without losing control.
* Close, pause, be, reflect.

Creativity / new 'language' / action, sound, body, words, material / playfulness.

Clearing out

Doing this, I try to come to terms with the challenge of writing about something that's hard to put into words: of an experience of a holistic artistic practice that involves the body, spoken and written word, drawing, sound, objects, to develop a shared … tssssss … *there it is again! Which word do I find for what I want to express? Language? No! It's more than that, it's like …* pfffffff … something in fact natural to human communication, as you may see in the way kids communicate before they have learnt to speak — before words, language, gain meaning. I relate to what I experienced in such an immediate way, and at the same time I'm puzzled, still trying to find words for this. Rather, I resist, struggle to pin it down in words — a necessity because books require texts or visual contributions — and I'm not an artist so I'm not going to start making drawings instead, for instance — but I do imagine myself with a recorder, walking around my

This is an experiment for me: the idea to interweave thoughts, reflections on an experience, and things you can hardly put into words — sounds, a sensation —, not only requires finding a different way of writing than I am used to. I decided to follow and try to translate some of the *Elemental Figures* developed throughout the *Choreo-graphic Figures* project, using them to create a structure for this text. This also means to free myself from how I think I am supposed to write, or what I believe is expected from me as a writer, wit(h)ness, curator. Let that go, try something new, open up to an experiment and see what happens. This is both exciting and unsettling, but nevertheless a liberating experience.

flat, along the streets, randomly recording, talking into it, singing, playing a tune, recording a noise, a sound, expressing surprise, or commenting on an observation — recording a flow of consciousness, untroubled, drifting and at the same time not letting go completely.

CLACK TRAPPP LICKKK
CLICKKK … *Focus, Jeanette!*

I've witnessed, in various performances and talks in the course of *Choreo-graphic Figures*, and learnt a couple of tools from this research project how to be, or to perceive, to act, think, if you want, in different modes or places of existence.

So, yes, right now, I guess I'm still in a mode of transition — back from an intense trip to Brazil, my impressions of it still very present. And I am feeding into this text, as if Emma, Mariella and Nikolaus and their 'sputniks' had travelled with me all this long way.

Okay, so it's time for a clearing out now.

This was just a warming up, a chattering about myself, becoming aware of what I'm doing, thinking, linking, assuming.

I run my fingers over the keyboard of my laptop. This is a clearing-out sound for me now. Tssschhh, chhussshhh, zzzzsh, how can I translate this sound into words, or simply letters of our alphabet? I think I'd really like to include phonetic spelling, this would make things much easier and clearer. And, at the same time, this would mean inviting another — international, or interrational — language (or translation of language) — open up the scene for other perceptions, sensations.

Okay. Clear. Let's start.

CLICK (like the shutter of a camera)

… at least I have to make a start … how … I'm really running out of time. This is not how it should be working, or how I thought it should be. But of course, in the end, it's as it always is with me: too late, or almost — maybe just in time, I always hope.

And then, on top of everything — trying to sort out my impressions, thoughts, and feeling about what I had experienced, or better: witnessed on multiple occasions over the last year in order to be able to comment on this and write something substantial about being in or becoming part of the *Choreo-graphic Figures* research project — this trip. Trip as in travelling, but also as in tripping over something. Well, it came unplanned and definitely triggered a good vibrating turbulence but also caused some mess (in terms of having to re-schedule things that I had only roughly scheduled in the first place), but this, at least, provided a certain kind of security of still being able to match ends, like deadlines for instance) and at the same time …

Six-hour Long Radical Score of Attention

How do I remember? What do I remember? What can I say about this — in words?
This was a thrilling experience, something I was looking forward to, and which was indeed very rewarding. My approach to the projected duration of the performance, six hours, was informed by recollections of evenings or afternoons, or whole days when, for instance, I had attended the screening of *As I Was Moving Ahead, Occasionally I Saw Brief Glimpses of Beauty,* a five-hour-film by Jonas Mekas at Metro Kino in the framework of the Viennale Festival 2000. I remember how irritating I found the break after 2 ½ hours; for me it could have just continued. It's like reading a really compelling book, 600 + pages and the way you are almost inevitably confronted with a sensation of void, of falling into an emotional chasm when it's over. Andy Warhol's *Empire*, David Claerbout's *Bordeaux Piece* — I LOVE the chance of being able to slowly tune in to a situation, go with the flow, break out, tune back again in another mood or mode, *be it.* That's, in my opinion, a unique quality of experiencing, perceiving, understanding, becoming. Togetherness.

Kissing. A kiss on my cheek, full of warmth, unexpected but nice. So nice that I automatically return the kiss; kiss Christine on her cheek. And then she kisses back. And I kiss her back. We smile. A big broad smile; you can't help yourself but smile and return this nice gesture. Then: stop. Good stop. Plopp. Aaaaah. Glance at each other: we're fine, it's good, now we can turn to something else. This was a culmination of paying attention that arose quite spontaneously and we had the moment to enjoy and let it fade out in our own time.

Repetition.

Repetition.

Repetition is learning.

Repetition is learning.

Learn by repeating. Learn through imitation. Imitating is learning. Imitating is learning through repetition. By repeating what one has observed, or experienced? Repetition over and over again, learning for instance how to put your foot on the ground (whether this is a move in a choreography for a performance or a small kid learning to walk), or how to start a conversation, and how to end it again: repetition is a way of learning. Once you get bored, or simply less anxious, more confident, relaxed, you know you know it. Then you can move onto step two or three, or jump a few. Nevertheless, repetition, I have to repeat myself, is a very good tool, precisely because it can cause boredom or, more than that, it can help to free your mind because you ALREADY KNOW or are familiar with a situation. You needn't think about what you're doing, it's automatic. And this is when it starts to become interesting again. Because you're free to try out something else, make new unknown steps.

Learn by repeating. Learn through imitation. Imitating is learning. Imitating is learning through repetition. By repeating what one has observed, or experienced? Repetition over and over again, learning for instance how to put your foot on the ground (whether this is a move in a choreography for a performance or a small kid learning to walk), or how to start a conversation, and how to end it again: repetition is a way of learning. Once you get bored, or simply less anxious, more confident, relaxed, you know you know it. Then you can move onto step two or three, or jump a few. Nevertheless, repetition, I have to repeat myself, is a very good tool, precisely because it can cause boredom or, more than that, it can help to free your mind because you ALREADY KNOW or are familiar with a situation. You needn't think about what you're doing, it's automatic. And this is when it starts to become interesting again. Because you're free to try out something else, make new unknown steps.

FLASHBACK.

First experience, first wit(h)nessing.

I'm curious but also shy. Try to take in all that is explained, understand, perceive. Everyone is invited to join in the 'warming up' — rather than long theoretical explanations, what really sticks in my mind is a kind of physical experience. Lying on the floor of the space. Breathe in, breathe out — slowly, close your eyes, etc. Almost like a yoga group. I'm not quite sure what to think of this but nevertheless join in, try to tune in. Try to let go the uncertainty that inescapably creeps in when you find yourself lying on your back, shoes off, breathing heavily but at the same time quietly (control *control!*) with a bunch of people you barely know.

It's kinda warm to start with. Well, it's May I think, springtime in Vienna. First time the sun comes out and REALLY WARMS. No cold winds. So I enter this space, am introduced to a group of people, and shortly afterwards we're asked to participate (if we want) in their 'warming-up' rituals (as I will call it for now, as this is what it appeared to be to me at the time; not knowing or sensing that this 'ritual' was actually more already: it was already forming a common language between three researchers from different disciplines, which indeed involve the body on very different levels of interaction, and of closeness). I feel uncomfortable, at first, not being used to this kind of interacting for quite a while: out of practice, so to say.

REFLECT

What I witnessed over the course of the *Choreo-graphic Figures* project coincided with some issues I had been discussing with the artist Manon de Boer while preparing and installing her exhibition at the Secession. We were talking about creativity, and the circumstances and conditions that propel setting free creative processes.
There are two aspects we talked about that I would like to point out in this context: the need, within the creative process, for *open-ended time* and a *carefree, untroubled mind*. Not only did they play a significant role for my perception as a wit(h)ness ,but, as I believe, for the project's development, too.

I deeply respond to both conditions — open-ended time and an untroubled mind —, probably because we live in a society and time that endangers or highly limits these experiences in an adult's everyday life that is structured by means of deadlines to be met, appointments, meetings, duties, responsibilities, taking care of things, situations, etc. It seems that this kind of freedom nowadays only exists in your childhood days (if you're a lucky child). What a shame! *But what happens when all you do is to function accordingly? Maybe it's good for your career. Maybe. Maybe not. Who says so? What if you decide "to rather not" (thanks, Bartleby, I love you for your persistence to 'prefer not' and in doing so sketching out, opening up for other life concepts, at least in my mind)? In this sense, the resistance, to* not *function accordingly but rather discover other opportunities, and cherish them, is in essence also a political question or stance of freeing oneself and paving one's way to a different being-in-the-world. So all these thoughts were on my mind at the time (and they still are, and in my striving to achieve freedom — in doing, thinking, being, becoming — I don't think they're going to go away) and, oh my, CLICKKLACK, what a delight, a leap-in-my-heart moment it was to experience and witness these things not only being addressed, but in fact coming together in the experimental performative practice that Emma, Mariella, and Nikolaus were developing and letting me be part of. This was it! Time just flowed. In their six-hour performance, I experienced moments of absolute delight, concentration, curiosity, playfulness as well as of my attention drifting, my thoughts being interrupted, or expectations surprised, and at times simply being bored, too. All was good. It was inspiring.*

The process-oriented approach that is characteristic of the *Choreo-graphic Figures* project is based on a notion of openness in terms of time as well as of performance. In her film *An Experiment in Leisure* (2016), Manon de Boer corresponded to the idea of an aimless temporality, an unrestricted time by means of reduction or what you could call 'emptying out': the imagery of a vast deserted landscape intersected by shots of workplace interiors — filmed almost like still lifes — shows so little motion, and with its only subtle changes the viewer may find him / herself on the brink of boredom, thoughts drifting off to other places — paradoxically stimulated by precisely this reduction to almost nothingness (in terms of activity). 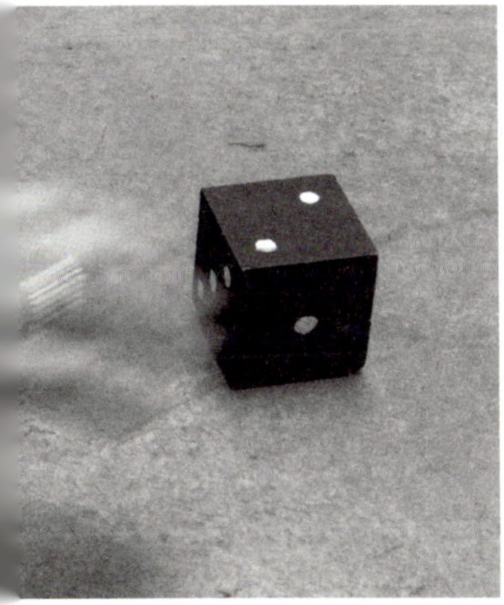
A specifically valuable quality of the *Choreo-graphic Figures' Method Labs,* to me, was to have plenty of time to unfold different states of mind — to tune in, be / come, connect, reflect and reverberate, step out, come back, ponder and wonder, fade over — as well as to experience a variety of temporalities and intensities of activeness. The delight of witnessing one of the agents exploring, with childlike curiosity, the acoustic qualities of bare fingers running over the painted surface of a wall, striding up and down, while another agent was sorting materials — tapes, paper rolls, string — quietly babbling along to him / herself, and yet another had rolled up on the floor, nestling their body to a makeshift cardboard structure, or was pushing objects around, making scribbles, was reading a text, seemingly endlessly repeating it, interacting with a guest: *How does it feel?*

P.A. Skantze

TAKE ME TO THE BRIDGE

For those of us whose training renders us makers, performers, teachers and writers, opportunity always knocks in the shape of an invitation to improvise, or a call or a demand or even the prompt embedded in scorn when someone refuses to condone something as intellectually paradoxical as improvisation. Like the gap, the caesura, the ravine, there is a moment, sometimes tiny and domestic — a lover's raised eyebrow, sometimes local and necessary — a moment when the weight of what must be done simply swamps everyone into silence — when one is invited to improvise, to begin speaking. To think quite clearly, 'I don't know what the fuck I just said; I don't know how the fuck to describe this; I don't know what the fuck we are going to do next to address this situation that is the world we inhabit', but I am willing to

'What did you think', a question that follows a spectator out of the theatre / auditorium / gallery into the night. Describing what we have seen, right away in the wake of making a performance together or later at the prompt of an interlocutor, becomes a craft of constructing a rope bridge swinging over the chasm of distance between the telling and the seeing. How durable the bridge needs to be depends on whether the person one is speaking to is making it as well from the other side. If he / she saw the performance then it will almost be enough to lob a single strand of double strength cord across and swing over. But if you who are recounting have to design the structure of an unseen, unheard, unwitnessed thing in the air, the bridge must bear more weight as the crossing demands more.

start braiding a rope for a bridge towards the other side. I will to do this in the absence of any certain sense of whether the bridge will hold, whether the middle will be more interesting than getting all the way across or how far away from the other side we actually are.

When this improvisation occurs in the act of speaking about a performance, the risk always exists that the improvisation might fall flat, a dangerous notion when you are constructing a bridge over a chasm. The need to know what we do think — how we experienced the performance, what are our reflections, considerations, critiques — depends as well on the give and take, the sway of the bridge, the cautious stepping out onto a discussion of the work.

Such invitations to tell what we saw currently arrive under the sign of 'feedback'. Once the provenance of a conversation between artists, 'what did you think, was it good?', this quiet, vulnerable exchange has gone culturally viral.[1]

Here, in our moment of clicking 'like', or visiting our webpage to give us your feedback on any and every little thing, how do we meet at the place of responding to the work we are doing, to the work we are seeing? How do we introduce the complex braid and weave without being distracted by the rushing noise of the tallying of scores or becoming entangled in the facile and injurious categorising of work all around us?

"Some people love to divide and classify, while others are bridge-makers — weaving relations that turn a divide into a living contrast, one whose power is to affect, to produce thinking and feeling."[2] Isabelle Stengers begins her delicate work of *Reclaiming Animism,* offering us the braid as 'a living contrast'. A living contrast speaks as powerfully to the acts of practice as research as to the artistic exchanges across disciplines and acts of response, acts we might think of as an attentive act of reanimation.

Stengers elucidates a practice of 'critical immanent attention', those words providing a kind of toolkit for how we tell each other what we saw/experienced/heard. Stengers herself performs in this essay her risk and her inheritance as a philosopher. She stands on the side of the disciplinary ravine marked philosophy — with its insistence on logic and reason — and writes of witches as a model in their "radically pragmatic experimenting with effects and consequences of what, as they know, is never innocuous and involves care, protection and experience."[3] 'A methodology of care', I have written, is at the heart of the practice of being a spectator.[4] When in that practice we are called to respond — what did you think? — then we must remember and invent. Invention is the art in the weaving. Description itself, particularly description in the service of recounting and collaborating, is a form of critical immanent attention.

* * *

BRIDGE: 'I'M A STRANGE KIND OF IN-BETWEEN THING'

As describing is critical immanent attention so singing is describing. When soul singer James Brown says 'take me to the bridge, Maceo' to Maceo Parker, the request is spiritual, spatial and pragmatic. Get me where I can cross over; weave me a swaying passage.

In the midst of this discussion of the writing in the air that is retelling, I invite my readers to sit down on the other side of the chasm while I tell you about *Desdemona*. Hear this, here we are in a hall, an auditorium in Southern California filled with texting youth. The production is still in rehearsal with Rokia Traoré on guitar, terrific musicians playing kora and guitar, backup singers transforming the space of the afterlife into a party.

The lighting on stage is simple, lots of bulbs. Blonde, thin Tina Benko plays Desdemona, she who has awoken into the between space of the afterlife, strange to her and to all of us, yet also strangely welcoming. We all dwell together in the suggestive gap, a space that "invites movement, running one's eye back and forth over what at first appeared a fixed grid, trying to see the new shapes forming out of the newly perceived curve in the boundaries, hearing some bit of sound that had before been pulsing underneath the recognizable chord."[5]

But as a spectator that night, to be honest, we did not all exist in the gap; in fact the students were restless and bored, and Shakespeare scholar Ayanna Thompson and I who had travelled from Washington DC and London to Los Angeles were tired and full, therefore, of dismay. Had we come all this way only to find that a trio of gloriousness that is the direction of Peter Sellars, the writing of Toni Morrison and the composition and singing of Rokia Traoré by way of Shakespeare would produce an uneven, too much white woman / girl speaking, too little recalibration of all that needs recalibrated across gender and race? Yes, that night, that is exactly what we experienced.

And here comes another braid in the rope bridge over this in-between, the in-between of two nights of seeing the same performance, the day that went between. The following night that began with Sellars saying "I can't believe you two came back." Who has time, the commitment, the zeal other than the makers to come back and see something again? What sense-memory of the night before sits in this in-between? That night, that second night, the hall was buzzing with excitement and expectation. The crowd was a crowd of curious spectators, you could tell. Curiosity may be the most deserted country of our time and the generations granted everything in their hands, so ready to hand, have somehow been stripped of the opportunity of the in-between that, as Fred Moten often says, invites you to get all up in there, or at least invites a confusion that can invite an invention.

On the second night, the weight on the stage had shifted, had been shifted by the makers of the performance. That night, that second night, Desdemona refashioned her world in the air; Morrison's insistence on telling the truth of the life of women, her insistence on having Traoré clarify bluntly for the naïve Desdemona the difference between an African servant and a little rich white girl's imagined friend. But, as importantly the balance, the shifting between had almost no rancour in it; the afterlife allowed for exploration. Without the need to fix or resolve in the afterlife, the striving for agreement drops away and discovery does not equal remorse, though injustices are indeed exposed.

As a spectator, I know I watched with critical immanent attention sharpened in the wake of the between, in the wake of the disappointment of before. As a spectator I knew how *Desdemona* played out and yet I had forgotten. We have blissfully short memories in this regard, the precise motions and shifting scenes blur, a word that has become an invitation, one dependent on the grid and the shift, on the thing outlined and the blurring that makes a not quite new thing, like the afterlife or a bridge swaying between it and us.

* * *

What did you think of the performance — *When* did you think it — How many minutes, hours, days, aeons went by before you could articulate, could describe, could tell? You could of course take a picture and send it, the need for description usurped by the photo. But the rope, the rope is made of words, and the braiding is complicated precisely because description is difficult, particularly description 'as an experience of meaning'. The "question is how to describe that experience ... whose provenance or emergence is not reducible to logical structure ... [description as] an experience of the passage ... perhaps it is the supplement of description that allows description; for description of the phenomenon or experience of ensemble is only adequate if it is also itself the phenomenon or experience of ensemble."[6] The work of trying to convey, be the conveyor, and let what is conveyed rest in the ear without trying to persuade the listener depends upon the cultivation of description, practising a form of 'critical immanent attention'.

In the process of conveying, one comes up against other possibilities in the exchange of responding to performances seen and performances made together: when the knot slips, when the interlocutor has her focus elsewhere, is impatient with my need to embroider that bit stage left with the bassoon since all she really wants to talk about is the fire-eater. I am thinking of a moment in the *Choreo-graphic Figures Summer Lab* when someone said to me, a delicious, annoyed sound to her voice, "the problem with working with objects is that they just won't disappear". One artist's built environment-performance-space meets another's longing for the sweep of a gesture that occurs, ends and is no more.[7]

Moten makes his critically demanding call for a description that is itself the phenomenon and experience of ensemble in writing, in a book. I offer the weaving of a discussion of how we tell each other about what we have seen in a printed text. *Choreo-graphic* itself has a gap in the middle inviting the braid of a descriptive rope bridge. The challenge is to begin without knowing, to improvise knowing the bridge is not a safety net. To use one's writing to describe in a critically immanent way, to let the sway surprise you and to remind you that the bridge depends on the hands and ears across the chasm.

---

1) From National Student Satisfaction surveys, which in the UK now will offer a measure from which a University can win the bronze, silver or gold medal of teaching — the higher the score of student satisfaction, the more the Universities can raise tuition, a breathtakingly cynical exercise — to the obligation to give evidence to Arts Funding Organisations whose elaborate feedback mechanisms seem ultimately to be the truly valuable commerce, eliding the power and integrity of artistic production.

2) Isabelle Stengers, 'Reclaiming Animism', in *e-flux Journal #36*, July 2012. www.e-flux.com/journal/36/61245/reclaiming-animism

3) Stengers, 2012.

4) P.A. Skantze, *Itinerant Spectator/Itinerant Spectacle*, New York: Punctum, 2013, p. 8.

5) P.A. Skantze, 'Shift Epistemologies: Gap Knowledge', in Marin Blaževic and Lada Čale Feldman (Eds.), *MISperformance — Essays in Shifting Perspectives*, Ljubljana: Maska, 2014.

6) Fred Moten, *In the Break: the Aesthetics of the Black Radical Tradition*, Minneapolis: University of Minnesota Press, 2003, p. 92.

7) The varieties of response often mask the difficult discussion we might have about taste: how some people will not respond to the prompt of improvisation until they have heard other people's opinions. Or someone will cut the carefully braided rope and let the entire bridge fall in scorn or in disinterest. But also the way that when we do specifically recreate a world of a performance for each other, things can shift. I have gone back to see companies I had dismissed and am glad I did on the basis of a conversation, a re-animation, critically immanent, which got me to the other side despite my doubts.

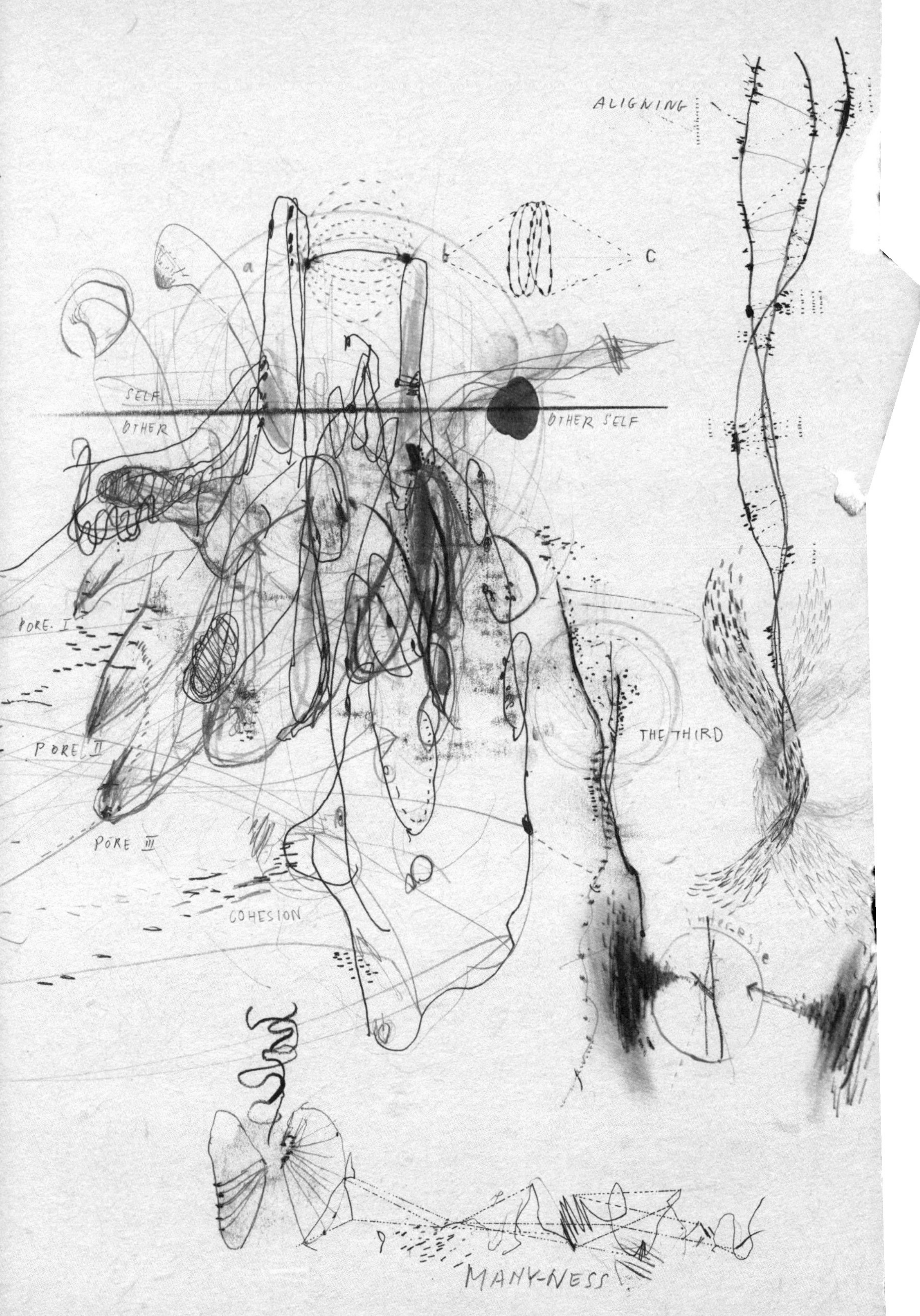
ALIGNING
a
b
c
SELF
OTHER
OTHER SELF
PORE. I
PORE II
PORE III
THE THIRD
COHESION
MANY-NESS

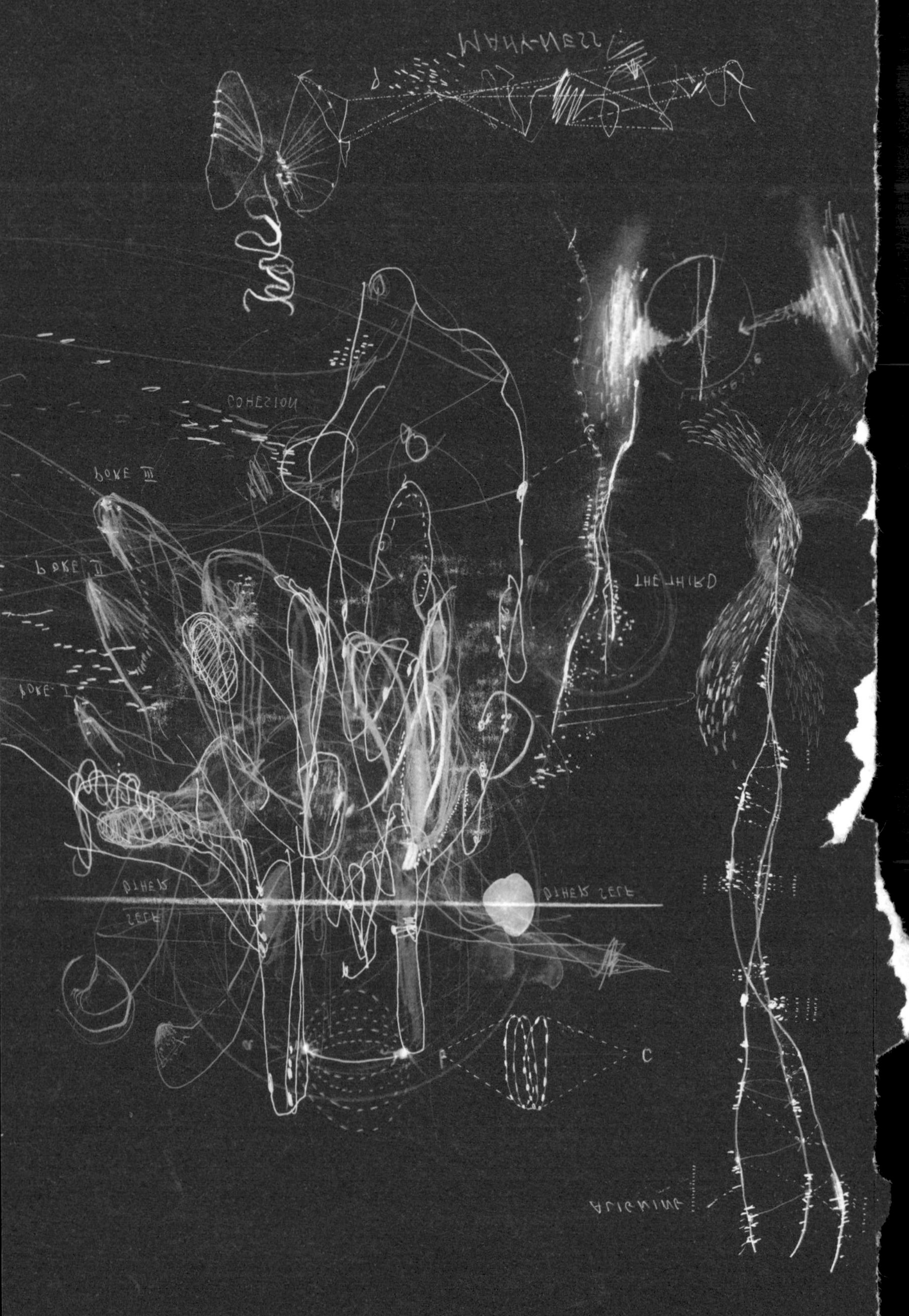
MANY-NESS
COHESION
POKE III
POKE II
POKE I
THE THIRD
OTHER
SELF
OTHER SELF
C
ALIGNING

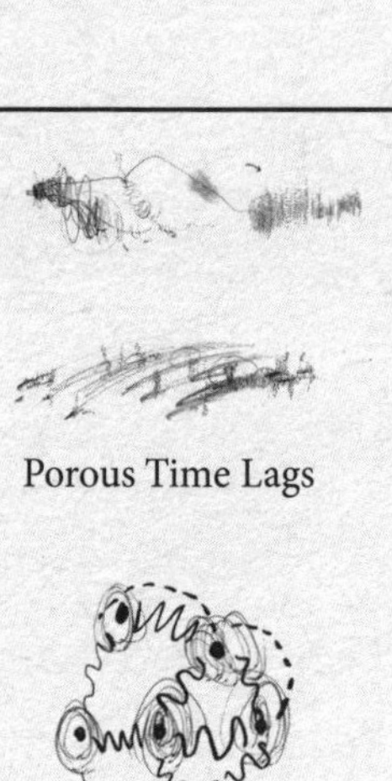

Porous Time Lags

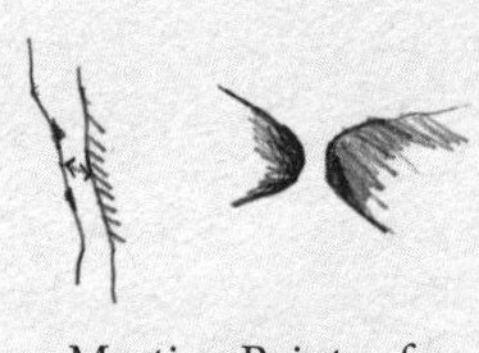

Meeting Points of Intransigence

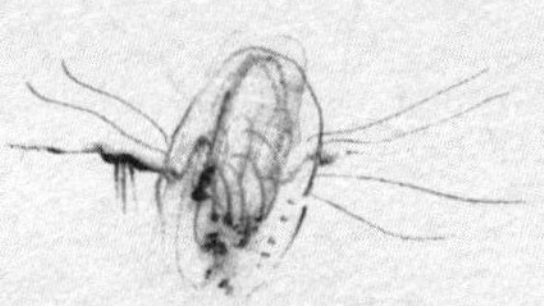

Conditions of Between-ness

Relational Attention

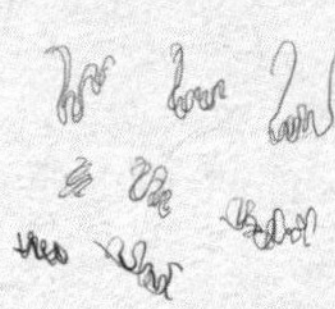

Folds of Intense Togetherness

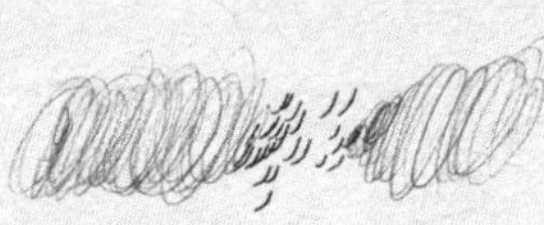

Rhythmic Interplay

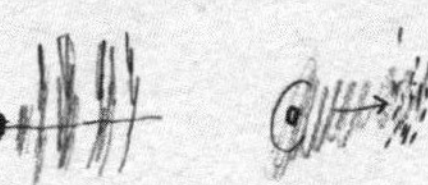

Ethical Sensitivity

Principles of Porosity and Periphery

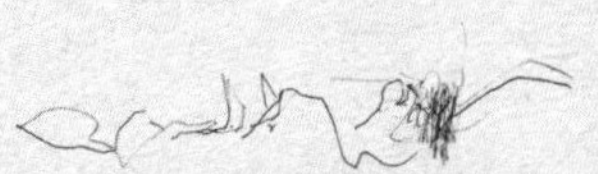

Correlational Moving Towards

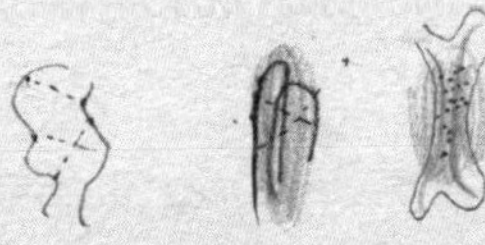

Aesthetic Affinities

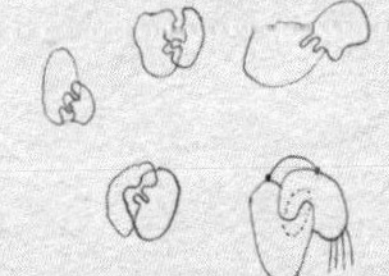

Culture of Solidarity

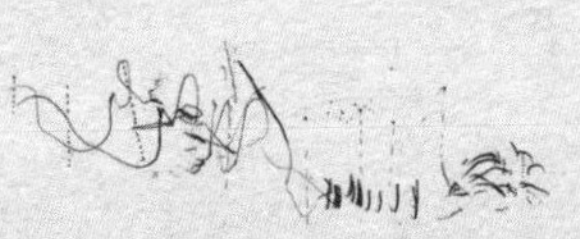

Dissonant Consonance

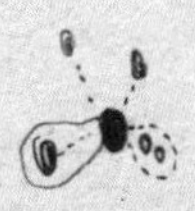

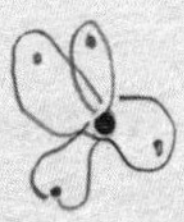

Tangible Experience of Collectivity

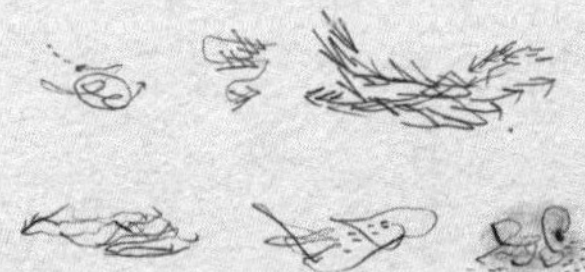

Shifts of Interweaving

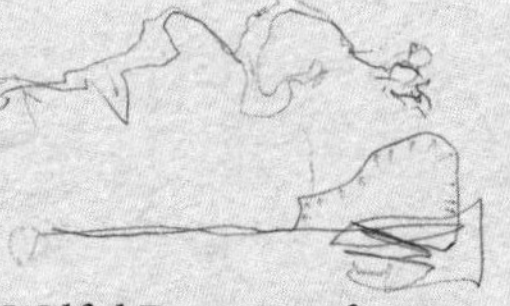

Wilful Deviation from the Line

KEY LINES
EMPATHETIC FIGURES

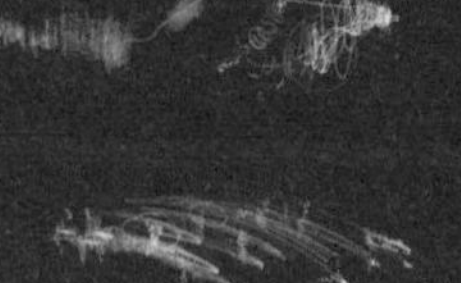
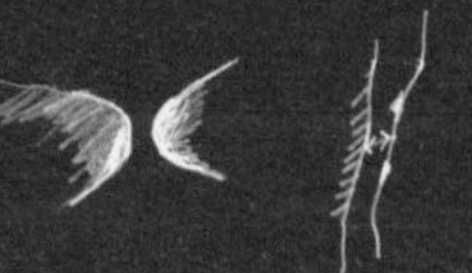
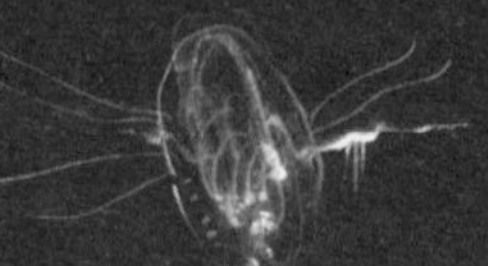
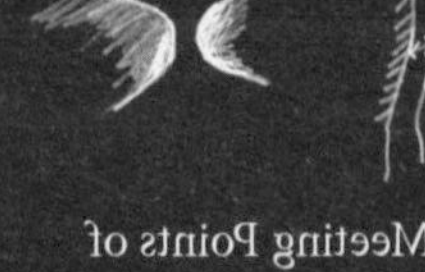

EMPATHETIC *Figures*

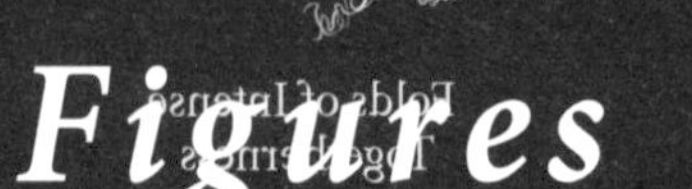
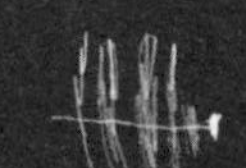
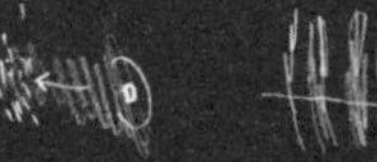
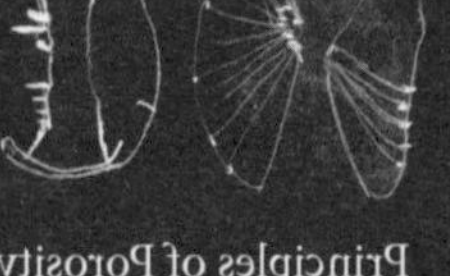
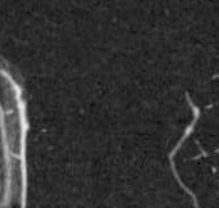
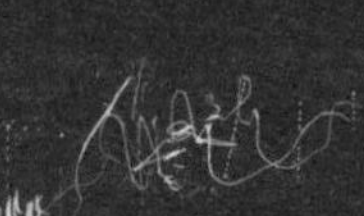
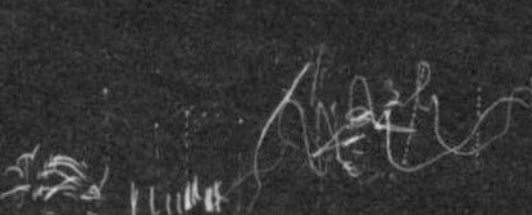
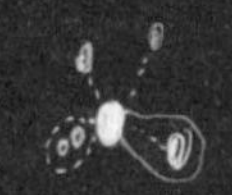
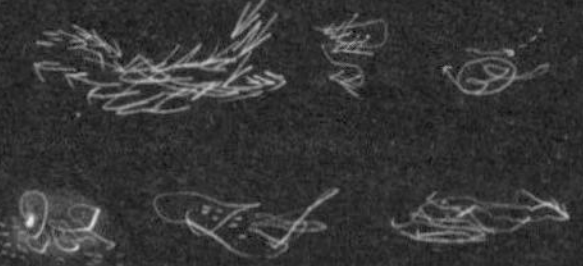
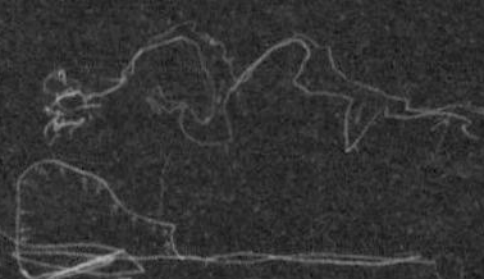

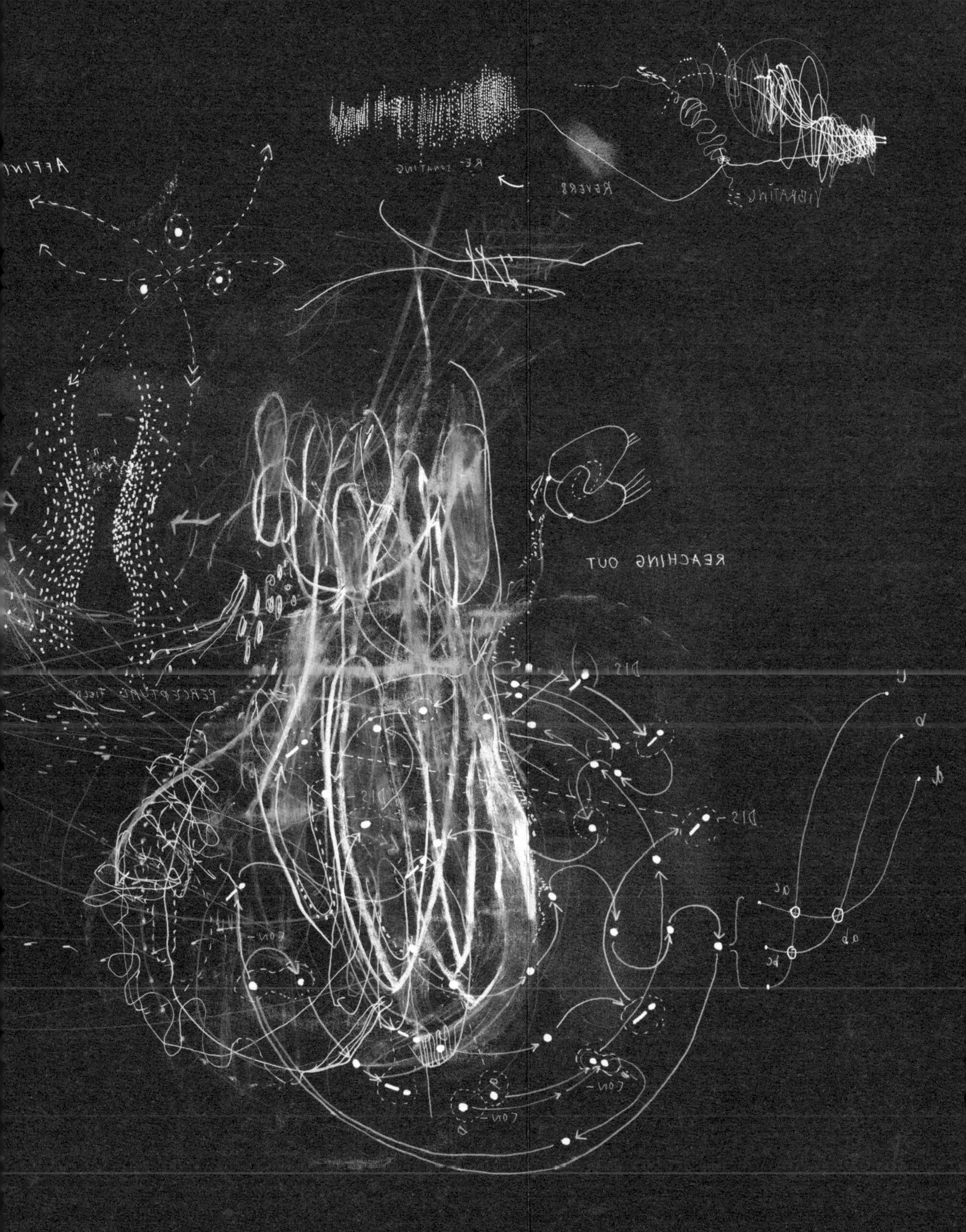
RE-SONATING
REVERB
VIBRATING
REACHING OUT
DIS-
CON-

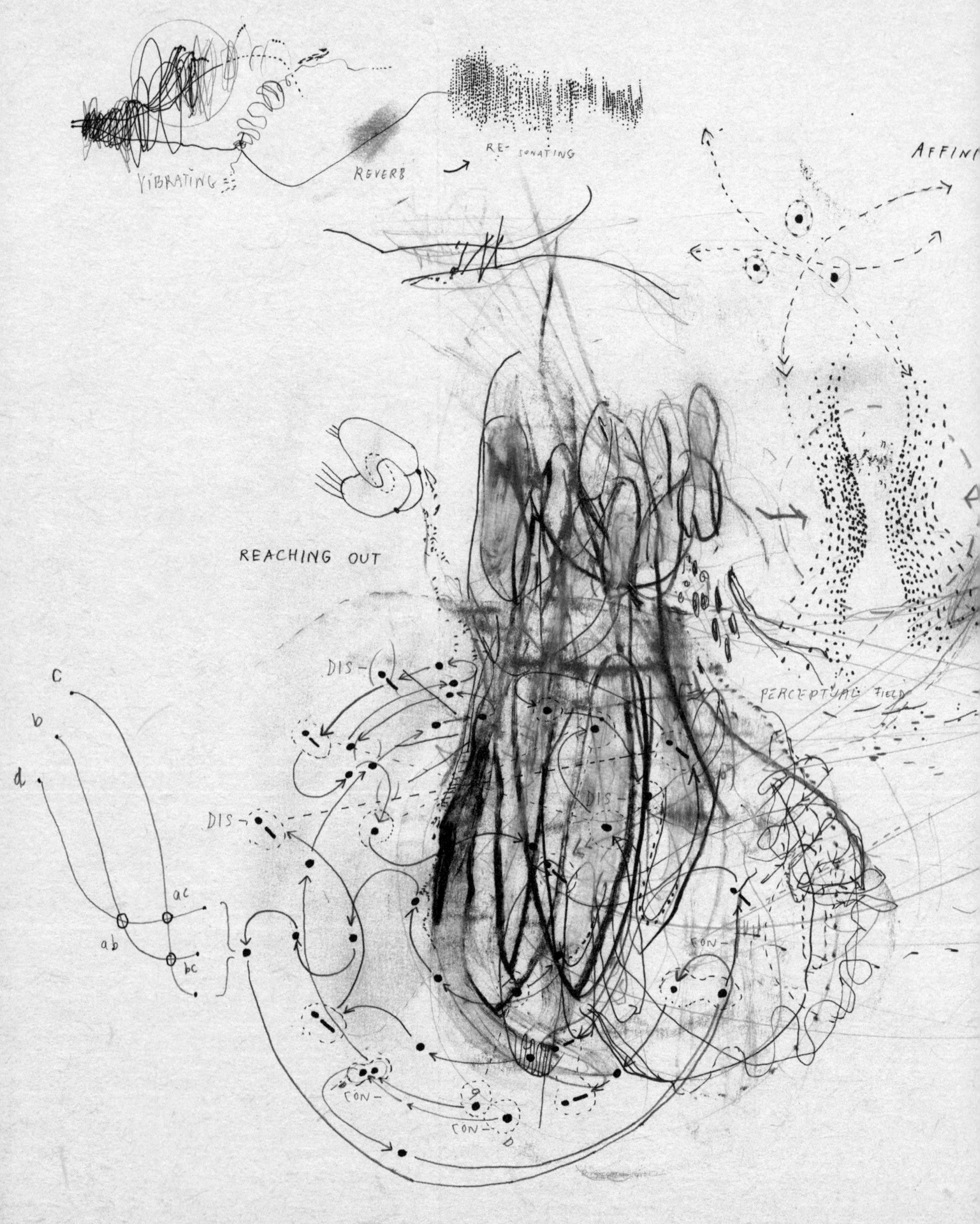

VIBRATING
REVERB
RE-SONATING
AFFINI
REACHING OUT
DIS-
DIS-
DIS-
PERCEPTUAL FIELD
CON-
CON-
CON-
c
b
d
ac
ab
bc

EMPATHETIC *Figures*

The *Empathetic Figures* give articulation to the meaning and weight of relations as generative forces within the making of aesthetic knowledge, make tangible the experience of working relationally with and between. Our diagramming of relations draws attention to the ethics of collaboration, the sensitivities and sensibilities of *being-with*.[1] These *figures* reflect on meeting points and moments of empathetic connection experienced within our collaborative artistic exploration, as well as the disparities and interferences emerging through excesses of meaning, points of intransigence and (in)translatability. We consider the crafting of relations through collaboration as an inherently micro-political, even ethico-aesthetic act, capable of cultivating new forms of social relation and solidarity. Neither exhaustive nor hierarchical, the three *figures* presented — *Vibrating Affinity, Wavering Convergence,* and *Consonance / Dissonance* — articulate a shift from the experienced intensity of *being-with one* to the *many,* or rather from the experience of the one (that is already the many) to the multitude.[2] Related closely to the principles of porosity and collectivity developed through our various *Practices of Attention,* we associate these *figures* with the prefixes *inter-, co-, com-, con-*, indicating the conditions of between-ness, with-ness, together-ness. Mapping of com-plex relations (from *com* — with, together, in association; and *plexere* — to weave, to braid, entwine, or even *plicare* — folded together), our diagramming reflects upon different states of interwoven-ness, the intermingling of self and other(s).

---

1) ⟶ *Practices of Wit(h)nessing* for reflection on the notion of *being-with.*

2) ⟶ *On Sedimentations of Sensitivities.*

Figure of VIBRATING AFFINITY

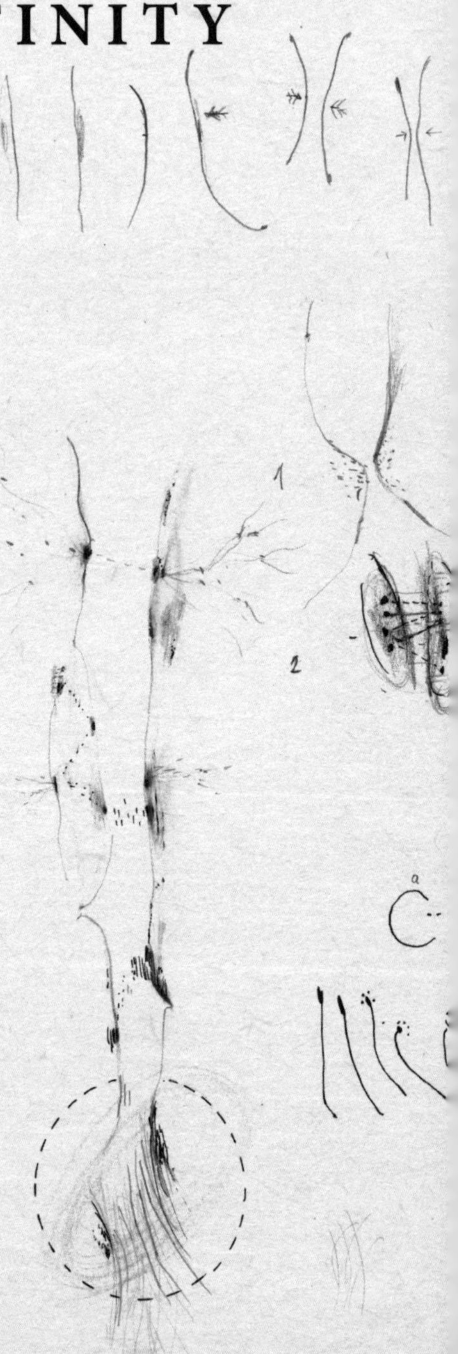

Dynamic of the dyad, magnetic coupling: bond of strong attraction within a wider field of forces. Shared intimacy of the one-to-one, between I *and* other. Attunement intensity, hone to the frequencies of a body beyond oneself. Dialogic encounter before words, conversational back and forth of movement, to and fro — first following, now leading, gentle drift towards synchronisation. Meeting point of two in action becoming as one. Empathetic precision. Self-contained mutuality. Symbiotic reciprocity. Sustained focus, in the moment, undistracted. Inter-subjective interdependence. Intent tending — towards tender togetherness, being-in-relation. Affinity not similarity — mirroring of affect, of attitude, not of form. Not just copying. Co-captivation. Commit to co-emergence, concentrated cohesion; micro unit of collaboration, of being-in-common.

Vital in its liveliness: vibrational pulse of living matter, wave of excitation over nerve or muscle fibre. From cellular trembling the principles of life-organising, as when two cells meet, meld, multiply. Materials make this tangible; amplify the imperceptible. A conduit for connection, mediating distance, materials become a means through which to reach towards. Rhythmic singularities intermingle becoming plural.

Arrived at, *it* happens. Involuntary impulse, shared sudden inclination towards action. Arising. By surprise, not contrived. Of one's own accord. Spontaneous affinity.

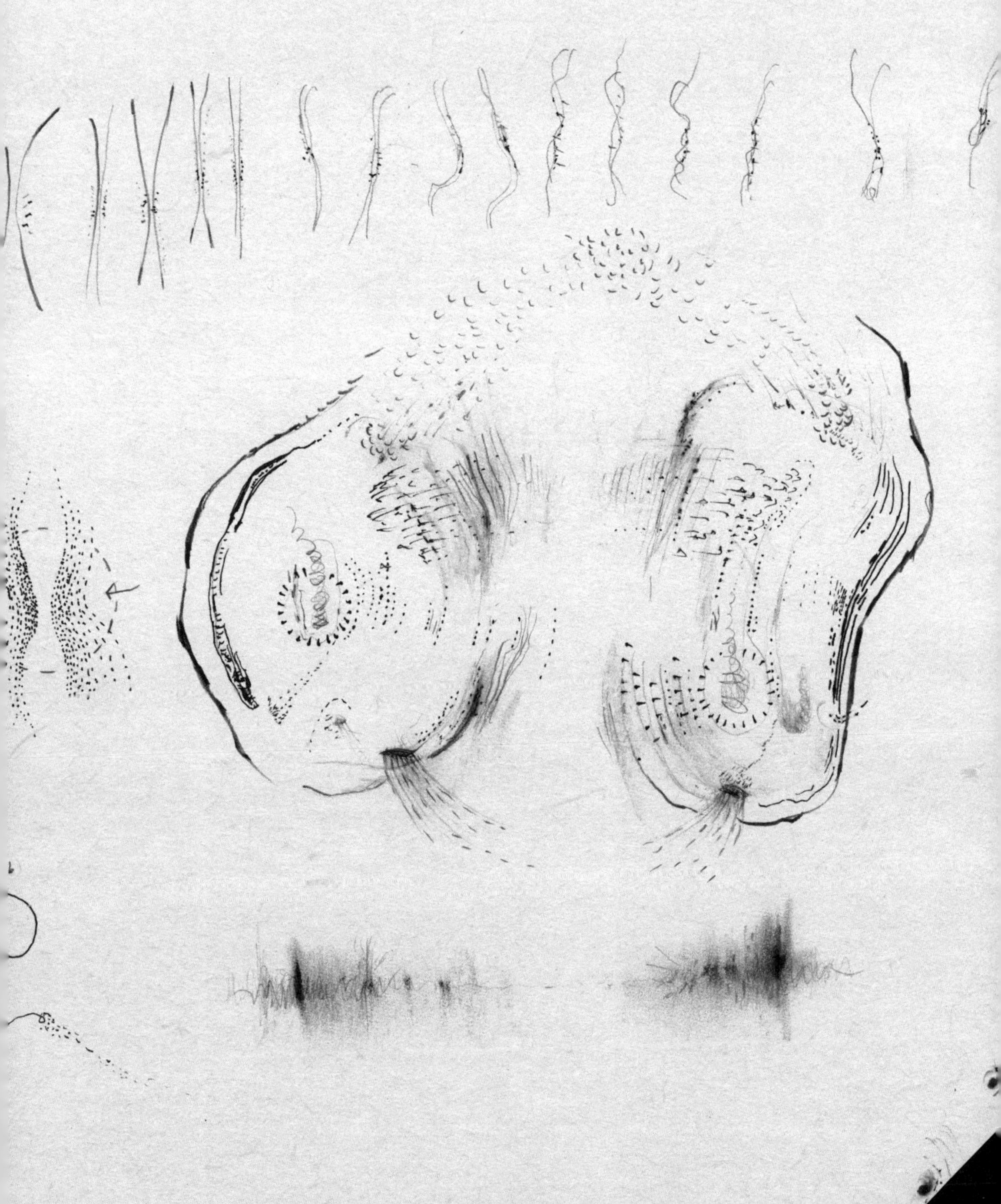

Figure of VIBRATING AFFINITY

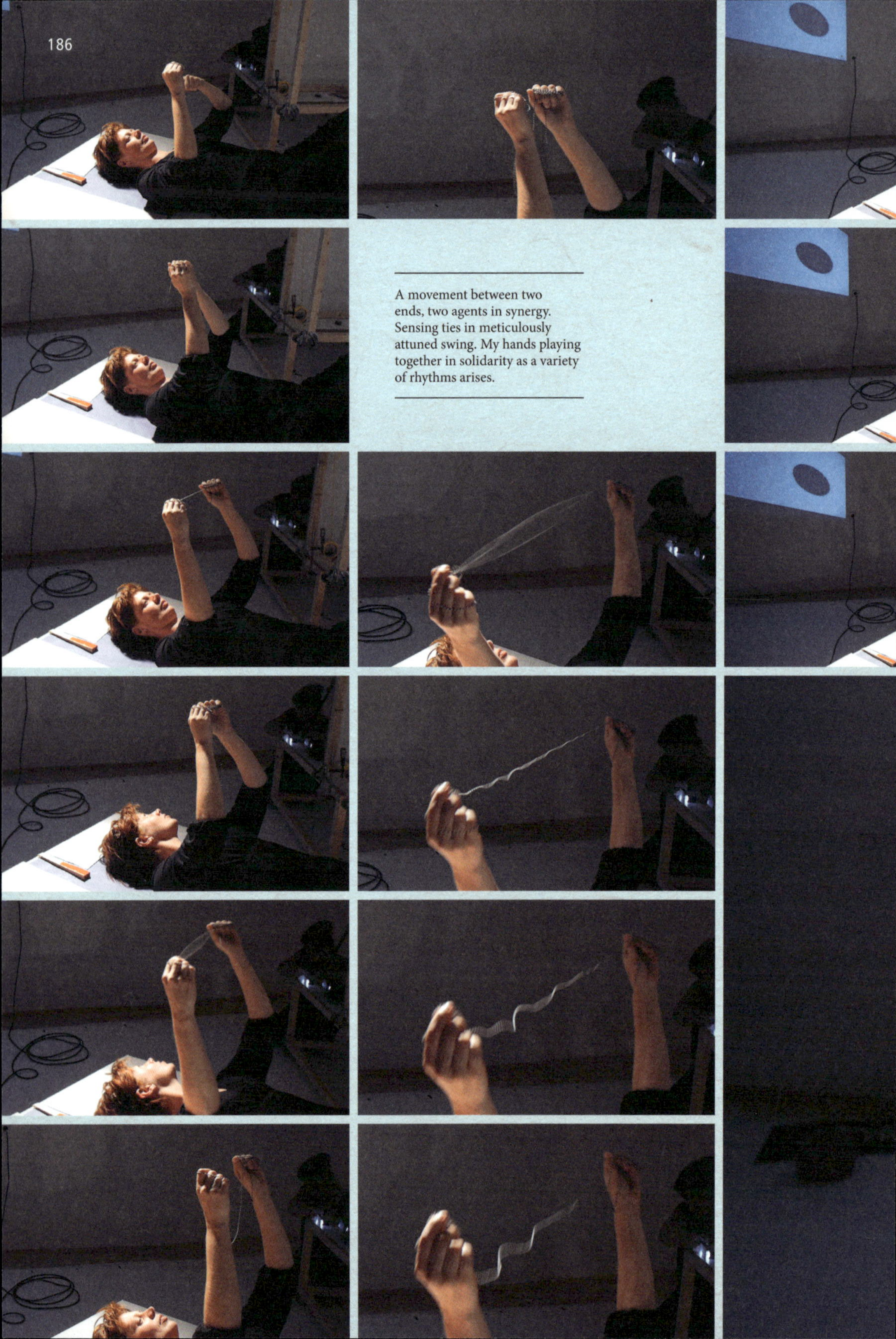

A movement between two ends, two agents in synergy. Sensing ties in meticulously attuned swing. My hands playing together in solidarity as a variety of rhythms arises.

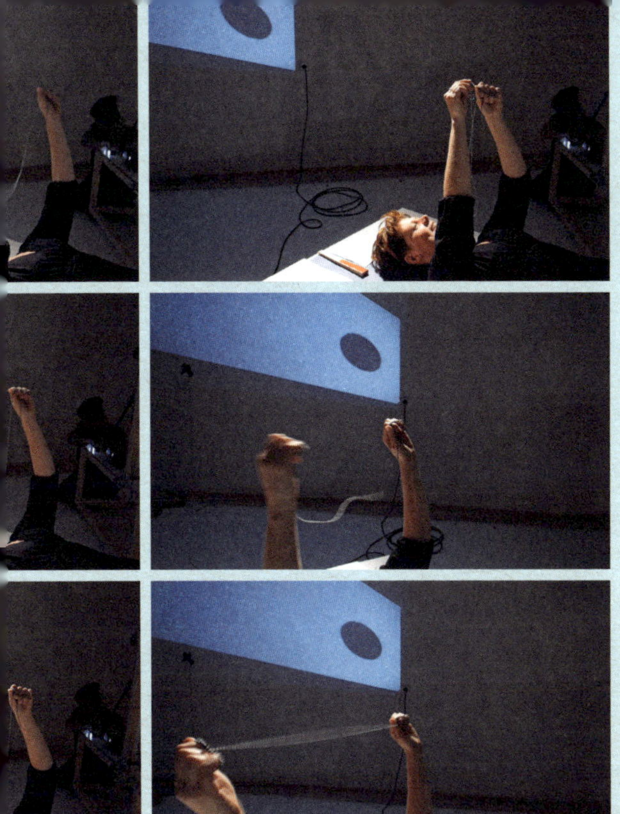

Shadows projected into the next movement as retrograde prospects. Clipped connections of past and future. Tangential.

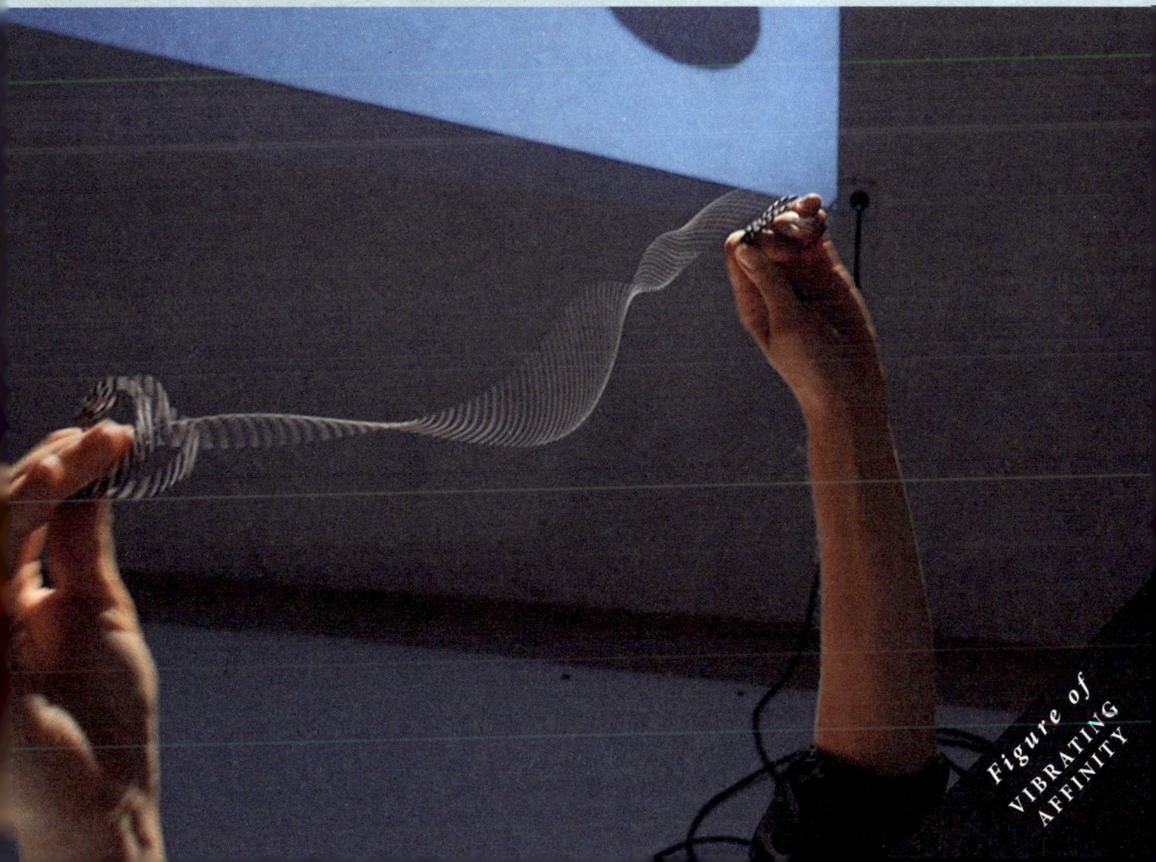

Figure of VIBRATING AFFINITY

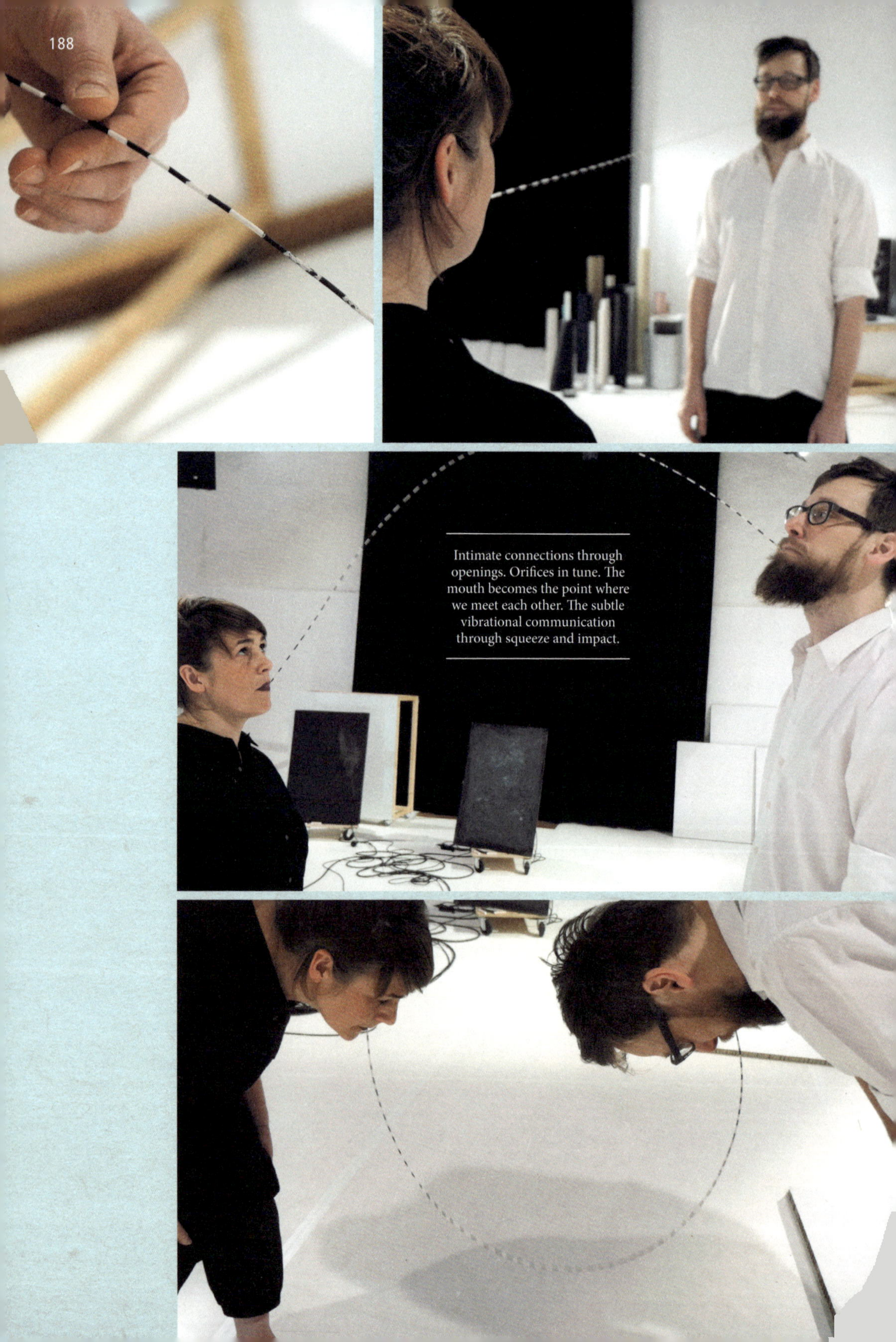

Intimate connections through openings. Orifices in tune. The mouth becomes the point where we meet each other. The subtle vibrational communication through squeeze and impact.

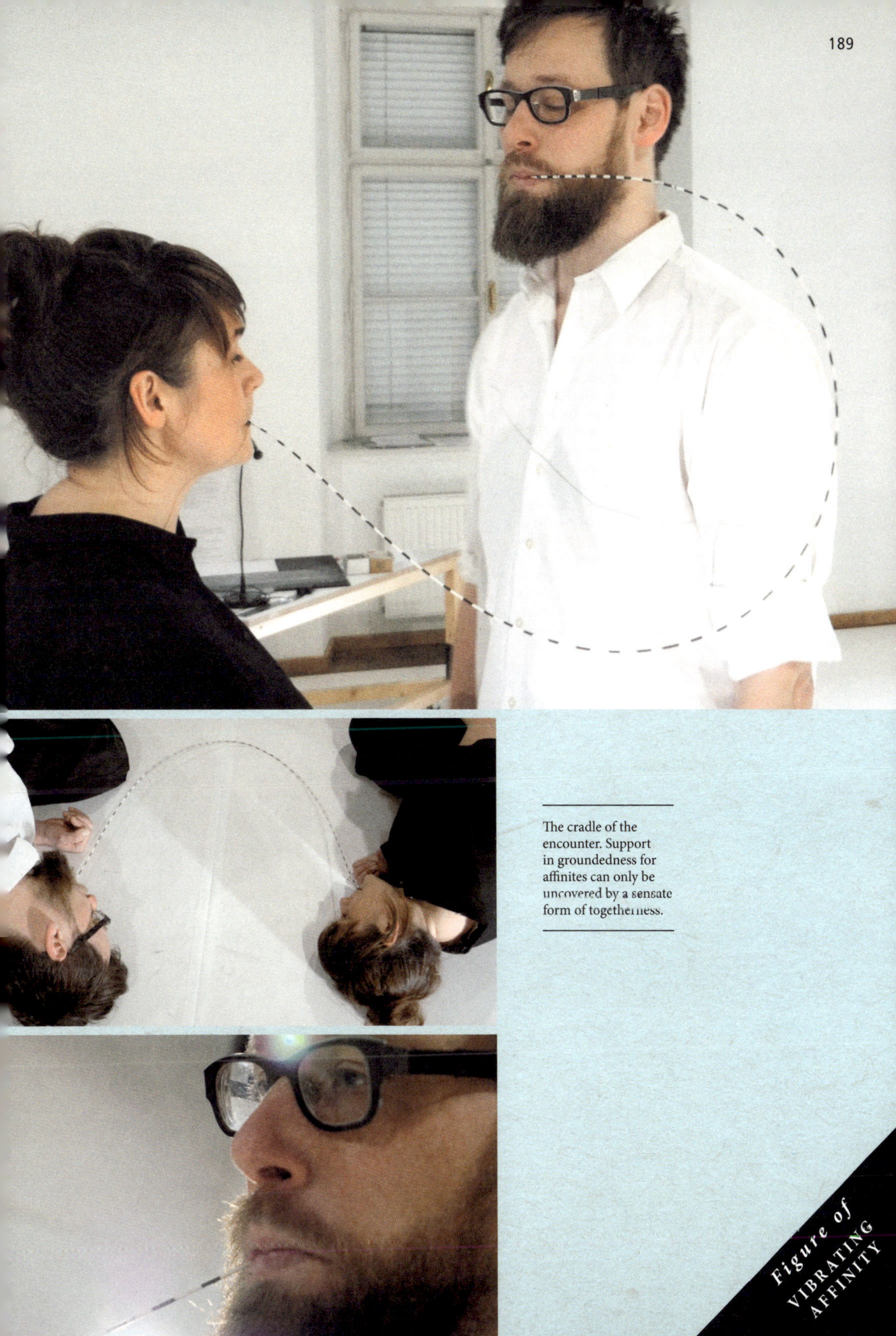

The cradle of the encounter. Support in groundedness for affinites can only be uncovered by a sensate form of togetherness.

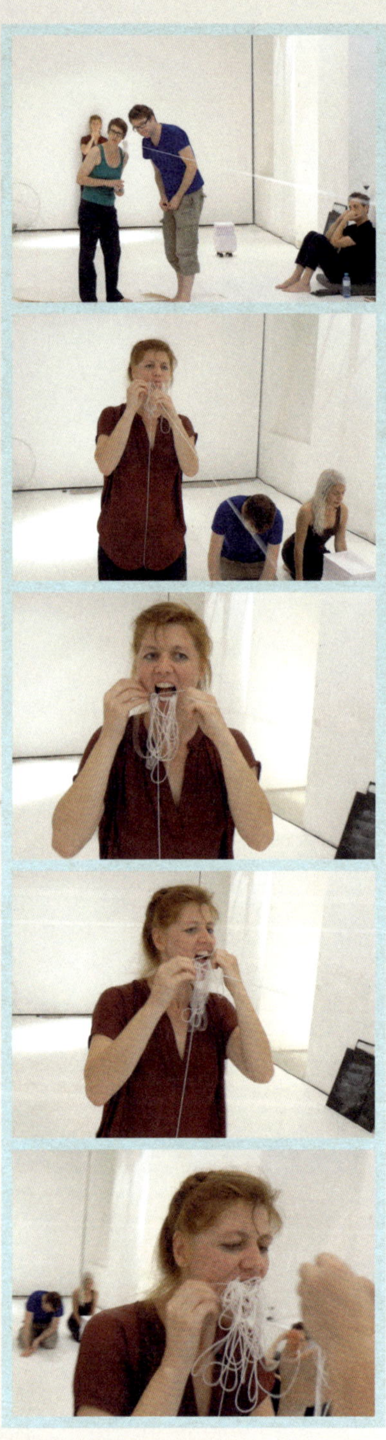

Feeling the reverberations in my teeth. My gaze follows the ripples, feeling convivial titillating. The depth of these sensations surprises me. My lips open in order to not speak. For not getting overwhelmed by the intimacy of this act.

The bassline — plucking the strings of connection. One frequency, attuned and unplugged. Vibrations and openings. A mouth full of entanglements.

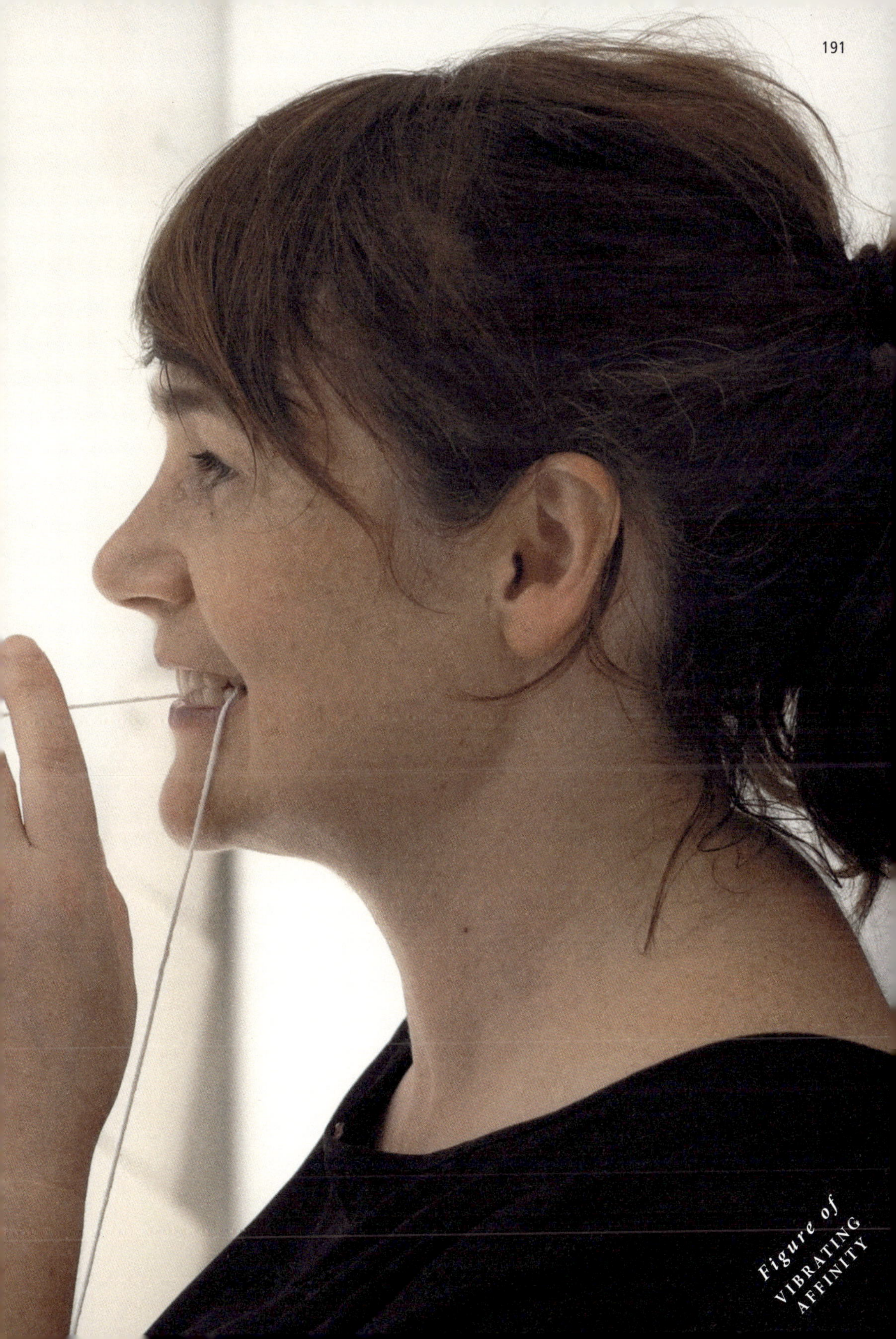

Figure of
VIBRATING
AFFINITY

Figure of WAVERING CONVERGENCE

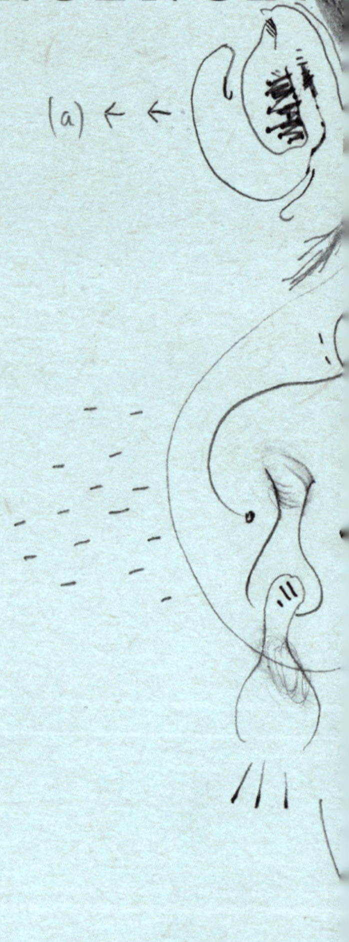

From dyad to triad: introduction of a third, *another* other. Another presence brings its own call of attention — expansion of relations beyond the duo, beyond the stability of a single coupling. Shared vibrations felt in togetherness, now unsettled. Unstable triad — the third creates imbalance, disrupts. Within the dynamic of a trio, in facing towards, lies the inescapable event also of facing away, gesture of turning *from*. The with-ness felt with one can distance another or leave out. Acts of intense togetherness between two become exclusive, excluding. To attend then whilst remaining available: ethical dilemma of being-in-relation, of collaboration with more-than-one. Absorption in shared action whilst still receptive to relations beyond, commitment made with openness to change. Avoid possession; resist the fixity of co-relation, practise shifts of attention in more than one direction.

There is a time to let go, loosen the affinity of a singular bond — extension of *being-with* to others beyond one. Wavering convergence: the inclination of attention first one way, then another. Incline — to bend towards; lean in, to be disposed to listen. Towards fluctuating coupling then — delicate dance between attraction and distraction, inclining and declining, allowing for new connections to emerge.

Or by playful revelation of unskilful means — activate the awkwardness, the turbulent energy of the push and pull. Eyes can wander; attention can be deviated, commitment swayed. Wilful obstruction of another's togetherness — prevention of stabilised relations. Vacillating back and forth, to waver — resist the binding of one relation above another, of *this* above *that*.

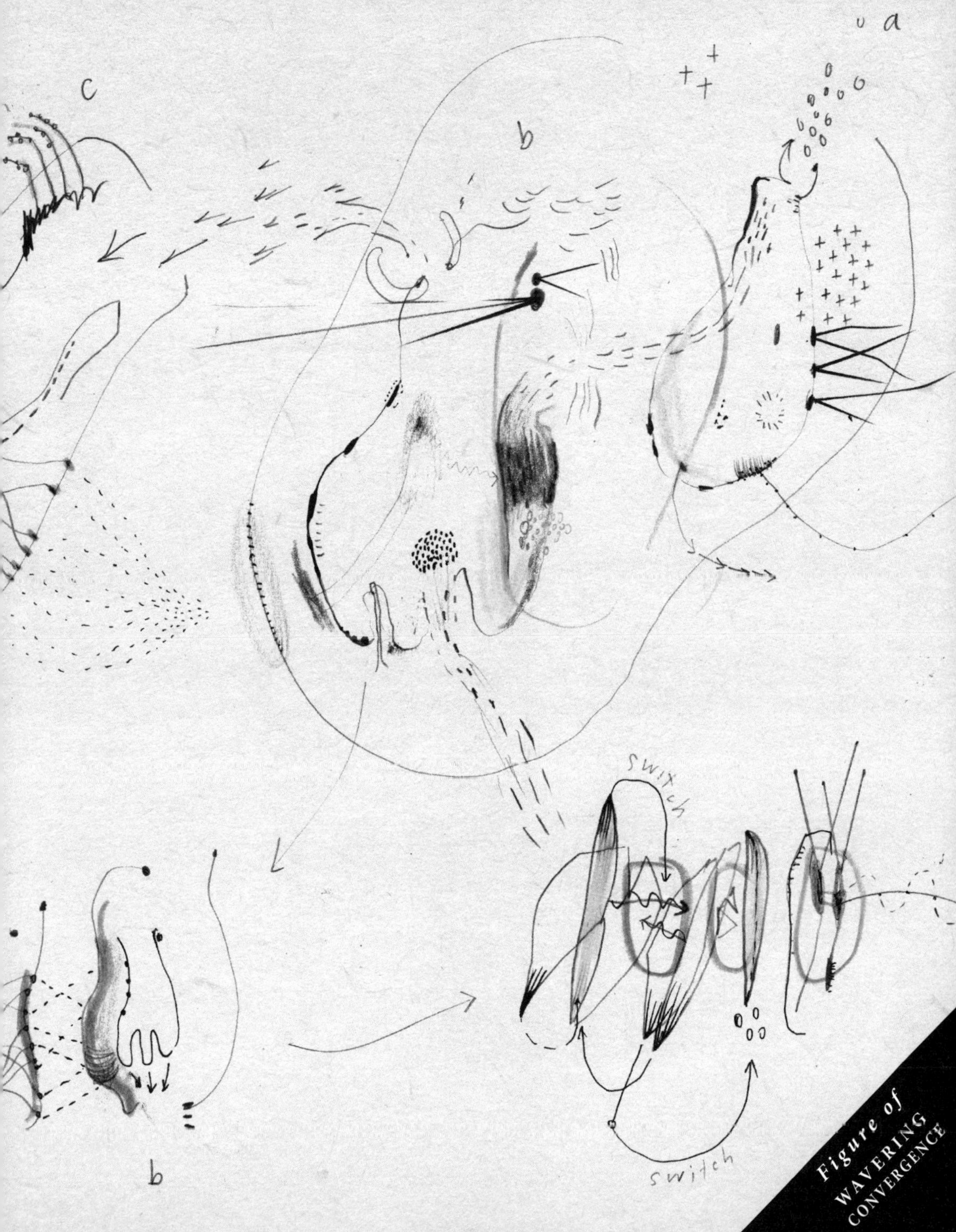
a
b
c
switch
switch
b
Figure of WAVERING CONVERGENCE

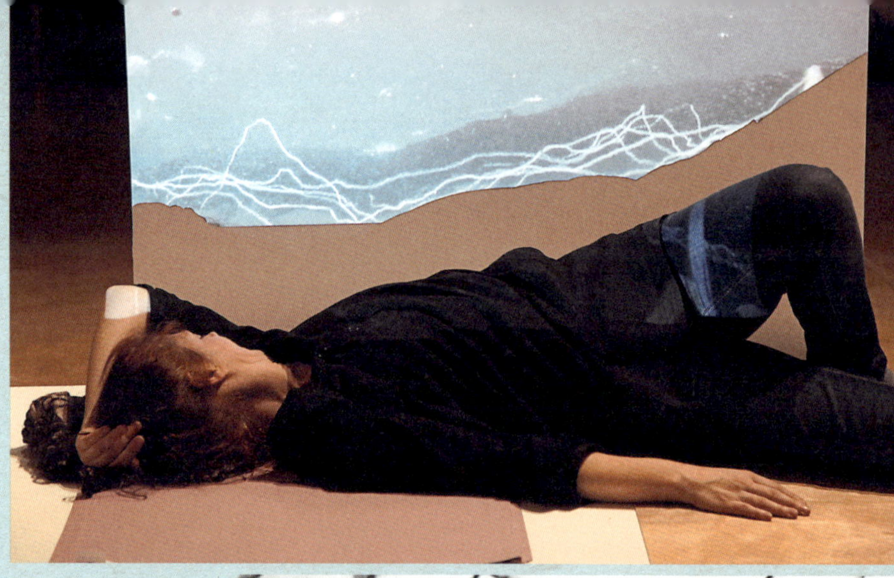

Touching the skin of the world with a sense of reaching out towards the immanent beyond. Through this extension I meet the other side of still the same being. A wave of breath. Light touch. Light touches. Warmth and intensity when the encounter takes place. But where is the place of the encounter between the body and the hand that carefully traces the body's outline in its changing rhythm?

A form in permanent transition, an organic mass that continually transforms — not only the delineation of its form, but by softly shifting spaces.

Squeezing, stretching, slowing the breath, sequencing, sliding, sinking, simmering, touching the shimmering light from the inner spheres. Sanctums.
A person's private retreat looms in the visceral rhythms of fluids and breath.

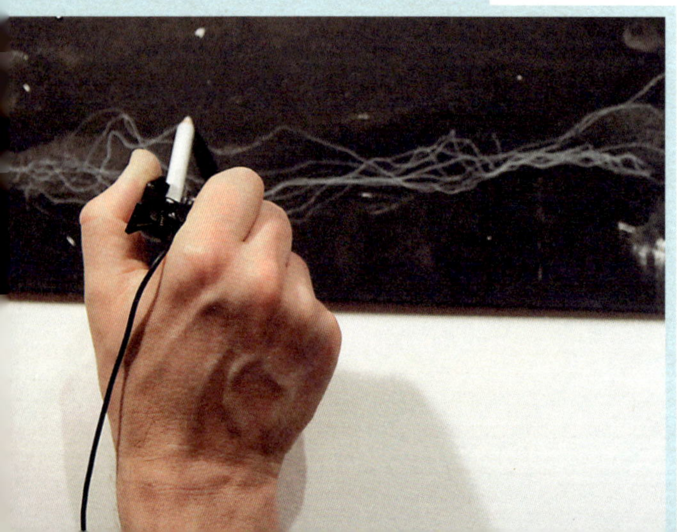

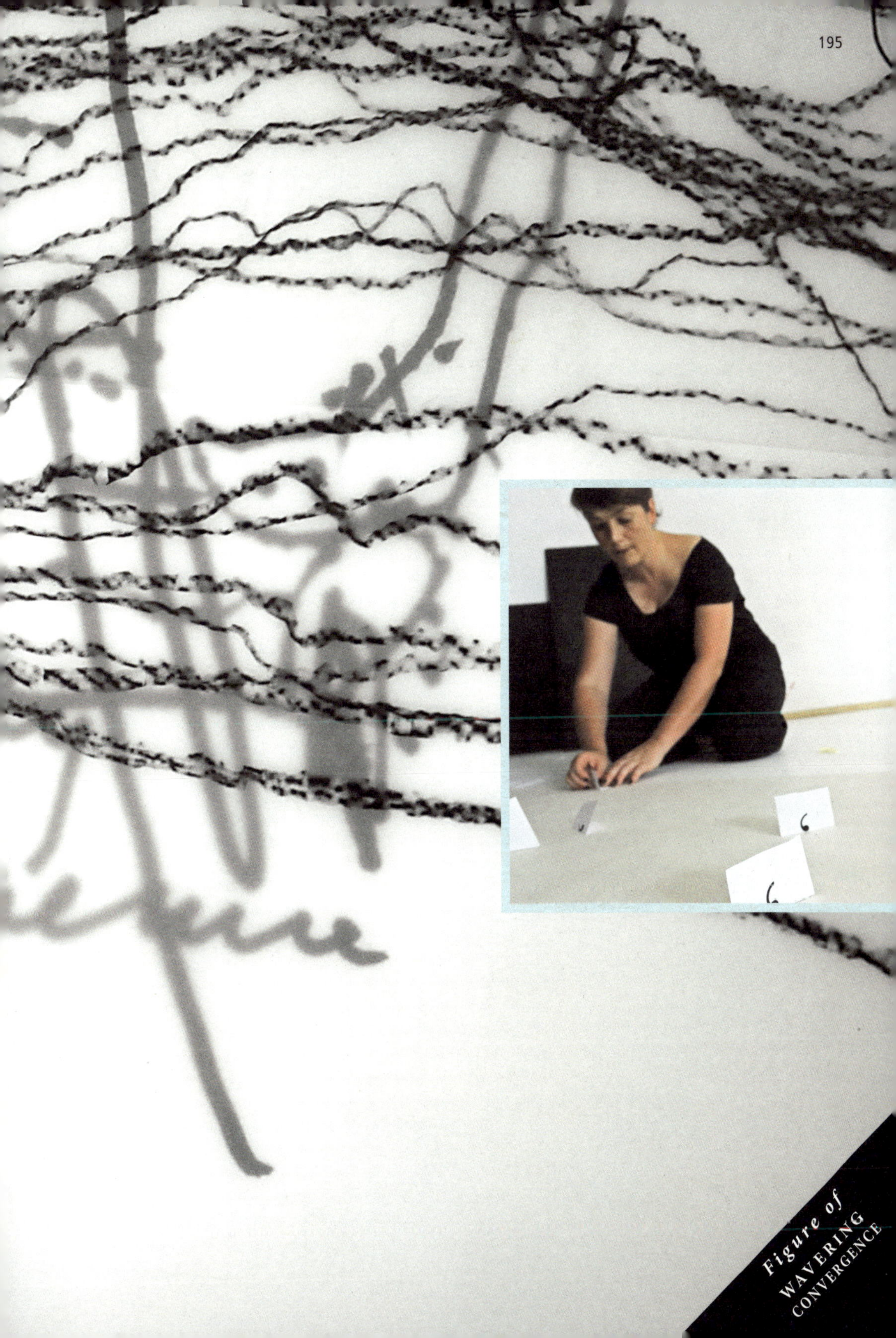
Figure of
WAVERING
CONVERGENCE

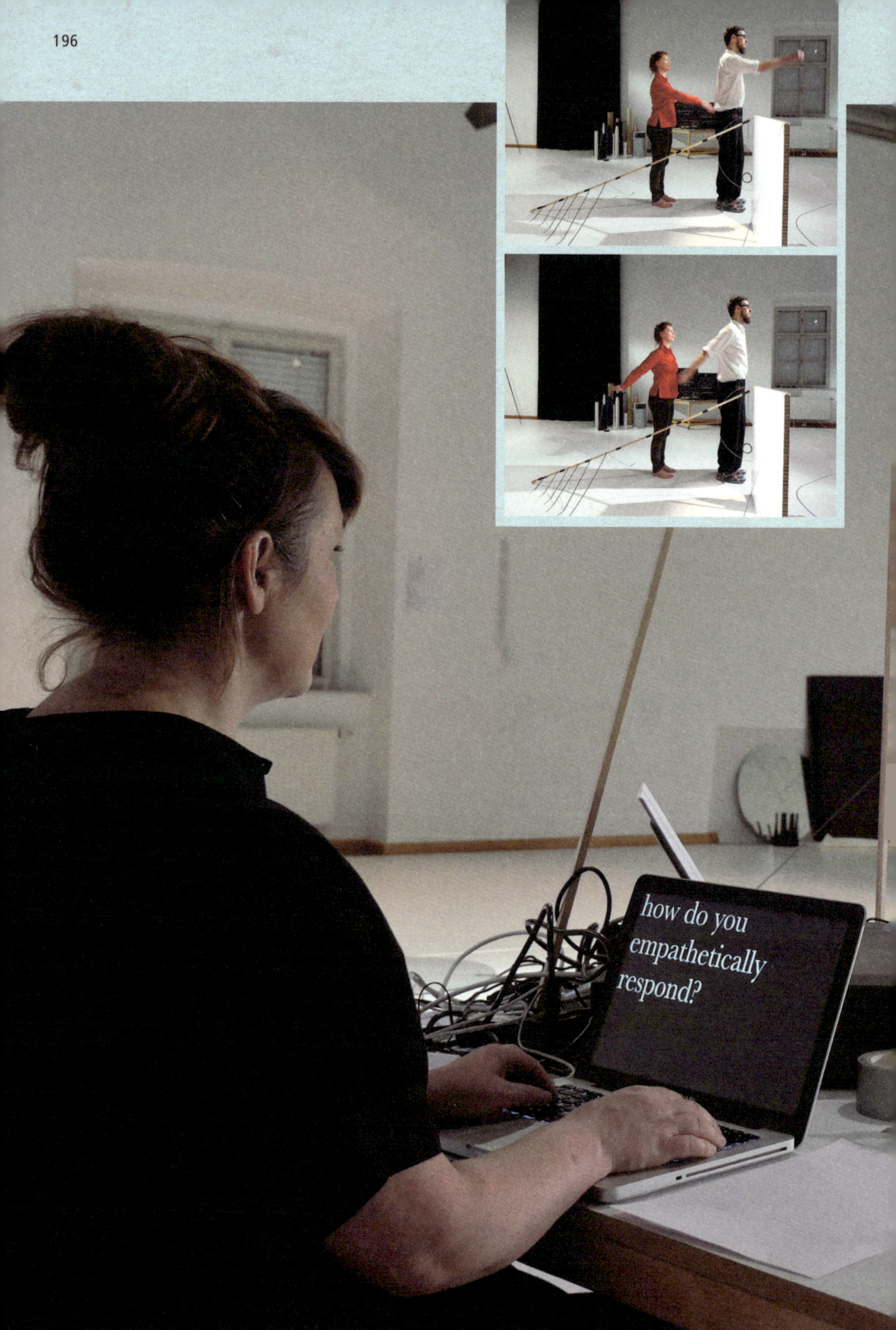
how do you
empathetically
respond?

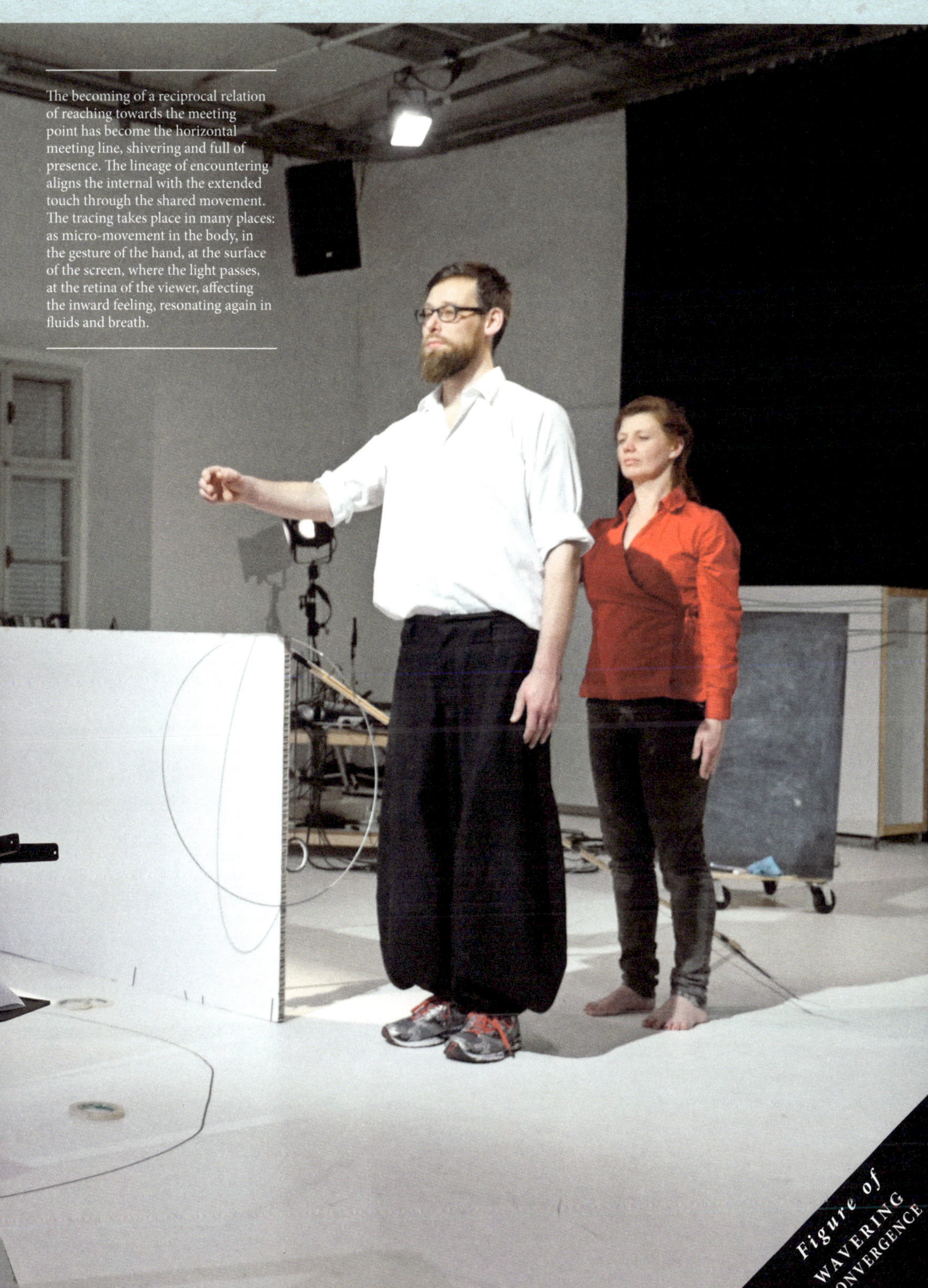

The becoming of a reciprocal relation of reaching towards the meeting point has become the horizontal meeting line, shivering and full of presence. The lineage of encountering aligns the internal with the extended touch through the shared movement. The tracing takes place in many places: as micro-movement in the body, in the gesture of the hand, at the surface of the screen, where the light passes, at the retina of the viewer, affecting the inward feeling, resonating again in fluids and breath.

Figure of WAVERING CONVERGENCE

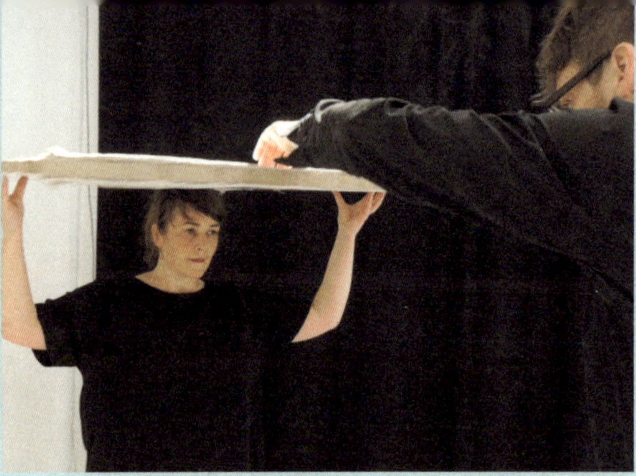

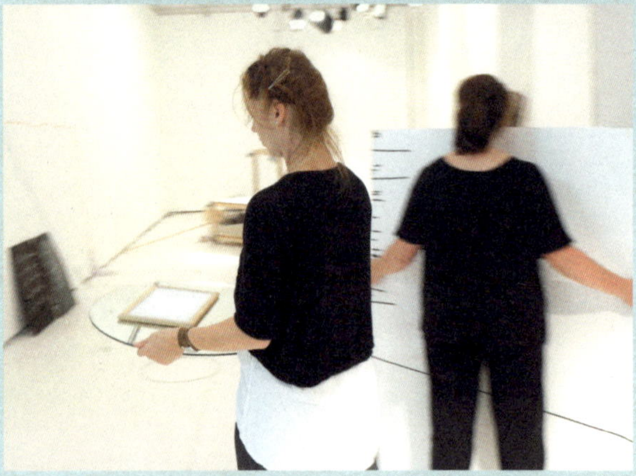

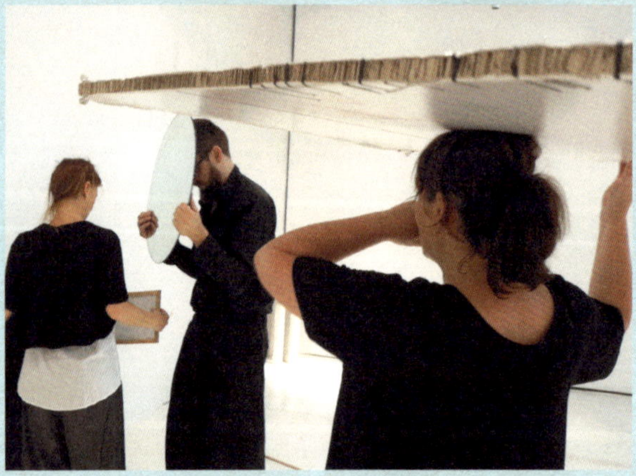

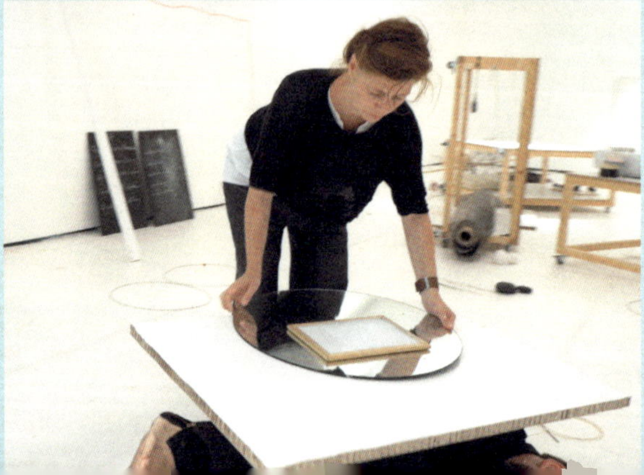

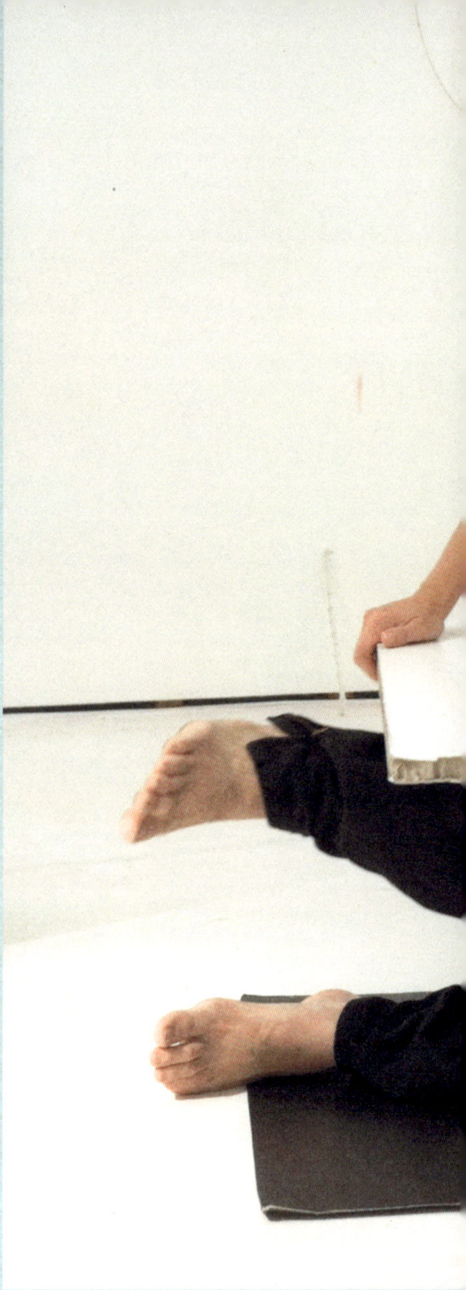

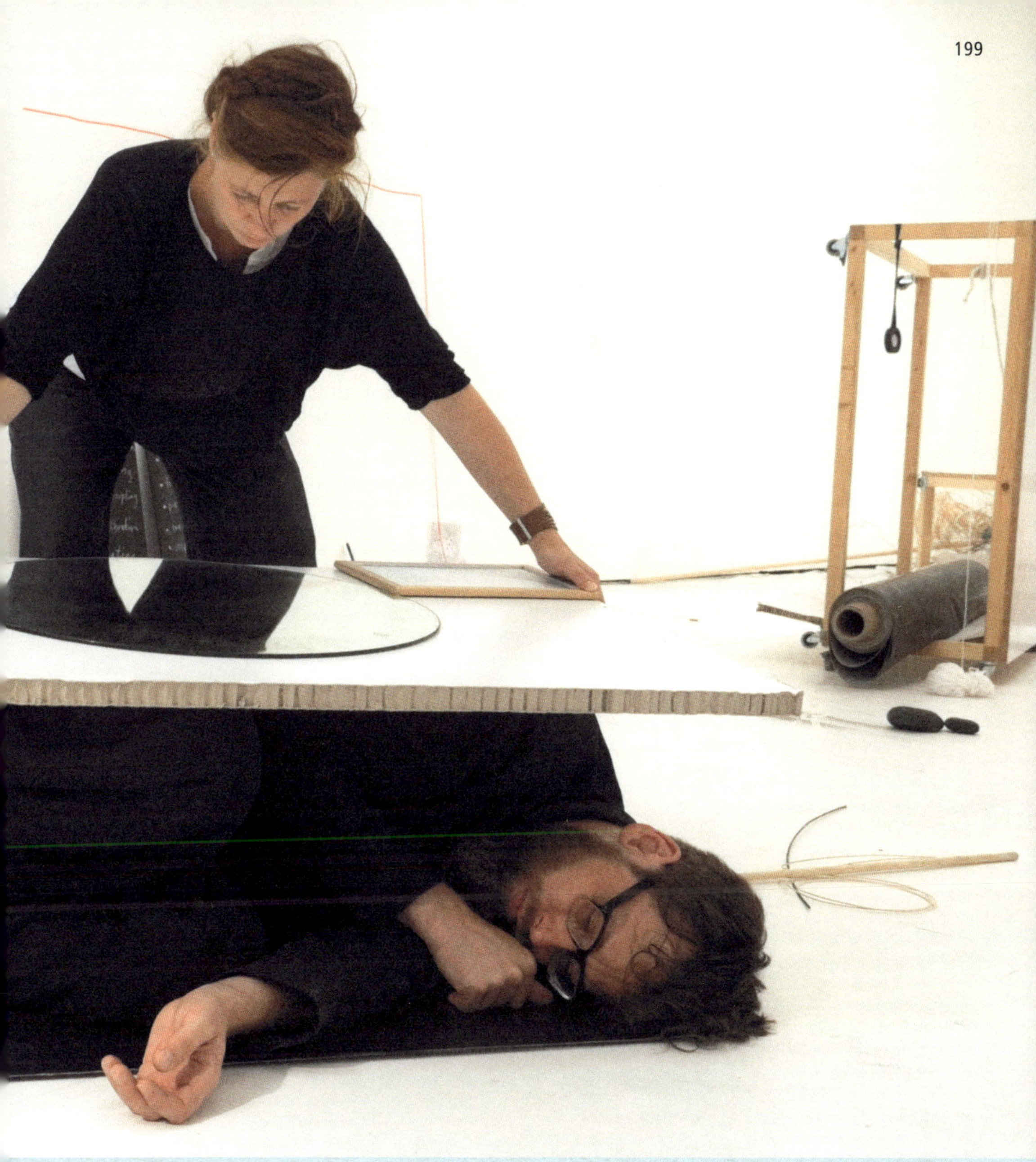

The wind within the body — the breath — entered through openings and the gentle resonances of togetherness. A meeting passes. No more tender turbulence. I move on.

Then, perceiving in action, to be moved, to work a way around. Thinking through the body, practising. Recognising … something is happening. How is it happening, how might that translate? The delicate line between proximity and distance, between intervening and destroying — the sensitivities of collaboration emerging between the lines. *Wavering Convergence.* The edges can get rough or blurred. Constantly negotiated in the process of making. Affective. Embodied. Relational.

Figure of WAVERING CONVERGENCE

Figure of CONSONANCE/DISSONANCE

Opening further the perceptual field towards the possibility of other relations, social reverberations, group dynamics. Widening of space, multiple agents—activate peripheral perception, extension of attention to the many. First establish a continuum—a wave pattern principle for movement in time and space; bodies in agreement become a ground, the conditions for experimental play. Ever-shifting modulations in motion: polyrhythmic interplay of divergent speeds and urgencies. Recognising connections, resonating with-ness, momentary coming together, multiple meeting points with others. Synchronicity—bond of co-experience; meaningful co-incidence, an act or fact of coinciding. Correspondence. Concurrence. Correlation. Co-relation. Intensity of seconds shared in mutual action. Yet fleeting, never lasting. Always in passing, not held. Resist agreement as flattening consensus, homogenising of rhythmic singularities to a singular beat, a uniform drill. Become attuned to the need for breaks and ruptures, obstacles for interrupting harmonious flow if practised without thought. Desirable dissonance, insistent instability: wilful deviation from the line.

Extension of sociality, relationality expands towards the inanimate, non-living matter. Recognising resemblance. Or more like prosthesis, materials make visible, amplify or sharpen the sense of human interactions. Re-lation anticipates trans-lation: foretaste of the transformative blurring of subject-object as much as between selves.

Always in transition, never settling, non-dualist resistance of the privileged term. Consonant dissonance, dissonant consonance: which is the qualifying and which the qualified? Perpetual passage: between connection and divergence; concentration and dispersion, synchronicity and a-synchronicity, continuity and dis-continuity, singular and the collective, the fluid falling in and out of time and space.

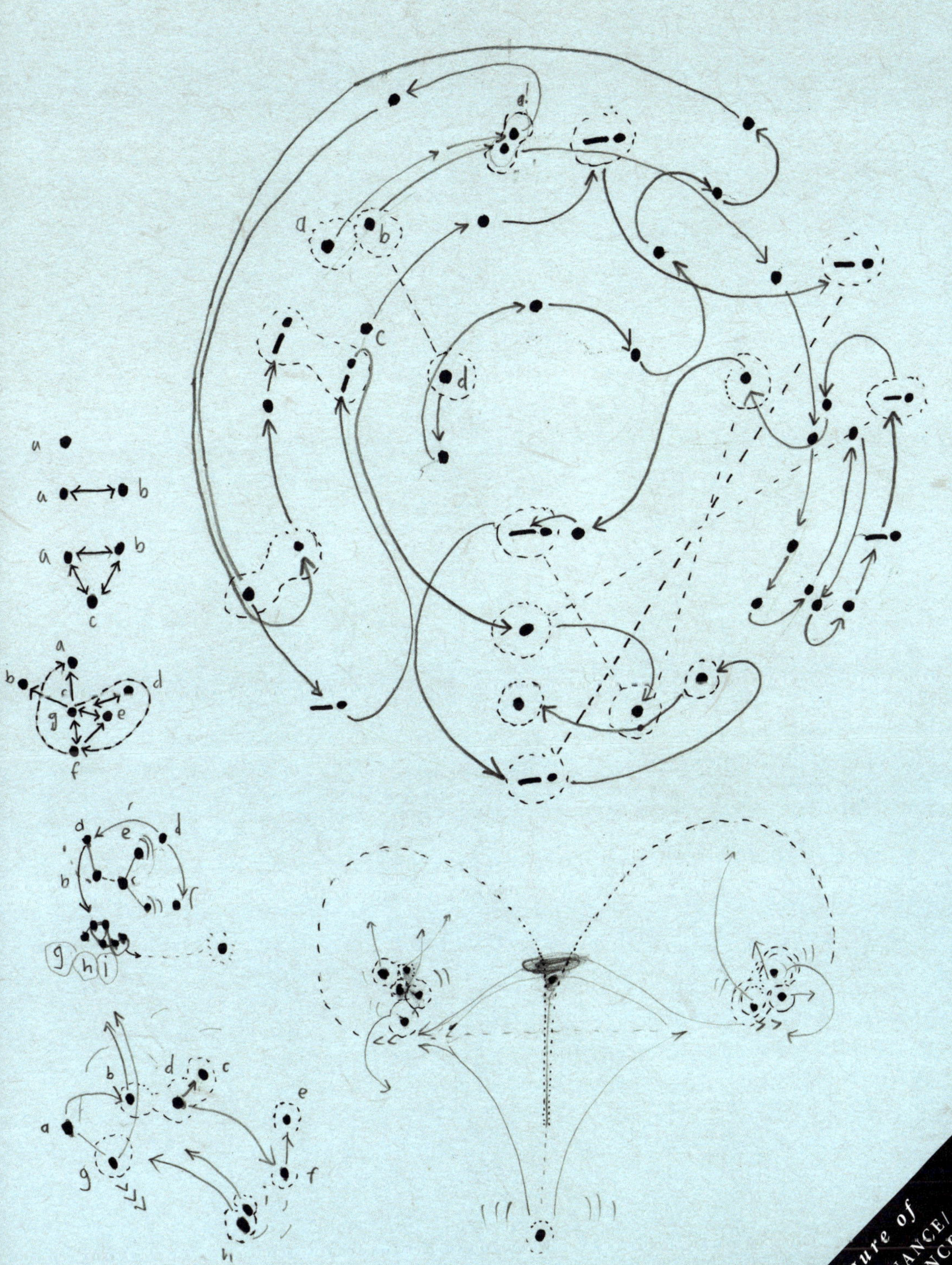

Figure of CONSONANCE/ DISSONANCE

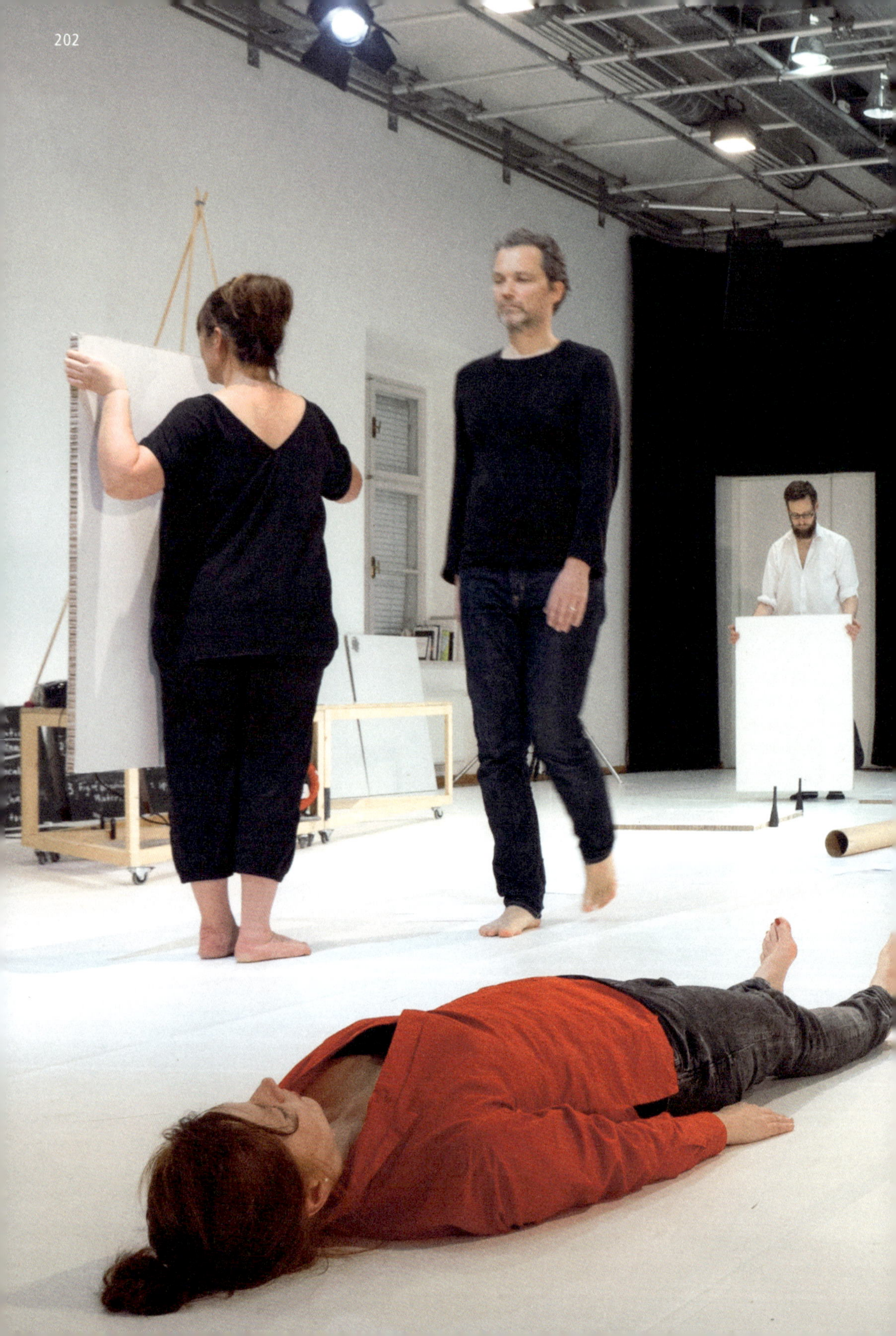

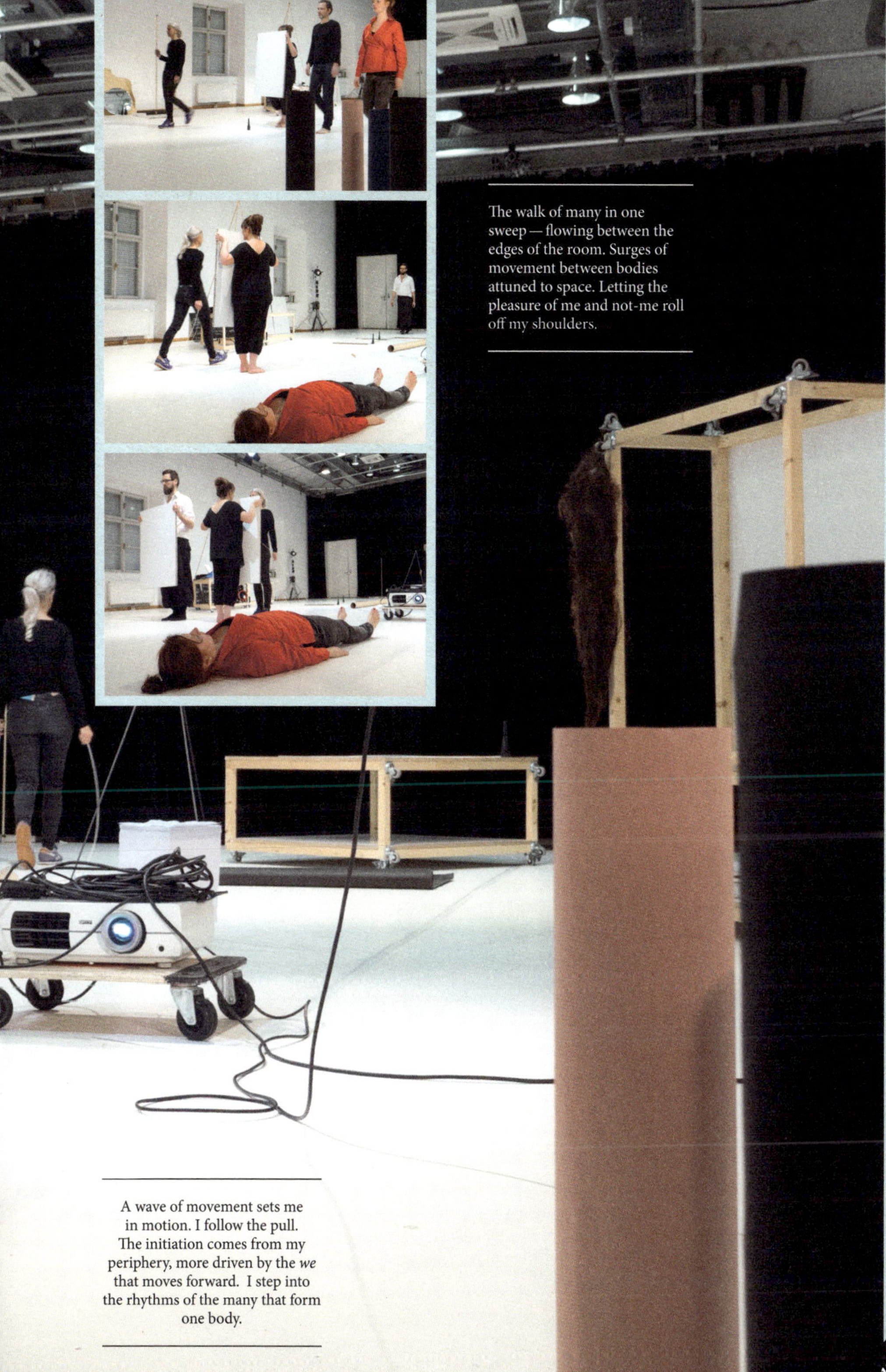

The walk of many in one sweep — flowing between the edges of the room. Surges of movement between bodies attuned to space. Letting the pleasure of me and not-me roll off my shoulders.

A wave of movement sets me in motion. I follow the pull. The initiation comes from my periphery, more driven by the *we* that moves forward. I step into the rhythms of the many that form one body.

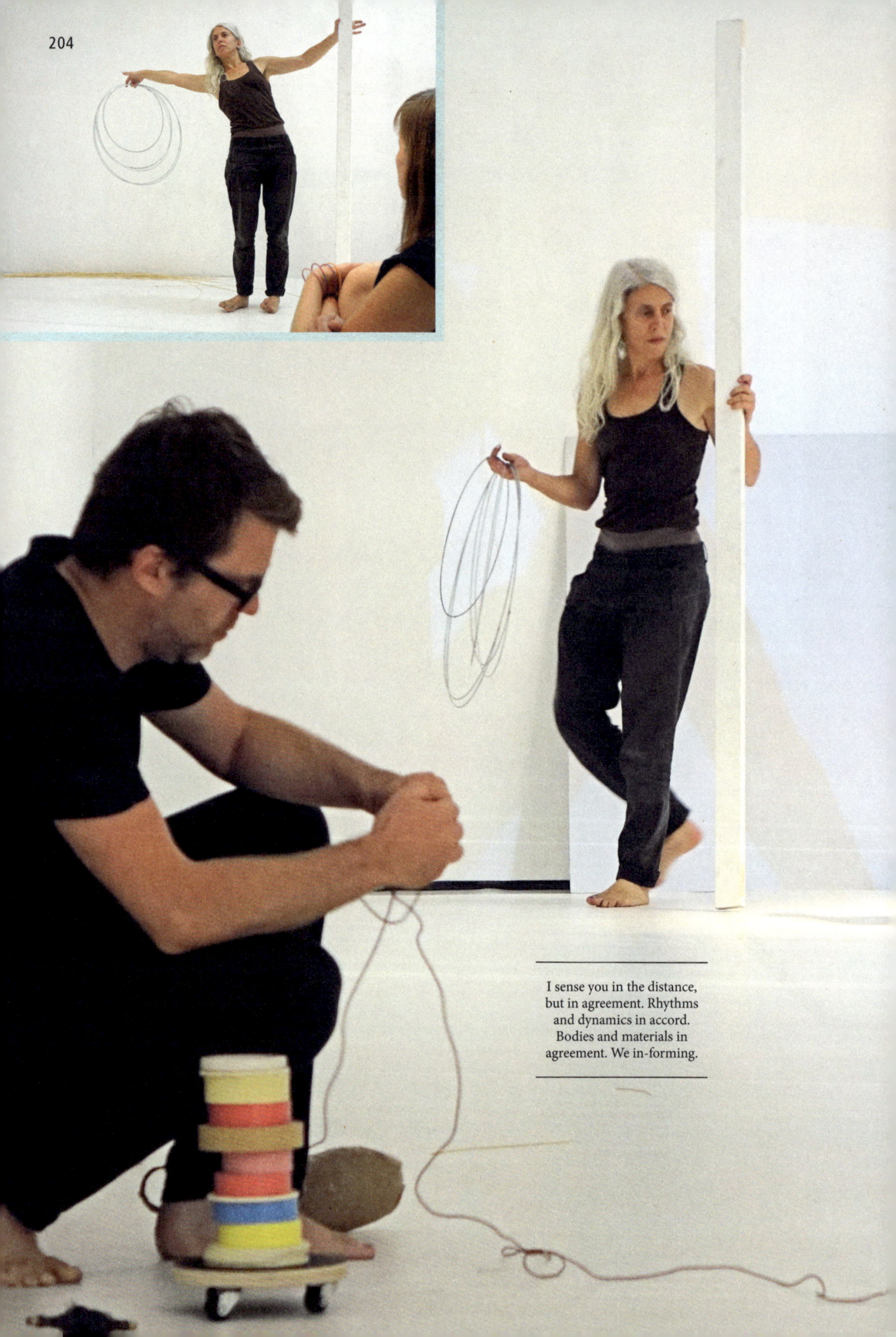

I sense you in the distance, but in agreement. Rhythms and dynamics in accord. Bodies and materials in agreement. We in-forming.

I sense you close, but open for negotiation. Standing still. Still standing. My gaze raised and ears attuned to feet. When to step forward? Deviations noticed. Dissonance enjoyed. Affirming togetherness as much as divide.

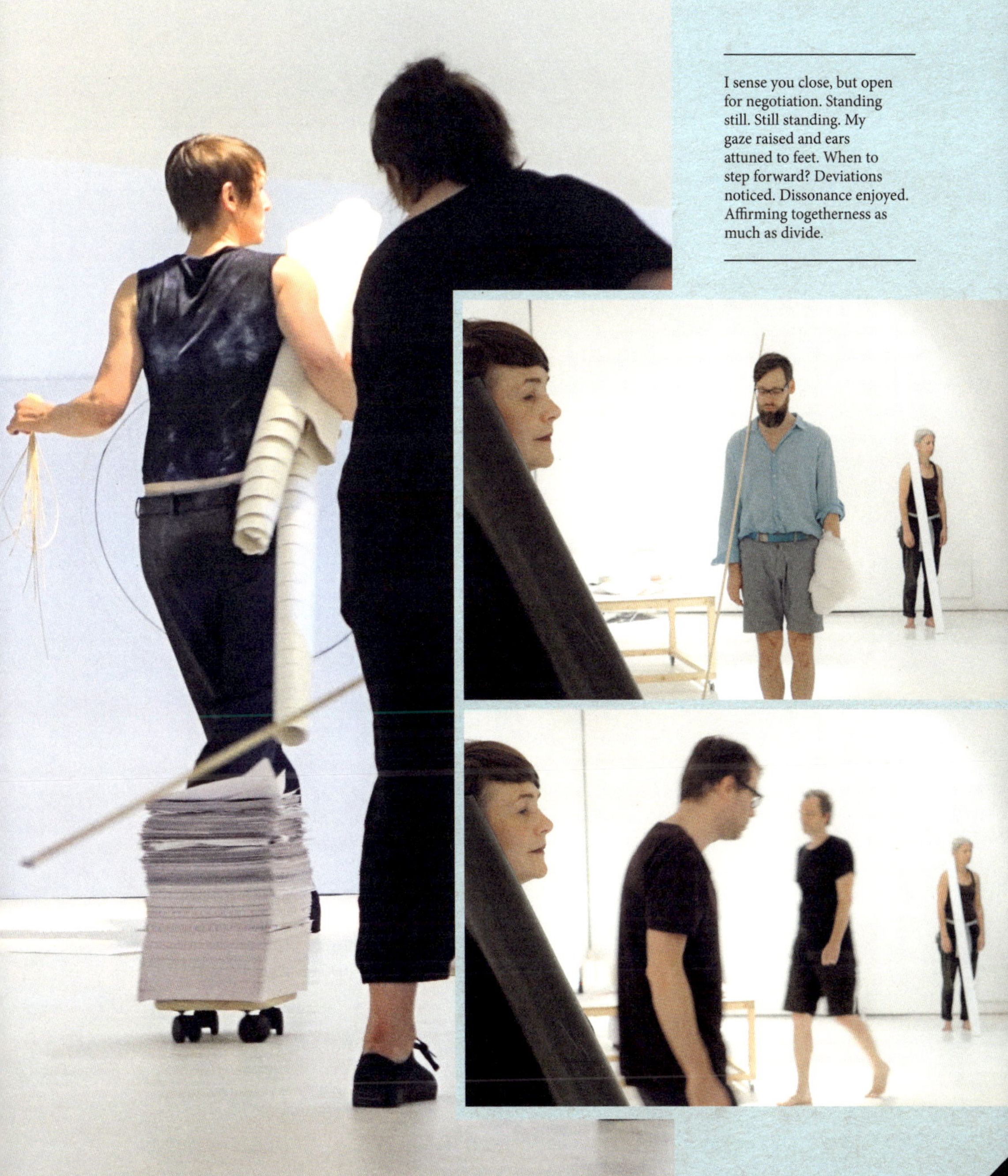

Figure of CONSONANCE/ DISSONANCE

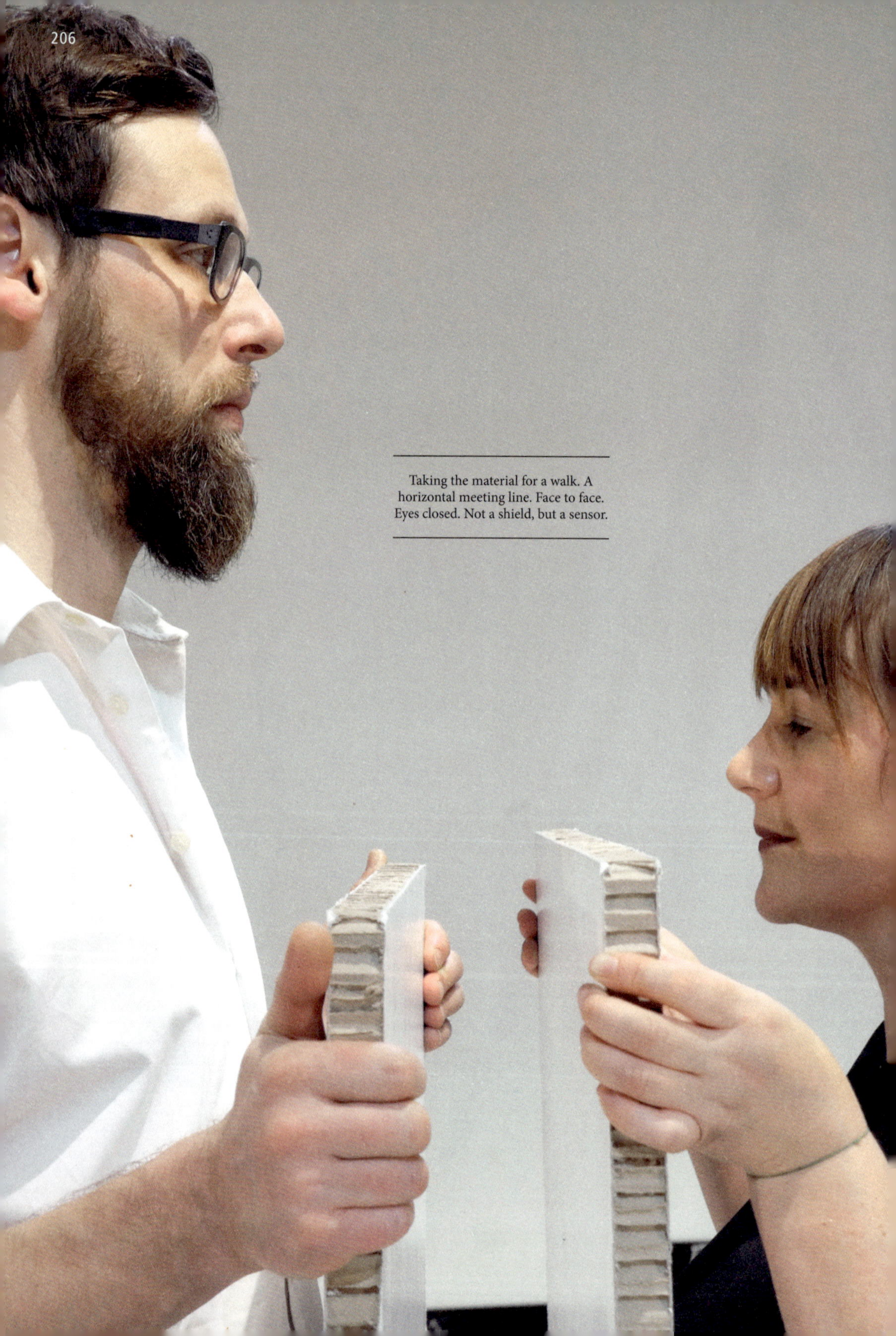

Taking the material for a walk. A horizontal meeting line. Face to face. Eyes closed. Not a shield, but a sensor.

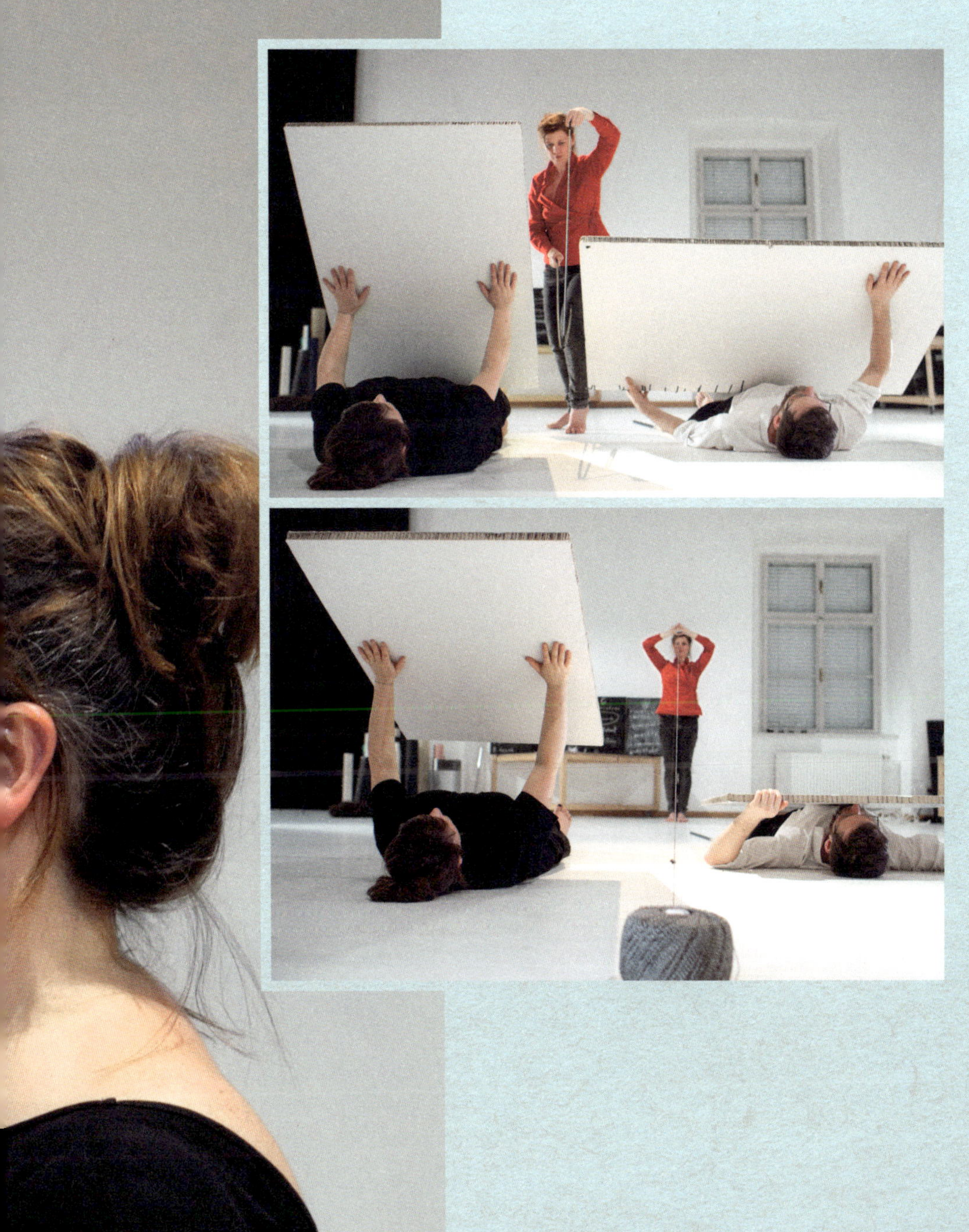

Figure of CONSONANCE/ DISSONANCE

SENSORIAL BODIES
FORCES — BODIES — SENSATIONS

Arno Böhler

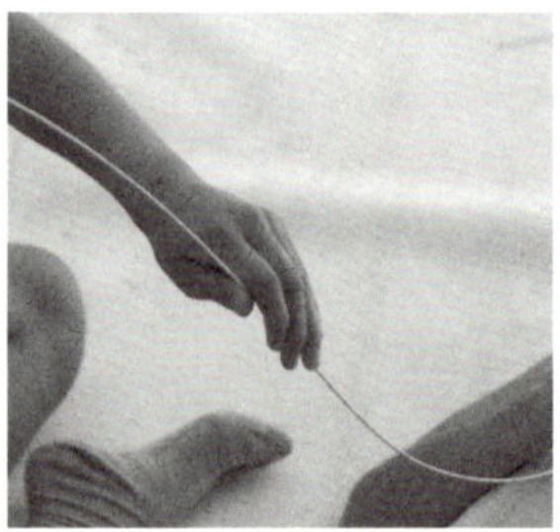

Logic of Sensation

In his book, *Francis Bacon: The Logic of Sensation,* Gilles Deleuze pinpoints the crucial problem with Bacon as *"the action of invisible forces on the body."*[1] That which Bacon's pictures capture is *touch* — sensations generated at the interface between affecting forces and affected bodies, exactly where both enter into *mutual reaction* with each other. Where they build up a junction at which both are there *at the same time*: intimately, within each other, affecting each other. Bodies — forces; forces — bodies. Interfaces — junctions — sensations.

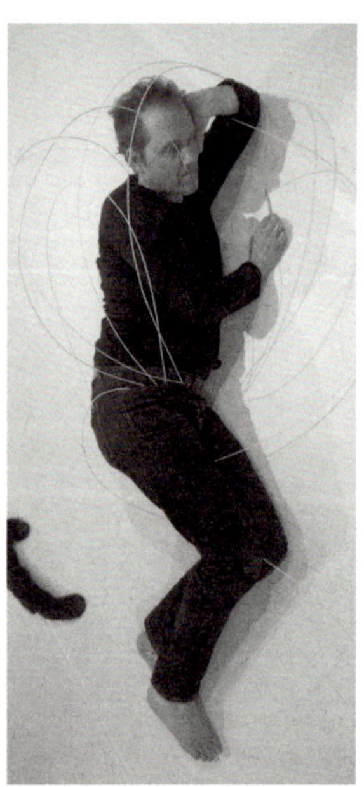

Figural Thinking

With recourse to a text by Jean-François Lyotard, Deleuze distinguishes this *figural concept* of figure from the classical *figurative concept* of figure.[2] In the figural sense, a figure is a "sensible form related to a sensation; it acts immediately upon the nervous system [...] at one and the same time I *become* in the sensation and something *happens* through the sensation, one through the other, one in the other."[3] Contrarily, in the figurative sense a figure *ends* at the surface of its body. It is regarded as *isolated* from the background surrounding it, as if it existed independently, 'per se', so to speak, and not as an *response* to it.

Becoming Skin / Becoming Flesh

According to the figural concept of figure, the surfaces of bodies become skin.[4] Sensitive zones which capture and make their surroundings perceptible *in a lived-body* by cross-linking them with all the fibres of flesh available to a body. Even if contact that goes under one's skin is perceived *in a lived-body*, the affected body definitely *not* only senses 'itself', i.e., a body isolated from its environment. Wherever sensations occur, that which takes place is rather the sensitive localisation of one's own corporeal

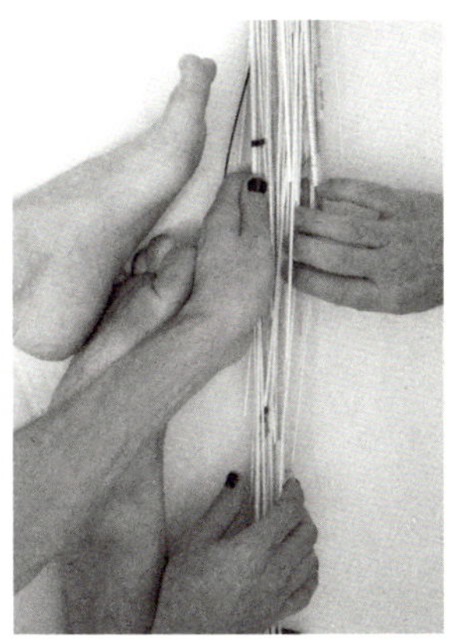

being-in-the-world to which a body is *exposed* at its physical surface everywhere in the world. Consequentially, feeling 'oneself' means perceiving oneself as a body *touched* by others, *exposed* to others *in the middle of the world*. One perceives one's being *towards others*, towards other human and non-human bodies, together with which one forms a *sensorial field* whenever one feels sensations. Therefore, sensations are not private phenomena. They are forms of *transport* into the world's world-wide-ness. Pores that provide us with a sensorial — as it were haptic approach — to the world's objects, which then allows us to have objects *before us* so that we then can regard them *objectively*.

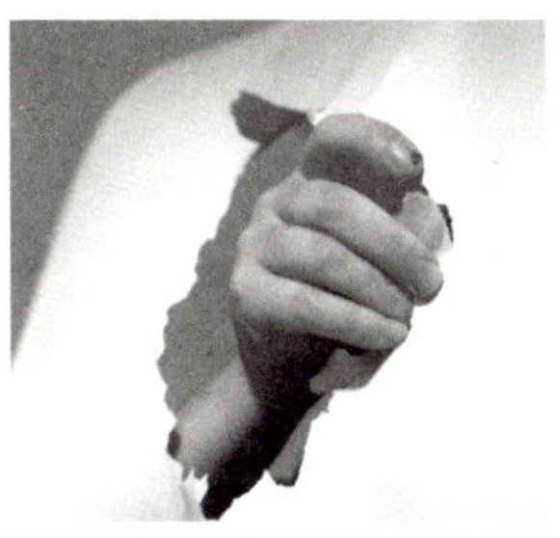

Images of Thought

In *Beyond Good and Evil*, Friedrich Nietzsche writes that 'I-think' and also the philosopher's *cogito* is always already based on an 'It-thinks' which *appraises the actual world conditions with regard to their relations of power and force*.[5] He utters these words from the *position* of the flesh, i.e., in the name of that sensitive zone which bodies share with other bodies in so far as they are directly affected by each other. Such a position is never neutral, because it appraises the relation to the world from the perspective of a *corporeal living being*: perspectively, interested, in resonance with all the other bodies with which a body maintains an *intensive* relationship. In this case, judgement is not rendered *on* the world from the bird's eye view of an untouched observer. In this case, the *conatus* — a body's will to self-preservation — articulated itself as a force, which again is located *in* the world, and therefore possesses a vital inter-est in its own physical survival *in the midst of the world*.[6]

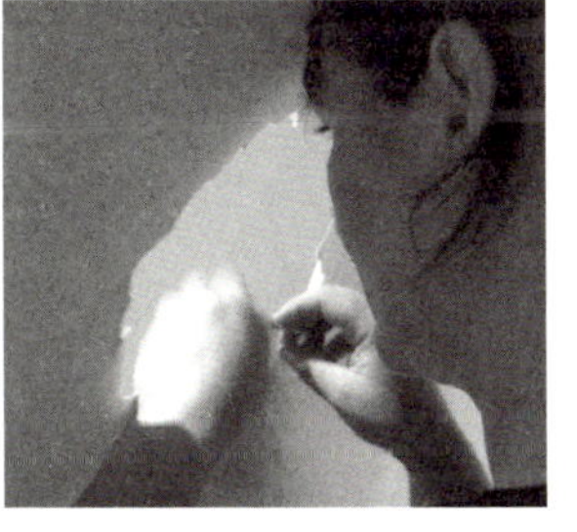

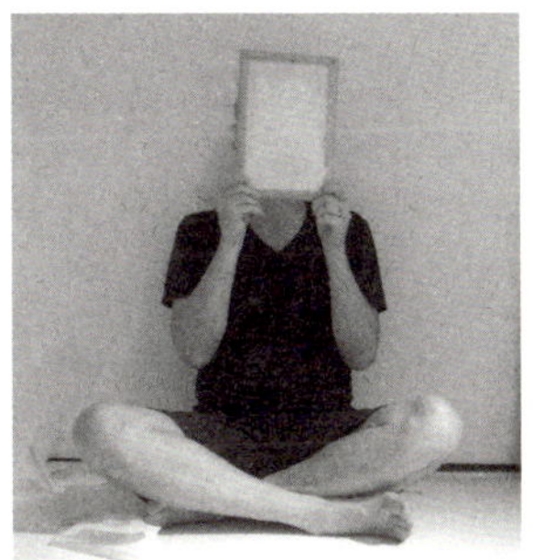

Witnesses

Being witness to such an experimental set-up (as experienced within the *Choreo-graphic Figures* project) actually does *not* mean observing the processes in which 'choreo-graphic figures' are immanent *from the outside*. One has to enter *into* the processes in which a *choreo-graphic figure* emerges, where — like in Bacon's mirror[7] — one has to engage with the balance of power in which one situatively finds oneself to be in a position to bear witness to what happens in such a 'research laboratory'.

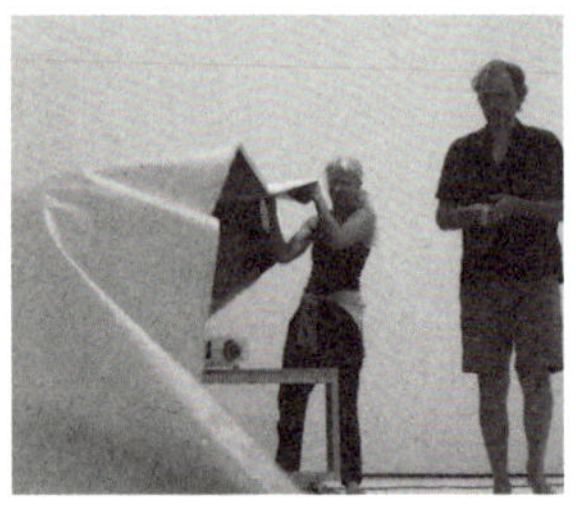

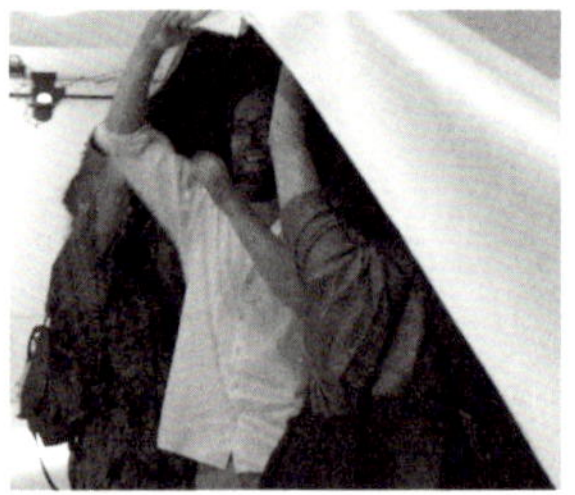

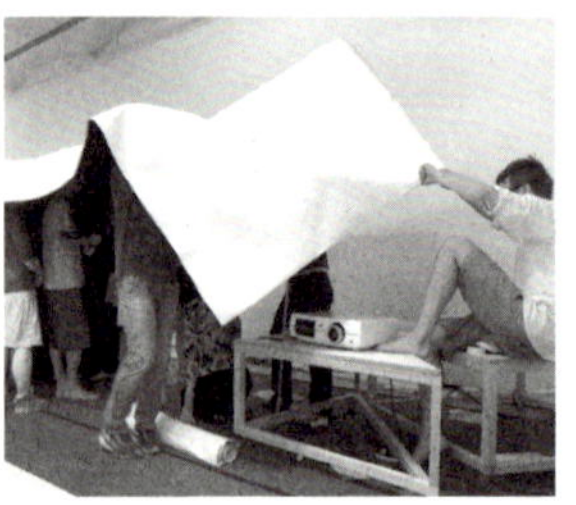

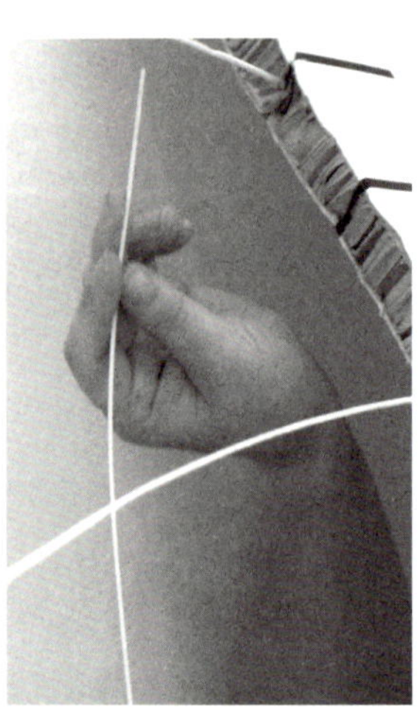

Gathering

For this reason, witnessing a *choreo-graphic* experiment requires an *intensive gathering* of the witnesses in the resonance field of the participating bodies. So to speak, the sensorial carpet that unfolds between the bodies in the space is atmospheric, the earthly meshwork out of which the individual bodies receive their movement impulses. When one engages with the emergence of *choreo-graphic figures,* one does not act strategically, one does not act in isolation, one acts out of the bodies' resonance field. Therefore, whoever witnesses a *choreo-graphic* situation cannot simply keep the world at arm's length in the 'good' old ascetic manner. One is part of the events, part of the bodies affecting each other. Skin — 'witness skin' — that in ec-static walkabout around itself captures the other bodies' world-wide-ness and incorporates it in its body's interior. It follows that such a figure of thought is "not a matter of reproducing and inventing forms", but of "capturing of forces."[8]

Choreo-graphic Figures

Choreo-graphic figures are *figural* in the sense discussed above. They present temporary 'solutions' resulting from the procedural interplay of the three components *force-body-sensation.* As a configuration of a power play issuing between bodies that are in sensorial contact with each other, a *choreo-graphic figure* never exists *outside* or *before* the temporary junction of these three components in time and space. Rather, in order to emerge it is dependent on the factual performance of concrete experimental arrangements which bring it into being. From this originates its 'practical' character. If the processes in which a *choreo-graphic figure* configures itself are not initiated, then it is not endowed with being. It lacks the *flesh* — that *virtual* moment which makes it an *intensive* field of vibrating *bodies*, which in-carnates it *in actu*.

Intensities

The space of *choreo-graphic figures* is not an empty stage on which figures perform for themselves, but a delirious space, a field of intensities. To be delirious etymologically means *getting out of one's groove (de-lirare), being thrown off the track*. The subject loses control over the situation it is in when it strikes up resonance with other bodies. It eludes its 'self'. Unexpectedly, two or more bodies find a play of relations with each other which surprises, by letting *potencies* of being-together and their *mutual reaction* flash up. Such *moments of event* are intriguing because in them astounding fields of intensity between bodies are set free.

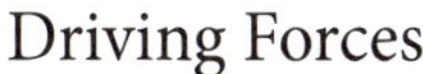

Driving Forces

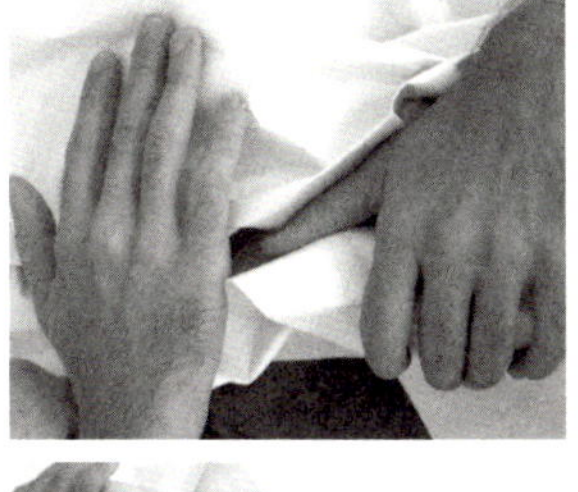

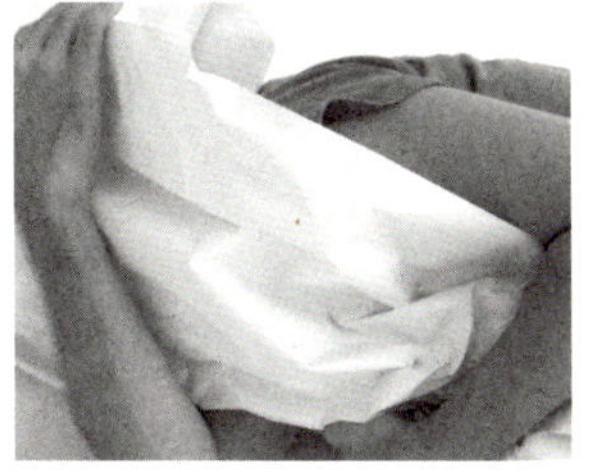

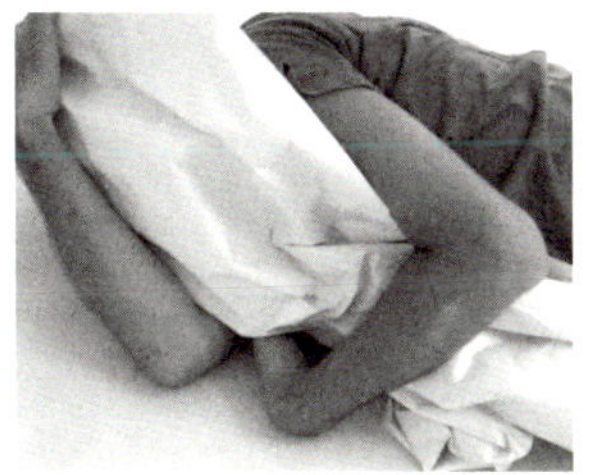

Choreo-graphic figures neither realise a previously determined intention nor an anticipated aim. Rather, in them *potencies* of mutual reaction with-each-other break into the regime of the visible. One moves on black ice. An unexpected figure emerges between bodies which puts them in an ec-stasy of heightened awareness regarding the constellation of forces in which they situatively find themselves. Since in such moments *virtual degrees of freedom* between the bodies are *set free*, they necessarily produce *joy*. This implies, at least from the perspective of Spinoza's *Ethics*, an *ethical-aesthetical* moment. When one makes the driving forces of a situation flash up and one's own body's neurons fire away, one paves the way for joy.

Earthly Beautiful

Such events are beautiful in the sense that for a moment they affirm our *earthly* life instead of letting us flee into transcendental worlds. Wherever research about the configuration of *choreo-graphic figures* is undertaken, one might sum up with Nietzsche's *Zarathustra, one remains true to the earth.*[9]

---

1) Gilles Deleuze, *Francis Bacon: The Logic of Sensation,* London / New York: Continuum, 2002, p. 41.

2) Deleuze, 2002, p. 2.

3) Deleuze, 2002, pp. 34-35.

4) Cf. Jean Luc-Nancy, *Corpus,* New York: Fordham University Press, 2008, p. 33, on the bodies' becoming skin.

5) Cf. especially Friedrich Nietzsche, *Beyond Good and Evil,* Oxford: Oxford University Press, [1886] 2008, No. 3, p. 7 and No. 17, pp. 17-18.

6) Spinoza determined *conatus* as a body's striving to preserve itself in its existence. Cf. Baruch Spinoza, *Ethics,* Oxford: Oxford University Press, [1677] 2000, Part III. Proposition 6 and 7, p. 171.

7) Deleuze, 2002, p. 19.

8) Deleuze, 2002, p. 56.

9) Friedrich Nietzsche, *Thus Spoke Zarathustra,* (Trans.) Graham Parkes, Oxford: Oxford University Press, [1883] 2005, No. 3, pp. 11-13.

TRIALOGUE:
On Sedimentations of Sensitivities

WHERE: This trialogue between **Emma Cocker (EC), Mariella Greil (MG)** and **Adrian Heathfield (AH)** took place in London, where Heathfield has collaborated on numerous projects with the photographer Hugo Glendinning, including *Transfigured Night: A Conversation with Alphonso Lingis*, 2013; *No Such Thing as Rest: A Walk with Brian Massumi*, 2013, and *Spirit Labour*, 2016, a visual essay that follows the creative practice of sculptor and performance artist Janine Antoni, her collaborations and conversations with the choreographer Anna Halprin and the writer Hélène Cixous.

WHEN: 25th October 2016.

HOW: The original 3-hour conversation has been edited to focus specifically on the ethical-aesthetic sensitivities of collaborative exploration, expanding attention from subject-to-subject relations towards an emergent ecology of radical coexistence beyond the anthropocentric.

EC: […] An underpinning question for our project is how to attend to the micro-level of sense-making within shared live exploration? How can you find systems of notation for sharing this usually hidden component within the artistic process, those micro-moments when 'something is happening', such as a decision to do something or a sense of an impulse or a desire to change tack?

MG: Insistence, commitment, conflict …

AH: … all that is arising in a space of collaboration between different bodies.

EC: How do you make tangible the register of sensation that usually operates just below the surface of making? How do you raise that to a level of awareness so that you can share it?

AH: So, this question would be different in every artistic project: to anatomise intuitive processes and to pressure them into linguistic forms. But to me, what is interesting about what you are doing is that this question is being reformulated in a complex trans-disciplinary space of relations, and between multiple sensibilities. That would be a tremendously useful resource for artists in relation to collaborative practices. If anything is hidden in this context then I think it is probably on the collaborative side of things. Because we have lived through a drastic shift in the conditions of cultural production — which has basically disallowed particular forms of sustained collaborative creative co-working — there is a certain imperative to articulate the social and political force of those energetics as their 'home' is disappearing.

MG: This points towards the established time-frames of collaboration. It needs physical co-presence; it needs an engagement and a commitment to a longer process in order to meet or bridge those experiences of intransigence, to stick with something, for trust-building, to open up towards a foreign practice encountered in the intimacy of studio space. Meeting another's practice, sharing that space together, can create a sense of discomfort. We have to wrestle with this.

EC: Unsettled space, unsettling of habits.

AH: It is hard to delineate and identify the idiosyncrasies and singularities of the human subjects in those interplays and the forces that they generate. Some persistent questions arise for me — does focusing on their figuring in some way diminish the weight of the specific relations in the interaction? How does one deal with the pre-given, the resistant and intransigent elements of all collaboration, which actually gets us, once we identify those, to a different kind of ethos? Non-idealistic. How to talk about stuck-ness, what passes through silence or inertia? One subject often produces the conditions in which their creativity can thrive: a terrain that a subject produces in order to enter and test their own limit conditions, a space where they are individuated. They are transforming themselves in contact with others. But, at the same time the creation of that space delimits the other's space. So, this interests me from an ethical perspective, which is to say that part of the work of collaboration is the recognition and acceptance of that delimitation. This takes us to a founding dimension of ethics: you do not *choose* the other. You must respond to the other that you do not choose. Once one recognises that, then one is in a very different space of contact and relation. What happens when we stop trying to overcome our resistances to each other, and enter a space of acceptance of our differences? I have found for instance, that in sustained collaborative practices, we don't even need to say things to have an articulated or agreed shared sense of what is happening, we just do things with each other. There is a level of implicit activation over longer durations, which creates very dense situations of emergence. To think about these dynamics takes us out of the framework of general eventhood and into a framework that is more about sustained life practices of experimentation.

EC: Within our project we have sustained collaboration, but it is also discontinuous. It never fully reaches a level of sustainable fluidity. By the fifth week, we get close to this condition that you are describing, where it is possible to intuit or be capable of dialogue without words. And then we stop. Through the process of working together and working side-by-side in the Method Lab *something happens*, but the discontinuous element in the project is …

AH: … generative.

EC: It shows up things that, within sustained collaborative practices might not be tangible.

AH: It sounds like you are trying to find a kind of *idiorrhythmy*, as Roland Barthes says in *How to Live Together.*[1] That is a rhythmic of relation that acknowledges the creative necessity of being together and being apart or being alone. Barthes was studying various monastic religious practices of isolation and contemplation. From those ancient forms of separation and communion he asked how one might establish some principles about the rhythms of these forms of experience and learning.

MG: These relationships from subject to subject but also subject to object stretch towards political implications with an ethical-aesthetic dimension, built on the ground of intensely listening — Jean-Luc Nancy speaks about it in the sense of sensory apprehension and the active "holding open of the work"[2] —, of connection with a resonance of humans or materials and the responsibility that comes with that. Materials bring their own dynamics; they might do things that you did not envision them to do. This confronted me with my choice of an ephemeral and less material practice, and my assumption of emptiness as productive. I guess it also points to this dilemma that capitalism confronts us with — how are we dealing with all that stuff that we are accumulating, that doesn't go away and that doesn't disappear. But in the Lab space, materials can transform, turn upside down, spill, dissipate, circulate … not as commodities, but as co-emergent agents.

AH: So this is a political and environmental concern that relates to our basic attitude towards materials, letting go of our control of things, moving towards being in *another relation* to things, more accepting of our equivalence. How one constitutes one's relations to material things and objects, how one thinks and acts in intimacy with them? This is quite a difficult terrain to encounter in collaborative practices.

EC: The process of *becoming material* or the transformation of material necessarily involves the dampening of one's own agency, to give rise to a kind of elevated material agency — there is a collaboration with the material. We have conceived different *species* of figures, for example, differentiating between *Empathetic Figures*, which are predominantly to do with social relations and *Transformative Figures*, which involve more explicit shifts of state. In some respects, the gap between these two groups is the space of ethics. What is the nature of this *being-with*? Or to make this more complex, we could ask: what is the nature of aesthetic enquiry involved in this *being-with*? How is the shaping of social relations a creative enquiry in-and-of itself with an aesthetic agenda, not just in the service of another kind of transformative practice?

AH: It is also very gendered, this investment in sociality and the labour of empathy, the invisible and 'subterranean' transfer of information that is necessary to continue living and living well. It has traditionally fallen to women and has been consigned as a female labour. It is a labour not acknowledged as being of value, and consequently our language for it is impoverished. In one of my recent collaborations with two women artists, Janine Antoni and Anna Halprin, I have been talking about this labour as a 'transgenerational spirited affinity'.[3] More broadly, I have been trying to think these agent-material relations as kinds of infrastructure for art and performance. This counters common concepts of the infrastructural as foundational, technical or material. I am not so interested in the micro-dynamics of emergence, but more in the macro-political significance of these affinities between people, and between people and things, these material engagements across time. When you look at these affinities and their surfacings in a historical perspective they are actually infrastructural. They transform our understandings of ways of making. They are the resource and the potential for new work.

MG: We use the word nano-political for those micro-movements and movement acts, curious how they branch out into society or the wider societal field.[4]

EC: Our *Empathetic Figures* are not exhaustive — we have only named three. The first — *Vibrating Affinity* — involves an intensity of meeting with one other person. There is this 'attunement' to borrow Daniel Stern's term, a process of following and leading, towards a quality of synchronicity.[5] The next figure — *Wavering Convergence* — addresses the dynamic emerging through the triad of our collaboration, where in facing the one you are necessarily turning away from the other. The final figure in this series is the *Figure of Consonance / Dissonance* which opens up the perceptual field further, towards the possibility of other relations, group dynamics. We were reading Emmanuel Levinas — reflecting on the intensity of facing another, and Luce Irigaray in relation to the preservation of the other's strangeness. How to avoid a model of assimilation or equivalence? Within collaboration, how might one allow the other to retain their sense of strangeness, whilst one's own integrity is also allowed to remain? There is a question of integrity and autonomy.

MG: Following Irigaray, this is not a model of relationality aimed at wholeness. You don't expect the other to complete or make you whole — it is a meeting of different qualities.

AH: What strikes me in these delineations is that they inevitably follow the distinctions between the two, the three and the many. So there is a kind of buried pyramid. At each level, what is revealed is that each is founded on the level 'beneath' it. *One is never one*. You are always in relation to some other. In the dyad, you may fantasise that you are not a triad, but the question of how you sustain your openness to the other is actually the question of how you recognise that you are never just two.

There is always the interloper, the third. There are always others in a relation that are profoundly affecting and transforming the course of one's ethical treatment of the relation. One is not just dealing in any case with the other, one is dealing with the *others of the other.* Similarly, in acknowledging the complexities of being three, the triad starts to understand that it is about a multitude of beings and relations and forces that pass through the three. In a way, all of this is about a passage towards the recognition of the many, or of many-ness. So the ethical question is reframed as how to sustain a relation while facing — while remaining open to the strangeness of — the many others, and in the condition of one's own 'many-ness'? To me, this would be *the* collaborative question.

EC: It is also to do with the relationship between making a *commitment to* and being *available for*. How does one commit to someone or something, but at the same time as being receptive to other encounters? How do you remain available?

AH: In the ideal situation the collective body allows for those contractions and expansions whilst retaining its creative consistencies. The struggle of collective labour is the struggle against sovereignty, the struggle against the sovereign individual, or the rooted integrity of the individual's creations, or the sovereignty of the collective itself, because it too can become a sovereign power very quickly. How to create practices that perturb the sovereignty of the collective? How do you attend to that *becoming sovereign* of the collective, in order to forestall or suspend it? The collective itself needs to remain unfinished so that its work — which never fully surfaces — can be taken on by others. These are questions that can also be pursued in terms of pedagogic practices. How do you transmit the imperative to learn rather than specific resolved objects of knowledge? How do you create pedagogic relations with others that do not replicate your aesthetics or values, but are invested in the continuance of epistemological urgencies, dynamic inclinations or qualities in the field of your questioning? So, an *ethics* of transmission.

EC: There is something in the space between ease and difficulty where collaboration emerges. Admittedly, I have previously tended to privilege the sense of difficulty or challenge, however, the idea of ease can have radical potential.

AH: And in the negotiation of those passages between ease and difficulty there is another question for both the individual and the collective: how do you manage inevitable processes of dis-identification whilst still retaining relation?

EC: Difficulty can involve a limit-investigation, to do with the edges, the point at which resistance and antagonism operate. It is frontier-based. However, what can get lost in that limit-experience is a range of experience that is *within range*. In certain visual arts practices, it seems that the privileged forms of social relation are often to do with antagonism, alienation, hostility, violence.

AH: Yes, the predominant model for understanding the value of participatory and social practice is basically an agonistic model. However, what doesn't happen in the *hurt space*, where one is polarised with the other, is the fluidity, multiplicity and complexity of a conversation. As soon as you establish an antagonism, seven or eight other positions or possibilities have fallen away. I don't think that is the optimal situation for transformation and change to happen.

EC: Points of difficulty are not necessarily transformative places, they can often be the places where our positions become reinstated, more fixed. How do you set up conditions in collaborations that are conducive or that give rise to difficult affects in the affirmative sense, which is different from simply making things difficult?

MG: I make a commitment to put myself in service of supporting the vitality of the process. This can be difficult or easy, painful or pleasurable, but it needs to keep moving. It is just something that is in *movement*.

AH: You might mutually decide that the thing you

all need is to press the collective conditions into a space of difficulty in order for them to be more fruitful. I guess it's always a case of trying to identify your communal reliances and asking how do they enliven the situation in its potential, and also how do they securitise, deaden, sanitise or depotentialise things?

EC: Since our *Empathetic Figures* explore forms of connection, one could question whether connection has been privileged above discontinuity, whether there is a value system of relations asserted through this investigation? In the recent *Documents of Contemporary Art* book on *Ethics*, the editor, Walead Beshty, states how historically the visual arts have some difficulty with practices that take the social as their material, because there is a lack of criteria for how to judge them.[6] Do you judge them on the basis of 'good relations' being made? Through what means can you make an aesthetic judgement on the nature of relations that have been established therein?

AH: Or not even aesthetic, but social and political judgements. How do you measure social transformation? In what time frame? What *is* the social good? Hugely contentious. I am interested in the idea of connection being privileged above disconnection or discontinuity, because it takes us to something I recognise in performance aesthetics over the last forty or fifty years: the relationality of non-relation. When one sees in a work the coexistence of things or elements in a world that cannot speak to each other, but nonetheless remain 'together'. I am interested in what can be learnt, in terms of aesthetics and ecology, from the coexistence of things that aren't in a supportive relation, aren't in a meaningful, transformative dialogue, but that do have a sustained 'incompatibility'.

MG: In a way you are articulating an aesthetics based on ethics, exploring an alternative paradigm, which feels to be an opening, a turning towards an ecology of radical coexistence, a differentiated articulation and composition of a space of immanence that is up for exploration.

AH: Well, the danger with privileging connection over disconnection is that you end up with sterile harmony. What you want to sustain in ethics or aesthetics is movement, change, friction and differentiation. That is what is happening in the social reality. You can't falsely produce static differences, which to me would be the tendency to jump to definitive antagonisms. As soon as you are in the antagonistic relation, you can't attend to the real differences that are in play, because you have actually consolidated those differences into fixed points.

MG: I wonder what would be the role of hospitality in such an aesthetics? Maybe it is not privileging connection, but rather the privileging of making oneself a space of hospitality for meeting other others, be it subjects or objects or other kinds of beings. Maybe it would even be the privileging of the opening up towards, as a reaching out, an actualising act. It is not even a site or a space in these kinds of territorial terms … it is more a deterritorialising practice.

AH: All of that is really important to an ethics of hosting, but the thinking on hospitality often emphasises the art of the host rather than the guest. So something of the mutuality of the situation is lost. There would be another ethics of being a good guest, with a slightly different set of questions. Hospitality tends to get figured through the terms of the one who has control of the real estate. Those that have a certain privilege. Why is it that *I* am hosting *you*? And, what is it that gives me the power to think of myself as your host? Then the whole host-guest relation is somehow in question. If we think hosting from a communist or non-anthropocentric perspective, we have to ask why is it that the host thinks of this place as *their* place? Why is the earth the human estate? It doesn't belong to us at all. So it seems hard to undo the perception of ownership of a place, from or within which I admit others, decide *who* is admissible. In creative practice at least, I'd rather ask how to be a good guest in a place that no one owns or has a prior claim to.

EC: The implications of how we think this *self-other* dynamic is interesting, because if I think about the rhetoric of opening oneself up to the other it is sometimes presented almost like opening the doors of one's house in a way. What would it be to conceive of the self not as a place that can be opened or that you have possession of? I don't know the etymology of hospitality, but maybe there is another word like communion which is perhaps more about reciprocity, a shared responsibility, where hospitality isn't gifted from one to the other, but is co-produced?

MG: The etymology of hospitality is linked to *hostis*, which is actually the enemy.[7]

EC: Hospital … hostage … somewhere between taking care and taking possession. I think that this notion of hospitality relates to questions that we have been exploring in relation to opening up our process to wider publics. And even the dilemma of what those 'wider publics' might be called: 'audience' does not feel sufficient. We have used the term 'wit(h)nessing'.[8]

MG: It is related back to Nancy's understanding of *being-with*. We were interested in this wordplay and a semantic shift between witness and wit(h)ness. There is the silent 'h' that makes all the difference, also being a German native speaker, the witness is predominantly associated to Holocaust or trials.

EC: Developed from the attention practices that we have cultivated within the project, we became interested in what you need to do in order to prepare yourself to be a witness or a wit(h)ness? How do you prepare to be the guest? Conventional cultural frameworks or protocols don't ask people to prepare when they come to an event. How do you prepare for an event?

AH: So you get into a condition where art making is also about spectatorial training. Creating a specific set of conditions for reception, which are also then rolled out as ways of being in the world or broader practices of attending to art. In terms of aesthetics, every good work is to some extent doing that, right? In the field of Participatory Art, I very much like what Paul Ramirez Jonas says — that he wants to ensure that the decision *not* to participate in his work is *as meaningful* as the decision to participate.[9] So, there is a moment or a process within the work, where the work is attending to its refusal or its rejection, deploying tactics to manage and make resonant that fall away from attention. In my own work this question has been posed most vitally in terms of performance in museal spaces, where the practice and conventions of attendance are based on perambulation: the 'audience' can walk away at any moment in time. So you have this spectator, who is highly mobile and who is also experiencing, receiving and speculating in general cultural conditions, which have now become highly distracted and accelerated. Very few people expect to attend to something for longer than a few minutes in order to have understood or have taken something from it. Then they are going to move on to the next thing. For artists working in that context, you often have this tension between an invited designated public for the work and another public, which is the public of the passer-by, the unbidden spectator. Then the question is how do you navigate those two quite different modes of attention to your work at the same time, how do you hook passers-by into more focused relations? I became fascinated in my recent curatorial work with these conditions of difficulty, which have some real questions within them about the affective convening of social space. One other thing I have noticed working across many different durational forms of performance — works that extend beyond normative institutional timeframes of reception — is that these durations create within their witness the desire to attend in a mirrored duration. You often see this in longer durational works: a small army of willing durational spectators. There is something about the excessive frame or impossible aspiration of endurance that pulls people into its spell.

EC: Within our work, there has been a desire to raise the performativity of things, and by that I mean objects … so that everything becomes an actor in a sense, privileged agencies in space. However, I was curious, because when you use the word ecological, it enables a way of thinking about things in other terms.

AH: Yes, because as soon as you get into this situation, assuming that you have the subject power over that thing to enable its agency to be raised or seen by others like you, you may have reiterated the problem. All things are actant. It is just that we find it hard to see that, given the duration in which they are actant. So, the duration of the agency of this table is less perceptible within the human duration. How to have a situation of its perceptibility, without us acting upon or over the thing?

EC: Rather than raising everything to the level of human agency, duration or performativity, there might be something to do with dampening or quietening our own habitual ways of doing things.

MG: When compositional sensibility is underway, stumbling over the phenomenon of a quality of listening to objects as subjects can introduce unprecedented experiences of togetherness. I think of deep listening practices in acoustics, navigating the exploratory space of being-with. It is not about tuning up or down your attention or our acting on things, but more tuning into a receptive quality of resonance.

AH: New materialism has had such a profound influence on contemporary critical thought and discourse, and is finding its way into aesthetic practices. No doubt in part because of the broader pressures on human consciousness of catastrophic planetary conditions. But I notice, for instance, that in drawing attention to the status of matter, its vibrant life or its agency, artists are inclined to choose materials within which there is already a *perceptible vibrancy*: things which are readily mobilised, changing or less substantive, because they are the ones easiest to agitate and ascribe actant qualities to. It is a little like the reliance in contemporary performance practices on slow time actions, as a means to re-tune attention and create an immediate feeling of significance. These are surface moves that quickly become tropes. Perhaps what I am trying to get at is the way that aesthetic choices can enter into a kind of subservience to readily circulating concepts. Something of the integrity of felt relations between artist, form, material and viewer gets lost.

EC: Dieter Mersch talks about how discursivity and methodology have emerged from theory and from science to be the dominant modes through which we construct episteme. He said that neither of these is suited to artistic practice; rather, the way that artistic — or perhaps even aesthetic — knowledge reveals itself is through *showing*. In some senses, we are interested in *showing*, perhaps even in making visible, the working-with theory done in an artistic sense. It is something to do with having the books to hand and engaging with theory as a tangible material, but not necessarily in the direction of discursivity. What does it mean to get the books out, to be wrestling with ideas, but not necessarily through close reading, but rather through a *material engagement*? There can also be a rather conservative position, which says that artists shouldn't engage in a certain theoretical domain. There is something about engaging with this sort of material that feels fundamental to our research practice.

AH: I have always been intrigued by bookshelves and the writing process: the presence of unopened books in relation to the act of writing and in particular, the silent presence of an unread text in the writer's labour. You must have had that moment, when you are stalled or frozen facing the screen, you are in a fog or a knot of concepts that you cannot untangle, and your eye goes straight to the place on the bookshelf where the answer is? Some kind of attuning to the transmissions contained within a volume, not taking place through signification or reading. So, tracing the place of material relations in the work of intuition.

MG: This applies also for encounters with people. There are those dynamics of maturing when you can — are ready to meet or re-meet — a person. Those kind of morphogenetic fields, that we are navigating on an everyday level, but also in the endeavour of trying to make sense of the world that comes to me most intensely in art practice.

AH: One thought I find useful and important in terms of any creative relation is that its utility is not to be found *now.* If there is something in a material relation that is forceful, it will recur or be made manifest at a later time. Radical impulses, even if they are suppressed, underrated or marginalised in specific ways, will have their resurgence. Just as things that are unleashed and articulated through you, sent off into the world, will have many other lives. They often come back to you much later in barely recognisable forms.

MG: There is something to be said for being at the margins. I think it really gives you another range of possibilities to not be at the centre of attention.

EC: There is also something in this discussion in relation to untranslatability. Admittedly, there is a dilemma in our project, at the heart of trying to translate the untranslatable. There is the possibility of complicity in making visible the thing that is normally not seen, in that once visible there is the capacity for it to be captured and commodified, especially through a discursive framework, which is more exchangeable in some respects.

MG: We were talking a bit about the way in which artistic research accelerates that tendency, the surplus that gets produced in the artistic-discursive field.

EC: One of the modes of 'writing', for lack of a better term, that we have been using in our project is that of recording our conversations and then using distillations of the transcripts to produce 'texts', mining the material for sense that was not tangible at the time, but later emerges as being important. On the one hand, this practice involves a certain kind of depersonalisation so the 'I' isn't the one that is authoring. But actually it is also a move towards an inter-subjective position, where the tone and nature of the language constructed emerges in the gaps between the persons speaking.

AH: So when you de-personalise your relation to a material, you come into contact with the impersonal, which is common and connective. If you can recognise or identify the impersonal conditions in a situation — within which you are experiencing things personally — you gain a different access to others, or others have a different access to you.

EC: Conversation can create the conditions for a certain kind of co-emergent thinking. There is something in that space of conversation that for me is aesthetic: conversation is an aesthetic terrain, a kind of aesthetic production.

AH: Yes, at its best you are in an *event of relation*, which is also an event of new thought. It's the birth of new thought in the world. You don't produce it, it happens through you. Jonathan Burrows has a great phrase for this in relation to the history of expressivity in dance; he says, "I am not interested in what it is that I can express. But, rather in submitting myself to a field of expression."[10] On one level this idea de-centres the expressive creative subject. Expression isn't something that is emergent from you, it is actually something ongoing anyway, that you allow to pass through you. Of course, something of you is then disclosed, which is not you, but somehow *more* you.

EC: And this I think feels very tangible in a conversation practice. Maybe there are certain things that you *want* to say … to a certain extent, they are rehearsed already or known, and then there are these *other things* that have quite a different dynamic.

AH: Perhaps these sayings have always been there, even though you have never said them before. They emerge in the event of relation. There is a strange immemorial quality to this kind of saying. It feels like you have always known it. It was always part of you; there, waiting to be said. At the same time, it is radically new. The pre-existent dimension of the new, which lets us know that it is an *otherwise* transmission: one coming from elsewhere.

EC: That is also *life* in a way, where you give over to life, in its most vibrant sense?

AH: Yes, that is life.

MG: It is also risky. There is no liveness without risk in the sense of constructive self-affirmation that we are practising by dedicating our time, energy and love to what we are doing. But it also speaks of an enormous amount of embedded trust.

EC: Risk in its most subtle and nuanced form, because I think that sometimes there is the idea that risk …

MG: … must be spectacular.

EC: Those subtler forms of risk are interesting, especially the ones that involve a *letting go*. Receptive forms of risk rather than active forms of risk, if that makes sense. I find them intriguing in the context of what we have been exploring. A different attitude to risk. Risk is often associated with spontaneity and action, danger and stepping out rather than a practice of opening and allowing in.

MG: Again, it is quite gendered I would say.

EC: Yes, it has the mark of the adventurer or explorer or the frontier-finder.

AH: Mundane heroism.

---

1) Roland Barthes, *How to Live Together: Novelistic Simulations of Some Everyday Spaces*, New York: Columbia University Press, 2013.

2) Jean-Luc Nancy, *Listening*, (Trans.) Charlotte Mandell, New York: Fordham University Press, 2007.

3) Cf. Hugo Glendinning and Adrian Heathfield (Dirs. and Eds.), *Spirit Labour*, 2016.

4) Nanopolitics group, *Nanopolitics Handbook*, Brooklyn: Minor Compositions, 2014. 'Nanofied' — between attention to the little (but not belittled) details (the word's root can be traced back to Greek *nanos*, 'a dwarf', but also *nana*, a child's word for 'grandmother' or, sometimes, 'nurse') and its nursing and development towards meaningful acts in the world. In our context we think of nanofied meaning as focused attention to the micro-particulars of artistic gestures (bodily-kinesthetic, verbal-linguistic, visual-spatial).

5) Daniel Stern, *Forms of Vitality: Exploring Dynamic Experience in Psychology, the Arts, Psychotherapy and Development*, Oxford and New York: Oxford University Press, 2010.

6) Walead Beshty, *Ethics*, London: Whitechapel Gallery, 2015.

7) Hospitality means the 'act of being hospitable', from Latin *hospitalitas* 'friendliness to guests', from *hospes* 'guest; host'. However, the etymology of the word 'guest' has a forked path as exactly those reciprocal duties of hospitality or a mutual exchange relationship also holds the potential for both options: strangers can be potential enemies (from Latin *hostis*) as well as guests.

8) → *Practices of Wit(h)nessing.*

9) www.paulramirezjonas.com

10) www.jonathanburrows.info

METHOD LAB:

POROUS BOUNDARIES

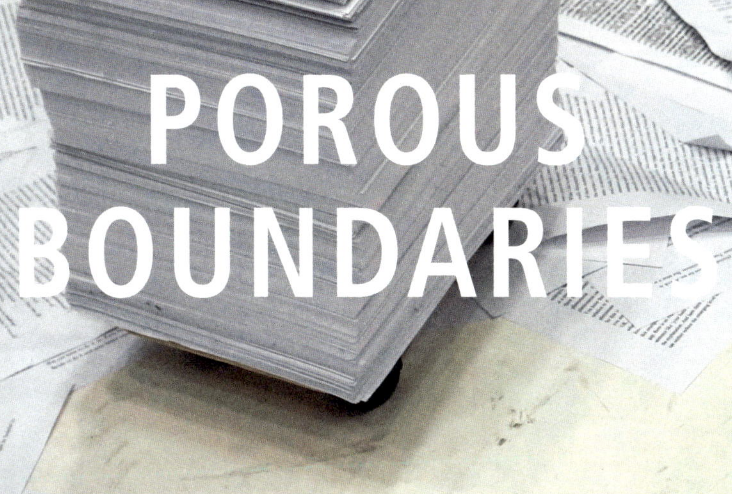

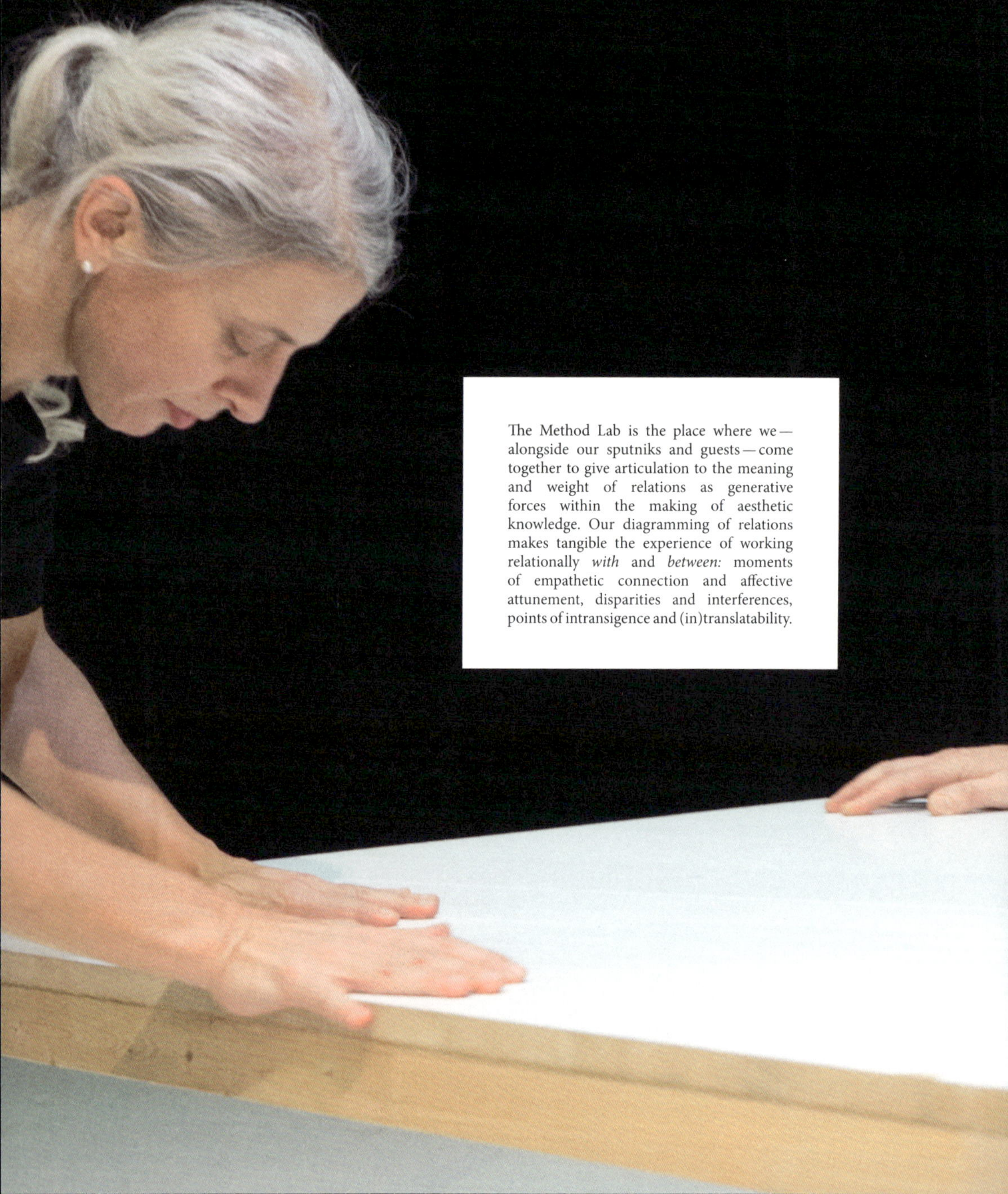

The Method Lab is the place where we—alongside our sputniks and guests—come together to give articulation to the meaning and weight of relations as generative forces within the making of aesthetic knowledge. Our diagramming of relations makes tangible the experience of working relationally *with* and *between:* moments of empathetic connection and affective attunement, disparities and interferences, points of intransigence and (in)translatability.

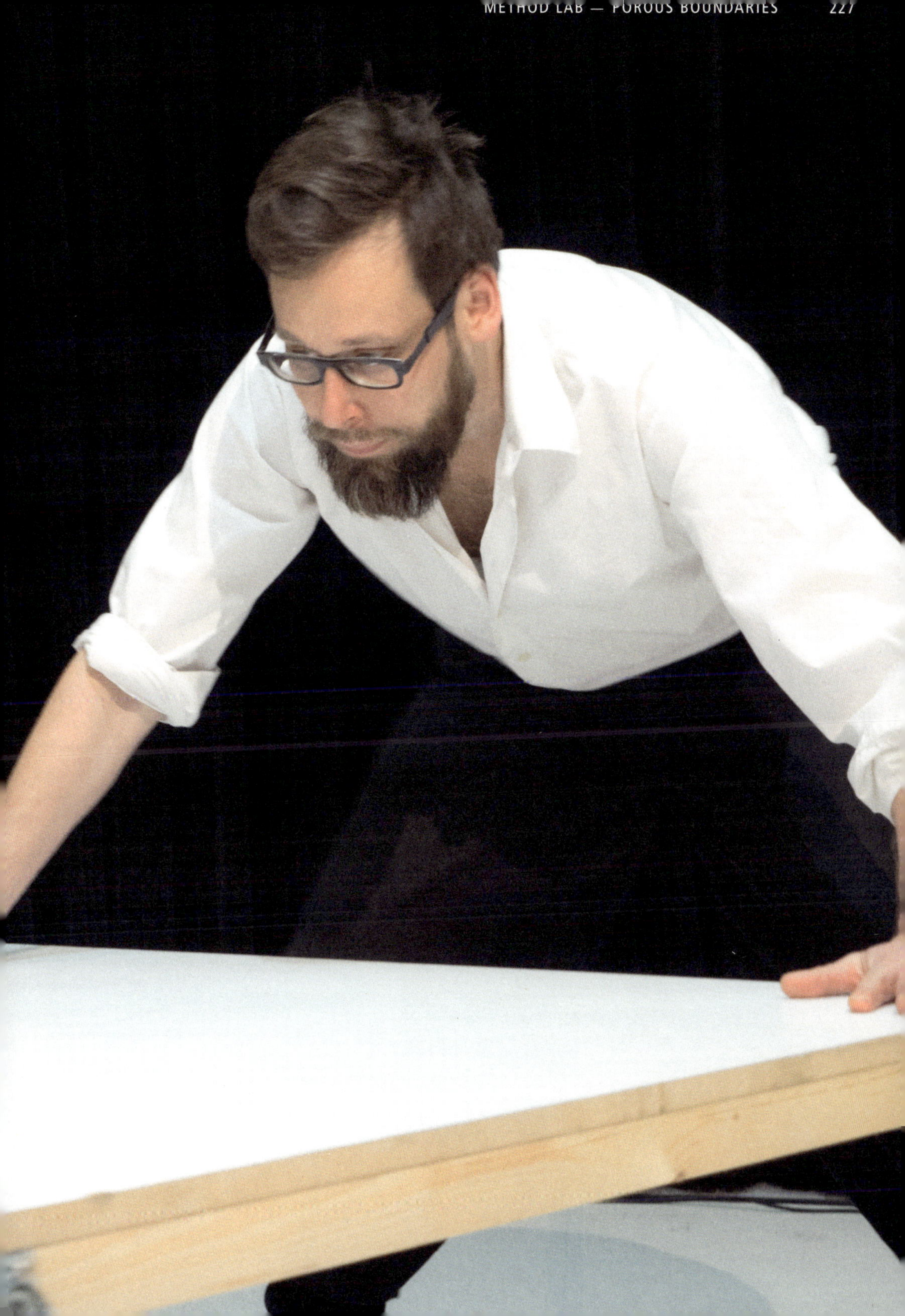

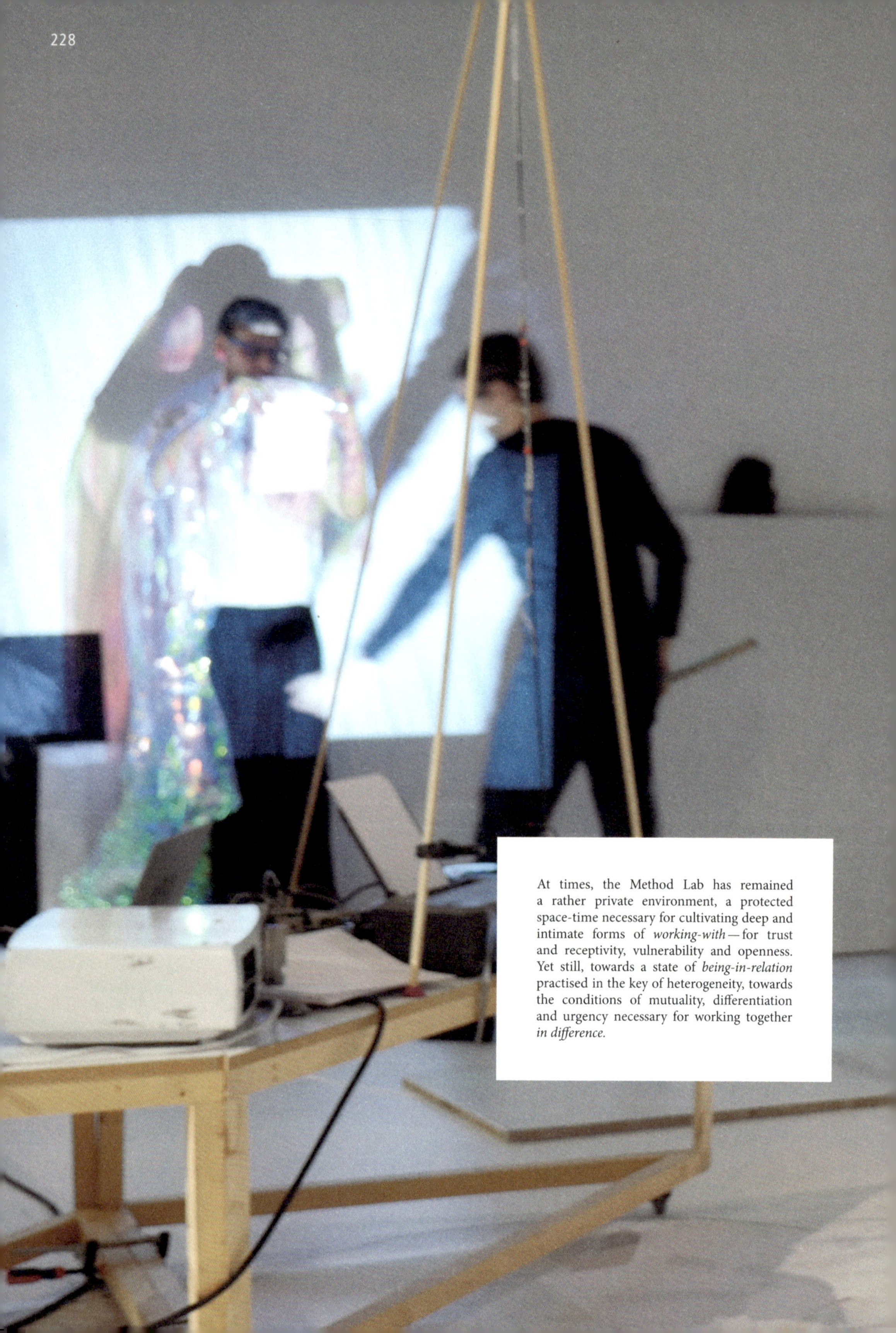

At times, the Method Lab has remained a rather private environment, a protected space-time necessary for cultivating deep and intimate forms of *working-with*—for trust and receptivity, vulnerability and openness. Yet still, towards a state of *being-in-relation* practised in the key of heterogeneity, towards the conditions of mutuality, differentiation and urgency necessary for working together *in difference*.

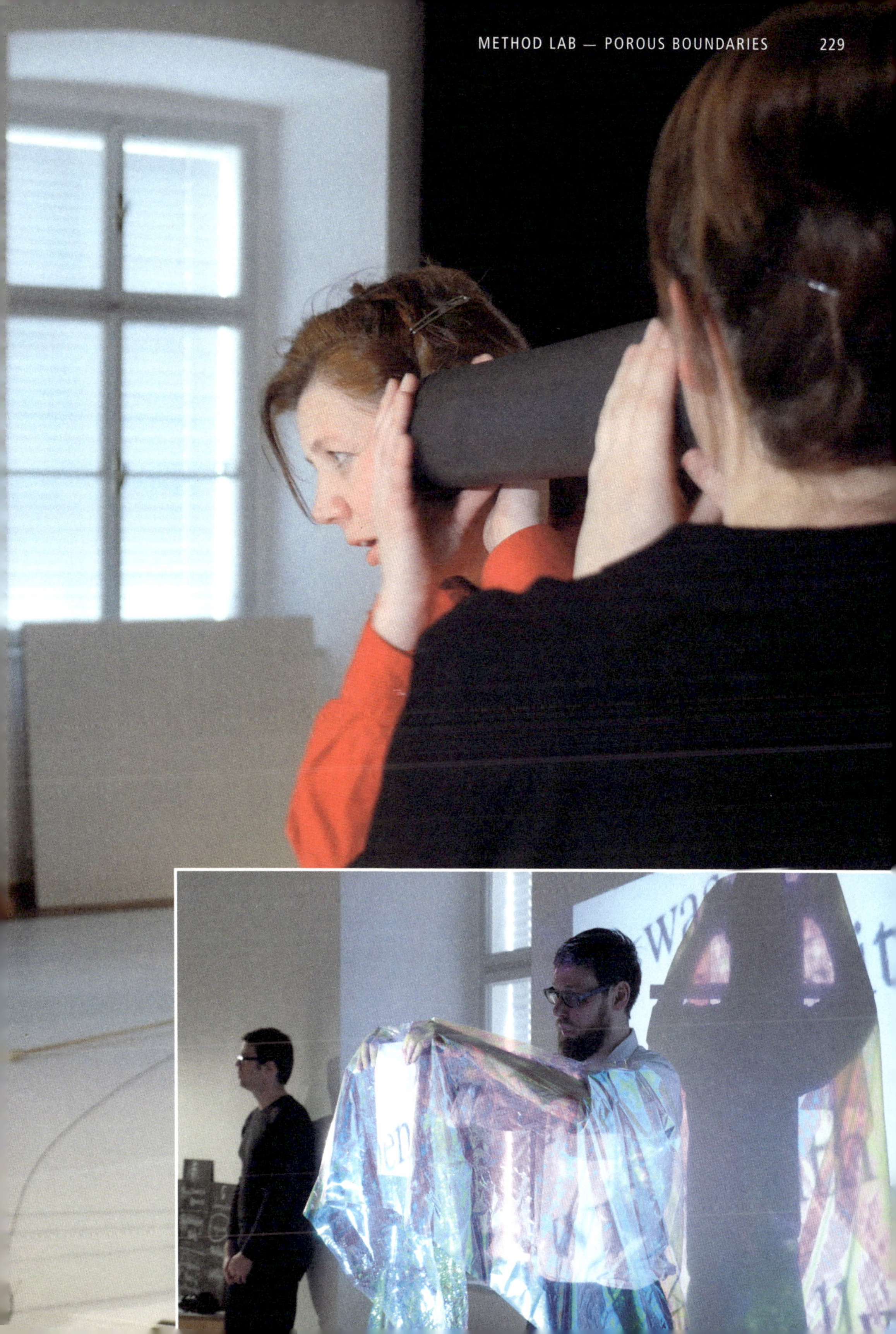

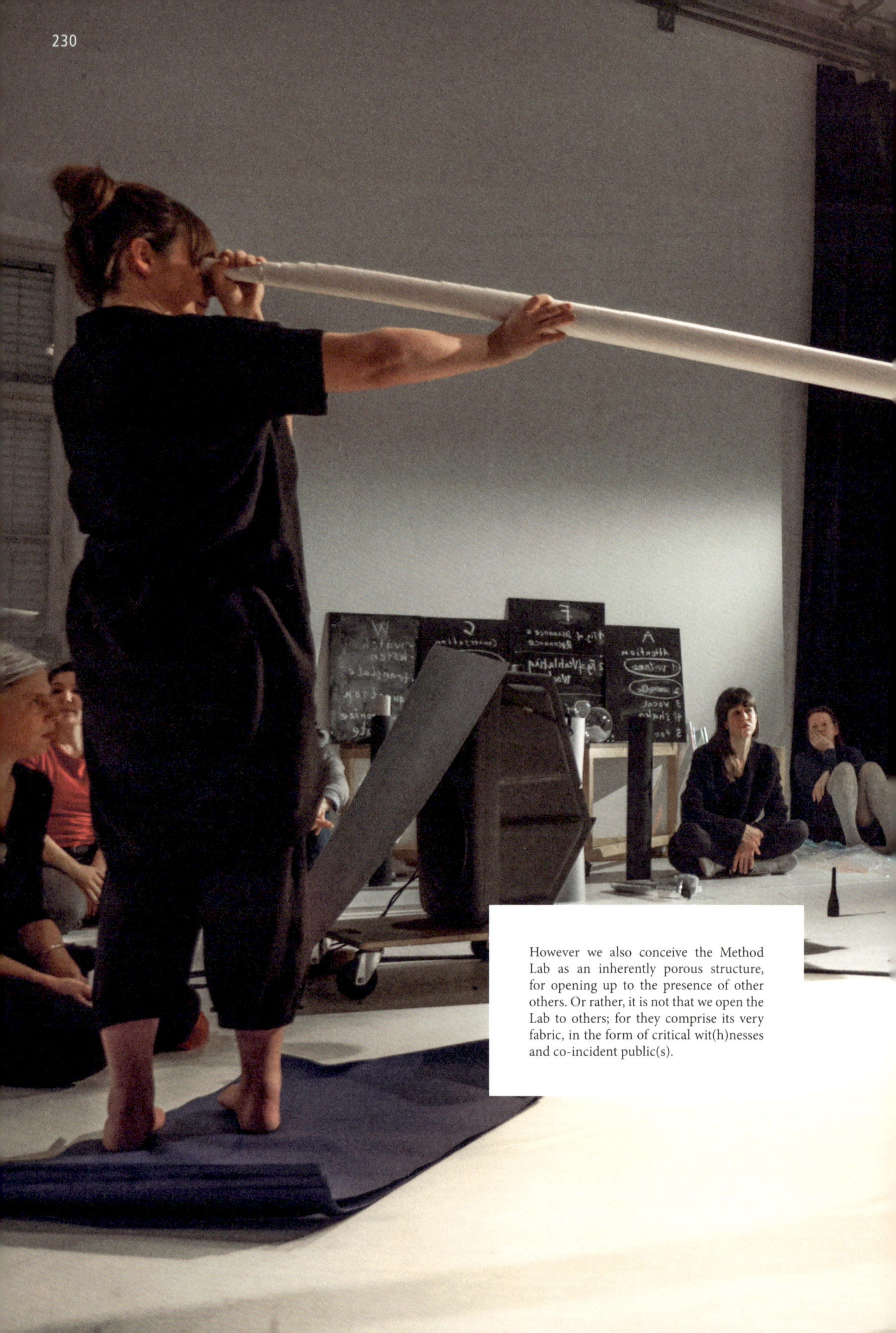

However we also conceive the Method Lab as an inherently porous structure, for opening up to the presence of other others. Or rather, it is not that we open the Lab to others; for they comprise its very fabric, in the form of critical wit(h)nesses and co-incident public(s).

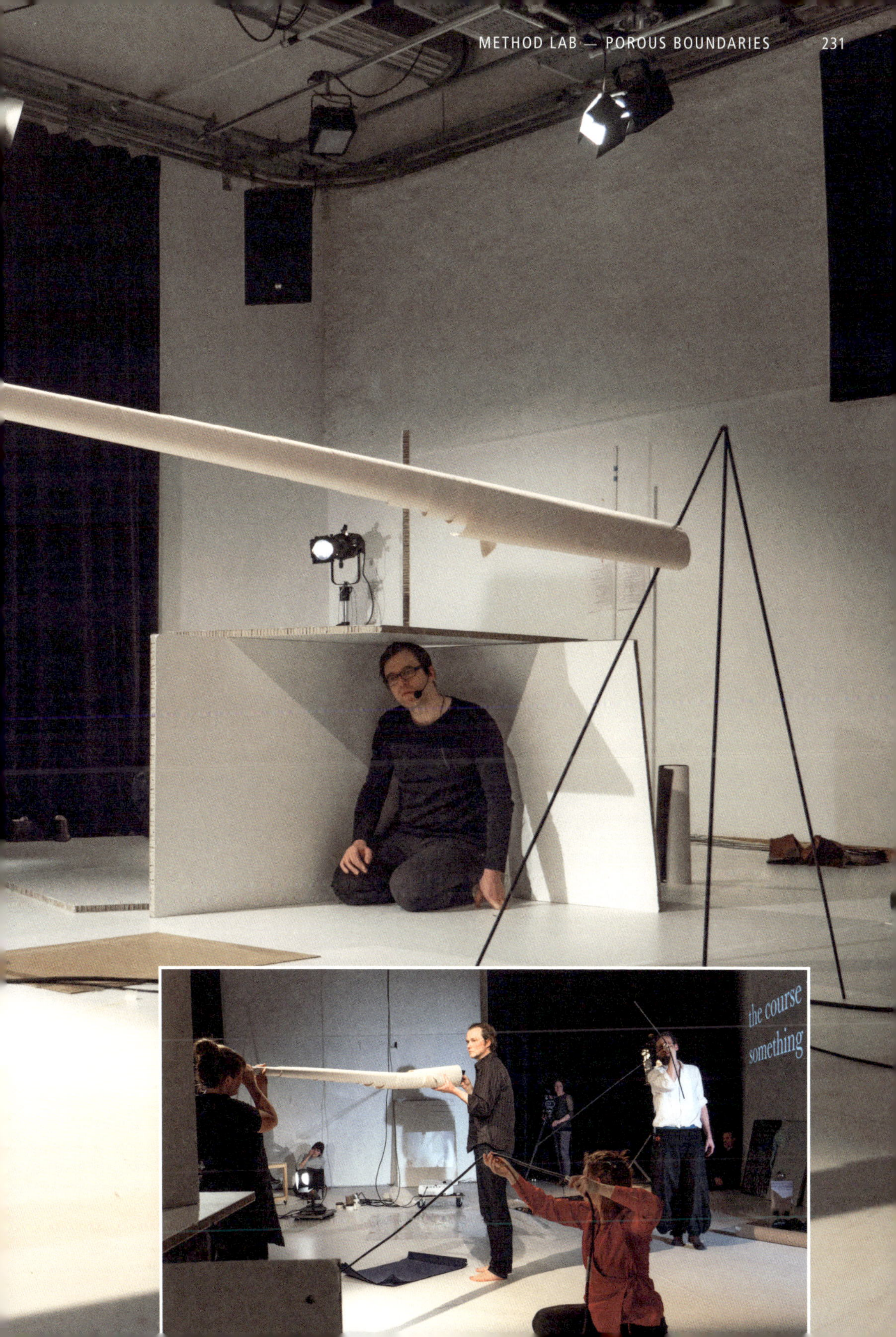
the course
something

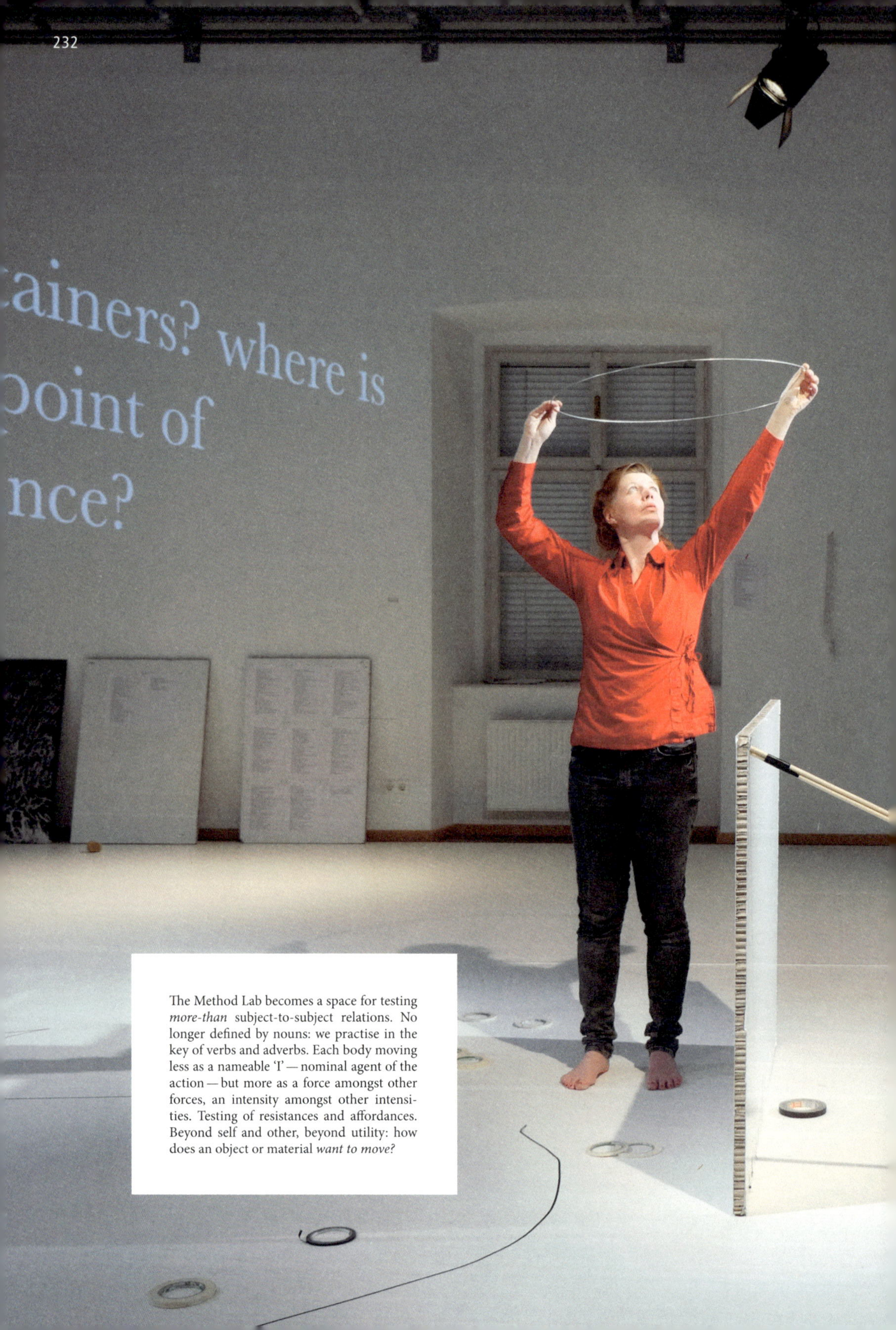

The Method Lab becomes a space for testing *more-than* subject-to-subject relations. No longer defined by nouns: we practise in the key of verbs and adverbs. Each body moving less as a nameable 'I' — nominal agent of the action — but more as a force amongst other forces, an intensity amongst other intensities. Testing of resistances and affordances. Beyond self and other, beyond utility: how does an object or material *want to move?*

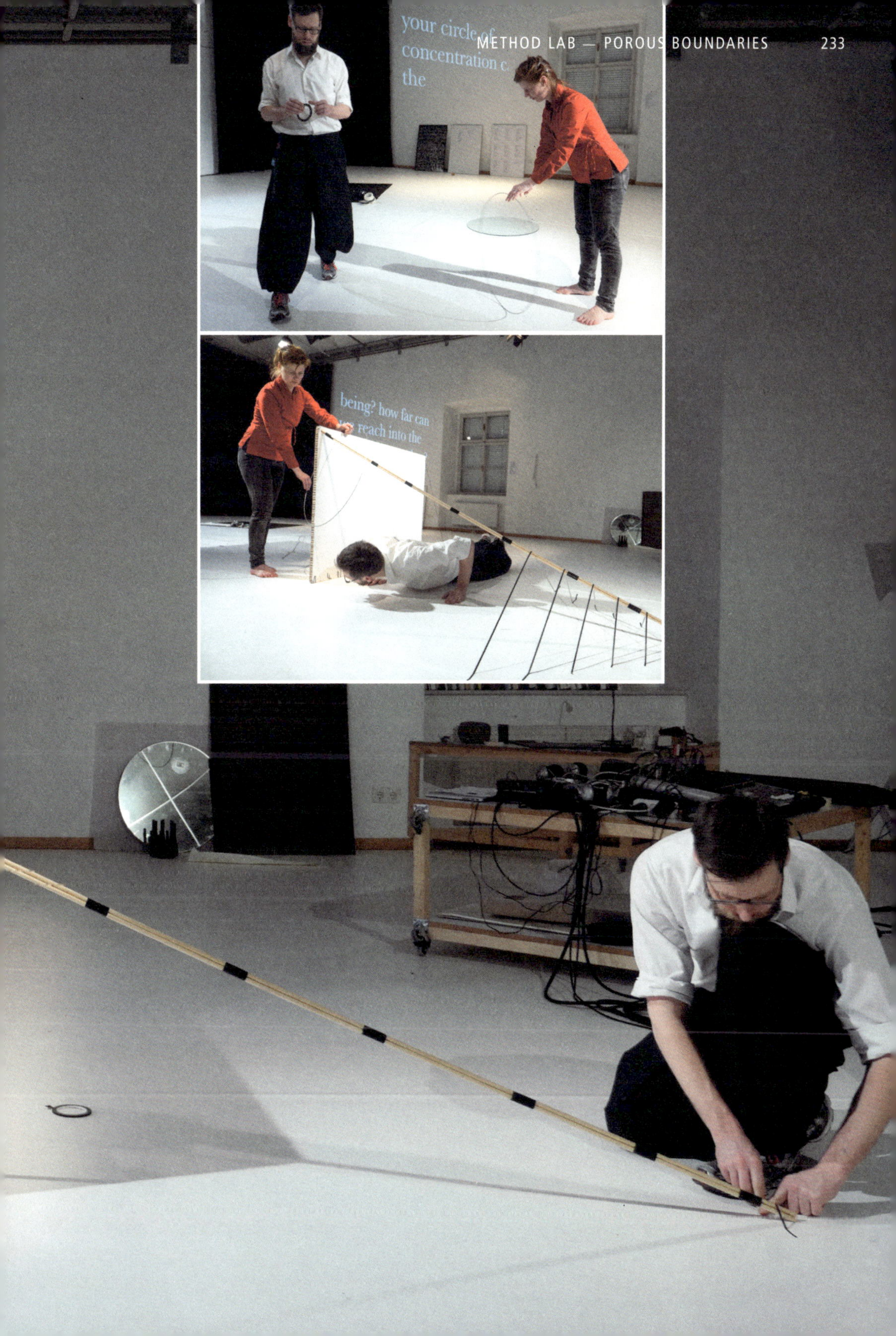
your circle of
concentration c
the
being? how far can
reach into the

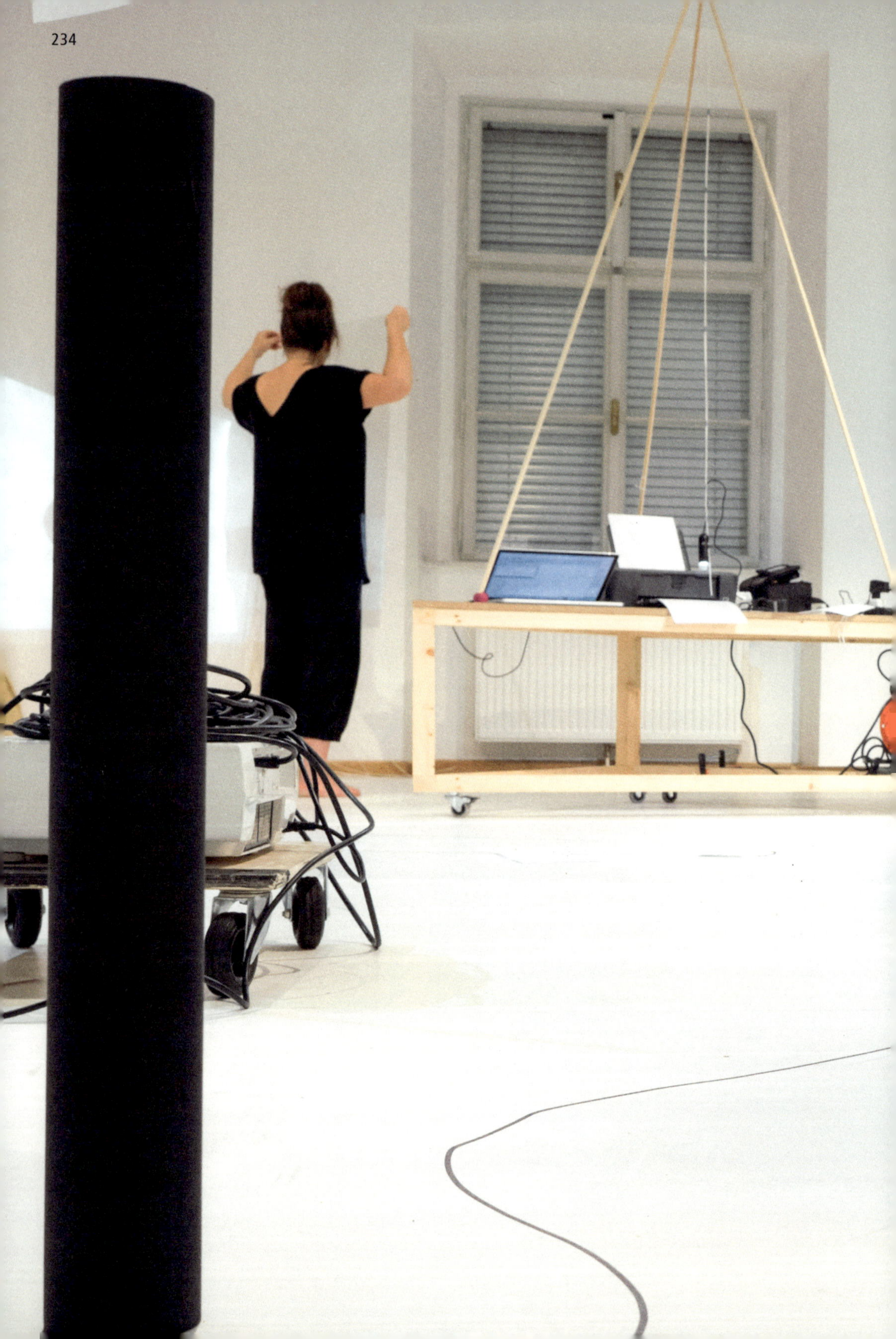

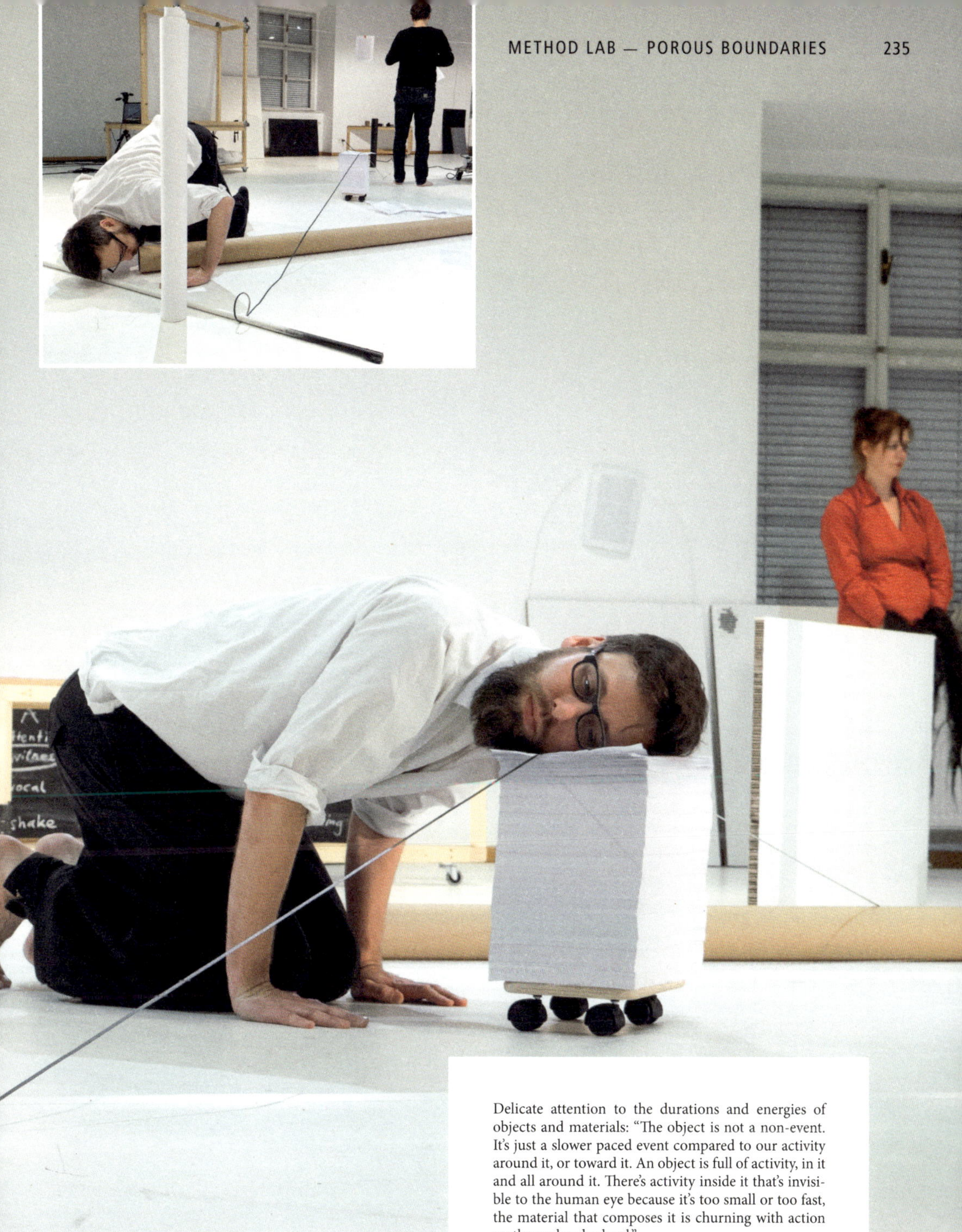

Delicate attention to the durations and energies of objects and materials: "The object is not a non-event. It's just a slower paced event compared to our activity around it, or toward it. An object is full of activity, in it and all around it. There's activity inside it that's invisible to the human eye because it's too small or too fast, the material that composes it is churning with action on the molecular level."

Brian Massumi, in Hugo Glendinning and Adrian Heathfield (Dirs. and Eds.), *No Such Thing as Rest: A Walk with Brian Massumi*, 2013, p. 4.

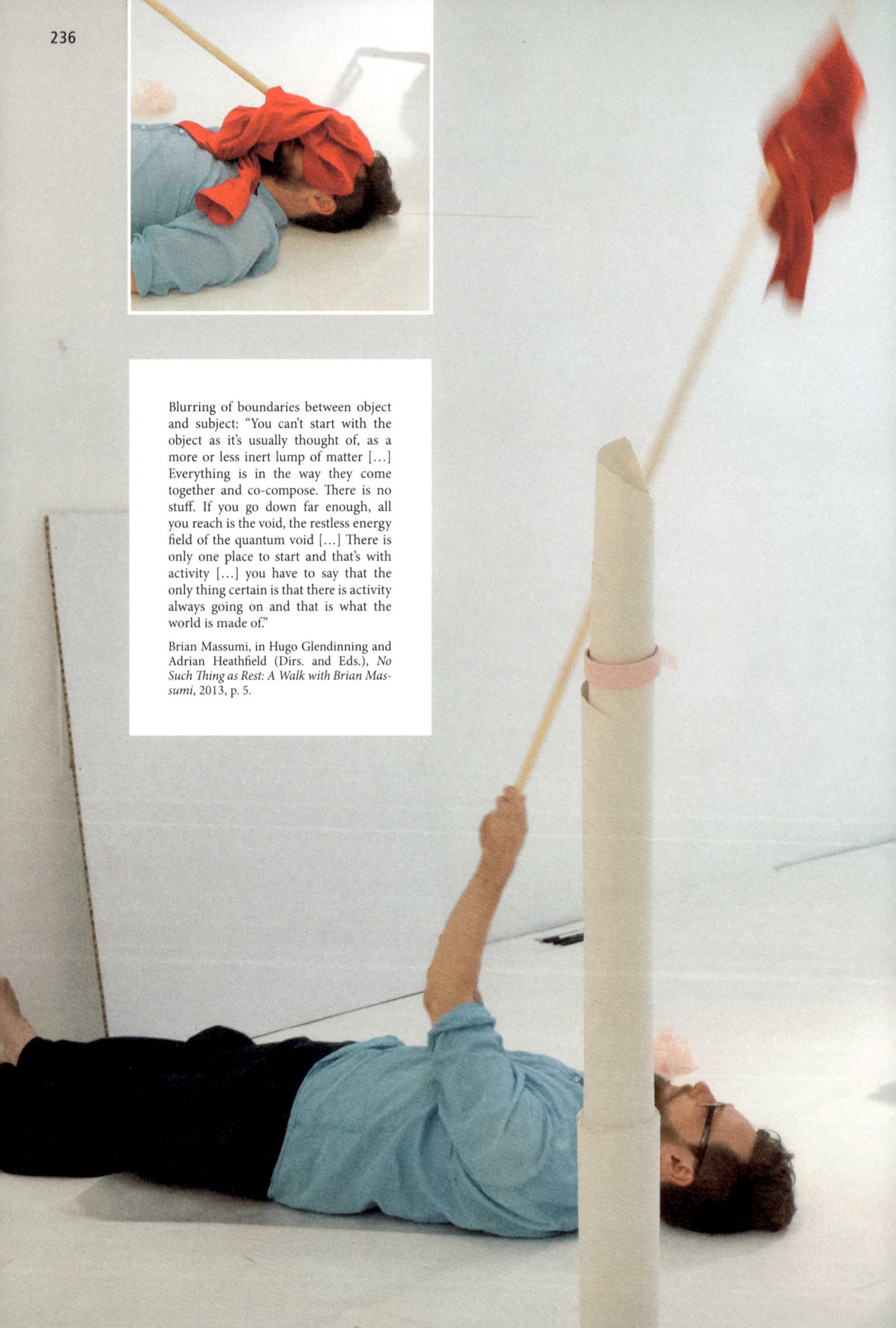

Blurring of boundaries between object and subject: "You can't start with the object as it's usually thought of, as a more or less inert lump of matter […] Everything is in the way they come together and co-compose. There is no stuff. If you go down far enough, all you reach is the void, the restless energy field of the quantum void […] There is only one place to start and that's with activity […] you have to say that the only thing certain is that there is activity always going on and that is what the world is made of."

Brian Massumi, in Hugo Glendinning and Adrian Heathfield (Dirs. and Eds.), *No Such Thing as Rest: A Walk with Brian Massumi*, 2013, p. 5.

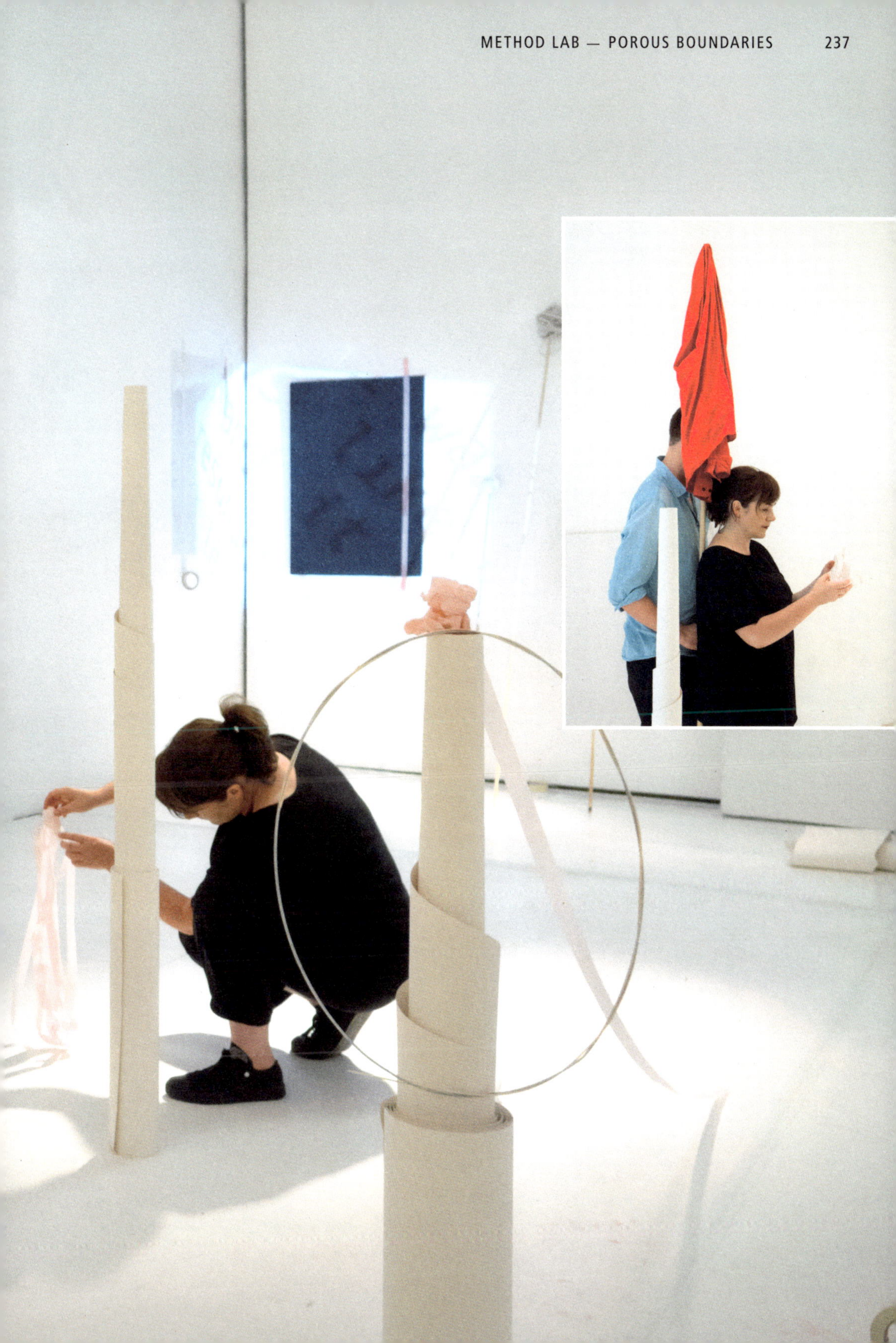

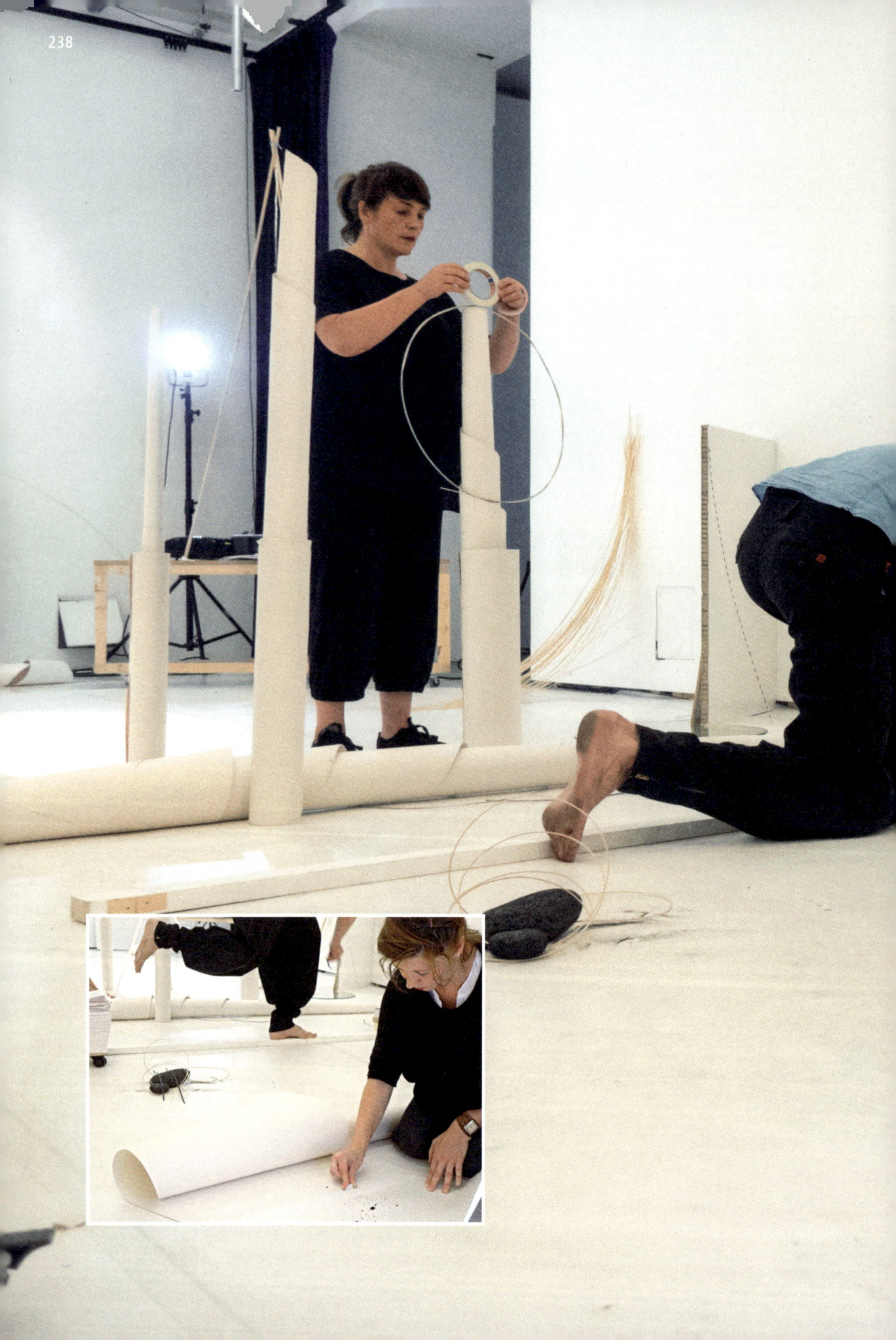

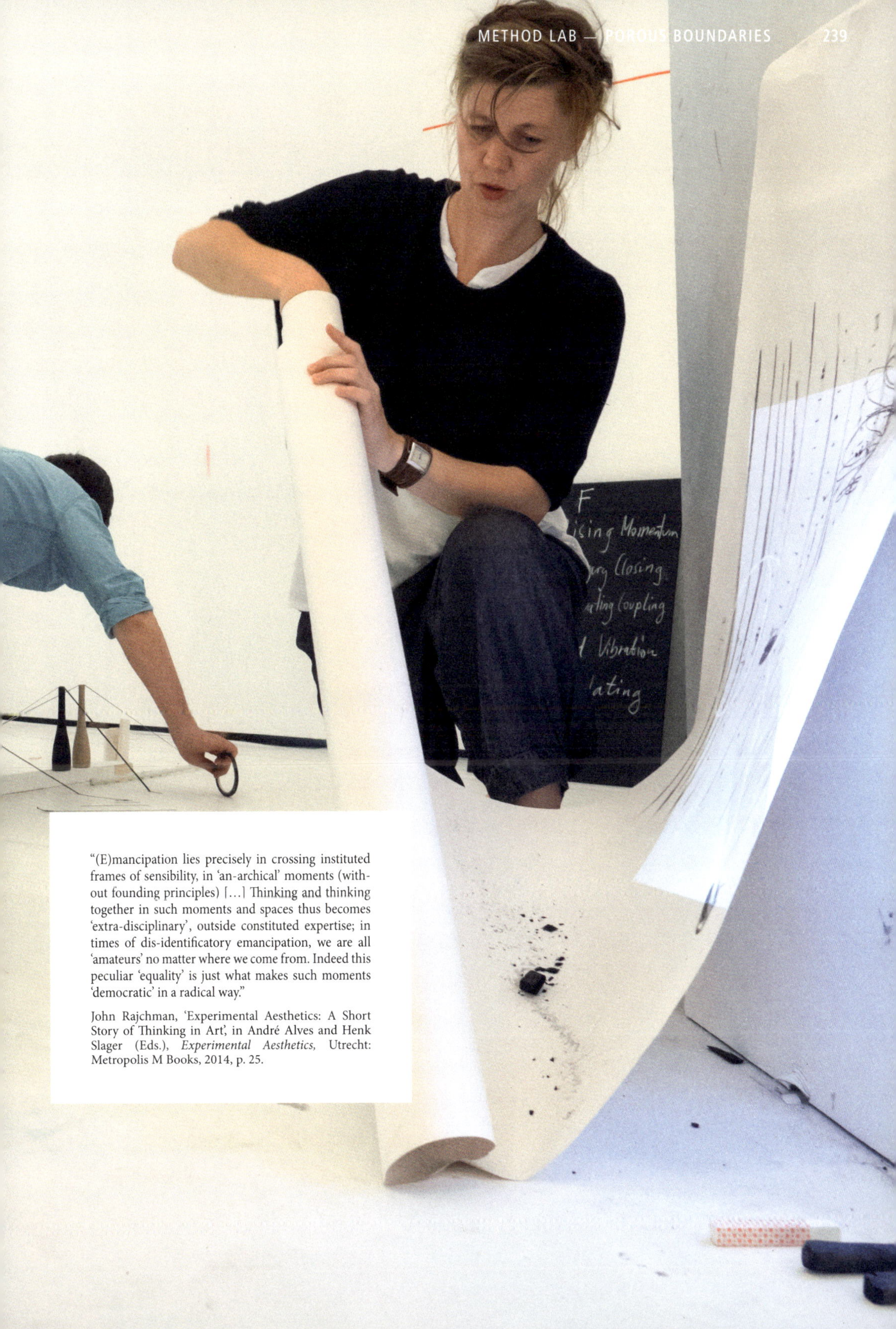

"(E)mancipation lies precisely in crossing instituted frames of sensibility, in 'an-archical' moments (without founding principles) […] Thinking and thinking together in such moments and spaces thus becomes 'extra-disciplinary', outside constituted expertise; in times of dis-identificatory emancipation, we are all 'amateurs' no matter where we come from. Indeed this peculiar 'equality' is just what makes such moments 'democratic' in a radical way."

John Rajchman, 'Experimental Aesthetics: A Short Story of Thinking in Art', in André Alves and Henk Slager (Eds.), *Experimental Aesthetics*, Utrecht: Metropolis M Books, 2014, p. 25.

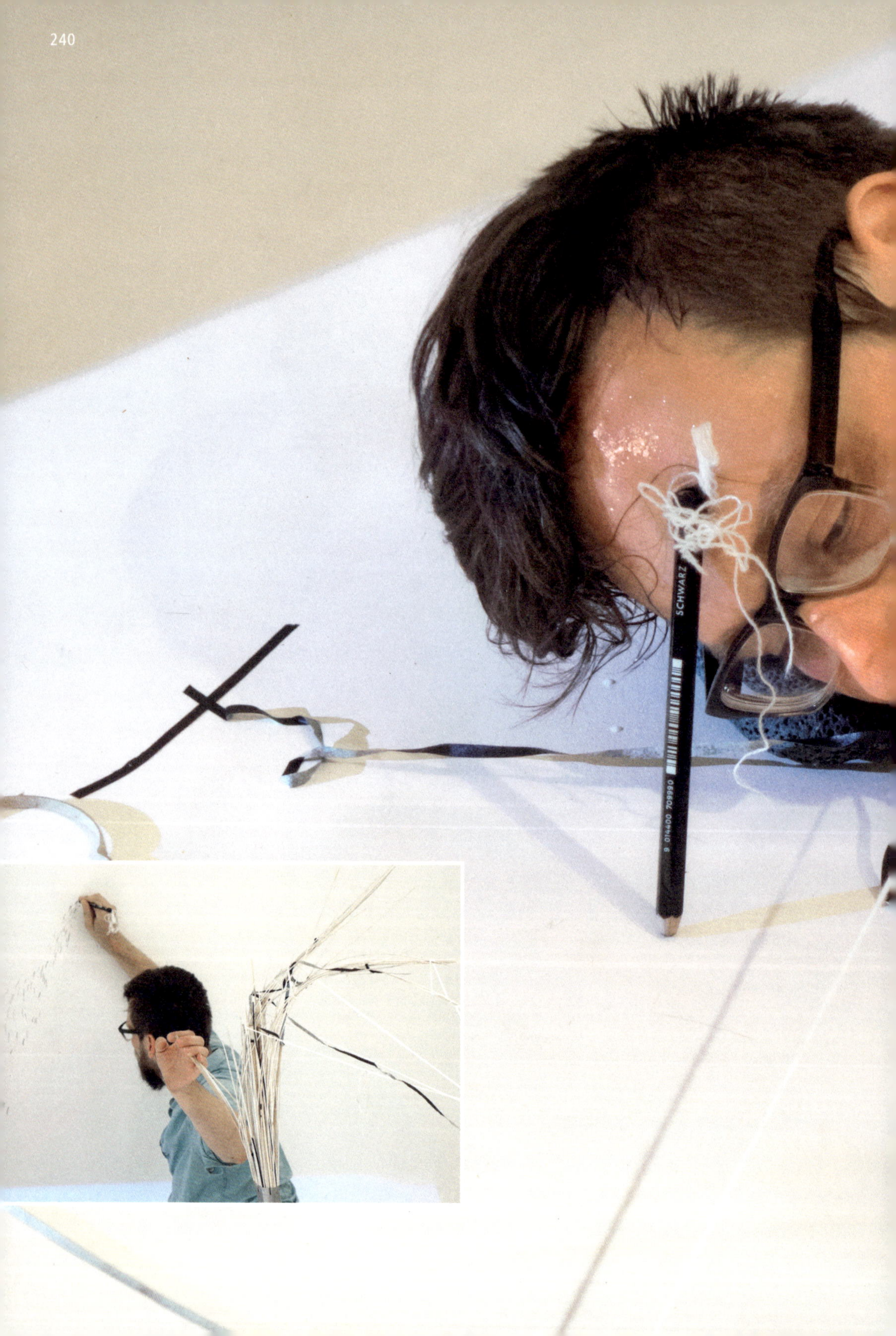
SCHWARZ
9 014400 709990

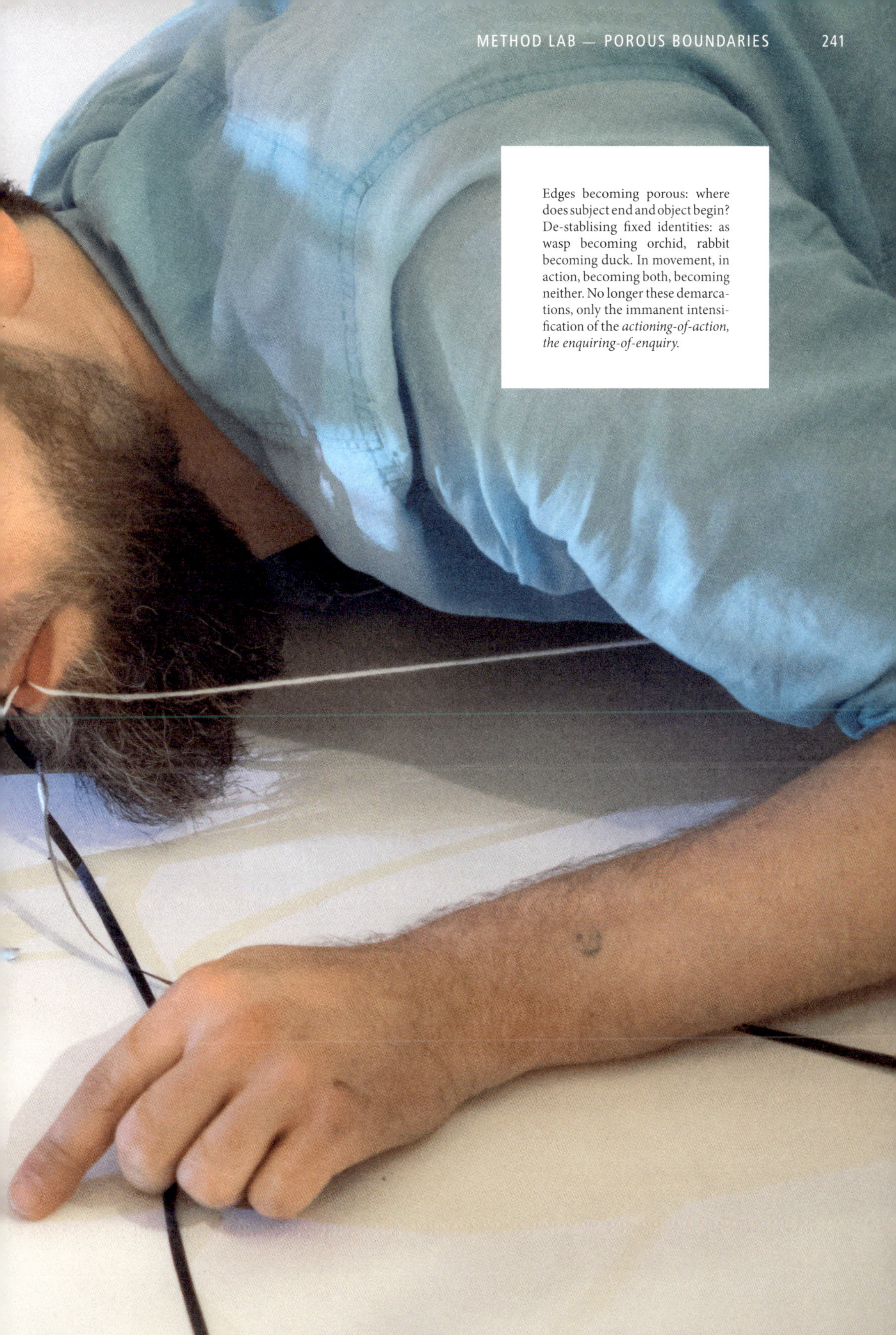

Edges becoming porous: where does subject end and object begin? De-stablising fixed identities: as wasp becoming orchid, rabbit becoming duck. In movement, in action, becoming both, becoming neither. No longer these demarcations, only the immanent intensification of the *actioning-of-action, the enquiring-of-enquiry.*

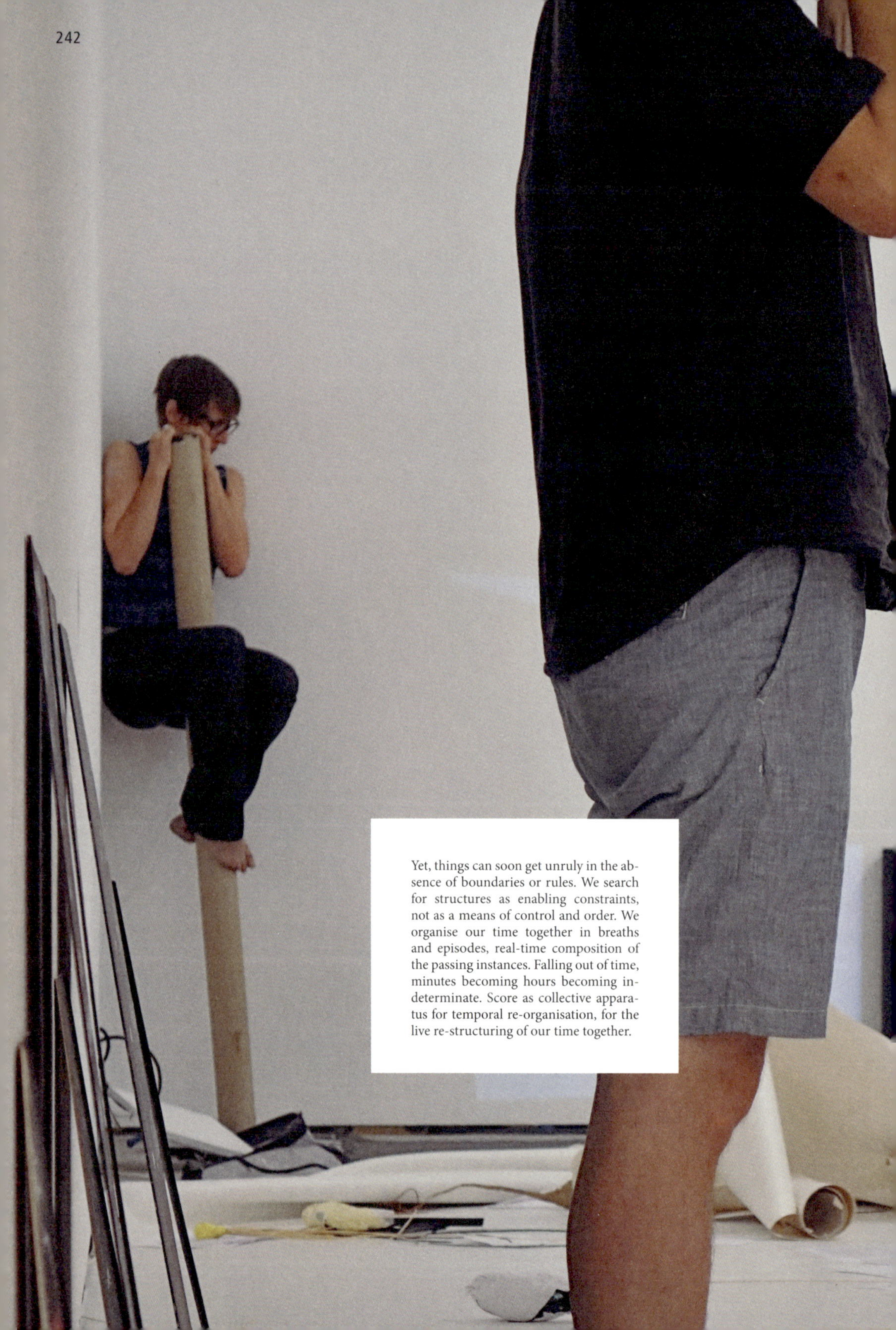

Yet, things can soon get unruly in the absence of boundaries or rules. We search for structures as enabling constraints, not as a means of control and order. We organise our time together in breaths and episodes, real-time composition of the passing instances. Falling out of time, minutes becoming hours becoming indeterminate. Score as collective apparatus for temporal re-organisation, for the live re-structuring of our time together.

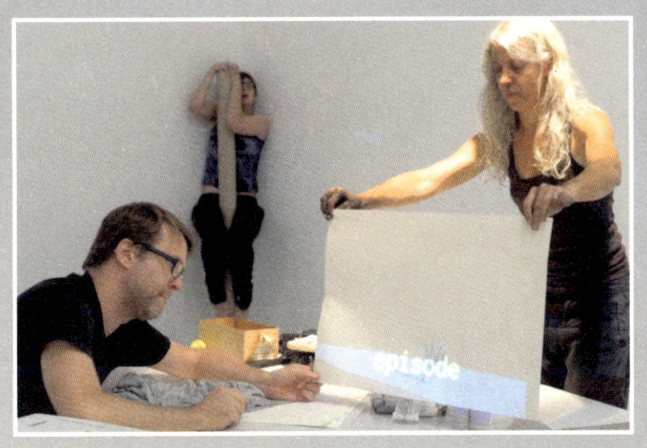
episode

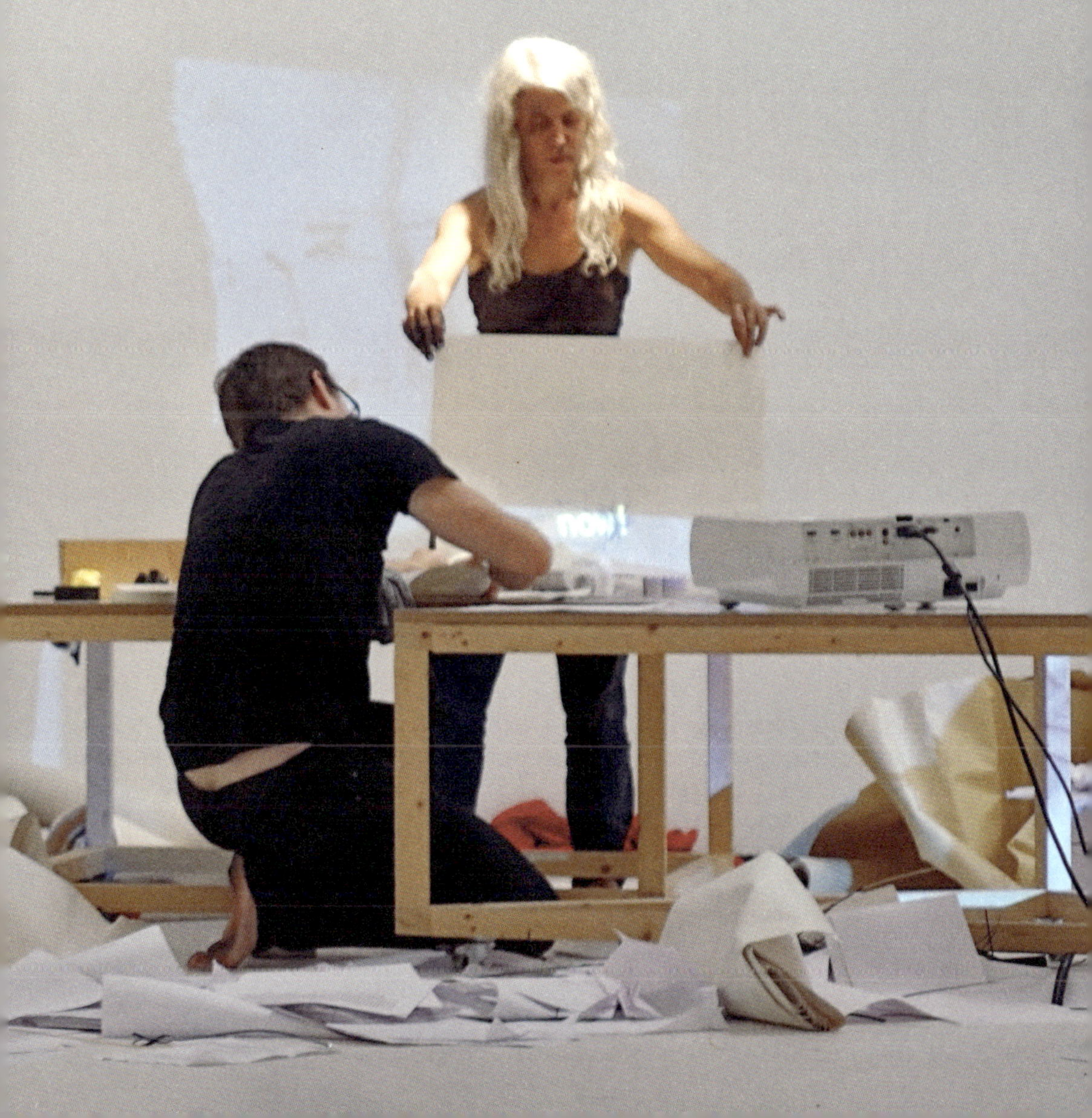

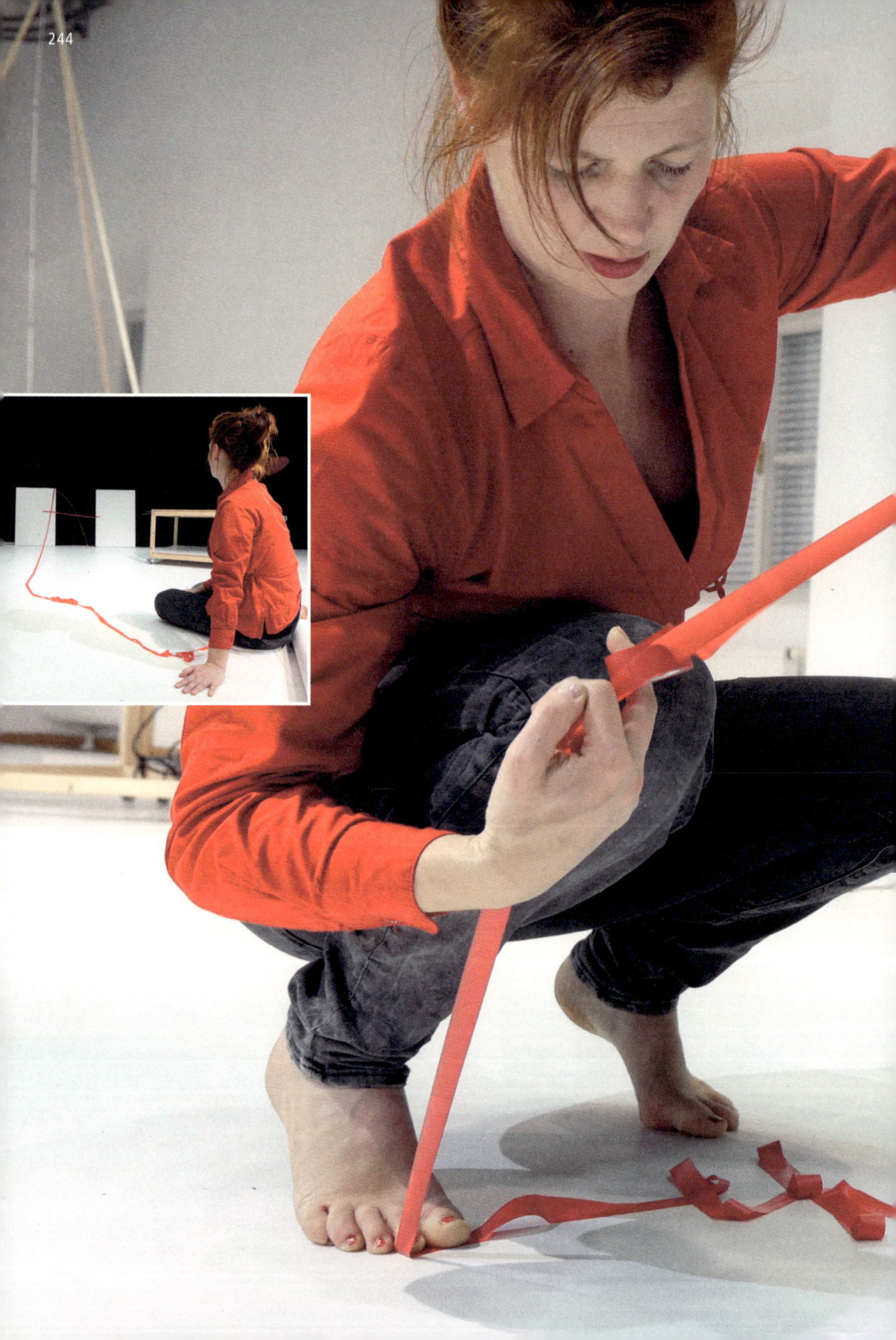

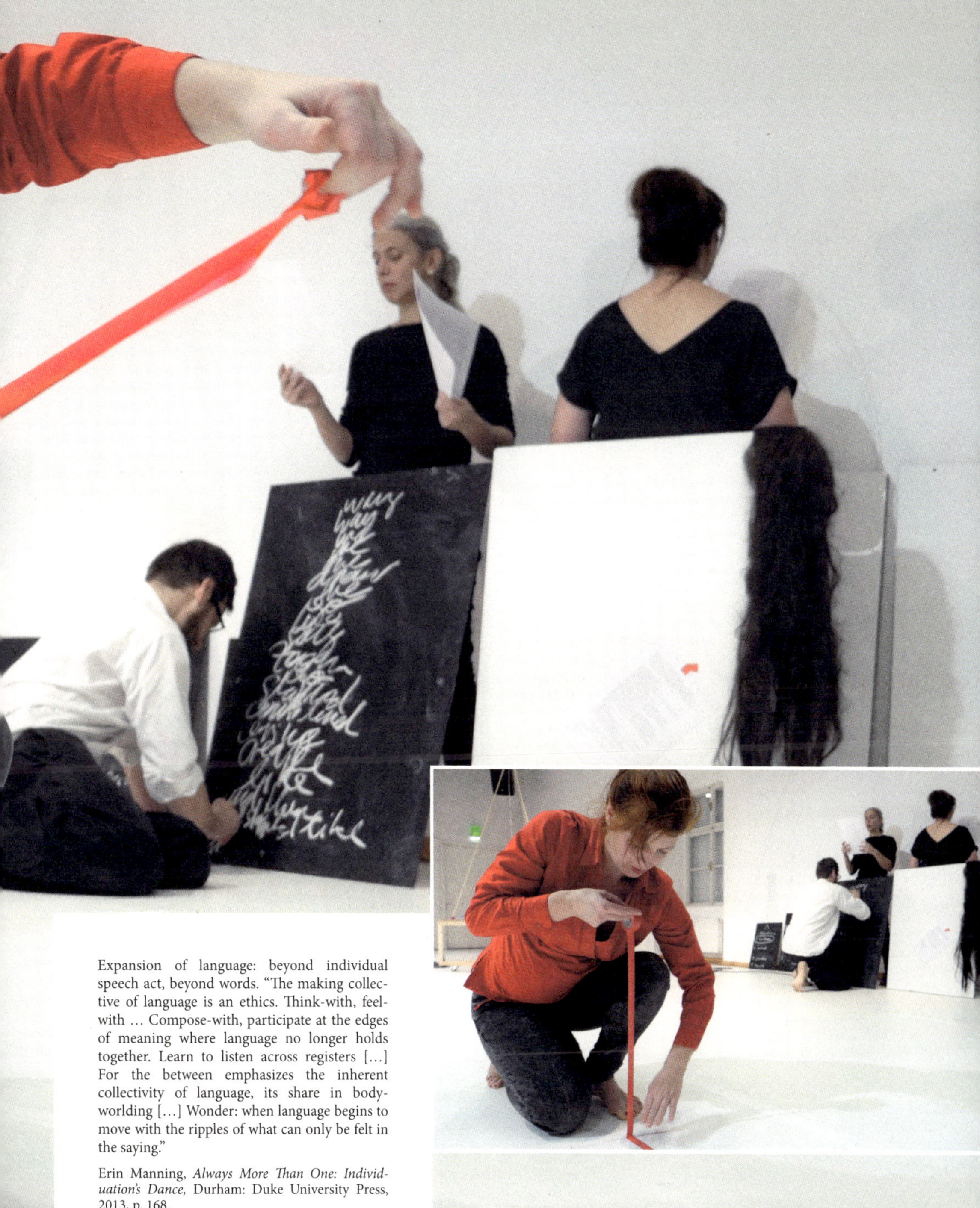

Expansion of language: beyond individual speech act, beyond words. “The making collective of language is an ethics. Think-with, feel-with … Compose-with, participate at the edges of meaning where language no longer holds together. Learn to listen across registers […] For the between emphasizes the inherent collectivity of language, its share in body-worlding […] Wonder: when language begins to move with the ripples of what can only be felt in the saying.”

Erin Manning, *Always More Than One: Individuation's Dance,* Durham: Duke University Press, 2013, p. 168.

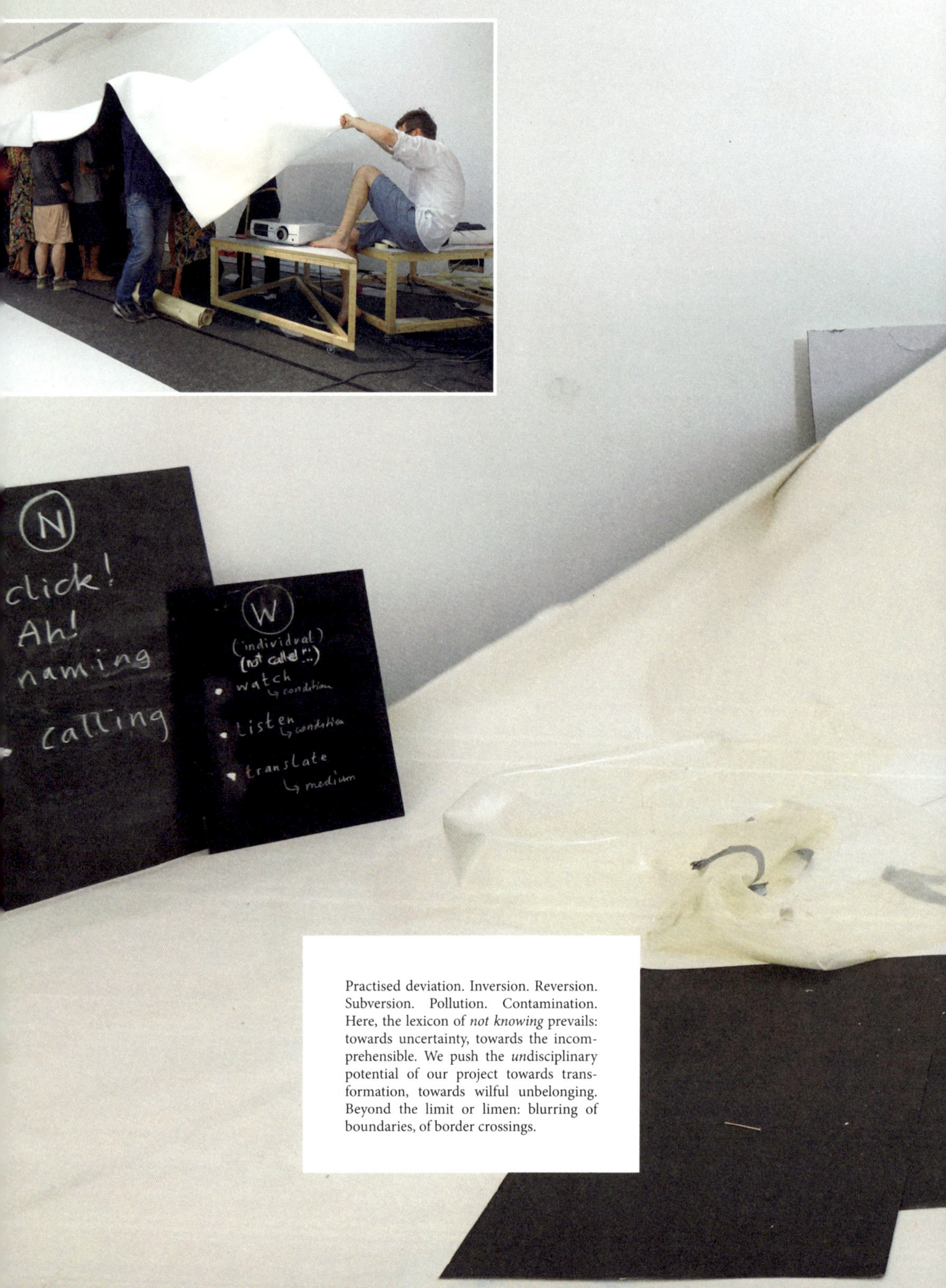

Practised deviation. Inversion. Reversion. Subversion. Pollution. Contamination. Here, the lexicon of *not knowing* prevails: towards uncertainty, towards the incomprehensible. We push the *un*disciplinary potential of our project towards transformation, towards wilful unbelonging. Beyond the limit or limen: blurring of boundaries, of border crossings.

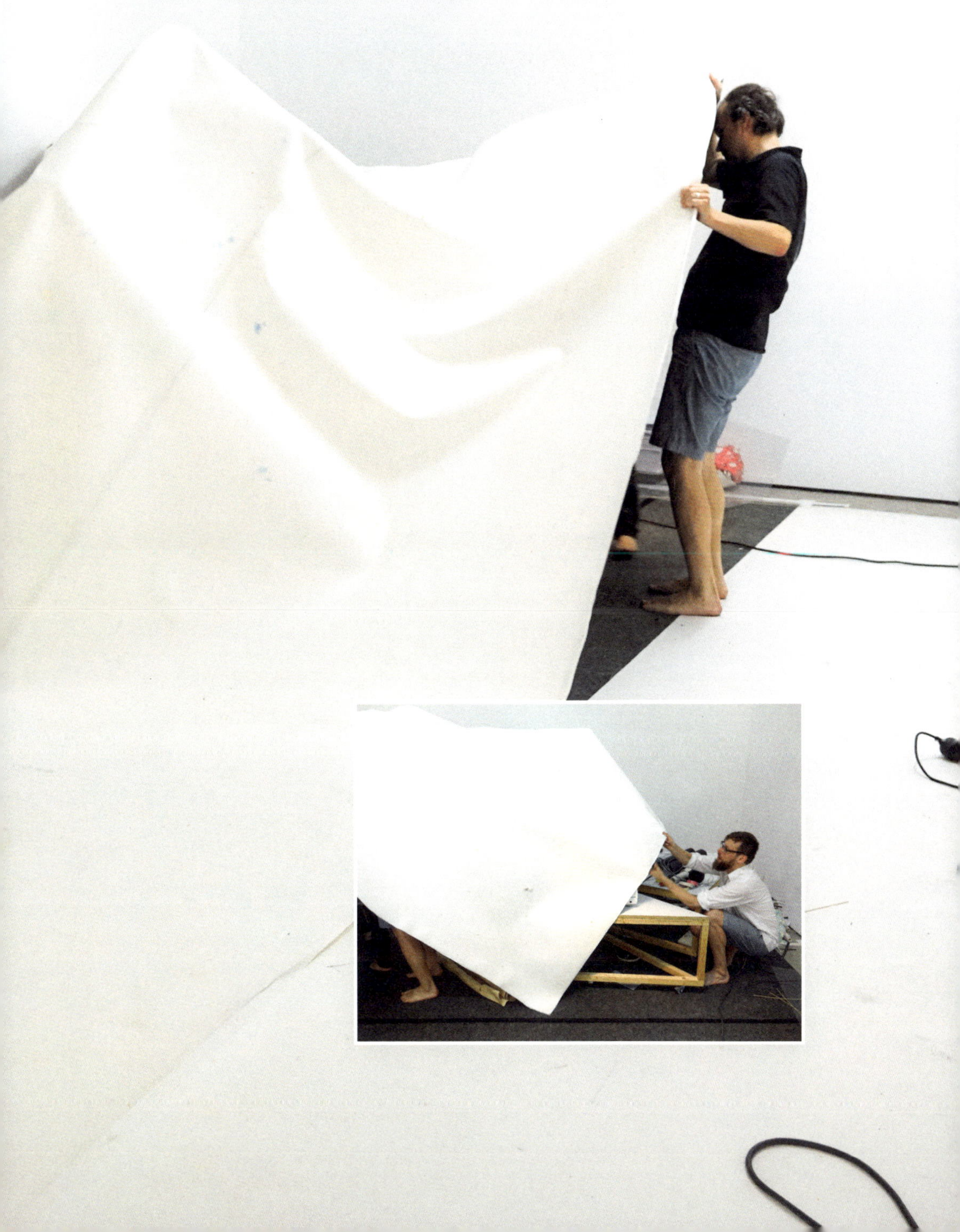

WHEN-NESS

Alongside *how-ness* and *where-ness*, the principle of *when-ness* has played a key role in our enquiry — it indicates towards the sense of the temporal, perhaps even temporalising dynamics within our artistic exploration.[1] In grammatical company with *what, where, why,* and *how*, the word *when* is often coupled with a demonstrative adverb: what — this; where — there; why — because; how — so; when — then. Whilst *when's* interrogative function refers to a point of time (*When* — meaning at what time? How long ago? How soon?), conceived as a synonym for *if*, *when* shifts to become conditional. *If* > *then* can become *when* > *then*. In these terms, *when* introduces the possibility of a cue or trigger, anticipating the circumstances or occasion upon which something will happen or occur. When this happens … then this will happen. Linear temporality of events unfolding — *this* follows *this*, game of consequence, of cause and effect. Here, *when* operates within the logic of *chronos,* the tick-tock of chronology. In this *chrono-temporality*, there is a species of *when* that points to the future (when this happens) as well as a — perhaps nostalgic — when of the past (*remember when*). However, one might also discern the *kairotic when,* the when of the present, the when of *now*. Less (con)sequential, instead focused towards the conditions of mutual arising — this is the *when* of the opening ready to be seized, of the opportunity that is not yet known. *When* of the specious moment: an indefinite period; a brief portion of time, an instant. An unpredictable *when* — not conditional in the strict causal sense of if-then (or *when-then*) but a rather more indeterminate '*when* the conditions are right' *something* will happen. Here, neither the conditions nor what arises can be fully known in advance.

This *when* exists outside the chronological continuum — it refers to a quality of timing, timeliness, perhaps even untimeliness. Indeed, the *when* of *kairos* is that of the right time; the opportune time, a time when anything could happen. A breach or rupture in the chronology of time allows something to emerge that could not have been predicted. Like when things intensify or come together in order to make a next step possible. The opening of opportunity's aperture in the situation is co-emergent with the opening up or receptivity of the individual in response; *kairos* thus refers to both the emergence of a temporal opening and the capacity or readiness of an individual to actively seize the opportunity therein. According to Daniel Stern, *kairos* refers to "the coming into being of a new state of things, and it happens in a moment of awareness."[2] He describes how the arising of this auspicious upsurge "can crash upon us like a wave, or appear almost without notice and then slip away like a sea swell."[3] Alternatively, philosopher Antonio Negri uses the term *kairòs* to describe a mode of immanent (and imminent) invention taking place at the limit of being: "being's act of leaning out over the void of time *to-come*, i.e. the adventure beyond the edge of time."[4] Conceived as an open-ended, immeasurable and revolutionary temporality (a moment of rupture and opening), for Negri "*kairòs* is an exemplary temporal point, because Being is opening up in time; and at each instant that it opens up it must be invented — it must invent itself. *Kairòs* is just this: the moment when the arrow of Being is shot, the moment of opening, the invention of Being on the edge of time."[5] The future that *kairos* ushers in is less the 'not yet' of the future conceived as a continuation of the present, but that of a radical discontinuity. For Simon O'Sullivan, Negri's *kairòs* can be pictured, "as an oblique line — a 'disjunctive synthesis' to use Deleuze and Guattari's terminology — away from the present (but, not, as it were, to an already determined future)."[6] Within this model, as O'Sullivan asserts, "language is creative and future orientated, an exploratory probe of sorts … The name is then a leap into the *to-come*"[7] (⟶ *Practices of Notation: Naming*). Indeed, Negri designates the term *kairòs* for the 'restless' instant where 'naming' and the 'thing named' emerge simultaneously (in time), a process he likens to the way that the poet, "vacillating, fixes the verse."[8]

We practise *when* in the generation and naming of our *figures* (⟶ *Figuring* >< *Figure*) — not so much a 'remember when', the recollection of how we did *this* and *this* and *this*, but rather through the shared quest for the right conditions, a *when-ness* that will give rise again to the *figure* but in a form that we don't yet fully know. So too, our notations strive to mark these very moments of *when-ness* (⟶ *Practices of Notation*). We mark or notate the moment *when* we have noticed 'something is happening'. *When-ness*, in the philosophical sense, relates to existence at a particular point or moment in time. Moment — linked to motion, but also to a sense of importance or weight. Moment: the contraction of movement, momentum. For Maxine Sheets-Johnstone, "[m]ovement creates a certain temporality and that temporality is qualitatively constituted"[9], where "temporality unfolds dynamically as 'qualities', 'contours', 'auras', 'intensities' and 'shadings'".[10] We mark the *when* of the *how*, the arising of a qualitative shift, synchronous to its evental arising, real-time. Marking time as much as marking space — marking of the *when* and the *how* and the *where*. An art of *knowing-when* as much as of *know-how*; yet, timeliness is not only a practice of speed and seizure, the grasping of opportunity. One must also learn to bide one's time. *When* can sometimes signal towards a practice of sitting back, waiting; allowing time and space to let things rest. An impulse does not always need to be followed; an opening does not always need to be filled. Practise the art of knowing when to say *when*, the when-ness of enough (⟶ *Figure of Temporary Closing*). There is the *kairos* of emergence and the *kairos* of closing, stopping, coming to a timely end. To call time — to catch one's breath, to come to a standstill, to hold back, to put on hold, to take a break, take a breather. This knowing *when* is bodily, embodied, felt in flesh and breath. Time can be measured in other ways than the clock — we organise our time together in breaths and episodes, real-time composition of the minutes and hours. At times, it can feel like we have fallen out of time, lost all sense of time spent in the process of live exploration, minutes becoming hours becoming indeterminate. Liminal time — no longer and not yet. *Undisciplinary* time — not so much the unruliness of bad timing or wrong timing, the untimeliness of a mistake or an error. Rather a sense of *time-less-ness*, suspension of the standardising beat of measured time, of time that must be utilised, not wasted (⟶ *Becoming Undisciplinary*). S/he who rules the time has power indeed, for the time-keeper sets the temporal frame for action. Yet, our explorations pulse with a temporality that has no singular keeper: we conceive our score system as a collective apparatus for temporal re-organisation, for the live re-structuring of our time together (⟶ *Embodied Diagrammatics*, ⟶ *How to Play the Score*).

---

1) The following pages present a list of 'whens' gleaned from our conversational transcripts, which in turn we have used within the context of our live explorations as playful provocations.

2) Daniel Stern, *The Present Moment in Psychotherapy and Everyday Life*, New York: W. W. Norton & Company, 2004, p. 7.

3) Stern, 2004. p. 25.

4) Antonio Negri, *Time for Revolution*, New York and London: Continuum, 2003, p. 156. The relation between *kairos* and artistic 'thinking-in-action' (including through the prism of Negri's philosophy) is addressed further within Emma Cocker's ongoing research. Cf. 'Kairos Time: The Performativity of Timing and Timeliness … Or, Between Biding One's Time and Knowing When to Act', PARSE conference *On Time*, 2015, 'Performing Thinking in Action: The Meletē of Live Coding', *International Journal of Performance Arts and Digital Media*, 'Live Coding', Vol. 12, Issue 2, 2016, pp. 102-116 and 'Time Criticality', co-authored chapter with Alan Blackwell, Geoff Cox, Thor Magnusson, Alex McLean, in *Live Coding: A Users Manual*, 2018.

5) Negri, *Negri on Negri: In Conversation with Anne Dufourmentelle*, New York and London: Routledge, 2004, p. 104.

6) Simon O'Sullivan, *On the Production of Subjectivity: Five Diagrams of the Finite-Infinite Relation*, Houndmills, Basingstoke, Hampshire and New York: Palgrave Macmillan, 2012, p. 119.

7) O'Sullivan, 2012, p. 122.

8) Negri, 2003, p. 157.

9) Maxine Sheets-Johnstone, *The Primacy of Movement*, 2nd edition, Amsterdam & Philadelphia: John Benjamins, 2011, p. 132.

10) Stuart Grant, Jodie McNeilly, Maeva Veerapen, citing Maxine Sheets-Johnstone in their introduction to *Performance and Temporalisation: Time Happens*, Houndmills, Basingstoke, Hampshire and New York: Palgrave Macmillan, 2014. p. 9.

When the work works > When you interrupt > When you break someone's solitary activity > When someth
yourself > When you are private > When we are performing > When there is an onlooker > When you exec
to not be in the spotlight > When I am working with text > When one mode of operating is starting and or
discussion is probably not worth it > When we have done this before > When I say what am I working o
don't want to be disturbed from > When you want a different kind of provocation > When I am writing > W
your body > When it is finished > When you don't hear > When it first happens > When you see the situa
When we talk about the form that this might take > When you put yourself into this uncomfortable situa
performance > When I am speaking > When you conceive of two things coming together > When they slip
polyphony > When you make a click > When you tune in > When you are looking > When I am do
you pay more attention to your own voice > When we make the clicks > When we look back > When all th
something else > When she moves it or touches it > When I use the term experiment > When I use the w
look again > When you hear yourself speak > When you are feeling lost > When you are out of the imag
emerge by chance > When things are arising unexpectedly > When something is happening > When the ri
it feels like it needs more nuance or clarification > When we talk about difference and repetition > When
first time you have said it or even thought it > When the tension is not obviously there > When we say notat
> When we are repeating the same thing > When it has more meaning > When you repeat a word > When
> When we are moving around and thinking > When you are lost in the context of what's happening or
to dissipate and become something else > When you are dealing with molecules of a process > When I s
When two lines meet > When I am doing movements in the space it is just the same as drawing > When
When we describe our processes using verbs > When there is a lot of turbulence > When I close my eye
have the feeling that some elements are coalescing and creating a certain constellation > When you
> When you start to let go > When we stop > When we use stop using nouns > When we talk about us
talking > When we break a rule > When you realise 'ah' now I know what I am doing in this room > When
group > When you are doing something else > When time shifts or the quality of time feels different > W
When something is coming into experience > When something is touching without actually touching > W
symmetrical > When a feeling is felt > When it starts to vanish > When we are crossing or stepping into
break > When we place an object in order to create a line > When you seeing it turning > When mass
have a special resonance > When the word becomes flesh > When you feel more present > When a *figur*
grasp something that is not graspable > When what is coming is wholly contingent > When you are lu
space > When all of that falls away and it becomes quite singular > When the conditions are right > When
touching > When you are walking a line and then you stop > When we mark a movement > When we re
When you cross the river > When you see synchronicity > When breath becomes synchronous > When bre
I make a gesture > When you get the sense of emptiness > When I talk about the body > When I talk ab
observe someone doing something > When we are ventilating words > When word becomes sound > Whe
like you need to enhance a moment > When 'something' happens > When you notice and mark > When
than a click > When you can name it > When you are watching > When I address my attention to my bre
conversation > When you give time to the other > When you are speaking beyond the space > When I finis
you imagine something for the first time > When it is more spontaneous, more wild > When the spirit is talk
evident > When you find a translation > When we speak > When one thing stops and another thing star
more than one > When we come together > When someone feels that their faith has left > When we talk ab
things are intensifying or coming together > When the energy is peeking > When there is a se

orking > When the work is not working > When the energy ebbs > When it starts again > When you are by
ction > When things peter out > When something is happening > When we move > When someone wants
ping > When people talk > When I say something > When we switch the recording device on > When the
en the other arrives > When I look at my notes > When someone might be engaged in something that they
1 the writing > When I am moving objects around the space > When you talk about being in the space with
ning > When you zoom into the body > When you give it a name > When we retreat into our disciplines >
then something happens > When we talk about emergence > When the *figures* are re-inhabited through
ync > When notations begin to happen > When you listen > When people begin to sing > When we sing in
ething > When you hear yourself speaking aloud > When you are standing up in front of a crowd > When
ditions connect > When we talk about the idea of the *milieu* > When the whole thing shifts and it becomes
hod > When you discover something > When I watch myself walking > When I remember > When you
en you feel something is changing > When you are listening to two conversations at once > When things
nent comes > When there is a small movement > When you are close to it > When you don't know > When
in a group > When you recognise that what you are describing is personal > When you speak and it is the
hen we say notion > When there is a point of focused discussion > When I am trying to do something silent
dedicating your full attention > When the other person is making a turn > When you are moving around
what else to do > When simply being together becomes collaborative > When collaborative activity starts
raw > When I start thinking about the idea of the body > When we talk about the metaphor of perfume >
an 'a' in front of something and it becomes the opposite of that word > When we go around in circles >
en things happen in the periphery of your vision > When you don't focus directly on anything > When you
nming at the surface > When you observe something > When we invite your attention > When you step in
ctuation as poetry > When language is liberated from being a carrier of information > When we stop
to recall it > When something opens up > When everybody turns in unison > When you feel part of the
see a sound wave > When you feel a capacity to disrupt > When it becomes too fixed > When we meet >
e is a level of *intention* at the limit of the shadow > When something could explode > When folds are
l that is brought by the others > When we share what was happening > When you pay attention > When we
pressed > When the momentum is getting slower > When we circulate around a word > When it starts to
ring > When we talk about the nature of lightness > When a dance of attention circulates > When we try to
ugh that something happens even though you do it for the first time > When a *figure* is emerging in the
ce the presence of consonance or dissonance > When you make a call > When things fall > When you are
hen you enter the *figure* > When you enter a force-field > When I am notating > When you call a *figure* >
omes asynchronous > When you focus on your spine > When I make a line > When I write a word > When
subject > When we say something is becoming material > When we are really working *with it* > When you
ctice of attention becomes a praxis > When we play with duration > When I hear you click > When you feel
for a notated mode > When the *figuring* is happening > When the click moves into something that is more
hen we invite someone to join us for a walk > When the *figure* of translation appears > When we practise
en you are forced to continue > When there is nothing else to say > When you are really thinking > When
ugh us > When you feel like you are on the same page > When we are at war > When the connection is too
en you think of the diagrammatic > When we put these things into the score > When we talk of *choreo-* as
-ness > When we talk about where-ness > When we say stop or enough > When we lie on the floor > When
nomentum > When it becomes most charged > When it is no longer > When we decide to stop.

Alex Arteaga

RESEARCHING AESTHETICALLY THE ROOTS OF AESTHETICS

AN ENQUIRY INTO FIGURE AND FIGURING

During the whole process of research set in motion by *Choreo-graphic Figures: Deviations from the Line*, I have been one of its *sputniks*: satellites moving around the main researchers at different distances — sometimes in the very core of their activities, sometimes far away, but always connected — broadcasting critical impulses as a response to what they have been developing and transmitting. This text is a reflection — another one, a kind of concluding one — on two main concepts of this project: *figure* and *figuring*.

In this short essay, I try to situate the concepts — of *figure* and *figuring* — in the framework of my ongoing research on aesthetics, or to be more precise on the 'roots' of aesthetics, that is, those constitutive, ineluctable and most fundamental aspects of the field of human activity that we distinguish from other spheres of action and designate with the term 'aesthetics' and occasionally, as one of its possible particularisations, 'art'. The attempt to define *figure* and *figuring* in this context allows me to encompass these terms in the conceptual meshwork that I am developing, and simultaneously to present the meaning that they have acquired in this project — at least, the meaning that they have been adopting for me from my perspective and through my participation as a *sputnik*. Furthermore, it makes it possible to characterise the research developed in this project as 'artistic research': an enquiry, as the essay title indicates, into the basis of aesthetics *by* aesthetic means.

The strategy I chose to address in the production of this text is to outline the main traits of my reflections on aesthetics and to situate the concepts of *figure* and *figuring* — and as relevant aspects of the latter also of 'noticing' and 'notating' — in this context. The brief description of my ideas about aesthetics is structured in three parts. The first refers to my core understanding of aesthetics as a variety of cognition, that is, as a network of processes that enables the emergence of selves and their worlds — of worlds and their selves. The second, developed in the framework set by the first, deals with my concepts of 'aesthetic conduct' — a variety of behaviour that allows for a mobilisation of the intrinsic cognitive power of aesthetics — and of 'transitional awareness' — a kind of attentiveness that makes possible a fluid circulation between aesthetic understanding and other cognitive types. And the third, based necessarily on the second, presents my notion of 'aesthetic research': a form of enquiry performed through the methodic organisation and actualisation of the aesthetic cognitive potentials.

In accordance with the original denotation of the term 'aesthetics' in the unfinished project of Alexander Baumgarten[1] or with its outline in Immanuel Kant's third Critique[2] — just to mention the beginning of a lineage of conceptual development — I understand aesthetics as a variety of cognition. This position situates cognition as the *raison d'être* of the differentiated field of human activity that we name aesthetics, and therefore of any possible interpretation of the term 'beauty' and of the conceptualisation and performance of practices of aesthetic or artistic formalisation. The term 'cognition' is not understood here as the language-based reflection on a given subject matter. Thus, the meaning of cognition here is not reduced to what we trivially formulate as to 'think about something'. I understand cognition as the activity of a living system — equally from a monocellular bacterium to a human being — in structural coupling with its environment, that is, co-creating a field of shared agency and reciprocal determination. Regarded from the perspective of the living being that I am referring to as cognitive agent — that is, changing from a third-person-perspective to a first-person-perspective — cognition would be defined here as the emergence of its domain of significance — its world — out of its interaction with the components of its surroundings. The living being co-constitutes its own world — a world-for-itself, for a self co-emerging with this world and thus a self-for-the-world — through its participation in this process of constitution. In other words, the living being simultaneously in-habits the world that it in-forms and this complex, dynamic and systemic process is what I denominate cognition.[3]

Obviously, the roots of aesthetics are to be found in this systemic network of processes and I postulate, *vice versa*, that aesthetics configures the very roots of this network of processes. I understand aesthetic cognition as the activities of the whole system — living-being-environment — constrained by the spontaneous, sensorimotor and emotional actions of the living being. In case that the living being is a human being, these actions — and their immediate results — are operatively present for itself. In order to deliver the entire definition I reformulate it thus: aesthetic cognition — the roots of aesthetics — is the spontaneous, sensorimotor, emotional and operatively present realisation of a viable coherence. I am going to spell out this dense formulation by specifying each term. Let us begin with 'spontaneous'. I use this word here with reference to its etymological origin: 'sponte sua', which denotes actions occurring 'out of their own motivation', 'out of themselves'. I ascribe the source of spontaneity to the very core of the emerging self of the agent that performed them: the *organisation* of the living being. In this context, a living being is differentiated from a non-living entity by its own form of organisation. The living system is *autopoietic* while the non-living thing is *heteropoietic*.[4] On this basis, 'spontaneous actions' are those that are brought about by the most basic development of our biological autonomy — our operational closure — in structural coupling with the actions of our environment.[5] Spontaneous actions, therefore, are not mediated by reflection and will. They are not target-oriented but motivated by our organic response to the perturbations of our surroundings. This definition of spontaneity has to be understood as a limit: on the one hand, because we are embodied, that is, physicochemical realisations of our form of organisation, habitualised expressions of a long phylogenetic and ontogenetic history; and on the other hand, because our reflection, will and target-oriented action also stem from our autopoietic organisation. In previous essays, I used the term 'passive' to designate these kind of actions, meaning actions we do — indubitably we are the ones who undertake these actions — that seem to 'happen', that seem to 'occur without us doing anything', that is, without us deciding to perform them and consequently not performing them on purpose. Passivity, thus, would designate here a variety of activity.[6]

The next terms to be specified are 'sensorimotor' and 'emotional'. They are to be understood in continuity with my interpretation of the word 'spontaneity', simultaneously as consequences and sources of our embodiment. Under 'sensorimotor and emotional' actions I understand actions determined by the coordination through our nervous system of our abilities to sense and to move, which is constitutive in the realisation of our organism, and by what moves our-selves as a whole 'out of our-selves'—e-motion—in touch with this exteriority. 'Sensorimotor' and 'emotional' are therefore specifications of 'spontaneity' in relation to our particular embodiment—our realisation as humans.

The following term of my definition of aesthetic cognition is 'operatively present'. If with the first attributes—spontaneous, sensorimotor and emotional—I tried to qualify the variety of actions and their enabling conditions, with 'operatively present' I am trying to express how these actions and their immediate consequences become manifest to us. My thesis is that they are not perceptually present for us but operatively.[7] That means that they do not appear explicitly, in a clearly contoured way, in a way we can point to them and discern them from other arising phenomena. They are not objectified. They are not constituted as objects through perception. They are not phenomena—or at least, not yet. On the contrary, they are implicit, intrinsic, indistinguishably embedded in our active 'being-in-the-world', constitutively integrated in our ceaseless, everyday life experience of the deep continuity between us—our-selves—and our worlds. This variety of presence also characterises the last two terms of my definition of (the roots of) aesthetics as cognition: 'viability' and 'coherence'. As my formulation shows—'a viable coherence'—both terms are intimately intertwined as they are with the rest of the formulation: 'the spontaneous, sensorimotor, emotional and operatively present realisation of a viable coherence'. The whole picture expressed through this articulation is the following: a living system moved by the embodiment of its own form of organisation interacts with the components of its surroundings and out of the constant actualisation of this field of shared agency, a whole system—living-being-surroundings—acquires signification for the living being. This signification has the structure of a whole: a form of coherent relationship among its parts and between parts and whole characterised by co-emergence and circular causality—the whole emerges from the very specific and dynamic relationships between parts, and the parts are constrained and thus co-determined by the whole.[8] This coherence is what I denominate 'environment' taking as its reference the German equivalent word—*Umwelt*: the world (*Welt*) around (*um-*)—meaning the actual surrounding domain of significance of and for the living unit. I postulate that this coherence appears for the living being operationally, that is, intrinsically in its own realisation, as viable for the living being—as possible to be lived, to be realised, to be 'walked through' (*via* = way). The autonomous cognitive agent to whom its world—and its own self—appears, realises simultaneously that this world is viable for it-self. I call this viability, 'sense', and agree with Francisco J. Varela that 'living is sense-making'[9]—although, in order to stress shared agency and co-emergence, I would rather put it this way: life is a meshwork of processes of emergence of sense.

I understand a *figure* to be an incipient formation in and of this viable coherence, a specification of the senseful environment of the subject to whom the *figure* appears, firstly and fundamentally in an operational way and by virtue of the sensorimotory and emotionally constrained interaction with the subject's surroundings. Let me develop this idea by taking the practices conceived and performed in the *Choreo-graphic Figures* project as a concrete case study. A group of artist-researchers perform simultaneously and in the same space, different actions interacting with one another and with an assortment of materials and artefacts. Although they do that in order to understand what a *figure* is and how it comes to be in a field of transdisciplinary artistic practice, they suspend this final goal — they leave it aside, they do not attend to it explicitly — and instead focus their attention primarily on the concrete actions that they are performing and secondarily on the possible emergence of new presences — *figures*. Let us look in detail to these two foci of awareness in order to outline their differences. The first focus of attention is set on the manipulated materials and artefacts. They appear as objects. They are clearly contoured and therefore graspable. They can be handled. They are used to undertake concrete, more or less target-oriented actions. They are perceptually constituted phenomena set in motion in the wide field of all possible intentional acts.[10] In contrast, a *figure* is present in a totally different way. It is not contoured, it is not graspable. We cannot move straight forward to it — it is not an 'it' — and put it under our control. It is not an object. It is not (yet) objectified, it is not (yet) constituted as a phenomenon — a phenomenon is always a singularity, a differentiated, discrete, segregated unit. In the case that a *figure* becomes explicit it always remains at the edge of its own explicitness. It is fragile, subtle, contingent, dubious, shady — in the shade of the objects and subjects that enable its presence. A *figure*, we could say, is proto-phenomenal, since it is endowed with the potentiality of becoming a phenomena, of being objectified, of ceasing to be silent, implicit in our handling with objects and interacting with other subjects and becomes explicit by means of a certain kind of awareness that I will describe later: 'transitional awareness'. It is not a phenomenon but depends on phenomena and their mutual dynamic relationships to emerge. A *figure* is a meshwork of qualities operatively present as a whole, that emerges out of a dynamic disposition of actions performed in interaction with phenomena. Phenomena and *figures* — intentionally objectified presences and operative presences — configure a system of co-emergence, in which phenomena compose the level of enabling conditions and figures the emergent field. Phenomena and *figures,* thus, are in a relation of mutual determination. *Figures* are specific tonalities of our environment, temporary regional particularisations of our current world that emerge by virtue of the same processes that constitute it: the constant actualisation of our dynamic and relational existence.

Having outlined the fundamental traits of a *figure* it is now time to address the question of its realisation: the *figuring*. I use the term 'realisation' here in its two meanings: to understand and to make, to produce. I am going to address the first significance on the basis of two further key concepts from my reflections on aesthetics: 'aesthetic conduct' and 'transitional awareness'. 'Aesthetic conduct' is a variety of behaviour. I choose the term 'conduct' to denominate it with reference to its etymology: to lead oneself (-duct), with others or other things (con-). The term 'con-duct' thus expresses the fundamental relational nature of our behaviour, the shared agency — shared between us and the components of our surroundings — which manifests in a more clear and intense way when behaving aesthetically. 'Passivity' — a concept I mentioned in relation to the 'spontaneity' that characterises aesthetic cognition — understood as the minimisation of will and target-oriented action, is the trait of behaviour which allows for an increase of our receptivity towards the agency of others — equally autonomous or heteronomous units — and is therefore the key for entering aesthetic conduct. By reducing our exclusive leading position in our interaction with the environment, by passing from control, manipulation and leadership to permeability, openness and receptivity, we come closer to our inclusive foundations: the spontaneous, sensorimotory and emotionally constrained co-emergence of our world and our-selves — we come closer to aesthetic cognition. Behaving in this way — this is not a 'state of mind', not even an 'attitude', but a variety of (inter)action — the first aspect of which I call the 'realisation of a *figure*' — *figuring* — can take place. I denominate it 'noticing'. Thanks to the variety of awareness that is triggered when behaving aesthetically we can 'notice' that a *figure* is emerging. I call this variety of awareness 'transitional awareness'. Its main feature is of providing a fluid and reciprocal relationship between the operational and the perceptual; between the implicit and the explicit, between the signless and the sign-based. Acting aesthetically — being in intimate touch with the most basic, bodily process of emergence of sense, of viable coherence — it is possible to constitute sign-based artefacts, for example 'names' — the name of a *figure* — which stand in deep continuity with the actual operative presences. This is not an operation of 'translation'. The operative presence remains operative — its operative character is constitutive and irreducible — and the intentional object configures an *analogon*, which is recognised as such, that is, *als stimmig*[11] — as adequate, as 'equal' — to the operative proto-phenomenon by the subject to which the *figure* appears. The one who co-constitutes the *figure* operationally notices it, that is, co-configures its analogon incipiently in the field of perception, and afterwards names it. In the case of the research on the emergence of *figures* through the aesthetic practices performed in the *Choreo-graphic Figures* project, 'naming' (⟶ *Practices of Notation: Naming*) was not an intrinsic moment of the perceptual constitution of the *figure* as it is the case when we, for example, see a bottle. In this regular case of perception we do not see something and then endow it with a name: the perceptual object emerges simultaneously as form and name — we directly and spontaneously see a bottle. In the case of 'noticing a *figure*', it arises as a vague — although in its vagueness also clear — presence. When this happened in the so called 'live explorations' of the *Choreo-graphic Figures* project, the researcher that noticed this presence 'marked' it. We agreed to use an oral-acoustical sign — a 'click' — as a minimal and basic mark (⟶ *Practices of Notation: Clicking*). The 'click' was thus the first and most reduced sign-based expression of a *figure,* the first sign in the process of its realisation. As such, the 'click' was the point of inflection between the operative and the phenomenal, enabling the possibility of naming and describing the *figure,* that is, the performance of further intentional acts based, as always the case, on perceptual constitution. The 'click' thus articulated the transition between noticing and the second basic aspect of the understanding of a *figure:* 'notating'. The 'click' was actually the minimal notation, the first and foundational sign of an incipient process of production and organisation of signs.

On this basis, that is, noticing the emergence of a *figure* through the collective and simultaneous performance of different aesthetic practices, marking its presence and naming it, a reflection on the conditions for its arising was possible. After finishing a session of *aesthetic* enquiry, another complementary variety of research — performed mostly in the medium of language and organised by practices of reflection like writing and dialogic exchange — allowed for the identification of the correlation between the performed actions and the emergence of the *figure.* This procedure connects both aspects of the *figuring,* that is, of the realisation of the *figure:* its understanding and its 'production'. I use quotation marks for this last term, because I think that a *figure* cannot really be produced. It cannot be made. It cannot be manufactured the same way we assemble a material or even an ideal thing. A *figure* is an emergent entity whose appearance cannot be completely under our control. The only possible way to contribute to its arising — we can only contribute to its arising but not produce it — is to identify, dispose and activate its enabling conditions: we can co-configure the constraints of a system of emergence. In the case of the emergence of *figures* in this research project, these conditions were provided through the selection of materials and artefacts to interact with, their disposition in space and the identification of individual and collective actions to be performed in this newly shaped surroundings. This configuration — defined through reflection on the basis of aesthetic practices and revised, confirmed or modified through the very same aesthetic practices, which allowed the identification of the *figure* and its enabling correlates — becomes part of a *figure.* A particular *figure* thus included the sense or experience of the *figure* — we often said: "we know what/how this *figure* feels like" — the name of the *figure* and the conditions that can facilitate its emergence. 'Can' because the intrinsic fragility of the *figure* confers instability and uncertainty to the whole system of emergence. The situation in which a *figure* can appear encompasses inevitably more factors — potentially reinforcing or disturbing — than those which can be foreseen; another proof of the embeddedness of the *figure* and the *figuring* in the logic of life.

I consider the enquiry on *figure* and *figuring* developed in the *Choreo-graphic Figures* project to be a process of aesthetic research.[12] Although this process has included practices that I will not denominate 'aesthetic' and therefore the research could be adequately categorised as 'hybrid', aesthetic practices have configured its foundations. To formulate it in a more radical way: the roots of this research project have been set on the roots of aesthetics — aesthetic cognition made available through aesthetic conduct and organised through aesthetic practices. The criterium that I am using here to consider a research process to be 'aesthetic' does not refer to the subject-matter of the enquiry, which in this case was as well fundamentally aesthetic, but to the practices that organise it, that is, to its methodology — to the systemic way of proceeding. *Figures* and the twofold defined process of *figuring* have been researched in this context through the conception, organisation and performance of 'aesthetic dispositives': chrono-topological arrangements of materials, artefacts, people and actions, addressed, handled and performed through aesthetic conduct in order to allow their respective agencies to develop inter-connectedly and to bring forth *figures* and the conditions for their intentional constitution and processing. Aesthetic research processes like the ones realised and exemplified in the *Choreo-graphic Figures* project make it possible to get in touch with the most fundamental processes of embodied and situated emergence of *sense* and, furthermore, to make them available for the production of *meaning*. Aesthetic research allows us to connect with our most basic and vital *understanding* — our operativity in our environments, the fluent, simultaneous and intimately intertwined realisation of our-selves and our-worlds — as the most solid and at the same time creative foundation for the configuration of positive knowledge.

---

1) Alexander Gottlieb Baumgarten, *Aesthetica*, Trajecti cis Viadrum, 1750.

2) Immanuel Kant, *Critik der Urtheilskraft*, Berlin, 1790.

3) Cf. Francisco J. Varela, 'Organism: a Meshwork of Selfless Selves', in Alfred I. Tauber, *Organism and the Origin of Self*, Dordrecht: Springer Netherlands, 1991, pp. 12-42, for a foundational description of this expanded concept of cognition.

4) Cf. Humberto R. Maturana and Francisco J. Varela, *Autopoiesis and Cognition: The Realization of the Living*, Dordrecht and Boston: D. Reidel Pub. Co., 1980, for a first formulation of the theory of autopoiesis.

5) Cf. Francisco J. Varela, *Principles of Biological Autonomy*, New York: North Holland, 1979, for a definition of the concept of 'operational closure' in this context.

6) I thematise this concept of passivity in two previous texts: 'Architektur der Verkörperung. Ein künstlerisches

Forschungsprojekt als phänomenologische Ästhetik' in Dieter Mersch (Ed.), *Internationales Jahrbuch für Medienphilosophie*, Berlin: De Gruyter, 2016, pp. 23-35 and 'Sensuous Knowledge. Making Sense through the Skin', in Mika Elo and Miika Luoto (Eds.), *Senses of Embodiment. Art, Technics, Media*, Bern: Peter Lang AG, Internationaler Verlag der Wissenschaften, 2014, pp. 85-96.

7) Cf. John J. Drummond, 'The structure of intentionality', in Rudolf Bernet, Donn Welton and Gina Zavota (Eds.), *Edmund Husserl: Critical Assessments of Leading Philosophers. Volume III, The Nexus of Phenomena: Intentionality, Perception and Temporality*, London: Routledge, 2005, for the concept of 'operational intentionality' ('fungierende Intentionalität').

8) Cf. Evan Thompson, *Mind in Life: Biology, Phenomenology and the Science of Mind*, Cambridge, Mass.: Belknap Press of Harvard University Press, 2007, especially Chapter 3, 'Autonomy and Emergence', for an exhaustive description of the concept of 'co-emergence'. Cf. Henri Bortoft, *The Wholeness of Nature: Goethe's Way of Science*, Edinburgh: Floris Books, 1996, for a grounded description of this concept of 'whole'.

9) Cf. Varela, 1991. Cf. also Francisco J. Varela, 'Patterns of Life: Intertwining Identity and Cognition', in *Brain and Cognition* 34, 1997, pp. 72-87 and Andreas Weber and Francisco J. Varela, 'Life after Kant: Natural Processes and the Autopoietic Foundations of Biological Individuality', in *Phenomenology and the Cognitive Sciences*, Vol. 1, Issue 2, 2002, pp. 97-125.

10) I use here the term 'intentionality' as defined by Franz Brentano as the aboutness of consciousness, and thus 'intentional acts' as all deeds of mind that, unavoidably, refer to something different from the mind itself, like for example perceptions (the perception of something), judgements (the judgement on something) or deductions (the deduction of something based on something else). Cf. Franz Brentano, *Psychology from an Empirical Standpoint*, London: Routledge and New York: Humanities Press, [1874] 1973.

11) The German adjective *stimmig* relates to the operation of tuning musical instruments (*stimmen*) and thus implies a relation of belonging to the same system of tuning (*Stimmungssystem*).

12) I prefer to use the term 'aesthetic' rather than 'artistic' to qualify this kind of research in order to potentially include in the research process and method all kind of practices that might be performed acting aesthetically and not only those considered to be artistic, that is, accepted as part of the art system.

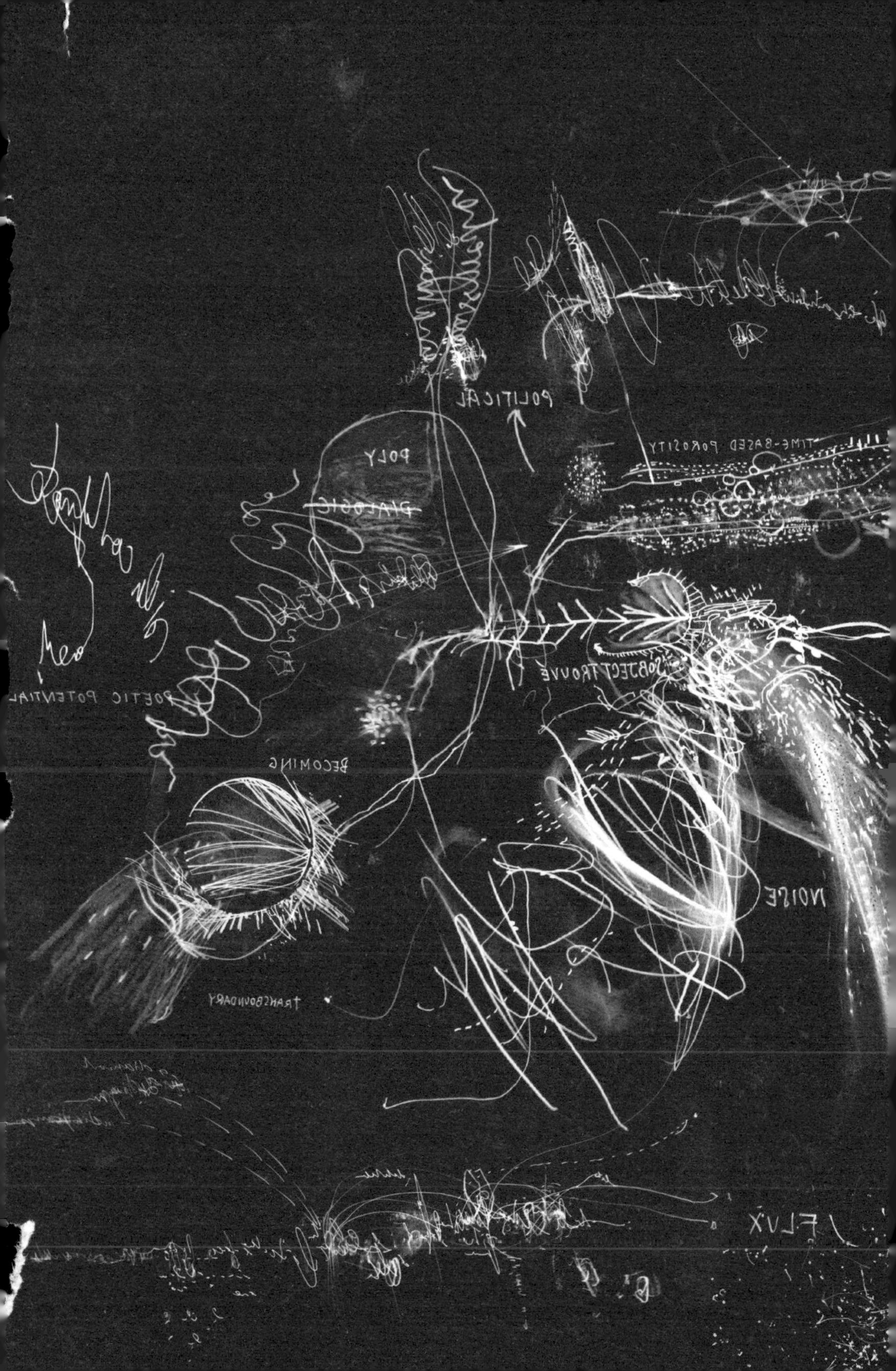
POLITICAL
TIME-BASED POROSITY
POLY
DIALOGIC
OBJECT TROUVE
POETIC POTENTIAL
BECOMING
NOISE
TRANSBOUNDARY
FLUX

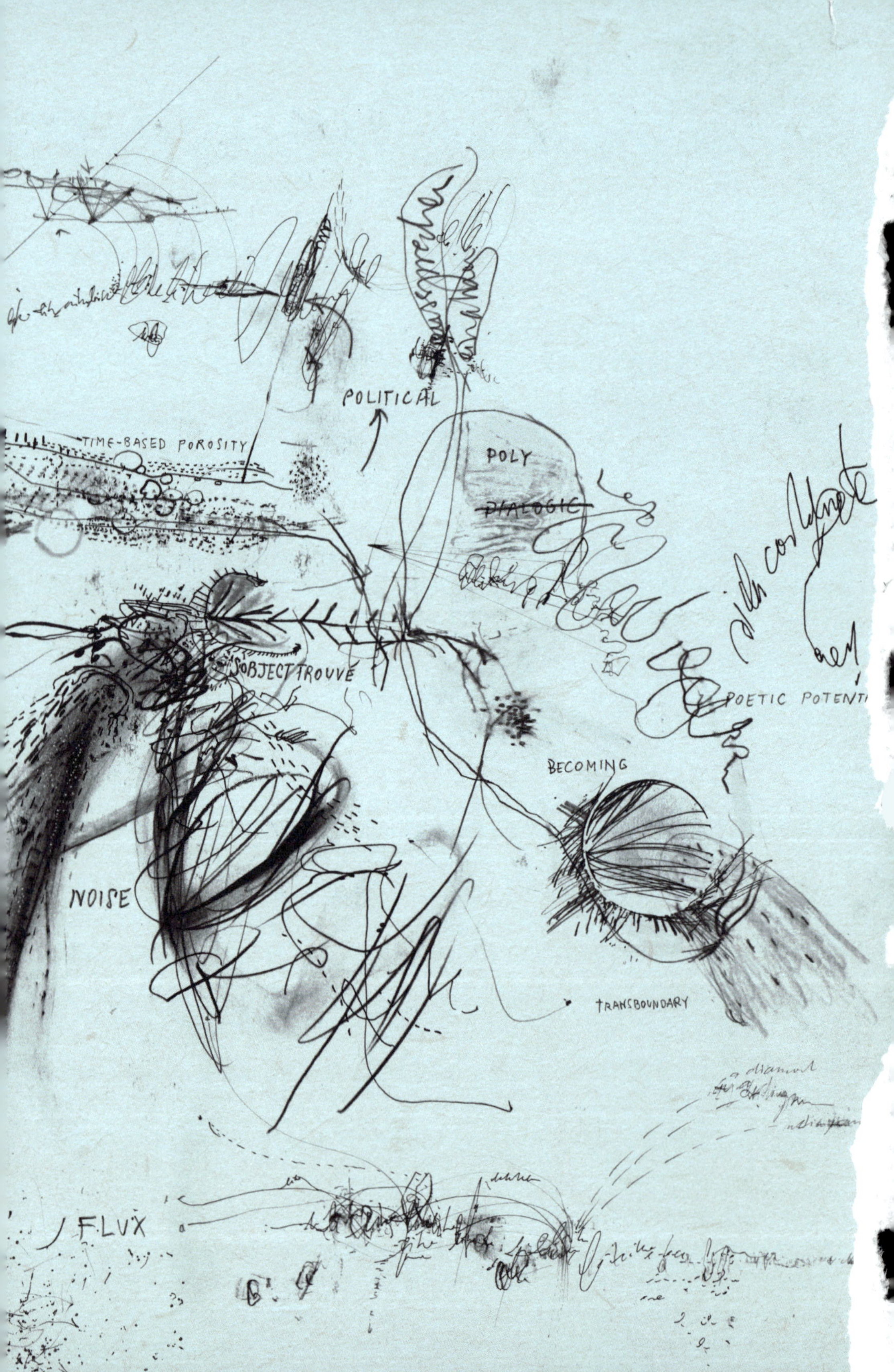
POLITICAL
TIME-BASED POROSITY
POLY
DIALOGIC
OBJECT TROUVÉ
POETIC POTENTI
BECOMING
NOISE
TRANSBOUNDARY
/ FLUX

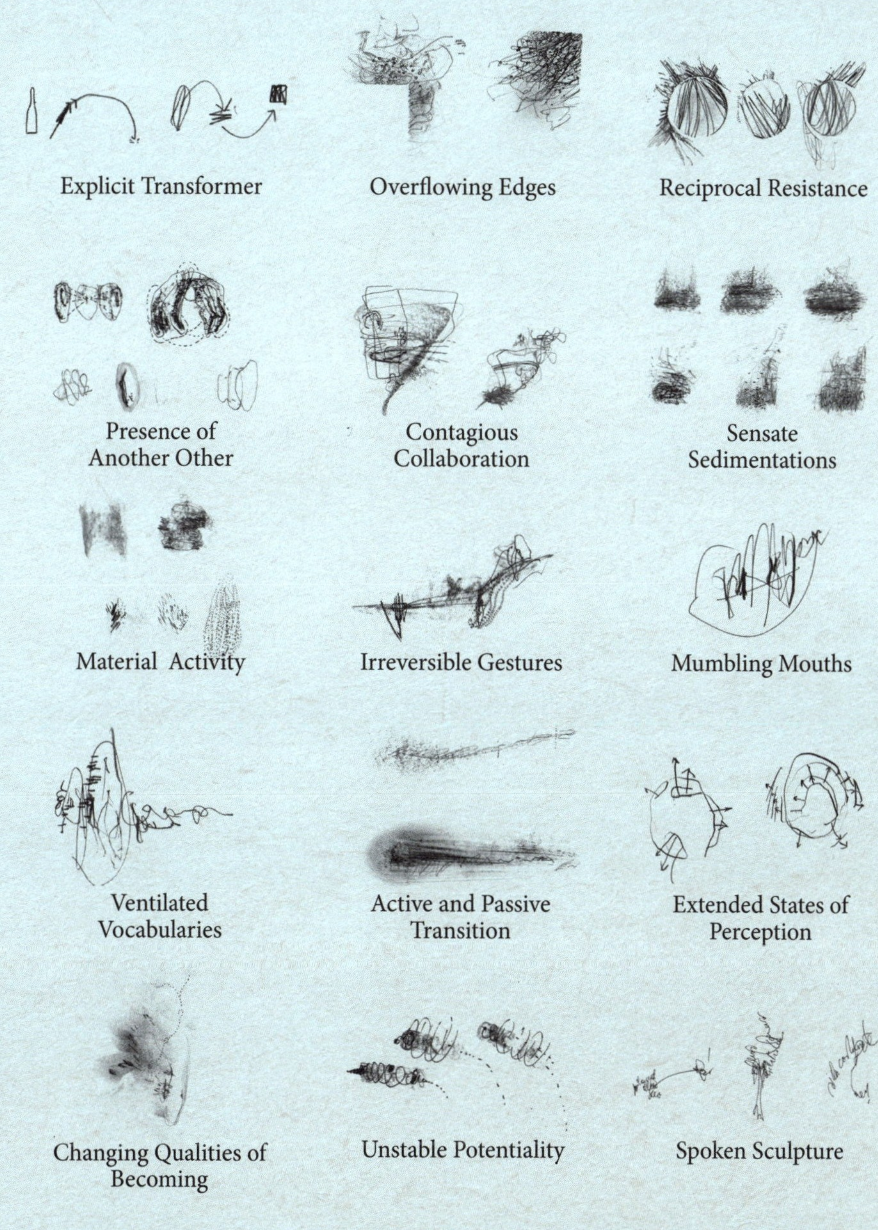

KEY LINES
TRANSFORMATIVE FIGURES

TRANSFORMATIVE *Figures*

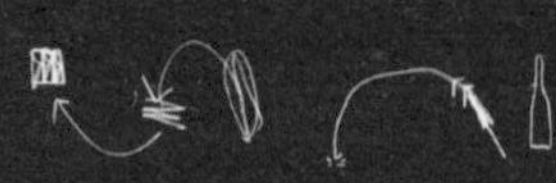

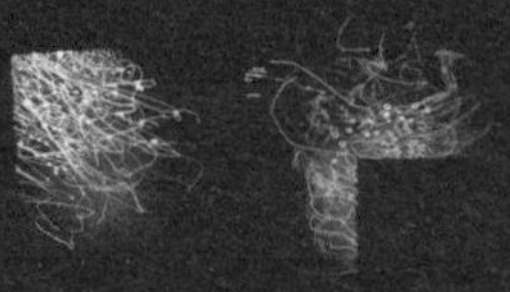

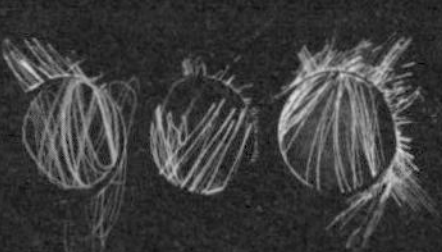

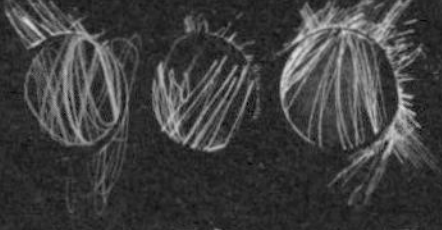

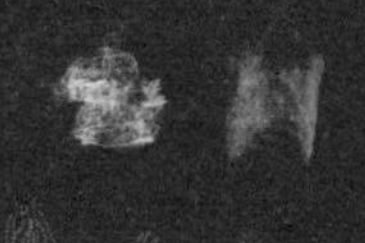

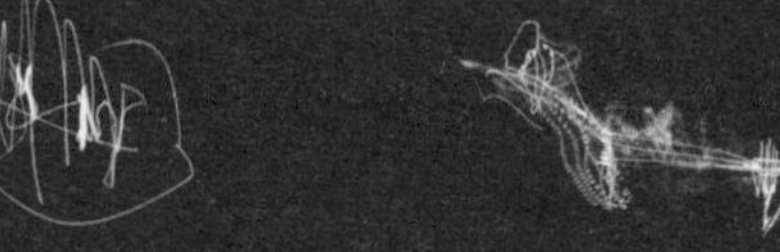

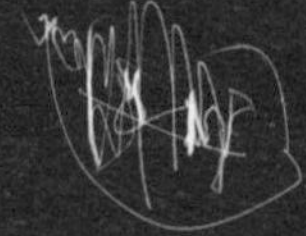

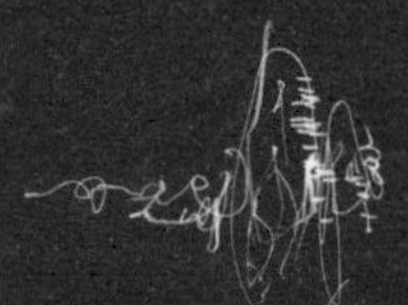

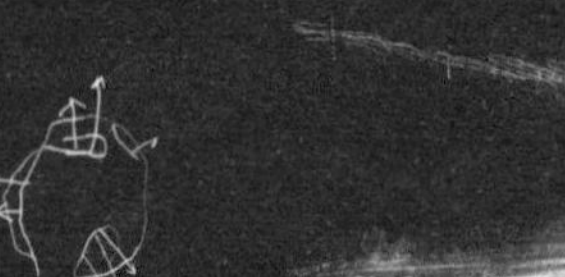

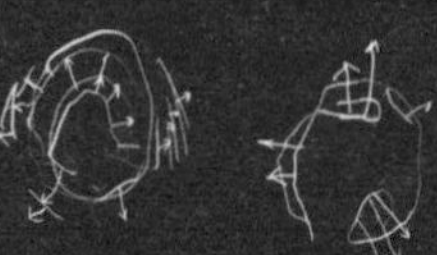

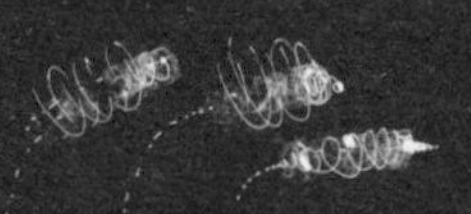

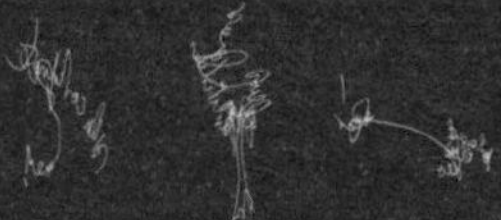

KEY LINES
TRANSFORMATIVE FIGURES

TRANSFORMATIVE *Figures*

The *Transformative Figures* are connected through the prefix *trans-* indicating movement across or through, the act of 'going beyond'. They each involve an explicit shift, change or even transformation in property, quality or state of being. Less interdisciplinary and rather *more than* disciplinary, our enquiry has evolved towards a vocabulary that reaches *beyond* the conventions, protocols and domains of our respective disciplines. By pressuring, translating and in turn expanding the gestures of choreography, of drawing and of writing — through the cross-contamination and friction within shared research — the gestural vocabulary of each discipline becomes hybridised and roughened, inflected or even infected by the gestures of the other(s). However, the boundary crossings that have emerged through our research have been more than disciplinary, involving the negotiation of various lines of demarcation, a radical shift from thinking in terms of binaries and dialectics, towards a condition of porosity, permeability, mutuality, reciprocity. Less a practice of trespass or of transgression, the three *figures* presented — *Ventilating Meaning, Becoming Material* and *Translational Flux* — involve a necessary process of deterritorialisation, perhaps even emancipation, dissolving or destabilising fixed meanings by collapsing the lines of distinction between activity / passivity, animate / inanimate, subject / object, self / world. Transformation is inherently bidirectional, moreover, irreversible: what transforms is also transformed. Our *figures* view transformation not as the destination, but rather as an unstable process of *becoming*. Always in transition: perpetual passage from the virtual to the actual, endless activation of potentiality.

Figure of VENTILATING MEANING

Before they can become material, words must first be rendered matter. Emptied of signification, evacuated of semantic sense. Collapse to sound, sonorous babble of emancipation. Dispersal. Disintegration. Release of language from itself: rhythmic and relational, a move beyond informational exchange. Beyond representation, beyond the symbolic: ventilation of the sign. Displace the agency of words to escape the regime of 'this means this'. Names can be forgotten, syntax lost, thrown to the wind. Not only words, but letting go of the meaning of things. Yet, language seems the most stable of things, so how to prevent it from becoming further solidified? Less towards density, but an enlivening through aeration; practice of resuscitation, revitalise through the bringing of air. Resuscitate: bring back to life, invigorate. Creating air holes, punctuation through the intervention of breath. Activate the intermediary zone between voice and exhalation. Hyperventilation. Not the proliferation of meaning towards meaninglessness, but a practice of sensuous soundings.

To ventilate: to winnow, fan, to set in motion — not towards action but affect. Aeration conceived as quality, not the production of air. Lightness. Levity. Still not yet mutual co-production, rather an affective doing of things with words. Turning over: rotation, inversion. Permutation. Repetition whisks up, froths. Agitation empties out. To expose to wind separates as with the wheat from chaff. To wind: *vente* — adventure at the limits of language, uplifting, slips, taking of flight and fall.

Beyond the self-expressivity of the speaking *I*: towards a practice of collective voicing, movement of words beyond the dialogic, beyond conversation. Passage. Relay. Circulation. Appropriation. Re-appropriation. Re-citing. Citing — again, again, an act of summoning, to call or rouse to action, towards meaning as the creation of the common.

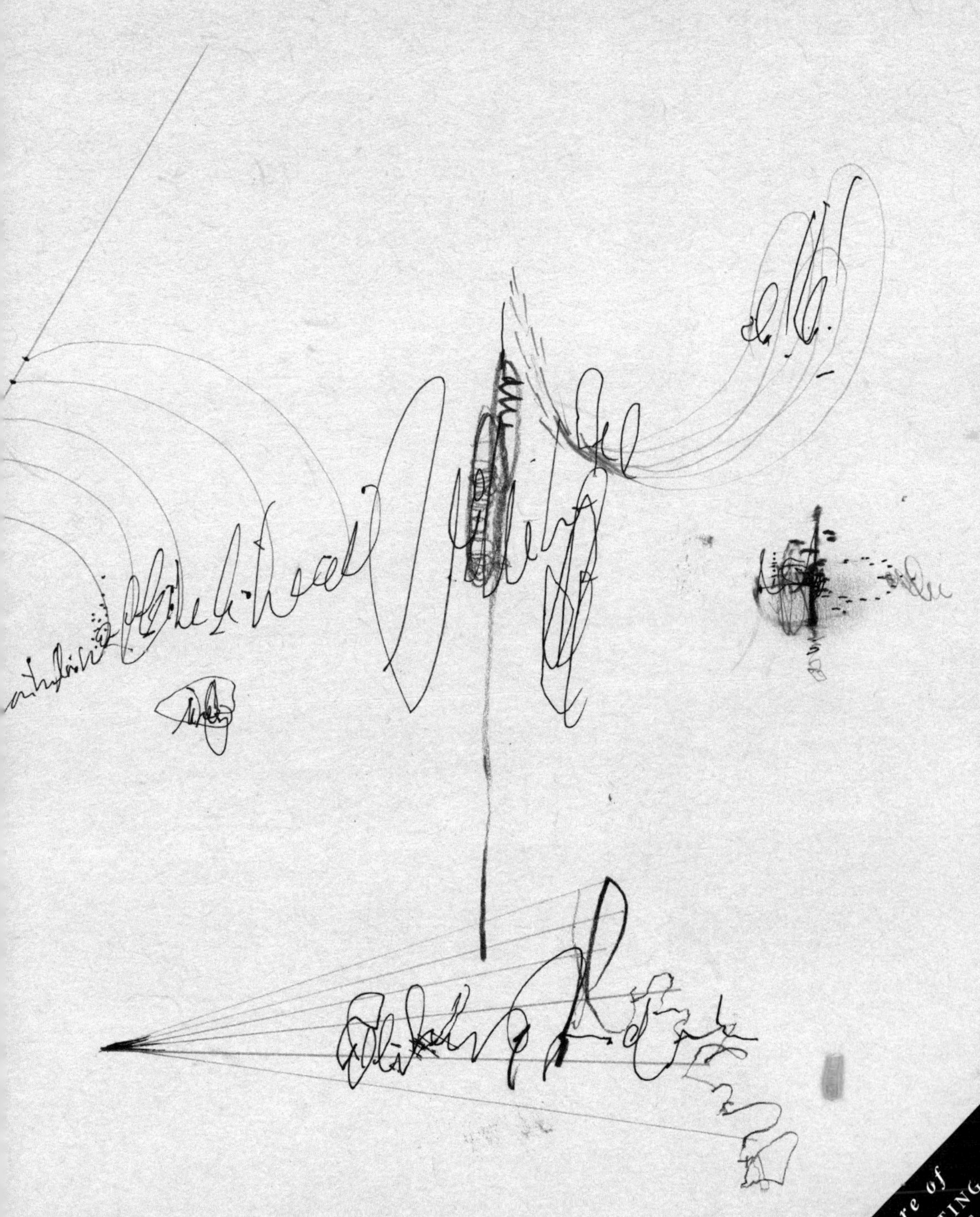

Figure of VENTILATING MEANING

Written words spat onto my face. I listen to the rhythms of the printing machine, buried under lists of likes.

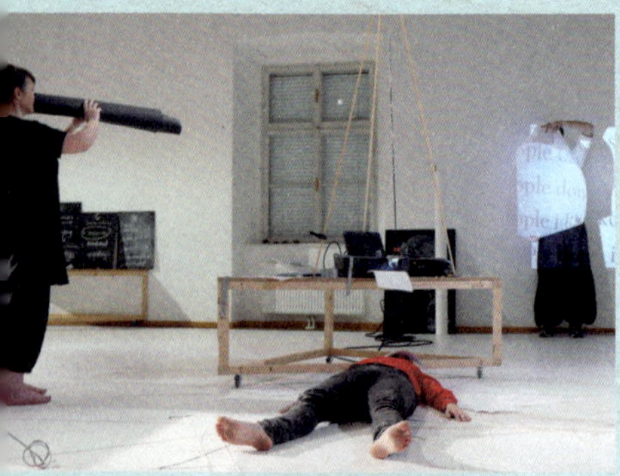

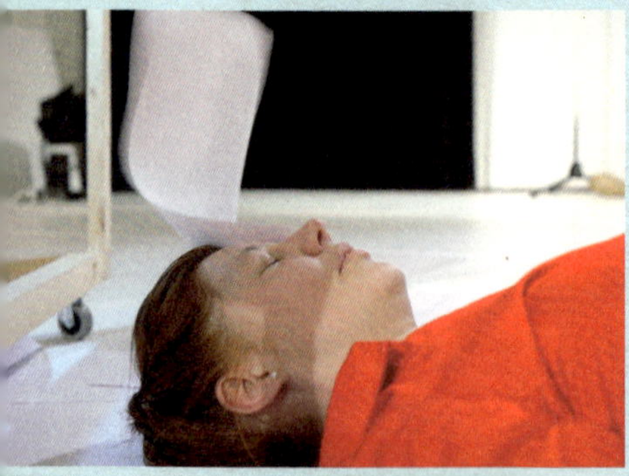

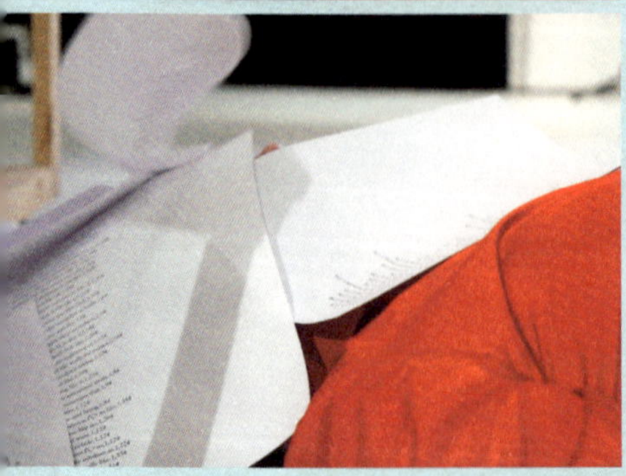

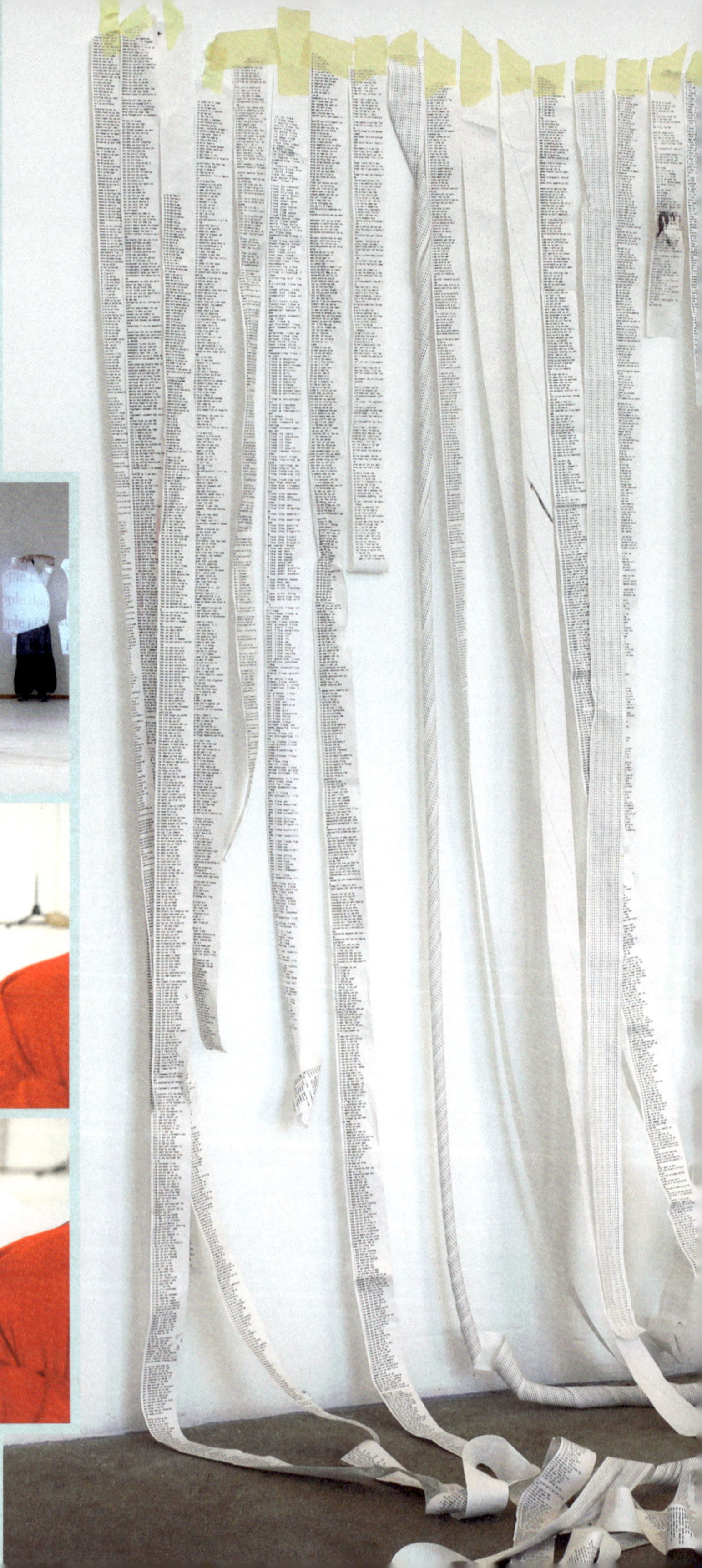

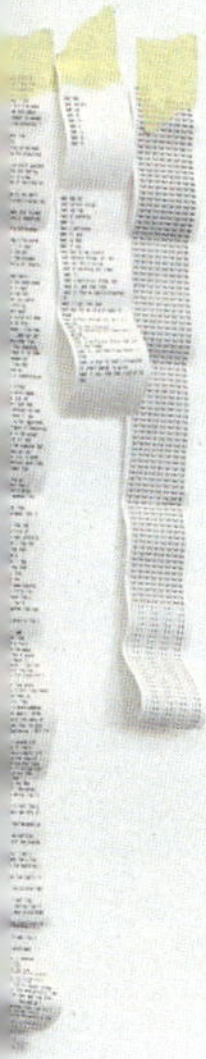

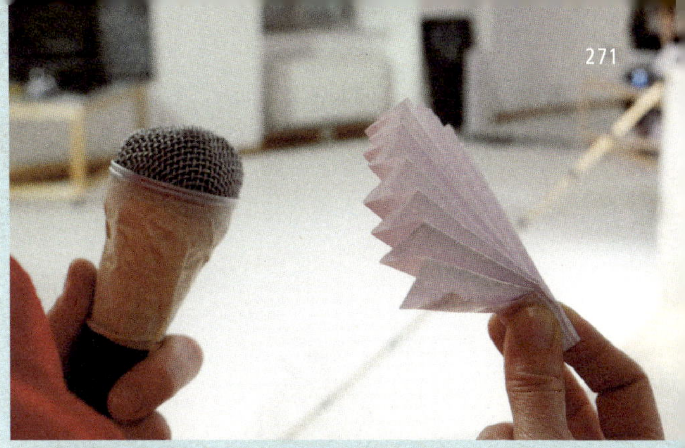

Ventilated sounds in the distance, a sideline. The undoing of meaning, instead stutter and systrophe. I feel the ephemeral solidification before I decide to let it go again.

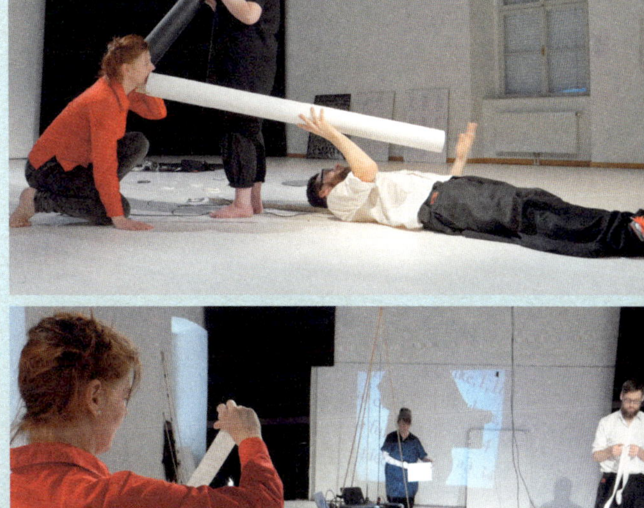

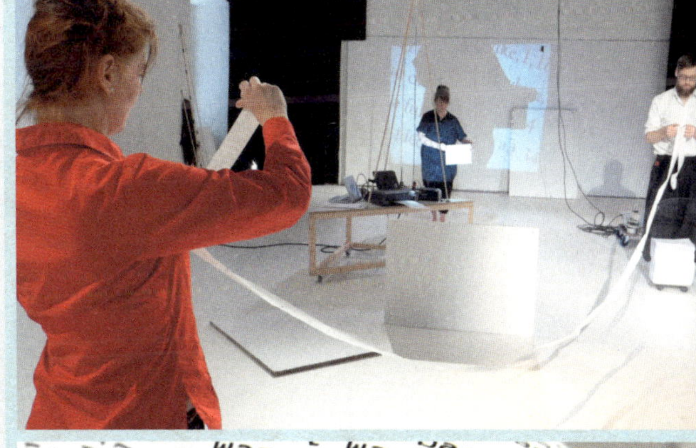

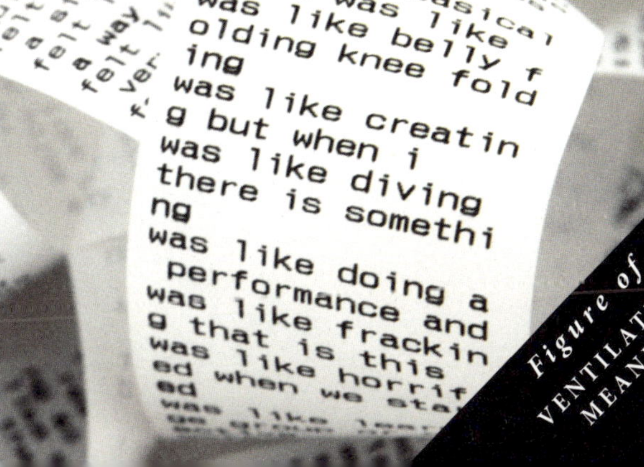

Figure of VENTILATING MEANING

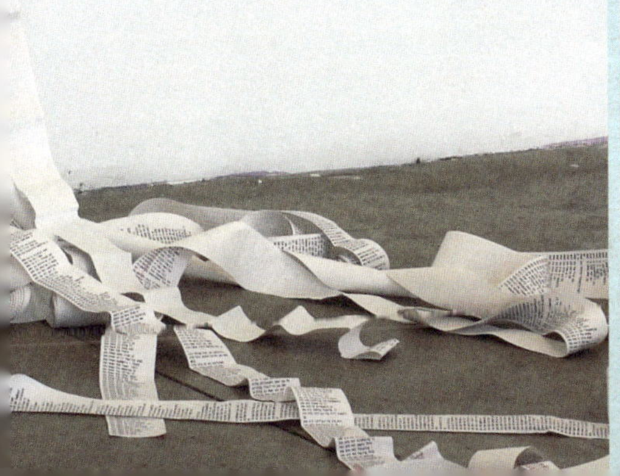

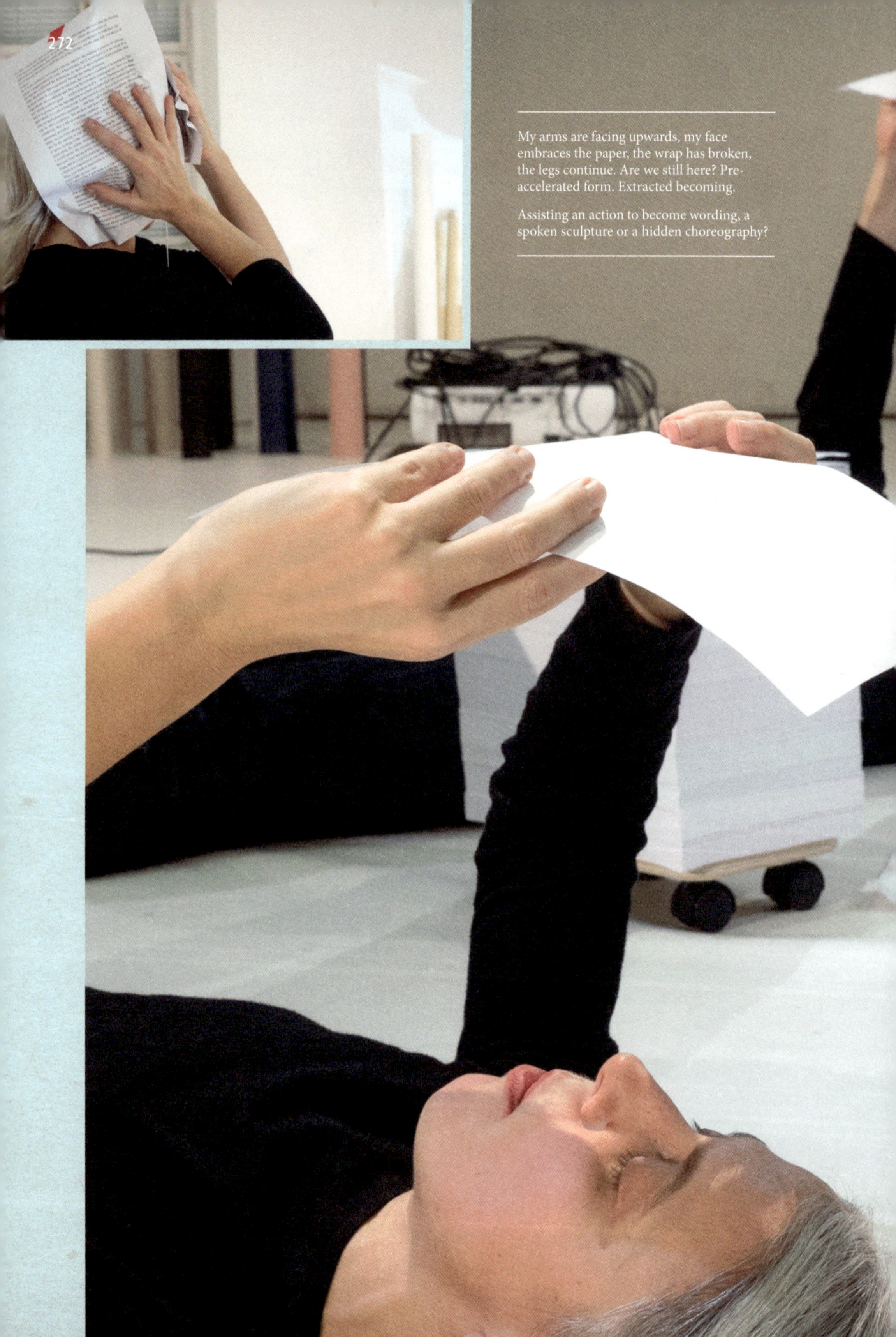

My arms are facing upwards, my face embraces the paper, the wrap has broken, the legs continue. Are we still here? Pre-accelerated form. Extracted becoming.

Assisting an action to become wording, a spoken sculpture or a hidden choreography?

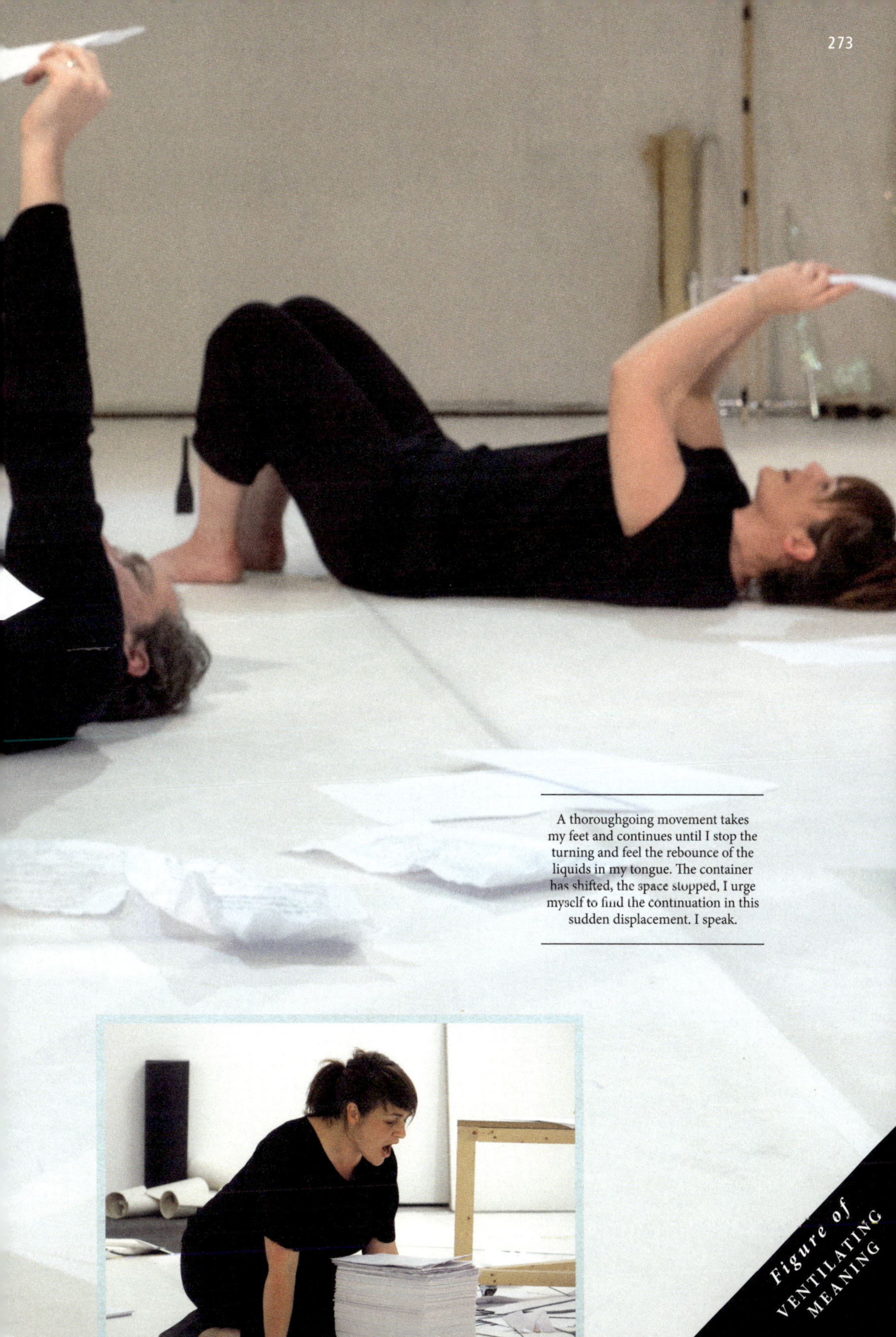

A thoroughgoing movement takes my feet and continues until I stop the turning and feel the rebounce of the liquids in my tongue. The container has shifted, the space stopped, I urge myself to find the continuation in this sudden displacement. I speak.

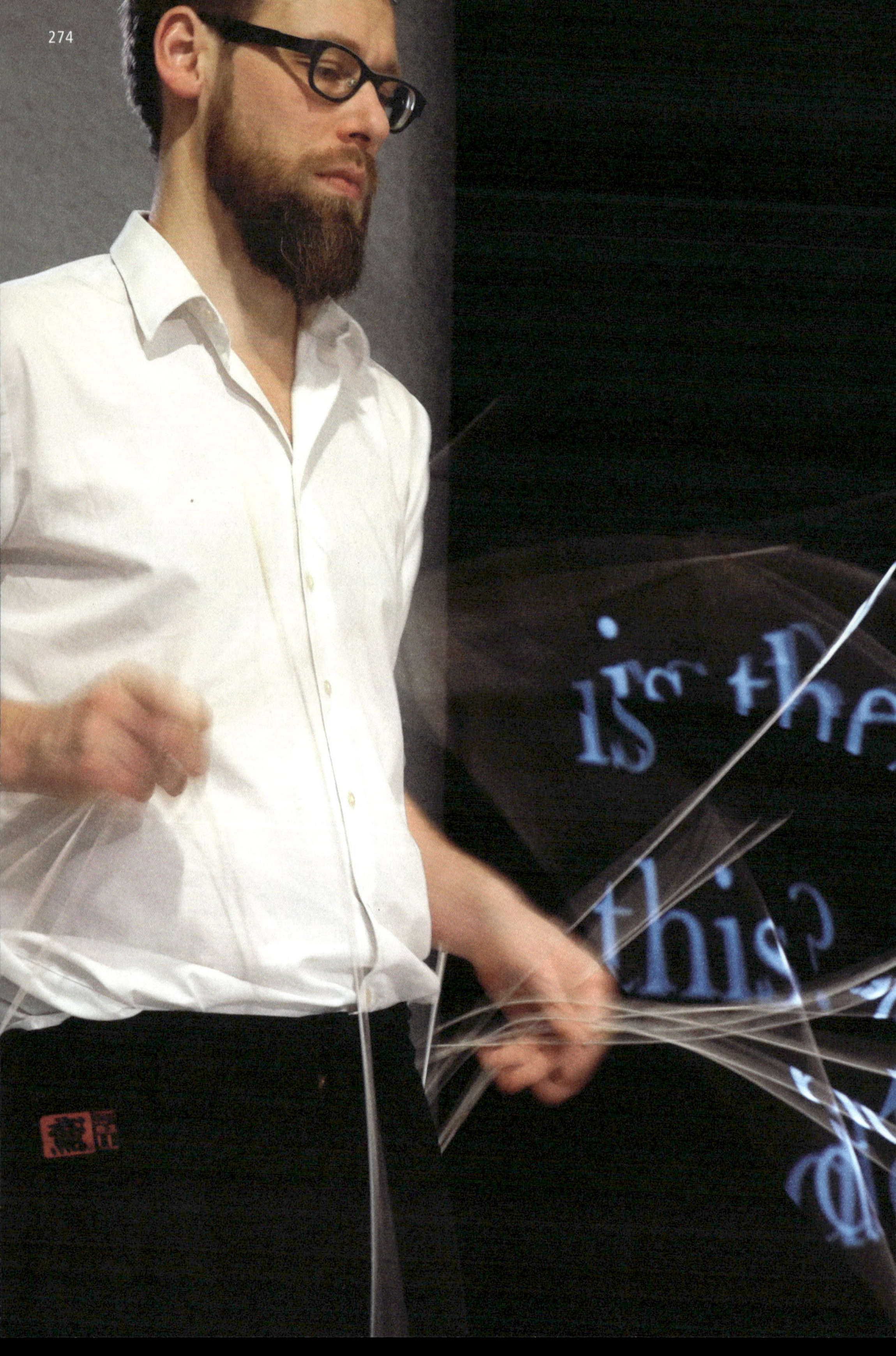
is
this?

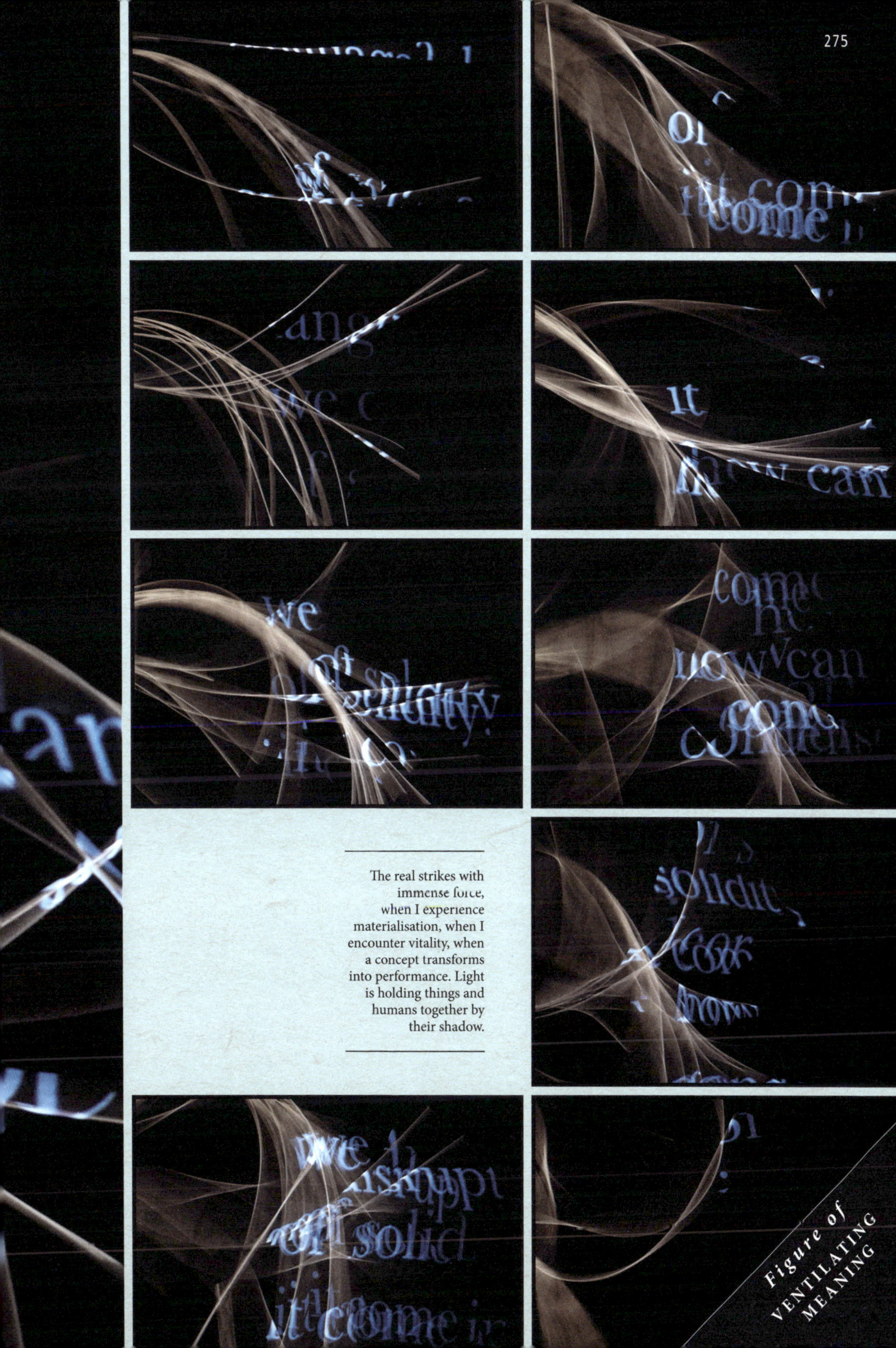

The real strikes with immense force, when I experience materialisation, when I encounter vitality, when a concept transforms into performance. Light is holding things and humans together by their shadow.

Figure of VENTILATING MEANING

Figure of BECOMING MATERIAL

Transformation of matter becoming material — categorical shift affected through the alchemy of play, movement and manipulation. Stay with it, commit. In time material unveils itself, reveals its unseen side, un-actualised potential. Going beyond the raw substance of stuff, beyond physical substrate. Slippery transition of the inanimate towards animation: awakening to a material's liveliness, its vitality or vibrancy, a sense of its pulse. Ritual estrangement: loosening the bonds of habitual utility or purpose. Emancipatory practice. Liberation of things from designated use or function. Through a process of de-familiarisation, familiar objects turn uncanny. Towards a state of working *with*, neither forcing nor bending a material against its will, but becoming attuned to its specific resistances, affordances. Not to dominate or overbear, not to master. To *work with* is to be *worked with*. In the working of matter towards material, one also becomes material. Reciprocally available — I for the material, material for the I. Dual directionality — towards a state of permeability, malleability and receptivity; to become open for the agency of the other.

The boundary between subject and object blurs. Deepening solidarity with materials calls for the densification of relations or of agency, the dampening or renouncing of one's will. Human becoming material, heightened physicality or solidity alongside increased passivity — the surrender of authorial intention creates the conditions for unexpected forms of mutuality, arising of shared spontaneous action, co-emergent.

Yet the condition of consistency, of un-differentiation, is not a move towards equivalence, if this serves only to homogenise, to render reductively the same. Rather the process of becoming material allows for negotiation between materials in their unpredictable singularity, released from the stranglehold of existing subject-object relations, opening towards new forms of entanglement.

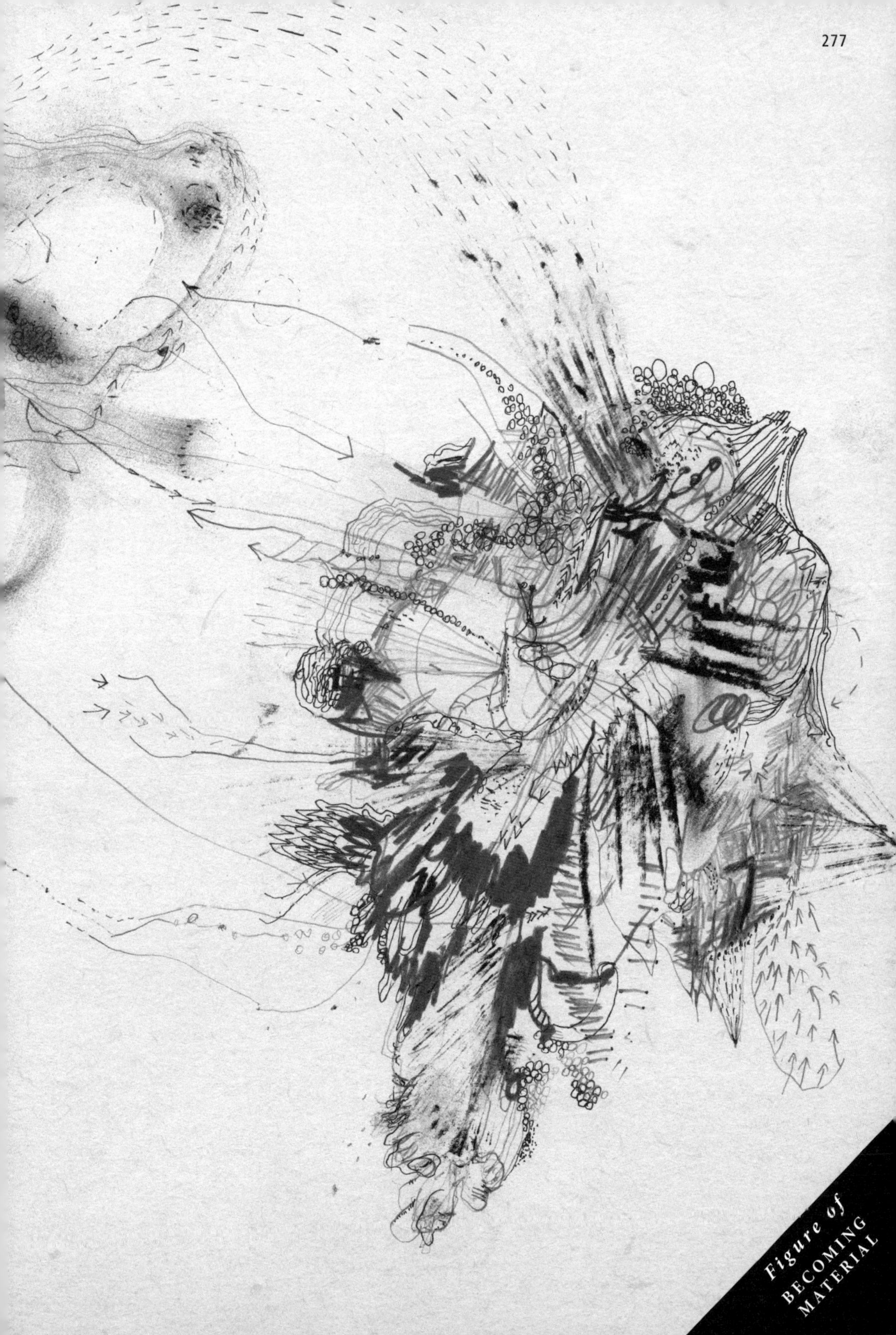
Figure of
BECOMING
MATERIAL

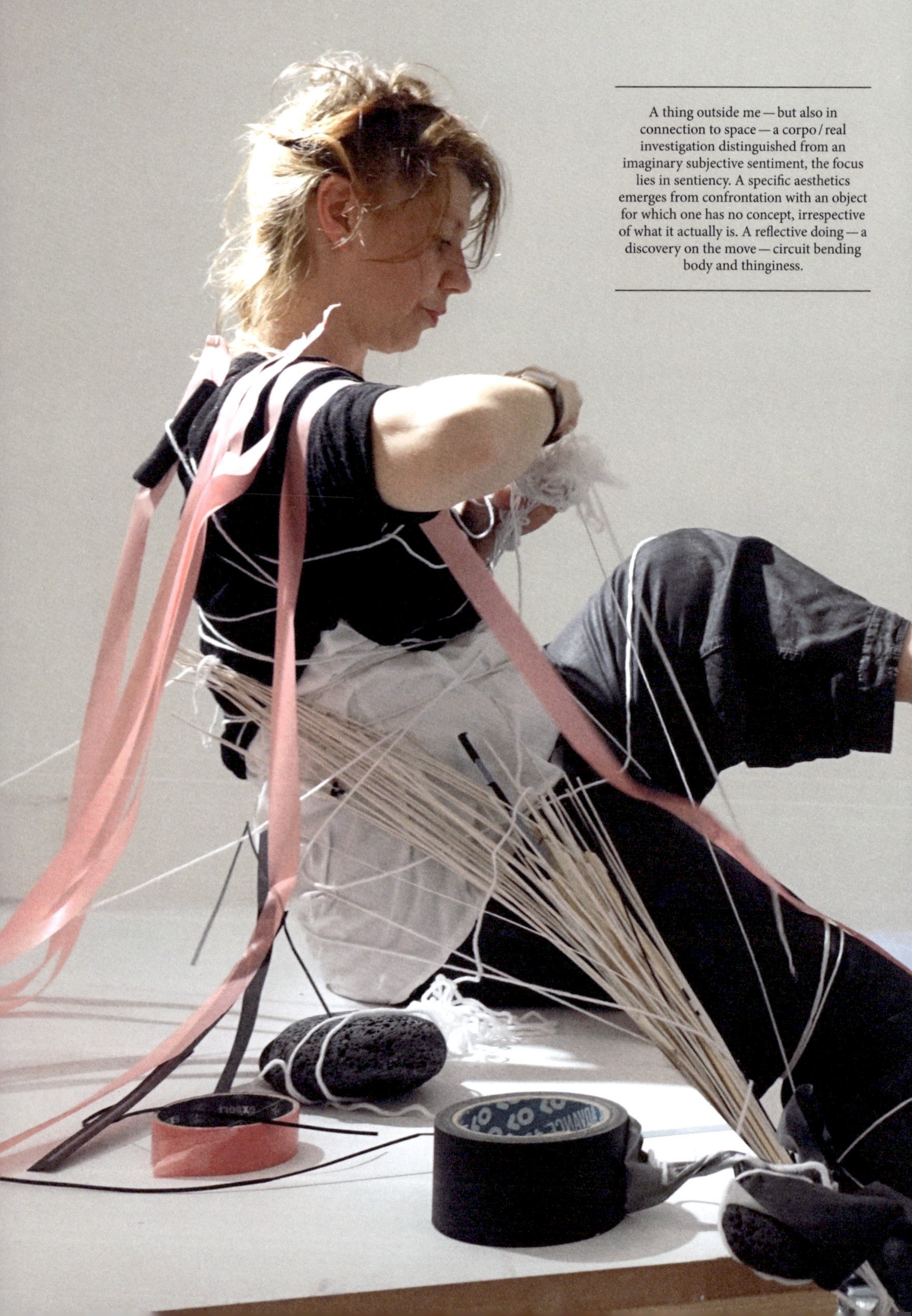

A thing outside me — but also in connection to space — a corpo / real investigation distinguished from an imaginary subjective sentiment, the focus lies in sentiency. A specific aesthetics emerges from confrontation with an object for which one has no concept, irrespective of what it actually is. A reflective doing — a discovery on the move — circuit bending body and thinginess.

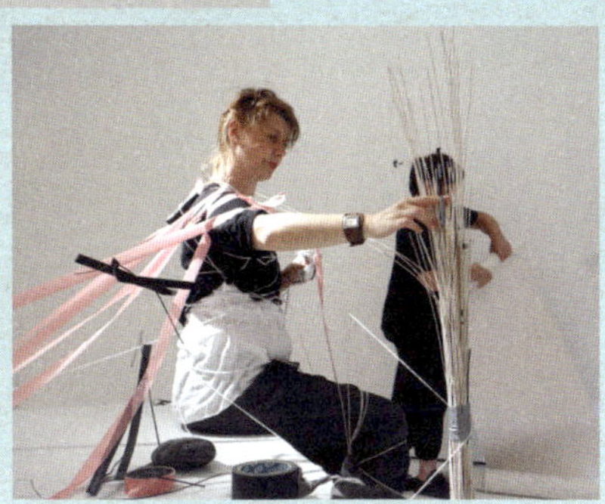

The diagrammatic space between my organs gently pulls me towards nanopolitical acts.

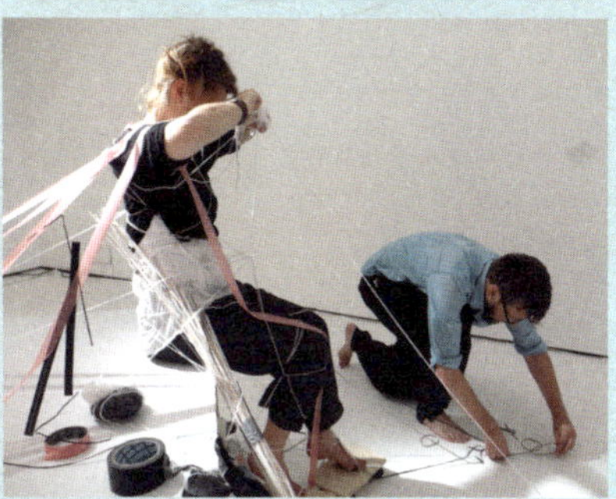

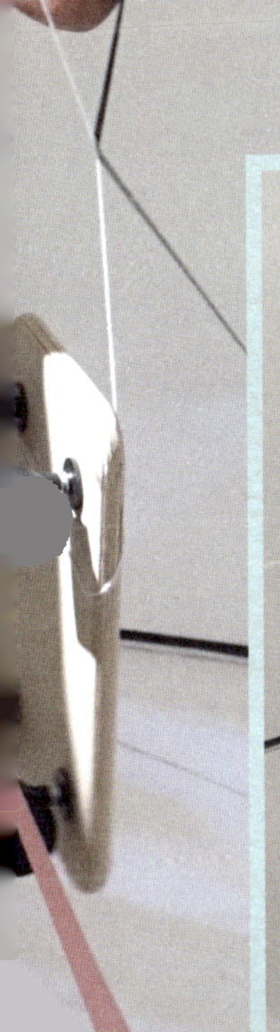

Matter matters. A body that moves. Shades of matter-of-factness. A more-than-body experience when we surrender to our sensibilities. I share the space with others: other bodies, other materials, other words.

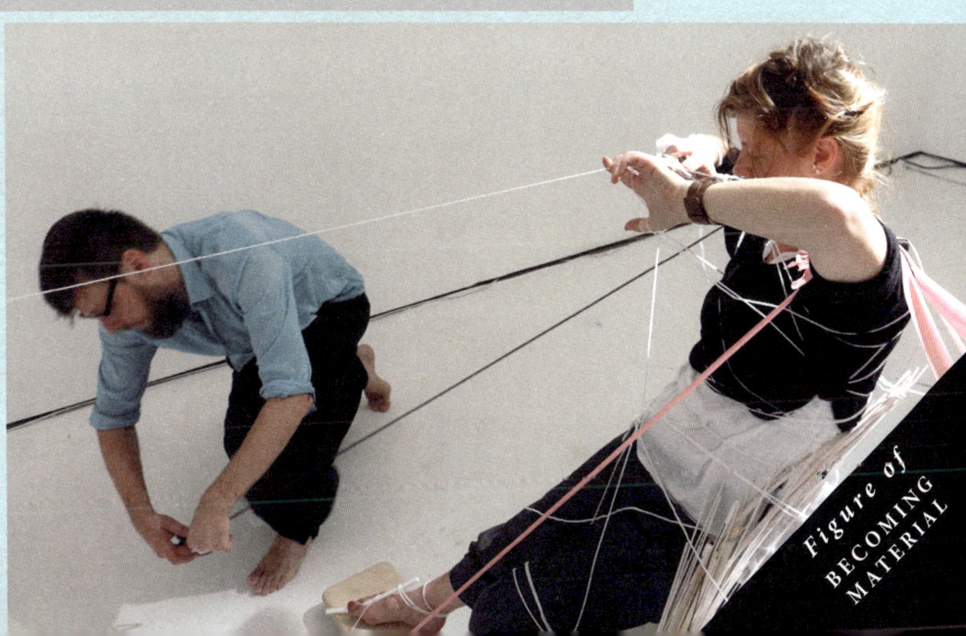

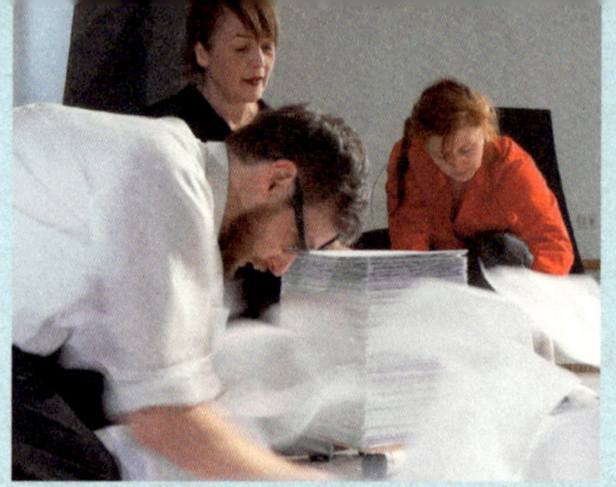

Every paper creases and is grown together with memory of the planet, the woods, the roots, its growths, its paper manufacturing history, and burns in the future. The feeling of my somatic memory — I crush the paper, rubbing it against its inside, wrapping it with the past moment when it still resisted my hand. Its folds and creases wrinkle up, becoming a light sculpture. Subatomic pleasures. I try to slip under the skin of the material, passing every point of its history, the paper's memory of having been printed with transcripted, condensed, collated, collective experience. The death of the paper in my hand proves its vitality.

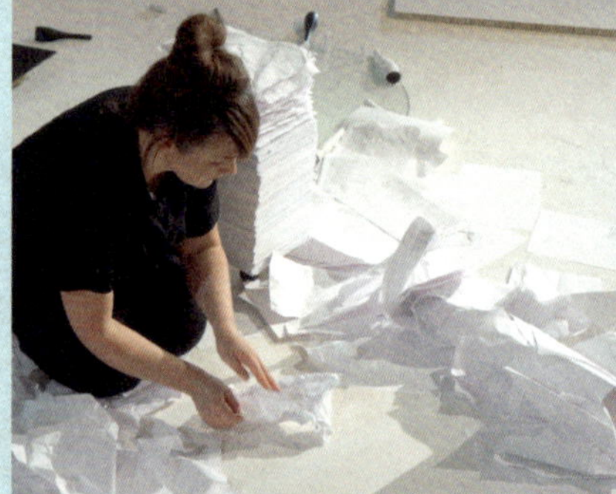

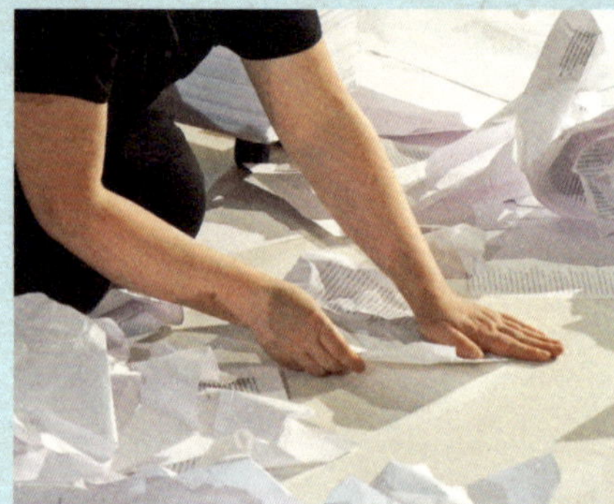

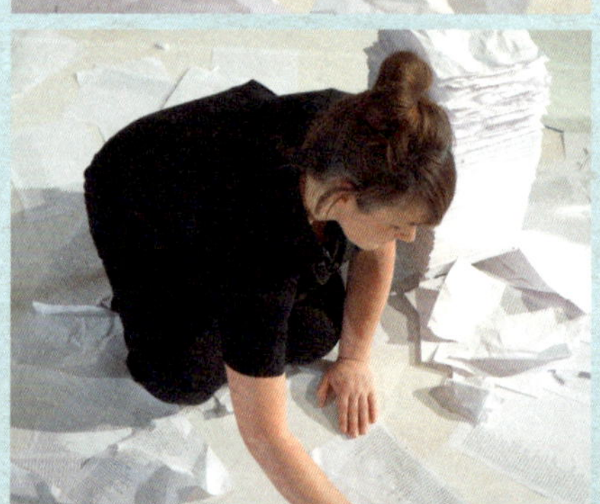

Working with the resistance of concrete materiality — second folding-in. Finding the emergence from the black substance. Unpacking the elasticity of materiality.

Second fold, first squeeze.

Layers of experiences crossfade and coalesce into something that has become a black substance with a peculiar texture, a quality, a relational intensity. No pre-informed conceptions concerning its function or use, its purpose. Purposiveness without purpose. Kant's third Critique resonates in the third crease.

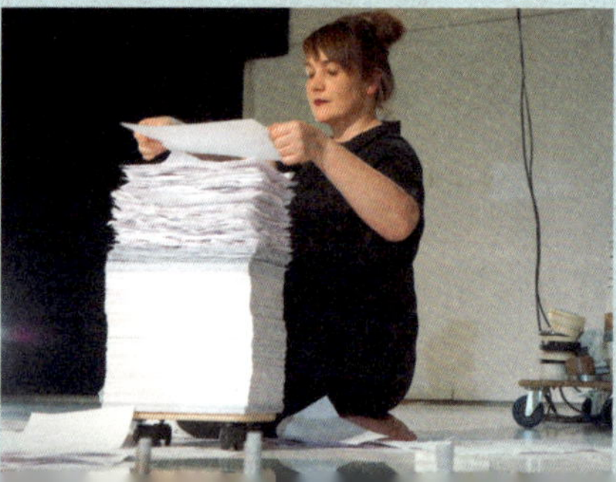

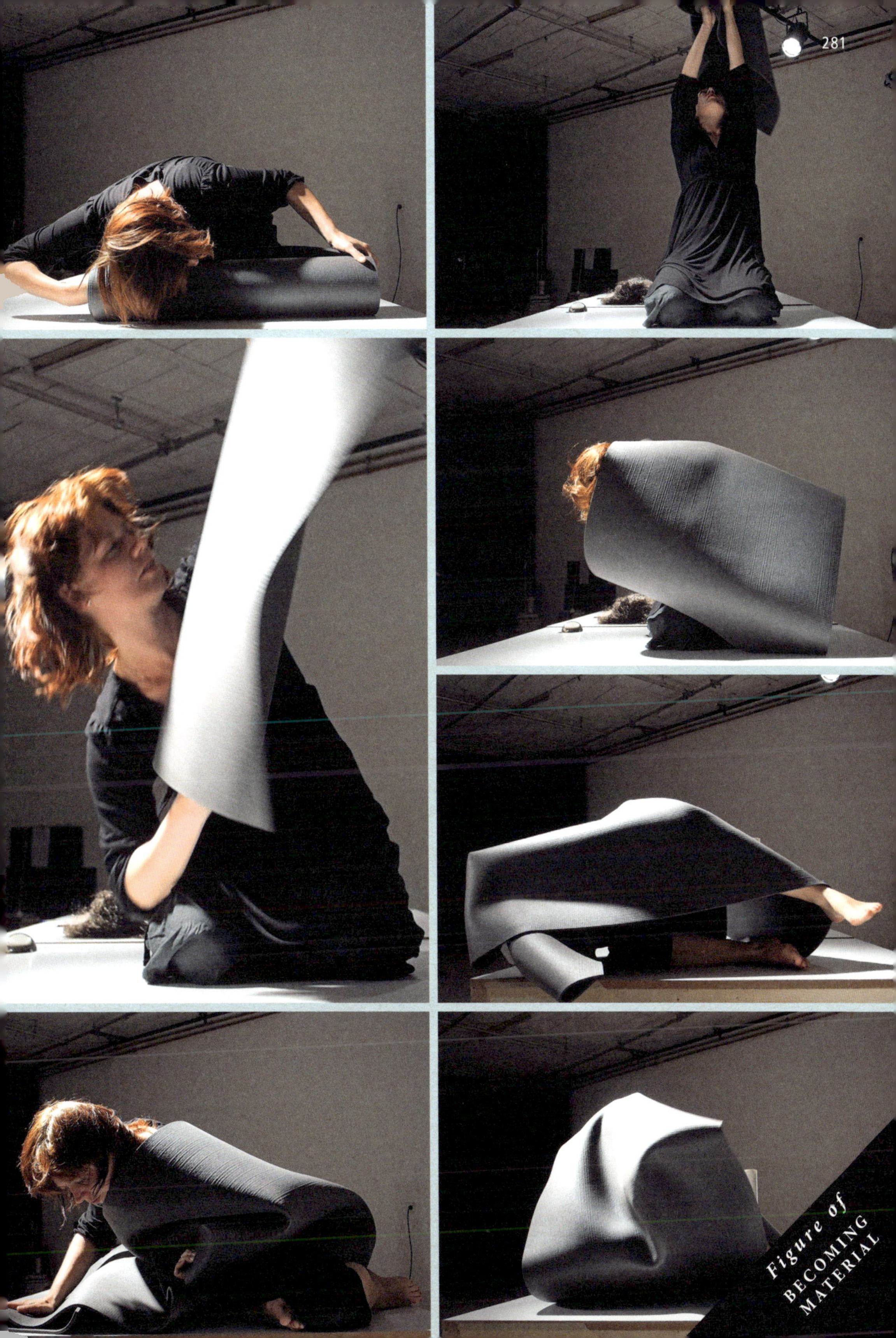
Figure of
BECOMING
MATERIAL

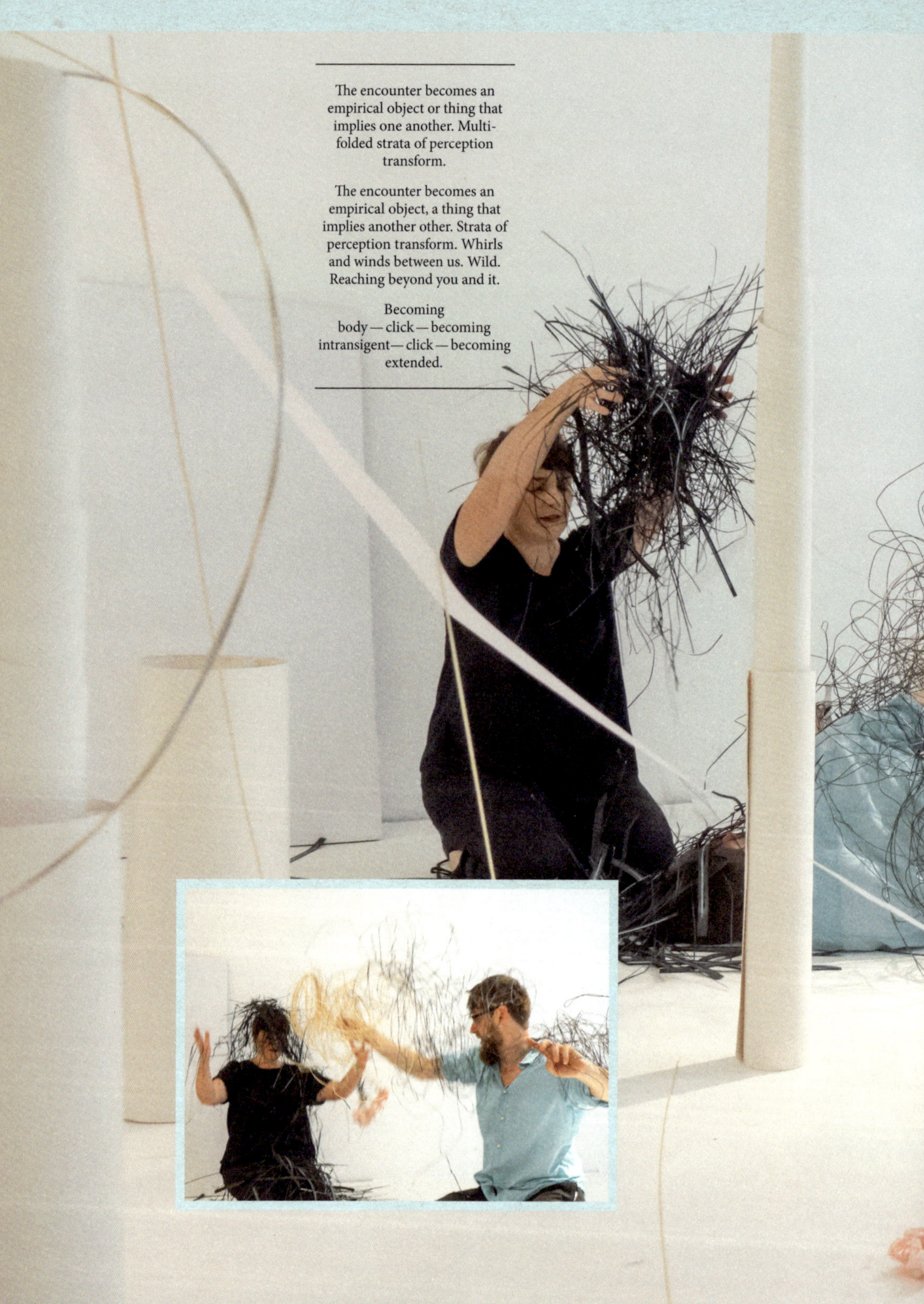

The encounter becomes an empirical object or thing that implies one another. Multi-folded strata of perception transform.

The encounter becomes an empirical object, a thing that implies another other. Strata of perception transform. Whirls and winds between us. Wild. Reaching beyond you and it.

Becoming
body — click — becoming
intransigent— click — becoming
extended.

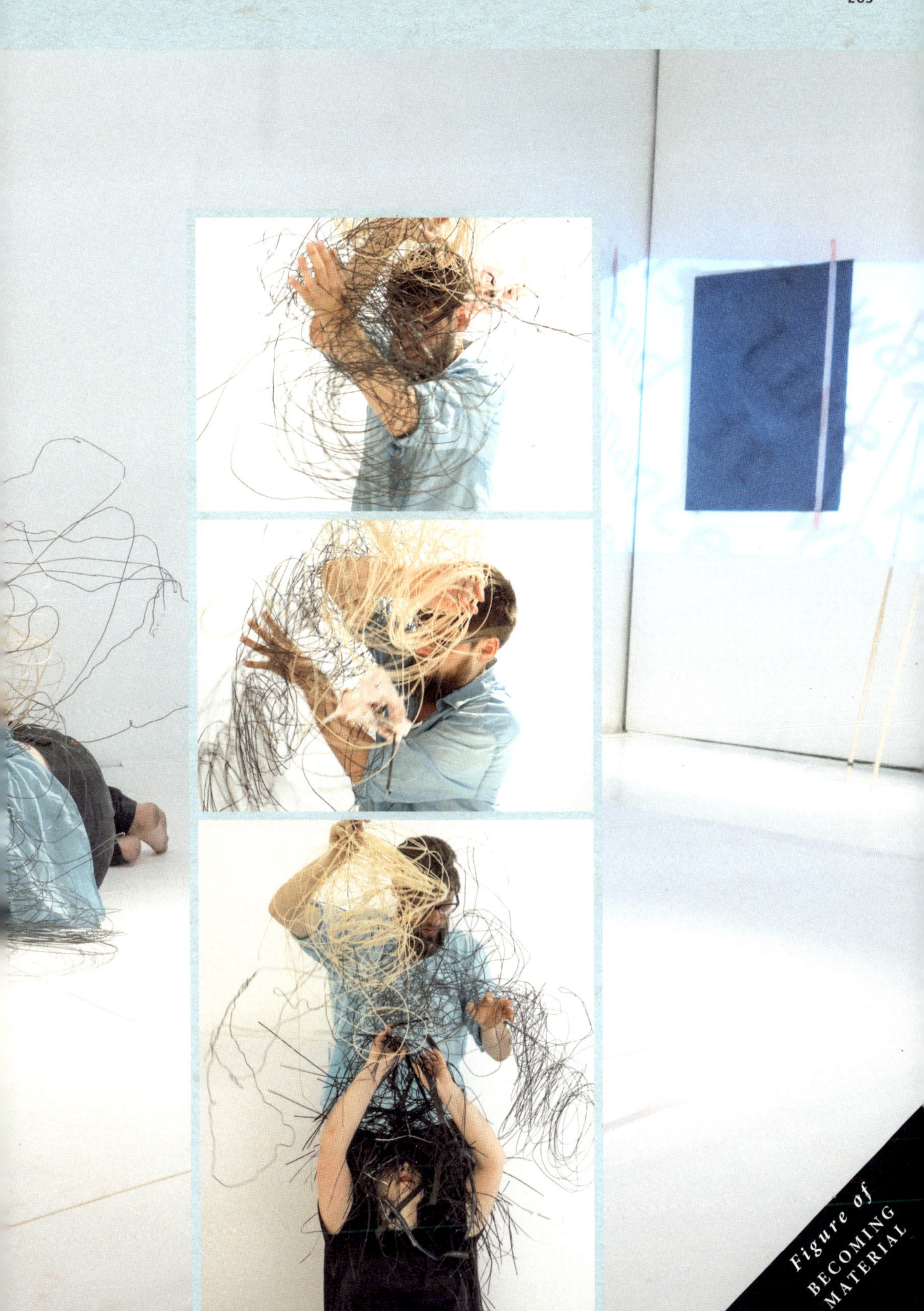
Figure of
BECOMING
MATERIAL

Figure of
TRANSLATIONAL FLUX

Relay of relations: the passage of conversion, crossing from one state to another. Iterations. Proliferations. To set in motion, fixed form dissolved towards a perpetual state of flux. Translate, transport — to carry over, to move, to convey from one place or language to another. Always in flight, never solidifying into stasis. Never settling on any singular form. Migratory movement from this to this to this, from one modality or medium to another: tactility of touch transcribed through trace, inscription shape-shifting towards the material, the spatial, relational, or sonorous. Bi-directionality of flow — *becoming* refusing the logic of linearity, the order of any prescribed route. Yet ever forward, onwards, for the process is irreversible, the original irrevocably altered. The accumulation of translations will not be forgotten or erased, indeed, the traveller does not return unchanged. Mutual reciprocity then: less acting as translator, the neutral intermediary between, rather through translation one is also translated, changed, transformed. In translating, not just bearing, also borne.

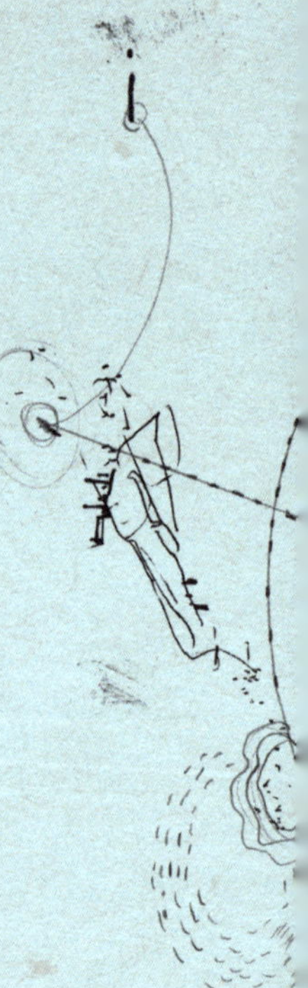

Navigating the journey from A to B, yet B still remains uncertain. In turn, A becomes defamiliarised. Mutual destabilisation: each becomes altered by the other. Transduction. Transmutation. Contamination. Interpretation. Reinvention. Crossing of a threshold or boundary, a rite of passage. What to let go? What is lost, what gained? What is smuggled over? Unavoidable mistranslation: accumulation of noise, of deficits and excess. Arising of the third thing as yet unknown.

Not translating, but translation arising. Not about likeness. Not the representational act of copying, mimesis or of mimicry. Through translation — fidelity to force not form. Retaining the quality of A whilst facilitating its alteration, a change in state — the keeping of its this-ness in other-ness. Maintaining enough identity, conditions of re-cognition. For finding it again, feeling it again. Going beyond whilst somehow getting closer. Translation is figuring, an experiential process of discovery: revelation of essence through translation, practising qualitative precision.

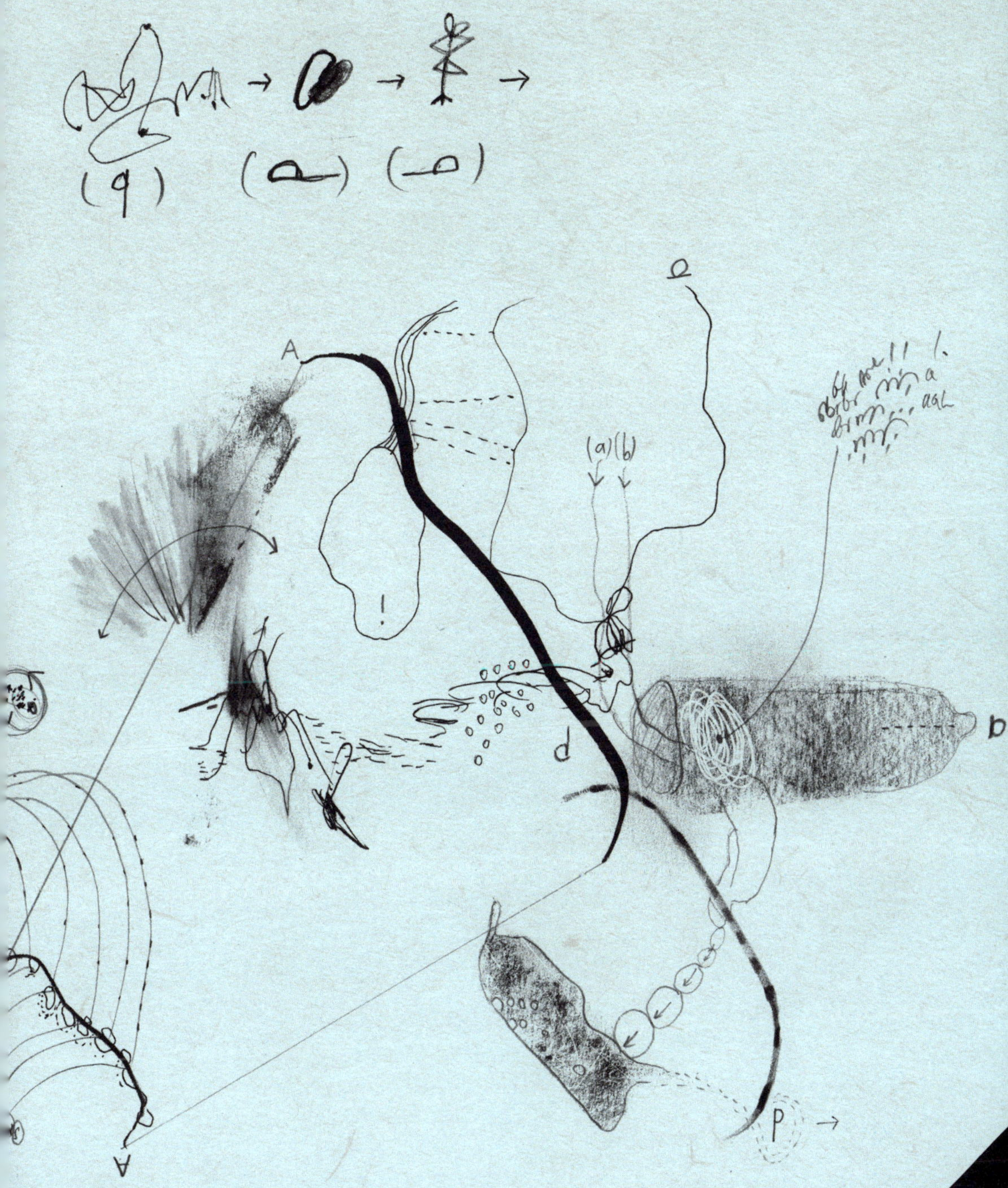

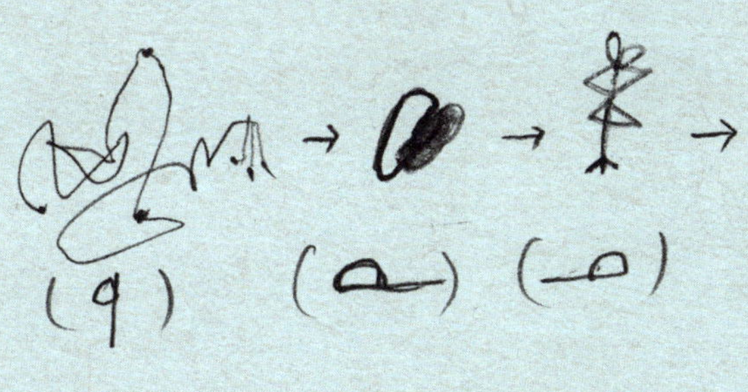

Figure of TRANSLATIONAL FLUX

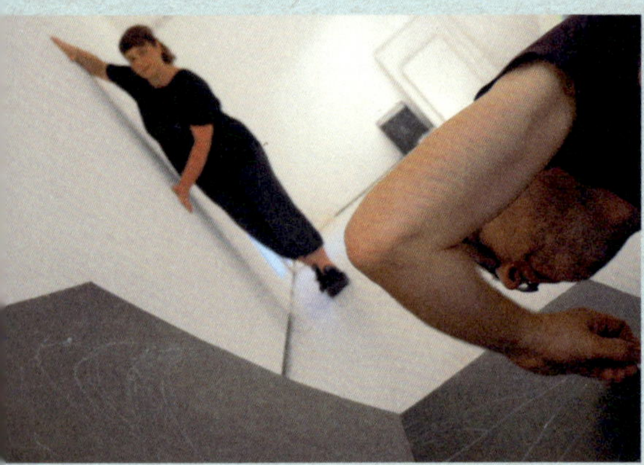

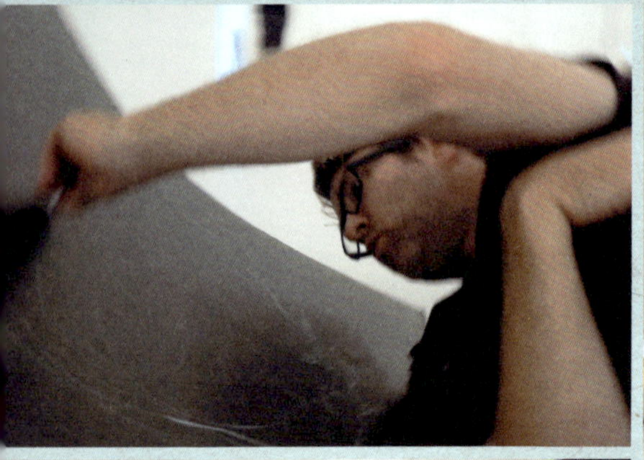

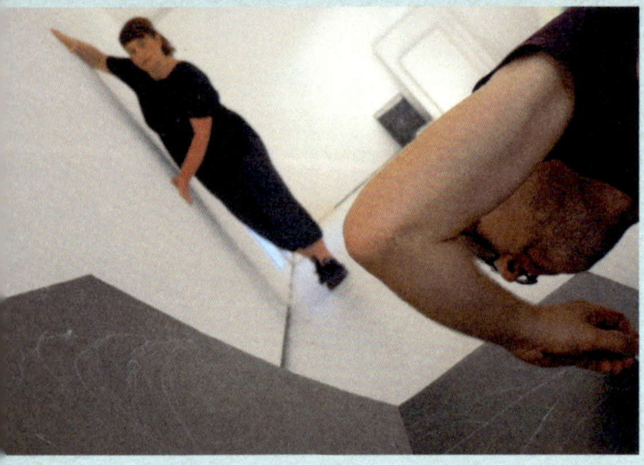

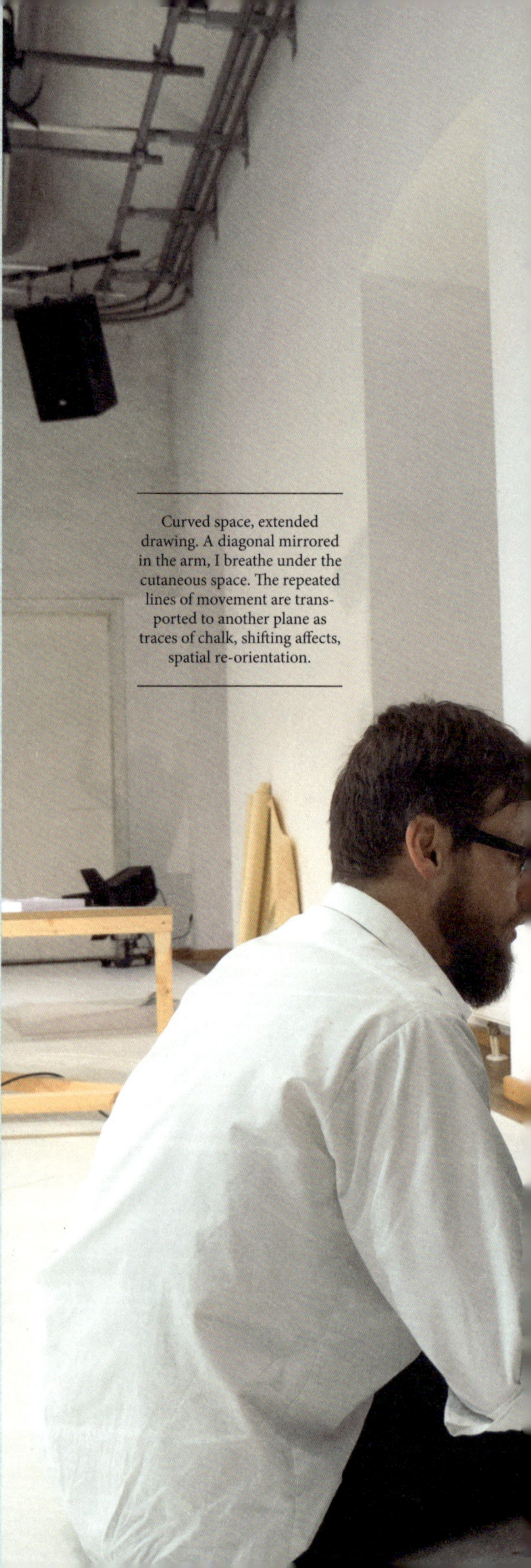

Curved space, extended drawing. A diagonal mirrored in the arm, I breathe under the cutaneous space. The repeated lines of movement are transported to another plane as traces of chalk, shifting affects, spatial re-orientation.

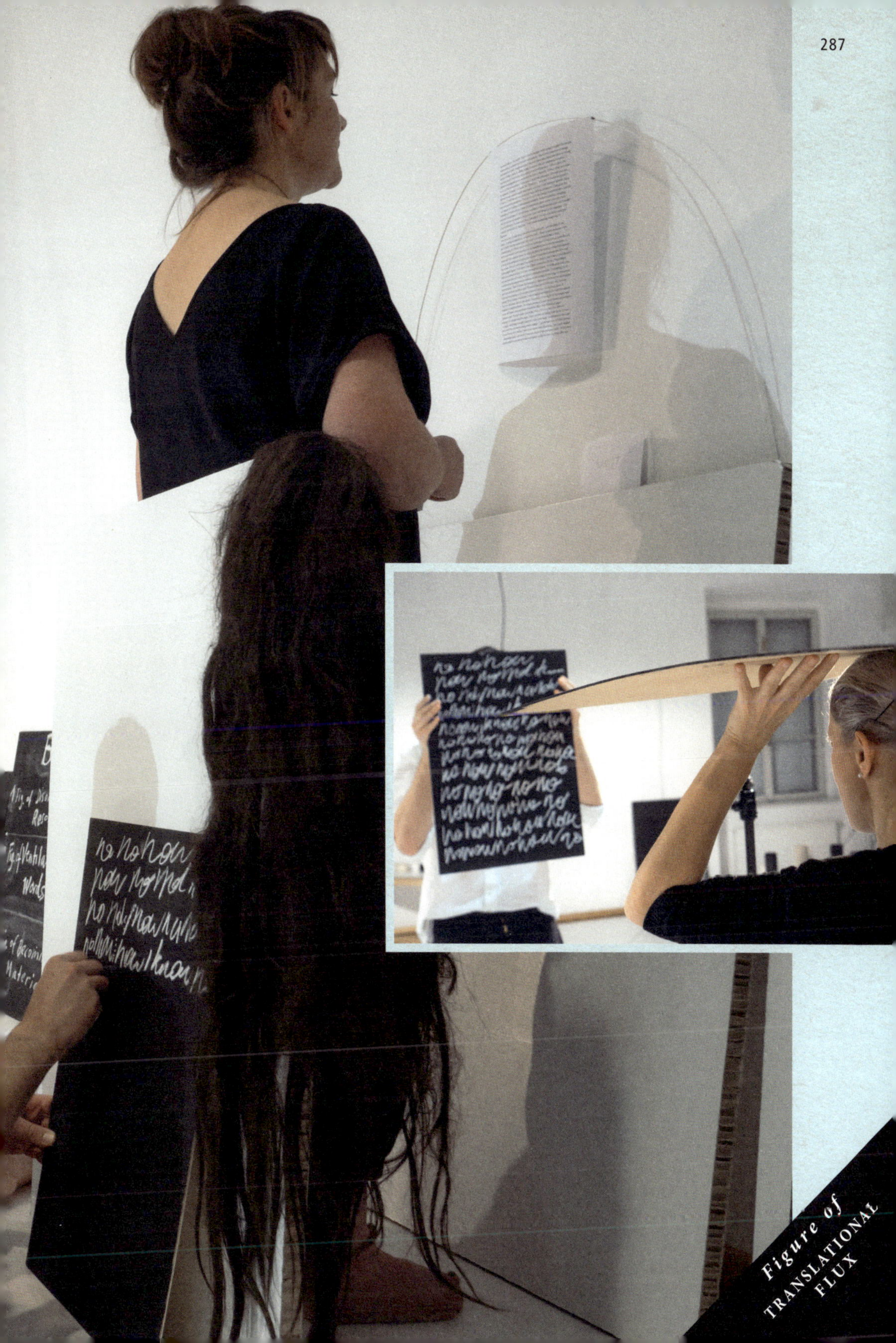

Figure of
TRANSLATIONAL
FLUX

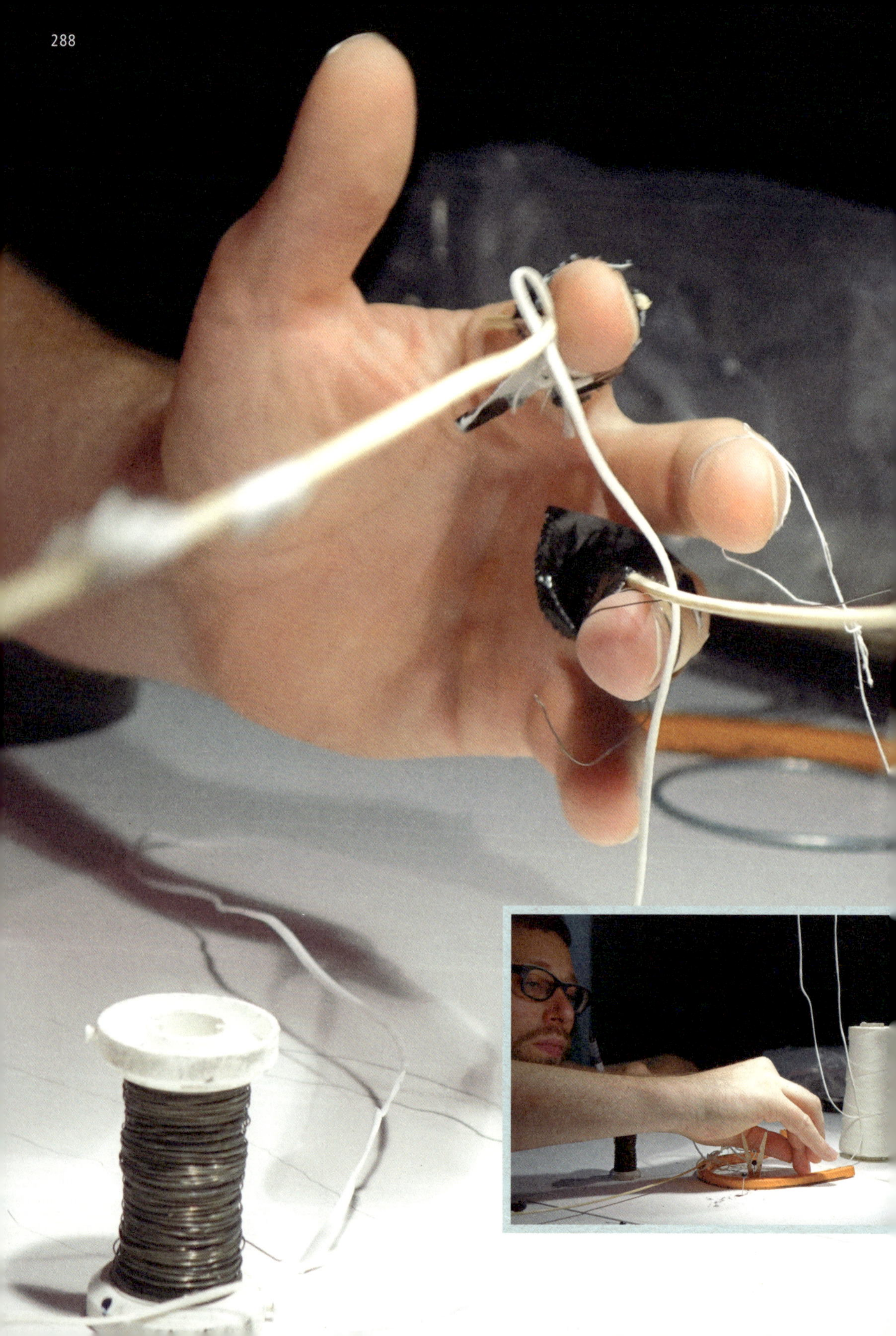

A slow, insisting movement is defending space beyond the visible, a deterritorialising movement. Try-outs on aesthetic grounds, cohabited forms. Yes, vitality again, the dynamics of form as remembered from *vita*, from life, through its *re-per-formance* and trans-substantiation.

Untold power emerges through practising trans-formation, trans-plantation, trans-scripture. The ecology is a delicate, subtle and micro-political one.

Sequence. Living knowledge, sensing space, moving affects. Laying bare. Crude. Gyration emanates through my body. Spiral. Acceleration. Extension. A wave of radical movements claims persistence and rigour. Start back. Trans-late.

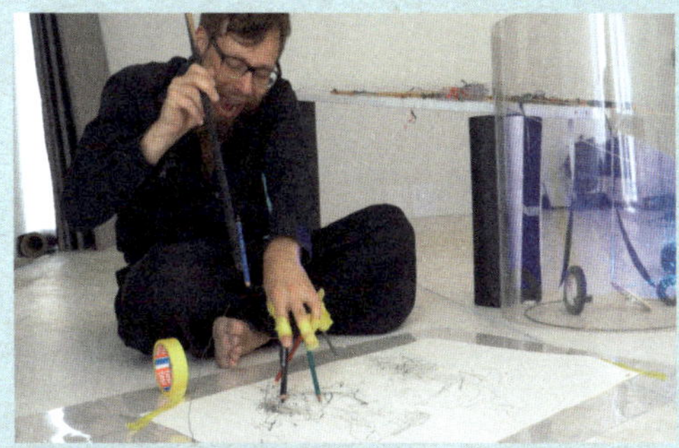

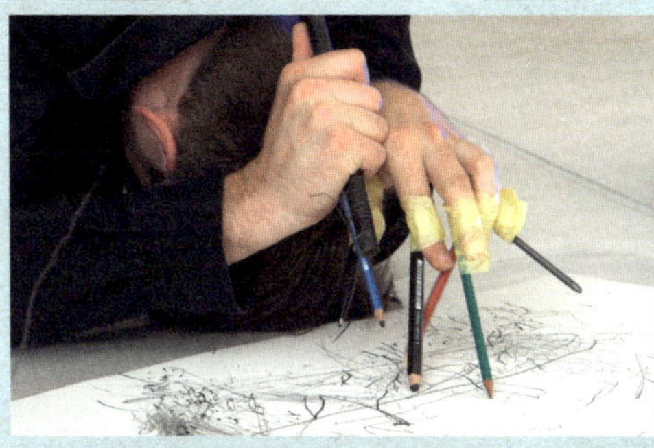

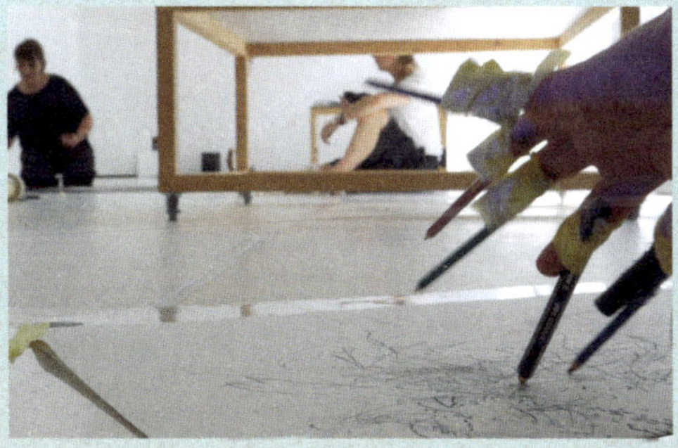

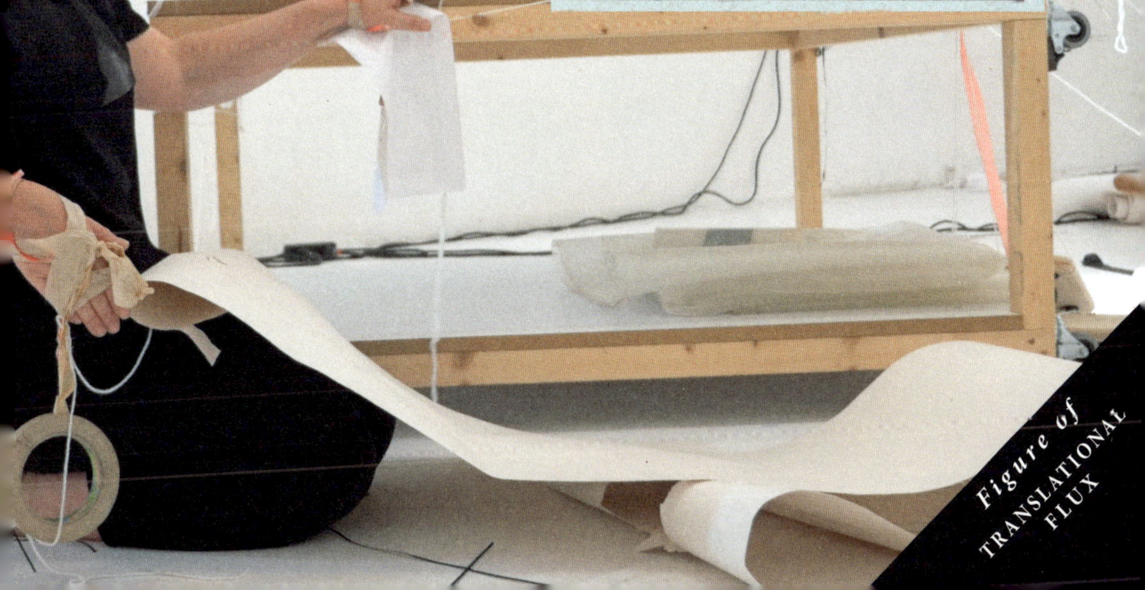

Figure of TRANSLATIONAL FLUX

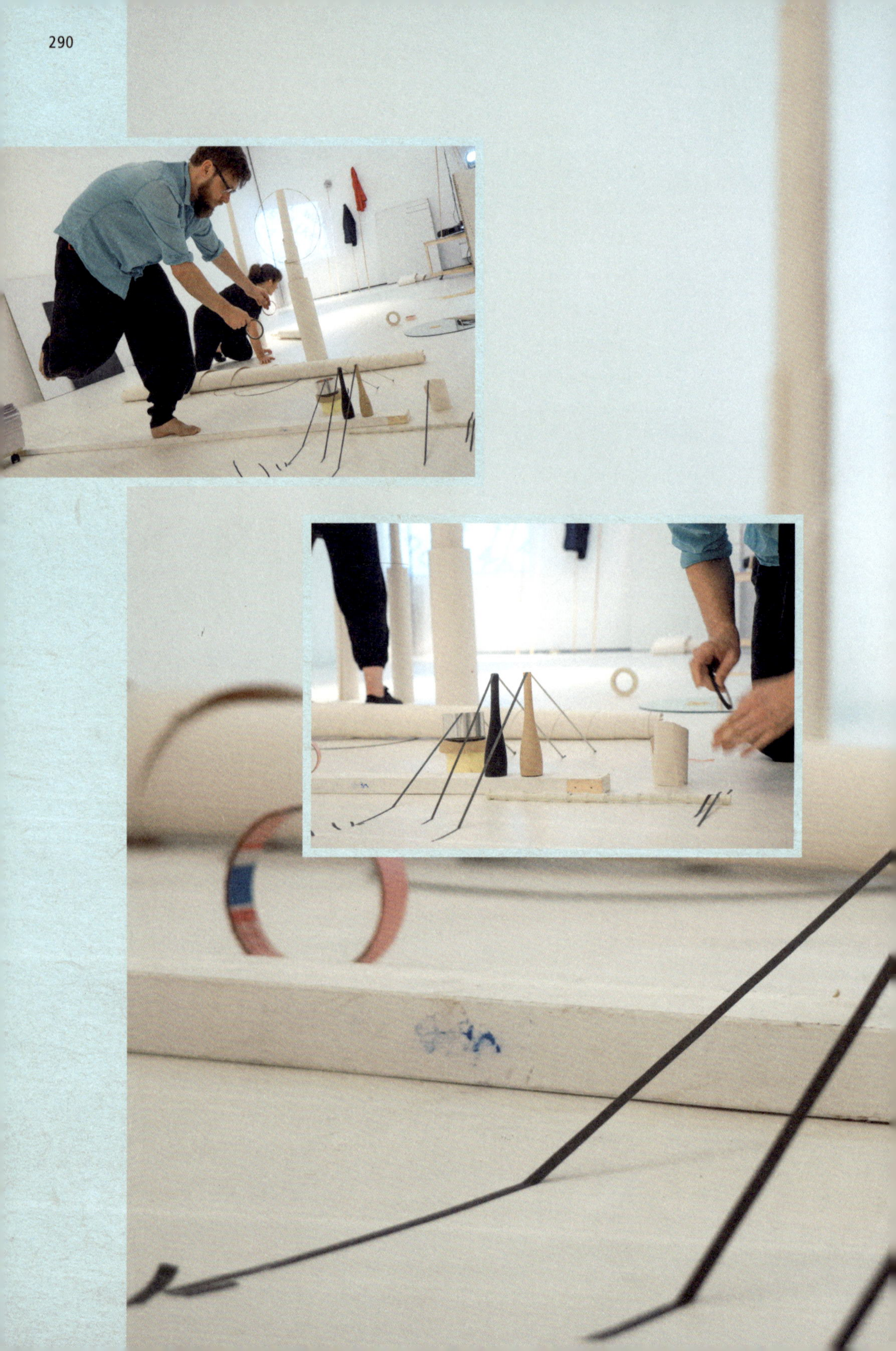

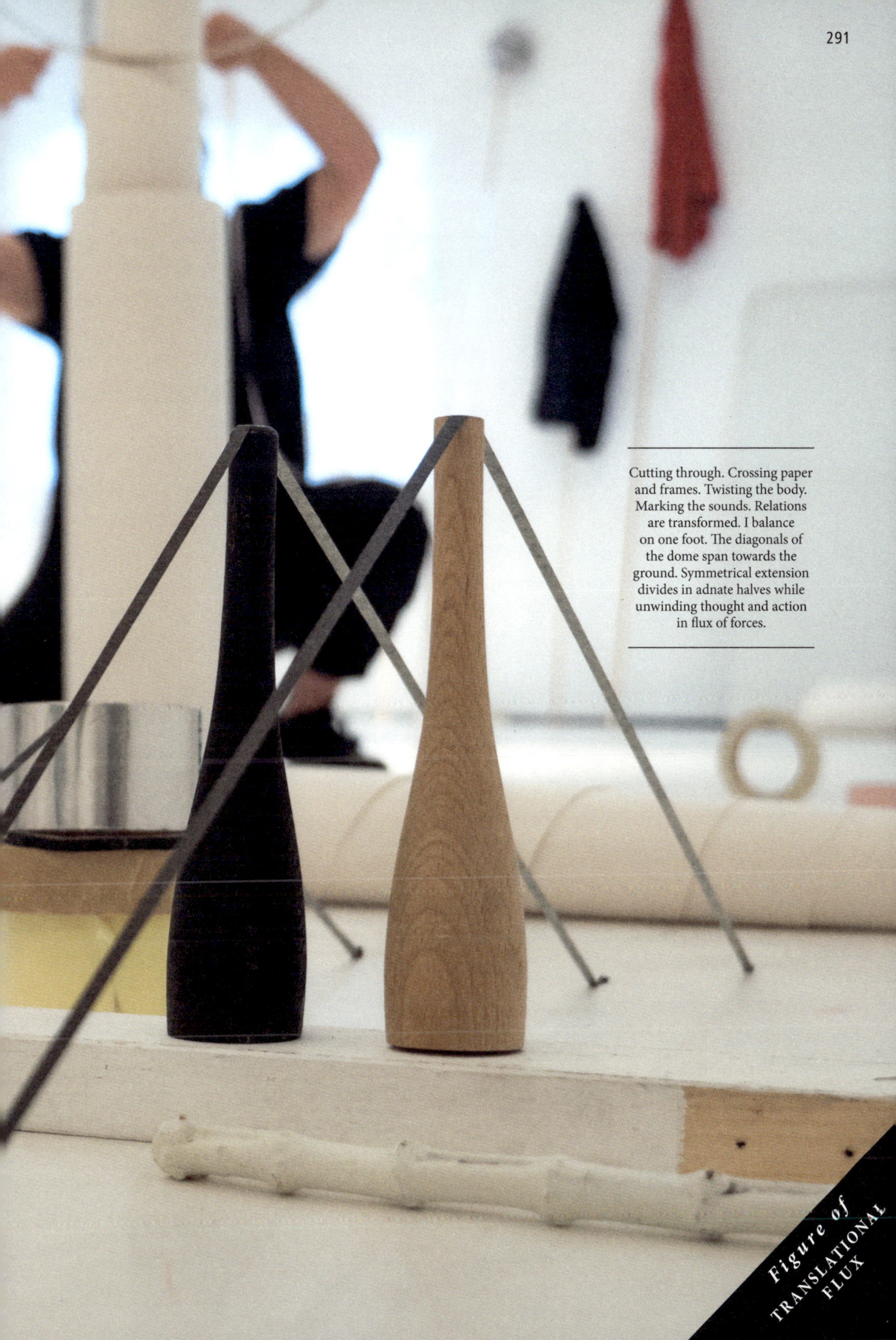

Cutting through. Crossing paper and frames. Twisting the body. Marking the sounds. Relations are transformed. I balance on one foot. The diagonals of the dome span towards the ground. Symmetrical extension divides in adnate halves while unwinding thought and action in flux of forces.

Figure of TRANSLATIONAL FLUX

PRINT OUT

Jörg Piringer

Beyond signification, hybrid languages emerge between human and machine: conversational transcripts computer-filtered through keyword search analysis, minimalist micro-scripts unfurl on printed receipts — stuttered and babbling, abstract and opaque, yet also mysterious, enigmatic.

ike
like
like
like
like
like
like
like
like
like
like
like
like

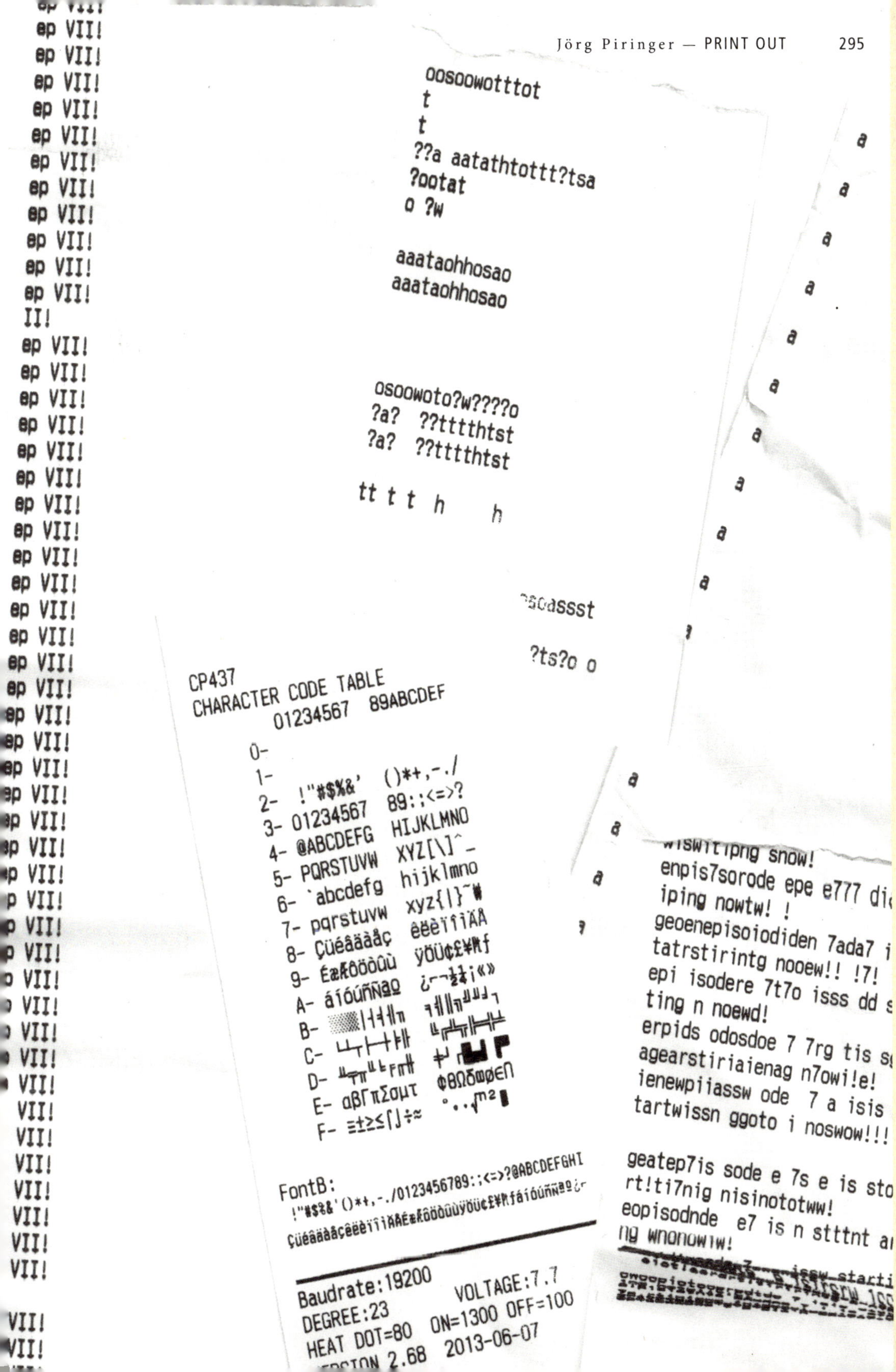

ep VII!
ep VII!
ep VII!
ep VII!
ep VII!
ep VII!
ep VII!
ep VII!
ep VII!
ep VII!
ep VII!
II!
ep VII!
ep VII!
ep VII!
ep VII!
ep VII!
ep VII!
ep VII!
ep VII!
ep VII!
ep VII!
ep VII!
ep VII!
ep VII!
ep VII!
ep VII!
ep VII!
ep VII!
ep VII!
p VII!
p VII!
p VII!
p VII!
p VII!
p VII!
VII!
VII!
VII!
VII!
VII!
VII!
VII!
VII!
VII!
VII!
VII!
VII!

VII!
VII!

oosoowotttot
t
t
??a aatathtottt?tsa
?ootat
o ?w

aaataohhosao
aaataohhosao

osoowoto?w????o
?a? ??tttthtst
?a? ??tttthtst

tt t t h h

?soasssst

?ts?o o

CP437
CHARACTER CODE TABLE
01234567 89ABCDEF

0-
1-
2- !"#$%&' ()*+,-./
3- 01234567 89:;<=>?
4- @ABCDEFG HIJKLMNO
5- PQRSTUVW XYZ[\]^_
6- `abcdefg hijklmno
7- pqrstuvw xyz{|}~⌂
8- Çüéâäàåç êëèïîìÄÅ
9- ÉæÆôöòûù ÿÖÜ¢£¥₧ƒ
A- áíóúñÑªº ¿⌐¬½¼¡«»
B- ░▒▓│┤╡╢╖ ╕╣║╗╝╜╛┐
C- └┴┬├─┼╞╟ ╚╔╩╦╠═╬╧
D- ╨╤╥╙╘╒╓╫ ╪┘┌█▄▌▐▀
E- αßΓπΣσµτ ΦΘΩδ∞φε∩
F- ≡±≥≤⌠⌡÷≈ °∙·√ⁿ²■

FontB:
!"#$%&'()*+,-./0123456789:;<=>?@ABCDEFGHI
ÇüéâäàåçêëèïîìÄÅÉæÆôöòûùÿÖÜ¢£¥₧ƒáíóúñÑªº¿⌐

Baudrate:19200
DEGREE:23 VOLTAGE:7.7
HEAT DOT=80 ON=1300 OFF=100
VERSION 2.68 2013-06-07

a
a
a
a
a
a
a
a
a
a
a
a
a
a
a
a

wiswitipng snow!
enpis7sorode epe e777 di
iping nowtw! !
geoenepisoiodiden 7ada7 i
tatrstirintg nooew!! !7!
epi isodere 7t7o isss dd s
ting n noewd!
erpids odosdoe 7 7rg tis s
agearstiriaienag n7owi!e!
ienewpiiassw ode 7 a isis
tartwissn ggoto i noswow!!!

geatep7is sode e 7s e is sto
rt!ti7nig nisinototww!
eopisodnde e7 is n stttnt a
ng wnonowiw!

OVERCHALLENGE AS AN ARTWORK

DEVIATIONS IN THE SYSTEM OF CULTURAL BOOKKEEPING

Helmut Ploebst

Matter, material, and 'matters' pose extreme challenges for the research on connections, inner and outer relations or conditions as well as their semiotic character, organisation, and performativity. Think of *quipu*, the Inca's knot writing system, whose messages could not be delivered without oral commentary, i.e., not without performative action. But also consider that the systematic application of characters between Peru and Mesopotamia obviously derives from the *bookkeeping* (the accounting) of historical cultures. Hence, writing and bureaucracy systems are similarly entangled as their supports: mediality and performativity.

Without communication there would be no matter, no material, and no objects (*things* and *themes*). Communications which enable the formation of matter already are autopoietic, that is, self-creating — sustaining systems in the sense of Humberto R. Maturana and Francisco J. Varela[1] — and from the observer's viewpoint, Paul Watzlawick's axiom (together with Janet H. Beavina and Don D. Jackson), according to which there can be no non-communication[2], applies here, too. This is not only because Heidegger's 'Nothing' metaphysically and semantic-performatively 'nihilates',[3] but also because any observation itself provides the absolutely absent with an immaterial presence: it communicates absence *per se*.

A small, blackened globe was noticed which only had to be associated with the likewise black writing boards at another place of the installation to make possible an enlightening deduction: from the observer's perspective, in the blackening (a 'superdense overwriting') of the object — determined to represent the Planet Earth as a surface model — the anti of presence (*Nichtung* — 'nihilation', derived from Jean-Paul Sartre's term 'néantisation'[4]) is translated into an anti of absence (*Nächtung* — 'nighting').

Underneath this globe's black overwriting there probably still are the continents, oceans, islands as well as the geographic coordinate system printed on it, which altogether can be read as the 'rough balance' of the manifestation of Planet Earth. The overwriting *Nächtung* of this balance — which is the result of a comprehensive booking process of findings about the shape of the Earth — frees the object with regard to *memory* or *association operations*: e.g., on the 'writing globe' as an equivalent of the registrative writing board, one could on the one hand reconstruct the original 'bookkeeping' including the balance, or on the other hand apply or inscribe deviating registers.

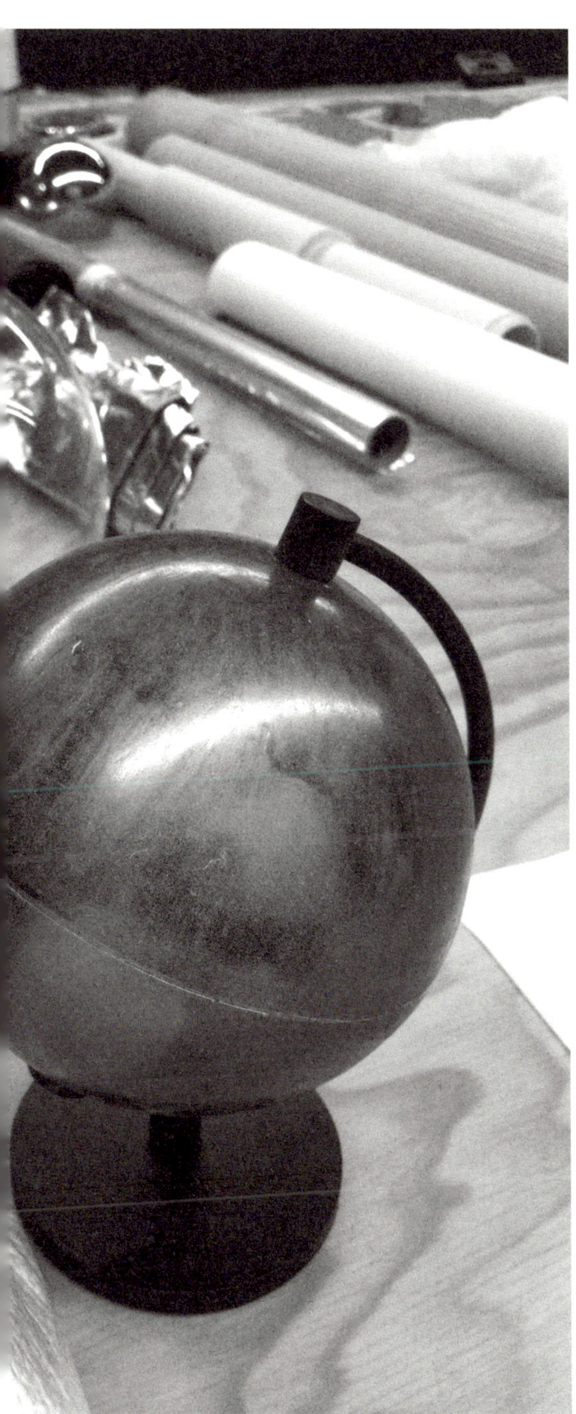

According to this, *memory operation* would be the basic pattern of any registrative bookkeeping from which the development of writing systems derives, and which in principle does not get changed by over-writing processes. *Deviant association operation* however creates a writing system that goes beyond the registration, calculation and balancing of the organisational, and first of all notates the imaginable and the thinkable. Bookkeeping in general does not enjoy a good reputation, which is why the sobering origin of writing systems from bureaucracy ('office regime') is cloaked in embarrassed silence. Very one-sidedly and without taking into account its deviant potential, the term 'bookkeeping' is associated with pedantry, doggedness, and narrow-mindedness.

The connection between bookkeeping — the estimation of things and their value relations — and critique — the estimation of value relations in social communication — seems evident.[5] Both require accuracy and revisal, if in different form. But only association-operative bookkeeping in the sense of 'keeping the book open' is suitable for critical balancing with regard to a dominant organisational or ideological system, while any memory-operative bookkeeping — even in its 'creative' form — always conforms to the regime.

Beyond this development of relations, bookkeeping also is related to scientific taxation, the sorting of matter, materials, and things, and the taxonomy of living beings. Without methodical appraisal — i.e., without verification and estimation — no form of bookkeeping, critique, or science would be able to fulfill its tasks. The etymological basis of the term 'taxonomy' is the Greek word τάξις (*táxis*). It mainly denotes a movement reaction of organisms triggered by exterior stimuli, an impulse of orientation in the perception of their environment. For the human body, τάξις is of existential importance: for its thinking as well as its acting. Orientation towards an exterior impulse is also constitutive for dance. The same holds true for all other forms of art in their unavoidable reactions to exterior stimuli. In the *deviations* of *Choreo-graphic Figures*, *τάξις* appeared to the observer as an instrument lending structure in dealing with materials with regard to 1) asymmetrically systematic deconstructions of existing object, text, and action classification systems (in the sense of their *Nächtung*); and 2) a complex choreography of *association operatively* devised registrations (arrangements, groupings, lists, and text collections).

In this place it should be emphasised that in *Choreo-graphic Figures* the traditional connection between creative artists and taxonomy was also worked off. An important detail, for the genesis of art as it is understood today could be represented classificatorily in its semiotic relations between image, sound, gesture and writing. This again entices one to the thesis that it was exactly the challenging of classification systems of characters by association operatively implemented *αταξίες* (*ataxíes* — disorders, irregularities) in modernity that created fissures between social order and systematic artistical deviance. Social orders principally orientate on memory operations, while artistic structuralisations tend to behave like association operations.

The social dismay that follows from this regarding the deviations of art, but also numerous phenomena of that which is perceived as nature and as sociality, oscillates between fascination and distress. With good reason, as the operations of subjective and social perception obviously behave mainly opportunistically. In other words: social observers do not behave neutrally but in a protectionist manner, which often creates an impression of incommensurability of observation matters. Even if that which appears incomparable or immeasurable quite obviously points out the inadequacy of observation methods.

Apparent immeasurabilities of deviances in autopoietic processes are especially disturbing, e.g., in communication — whose complexity overtaxes the area of science dedicated to it — but not the arts. In the artistic research project *Choreo-graphic Figures* this non-overtaxation by communicative autopoiesis was quite recognisable. The arts' 'lines of argument' happen via representations which appear as systemic approximation models to social communication — and not, like in science, by attempts to depict reality through exemplary models, to register it and subsequently render it conclusive.

In 'arts-based research', the alleged incommensurability of scientific and artistic methods is not abolished by making science become artistic, or art scientific. The decisive factor is, or would be the observation of communicative confluences in the artistic-scientific laboratory: e.g., by investigating how the *over-challenging* of a scientific method by complex communicative dynamics presents itself as an *artwork*. For instance, as a *choreo-graphy* as sketched in *Choreo-graphic Figures*. The materials and objects organised here — the globe mentioned above just being one object among many — changed so clearly under changing relations and conditions that the object, the material, the body receded behind these connections. However, the *τάξις* and αταξίες occurring in one and the same system — the orientation towards exterior impulses under irregular conditions — is a basic requirement of autopoiesis. With regard to communication this can easily be shown by the attempt to join Karen Barad's argument that relations do not need relata with Niklas Luhmann's statement that communication does not need communicators.

Here it possibly may turn out that the agentiality of agents (*relata*, communicators) could be more insignificant than society is ready to imagine. For the agents would only be phenomena created and changed by relations. All the materials that appeared in the laboratory of *Choreo-graphic Figures* thus would have a medial and performative relationship with the agents implementing them and themselves. Which again makes autopoiesis come into play. For it can especially be interpreted as a self-creating and self-sustaining *dynamic of relations*. This makes it a meta-system, as the principle of relationality would also be preserved if large relational systems — e.g., like that of social communication — were to break down.

Among other things, this is a disturbance of the bureaucratic-bookkeeping idea that societies could be permanently organised by memory-operative ordering structures. But it was entirely unplanned that the writing system originating from historical bookkeeping would eventually create literature, change materials, shift meanings, redefine societies. All this under the premises of deviation, the interactions of τάξις and ἀταξία in the memory- and association-operative registrations of social communication, this autopoiesis of relations which can also be exemplified as *Choreo-graphic Figures*.

---

1) Cf. Humberto R. Maturana and Francisco J. Varela, *The Tree of Knowledge: The Biological Roots of Human Understanding*, Boston: Shambhala Publications, 1987.

2) Paul Watzlawick, Janet H. Beavin, Don D. Jackson, *Menschliche Kommunikation. Formen, Störungen, Paradoxien*, Bern: Huber, 2007, pp. 53-70.

3) Martin Heidegger, 'Was ist Metaphysik?', reprinted in *Wegmarken*, 2nd edition, Frankfurt a. M.: Klostermann, 1978, p. 113.

4) Cf. Jean-Paul Sartre, *Das Sein und das Nichts. Versuch einer phänomenologischen Ontologie*, Hamburg: Rowohlt, 1976, p. 56.

5) The term 'Beckmesserei' (English: *carping*) derives from the character Sixtus Beckmesser in Richard Wagner's *Meistersinger* (1868), which the anti-Semitic composer employed to attack the Jewish music critic Eduard Hanslick. Wagner was later Hitler's hero because of his anti-Semitism, but especially because his total-work-of-art 'bookkeeping' had already precalculated the annihilating emotional balance of National Socialist ideology. Wagner's spectacular work largely aims at a speculative rebalancing of ancient mythologies and so correlates with 'creative bookkeeping', i.e., the manipulation of accounts.

ASPECTS OF UNDISCIPLINARY LISTENING

Werner Moebius

in

In reference to my sound practice, I have developed a visual process description revealing listening modes behind figuration.[1]

The sequence of images and words stems from a self-reflective process attending to pre-conditioned, sensate perceptual frameworks and the activity of listening as a primary field for artistic articulation. Listening itself becomes an instrument rather than the production of sound. It is a radical dedication to the present (*dem Vorfindlichen*), to receptivity, auditory sensibility and the unearthing of correlations.

There are various diagrammatic currents (within each image) in the visual process description opening up one's awareness for vital forms of listening (⟶ *Attention Practices: Listening*):

between precondition — recognise
between block — enhance
between delay — reverb

In sound contexts, it is the doing *through* or *with* de-lays, re-sonances and re-verberations both as signal processes but also in the felt sense (⟶ *Elemental Figures* in relation to prefixes de- / re-), both in terms of machine and affect.

Listening Modes Behind Figuration

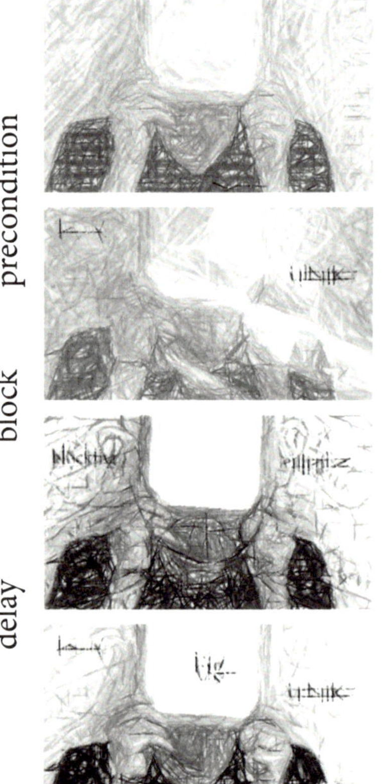

1) This contribution was developed in nexus to a durational performance of *Choreo-graphic Figures* in the framework of Visual Arts X Dance, ImPulsTanz Festival, 2016.

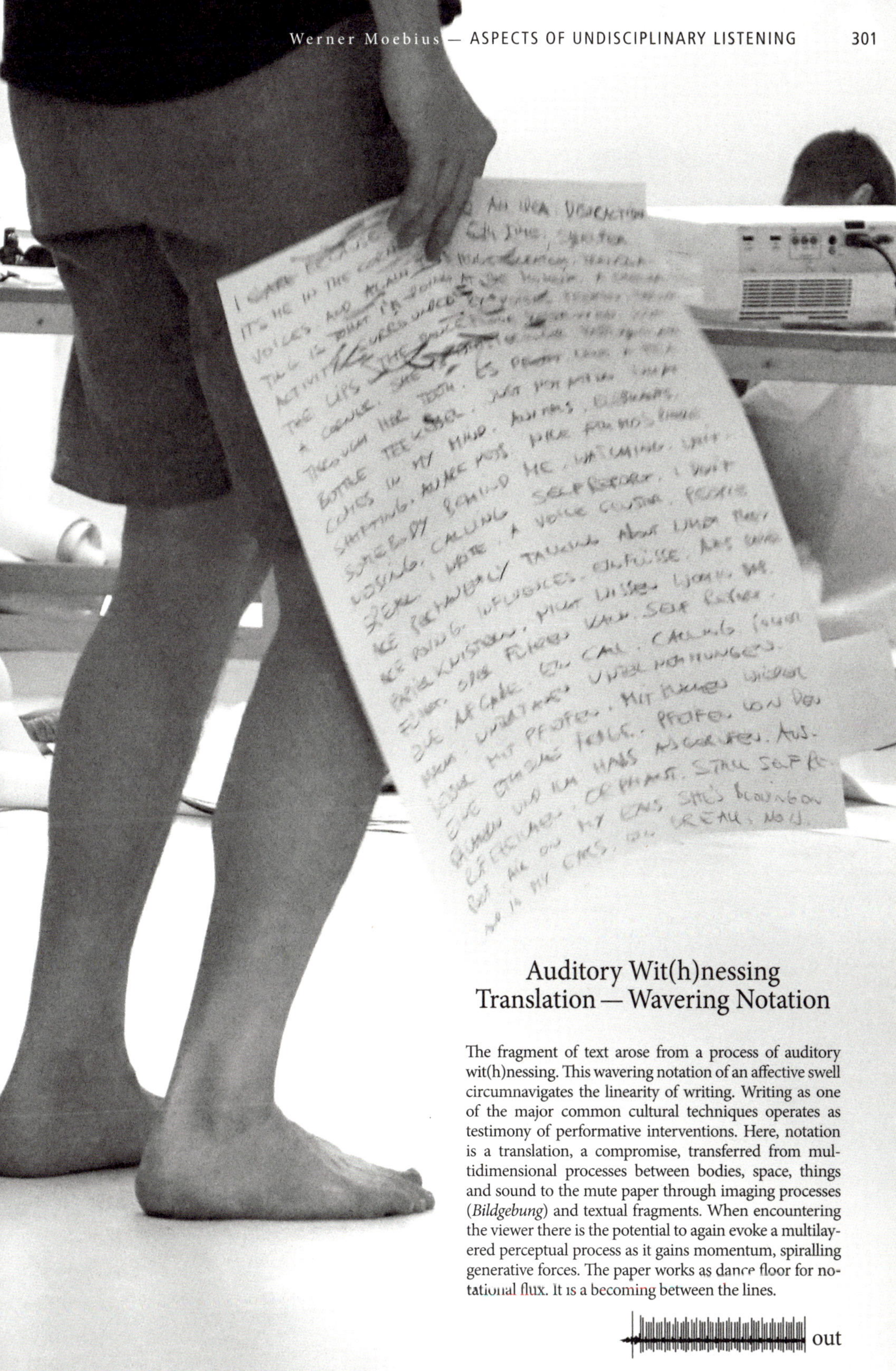

Auditory Wit(h)nessing Translation — Wavering Notation

The fragment of text arose from a process of auditory wit(h)nessing. This wavering notation of an affective swell circumnavigates the linearity of writing. Writing as one of the major common cultural techniques operates as testimony of performative interventions. Here, notation is a translation, a compromise, transferred from multidimensional processes between bodies, space, things and sound to the mute paper through imaging processes (*Bildgebung*) and textual fragments. When encountering the viewer there is the potential to again evoke a multilayered perceptual process as it gains momentum, spiralling generative forces. The paper works as dance floor for notational flux. It is a becoming between the lines.

out

THE RIDDLE OF THE SCORE:
A LESSON FROM THE PAST

Karin Harrasser

Some time ago, I became interested in the musical practices of Jesuit missionaries in Latin America. My first research trip brought me to Concepción, a small town in the Bolivian *llanos* (in the Eastern lowlands). It hosts an archive of musical scores from the eighteenth and nineteenth centuries containing approximately 3100 folios, predominantly of European Baroque music. The scores were archived and made accessible only during the last twenty years. Before that, people from local villages had kept them privately, sometimes over centuries. Some scores had been copied time and again after the expulsion of the Jesuits (1767) from South America, and sources from the nineteenth century testify that they were still in use around 1840. The former missionary complex of Concepción also hosts a small museum that documents the history of the town. Between 1690 and 1767, various indigenous groups converted, or rather, were converted to Christianity and were resettled into towns, now known as *reducciones*.

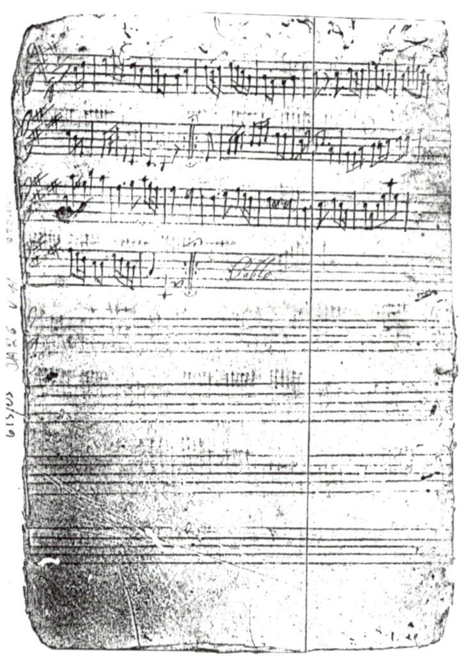

Minuet in A-major, R 82, f 44 V, Archivo Musical de Chiquitos

The whole constellation is quite complicated in terms of politics of signs and politics of scores. Obviously, the only things I could possibly study are the documents and scores left behind by the Jesuits — this includes reports, letters, statistics, etc. But are not the main things missing in these written testimonials here, the bodies, the practices, the voices of the indigenous people, of the Chiquitos, who were drawn into a new religion, into a new form of community, into a new cultural world?

I want to study one score to unfold the **tension between written score and (colonial) experience.** The sheet, in quite a bad shape, but readable, contains a Minuet in A-major. Supposedly it is from the late eighteenth century. The writer used preprinted sheet music — the writing material must have been ordered and shipped to this rather remote place back then. The notes are handwritten, and when played it becomes obvious that the tune is somehow in an Italian tradition, although **it contains some rhythmic particularities.** The name Pablo is written behind the double bar. This is where the riddles start: Who was Pablo? Did he write the minuet? Was it written for him; then, by whom? Was it just his copy of a (well-known or not so well-known) piece used in a performance? Where and when was the piece performed? The Jesuit missionaries were of course interested in establishing a soundscape suitable for solemn liturgy, but a minuet? Was it performed on the *plaza mayor* on a Saturday night, and the Chiquitos danced to it? Or was it a gift to some visiting Spanish official to prove how civilised the King's subjects were? We do have quite some reports about the rich musical life of the *reductions (reducciones)* but all of them are biased, written by Europeans who were astonished and pleased by the abundance and quality of musical performance. We know nothing about those who performed the music and dance. Did they enjoy it at all? Also, of course, we don't **know how the score was put into practice.** What instrument was used, was it played solo or in a group? **How much deviation was allowed or even desired?** (We know that Baroque music was not notated as 'exactly' as European music of later days). Or was the whole thing just a little writing exercise for someone who learned copying scores? Does an 'original' exist and where is it then? Some researchers of the scores even put forward the idea that the scores were not used as support for musical performance at all. It is thought that the mere writing and storing of the scores could have been an act of faith, some sacral act to remember the Jesuit's presence after they had to leave. We can see that with the humble little score the whole drama of cultural dominance of the West leaps into our face. Still, those scores are the only **witnesses of a process** that — violent as it might have been — created a link between me, an heir of the colonisers, and those who were drawn into globality back then.

We cannot fill in the bodies, the suffering, the joy, the proper experience of the Chiquitos back then. But probably we can start by honouring the dead who have not left letters and reports. I therefore dedicate this text to Pablo. I practised the piece on the Viola da Gamba while I was writing this. It is quite hard to play for an inexperienced musician like me. I cannot answer any of the questions that are raised by the little score but I can try to play it. **The answers might remain unanswered** but they can be ghostly guides to our colonial past and present.

SCORE IT!

Lilia Mestre

This text is written from the point of view of my participation in the research project Choreo-graphic Figures: Deviations from the Line. *The experience contributed greatly to my investigation on scores, entitled* ScoreScapes, *as a learning-through-practice tool. Through the lens of scores, we as artists propose to question the discursiveness of art practice. More precisely, this text wishes to underline the importance of the experiential as a thinking partner, by bearing witness to affective relations as guidelines for an understanding of the self and the collective.*

Imagine there is a space (the studio, a section of a street, a body part), imagine there is a time frame (ten days, three years, one hour), imagine there are things (objects, movements, words), imagine there are people (artists, philosophers, audiences) … Imagine you can 'categorise' momentarily your mode of acting in relation to all these elements. Imagine you name these categories: practices, modes of attention … and subdivide them into other categories which you also name. Imagine you can select the way one behaves in space by calling out one of them. Imagine that in the middle of an action, someone else will call out another category and that the situation will change, orienting you towards other relations with things.

Thinking scores as the mode of organisation of space, time and action in a given situation makes us engage in a particular way of thinking relationally. Once the focus of the score is oriented towards bringing together different elements, the practice of the score can be seen as a laboratory, a study environment, a place to provoke and observe events. As a research tool, the making of scores obliges us to assemble a precise choice of elements in order to investigate their function within a system of operations. In *Choreo-graphic Figures: Deviations from the Line*, the score operates simultaneously as a way to practise and to observe the practice.The score contains both potentials: it instigates performative acts and simultaneously facilitates the analyses of those acts. Throughout the reformulation of the score and its consequent practise, we as researchers analyse and elaborate on the possibility or impossibility of a system of notation enabled by the performative act. In a continuous manner we adapt, change and introduce new parameters, take away others, creating a multitude of possibilities for the study of performativity as a system of notation as such.

Imagine writing, reading, playing, writing, reading …

In the classic sense, a score is a written *partition* that enables the repetition and interpretation of a piece of music. It is an autonomous construction that is activated through reading and through playing. Within our research, the score as a partition is the point of departure to challenge, tweak, touch upon and put art practices into motion. When stripping the score to its elementary set of conditions, we engage in a process of writing modes of interaction between elements. One has to read and play out, to explore the resonance of the score in one's own skin. The score is a set-up that has to be (re)enacted.
As when drawing a map, we rely on paper and a pen to sketch the basic outline. Gradually, we add concerns, players, objects, environmental conditions, notions of time and space, modes of interaction, notation principles and alertness. It is a continuous process of going back and forth in a hermeneutical manner. The score as a written device enables the observation and thinking of interaction. And interaction then becomes a way of writing, a way of making sense, a way of understanding and experiencing our relation to what surrounds us, an attempt to communicate, to shed light on the subjectivity of our humanness.

Imagine we are bodies of affect. Imagine that we react, interact at every second of our existence with the existence of everything we encounter. Imagine we are aware of an infinitesimal part of that interaction. Imagine a universe of exploration is possible. Imagine we like it and we are not afraid. Imagine that this excites potential. Imagine play.

Choreo-graphic Figures: Deviations from the Line uses scoring as a mode of interaction that integrates and makes visible the ruling system as an invitation to play. The research questions are an integral part of the score and pinpoint the concerns that the researchers are looking for. Is it possible to be in the paradox of improvisation and formalisation simultaneously? And is it possible to share these conditions with the audience? A central concern in the research is the development of modes of being together, with our individual backgrounds, moods, sensibilities and that all visitors of the practice (practitioners or 'viewers') are invited to observe and play. The score manifests the way that the researchers envisage a life-art laboratory for multidisciplinary practices and plurifocal presences. An attempt to shift from an art-to-look-at to an art-to-experience.

In this case, as in many others, the score proposes a form of sociability. It becomes an artificial organism seeking for its survival, for its sustainability. It is a venture to articulate our artificial nature through the recreation of a time-space relational environment. Where are we? In a laboratory that is set up for studying of the performativity inherent in the gesture, the word, the line, the eye, the mind, the guts and anywhere else. We are in a constructed framework exhibiting an ecology of affect between the ruling system and the players, audience included. We are all part of it and we all contribute in one way or another to the life-vitality of this observatory with the knowledge we have gathered so far. In the end, this micro-landscape searching for its borders wants to create an interface of awareness for the sensible.

Imagine life transpires through underneath currents. One moves through space alone-together like in an apartment building, like in the forest.

And we are not alone. A score is a control device, it is a perverse partner. It dictates ways of functioning, modes of presence. It is a self-regulator, a self-dictator. It makes one be here-and-now in an extreme state of alertness. The stricter the score, the more it frames its reading and interpretation but, the more it provokes trouble and friction. There is an inherent form of resistance in creating boundaries to then break, in wanting to test out parameters. The impossibility of the fulfilment of the tasks imposed by scores (since the since the word and its enunciation always propose certainty) and the obsessive behaviour it induces in the players (since we are driven by the desire to play) are symptoms of the disparate condition of the relationship between law and nature. The eternal quest to understand and the eternal impossibility of achieving, leaves us with the wonderful possibility of experimenting.

Imagine that the becoming of the subject takes place in experiences of interiorisation and exteriorisation of the world. Imagine the subject as an agent of change, which through its own transformation in the collective terrain, participates actively in the collective. Imagine the arts as a manifestation of that transformation and that transformation as a form of political engagement.

By banging our heads against or caressing the enforced walls of the score, we produce poetics. Poetics are used here as the capacity to produce the ephemeral and ineffable, what is fleeting. How do we implement this? The formal aspect of the score does not condition the timing of the practice. It allows for improvisational stretches, for example, between one and six hours, where all present are in a state of indeterminacy, constantly assisting the variables of relation between things. Repetition is not about doing the same thing, even though that happens to a certain extent, but about the difference of doing it again. The unexpected and unforeseen event is always a surprising call to pay attention to the performative aspect of art, to the condition of its existence as experiential, ephemeral event.

"… the ephemeral is not what has just passed (away), but that which, because it passes, haunts the very second of the present with its potential return. Ephemerality impregnates the interstices of time with a messianic dimension, thanks to which the past reveals itself to be not simply made of whatever is gone from the present time, but as a dimension of potentiality of matter deeply woven into the fabric of the future. Ephemerality is already dance's afterlife, the promise of an incalculable return without profit."[1]

The poetic machine is a paradox between the extreme precision of the score and the unpredictability of the events that are produced. This formal paradox allows the emergence of aesthetics and ethical concerns, giving place to imagining possible worlds. Importantly, the emerging events have an autonomy of their own because they are in relation to conditions that are not subjective. Something is happening in relation to another thing and another thing and another thing. The viewer might not even be able to see it all. The poetic machine also has its agency beyond the visible and in a heightened sense of presence beyond ownership.

Imagine the now is the condition of the present in presence, and where things happen. There is no time after all. At this moment, we are all here.

To work with scores allows us to constantly follow up and evaluate these relationships. The score evolutions are guidelines for the progress of the study and facilitate a chronological trajectory of the research. To make scores is also to produce documents in order to observe the paradigms that are at stake while making art.

At this stage, I can make a connection to my research on scores as a pedagogical tool developed in the frame of the Post-Master on artistic research at a.pass (advanced performance and scenography studies) in Brussels. *ScoreScapes* creates a framework that brings together diverse artistic practices to 'speak' to each other without having a common constraint in terms of content or form. To find systems of interaction where different aesthetic experiences cohabitate, complement, disagree and motivate *thirdness* together with the possibility to trace it. Like a maze of potentials hovering over us participants of the score.

The aim of these scores is to bring into conversation the principles of each of the participants' work, not as a conclusion but as a process-based practice. The scores are seen as thinking partners that allow us to see art practice (experience) as a discursive component of our intellectual lives as much as an essential useless potential that feeds life.

---

1) André Lepecki, *Singularities — Dance in the Age of Performance*, Abington, Oxon and New York: Routledge, 2016, p. 14.

WHERE-NESS

Alongside *how-ness* and *when-ness*, the principle of *where-ness* has played a key role in our enquiry — it indicates towards the environmental-spatial-relational dynamics within our artistic exploration. *Where* — at what place: the spot or site, the situation, position or location. Conceived in geographical, topographical or even cartographical terms, *where* can be demarcated according to coordinates on a map, plotted in terms of latitude and longitude, measured by metre and by rule. Where am I? You are here. The imperative of mapping is one of marking things in space, establishing proximity and distance, an art of triangulation where *here* (this) is determined through its relation to *there* (that). In these terms, *where* is a practice of orientation, alignment. *Dead reckoning*: calculating one's position from a previously determined point — orientation through what is known and stable, yet a practice also prone to cumulative error. We can plot our position in space through the movement of the stars and sun, the orbit of the moon. Over time, we have devised devices to better orient ourselves, technologies of enhanced emplacement — the celestial globe and quadrant, compass and GPS. However, as our locations and lives have become more mapped out, for Zygmunt Bauman, "nothing that happens in any part of the planet can actually, or at least potentially, stay in an *intellectual* 'outside'. No *terra null*, no blank spots on the mental map, no unknown, let alone unknowable, lands and peoples."[1]

Yet, whilst the traditional map asserts a sense of authoritarian truth claim about how the world *is*, the artists' map often seeks to disrupt this normative logic, operating as a 'countermand' to the habitual complicity of conventional cartographical practices.[2] Indeed, according to Lize Mogel and Alexis Bhagat, "if the map is an instrument of power, then that power is available to whoever wields it. The map is available as a tool for liberation as much as for exploitation."[3] Here, mapping becomes a means of self-organisation, a tactical' or even diagrammatic tool used for self-mobilisation, self-liberation.[4] Rather than for emplacement and orientation, maps and guides can be used for the purposes of 'getting lost', for de-familiarisation and misdirection as much as for finding one's way, less for arriving than for playful *dérive*. "Play with distances", invites Georges Perec, "prepare a journey that would enable you to visit or pass all the places that are 314.60 kilometers from your house. Look up the route you've followed on an atlas or army map."[5] Or by refusing the strategic logic of panoptic overview, space can be negotiated from within, routes through a landscape felt and remembered through its imprint upon our limbs. Alternatively, "Navigational aids and maps might be misused for wilful disorientation (where) to wander wills towards remaining unfixed, towards the condition of unbelonging."[6] Un-homing: *unheimliche*—to render the familiar strange. Drawing on Henri Bergson's writing, Catherine Clément explores the *syncopatic* 'leaps and jolts' of the 'creative arc' using the metaphor of the *renunçiant* who leaves the village (known, closed, static, inalterable) for the forest (unknown, "transformed by the vital impetus, obeying nothing."[7]) Towards the space of the not yet known: spaciousness conceived as prerequisite for creative thought and act, ring-fenced space and time beyond utility or habit.

Yet, paradoxically it is sometimes necessary to demarcate a space open or autonomous. A protected or protective space: a sacred site, a magic circle—surrounding surroundings, encircling, encompassing, enclosed. A liminal zone of ritual encounter, where 'normal' rules are suspended or subverted, where emergent ways of operating must be negotiated, inviting the playful and experimental (⟶ *Becoming Undisciplinary*). Beyond utopian: not a no-where, no-place, imaginable yet uninhabitable. Not the idealist's space of perfect and harmonious relations, which can all too quickly become entropic or stifle, protective moral codes arising for maintaining the equilibrium or status quo. Not a *non-place* of endless transience and passage through, with no potential for cultivating the common.[8] Rather towards the *heterotopian* (*héteros*—other, another, different), spaces of *otherness,* the conditions of the radically non-hegemonic. For Michel Foucault 'heterotopia' describes an "effectively enacted utopia in which the real sites, all the other real sites that can be found within the culture, are simultaneously represented, contested, and inverted."[9] Not a retreat or escape from society but rather a crucible wherein its systems of organisation—everyday practices of sleeping, breathing, walking and conversation, ways of *being-with* others, relations to materials, objects and things—might be taken apart, anatomised and playfully reconfigured (⟶ *Embodied Diagrammatics,* ⟶ *How to Play the Score*). Foucault outlines various "heterotopias of deviation: those in which individuals whose behavior is deviant in relation to the required mean or norm are placed."[10] He further argues, "The heterotopia is capable of juxtaposing in a single real place several spaces, several sites that are in themselves incompatible."[11] Site of disciplinary deviance, beyond the means or norms of our respective practices, we call for our heterotopia: *Method Lab* (⟶ *Method Lab: A Relational Milieu,* ⟶ *Method Lab: Porous Boundaries*). *Method Lab* is our *milieu*: a middle place, a medial place—an in-between space that is always *more-than-one.*[12]

Our *Method Lab*—following Foucault—is "a heterogeneous space … we do not live in a kind of void, inside of which we could place individuals and things … that could be colored with diverse shades of light, we live inside a set of relations that delineates sites which are irreducible to one another and absolutely not superimposable."[13] Whilst we attend to the ground—grounding, to what is *infra* and immanent, to the *beneath* and *below*—our ground is not an empty stage across which the dancer dances, a blank page upon which the artist draws, the writer writes. Our *where* is never neutral — since the *figure* cannot be disentangled from the ground — but rather a 'practised place' or 'taking place', constituted in and through practice. For Michel de Certeau, whilst 'place' indicates "stability", "Space occurs as the effect produced by the operations that orient it, situate it, temporalize it, and make it function in a polyvalent unity of conflictual programs or contractual proximities [...] space is like the word when it is spoken, that is, when it is caught in the ambiguity of actualization."[14] Indeed, etymologically, *world* draws its origins from the Old English *worold*, meaning human existence and the affairs of life. For Erin Manning, 'worlding', "involves the generating of a field that is co-constituted by all the pastnesses and futurities that compose it."[15] Rhythmic relation of past and future, spatial stretch from macro to micro, from the navigation of space by stars to the nanospace of the minor or universe within. Lie down. Feel the weight of your body on the ground. "Let us close our eyes", invites Hélène Cixous, "Where do we go? Into the other world ... The other side. An eyelid, a membrane, separates two kingdoms."[16] Velvet space behind the eyes: of quiet daydreaming or of reverie. For Gaston Bachelard, the 'intimate immensity' within is imagined akin to deepest sea or sacred forest: we are the "Sensitive inhabitants of the forests of ourselves."[17] Then, towards a *where* that welcomes the 'idiorrhythmy' of *being-with* alongside *being-apart:* where sociality includes the solitary, the production of a common that preserves the conditions of difference (⟶ *Trialogue: On Sedimentations of Sensitivities*).[18] What follows is a list of 'wheres' gleaned from our conversational transcripts that, in turn, might be conceived as describing the various conditions of our *Method Lab,* the heterogeneous where of our research enquiry.

---

1) Zygmunt Bauman, *Liquid Times: Living in an Age of Uncertainty*, Cambridge: Polity Press, 2007, p. 5.

2) Cf. Katharine Harmon, *The Map as Art: Contemporary Artists Explore Cartography*, New York: Princeton Architectural Press, 2009.

3) Lize Mogel and Alexis Bhagat, *An Atlas of Radical Cartography*, Los Angeles: Journal of Aesthetics & Protest Press, 2007, p. 7.

4) For the *Institute of Applied Autonomy*, "tactical cartographies" are "less a methodology than an orientation [...] they are political machines that work on power relations." Institute of Applied Autonomy, 'Tactical Cartographies', in Mogel and Bhagat, 2007, pp. 29-30.

5) Georges Perec, *Species of Spaces and Other Pieces*, London: Penguin Books, 1997, p. 85.

6) Emma Cocker, 'Drift', in *The Yes of the No*, Sheffield: Site Gallery, 2016, p. 62. Cf. Peter Wollen, 'Mappings: Situationist and / or Conceptualists' in Michael Newman and Jon Bird (Eds.), *Rewriting Conceptual Art*, London: Reaktion Books, 1999, pp. 27-46 and Thomas F. McDonough, 'Situationist Space', *October* 67, Winter 1994, pp. 58-77, on Situationist mapping practices and the *dérive*.

7) Catherine Clément, *Syncope: The Philosophy of Rapture*, Minneapolis: University of Minnesota Press, 1994, p. 173.

8) Cf. Marc Augé, *Non-Places: Introduction to an Anthropology of Supermodernity*, London and New York: Verso, 2006.

9) Michel Foucault, 'Of Other Spaces', (Trans.) Jay Miskowiec, in *Diacritics* 16, No. 1, Spring, 1986, p. 24. Originally published as 'Des Espaces Autres' in *Architecture-Movement-Continuité*, October 1984. The text is based on a lecture given by Foucault in 1967.

10) Foucault, 1986, p. 25.

11) Foucault, 1986, p. 25.

12) Cf. Erin Manning, *Always More Than One: Individuation's Dance*, Durham: Duke University Press, 2013.

13) Foucault, 1986, p. 23.

14) Michel de Certeau, *The Practice of Everyday Life*, Berkeley: University of California Press, 1984, p. 117.

15) Manning, 2013, p. 22.

16) Hélène Cixous, *Stigmata: Escaping Texts*, London: Routledge, 1998, p. 140.

17) Gaston Bachelard, *The Poetics of Space: A Classic Look at How We Experience Intimate Places*, Boston: Beacon Press, 1994, p. 187.

18) Cf. Roland Barthes, *How to Live Together: Novelistic Simulations of Some Everyday Spaces*, New York: Columbia University Press, 2013.

Where something opens … Where something emerges … Where something starts … Where you can n
we individually work together … Where we try to find the words … Where a vocabulary will emerge
Where there is scope for dialogue … Where there is patience … Where you can interrupt … Where th
relation between resistance and integrity is negotiated … Where there are connections within practices
… Where there is difference … Where we do not dissolve discipline, but also go beyond … Where
expanded is privileged as the way of working … Where you very much tune in to the other's process … Wh
… Where we see the potential to open things up … Where we make a spaceby establishing a bracket … Wh
… Where we create this tension field … Where we extend into space … Where we can meet and cr
trans- … Where air flows or ocean currents meet … Where we move between close connection and shift
Where we try something out … Where we follow our nose … Where we listen with intensity … Where we
can play more … Where gesture comes into play … Where the choreo-graphic comes into play … Where
coming … Where the doing is happening … Where the thinking is coming … Where we are forming thou
… Where we can start and stop … Where there is light and shade … Where molecules couple in unexpe
the outbreath and the inbreath … Where the boundary of inside / outside begins to blur … Where we wo
… Where we stay with something … Where we stay with something such that its habitual functions d
its potential, reveals its affordances … Where we forget about the utilitarian aspect of things … Where
molten condition or state … Where we allow the mud to settle … Where it tilts into an unknown … Wh
… Where something is taking form … Where things falls apart or become another … Where someth
advocate reading as a physical activity … Where there are bodies lying on the floor reading … Where thi
become illegible … Where there are maybe two or three words that keep getting changed and then chan
the other begins … Where we just notice the words … Where we decide that is out and this is in … Wh
to it … Where you get a field of language … Where we can find a poetics in speech … Where language ta
write … Where poetry arises by itself … Where the verb is … Where we try to hear fragments of languag
… Where it draws you … Where we wait … Where chronological time is suspended or put on hold … Wh
and a horizontal axis of time-space … Where *kairos* and *chronos* have to make a contract with each othe
there is a similar vocabulary through different actions … Where it is different every time … Where questi
Where we reach towards another's attention … Where I feel most like 'I am' … Where we are more than
things can emerge … Where there is something going on inside … Where you have little epiphanies … Wh
we are looking for certain emergences … Where there is intensification … Where we felt a certain form
shifts to happen … Where intensities or qualities are transformed … Where matter is compressed, gravity
… Where we explore qualities of vitality … Where vibration is a manifestation of this vitality … Where
new … Where we become aware of the peripheral activity … Where you can get in relation to it … Wh
becomes the performer … Where something might be happening behind me … Where some of the decisi
doorways into other details … Where we can access these other dimensions … Where ritual is still pres
happens … Where the *figuring* is incarnate … Where the shift from *figuring* to *figure* happens … Wh
naming is emerging … Where the emergence of the name and the thing named co-incide (in time) … Wh
means saying no to territory … Where you create the epistemology that supports the process … Wh
another body … Where two things come together … Where world and self intermingle … Where subato
constraint and an expanded form … Where those rhizomatic structures can be built … Where things
focused … Where we are really tuning into the sense of how … Where there is no framing from us ab
constantly remapping space … Where all the basic functions of living are re-configured

other … Where we work collectively and work apart … Where we tune in to the other's process … Where ere we enter things … Where we are all together, doing what we do … Where we all feel challenged … ›ace for misunderstanding … Where we don't have to agree on things and still collaborate … Where the ht otherwise seem dissimilar … Where one does not obliterate the other … Where we find the common g comes to an end and another thing starts … Where there is consonance and dissonance … Where the possibilities were emerging … Where we have no reference points … Where there is a sort of pixilation space is open for something-to-come … Where there is no fixed point … Where there are no clear borders hms … Where different directions meet … Where thinking is a feeling … Where it is between inter- and raction … Where the connections and resonances and proximities and distances are more readable … sted for longer … Where we feel compelled or bound to the thing … Where it feels exciting … Where we gic is happening … Where we are discovering things … Where we are reflective … Where the phrasing is le in an activity … Where we get oriented … Where we do lots of rotations … Where we plot a landscape s … Where opposing categories fall together … Where anyone can move anything … Where we follow e something unfold through endurance … Where there is a commitment … Where it is about a promise y … Where things reveal a different kind of resistance or tension or movement … Where a material shows te another form of attention … Where things are melted down and warmed up … Where we reach a an get lost … Where the confusion starts to enter … Where it begins to open … Where we cross the water pens … Where things draw you … Where you find a question and allow it to guide you … Where we be read from more than one perspective … Where language starts … Where words are introduced and k … Where we are talking talking talking … Where is not always possible to tell where one voice stops and one can move anything … Where the sense of signification dissipates … Where there is a kind of flavour he air … Where we talk about poetry as the liberation of language … Where the many things actually all are being spoken … Where the fragment contains the whole … Where intuition is a condition of truth gs slip out of sync … Where there is a time lag … Where there is link between a vertical axis of pitch-base ere we are playing with the 'now, not now, now' … Where we might want to repeat something … Where ideas get further turned over … Where we get to the not yet known … Where it is not so clear-cut … Vhere we are co-producing an experience … Where we create enough energy in order to lift off … Where catch the moment … Where there is most resonance … Where everything hangs in the balance … Where sence … Where there is another form of presence that is not perceptual … Where we invite perception s are one … Where the before and the between of movement coincide … Where we become the material ctise a sharpness of noticing … Where notation happens … Where the notation transforms into something e is a quality of alertness to the call of others … Where we have somebody witness … Where the audience ome more visible … Where we watch in space … Where you still grasp the whole thing but there are also Vhere the unpredictable arises … Where things are on the verge of coming into being … Where *figuring* gs are recognisable yet entirely motile at the same time … Where you circle a certain *figure* … Where the name the thing that we walk away from … Where space and figure intercut … Where deterritorialisation rdances are neither objective nor subjective … Where the example is not the thing … Where a body meets ticles and the macro or the larger organisation come together … Where there is a dialogue between brought into different relation or connection … Where those transformative, qualitative compositions are t we have done … Where *no-how* is operational … Where there is a shift in politics … Where we are ere we play with systems of organisation … Where a game of re-organisation can start …

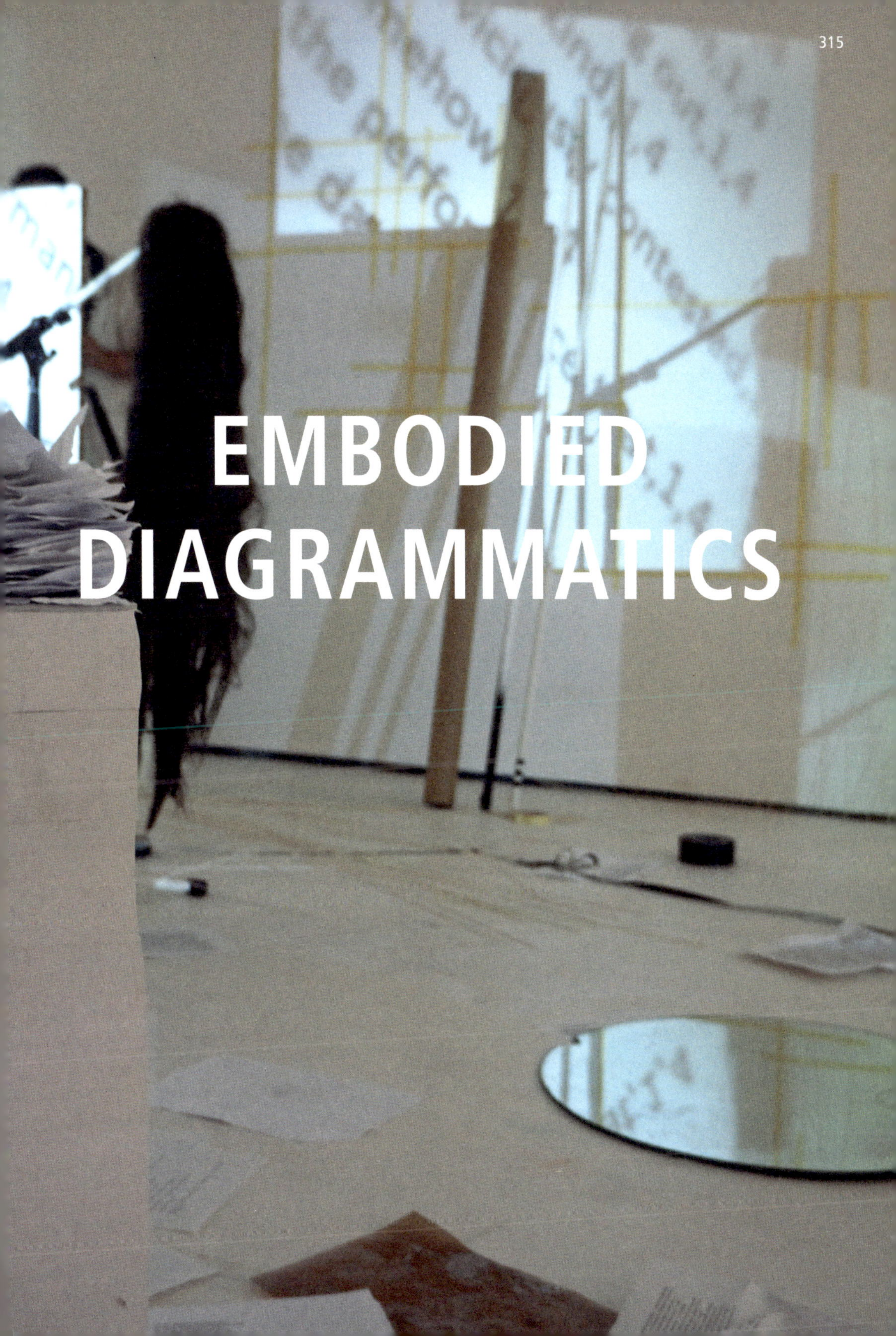

EMBODIED DIAGRAMMATICS

EMBODIED DIAGRAMMATICS

Choreo-graphic Figures: Deviations from the Line seeks to enrich and expand a vocabulary for reflecting on artistic process itself, going beyond an account of 'how to' — a description of practical ways of doing things with an operative 'how > so' emphasis on technics and techniques — in order to address the *how-ness*, the *micro-level* of vitality dynamics and affects within the process of process itself. We ask: how might specific focus on the micro-dynamics of artistic endeavour provide new insights in relation to artistic research, through emphasis on the qualitative nature of vitality, force and intensity within the creative process, rather than on its operational procedures and resulting products? How does this modality of attention expand the conceptual parameters through which artistic — even aesthetic — research is practised?[1] If, as Vilém Flusser states, "the gesture of searching is the model for all our gestures"[2], then how might attending to the micro-gestures of artistic (re)searching shape and inform our relationships with others, our own intermingling with the world? In this sense, attending to the specificity of artistic (re)searching is conceived as an intrinsic part of a wider ethico-aesthetic project, where the modalities of being and behaving practised within the context of artistic exploration might in turn give rise to new ways of practising the self, the production of a critical, self-reflexive subject capable of understanding its own enmeshing within a wider ecology, co-constituting new realities made possible through this realisation.[3] Indeed, as Henk Borgdorff argues, "Artistic research is therefore not just embedded in artistic and academic contexts, and it focuses not just on what is enacted in creative process and embodied in art products, but it also engages with who we are and where we stand."[4]

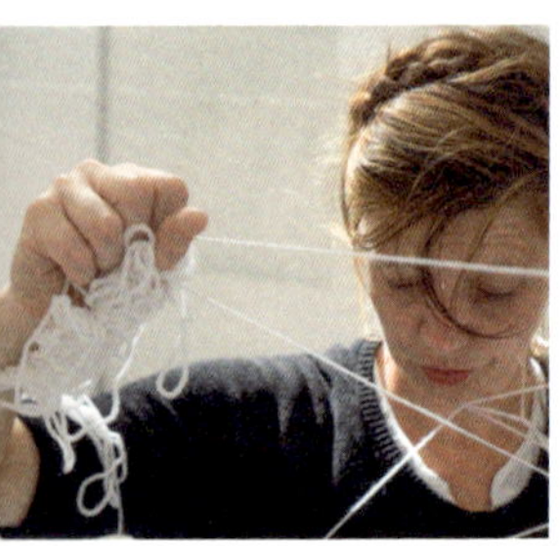

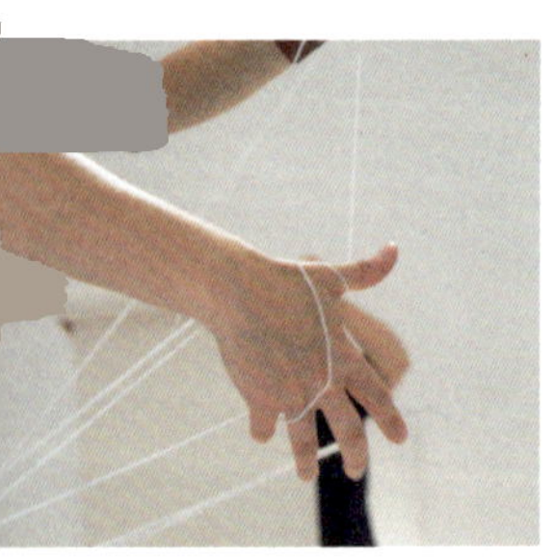

Our focus on the relation between the event of *figuring* and emergence of *figures* experienced within artistic endeavour is thus not only about artistic process, not only concerned with augmenting understanding for a specific epistemological field of practice. Daniel Stern argues that we should further explore dynamic forms of vitality — conceived as the "manifestation of life, of being alive"[5] — for it is through this barely recognisable realm of sensation that we cultivate greater possibilities for inter-subjective experience, a deeper capacity for "'implicit relational knowing' (how we implicitly know how 'to be with'...)."[6] Beyond focusing on the 'what' and the 'why' of experience and existence, for Stern, it is through addressing the *how-ness* of vitality dynamics that we develop spontaneous and receptive — cross and metamodal — ways of being in the world, in turn enabling creative responses to new situations as they arise, "in the moment-to-moment process of adaption and enactment."[7] Indeed, for Brian Massumi,"Politically, thinking on this affective, germinal level of events in the making, suggests that we can create collective platforms for experimentation at the level of our shared belief in the world. In other words, we can experiment with techniques that bring people together, leaving behind their subject positions, suspending their personal beliefs, their doctrines, but bringing with them, what moves them."[8] Herein he argues, emerges the potential of a "germinal politics".[9] Or else, as Erin Manning asserts, to focus on the 'minor gesture' is to attend to the "force that makes the lines tremble that compose the everyday, the lines, both structural and fragmentary, that articulate how else experience can come to expression."[10]

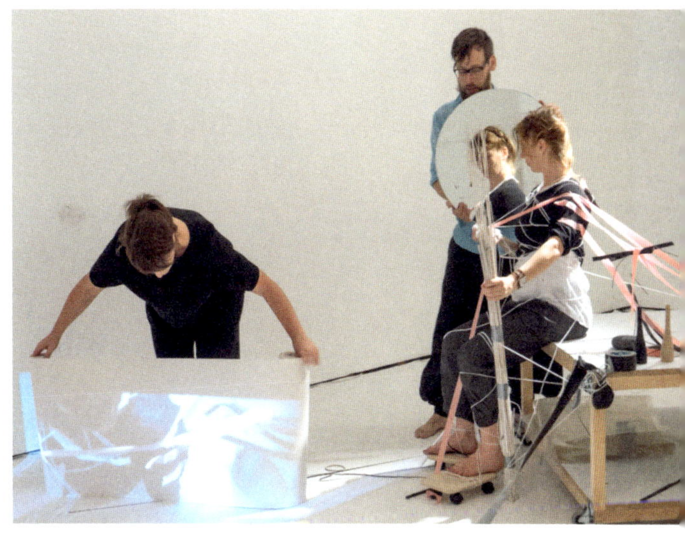

But, what — or rather *how* — is the critical specificity of artistic *knowing-thinking-feeling* in relation to our understanding of these vitality forces and affects? Why explore this realm of experience through artistic research rather than another research modality? Significantly, for Stern the reason is three-fold: first, "the arts provide an excellent example of how arousal-related vitality forms work on us [...] We are moved ... from moment to moment as well as over longer stretches of time. Tensions, forces, and excitement rise and fall. The time-based arts are largely about the dynamics of experiences. Vitality forms are the working

Beyond attending to the qualitative sense of *how-ness*, our research asks 'how else'? How does artistic research support the production of ourselves, our subjectivity — our being-with others, our being-in-the-world — as *otherwise*? Here, the initial speculative 'what if' direction of our enquiry shifts towards the imperative 'what for', where the deterritorialisation and hybridity of knowledge and opening of disciplinary borders can be argued to have implicit nano-political as well as aesthetic implications for both art and society.[11]

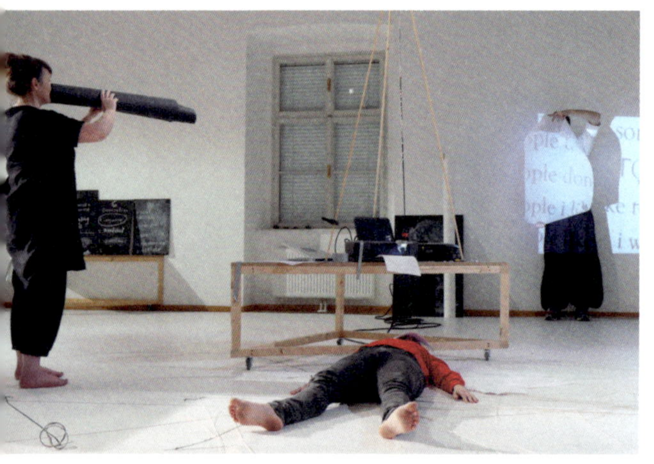

experiential units."[12] Secondly, he asserts that the arts provide a 'relatively purified form' through which to study 'vitality forms': "pure in the sense that the dynamic features of a performance have usually been amplified, refined, and rehearsed repeatedly. They are pure also, because … vitality dynamics can be relatively disentangled from the contingencies or storylines of daily life."[13] Finally, for Stern, the metamodal nature of art practice is uniquely positioned to offer new insights into the phenomena of vitality dynamics, since "vitality forms are not readily describable in words or mathematics. Moreover, when they are so described, and they can be, they lose most of their ability to evoke."[14] Art is experiential: it presents, shows or enacts the phenomena of vitality dynamics rather than attempting to represent or describe.

Choreo-graphic Figures: Deviations from the Line generates experiential, embodied reflections from within the artistic process, evidencing art's capacity to give rise to specific vitality dynamics that in turn are attended to, focused and articulated in and through the process of artistic exploration itself. Our *Method Lab* operates as a microcosm of wider society and its various vitalities, approached as a 'prism' or even a kind of 'petri dish' from within which we might observe and explore emergent vitality affects in a 'relatively purified form' (⟶ *Where-ness*). However, central to our enquiry has been an attempt not only to observe and identify, but also — as Stern asserts — to amplify and refine the specific qualitative vitalities of our various *figures* through repeated testing and experimentation. Whilst *figure* is the term that we use for referring to a 'local' instance of *figuring* incarnating as content modality — the point at which *figuring* becomes recognisable, even nameable — our intent has been towards the production of *choreo-graphic figures* within which there is more than one arising of a *figure figuring*. Yet, herein lies a dilemma, for how might we revisit and reactivate the qualities of specific *figures*, whilst also retaining or returning a sense of their dynamic vitality? How do we avoid, as Alva Noë cautions, our *figures* from becoming empty "symbolisations of an idea"; at worst, a 'hollow shell' dispossessed of its aliveness?[15] (⟶ *Fragile Figures*)

In this essay, we account for different ways that we have activated the *embodied diagrammatics* of the *choreo-graphic figure* as our enquiry has evolved, alongside some contextualisation of our own experiments in and through practice in relation to a wider ecology of 'diagrammatic praxis'.[16] In the first phase of our enquiry, we attempted to amplify, refine and reconfigure new relations between emergent *figures* through the use of a score, which we would activate in hope of re-encountering or re-meeting the originary dynamic vitalities of our identified *figures*. For example, during the process of open live exploration we would mark the event of *figuring* and the emergence of *figures* using various notation systems. Initially, we developed a system of 'clicking' (⟶ *Practices of Notation: Clicking*) where we each make an audible sound (a vocal 'click') to acknowledge the experience of a qualitative shift in awareness or affordance, for identifying that 'something is happening' at the level of vitality or emergence. At times, this process of 'notated' live exploration was recorded on video: the function of video being indexical, to simply capture the 'clicks' in the context of their production. By watching the video documentation back together — re-collecting and reflecting on the experience of notation — we were able to further qualify or even name the shifts in awareness, vitality or affordance marked by each 'click'. These emergent named *figures* were subsequently brought into new diagrammatic relation through a scored sequence, with the view that through performing the score, the *figures* could be re-incarnated with *figuring's* vitality returned. This potentiality of divergent forces 'put together' or composed through qualitative relation reflects what Petra Sabisch refers to as 'differential composition', "which undoes, each time anew, the preliminary split between movement and language, sensation and signification."[17]

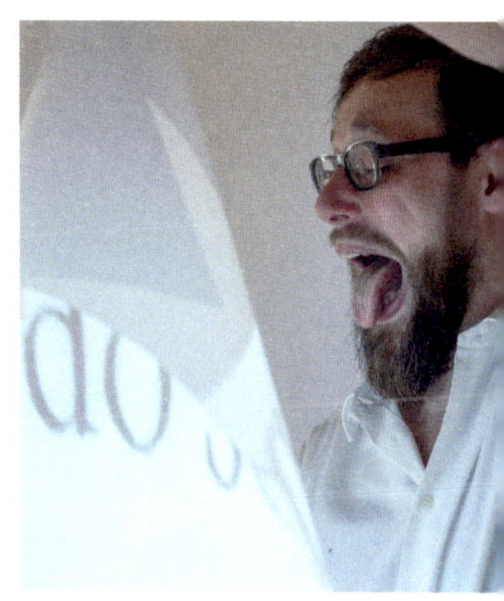

Significantly, the process of scoring and re-performing our *figures* required a radical *letting go* of the original form in order to per-form it again, where in Erin Manning's terms, "to begin is to begin again, differently, impossibly, impractically. It is to begin not with the form but with the force of the more-than as articulated by the welling diagram the event calls forth."[18] In the moment of its figuration, all previous iterations of the *figure* must be unlearnt or forgotten so that it can be transformed. A deformation or defiguring of the *figure* that necessarily prefigures figuration, an emptying out so that it can be refilled with life once more. For Dieter Mersch, "The figure in the sense of figuration consequentially 'keeps'

itself in persistent 'transience'. On the whole it is a movement without state." He argues that, the "reciprocal dialectics of figuration and defiguration" involve a process of "continuous transfiguration, processuality in itself" focused on "the permanence of a 'formative' that is formation and flux in one" (⟶ *Figuration / Defiguration*). Indeed, our *choreo-graphic figures* are not re-presentational diagrams: they are not outlines or instructions that define or describe a set of predetermined actions or operations.[19] Here, as Manning suggests, "The diagram does not pre-exist its shaping [...] The diagram that may have seemed to be an individual form now reveals itself to be an emergent multiplicity."[20]

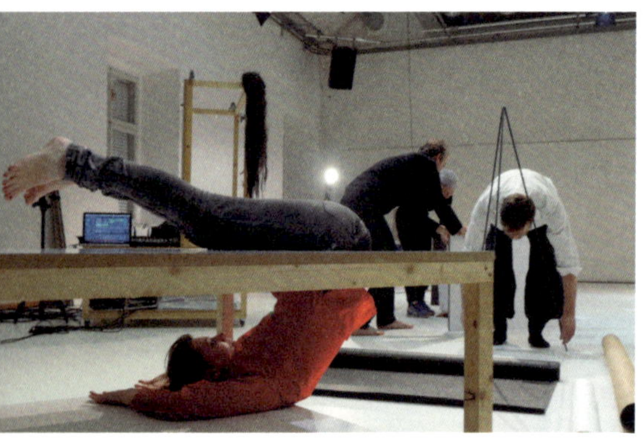

In attempting to re-meet an existing *figure,* one must re-find a way of finding it again in its vitality: this is not simply a case of repetition. For, as Manning elaborates, "No movement can be cued, aligned to or performed in the same way twice [...] What emerges as a dance of attention cannot be replicated. It is not a thing, a form."[21] Likewise, Alex Arteaga reflects on our *figures* thus: "We cannot move straight forward to it — it is not an 'it'" (⟶ *Researching Aesthetically the Roots of Aesthetics*). So how does one reactivate the *embodied diagrammatics* of the scored *choreo-graphic figure,* so as to reencounter or re-find the experience of its dynamic vitalities? For Manning, what is required is the ecology of a 'diagrammatic praxis' where, "Spacing and bodying transindividuate, fashioning a multiple singularity: a body-diagrammatic. The body-diagrammatic is a procedural 'I' that stands not for the subject but for individuation ... making felt the merging of topological registers of co-constitution: space-body-ing, time-spacing."[22] She uses the term *biogram,* for describing a 'becoming-body' that "has no fixed form"[23], that "makes itself felt in the intensive passage from one intensity — one series — to another ... The *biogram* cannot represent anything because it has no pregiven form ... The biogram propels a process of determining that always resists final form."[24] Whilst the concept of — or even previous iterations of — a given *figure* might pre-exist (⟶ *Figures*), the process of figuration is always immanent to its per-forming.

Can we re-embody or re-incarnate our diagramming of the *figure* through the practice of figuration, a "mode of existence" that finds "within the practice the singularity that gives it its diagrammatic force."[25] Our first phase of 'diagrammatic praxis' involved attending to the emergent *figuring figures* within a process of open aesthetic exploration, then creating new diagrammatic relations through the scoring, sequencing and re-performing of these different 'content modalities'. This initial practice of scoring for live per-forming focused on moving through forms while re-finding relational-choreographic content. Significantly, it enabled us to recognise and 'name' those *figures* emerging and recurring within the context of our shared exploration, which we have since been able to further organise into related fields (⟶ *Elemental Figures*, *Empathetic Figures*, *Transformative Figures*). However, rather than continue to amplify and refine — even 'purify' — the vitality force of our *figures* through 'repeated rehearsing' (as Stern suggests happens within the field of performance), the direction of our enquiry shifted in orientation. Whilst we were able to articulate the qualities of a *figure* and even identify concrete examples of its articulation, we became curious what it might mean not to fix or pre-designate the 'content modality', the specific form that a *figure* should take. How might we attend to the vitality dynamics of a specific *figure,* attempting to reactivate its qualities without predetermining *how* it might appear? How do we 'let go' of our preconceptions of what a specific *figure* 'looks like', attending rather more to how it 'feels'?

Prompted by this questioning, we developed a second model of diagrammatic praxis, which has involved the evolution of a different kind of score system for bringing-into-relation, as well as for giving rise to unexpected interactional constellations of — both known and not-yet-known — *figures* through live activation and play. Our shared intent was to find a way of scoring that could enable a process of exploratory real-time composition through which we might activate new articulations of *figuring figures* rather than reactivating existing forms that we already knew. Here then, our use of the score no longer functioned for organising or sequencing known *figures* in advance of their per-forming, nor was it used as a tool of reflection for retrospectively recollecting and recalling what has been. Rather, we began to develop the framework for a 'radical score of attention' conceived as an enabling — tactical rather than strategic — 'collective apparatus', a tool or even *dispositif* for foregrounding artistic compositional decision-making processes as a

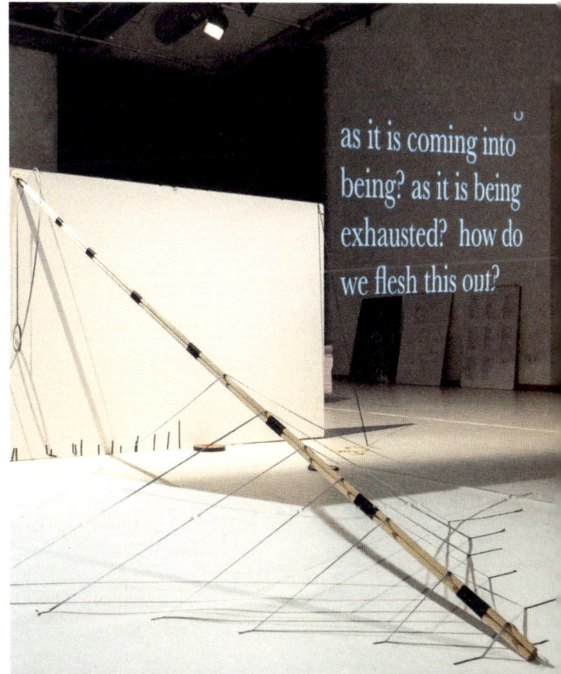

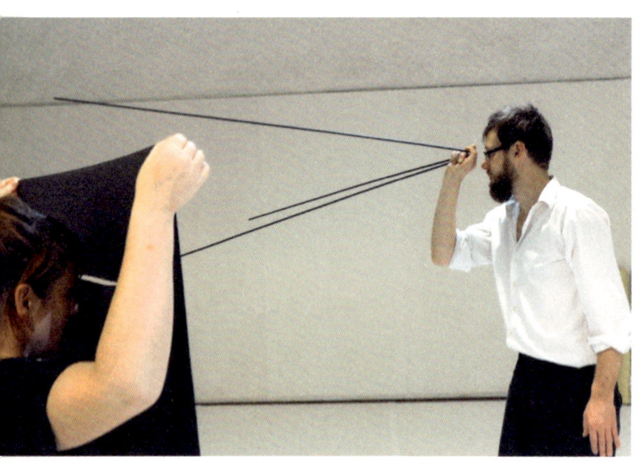

live event, capable of generating as yet unknown *figuring figures* 'en acte'.[26] How can we create the conditions for organic self-organisation or *organism-relation* that emerges from within, rather than being imposed from above or from outside? How can we develop a score that activates 'thinking-in-action', where the 'vitality contour' of a live exploration evolves through specifically attending to the emergent vitalities therein? Towards a practice of scoring then, where the organisation of live exploration is immanent to the unfolding process rather than anterior, towards an organisation that is *kairotic* rather than conceived sequentially in advance (⟶ *When-ness*).

We began to develop and test an experimental modular or permutational — even rhizomatic — score system for organising our process of aesthetic enquiry through the bringing-into-relation of different fields of practice. By this point, we had already identified and named specific practices (⟶ *Practices of Attention, Notation, Conversation, Wit(h)nessing*) and *figures* (⟶ *Figures*), but had not yet explicitly explored their relation. So too, within this publication we have thus far elaborated on these different elements within our enquiry: the various 'preludes' introduce the qualities and characteristics of both our practices and *figures*, whilst concrete examples or variations show how these have previously manifested within our practice. However, it is through the use of 'score' — conceived as a 'research tool' — that we were able to specifically test how the various 'practices' might impact upon the process of artistic exploration, as a means for sharpening, focusing or redirecting attention towards the event of *figuring* and emergence of *figures*. Here, as Lilia Mestre states, "Thinking scores as the mode of organisation of space, time, action in a given situation makes us engage in a particular way of thinking relationally" (⟶ *Score It!*). The development of a 'score system' enabled us to closely attend to the relational conditions for the arising of specific named *figures*: live exploration focused through the prism of various practices.

Significantly, within this second diagrammatic system of scoring, the *form* that a *figure* takes has not been predetermined from the outset, but rather it becomes recognisable through the arising of its qualities during the process of exploration. For Alex Arteaga "In the case that a *figure* becomes explicit it always remains at the edge of its own explicitness. It is fragile, subtle, contingent, dubious, shady — in the shade of the objects and subjects that enable its presence." (⟶ *Researching Aesthetically the Roots of Aesthetics*). Whilst previous 'examples' of a *figure* might indeed help to indicate the conditions needed for a *figure's* arising, they do not define what the *figure* is, nor do they guarantee its return (⟶ Alva Noë, *Fragile Figures*). The 'call' for a specific *figure* is thus for the conditions of the *figure's* arising, wherein we collectively strive to generate the qualities associated with that *figure*. We ask: how are the conditions that give rise to the emergence of a *figure*? How does the *figure* come into being, how does it *become*? What conditions are prerequisite; moreover, how might the *figuring figure* require conditions that are contingent and unpredictable, which cannot be diagrammed in advance? In one sense, our enquiry is one of exploring the germinal conditions for the arising of specific *figuring figures*, refining and amplifying the qualitative vitality dynamics emerging therein as a means for shedding new light on the process of collaborative artistic exploration, where as Mestre asserts, "the score operates simultaneously as a way to practise and to observe the practice." (⟶ *Score It!*) In these terms too, the qualitative descriptions of our *figures* and the documentation of previous examples within this publication are not conceived as a 'how to' guide — as instructions or ingredients — but rather as the diagramming of possibility; moreover, as provocation for deviation from the line.

Whilst we share our score system in lieu of an *Epilogue* (⟶ *How to Play the Score*), below is an account of *how* it has been practised in concrete terms. Prior to an exploration, we select which practices and *figures* we want to explore, making a visible note of these on a series of blackboards. We then enter a designated time period of shared exploration, where the invitation is to 'call' (⟶ *Practices of Notation: Calling*) different named fields of practice into play. You could begin like this: let's say someone *calls* for the ⟶ *Figure of Becoming Material*. Since you and 'fellow explorers' all know the qualities of this *figure*, you can collectively begin a process of exploration in the hope of giving rise to its emergence. Continue to explore together — in time, maybe the *figure* shows up, maybe not. Perhaps a ⟶ *Practice of Attention* would help to refine your collective sensitivity to the material transformation inherent within this *figure*: someone calls for the practice of ⟶ *Touching*. Haptic awareness now heightened, you could

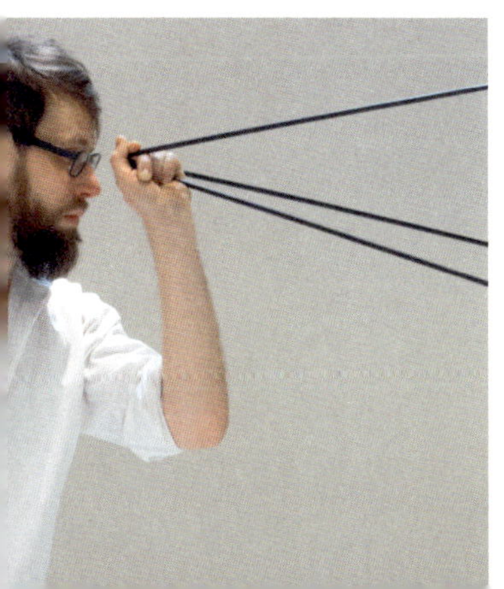

collectively return to exploring the arising conditions of —➤ *Becoming Material*. Alternatively, another *figure* or another practice might be called. The process continues (—➤ *How to Play the Score*).

Counter-intuitively perhaps, the more 'open' our score has become, the more precisely we have needed to articulate the specificity of its various elements. As Mestre argues, "the making of scores obliges us to assemble a precise choice of elements in order to investigate their function within a system of operations." (—➤ *Score It!*) Indeed, the evolution of this second model of diagrammatic praxis necessitated that we attempt to clarify — even categorise — the various intensities, energies and experiential emergences within our process of exploration, defining the qualities and attributes of differentiated *figures* (—➤ *Elemental, Empathetic, Transformative*), establishing the specificity of each of our various practices (—➤ *Practices of Attention, Notation, Conversation, Wit(h)nessing*). However, the attempt to create different categories — whether of *figures* or of practices — is not one of order or control, for fixing or delimiting the contingent process of creative exploration through labels and names; rather, we conceive the act of separation as a precondition for reconfiguration and reconnection. We consider the act of hyphenation evident in the *choreo-graphic* as an act of separation in order to conceive a new relationality between the constitutive parts.

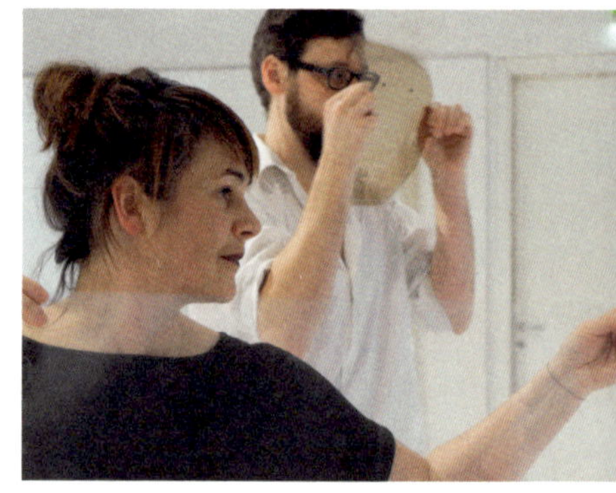

Indeed, paradoxically, the more we have strived to establish criteria for differentiation, the more interconnected, interwoven or even porous our taxonomic categories seem to become. However, this is not to suggest the futility or foolhardiness of our labour: it is not that reconnection or interconnection happens in spite of our attempts to separate or categorise. Rather, our process of anatomising process reveals there to be deeper connections and relations between the various 'parts'. Moreover, our practice of categorisation operates first as one of wilful or even subversive disorganisation, a means for de-stabilising or unsettling those habitual processes of — often imperceptible or undeclared — organisation that structure our ways of doing things (both within artistic exploration and our relations with others), so that we might observe *how* they organise us; moreover, in turn, how they might be reorganised. For Alva Noë, art is a "strange tool" through which we might engage, "with the ways our practices, techniques, and technologies organize us, and it is finally, a way to understand our organization and inevitably, to reorganize ourselves."[27] He argues that art and philosophy are "really species of a common genus whose preoccupation is with the ways we are organized and with the possibility of reorganizing ourselves."[28] Noë outlines various 'everyday practices' according to which the temporal and relationship-building dynamics of our lives are organised through the interplay of attention and negotiation, listening and responding, paying attention and losing focus, action and inaction. These organising practices are those habitual activities — often implicit rather than necessarily explicit — that shape and structure our ways of being and behaving at a biological level of embodiment. To a certain extent, many of our 'practices' might be conceived in such terms: walking, breathing, voicing, sleeping, touching, reading, naming, conversing, watching, listening, translating. However, within our enquiry they are 'offset slightly' such that they become disentangled from their everyday use or function, and instead have the capacity to be tested and explored within the frame of aesthetic exploration. Likewise, Noë uses 'choreography' as a 'stand-in' for reflecting more broadly on how art practices "seek to bring out and exhibit, to disclose and to illuminate, aspects of the way that we find ourselves organized."[29] Choreography, by which Noë means *all art*, is that which makes visible or attends to the system of organisation itself; moreover, remains 'bent' on its reorganisation. By bringing our practices into the score, we interrogate how they organise us alongside how we might activate them in new relation.

For Henk Borgdorff, artistic research can be conceived according to two different perspectives: "a constructivist and a hermeneutic perspective."[30] He argues that, "the hermeneutic perspective assumes that artistic practices and artworks disclose the world to us. The world-revealing power of art lies in its ability to offer us those new vistas, experiences and insights that affect our relationship with the world and with ourselves."[31] Alternatively, for Borgdorff, the "constructivist perspective holds

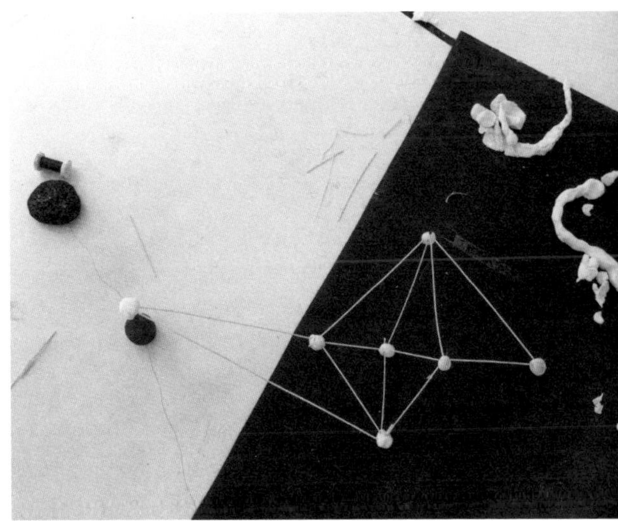

that objects and events actually become constituted in and through artworks and artistic actions. Only in and through art do we see what landscapes, soundworlds, histories, emotions, relations, interests and movements really are or could be. Here lies the performative and critical power of art. It does not represent things, it presents them, thereby making the world into what it is or could be."[32] In one sense, our own enquiry simultaneously operates in both "world-revealing" and "world-constituting" modalities. First, our 'complex' of practices are deployed as a means for identifying, revealing and offering new insights into the dynamic vitality affects emerging within collaborative artistic process, as well as giving tangible expression to the ways in which we organise and are organised. Adrian Heathfield points out the delicate ethical implications of relational 'organisation' when he states, "One subject often produces the conditions in which their creativity can thrive: a terrain that a subject produces in order to enter and test their own limit conditions, a space where they are individuated [...] But, at the same time the creation of that space delimits the other's space ... the work of collaboration is the recognition and acceptance of that delimitation" (⟶ *On Sedimentations of Sensitivities*). In one sense then, our *figures* focus on these fragile dynamics of organisation within artistic collaboration.

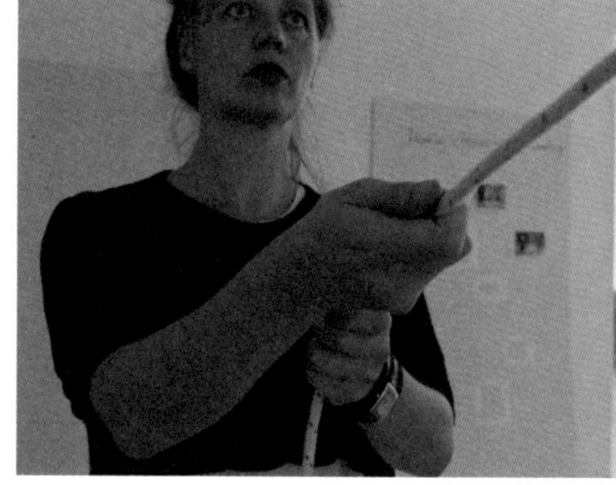

However, beyond revelation or disclosure, our use of the score seeks also to constitute new—experimental—ways in which we can become re-organised, through the diagrammatic interplay between our different categories of practice. In one sense, our adoption of a diagrammatic paradigm as a practice of ethico-aesthetic reorganisation can be conceived as practical articulation of Gilles Deleuze and Félix Guattari's concept of the rhizome (as map) that "is open and connectable in all of its dimensions; it is detachable, reversible, susceptible to constant modification. It can be torn, reversed, adapted to any kind of mounting, reworked by an individual, group, or social formation. It can be drawn on a wall, conceived of as a work of art, constructed as a political action or as a meditation [...] A map has multiple entryways, as opposed to the tracing, which always comes back 'to the same.'"[33] As Simon O'Sullivan elaborates, "The rhizome, as a map, is to do with experimentation. It does not trace something that came before (again no *re*presentation) rather it actively creates the terrain it maps — setting out the coordination points for worlds-in-progress, for subjectivities-to-come."[34] He asserts that this involves, "the creative mapping of our connections and potentialities, a mapping that pays attention to regions of intensity (the distribution of affects) and to trajectories of future becomings, as well as to those already delineated continents of representation and signification."[35] Within a rhizomatic diagrammatic model, there is no centre; all parts have the capacity to be connected to all parts, any point can be broken and reattached to another. The diagrammatic of the rhizome seemingly resists attempts to isolate or separate its individual nodal points from their entanglement, for as Deleuze and Guattari assert, "A rhizome may be broken, shattered at a given spot, but it will start up again on one of its old lines, or on new lines."[36] So too, we consider our acts of separation and categorisation as a means for activating new connections. Deleuze and Guattari offer a recommendation for operating rhizomatically: "Lodge yourself on a stratum, experiment with the opportunities it offers, find an advantageous point on it, find potential movements of deterritorialization, possible lines of flight, experience them, produce flow conjunctions here and there, try out continuums of intensity segment by segment [...] It is through a meticulous relation with the strata that one succeeds in freeing lines of flight."[37]

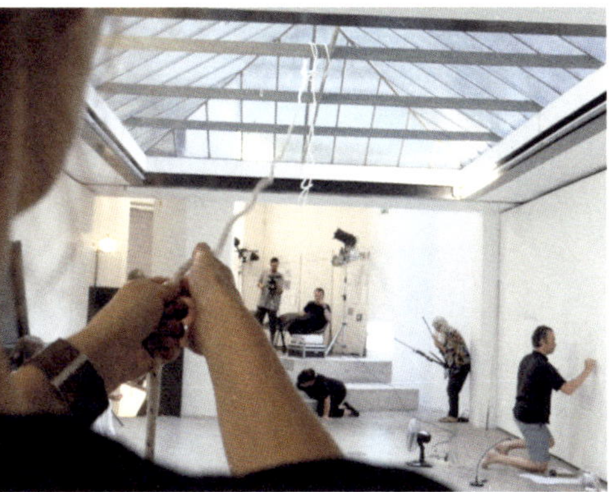

We ask: how can we create the germinal conditions for rhizomatic diagrammatics to arise? As Deleuze asks: "How does actualization occur [...] Beneath the actual qualities and extensities, species and parts, there are spatio-temporal dynamisms. These are the actualizing, differentiating agencies."[38] How do we constitute our relational milieu as an ecological 'rhizosphere'?[39] We anatomise and separate the practices and dynamics that specifically comprise the process of collaborative artistic exploration in order to test how they might be diagrammatically reconfigured otherwise, unexpectedly; in turn, how we ourselves also might be configured differently in and through this experience. Parallel to the model of the rhizome, we conceive our score and the milieu constituted through its very activation in *ecosophical* terms. Félix Guattari outlines an "ethico-aesthetic aegis of an ecosophy" — comprising the 'three ecologies' of "environment, social relations and human subjectivity"[40] — involving the cultivation of an *ecological* praxis, "specific practices that will modify and reinvent the ways in which we live [...] it will be a question of literally reconstructing the modalities of 'group-being' [*l'être-en-groupe*], not only through 'communicational' interventions but through existential mutations driven by the motor of subjectivity."[41] He argues that we "need new social and aesthetic practices, new practice of the Self in relation to the other, to the foreign, the strange ... we will only escape from the major crises of our era through the articulation of: — a nascent subjectivity; — a constantly mutating socius; — an environment in the process of being reinvented."[42] The notion of an ecology or even ecosystem of practices resonates with our conceptualisation of the score: we conceive it as a *living* organism more than a system of organisation. It pulses with a sense of liveness, aliveness; it has the capacity to develop and grow.

Our *embodied diagrammatics* attend to the rhythmic interplay of heterogeneous durations in the constitution of ethical relations, revealing a sense of polyrhythmic or even idiorhythmic micro-temporalities operating between, beneath and below the more 'readable' temporal dynamics of chronological — perhaps even anthropocentric — time.[43] Here, as Henri Bergson asserts, "In reality there is no one rhythm of duration; it is possible to imagine many rhythms which, slower or faster, measure the degree of tension of different kinds of consciousness."[44] Indeed, it is not a case of attempting to zoom in to different durational intensities, nor even between micro and macro levels of awareness; rather more, towards developing a practice capable of attending to — or at least acknowledging — their simultaneity. The embodied diagrammatics of our score enables the deepening of attention towards a level of vitality operating beneath or below a 'structural' level of organisation; in turn, providing a framework for bringing-into-relation different practices as a means of re-organisation, as a diagrammatic praxis for ethico-aesthetic experimentation. The focus of our enquiry thus expands from attending to the *how-ness* — the qualitative-processual dynamics — within shared collaborative exploration, towards the evolution of a 'score system' for the experimental testing of 'how else'. However, the score is not the outcome of our research enquiry, for its 'knowledge' can only be activated *en acte,* as a live and living process of exploration. The score is the means and not the end; or else, it is a "means without end"[45] for ours is an unfinished and unfinishable enquiry. This inconclusiveness is not a mark of failure nor futility however, rather a characteristic of both artistic research and also of play, where as Roger Caillois states, "what to begin with seems to be a situation susceptible to indefinite repetitions turns out to be capable of producing ever new combinations."[46] Here, "At the end of the game, all can and must start over again."[47] (⟶ *How to Play the Score*).

1) ⟶ Alex Arteaga, *Researching Aesthetically the Roots of Aesthetics.*

2) Vilém Flusser, *Gestures,* Minneapolis: University of Minnesota Press, 2014, p. 159.

3) The term 'ethico-aesthetic' is attributed to Félix Guattari. Cf. *Chaosmosis: An Ethico-Aesthetic Paradigm,* Sydney: Power Publications, 1995. Cf. also Gilles Deleuze, 'Life as a Work of Art', in *Negotiations: 1972-1990,* New York: Columbia University Press, 1995; Michel Foucault, *The Hermeneutics of the Subject, Lectures at the College de France 1981-1982,* New York: Picador, 2001. Cf. Baruch Spinoza, *Ethics,* Oxford: Oxford University Press, [1677] 2000 and Gilles Deleuze, *Spinoza Practical Philosophy* (Trans.) Robert Hurley, San Francisco: City Lights Books, 1988.

4) Henk Borgdorff, 'The Production of Knowledge in Artistic Research', in Michael Biggs and Henrik Karlsson (Eds.), *The Routledge Companion to Research in the Arts,* London: Routledge, 2011, p. 51.

5) Daniel Stern, *Forms of Vitality: Exploring Dynamic Experience in Psychology, the Arts, Psychotherapy, and Development,* Oxford and New York: Oxford University Press, 2010, p. 3.

6) Stern, 2010, p. 11.

7) Stern, 2010, p. 15.

8) Brian Massumi, in Hugo Glendinning and Adrian Heathfield (Dirs. and Eds.), *No Such Thing as Rest: A Walk with Brian Massumi,* 2013, p. 28.

9) Massumi, 2013, p. 28.

10) Erin Manning, *The Minor Gesture,* Durham: Duke University Press, 2016, p. 7.

11) Cf. Nanopolitics group, *Nanopolitics Handbook,* Brooklyn: Minor Compositions, 2014.

12) Stern, 2010, p. 75.

13) Stern, 2010, p. 75.

14) Stern, 2010, p. 98.

15) Cf. also Karin Harrasser, 'Drawing Interest Recording Vitality', in Nikolaus Gansterer (Ed.), *Drawing a Hypothesis: Figures of Thought,* Vienna and New York: Springer, 2011, pp. 109-120.

16) Cf. Erin Manning, *Always More Than One: Individuation's Dance,* Durham: Duke University Press, 2013.

17) Petra Sabisch, *Choreographing Relations: Practical Philosophy and Contemporary Choreography,* Munich: epodium, 2011, p. 129. Cf. Chapter on 'Articulation', especially 2.2.2. 'How to Make Sense with Differential Compositions: Towards a Topology of Articulations', pp. 129-143.

18) Manning, 2013, p. 147.

19) Cf. Susanne Leeb, 'A Line with Variable Direction, which Traces No Contour, and Delimits No Form', pp. 29-42, for differentiation of representational and non-representational modalities of diagrammatic practice; Gerhard Dirmoser, 'Figures of Thought' and 'Collection of Figures of Thought', pp. 153-176, both in Gansterer (Ed.), *Drawing a Hypothesis: Figures of Thought,* Vienna and New York: Springer, 2011. John Rajchman, 'Diagram and Diagnosis', in Elizabeth Grosz, (Ed.) *Becomings: Explorations in Time, Memory, and Futures,* Ithaca: Cornell University Press, 1999, pp. 42-54.

20) Manning, 2013, p. 134.

21) Manning, 2013, p. 142.

22) Manning, 2013, p. 134.

23) Manning, *Relationscapes: Movement, Art, Philosophy,* Cambridge, Mass. and London: MIT Press, 2009, p. 125.

24) Manning, 2009, p. 125.

25) Manning, 2013, p. 141.

26) Cf. Giorgio Agamben, *What is an Apparatus?,* Stanford: Stanford University Press, 2009. Cf. Michel Foucault, *Power/Knowledge: Selected Interviews and Other Writings, 1972-1977,* (Ed. and Trans.) Colin Gordon, New York: Pantheon Books, 1980.

27) Noë, 2015, p. xiii.

28) Noë, 2015, p. xiii.

29) Noë, 2015, p. 16.

30) Borgdorff, 2011, p. 61.

31) Borgdorff, 2011, p. 61.

32) Borgdorff, 2011, p. 61.

33) Deleuze and Guattari, 2004, p. 12.

34) Simon O'Sullivan, *Art Encounters Deleuze and Guattari,* Basingstoke: Palgrave Macmillan, 2007, p. 35.

35) O'Sullivan, 2007, p. 36.

36) Deleuze and Guattari, 2004, p. 10.

37) Deleuze and Guattari, 2004, p. 178.

38) Deleuze, *Difference and Repetition,* (Trans.) Paul Patton, London and New York: Bloomsbury Academic, 2014, p. 278.

39) Cf. Mary Zamberlin, *Rhizosphere: Gilles Deleuze and the 'Minor' American Writing of William James,* London and New York: Routledge, 2014.

40) Félix Guattari, *The Three Ecologies,* London: Bloomsbury Academic, 2014. p. 18.

41) Guattari, 2014, p. 22.

42) Guattari, 2014, pp. 46-47.

43) Cf. Roland Barthes, *How to Live Together: Novelistic Simulations of Some Everyday Spaces,* New York: Columbia University Press, 2013; Henri Lefebvre, *Rhythmanalysis: Space, Time, and Everyday Life,* London: Bloomsbury Academic, 2015.

44) Henri Bergson, *Matter and Memory,* (Trans.) Nancy Margaret Paul and William Scott Palmer, New York: Dover Publications, [1896] 2004, p. 275.

45) Giorgio Agamben, *Means without End: Notes on Politics,* Minneapolis: University of Minnesota Press, 2008.

46) Roger Caillois, *Man, Play and Games,* (Trans.) Meyer Barash, Urbana and Chicago: University of Illinois Press, 2001, p. 30.

47) Caillois, 2001, p. 5.

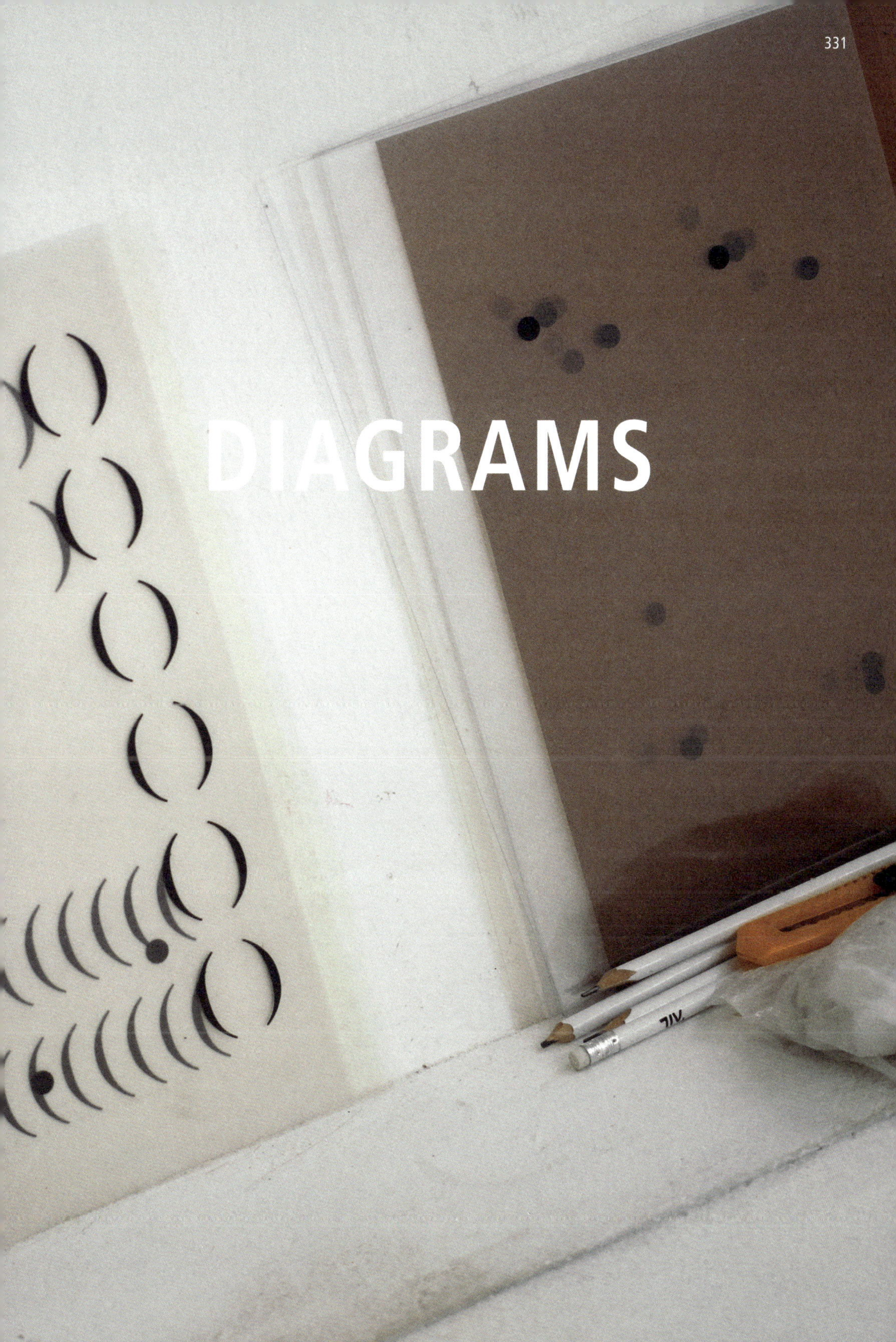

DIAGRAMS

is one

self

by thoughts

h

no

matter

plu

points

ex ing

draw in g

lettin g be dra

per ceptions

t

tat

on

ist

flow

feelings

following

here

eye can no longer see

say

ly

hand

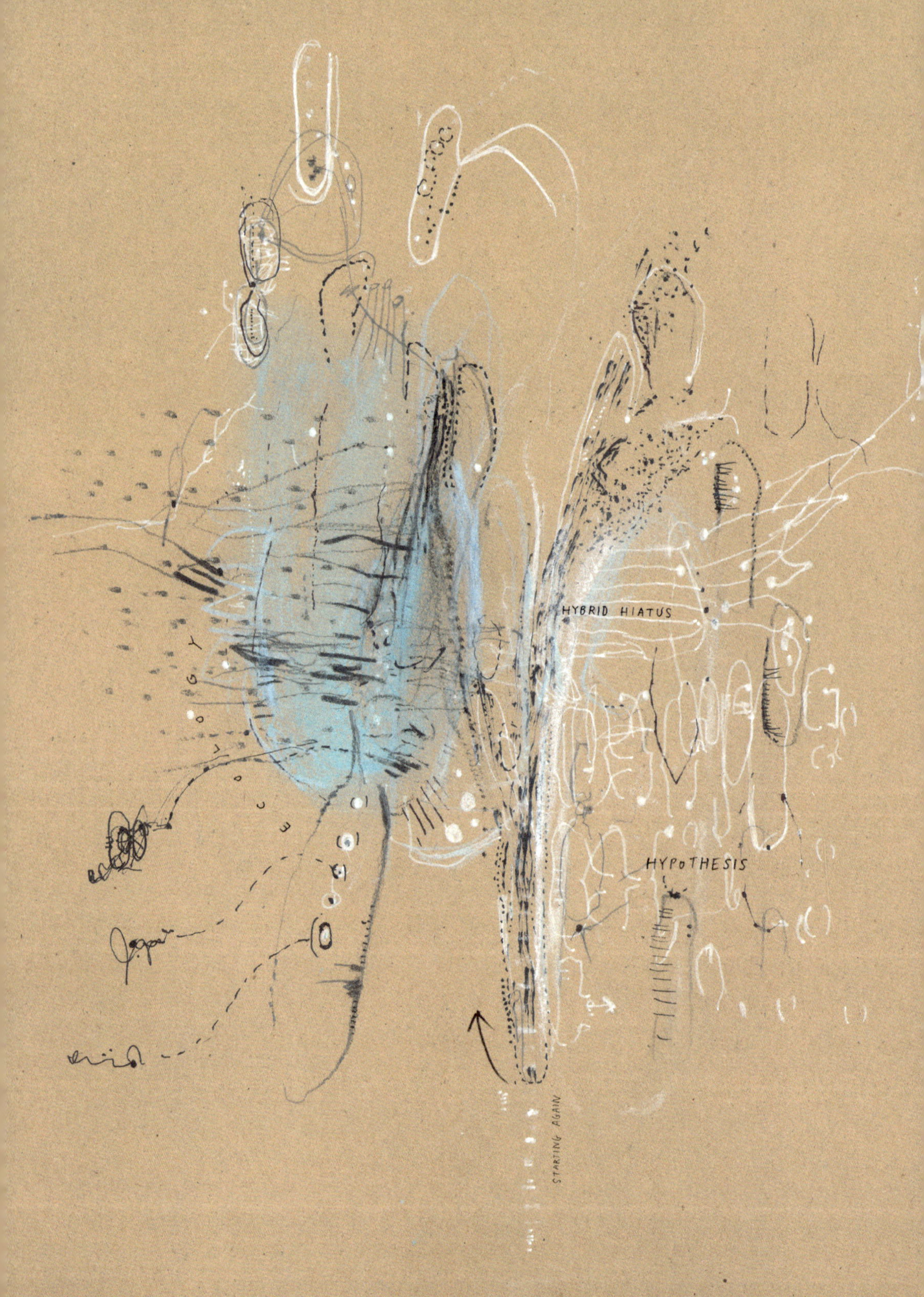
HYBRID HIATUS
HYPOTHESIS
STARTING AGAIN

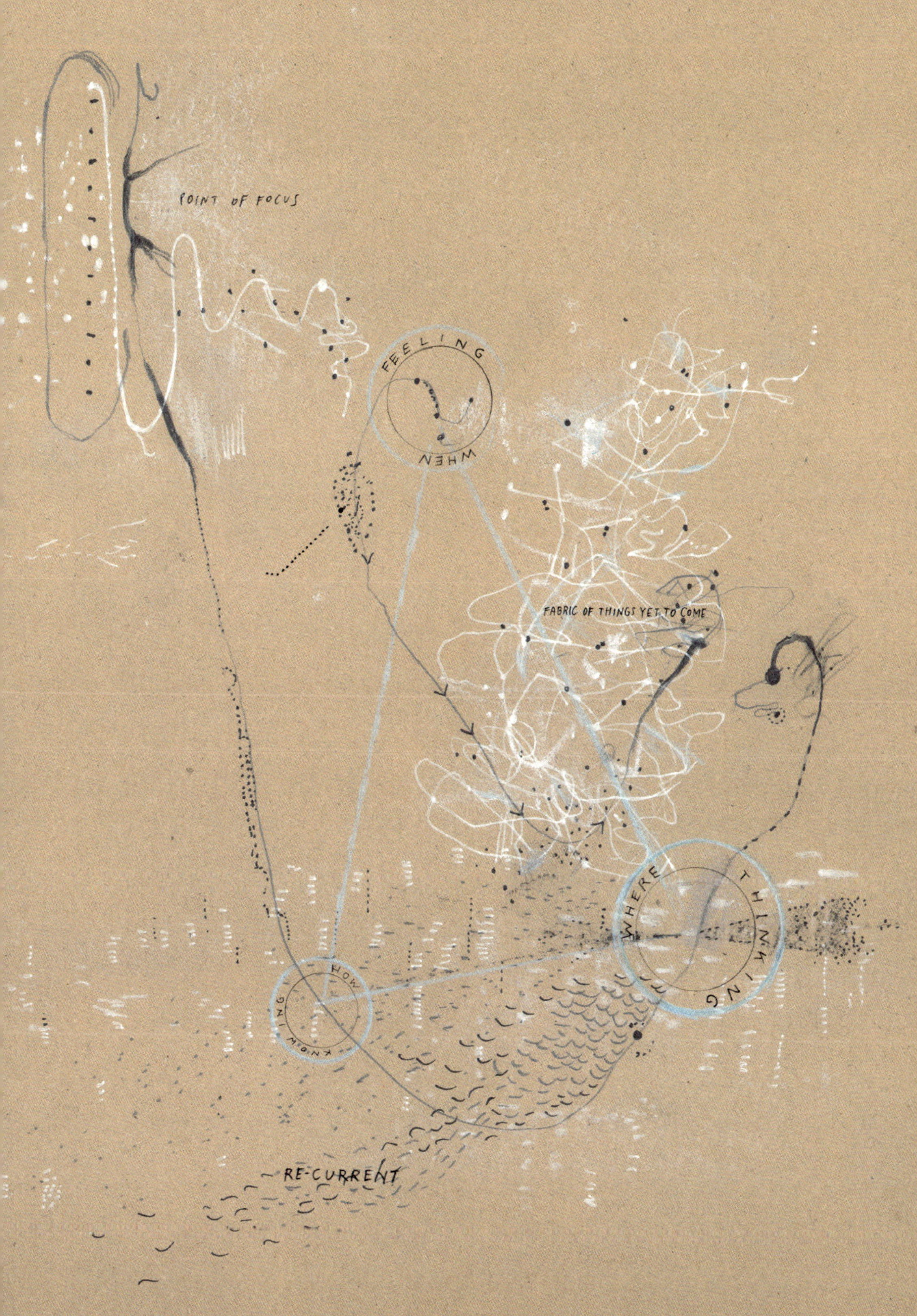
POINT OF FOCUS
FEELING
WHEN
FABRIC OF THINGS YET TO COME
WHERE
THINKING
HOW
KNOWING
RE-CURRENT

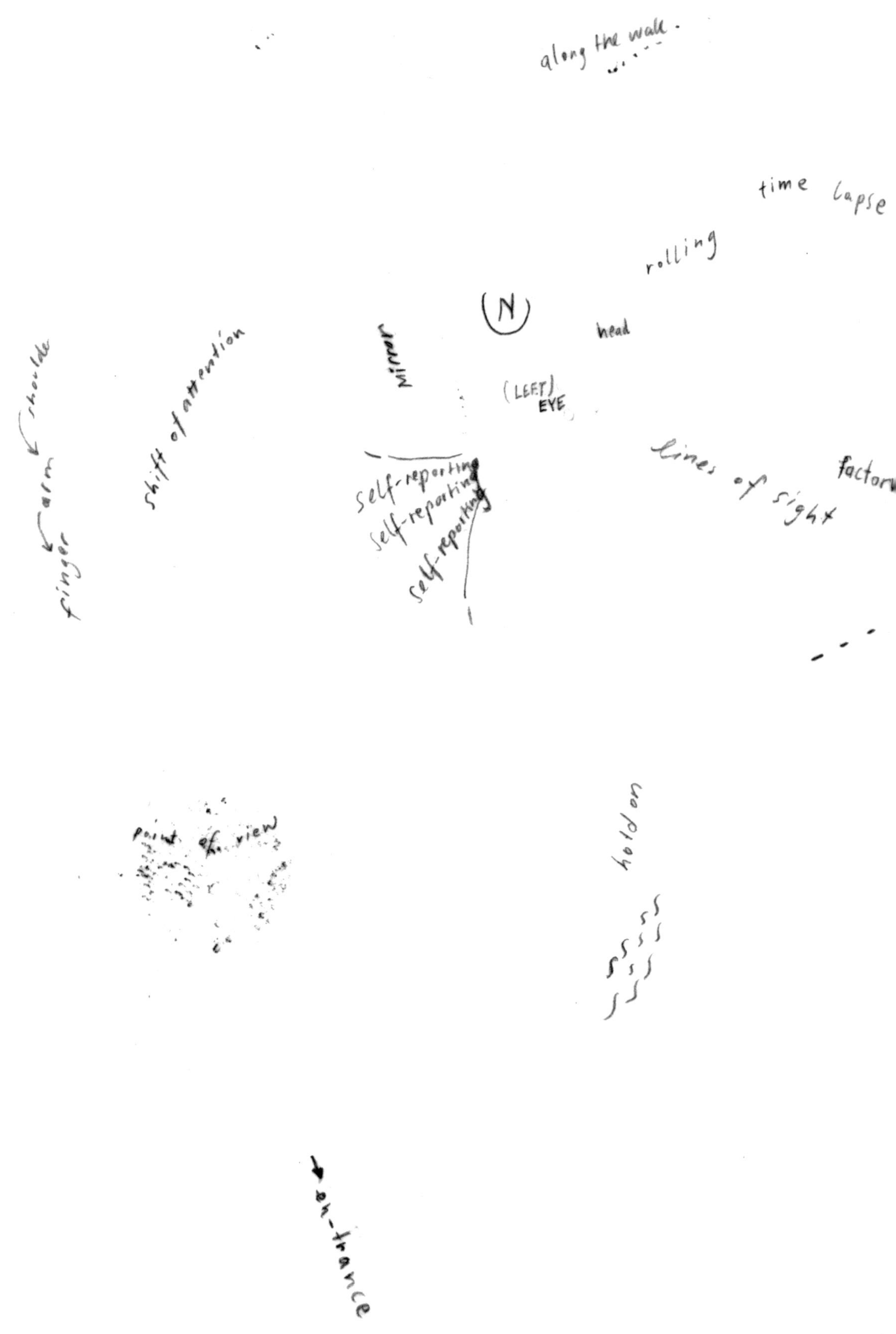

along the wall.
time lapse
rolling
N
head
mirror
(LEFT)
EYE
shift of attention
shoulde
arm
finger
self-reporting
self-reporting
self-reporting
lines of sight
factor
point of view
hold on
en-trance

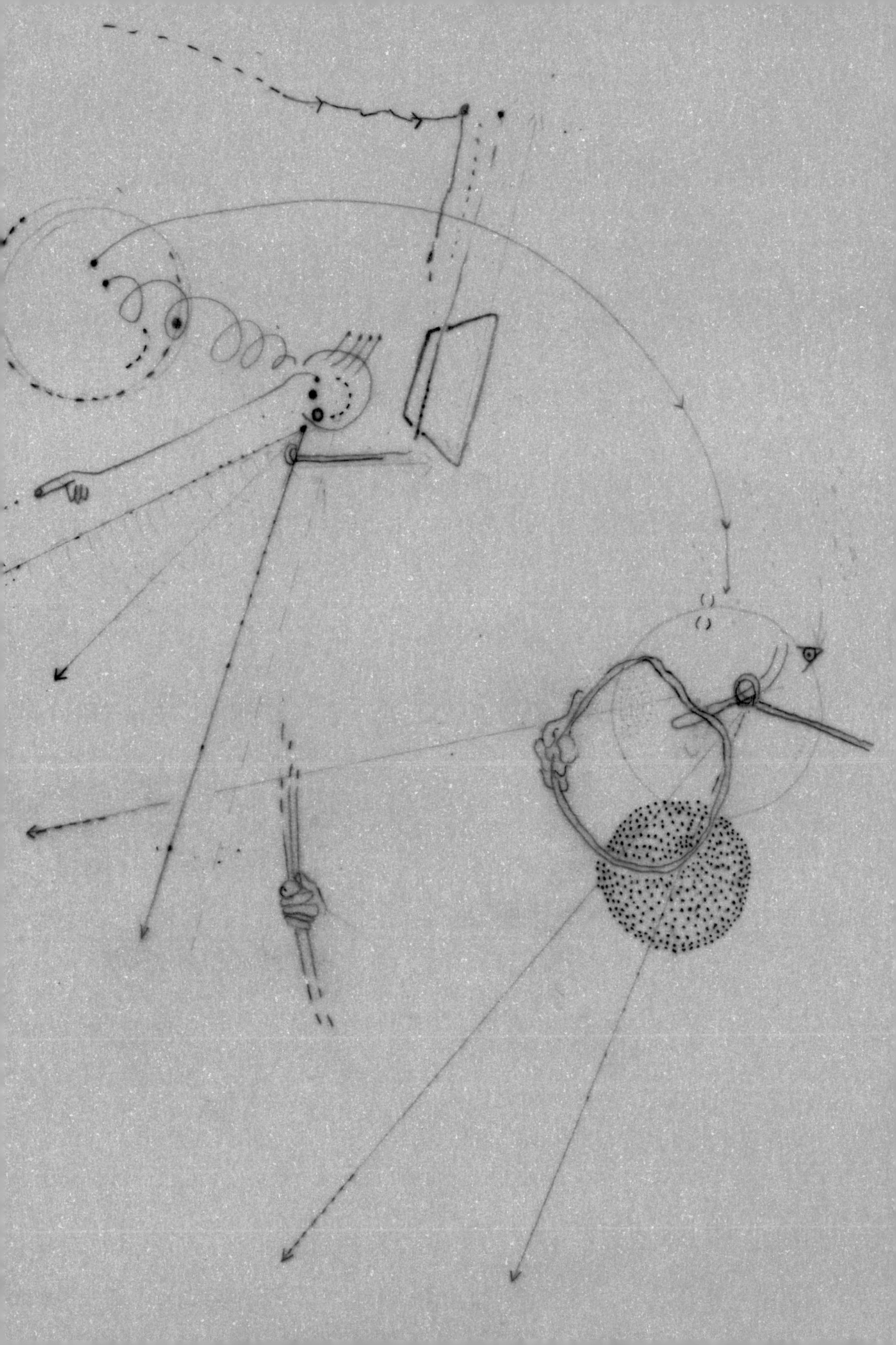

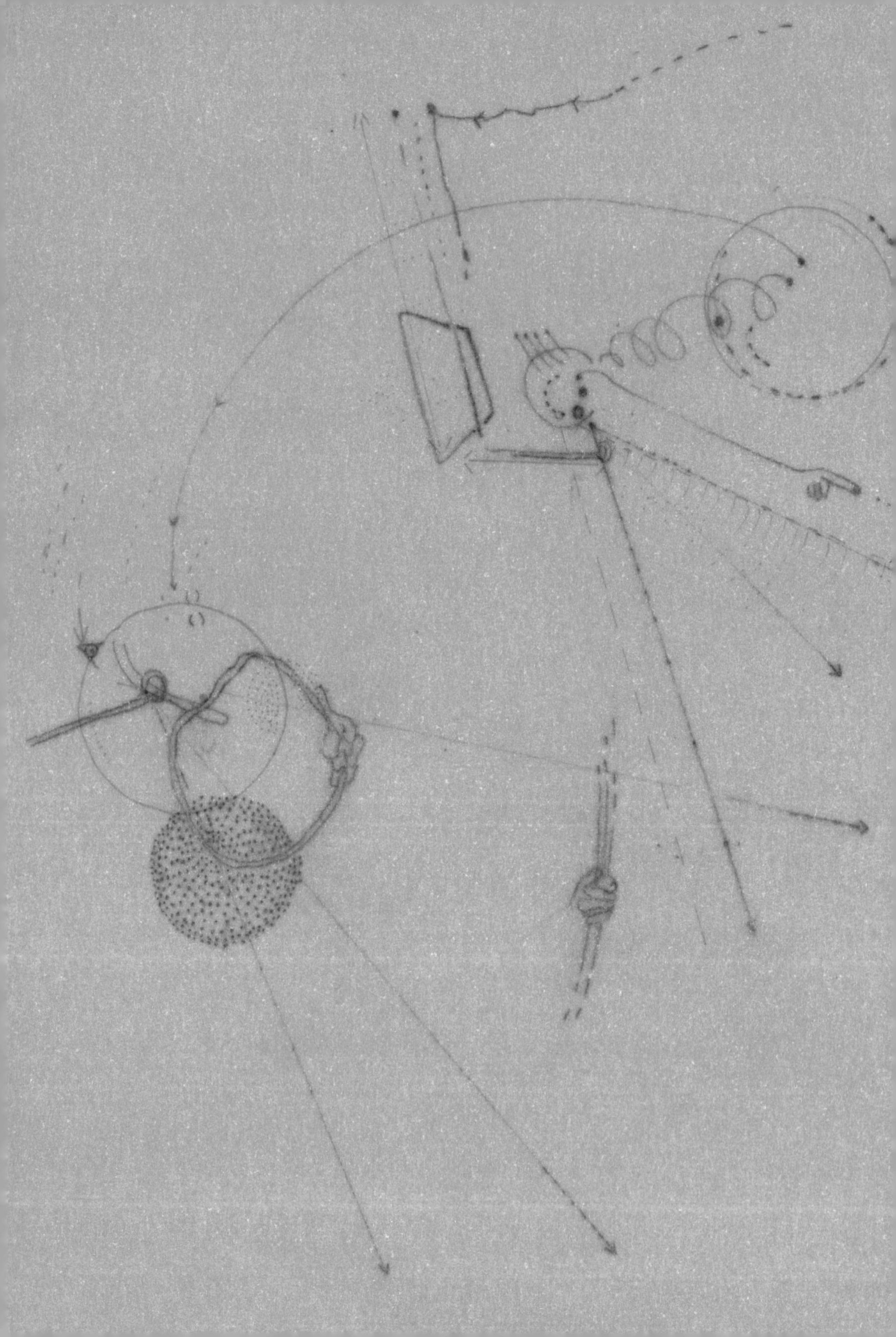

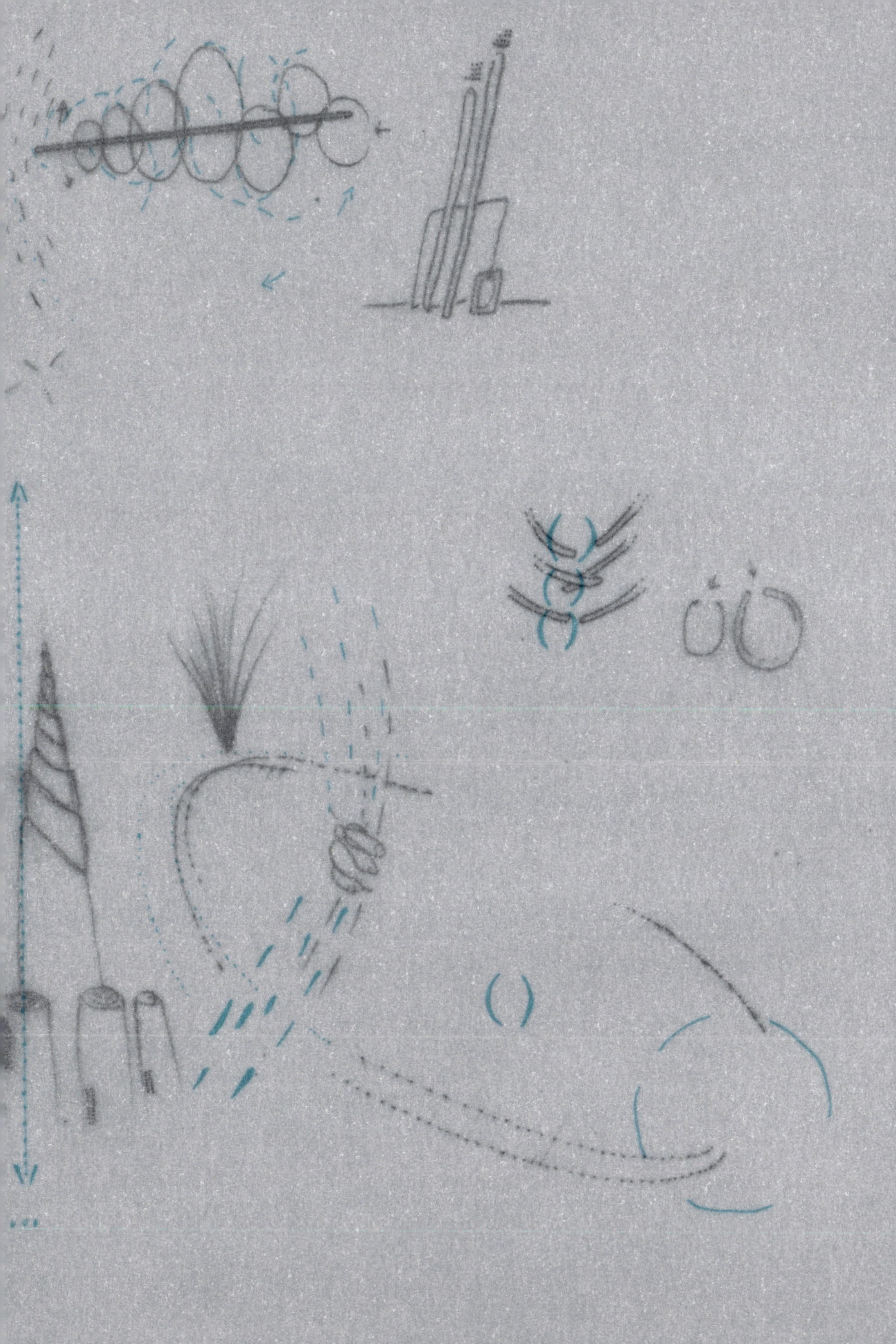

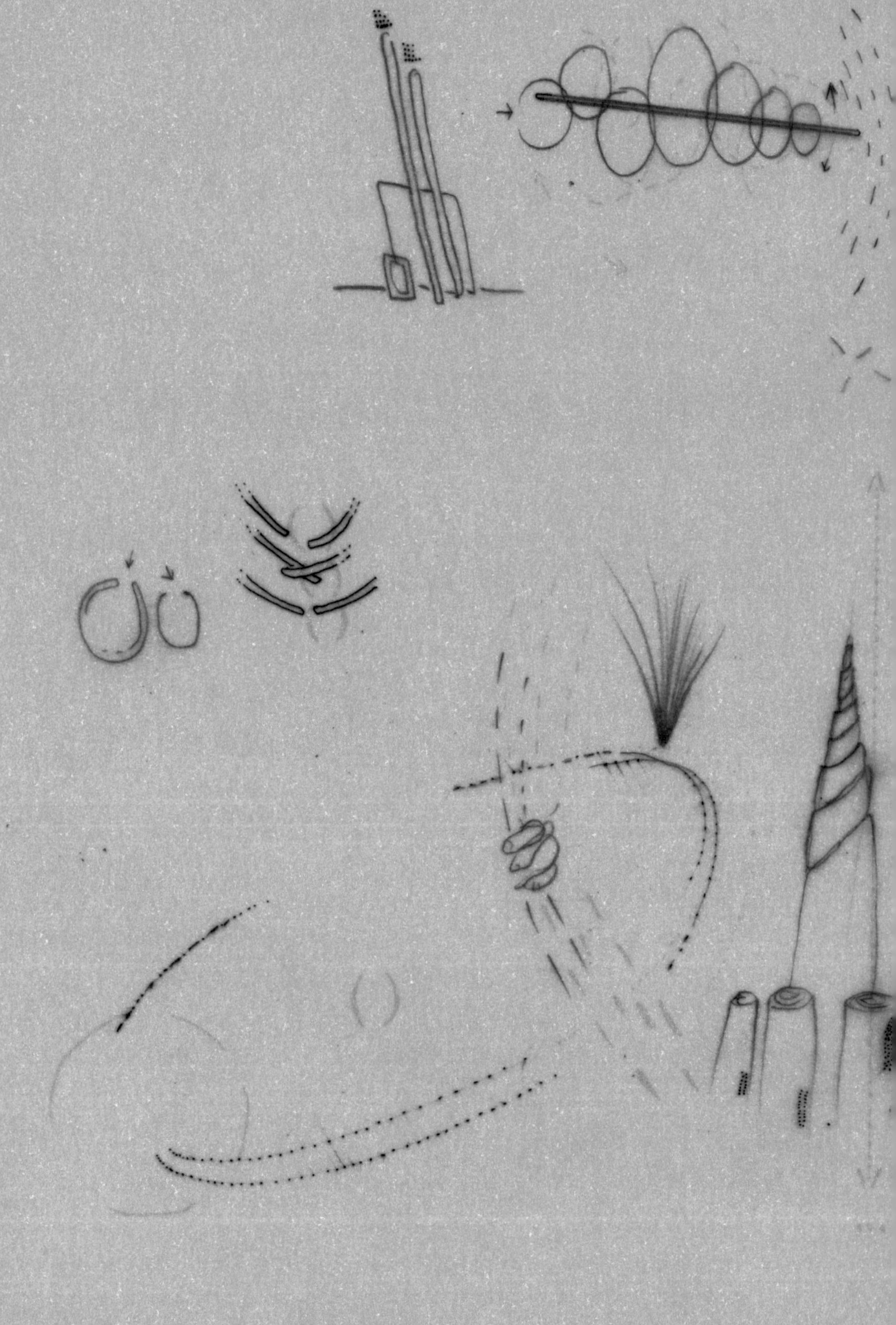

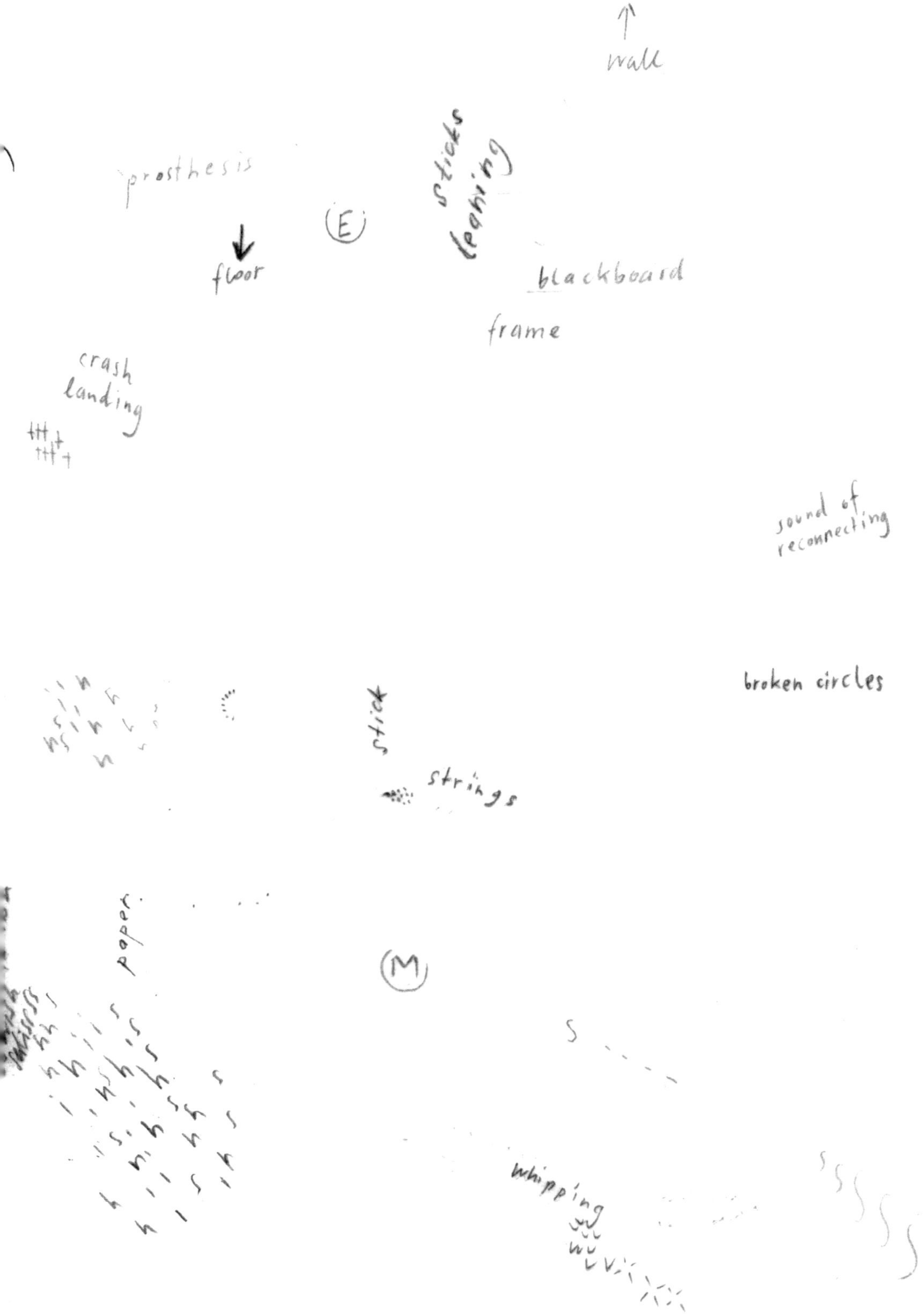

wall

prosthesis

sticks leaning

(E)

floor

blackboard

frame

crash landing

sound of reconnecting

broken circles

stick

strings

paper

(M)

whipping

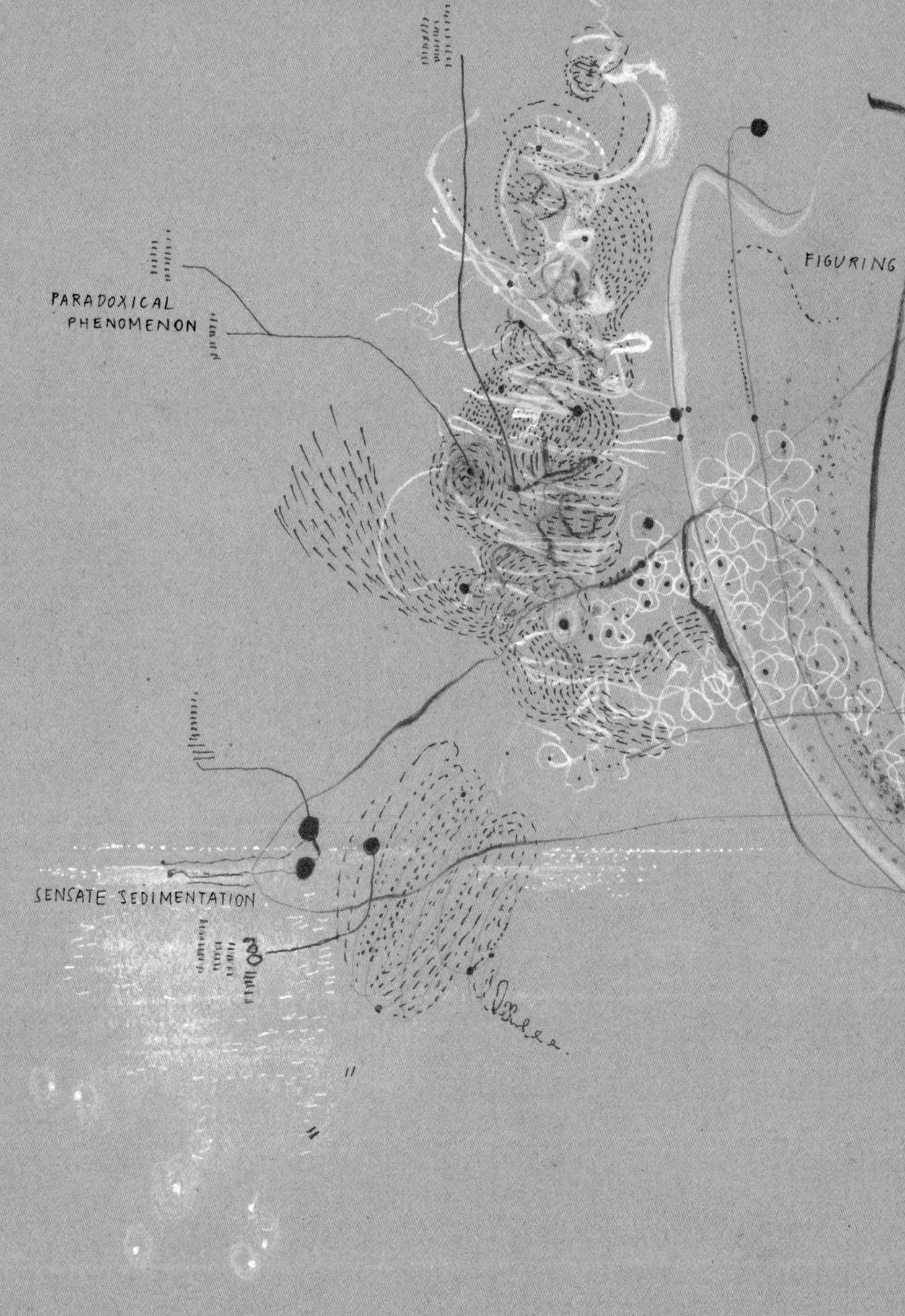
PARADOXICAL
PHENOMENON
FIGURING
SENSATE SEDIMENTATION

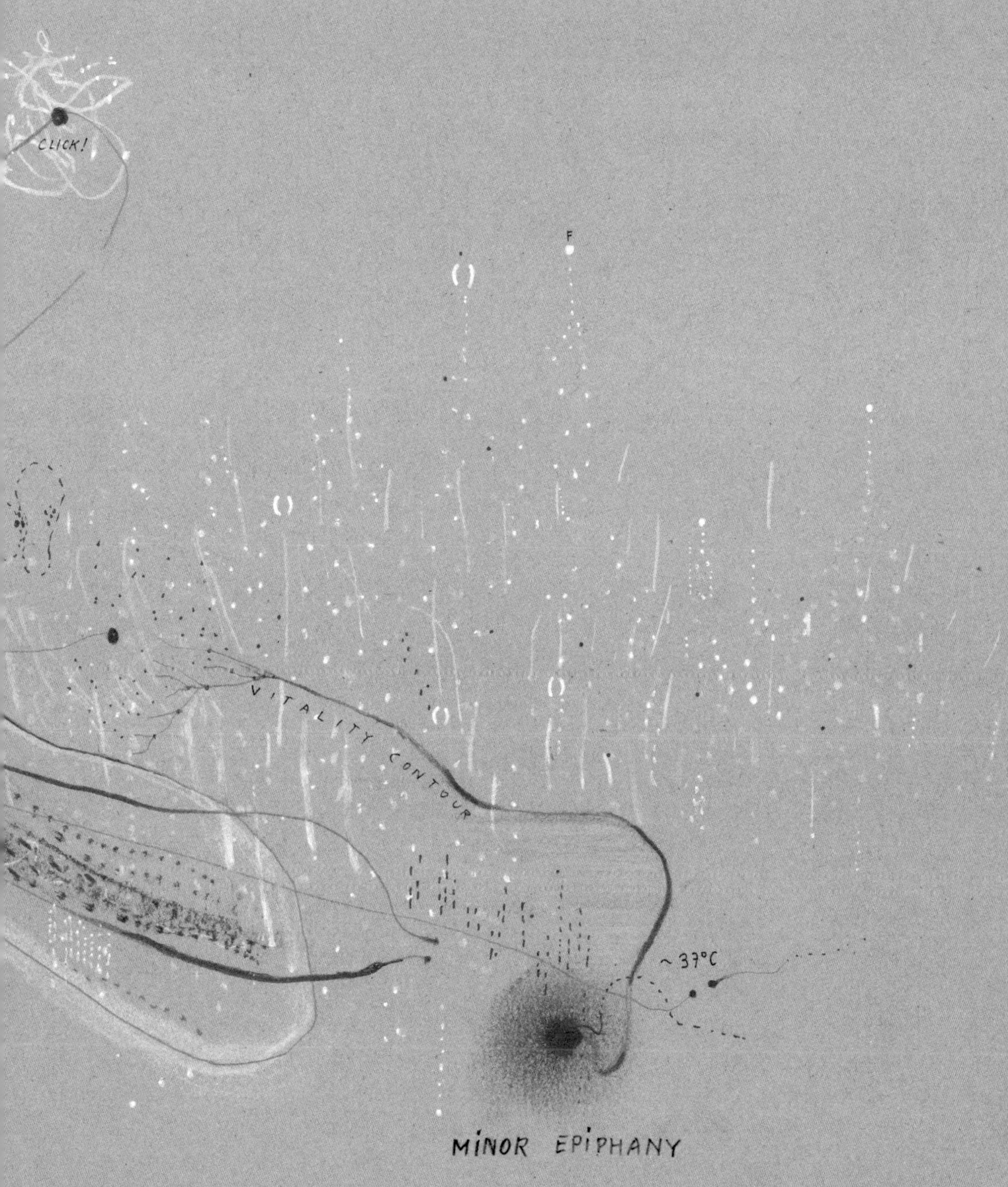
CLICK!
F
VITALITY CONTOUR
~37°C
MINOR EPIPHANY

suddenly
suddenly
secondly ---
actually
like

--- completely
like

tasting
actually -frequently
like a

a
a a a
a a a a
a a a
a a a
a a
a
a a
a
a a
a

like
like
like love

field of silence

43788
9 4784
4783
71 3 4326
4 41245
2 4276
3 4377
8 443
98 9 45
42
4 42

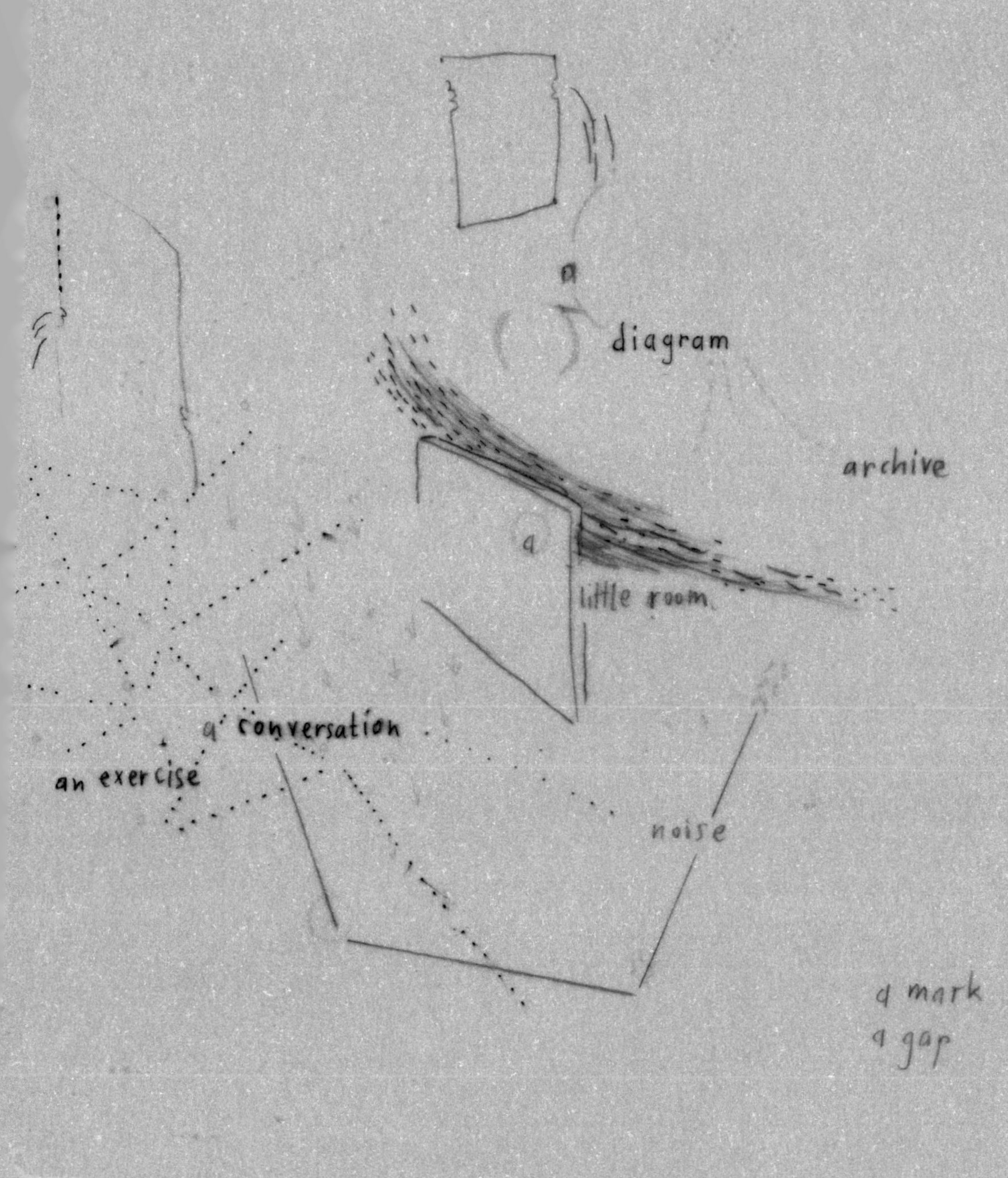
a
diagram
archive
a
little room
a conversation
an exercise
noise
a mark
a gap

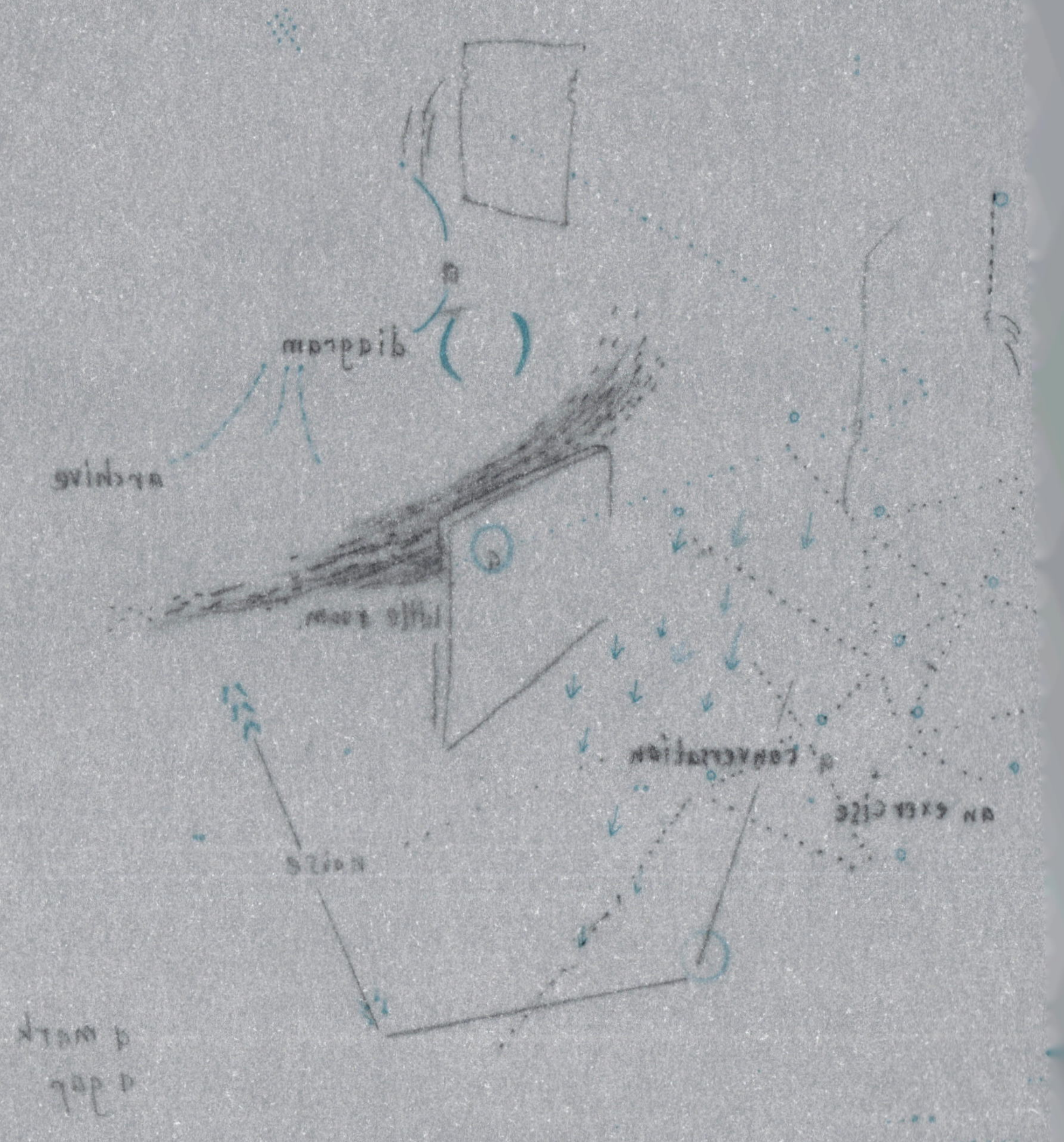

diagram

archive

little room

a conversation

an exercise

noise

a mark

a gap

a bird
board

a miracle

in time

Like a mirror

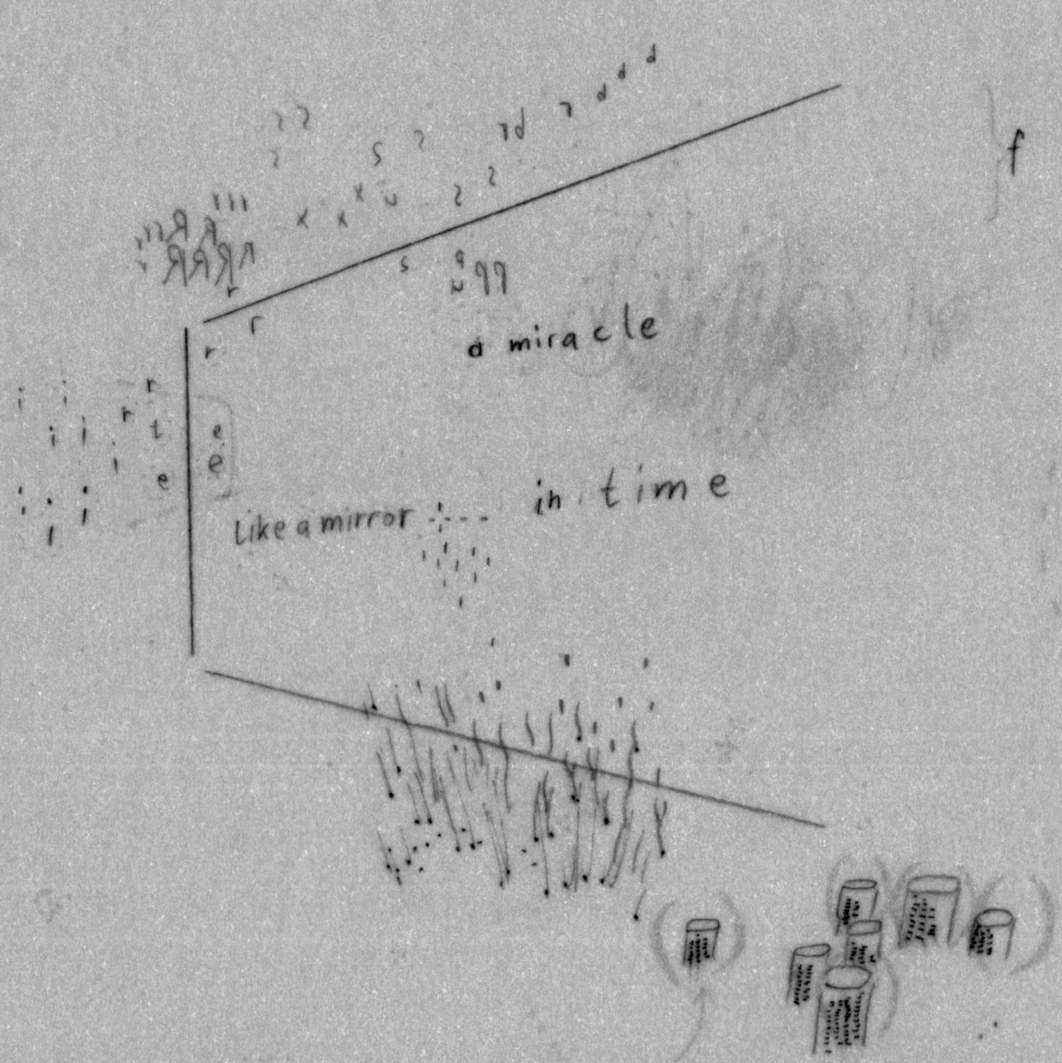
a bird
board
f
a miracle
in time
Like a mirror

a mark
(whispered)

researching
repeating
repetition

opening

a curve taking another direction

blind spotting

like done
by a machine

s
s
slike
slike
slide
slide sliding

more like a ground

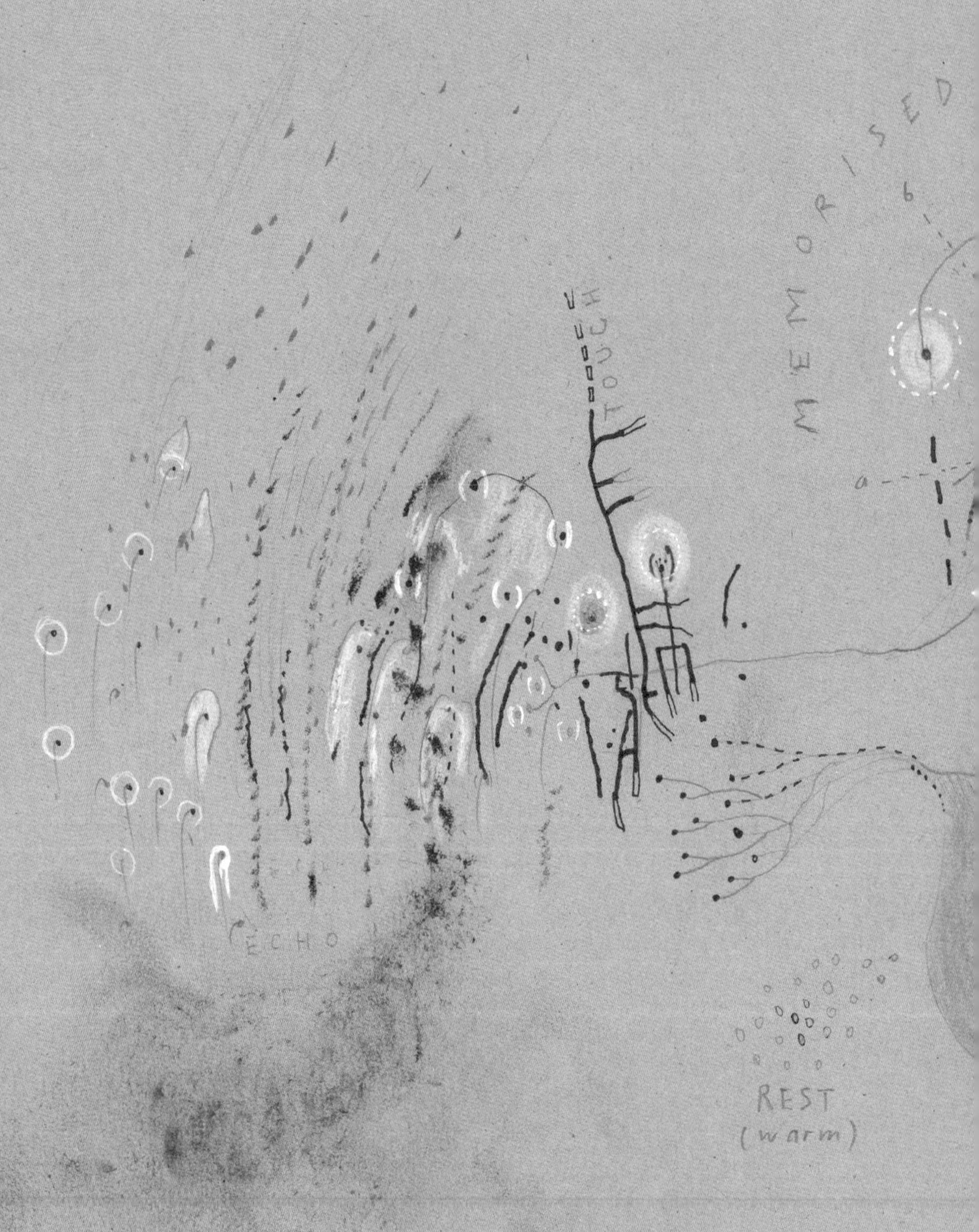

← what was

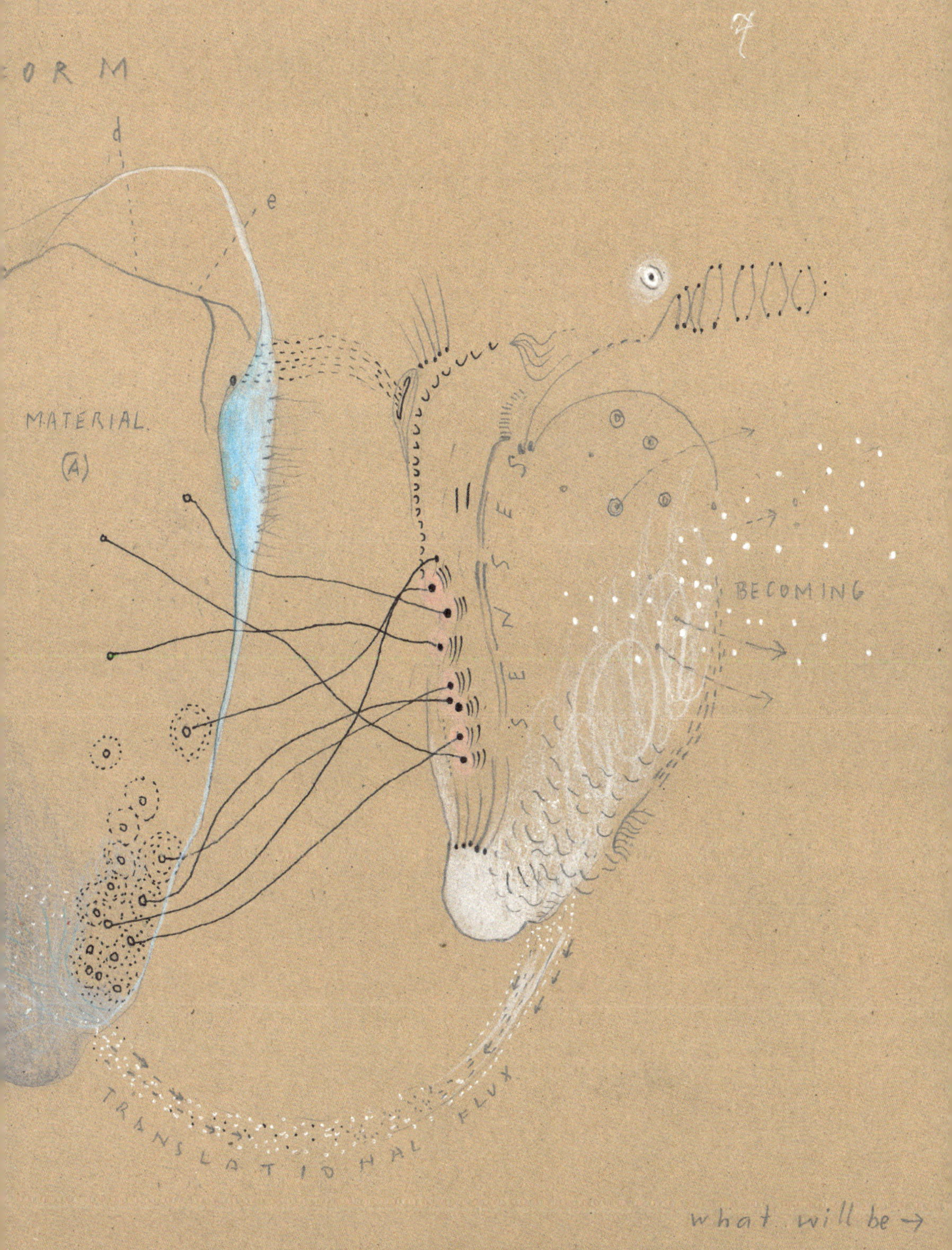

7

ORM

d

e

MATERIAL

(A)

SENSE

BECOMING

TRANSLATIONAL FLUX

what will be →

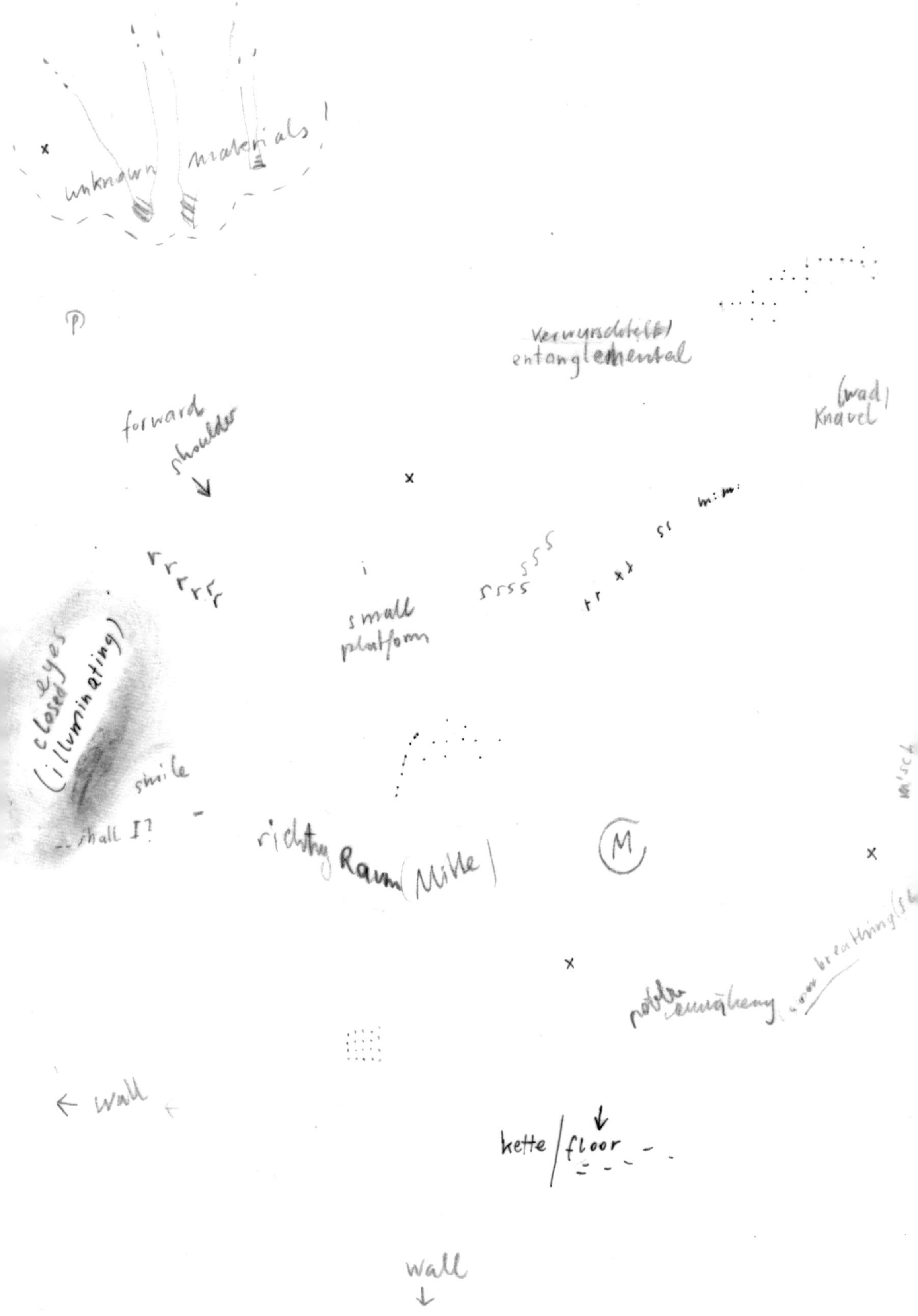

unknown materials!

P

verwurschtelt
entanglemental

(wad)
Knavel

forward shoulder

rrrrrr

i

small platform

ssss sss

rr xx

ss

m: m:

closed eyes
(illuminating)

smile

.. shall I?

richtung Raum (Mitte)

M

nobler annäherung

breathing

← wall

kette / floor

wall
↓

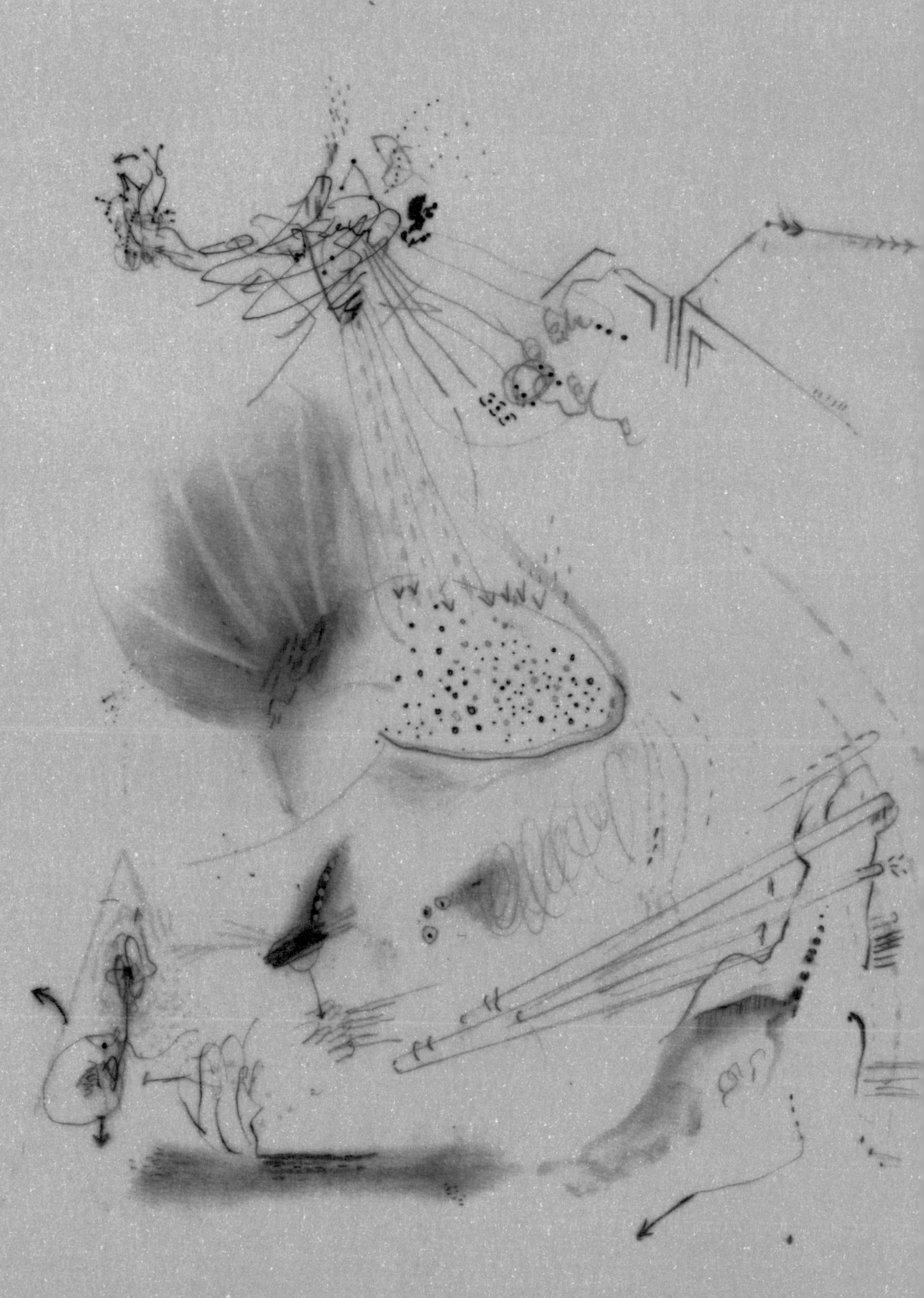

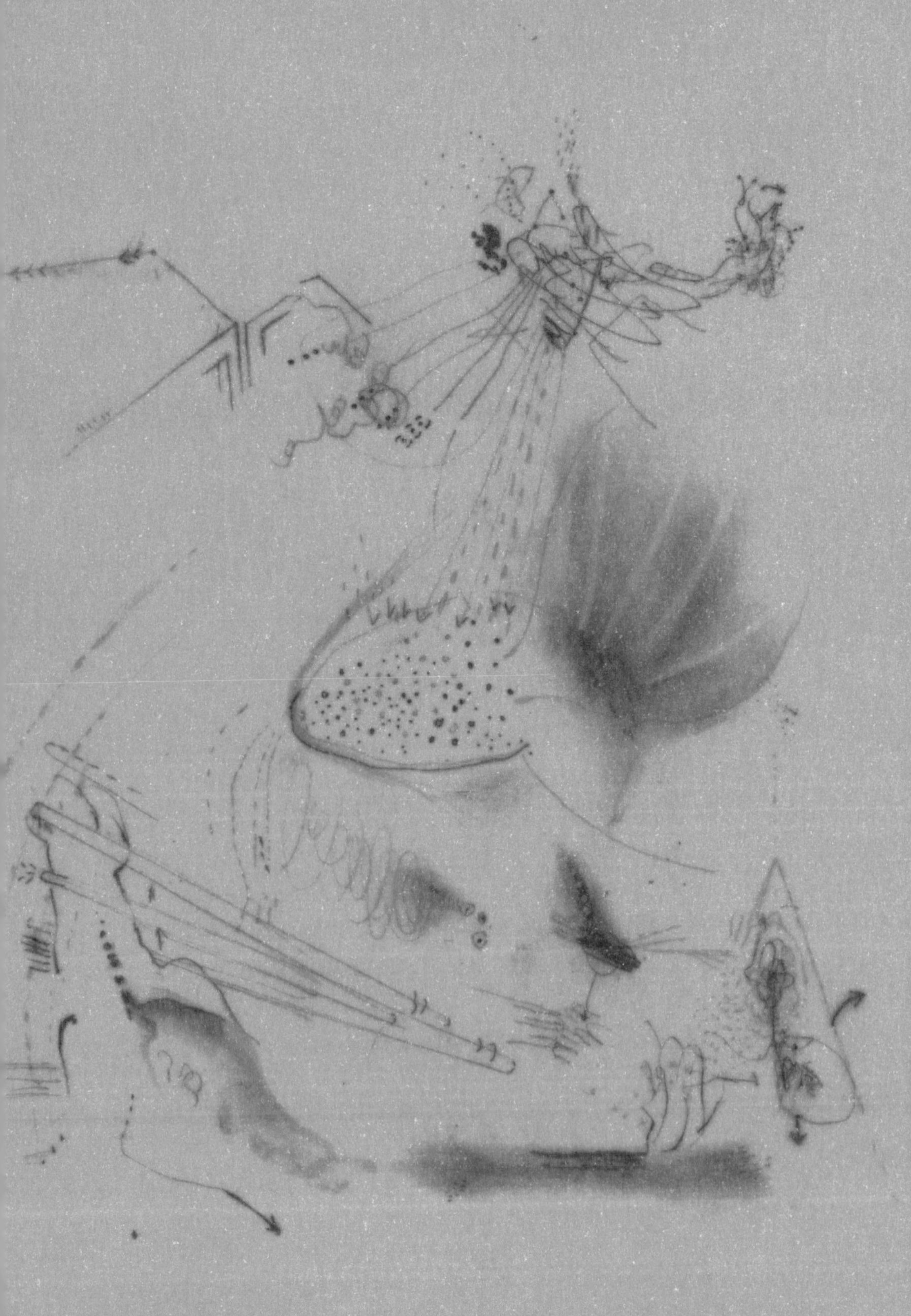

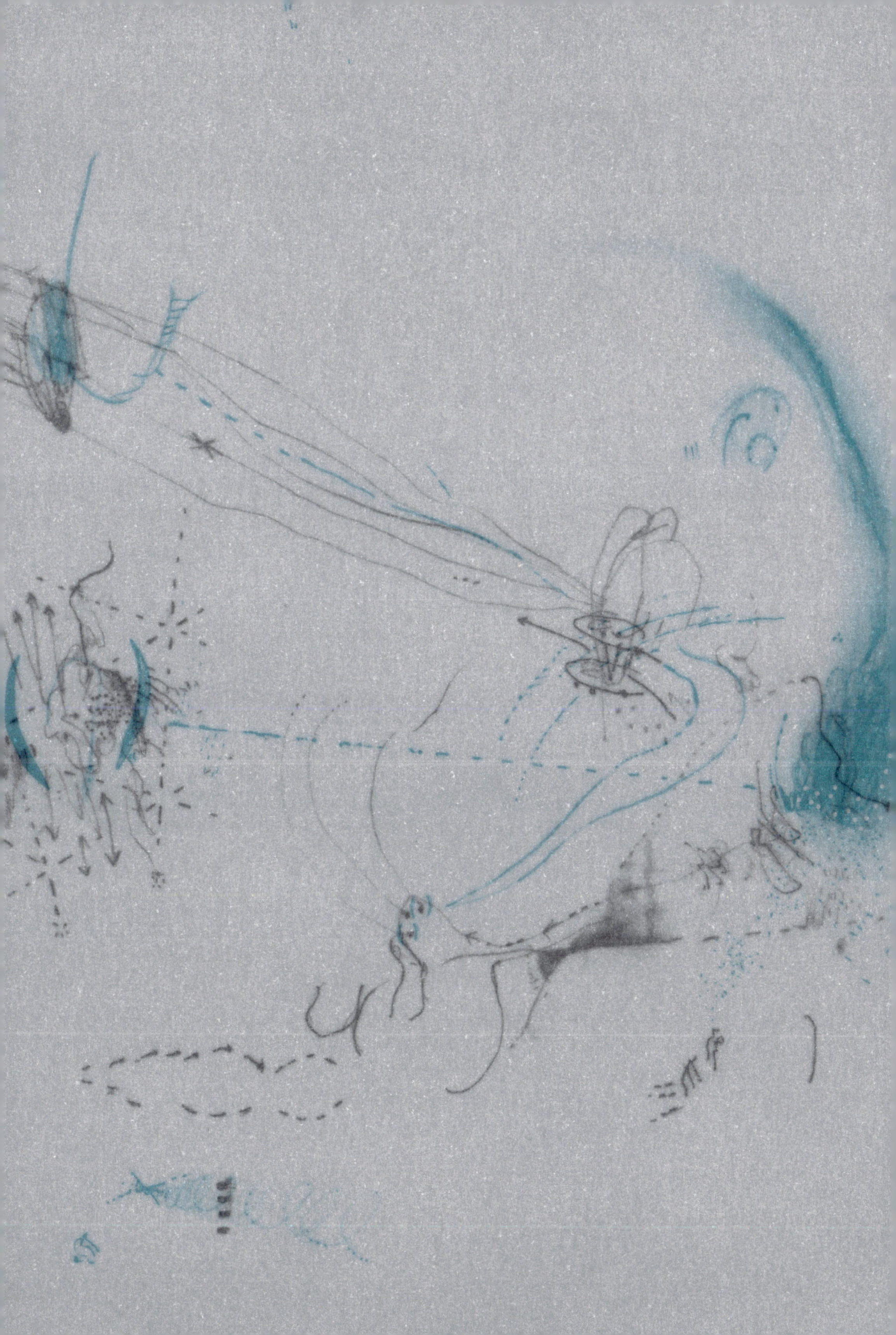

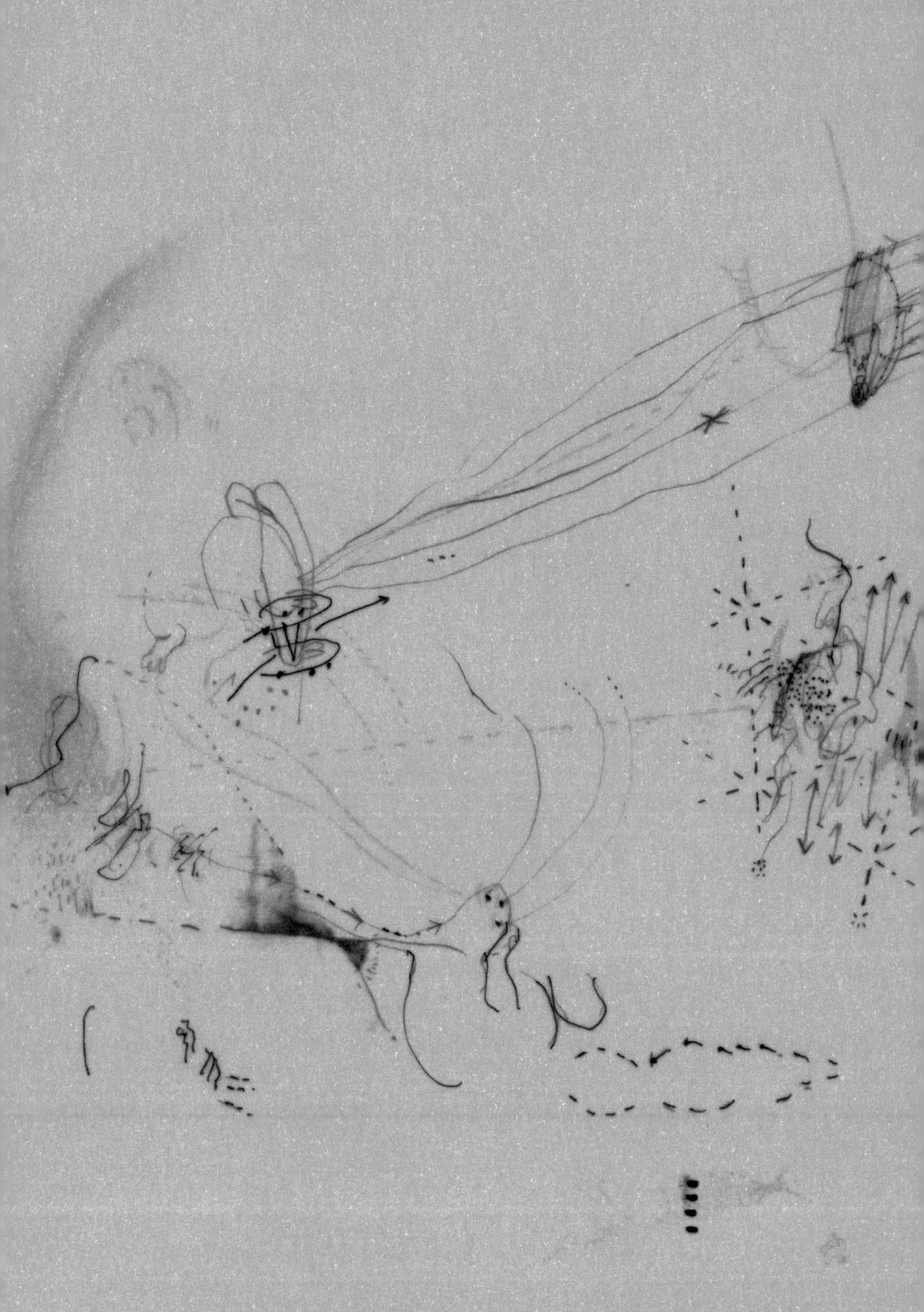

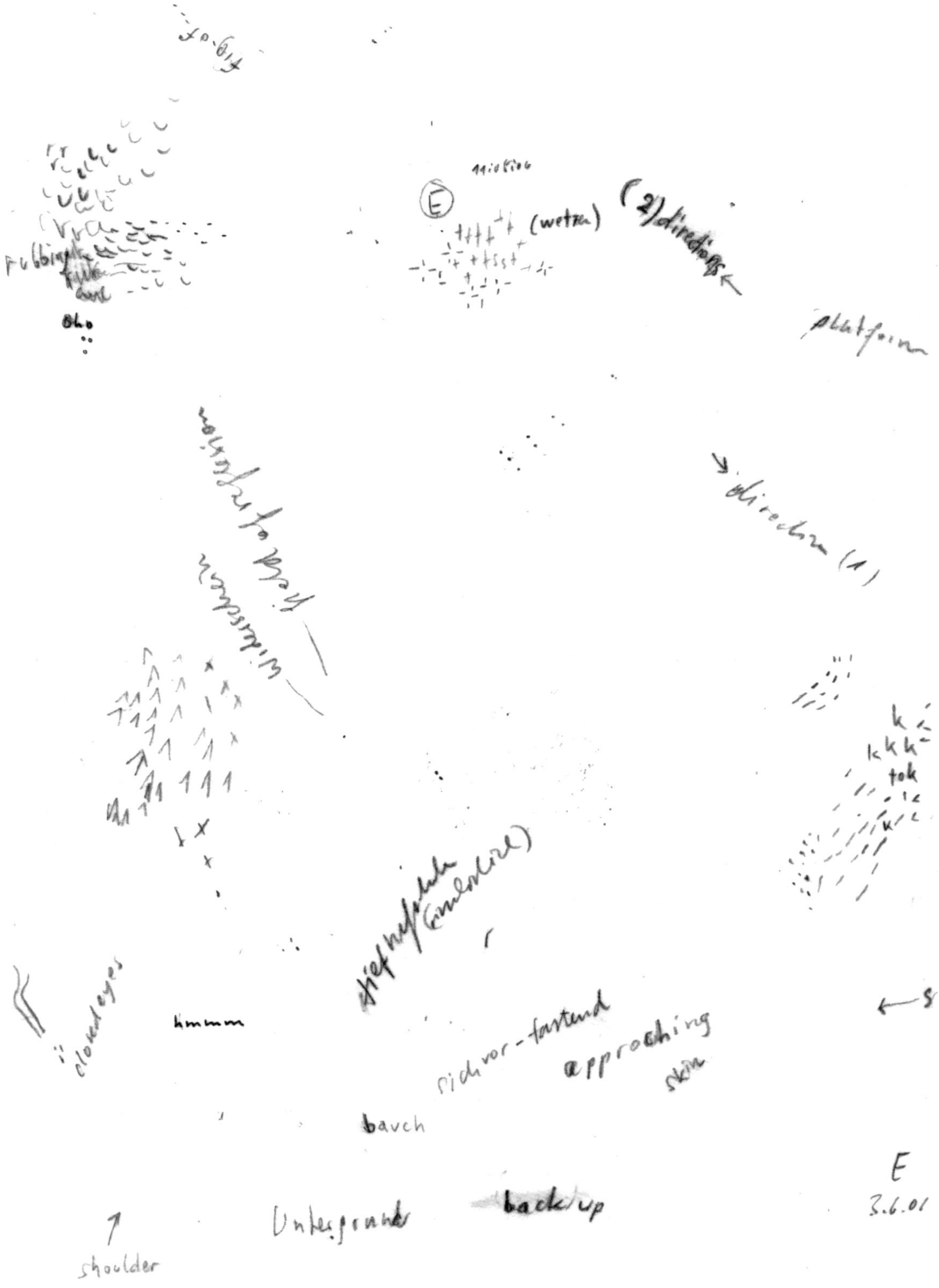

fig. of.

rubbing fallen card

Oho

nicking

E

(wetra)

(2) directions

platform

field of reflexion

widerstehen

direction (1)

k
kkk
tok

tiefschwebende (empfundene)

closed eyes

hmmm

sich vor-tastend

approaching

skin

← s

bauch

E
3.6.01

back/up

Untergrund

shoulder

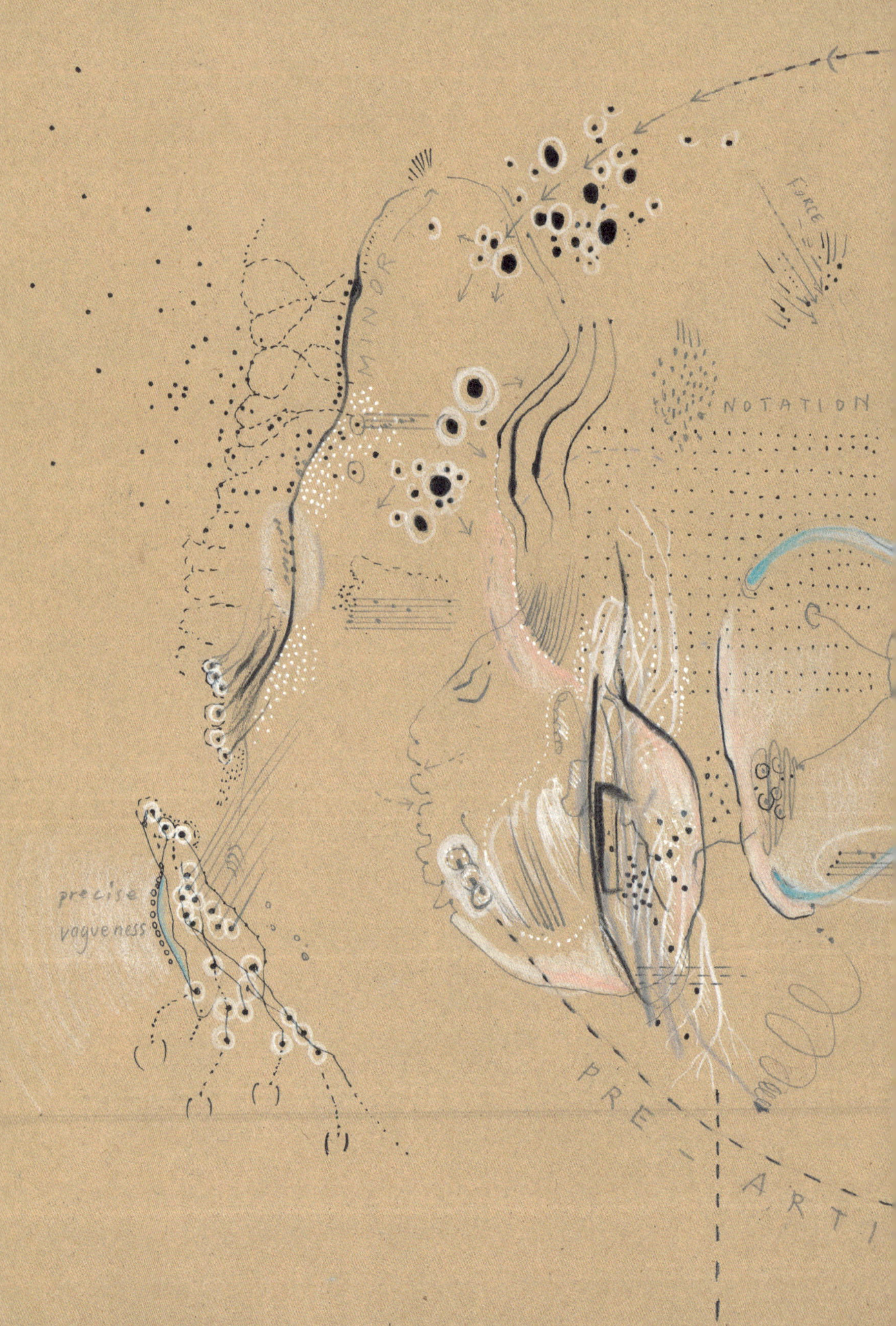

MINOR
FORCE
NOTATION
precise
vagueness
PRE
ARTI

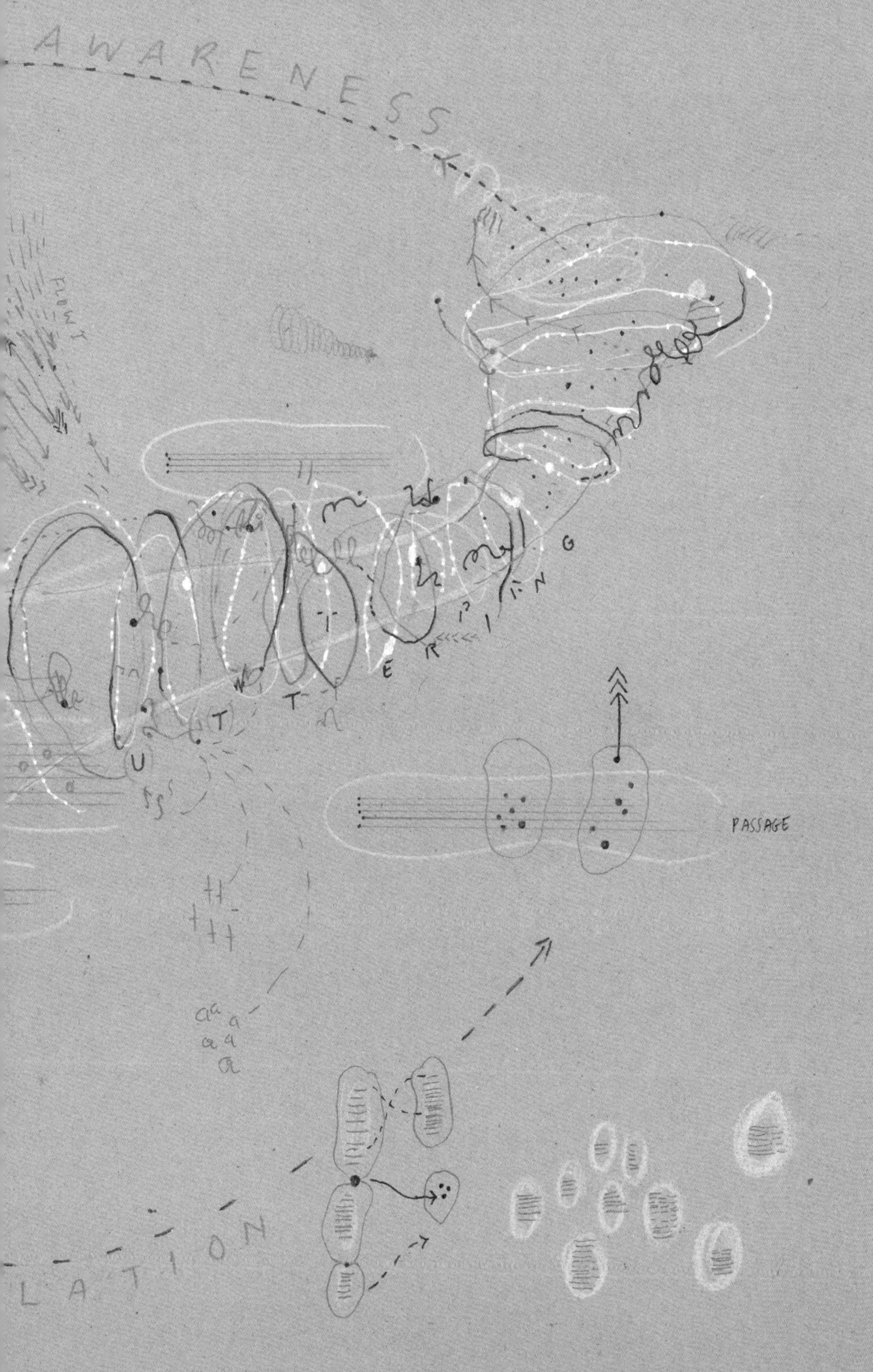
AWARENESS
FLOW
PASSAGE
LATION

and
ing

n

sense

u
o

y y

p n

J d

sss S

n

n n n
n

n

~~talking~~

~~drawing~~

end. (ing

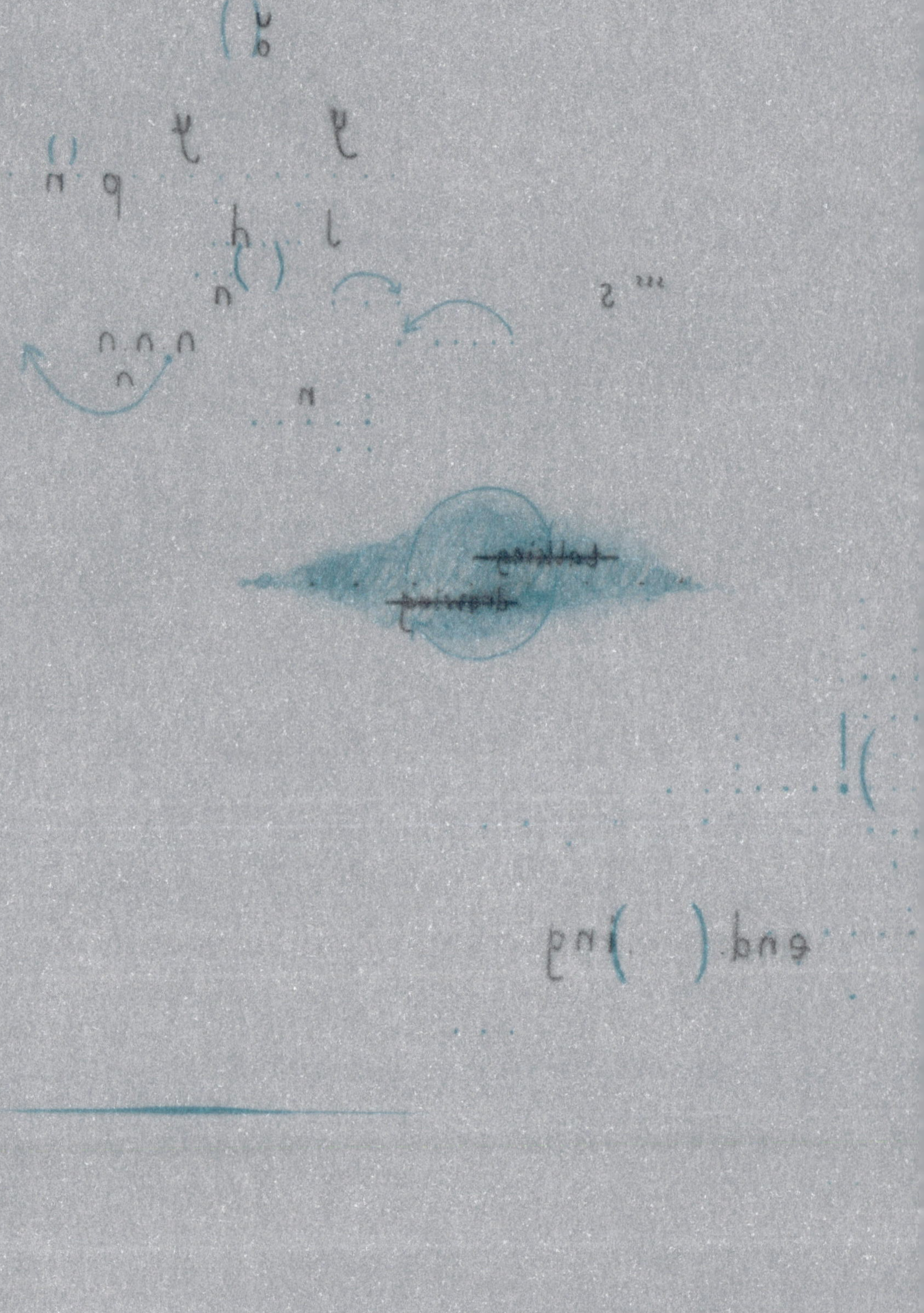

~~talking~~

~~drawing~~

end ( ) ing

e e e e e e[e]

e

e ee

e

~~thinking~~

~~writing~~

V

o W

TRIALOGUE: *Thinking-Making in Relation*

WHERE: This trialogue between **Catherine de Zegher (CdZ)**, **Nikolaus Gansterer (NG)** and **Erin Manning (EM)** took place in the nexus of the exhibition *The Minor Gesture* at MSK, Museum of Fine Arts in Ghent, Belgium, curated by Catherine de Zegher in 2016. It followed the performance *A Translecture on Minor Gestures in 16 Movements* combining spoken lecture (Manning) and expanded live drawing (Gansterer) further exploring the notion of *The Minor Gesture*.[1]

WHEN: 23rd June 2016

HOW: The original conversation has been edited through focus specifically on ideas of translation, improvisation, collaboration, intuition and the micro-politics of the *minor gesture*.

CdZ: [...] There are many points of connection within our work. For me, what is most apparent within each oeuvre is this attempt to reach out to the other; in their choreographic work Selma and Sofiane Ouissi speak of *'se projeter dans l'autre'*.[2] Trying to connect not by empathising but by not feeling alone in the relation.

EM: What I notice is that our thinking-making is made stronger *in relation*. And that's something I see in the artists who you surround yourself with, Catherine. What we encounter in this exhibition, *The Minor Gesture*, is less a set of artworks than the quality of an encounter. There are works, of course, but the works themselves orient toward the minor, opening up pathways for collective experimentation. What is being foregrounded is less the separated-out work of each artist than a collective conversation. To work at this level requires curiosity about the process of art, about the gestures that populate that process. This process that is gathered together is palpable both in the works that foreground process and in the quality of expression foregrounded by those which have found form, yet are still populated with the kind of uneasiness with form that I think of as the minor gesture. When you talk about the process of curating, you touch on an important difference between the *making of an exhibition* and the *staging of a field of relation*. Perhaps what emerges from the second is that the 'exhibition' becomes a turning point, an opening toward new ways of participating in each others' processes, and, equally important, an attunement to the differential of the minor gestures populating not only the work but the emergent collaboration.

NG: For me, the notion of 'what an exhibition is' becomes really expanded in *The Minor Gesture*. More towards *exposition*, meaning 'putting forth something', more *ex-posing* than ex-hibiting, less showing what you already know rather than posing a question that you want to share with others. It needs these moments of activation. The work is actualised to become alive, in reference to what is 'here and now': through the space, through the visitors, through various presences. You said that the gesture of curating was also a form of caring?

CdZ: Yes, absolutely. For me it relates to *cura*.

NG: From *curare*. To cure.

CdZ: In all these practices, you can see forms of caring — whether in drawing, textiles, or the recording of primary gestures in dance and film — yet they are all different. But there is always *a gesture of reaching out to the other*. Perhaps the reason I am fascinated with drawing is because it captures this outward gesture incredibly well. In fact, your translecture, Nikolaus and Erin, materialises what I theorised for a while [...] Let me clarify: when a child reaches out for the mother and, for the first time, instead touches and marks the paper surface with a pencil given by the mother, the child can find a response her / himself. This time it is not the response from the mother but the child's own response. Consequently, the outward gesture binds you as much as it makes you independent. At the same time, the outward movement of the hand remains a gesture of the desire to connect, with the environment, with the other. It is always both binding and separating. You could think of this in relation to your translecture, where each artist has their own work, in keeping with their own individuality, but it happens in relation to the other. It is rather about subjectivity-in-relation. In the translecture, the abstract becomes materialised, words and thoughts become visible through the drawing — thus *through* the other, in the encounter, which is quite unique. I have never seen anybody doing this. It's a step further in art history.

EM: What also fascinates me about your concept of the translecture is the relationship between the choreographic and the improvisatory. One needs the other. Nikolaus, you're working with the materiality of the objects and the compositional propositions they potentialise, and I am working with the materiality of sound, of words, of concepts. And we're both being moved by those singular materialities which are connecting in the relational field of voice and movement. But even though my words are pre-scripted and your work is emergent, there is nonetheless a quality of transversality that is wholly emergent in the event. It was particularly rich, I think — having just done this for the first time — the way the words didn't take over, as language can be very determining in these kinds of situations.

CdZ: I was also fascinated by the way Nikolaus was showing us all his materials in the projection during the translecture. The form, the ink, the water — so for you there's a connection with different materials? How do you feel them? How do you know what you want to take at a certain moment?

NG: The translectures have developed from the act of drawing to bringing more and more material qualities into it. Recently, in a translecture in Vienna with the philosopher Dieter Mersch, there was a moment when he spoke about the Dionysian and the Apollonian principles, when the paper and every single item were flooded by ink and the whole thing became a real mess.[3] So it turned into a real Dionysian moment happening in front of us. And it was not planned at all. So, for me it's better to have an ensemble or a register of materials at hand. And then I trust my intuition to take them and to work with them on the table as a model and from there to take things back into the space. This has become more elaborate in the last three years. Recently, I've been more interested in 'showing' that I'm not showing everything. Rather, in the mediated image things are always missing, remain un-shown. Together, the live experience and the projection form a kind of expanded drawing.

CdZ: It is drawing.

EM: I think this relates to the concept of intuition in Bergson's writing, which is associated with the rigour of a process.[4] And there's an incredible rigour to that intuition that you both have. It comes from years and years of modes of perception and modes of feeling, qualities of experience.

CdZ: Well, intuition is linked to the environment: to time and space, and to flow. To let it flow and not stop it. You have to follow the intuition — you cannot stop it, because then it doesn't work anymore.

EM: I would say that in this exhibition you feel the quality of that intuition very strongly: your sense of composition across minor gestures is very strong. The qualities across the works resonate — qualities of listening, the care for the relation, the curiosity about other tendencies and gestures.

NG: The practice of translecturing is also guided by the question of how to translate one reality into another ... how to bring it to a form of being in the moment ... drawing live-diagrams of the now.

EM: The drawing of diagrams is very interesting in the context of my work *Threadways,* which I also think of as drawing. This rethinking of what drawing can do has come from our collaborations, Catherine — you've expanded drawing for me to include movement, which has given me a keener sense of how drawing can also hold a certain quality of orientation. The technique that I used for *Threadways* is an old Belgian technique called *drawing thread,* which involves pulling thread from an existing weave and then creating patterns in the weave from the thread's absence. While I didn't reproduce the technique faithfully, it remains interesting to note the connection between drawing as a kind of pulling and reorienting by subtraction and drawing the collective movement of creating new pathways. In a sense, all of our works activate orientations that come into relation through the exhibition, for example, through adding, pulling, subtracting. What your way of creating an exhibition allows for, I think, is this two-phased orientation that invites us to come with an orienting gesture but without a full sense of how it will move us collectively?

CdZ: And to do the same thing again — it's never finished and it's never complete.

EM: So it carries its flow with it, and that's the fragility that I like in art.

CdZ: Exactly, and this is what I often find problematic about exhibitions: the idea of completion. Of course, they are not complete. Once exhibitions open to the public, they are over and again interpreted by audiences; they become the subject of alteration, because everybody has their own interpretation. Do you know that the word 'drawing' in English has a myriad of meanings? Drawing in. Drawing out. Drawing from ... many, many definitions. The Flemish *tekenen* is more like the German, right?

NG: In the verb *zeichnen,* there is *das Zeichen,* the 'sign' in it carrying the meaning of a mark, a sign, a signal, a symbol, a figure, a token, a note and even an omen. Maybe drawing as something assuming shape whilst appearing, *ap-paraître* literally means *etwas er-scheint,* or 'is coming into view', which seems to shine and shimmer, that plays with appearances and oscillates between seeing, thinking, remembering and imagining. But in German, *zeichnen* also has the meaning of *zeigen,* to show something — a gesture of showing. Drawing as showing is also carries the meaning of *zeihen,* to accuse or *anklagen*: to put the finger on something or somebody — to raise or lift a finger — to point out, to question, to search, *chercher* and *re-chercher,* again and again.

EM: This allows us to think of the materiality of drawing: how drawing orients the material itself.

CdZ: I have learnt to look at the material differently because of artists like Annie Albers or Anna Maria Maiolino who work intensely 'with' the materials. They allow the materials to reciprocate; it is as if they speak: 'Let us also do our thing!' It's almost close to the animate. But we lost this connection in the twentieth century; nothing is animate any longer.

EM: But everything is animate, alive with a certain quality of the *more-than* that populates it.

CdZ: I think what you are all trying to do is to show that the material is alive.

NG: That is exactly the state of mind I sink into when doing a translecture. Suddenly, the meaning of objects is shifting and objects start to communicate with me. This awareness for *the other* comes through that other state of mind where I am a bit *ent-rückt.* The German word for being engrossed, or absorbed in a situation, like a form of trance, entering something. I have to create this *interspace* in me where *we* meet.

CdZ: So it's even *ex*, out of the body, or reaching towards?

NG: Not so much *out of* the body, more *becoming the body*. This is something I learnt from the philosopher Arno Böhler referring to Nietzsche's concept of *über*, in the *Über-mensch*, where he was not at all talking about a Super-man! It's not the big, and the ever bigger, the superior, it is the very minor. It's something inside and between us. Immanence. Here and now. It's becoming aware of all the capabilities and materials that you have, which is your potential.

CdZ: But it's also the capability of touch.

NG: Exactly … and being touched.

CdZ: To me the translecture was very physical, where you touch *the other* … I think, for me at least, I always saw things more literally and now I can see them, not to say on another level, but in an enriching way.

EM: I often think about our scales of experience. Our bodies give us a certain account of experience because they have a very particular scale. They make it appear to us, for example, that the spaces around us are stable because the scale of movement in our bodies is much quicker than the concrete around us. But if we're capable of experimenting across different scales, then we begin to go into the place where you can *phase in and out* of different kinds of scales, which we do anyway. And children do it absolutely intuitively. You know, they get close to the earth with their eyes, they get close to things. The question for me would be: what: are the conditions that allow this shift in scale? There's something about the voice being capable of activating a scale of experience. This museum is also very interesting. It has a quality of light and sound that is very particular given the high ceilings, the stone structure and the skylights. It really allows things to happen. Because you can do the same work in a place that has different conditions without these phasings in and out of scale becoming perceptible in the same way.

CdZ: There is an environmental element that we never think of: the bad weather, the rain and the sun alternately shining through the glass ceiling, that constantly change the light.

EM: The environment and its complex materialities always participate in the drawings we engender, and if we give these materialities the space to make themselves felt, others will feel them too. This then allows attention to be distributed a little differently, moving away from the sole focus on the human into a more distributed focus. In my experience, when attention dances in this way, the work is doing its work. At that moment, all of us are participants in a process that is, to a large extent, unfolding collectively, despite pre-existing choreographic orientations […] I really struggle with the way the human tends to see him / herself as the centre of experience. This is of course not just in art. I often wonder what it is that makes us believe that something is ours; that a country is ours? Or that *a life* is ours? And, you know, about that concept, just before Deleuze jumped out of a window and killed himself, he wrote that tiny four-page piece called 'Immanence: A Life' that I cite in my book *The Minor Gesture*.[5] He writes that there is a quality of life that exceeds us. He calls this *a* life. *A* life moves through us to connect to this life, but always also exceeds us, tuning experience to the *more-than*.

CdZ: When you speak about the *more-than* […], it reminds me of the pond that I live next to. The water in the pond is never the same. It never has the same level. It goes up and down. Most people put a layer of plastic at the bottom of a pond so that the water cannot move any longer, to keep the water from passing through. But in natural ponds, the water is never the same. It flows: it flows under the earth; it comes up by chance in this pond. And then it flows further down to the sea. It flows everywhere under the earth, up, then it goes away again. The thing is that you cannot control it. I have a choice: do I control it and put a plastic layer in the pond and it will then always remain the same, or do I let it move? And evidently, I wish to let it move because it's also much more pure, healthier. But, of course, we try to control it. And sometimes this is very problematic. This urge to dominate its flowing brings about all kinds of economic and ecological issues.

NG: I think that's where the minor gesture starts to work, when you allow this responding to happen, when you become aware of all these little things. That's also what we do within the *Choreo-graphic Figures* project: becoming aware of these little, minor gestures. We call it *figuring* — these micro-moments when your attention reaches a tiny peak. We started to give these tiny *figurings* names, that is, when they melt into a recognisable form. Indeed, there are so many figures happening — here and now! We decided to work with the term of the *figure* rather than with the term *gesture*. But what is the difference, and how could these terms come together? I realised that with *gesture* we still tend to think very much of the hand. And I prefer to think of the gesture as of the whole body.

CdZ: Do we then speak of the *corporeal*?

NG: Each of these words brings a different connotation.

EM: Concerning gestures, I don't see them necessarily as tied to a body-part. I see them as that which punctuates a movement proposition, activating a worlding. These can be movements that affect a body, but they can just as well be material movements, or environmental movements. The concept of 'the minor gesture' as I've defined it is very influenced by the idea of 'minor literatures', which is a concept Gilles Deleuze and Félix Guattari developed in relationship to Kafka's writing.[6] For them, a minor literature is not a 'small' literature but a literature that cuts through what it means to be literary, orienting literature in ways that trouble the major ways in which it tends to define itself. Deleuze and Guattari also write about the capacity to be 'a minor speaker'. And they don't mean *less,* they mean that your language cuts through language, unseating language as it tends to be used or heard. This unseating activates a certain line of flight within the practice of literature that has the capacity to make visible the minoritarian tendencies in thought or in writing. When I was writing *The Minor Gesture,* I was thinking what's the difference between a minor literature and a minor gesture? I brought in the concept of gesture because I wanted to foreground the punctuality of a certain kind of minoritarian tendency. In the context of the minor gesture, what I am looking at are the ways a process is populated by tendencies toward variation. I don't believe that you can craft a minor gesture, but I do believe you can create conditions for it to emerge or become perceptible. The minor gesture, in the way I understand it, has a capacity to make felt a shift, a variation in experience that deeply alters the ecology of that experience. The question is then: can it be followed? This is where art can and does make a difference. Art practice is one of the ways through which the opening that a minor gesture activates can be followed. Art for me is not about replaying the stakes of macro-politics but about orienting tendencies that create follow-on effects in experience that affect what moves the political at its core. In this sense, art is proto-political, affecting what can come. When Deleuze and Guattari talk about the macro and the micro, they say, 'don't think of the micro as small'. The micro is a qualitative variation that cuts through the macro-political. Like the micro, the minor moves across scales — it's transversal. It moves through. Sure, it's often imperceptible or on the edge of feeling, but that doesn't make it any less powerful. And so I think, that there is definitely a similarity between what you're thinking of as the *figure* and how I am conceiving of the *minor gesture*. If I were talking specifically about the choreographic, I don't think I would use 'gesture', because there would be too much of a tendency to think about the body, just this body.

CdZ: Like the memorable gesture of the Chinese student in Tiananmen Square in front of the military tank. That, for me, is really a minor gesture. It came out of nowhere, from a student who suddenly was not afraid of anything. Nobody even knows what happened to him afterwards. But the repercussions of this minor gesture were enormous.

EM: Exactly! And people will think of that gesture as grand, but it wasn't grand. That's a good point.

CdZ: What fascinates me most in all the years that I've been working with artists on exhibitions is how things come to me, come together and how things somehow fall into place and present connections and coherence. It is as if I don't have to do anything, I just have to let it happen [...] In the process, I am intrigued by objects that make it towards me. It's the relation of people. It's the relation of objects. It's a beautiful confluence of circumstance, of moments, of conversation, of dialogue and suddenly it all falls into place and seems perfect [...] I love working in relation. But no one can get blocked, because then the whole undertaking falls apart. We only come into being-in-relation, no? [...] I have a sense that I really need other people to come-into-being. I mean, to evolve, to exist, to see the world more clearly, to give more purpose to existence, all of that. It can only happen through and with others.

EM: Absolutely. But working as I do in a collaborative environment at *SenseLab* that explores the interstice of activism, art and philosophy, I also want to register the importance of dissonance.[7] Working in this kind of context, I've learned that there is a way in which the capture of a process by discord or disorientation also contributes to the relation as long as the collaborative potential is not personalised—as long as its the work that remains the focus. I am very interested in the collaborative force of difference. What we have here is a bit different since you, Catherine, have created the ground for a collaboration that begins in the midst of a shared orientation. This is one of the strengths of your approach, I find: your attention to the conditions of different processes coming together. This leads us back to the gesture of the curator, which in this case involves creating the context to catch us in the middle, in the middling of a process still underway. You've made a career of catching artists in that middling, I would say. This is very important because it allows for a different kind of interaction amongst artists. When I speak of the work we do at *SenseLab* and of our sense that difference or dissonance is also an active component of working relationally, I should emphasise that the conditions are quite different. First, we don't come together on the merits of our individual work, but instead collaborate to generate new ways of working together around issues and practices that exceed any one participant's capacity. This kind of work requires a long-term commitment to collective exploration and the creation of an ethos of trust in the work itself. An exhibition context is different because it begins, in a sense, with the force of our own contribution (our own work, our own career as artists), which makes it much more difficult to activate an emergent solidarity. This is what I think your experiments toward new ways of bringing artists together is capable of achieving, and it's definitely what we see here.

CdZ: The translecture also allows an idea to be developed and taken up again and again. It's like in drawing and writing. It's developed and it's taken up, it's repeated, it's reframed. So you don't need to follow every word. It took me some time to accept that we cannot understand all texts at once. At first I wanted to understand everything at once, and then of course, you read something and you don't understand everything. You want to give up. Instead you have to accept, it's again this flow, you just have to let it happen. But, as I said at the beginning of our trialogue, the thing that has fascinated me most in the last days is this really common sensibility or sensitivity towards how '*se projeter*' ... And I have a sense that this is still not the right word: '*Comment se projeter dans l'autre*'. But in French, there aren't a lot of possibilities. Because it's not about appropriating the other, it's not about being the other, but it's something else, which I think the translecture in a way formulates more adequately. Actually, maybe we still don't have words in our language to speak about what we're speaking about.

EM: Someone said to me you really need to separate the text and the drawing, because then you really get the lecture and you really get the drawing. But it's exactly not about that. As I understand it, the translecture is about the quality and at the same time about the impossibility of mingling them. It is an experience of the middling that forces you to face the incapacity to stand outside the event. In this case, the echo created a kind of fourth character, a force that affected all of us. I felt uncertain because I could hear myself speak in a tonality that was just on the side of the ineffable, and I knew that you might be having difficulty hearing me [...] So all of us were attuning differently to the sound of our coming together across language and drawing [...] I think it's because we both collaborate a lot in general. And we met each other in that ethos of collaboration. There was immediately a sense of care for the work, and for our contribution to its coming to expression [...] I felt like it was important that attention be focused on the rhythms of your composition. If I moved, you tended to move as well, almost always. It was almost like the movement of waves in the water. I loved the quality of responsiveness. Similarly, if the rhythm of your composition calmed, I felt an invitation that allowed me to enter. There was a lot more happening, I think, than what was necessarily perceived.

CdZ: In fact, what we often do in our society is to erode the content of the work and turn it into a commercial object. That's mostly what our society is doing. It's commercialising everything. And it's incredible if you think about it. Where is there still a space where this is not happening? In effect, I hope that I can create that space a bit.

NG: Could it be that a minor gesture cannot or resists to be commercialised?

EM: It resists capture. It creates its own value. I think that the minor gesture really resists and I think that's what makes it a gesture: this resistance. It resists because it's far too complex. It creates an orientation that needs to be followed. It activates a revaluation.

---

1) The exhibition took place in the framework of the Creative Europe project *Manufactories of Caring Space-Time,* a cooperation between MSK, Museum of Fine Arts, Ghent, Belgium; FRAC Lorraine Metz, France and Fundació Antoni Tàpies, Barcelona, Spain and presented large-scale installations by artists Selma and Sofiane Ouissi, Nikolaus Gansterer and Erin Manning. In addition, Gansterer and Manning were invited to develop a translecture performance together. Cf. Nikolaus Gansterer, www.gansterer.org/translectures for further contextualisation of the 'translecture' model. Cf. Erin Manning, *The Minor Gesture,* Durham: Duke University Press, 2016. For further contextualisation of curating forms of expanded drawing: Cf. Catherine de Zegher, *On Line: Drawing through the Twentieth Century,* Museum of Modern Art, New York (21.11.2010-7.2.2011. Exhib. cat.); Catherine de Zegher, Griselda Pollock, and Everlyn Nicodemus, *Women's Work Is Never Done: An Anthology,* Ghent: Asamer, 2014.

2) This phrase is borrowed from a conversation with artists-choreographers Selma and Sofiane Ouissi, who consider the power of minor gestures to transcend boundaries, social differences, and linguistic barriers. Both poetic and political, their creations record nonverbal language and create new modes of cohabitation based on cooperation, attention, and exchange with the other. Their research on vital gestures is an opportunity to take the time to listen and visualise life stories marginalised by the dominant discourse. Making use of video, choreography, illustration and installation, they invite the audience to reach out to an other through a gesture of shared emotion and experience. Personal gestures are transformed into a collective notation. Like memory, the body is a site and an archive of lived experience, which may shed light on the individual in their subtlety.

3) Cf. Nikolaus Gansterer and Dieter Mersch, *A Translecture on Nietzsche Diagrams,* performed on 26.11.2015 at Tanzquartier Wien, in the framework of the research project *Artist Philosophers. Philosophy as Arts-Based Research* led by Arno Böhler and Susanne Valerie Granzer. http://homepage.univie.ac.at/arno.boehler/php

4) Cf. Henri Bergson, *Matter and Memory,* (Trans.) Nancy Margaret Paul and William Scott Palmer, New York: Dover Publications, [1896] 2004.

5) Gilles Deleuze, in *Pure Immanence: Essays on a Life,* New York: Zone Books, [1995] 2005.

6) Gilles Deleuze and Félix Guattari, *Kafka: Toward a Minor Literature,* Minneapolis: University of Minnesota Press, 2012.

7) Founded by Erin Manning in 2004, *SenseLab* is a laboratory for thought in motion. Based in Montreal, it is an international network of artists and academics, writers and makers, from a wide diversity of fields, working together at the crossroads of philosophy, art, and activism. www.senselab.ca

FRAGILE FIGURES

Alva Noë

Is there vision and action, thought and perception, outside the orbit of figures? Or are figures — the clichés and outlines and notations and ideas of things — inescapable? Can there be a dance, or a painting, without figures? Can there be a consciousness of ourselves and others that is not pinned down around the edges by empty figures of ourselves?

Francis Picabia's *Sad Figure* is a first source. There is no recognisable figure or form in this blue painting. A figure in a painting is a visible human form, not to say an actual person. Figurative painting, as the term is used, puts whole scenes, or worlds, on display. But there's no figure, and nothing figurative in Picabia's painting. Until there is! Once the figure makes its appearance, it can no longer be ignored. And it changes everything. The picture is now brought to order around the bent and brooding form. Up is now up and down is now down, and it is easy to pick out the distinctly human bearing.

Picabia's puzzle picture — there is to me something childish about it — lets us notice, or bring out, some characteristics of the figure. One is that it is formal. It's a shape, an outline, a pattern, or arrangement. A second is that it is fragile. The figure is something that you can make out in the night, in the shadow or the silhouette, or in the blocky shapes of Picabia's painting. A figure, in a way, is a shell-like thing, an apparition, and it does not always succeed in showing up. Either because it is too weak — the faintest discontinuities or marks or suggestions. Or because we are too indifferent, or undiscerning in our looking, or our curiosity. The lazy visitor to the gallery cannot see the sad figure in Picabia's rendering.

A triangle drawn cleanly on the blackboard is a second source. A triangle is a three-sided, closed, plane figure. Here, the formal element is on full display. But there is less fragility. A drawing realises the triangle by conforming to its rule. And its rule specifies, precisely, a form, that is to say, a figure. It makes no difference that the hand-drawn lines are shaky, or that they do not join neatly at the vertex. A triangle is the symbolisation of an idea, of a form, and what you see is a concept, not a thing. If Picabia's *Sad Figure* is fragile and empirical, the figure of the geometer is fixed and *a priori.*

Which brings us to a third feature common to everything that is figure. A figure is an essence. It is the idea of a thing; its characteristic look or mark or formula. These two sources also remind us that figure is at once a perceptual accomplishment (we make it out), and also a graphical one (we make it, we cut it, we draw it). So in the figure we have doing and undergoing the affects of what we do. A figure is always a glimpse opened up by an action. It is an opportunity. For recognition. But also for more figuring.

We say: "That man cuts a dashing figure." Or: "She has a great figure." These are themselves clichés, that is, figures of speech. We have said these, or written these down, so often, that they are like grooves in the surface of our talking, like the figure-of-eight of the figure skater. These hollow phrases — "she has a great figure!"; "he cuts a dashing figure!" — refer to standing or status more than to quality. What does it mean to say her figure is great? The phrase "great figure" is not one with a fixed meaning. These are shell-phrases — figures — for naming the shell-like form which is the human figure.

Hollow. Yes. Empty. But not without meaning or importance. Who doesn't want to cut a dashing figure? Who does not want to have a great figure? And we all know exactly what is meant when we speak of the important figures of history, such as Napoleon, Bismarck, Queen Elizabeth. These are influential or learned or powerful or accomplished people. But we know them not as people, but only, or mostly, as figures, as summed up by a list of facts and, no pun intended, figures. These grammatical usages are a third source. Here is a fourth: to be good with numbers is to be good with figures; to solve a problem, especially a mathematical problem, is to figure it out. But a figure, in this setting, is a numeral. A numeral, such as a hand-written 4, is not only a recognisable visible pattern of lines (a figure), it is also the product of a definite recipe of movements. In English, first you make the vertical line, from the top down. Then, again starting from the top, you make the left-pointing downward sloping line with its right turning horizontal crossing back over the vertical. The figure we see is a traced action. And we actually experience this fact, at least implicitly. To encounter a written number is to perceive a human figure at work in the background. One figure makes another.

And this brings out once again the fact that figures — organised, recognisable, law-abiding patterns or forms — are both perceptual objects and habitual action or movement schemata. We see them. We make them. They require skilful hand and knowledgeable eye. They are forms or essences that are given only ever in the exterior shell or husk of a thing. A figure is what we see, what we take in, what we write down or sketch. Figures are a kind of artifact. We make them. They are meaningful. To choreograph the figure, then, is to start with the outlines we read and make and know in the hope that maybe here, finally, we can unlearn them and so make our escape.

MEASURES FOR CREATING SPACE

A diagrammatic remix by Gerhard Dirmoser
Text by Christopher Dell

Agency for measures creating space / *Agentur für raumschaffende Maßnahmen*
An experimental system of elementary action patterns / Space as a medium of diagrammatics / Expansive structures as a medium of spatial perception

In my contribution, I create a diagrammatic remix of writing by Christopher Dell — Das Urbane (*2014*) [UR]; Die Stadt als offene Partitur (*2016*) [OP]; Die Epistemologie der Stadt (*2016*) [ES] — *whose experiences as a musician as well as his performative / diagrammatic approach to urban development offer intriguing language material for contextualising performance explorations by Cocker / Gansterer / Greil, and to open the image material (wholly in the sense of Boris Nieslony). Minimal modifications of Dell's original texts are marked with (*).*

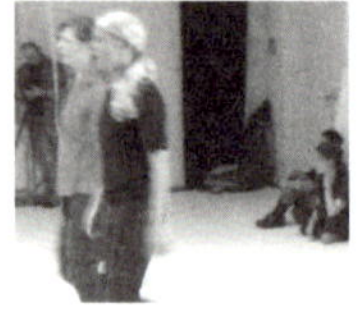

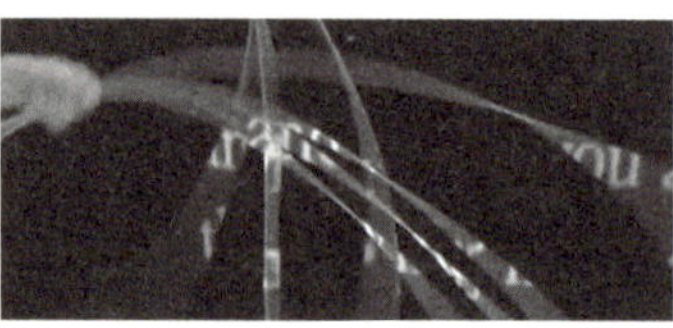

Rhythm

"If a rhythm is not a place but only occupies a place, where then is the rhythm? [...] the issue is the time-based and performative circuitry of different actors as spatial production." (UR / p. 272)

Spatial production

"Human produces space" (UR / p. 8)
"The urban is form: the space of encounter, gathering, and simultaneity. This form has no specific content, but is a centre and attractor of life." (UR / p. 272)

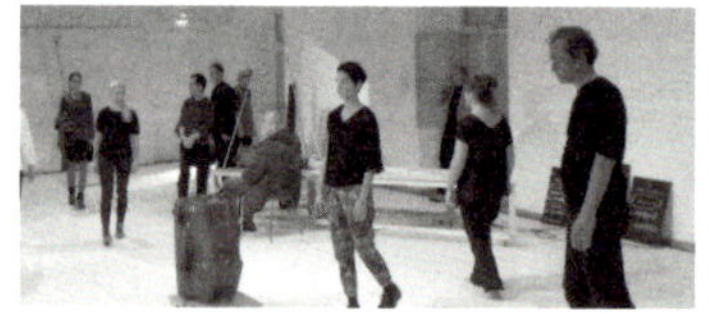

Spatial production as improvisation

"This leads to the field of discussion of spatial production as improvisation." (UR / p. 275)

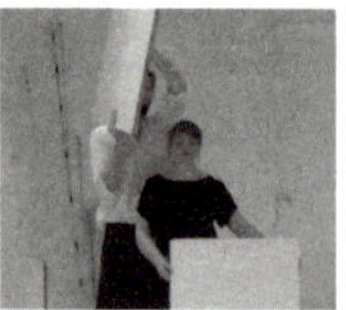

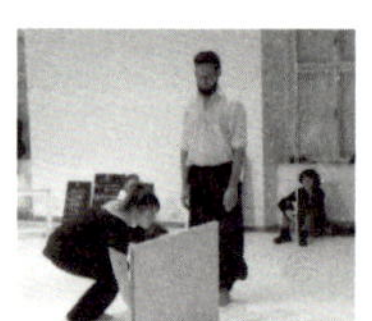

Live(d) space / *gelebter Raum*

"In the urban, however, the mental and the social in practice converge: as moments of developed, conceived, perceived, and experienced space (*l'espace concu, percu et vécu*)." Cf. Henri Lefebvre, *The Production of Space*, Oxford: Blackwell, 1991. (UR / p. 274)

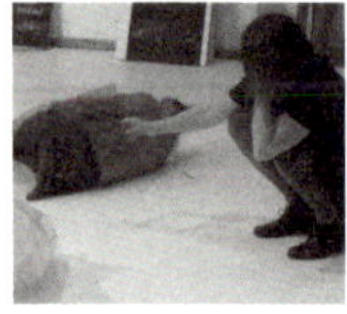

Cluster of actions

"The totality of the urban shows itself neither as that of an object expressed by mass and volume, nor as an idea, but as a *cluster* of actions which permanently let flow the concentration of its activity but never hold on to a state, and change through new forms of concentration." (UR / p. 273)

Experimental system

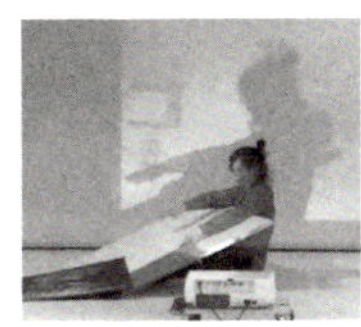

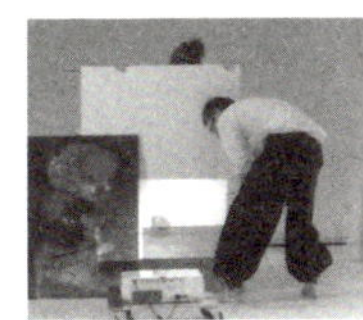

"The aim would be a form for the form, an experimental system which actually creates that form enabling us to formulate the questions *(of diagrammatics*)* […] we would like to answer. An urbano-clash, so to speak, that makes the orders of the urban *(or different media*)* clash in order to elicit from their fragmentation and islandisation the hidden vectors and things of people." (UR / p. 274)

Disclosure of structures

"The core of the investigation *(of diagrammatics*)* of the urban is formed less by experiences per se, but rather by disclosure of the structures of experiences as style; not events, but the ability to dispose oneself in various perspectives towards situations in order to access — in different constellations, assemblages, collectives — options for acting with regard to possible futures."(UR / p. 276)

Open score

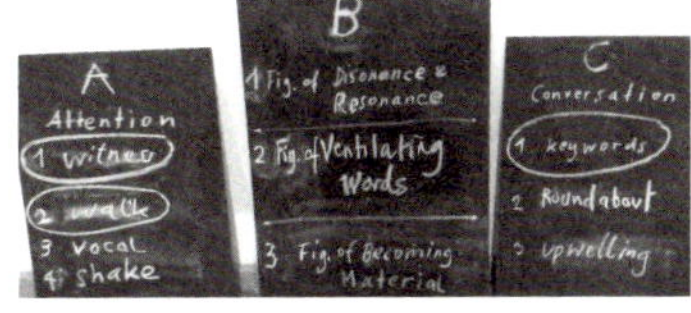

"Let us take a closer look at the term score [Partitur]: Etymologically, the German word derives from the Latin *(s)partire,* meaning to distribute or spatialise. Thus, the score is always connected with the technique (which should be conceived topologically) of visual arrangement of time […] (I)n the open score we face a kind of notation that firstly no longer only has the function of storing music, but aims at the entire structuring and the activation of actions in principle. Secondly, the open score is no longer ruled by the dictum of representational precedence." (OP / p. 37)

"Therefore the issue is not so much what is or is not representable in open scores, or what range and boundaries they possess, but firstly, what their specific development potentials consist of; secondly, in which aspects they go beyond other representational media; thirdly, what the practice of fabricating objects consists of which one can call notation; and fourthly, whether — yet more radically thought according to Latour — things can in principle be conceived as scripts." (OP / p. 38)

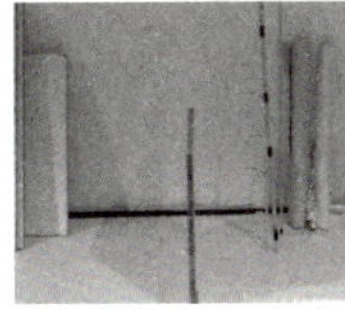

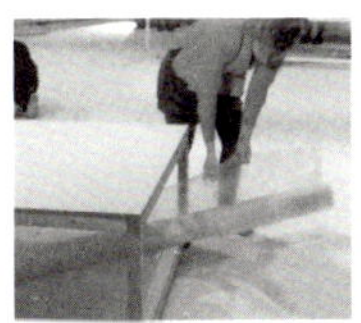

"From Latour's train of thoughts follows not only that things act, but also — and perhaps even more important — that artefacts feature the ontology of recording devices. What does this mean? It says that we also can read artefacts as forms of writing in which schemes of action are embedded. Things quasi store scripts of the operations accorded to them." (OP / p. 107)

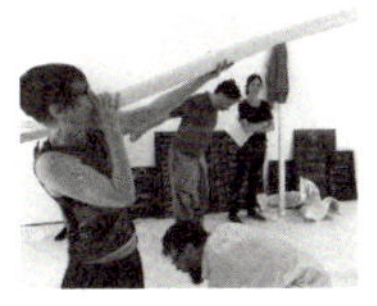

"With this turn of *notative* logic towards assemblies, cut-ups, fabrics of relations and serial circuitry […] notation no longer is about the differentiation of abstraction and figuration, mechanism and organism […] With the open score, the cultural technique of notation becomes productive with regard to itself, advances to being part of research and experiment. Although such notation refers to the serial topology of structural elements, it does not so much determine points but rather draws lines or trails that open up a relational space of being in-between, of that which is in one's interest." (OP / p. 53)

Arrangements

"A diagrammatic approach to the world initially means practising one's ability to register arrangements of people and things in their relationality, disassemble them into their structural components in order to deduce new connection points, and thus be able to make them newly convenable, and rearrange or recompile them." (OP / p. 34)

On the diagrammatics of open scores

"Let us focus even more on the diagrammatics of open scores, and specify: Performative diagrams are discontinuous and cannot be totalised. They deal with the specificity of situations, spaces, places and their proceedings and structures: <a map is about performance>, Deleuze writes. [...] Open scores notate temporally and sequentially as well as spatially, i.e., as an arrangement and relation of elements and dynamics. They operate in the musical-graphic and diagrammatic-medial mode preferentially beyond the system of symbols and representation of (written) language. This means that they can be understood as diagrams, and that they follow a diagrammatic logic."(OP / p. 103)
"As the open scores of (George) Brecht and (Cedric) Price demonstrate, the performative practice of writing only becomes recognisable if it is conceived as suspended meaningfulness, which performatively opens up reading as continued writing, and thus eventually makes the event in its indeterminacy possible."(OP / p. 107)

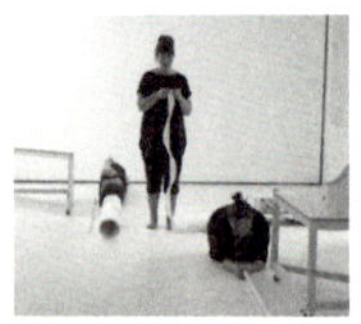

Organisation of the event

"While (John) Cage practised the eventualisation of music, Brecht undertook the musicalisation of the event, and Price its spatialisation. They continued to share the question of the organisation of the event as a process." (OP / p. 37)

Word events

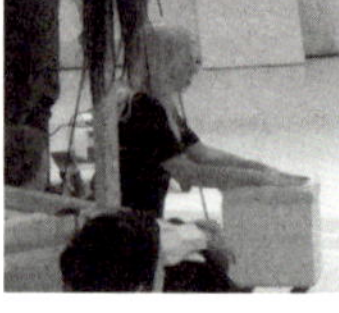

"In orientation towards the materiality of the situation itself, Brecht's *Word Events* open up the concept of work regarding the performative manifestation of events. However, the material of notational diagrammatics is always endowed with something indeterminate, intangible, whose discovery as a constructive resource already marked the central point of the diagrammatics of Dada. The here explicit inconclusiveness of the work, its turning towards the process, does not form a negation of construction, but a shift which elevates contingency to a productive principle, puts disorder in the place of the linear product of work, and not only allows the non-intentional components of events as a structural element, but quasi forces them. Thus the actually musical articulates itself in the meta-area: Aspects of transposition, variation, and modulation. Word events operate as diagrammatic triggers for transfer processes, allowing one to realise tableaus of relations in ever new circuitry." (OP / p. 63)

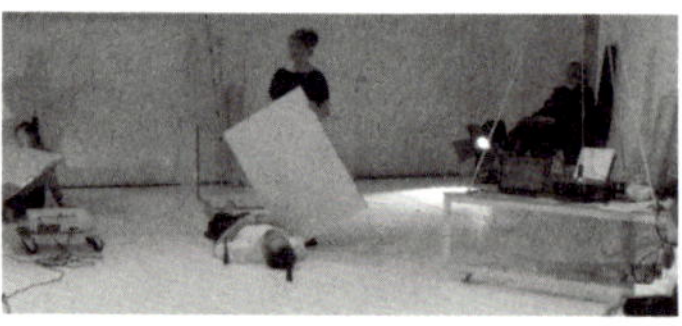

Order of neighbourhood

"The question whether it is the rule that lends the diagram its form or whether it is the diagram that creates the rule, in our approach is subordinate ... For the diagram is not created by planning but by threshold work, it is not lateral or vertical, but transversal; its rules are located on the same level as itself. So, what forms a diagram is the performativity of its strategic qualities. It follows that a procedure of transition and variation has to be described which out of the topology of points creates a temporally ... heterogeneous as well as diversified order of neighbourhood." (OP / p. 49)

Model of a life score

"*Lebenspartitur* (life score) describes a specific form of score which is to be understood not only as a hint at a process of perception, but also as representation *according to life*. [...] Against this background, Brecht's work can be specified as a score-based approach to everyday life, which through its focus on the conditionality of situations regarding usage and action releases their performativity: Event scores manifest a practice on the experience of the present." (OP / p. 86)

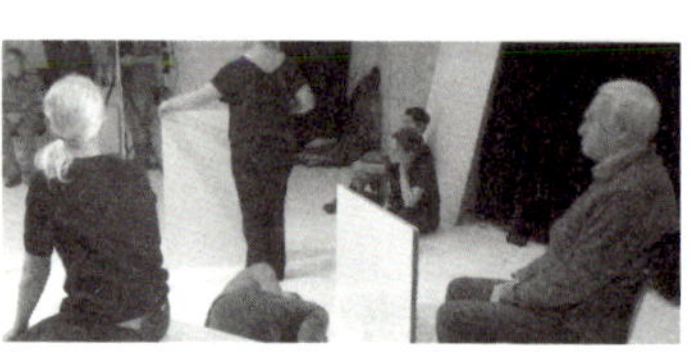

"One can say that Brecht projects the performative as a score (i.e., as a diagrammatically designed conception and framing) onto everyday life, and thus carries out the ontological shift from object to process, from stasis to becoming, which eventually makes its performative constituted- and produced-ness visible." (OP / p. 88)

Indeterminate scores vs. representation

"In view of this it is considered essential for the medial classification of indeterminate scores that they subvert the common sender-receiver model as much as they make concepts of success or failure become obsolete. In return, the scores themselves expose perception as an action which they endue with indeterminacy. Here, the methodical aspect of indeterminacy especially becomes a motor of the performative, henceforth to count as the premise for the possibility of experience." (OP / p. 107)

"Representation in this case has the task not only of putting the process of the event into operation and keeping it in operation, but also and specifically not to lapse into determining designation and to resist being determined conclusively. Every performative practice that is simultaneously indeterminate, takes place constructively, and is localised spatially and temporally, here shows an obvious relation with open notation. Its unfolding is writing-reading and reading-writing at the same time. Hints at an example are given by Heinz-Klaus Metzger who attaches the score's indeterminacy in experimental music to the variable reading while playing, thus firstly breaking up the teleology of common notation, and secondly pointing out the nomadic, geo-topological process of the diagrammatic work of writing-reading." (OP / p. 108)

"Diagrams do not operate with representations of things, but with representations of relations between things." (OP / p. 117)

Re-configurations

"In this way diagrammatic representations provide space for an infinite number of re-configurations of a relational and proportional structure, i.e., they enable the testing of new configurations […]. This is also called the principle of virtuality." (OP / p. 104)

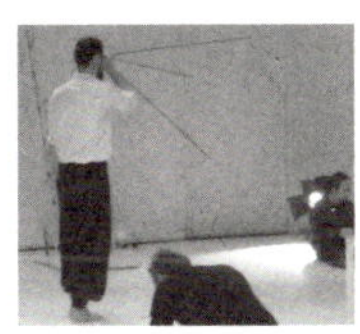

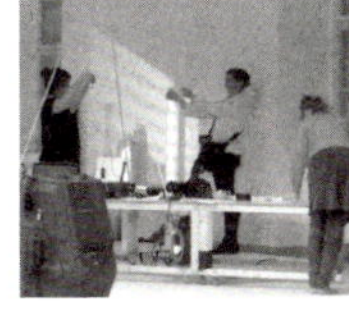

Perspective / projection / prospects

"Meaning alone — as producing — remains bound to non-precedence, and the production of sense to the relationality between the materiality of signs and physical implementation." (OP / p. 110)

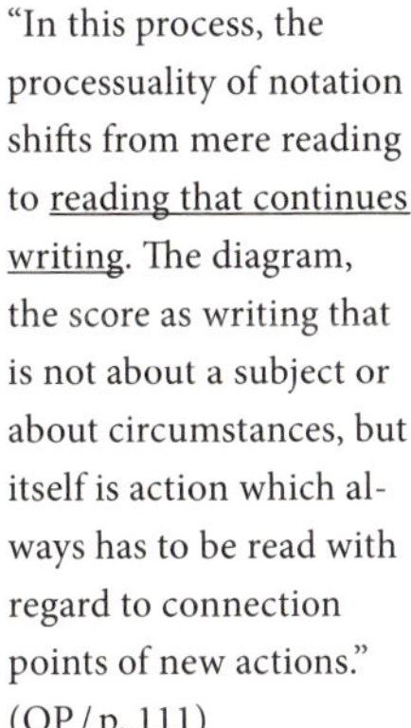

"In this process, the processuality of notation shifts from mere reading to reading that continues writing. The diagram, the score as writing that is not about a subject or about circumstances, but itself is action which always has to be read with regard to connection points of new actions." (OP / p. 111)

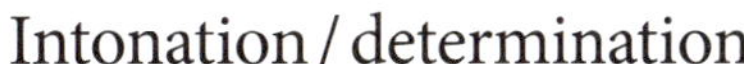

Intonation / determination

"Diagrammatics thus could be regarded as the notation of musically conceived territories where the transition from composition to improvisation becomes apparent as a vanishing line that leaves fixated, prefigured forms behind without sinking into uncritical randomness." (OP / p. 112)

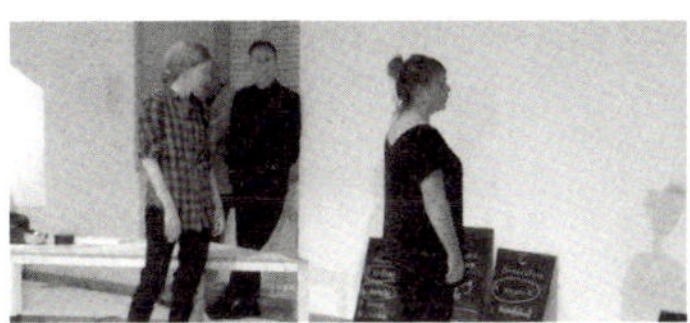

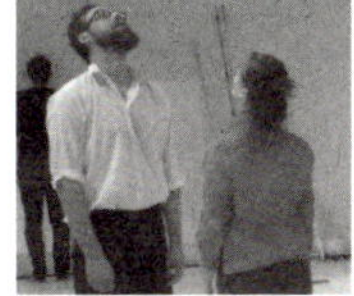

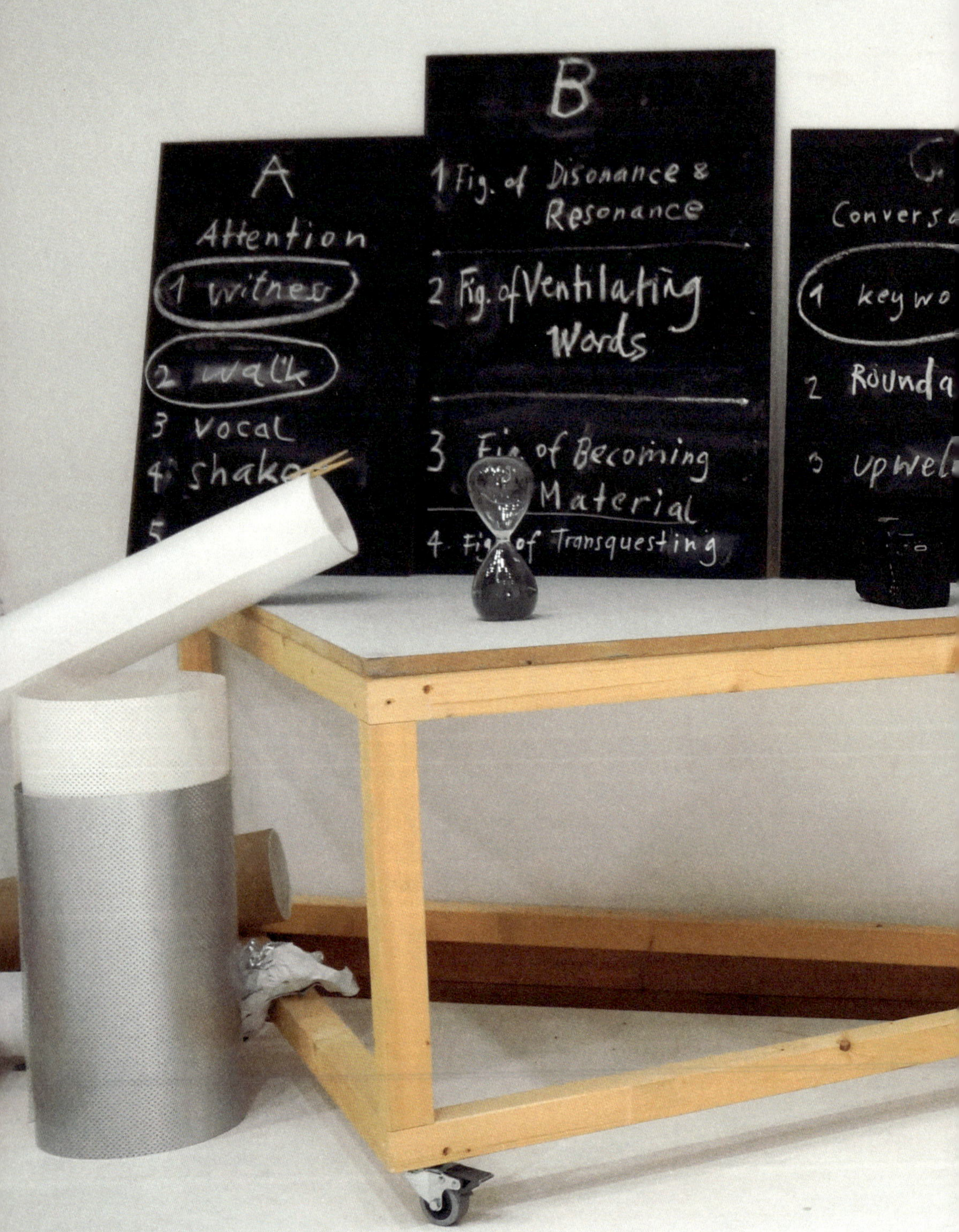

A
Attention
1 witness
2 walk
3 vocal
B
1 Fig. of Disonance &
Resonance
2 Fig. of Ventilating
Words
Material
4. of Transquesting

EPILOGUE

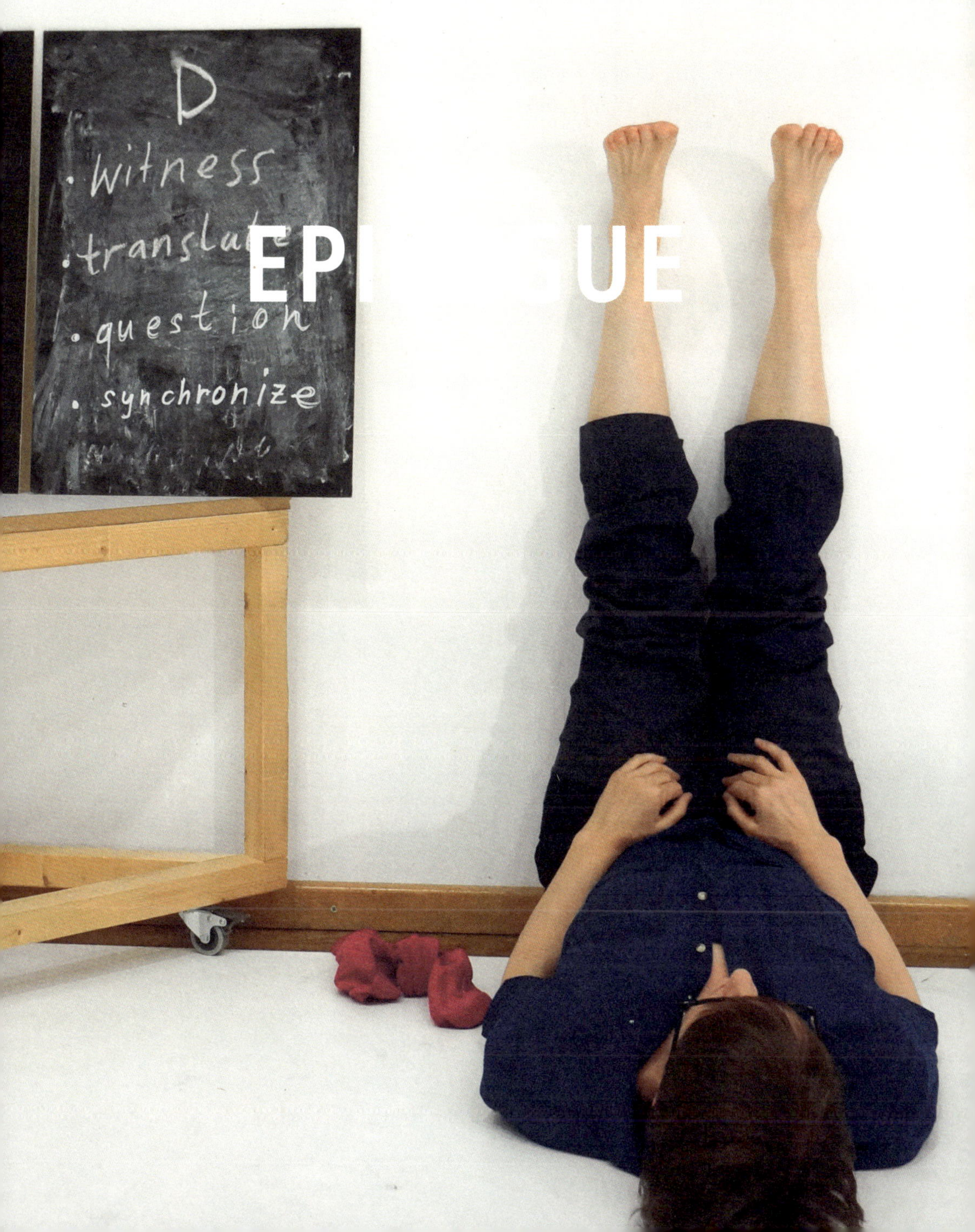

HOW TO PLAY

We draw our ending less as a conclusion or epilogue, but rather with an opening, an invitation to play. Our afterword — that 'after words', we make the *call* once more for exploration in-and-through artistic practice. Our research enquiry is perhaps best experienced through the experience of live exploration itself, practised or even played at the level of embodiment rather than only read in the pages of a book. Our score is one means — a vehicle or apparatus — for bringing into relation the various practices and *figures* outlined in the publication (see list), a device for foregrounding artistic compositional decision-making processes as a live event.

Before beginning this live exploration, you will need to have some familiarity with the characteristics and variations of the different practices (⟶ *Practices of Attention*, ⟶ *Notation*, ⟶ *Conversation*, ⟶ *Wit(h)nessing*), as well as a clear sense of the quality, vitality or atmosphere of different *figures*. We have elaborated the qualities of nine specific *figures* (⟶ *Elemental, Empathetic, Transformative Figures*), but there is an infinite list of potential others. It could help to have some understanding of the wider conceptual frame for the exploration (⟶ *Figuring* >< *Figure*, ⟶ *Embodied Diagrammatics*); however, the score can also be played without prior knowledge, understood through the experience itself.

To begin, choose which practices and *figures* you want to explore; it could help to make a visible note of your selection as a point of reference during the exploration (for example, write them down on the wall or on blackboards which are easy to 're-set').

VARIATIONS

Initially, you might choose only one or two options from each of the categories (F), (A), (N), (C), (W). The number can be gradually built up over time, with practise.

* Or, you might choose to explore the relation between the *figures* and specific practices (F) and (A) or (F) and (C).
* Or, you might choose to practise in a notated or non-notated form, i.e., with or without the (N) practices.
* Or, you might choose to divide your group of fellow explorers so that some explore the (F), (A), (C), (N) and some focus on (W). These roles can be swapped.

SETTING THE PARAMETERS

* **Where:** Decide on a space, location or environment within which to undertake your live exploration. This could range from a closed space such as a studio or rehearsal space, to an open space in the public domain — a park, a plaza, a promenade, or else perhaps a forest, a mountaintop or beach. You will also need to decide what kind of materials, resources, even technologies, are required as part of your exploration. This will depend upon the nature of your practice(s).
* **When:** Decide a length of time for your exploration — set an alarm, use an hourglass, or allocate a timekeeper. The minimum amount of time needed is around 30 minutes but the maximum is open. You could experiment with different lengths of time, e.g. 30 minutes, 60 minutes, 90 minutes, 180 minutes, 360 minutes … [and so on]. How much time is required to create the necessary level of attention and focus? When is enough, how much time is too much — the point at which exhaustion becomes an obstacle or distraction?
* **How:** Since the live exploration requires heightened awareness and attunement to the qualitative-processual dynamics of howness, consider how you might need to warm up, tune in or generally prepare yourself and the space before beginning the exploration itself.

THE SCORE

FIGURES	PRACTICES			
(F) FIGURES	(A) ATTENTION	(N) NOTATION	(C) CONVERSATION	(W) WIT(H)NESSING
Clearing and Emptying Out	Breathing	Clicking	Dialogic	Watching
Spiralling Momentum	Passing On	Affirming	Keywords	Listening
Temporary Closing	Reading	Naming	Wild Talk	Translating
Vibrating Affinity	Self-Reporting	Calling	Upwelling	
Wavering Convergence	Shaking			
Consonance / Dissonance	Sleeping			
Ventilating Meaning	Touching			
Becoming Material	Transquesting			
Translational Flux	Voicing			
	Walking			

HOW TO BEGIN:

* Just start. You could decide on a specific *figure* or practice to begin with, or else begin with a period of open exploration.
* *Timed shifts of attention*: you could decide to move between the *figures* and practices at set times.
* *Called shifts of attention:* you could decide to move between the *figures* and practices when the time feels right (⟶ *Calling*). Any person can call at any time for a specific *figure* or practice. Fellow explorers should honour the call and shift their attention, though not rush to finish what they are engaged with.

VARIATION

Episodes: During long periods of live exploration it can help to provide a further sense of structure or shape to the passage of time — we call these *episodes.* One person becomes the timekeeper for a specific episode: they decide when a new episode begins and when it ends. Keep a record of the episodes — the start and end time, the sequence of practices and *figures.* An episode could be very short or very long. Different episodes can have very different vitality contours (to draw on Daniel Stern's term), their distinctive vectors of energy taking the form of curves and arcs, rising and ebbing, fluctuating waves of intensity.

Enjoy playing!

APPENDIX

BIBLIOGRAPHY

Giorgio Agamben, *Remnants of Auschwitz: The Witness and the Archive*, New York: Zone Books, 1999.

Giorgio Agamben, *The Coming Community*, (Trans.) Michael Hardt, Minneapolis and London: University of Minnesota Press, [1993] 2007.

Giorgio Agamben, *Means without End: Notes on Politics*, Minneapolis: University of Minnesota Press, [2000] 2008.

Giorgio Agamben, *What is an Apparatus?*, Stanford: Stanford University Press, 2009.

Alex Arteaga, 'Sensuous Knowledge. Making Sense through the Skin', in Mika Elo and Miika Luoto (Eds.), *Senses of Embodiment. Art, Technics, Media*, Bern: Peter Lang AG, Internationaler Verlag der Wissenschaften, 2014, pp. 85-96.

Alex Arteaga, 'Architektur der Verkörperung. Ein künstlerisches Forschungsprojekt als phänomenologische Ästhetik', in Dieter Mersch (Ed.), *Internationales Jahrbuch für Medienphilosophie*, Berlin: De Gruyter, 2016, pp. 23-35.

Erich Auerbach, 'Figura', in *Archivum Romanticum*, Vol. 22, 1938, pp. 436–489.

Marc Augé, *Non-Places: Introduction to an Anthropology of Supermodernity*, London and New York: Verso, 2006.

J. L. Austin, *How to Do things With Words: the William James Lectures Delivered at Harvard University*, Oxford: Oxford University Press, [1962] 2009.

Gaston Bachelard, *The Poetics of Space: A Classic Look at How We Experience Intimate Places*, Boston: Beacon Press, 1994.

Alain Badiou, *Handbook of Inaesthetics*, Stanford: Stanford University Press, 2005.

Alain Badiou, *Being and Event*, London and New York: Continuum, 2005.

Roland Barthes, *How to Live Together: Novelistic Simulations of Some Everyday Spaces*, New York: Columbia University Press, 2013.

Zygmunt Bauman, *Liquid Times: Living in an Age of Uncertainty*, Cambridge: Polity Press, 2007.

Alexander Gottlieb Baumgarten, *Aesthetica*, Trajecti cis Viadrum, 1750.

Samuel Beckett, *Molloy, Malone Dies, The Unnamable*, London: Calder, 1994.

Franco 'Bifo' Berardi, *The Uprising: On Poetry and Finance*, Los Angeles: semiotext(e), 2012.

Henri Bergson, *Matter and Memory*, (Trans.) Nancy Margaret Paul and William Scott Palmer, New York: Dover Publications, [1896] 2004.

Walead Beshty, *Ethics*, London: Whitechapel Gallery, 2015.

Claire Bishop, *Artificial Hells, Participatory Art and the Politics of Spectatorship*, London: Verso, 2012.

Karl-Heinz Bohrer, 'Dionysos. Eine Ästhetik des Erscheinens', in Mira Fliescher, Fabian Goppelsröder, Dieter Mersch (Eds.), *Sichtbarkeiten 1: Erscheinen*, Berlin / Zurich: Diaphanes, 2013, pp. 13–38.

Yves-Alain Bois and Rosalind E. Krauss, *Formless: a User's Guide*, New York: Zone Books, 1999.

Henk Borgdorff, 'The Production of Knowledge in Artistic Research', in Michael Biggs and Henrik Karlsson (Eds.), *The Routledge Companion to Research in the Arts*, London: Routledge, 2011, pp. 44-63.

Simone Boria, Tim Boykett, Andreas Dekrout, Heather Kelly, Marta Peirano, Robert Rotenberg, Elisabeth Schimana (Eds.), *On Turtles and Dragons and the Dangerous Quest for a Media Art Notation System*, Linz: Times Up Press, 2012.

Henri Bortoft, *The Wholeness of Nature: Goethe's Way of Science*, Edinburgh: Floris Books, 1996.

Nicolas Bourriaud, *Relational Aesthetics*, Dijon: Les Presses Du Réel, 1998.

Rosi Braidotti, *Transpositions*, Cambridge: Polity Press, 2012.

Gabriele Brandstetter, Sibylle Peters, *de figura — Rhetorik — Bewegung — Gestalt*, München: Wilhelm Fink, 2002.

Gabriele Brandstetter, Gottfried Boehm, Achatz von Müller, *Figur und Figuration: Studien zu Wahrnehmung und Wissen*, München: Wilhelm Fink, 2007.

Franz Brentano, *Psychology from an Empirical Standpoint*, London: Routledge and New York: Humanities Press, [1874] 1973.

Martin Buber, *I and Thou*, New York: Scribner, 1958.

John Cage, *Silence: Lectures and Writings*, Middletown: Wesley University Press, 1973.

Roger Caillois, *Man, Play and Games*, (Trans.) Meyer Barash, Urbana and Chicago: University of Illinois Press, [1958] 2001.

Hélène Cixous, *Stigmata: Escaping Texts*, London and New York: Routledge, 2005.

Hélène Cixous and Catherine Clémente, *The Newly Born Woman*, (Trans.) Betsy Wing, Minneapolis: University of Minnesota Press, 1986.

Catherine Clément, *Syncope: The Philosophy of Rapture*, Minneapolis: University of Minnesota Press, 1994.

Emma Cocker, 'Moves Towards the Incomprehensible Wild', in *Art and Research*, Vol. 4, No. 1, Summer 2011. [Accessed at www.artandresearch.org.uk/v4n1/cocker.php]

Emma Cocker, 'Border Crossings — Practices for Beating the Bounds', in Hazel Andrews and Les Roberts (Eds.), *Liminal Landscapes: Travel, Experience and Spaces In-between*, Hoboken: Taylor & Francis, 2012, pp. 50-66.

Emma Cocker, 'Live Notation: Reflections on a Kairotic Practice', in Ric Allsopp and Jerome Fletcher (Eds.), in *Performance Research, 'On Writing and Digital Media'*, Vol. 18, Issue 5, 2013, pp. 69-76.

Emma Cocker, 'Tactics for Not Knowing: Preparing for the Unexpected', in Elizabeth Fisher and Rebecca Fortnum (Eds.), *On Not Knowing: How Artists Think*, London: Black Dog, 2013, pp. 126-135.

Emma Cocker, 'Looking for Loopholes: Cartographies of Escape', in Karen Bishop (Ed.), *Cartographies of Exile: A New Spatial Literacy*, New York: Routledge, 2016, pp. 228-248.

Emma Cocker, *The Yes of the No*, Sheffield: Site Gallery, 2016.

Emma Cocker, 'Performing Thinking in Action: The Meletē of Live Coding', in Thor Magnusson and Kate Sicchio (Eds.), *International Journal of Performance Arts and Digital Media, 'Live Coding'*, Vol. 12, Issue 2, 2016, pp. 102-116.

Emma Cocker, 'Writing without Writing: Conversation as Material', in Katja Hilevaara and Emily Orley (Eds.), *The Creative Critic: Writing As / About Practice*, London: Routledge, 2017.

Emma Cocker, Nikolaus Gansterer, Mariella Greil, 'Choreo-graphic Figures: Beginnings and Emergences', in Annette Arlander and Markus Kuikka (Eds.), in *RUUKKU, On Process*, 2015. [Accessed at www.researchcatalogue.net/view/132472/132473]

Emma Cocker, Nikolaus Gansterer, Mariella Greil, 'Notion of Notation >< Notation of Notion', in Scott deLahunta, Kim Vincs and Sarah Whatley (Eds.), *Performance Research*, 'On An/Notations', Vol. 20, Issue 6, Winter 2015, pp. 53-57.

Emma Cocker, Nikolaus Gansterer, Mariella Greil, 'Choreographic Figures: Vitality Gestures and Embodied Diagrammatics', in Alexander Gerner and Irene Mittelberg (Eds.), *Body Diagrams*, 'Gesture Studies', Amsterdam: John Benjamins Publishing, 2017.

Michel de Certeau, *The Practice of Everyday Life*, Berkeley: University of California Press, 1984.

Gilles Deleuze, *Spinoza: Practical Philosophy*, (Trans.) Robert Hurley, San Francisco: City Lights Books, 1988.

Gilles Deleuze, *Negotiations: 1972-1990*, New York: Columbia University Press, 1995.

Gilles Deleuze, *Foucault*, (Trans.) Sean Hand, Minneapolis: University of Minnesota Press, 1999.

Gilles Deleuze, *Francis Bacon: The Logic of Sensation*, London and New York: Continuum, 2002.

Gilles Deleuze and Félix Guattari, *A Thousand Plateaus*, (Trans.) Brian Massumi, London: Continuum, 2004.

Gilles Deleuze and Félix Guattari, *Kafka: Toward a Minor Literature*, Minneapolis: University of Minnesota Press, 2012.

Gilles Deleuze, *Difference and Repetition*, (Trans.) Paul Patton, London and New York: Bloomsbury Academic, 2014.

Gilles Deleuze, 'Lecture Transcripts on Spinoza's Concept of Affect', *Cours Vincennes*, 24.01.1978. www.webdeleuze.com/textes/14

Christopher Dell, *Das Urbane*, Berlin: Jovis, 2014.

Christopher Dell, *Die Epistemologie der Stadt*, Bielefeld: Transcript Verlag, 2016.

Christopher Dell, *Die Stadt als offene Partitur*, Zurich: Lars Müller Publishers, 2016.

Paul de Man, *Resistance to Theory*, Minneapolis: University of Minnesota Press, 1986.

Jacques Derrida, 'Die Struktur, das Zeichen und das Spiel im Diskurs der Wissenschaft vom Menschen', in Jacques Derrida, *Die Schrift und die Differenz*, Frankfurt a. M.: Suhrkamp, 1976, pp. 422-442.

Jacques Derrida, *Chōra*, Vienna: Passagen Verlag, 1990.

Jacques Derrida, *Politics of Friendship*, (Trans.) George Collins, London and New York: Verso, [1994] 2005.

Christine De Smedt, *4 Choreographic Portraits*, les ballets C de la B, 2012. [Accessed at https://issuu.com/irisraspoet/docs/4choreographicportraits_eng]

Gerhard Dirmoser, 'Figures of Thought' and 'Collection of Figures of Thought', in Nikolaus Gansterer (Ed.), *Drawing a Hypothesis: Figures of Thought*, Vienna and New York: Springer, 2011, pp. 153-176.

John J. Drummond, 'The Structure of Intentionality', in Rudolf Bernet, Donn Welton and Gina Zavota (Eds.), *Edmund Husserl: Critical Assessments of Leading Philosophers. Volume III, The Nexus of Phenomena: Intentionality, Perception and Temporality*, London: Routledge, 2005.

Bracha L. Ettinger, *Intimacy, Wit(h)nessing and Non-Abandonment* [Accessed at http://jordancrandall.com/main/+UNDERFIRE/site/files/q-node-562.html]

Bracha L. Ettinger, *The Matrixial Borderspace*, Minneapolis: University of Minnesota Press, 2006.

Erika Fischer-Lichte, *The Transformative Power of Performance: a New Aesthetics*, New York: Routledge, 2008.

Elizabeth Fisher and Rebecca Fortnum (Eds.), *On Not Knowing: How Artists Think*, London: Black Dog, 2013.

Vilém Flusser, *Gestures*, Minneapolis: University of Minnesota Press, [1991] 2014.

Michel Foucault, *Power/Knowledge: Selected Interviews and Other Writings, 1972-1977*, (Ed. and Trans.) Colin Gordon, New York: Pantheon Books, 1980.

Michel Foucault, 'Of Other Spaces', (Trans.) Jay Miskowiec, *Diacritics 16*, No. 1, Spring 1986, pp. 22-27.

Michel Foucault, 'Was ist ein Autor?', in Fotis Jannidis, Gerhard Lauer, Matías Martínez (Eds.), *Texte zur Theorie der Autorschaft*, Stuttgart: Reclam, 2000. ['Qu'est-ce qu'un auteur?', in *Dits et Écrits*, Vol. 1: 1954-1969, Paris: Gallimard, 1994].

Michel Foucault, *The Hermeneutics of the Subject, Lectures at the College de France 1981-1982*, New York: Picador, 2001.

Paulo Friere, *Pedagogy of the Oppressed*, London and New York: Bloomsbury Academic, [1968] 2014.

Nikolaus Gansterer (Ed.), *Drawing a Hypothesis: Figures of Thought*, Vienna and New York: Springer, 2011.

Clifford Geertz, 'Thick Description: Toward an Interpretive Theory of Culture', in *The Interpretation of Cultures: Selected Essays*, New York: Basic Books, 1973, pp. 3-30.

Liam Gillick and Maria Lind (Eds.), *Curating with Light Luggage: A Symposium*, Frankfurt a. M.: Revolver, 2004.

Hugo Glendinning and Adrian Heathfield (Dirs. and Eds.), *No Such Thing as Rest: A Walk with Brian Massumi*, [PDF transcript], 2013. [Accessed at www.adrianheathfield.net/project/no-such-thing-as-rest].

Hugo Glendinning and Adrian Heathfield (Dirs. and Eds.), *Transfigured Night: A Conversation with Alphonso Lingis*, 2015.

Hugo Glendinning and Adrian Heathfield (Dir. and Eds.), *Spirit Labour*, 2016.

Stuart Grant, Jodie McNeilly, Maeva Veerapen, *Performance and Temporalisation: Time Happens*, Houndmills, Basingstoke, Hampshire and New York: Palgrave Macmillan, 2014.

Mariella Greil and Martina Ruhsam, 'Postconsensual Collaboration. A Shared Lecture on Plurality and the Choreographic', in *On Collaboration II Symposium*, London: Middlesex University, 2013.

Mariella Greil and Vera Sander, 'On Practices of Shining Back', in *(per)forming feedback*, published by Centre for Contemporary Dance Cologne, in collaboration with the Federal Ministry of Education and Research and the Dance Education Biennale, 2016, pp. 22-27.

Elizabeth Grosz (Ed.), *Becomings: Exploration in Time, Memory and Futures*, Ithaca and London: Cornell University Press, 1999.

Félix Guattari, *Chaosmosis: An Ethico-Aesthetic Paradigm*, Sydney: Power Publications, 1995.

Félix Guattari, *The Three Ecologies*, London: Bloomsbury Academic, 2014.

David Halliburton, *Poetic Thinking: an Approach to Heidegger*, Chicago: University of Chicago Press, 1981.

Katharine Harmon, *The Map as Art: Contemporary Artists Explore Cartography*, New York: Princeton Architectural Press, 2009.

Karin Harrasser, 'Drawing Interest Recording Vitality', in Nikolaus Gansterer, (Ed.) *Drawing a Hypothesis: Figures of Thought*, Vienna and New York: Springer, 2011, pp. 109-120.

Deborah Hay, *My Body the Buddhist*, Hannover, New Hampshire: Wesleyan University Press, 2000.

Adrian Heathfield, 'Coming Undone', in *It's an Earthquake in My Heart: A Reading Companion*, Chicago: Goat Island, 2001. [Accessed at www. adrianheathfield.net/project/coming-undone]

Martin Heidegger, *Being and Time*, New York: Harper, 1962.

Martin Heidegger, 'Was ist Metaphysik?', reprinted in *Wegmarken*, 2nd edition, Frankfurt a. M.: Klostermann, 1978.

Martin Heidegger, *The Basic Problems of Phenomenology*, Bloomington and Indianapolis: Indiana University Press, 1988.

Martin Heidegger, 'The Age of the World Picture', in Julian Young and Kenneth Haynes (Eds. and Trans.), *Off the Beaten Track*, Cambridge: Cambridge University Press, 2002.

Luce Irigaray, 'This Sex Which Is Not One', in Elaine Marks and Isabelle De Courtivron (Eds.), *New French Feminisms*, Massachusetts: University of Massachusetts Press, 1980, pp. 99-106.

Luce Irigaray, *The Way of Love*, London and New York: Continuum, 2002.

William James, *Essays in Radical Empiricism*, New York: Dover Publication, [1912] 2003.

Rachel Jones, *Irigaray: Towards a Sexuate Philosophy*, Oxford: Wiley, 2013.

Immanuel Kant, *Critik der Urtheilskraft*, Berlin, 1790.

Gabriele Klein and Sandra Noeth, *Emerging Bodies — The Performance of Worldmaking in Dance and Choreography*, Berlin: De Gruyter, 2011.

Heinrich von Kleist, "On the Gradual Formation of Thoughts in the Process of Speech', in *Werke in einem Band*, (Trans.) Christoph Harbsmeier, Munich: Carl Hanser, [1878] 1996.

Kenneth Knoespel, 'Diagrammatic Writing and the Configuration of Space', in Gilles Châtelet, *Figuring Space: Philosophy, Mathematics and Physics*, Dordrecht: Kluwer, Academic, 2000 pp. ix- xxiii.

Julia Kristeva, *Powers of Horror: an Essay on Abjection*, New York: Columbia University Press, 1982.

Brandon LaBelle, *Lexicon of the Mouth: Poetics and Politics of Voice and the Oral Imaginary*, London and New York: Bloomsbury Academic, 2014.

Susanne Leeb, 'A Line with Variable Direction, which Traces No Contour, and Delimits No Form', in Nikolaus Gansterer (Ed.), *Drawing a Hypothesis: Figures of Thought*, Vienna and New York, 2011, pp. 29-42.

Henri Lefebvre, *Rhythmanalysis: Space, Time, and Everyday Life*, London: Bloomsbury Academic, 2015.

André Lepecki, *Singularities — Dance in the Age of Performance*, Abington, Oxon and New York: Routledge, 2016.

Emmanuel Levinas, *Entre Nous: On Thinking-of-the-Other*, New York: Columbia University Press, 1998.

Clarice Lispector, *Agua Viva*, London: Penguin Classics, 2014.

Jean-François Lyotard, *What to Paint?*, Leuven: Leuven University Press, [1987] 2012.

Sarat Maharaj, 'Xeno-epistemics: Makeshift Kit for Sounding Visual Art as Knowledge Production and the Retinal Regimes', in Okwui Enwezor (Ed.), *Documenta 11, Platform 5 Catalogue*, Ostfildern-Ruit: Hatje Cantz, 2002, pp. 71-84.

Sarat Maharaj, Stopgap Notes on "Method" in Visual Art as Knowledge Production', in *Art + Research*, Vol. 2, No. 2, Spring 2009. [Accessed at www.artandresearch.org.uk/v2n2/maharaj.html]

Sarat Maharaj and Francisco J. Varela, 'Ahamkara: Particules Élémentaires of First-person Consciousness', in Florian Dombois, Ute Meta Bauer, Claudia Mareis, Michael Schwab (Eds.), *Intellectual Birdhouse: Artistic Practice as Research*, Amsterdam: Rodopi, 2011, pp. 65-86.

Sarat Maharaj, 'What the Thunder Said: Toward a Scouting Report on "Art as a Thinking Process"', in Mara Ambrožič and Angela Vettese (Eds.), *Art as a Thinking Process: Visual Forms of Knowledge Production*, Berlin: Sternberg Press, 2013, pp. 154-161.

Erin Manning, *Relationscapes: Movement, Art, Philosophy*, Cambridge, Mass. and London, MIT Press, 2009.

Erin Manning, *Always More Than One: Individuation's Dance*, Durham: Duke University Press, 2013.

Erin Manning, *The Minor Gesture*, Durham: Duke University Press, 2016.

Erin Manning and Brian Massumi, *Thought in the Act: Passages in the Ecology of Experience*, Minneapolis: University of Minnesota Press, 2014.

Humberto R. Maturana and Francisco J. Varela, *Autopoiesis and Cognition: The Realization of the Living*, Dordrecht and Boston: D. Reidel Pub. Co., 1980.

Humberto R. Maturana and Francisco J. Varela, *The Tree of Knowledge: The Biological Roots of Human Understanding*, Boston: Shambhala Publications, 1987.

Derek McCormack, 'Thinking Spaces for Research-Creation', *Inflexions*, Vol. 1 No. 1. [Accessed at www.senselab.ca/inflexions/htm/node/McCormack2.html].

Thomas F. McDonough, 'Situationist Space', *October* 67, Winter 1994, pp. 58-77.

Dieter Mersch, 'Tertium datur. Einleitung in eine negative Medientheorie', in Stephan Münker, Alexander Roesler (Eds.), *Was ist ein Medium*, Frankfurt a. M.: Suhrkamp, 2008, pp. 304-321.

Dieter Mersch, 'Ästhetik des Rausches und der Rausch der Differenz. Produktionsästhetik mit Nietzsche', in Thomas Strässle, Simon Zumsteg (Eds.), *Trunkenheit: Kulturen des Rausches*, Amsterdam and New York: Rodopi, 2008.

Dieter Mersch, *Epistemologies of Aesthetics*, Zurich and Berlin: Diaphanes, 2015.

Lilia Mestre, *Writing Scores*, Brussels: a.pass (advanced performance and scenography studies), 2014.

Catherine Mills, *The Philosophy of Giorgio Agamben*, Stocksfield: Acumen, 2008.

W.J.T. Mitchell, 'Interdisciplinarity and Visual Culture', in *Art Bulletin*, 'Inter / disciplinarity', December 1995, pp. 540-544.

Lize Mogel and Alexis Bhagat, *An Atlas of Radical Cartography*, Los Angeles: Journal of Aesthetics & Protest Press, 2007.

Fred Moten, *In the Break: the Aesthetics of the Black Radical Tradition*, Minneapolis: University of Minnesota Press, 2003.

Pia Müller-Tamm, Gottfried Boehm, *Henri Matisse: Figur, Farbe, Raum*, Ostfildern-Ruit: Hatje Cantz, 2005.

Jean-Luc Nancy, 'Un souffle / Ein Hauch', in Nicolas Berg, Jess Jochimsen, and Bernd Stiegler (Eds.), *Shoah. Formen der Erinnerung. Geschichte, Philosophie, Literatur, Kunst*, Munich: Wilhem Fink, 1996.

Jean-Luc Nancy, *Being Singular Plural*, Stanford: Stanford University Press, 2000.

Jean-Luc Nancy, *Listening*, (Trans.) Charlotte Mandell, New York: Fordham University Press, 2007.

Jean-Luc Nancy, *Corpus*, New York: Fordham University Press, 2008.

Nanopolitics Handbook, Brooklyn: Minor Compositions, 2014.

Antonio Negri, *Time for Revolution*, New York and London: Continuum, 2003.

Antonio Negri, *Negri on Negri: in Conversation with Anne Dufourmentelle*, New York and London: Routledge, 2004.

Friedrich Nietzsche, *Thus Spoke Zarathustra*, (Trans.) Graham Parkes, Oxford: Oxford University Press, 2005.

Friedrich Nietzsche, *Beyond Good and Evil*, Oxford: Oxford University Press, [1886] 2008.

Alva Noë, *Strange Tools — Art and Human Nature*, New York: Hill and Wang, 2015.

Simon O'Sullivan, *Art Encounters, Deleuze and Guattari, Thought Beyond Representation*, Basingstoke: Palgrave Macmillan, 2006.

Simon O'Sullivan, *On the Production of Subjectivity: Five Diagrams of the Finite-Infinite Relation*, Houndmills, Basingstoke, Hampshire and New York: Palgrave Macmillan, 2012.

Erwin Panofsky, *Idea. Ein Beitrag zur Begriffsgeschichte der älteren Kunsttheorie*, Berlin, [1924] 2014.

Georges Perec, *Species of Spaces and Other Pieces*, London: Penguin Books, [1974] 1997.

Peggy Phelan, *Unmarked — The Politics of Performance*, London and New York: Routledge, 1993.

John Rajchman, 'Experimental Aesthetics: A Short Story of Thinking in Art', in André Alves and Henk Slager (Eds.), *Experimental Aesthetics*, Utrecht: Metropolis M Books, 2014, pp. 24-29.

Jacques Rancière, *Aisthesis: Scenes from the Aesthetic Regime of Art*, London and New York: Verso Books, 2013.

Theodor Reik, *Listening with the Third Ear: The Inner Experience of the Psychoanalyst*, New York: Farrar, Straus, and Giroux, [1948] 1993.

Hester Reeve and Tom Hall, 'Slow Coding, Slow Doing, Slow Listening, Slow Performance', in *International Conference on Live Coding*, Leeds, 2015.

Paul Ricoeur, *On Translation*, London and New York: Routledge, 2006.

Irit Rogoff, *Terra Infirma, Geography's Visual Culture*, London and New York: Routledge, 2000.

Irit Rogoff, 'Without: A Conversation-Interview with Peggy Phelan', in *Art Journal*, Fall, 2001, pp. 34-41.

Martina Ruhsam, 'I Want to Work with You Because I Can Speak for Myself: The Potential of Postconsensual Collaboration in Choreographic Practice' in Noyale Colin, Stefanie Sachsenmaier (Eds.), *Collaboration in Performance Practice: Premises, Workings and Failures*, Basingstoke: Palgrave Macmillan, 2016, pp. 75-92.

Petra Sabisch, *Choreographing Relations: Practical Philosophy and Contemporary Choreography*, Munich: epodium, 2011.

Jean-Paul Sartre, *Das Sein und das Nichts. Versuch einer phänomenologischen Ontologie*, Hamburg: Rowohlt, 1976.

Michael Schwab and Henk Borgdorff (Eds.), *The Exposition of Artistic Research: Publishing Art in Academia*, Leiden: Leiden University Press, 2014.

Maxine Sheets-Johnstone, *The Primacy of Movement*, 2nd edition, Amsterdam & Philadelphia: John Benjamins, 2011.

P.A. Skantze, *Itinerant Spectator / Itinerant Spectacle*, Brooklyn, New York: Punctum Books, 2013.

P.A. Skantze, 'Shift Epistemologies: Gap Knowledge', in Marin Blaževic and Lada Čale Feldman (Eds.), *MISperformance — Essays in Shifting Perspectives*, Ljubljana: Maska, 2014, pp. 245-254.

Henk Slager, *The Pleasure of Research*, Ostfildern-Ruit: Hatje Cantz, 2015.

Paolo Soleri, *Entry #34 — 'Howness', What if? Quaderno 2 — Space as Reality*, Scottsdale: Cosanti Press, 2004.

Baruch Spinoza, *Ethics*, Oxford: Oxford University Press, [1677] 2000.

Serge Stauffer, *Kunst als Forschung*, Zurich: Scheidegger & Spiess, 2013.

Isabelle Stengers, 'Reclaiming Animism', *e-flux Journal* #36, July 2012. [Accessed at www.e-flux.com/journal/36/61245/reclaiminganimism]

Daniel Stern, *The Present Moment in Psychotherapy and Everyday Life*, New York: W. W. Norton & Company, 2004.

Daniel Stern, *Forms of Vitality: Exploring Dynamic Experience in Psychology, the Arts, Psychotherapy and Development*, Oxford and New York: Oxford University Press, 2010.

Evan Thompson, *Mind in Life: Biology, Phenomenology and the Science of Mind*, Cambridge, Mass.: Belknap Press of Harvard University Press, 2007.

Victor Turner, *The Ritual Process: Structure and Anti-Structure*, Chicago: Aldine Publishing, 1969.

Victor Turner, *From Ritual to Theatre: The Human Seriousness of Play*, New York: Performing Arts Journal Publications, 1982.

Francisco J. Varela, *Principles of Biological Autonomy*, New York: North Holland, 1979.

Francisco J. Varela, 'Organism: a Meshwork of Selfless Selves', in Alfred I. Tauber, *Organism and the Origin of Self*, Dordrecht: Springer Netherlands, 1991, pp. 12-42.

Francisco J. Varela, 'Patterns of Life: Intertwining Identity and Cognition', in *Brain and Cognition 34*, 1997, pp. 72-87.

Francisco J. Varela, *Ethical Know-How: Action, Wisdom and Cognition*, Stanford: Stanford University Press, 1999.

Eric Voegelin, *Anamnesis. Zur Theorie der Geschichte und Politik*, Munich and Freiburg: Verlag Karl Alber, 2005.

Thomas Carl Wall, *Radical Passivity: Levinas, Blanchot and Agamben*, New York: SUNY Press, 1999.

Paul Watzlawick, Janet H. Beavin, Don D. Jackson, *Menschliche Kommunikation. Formen, Störungen, Paradoxien*, Bern: Huber, 2007, pp. 53-70.

Andreas Weber and Francisco J. Varela, 'Life after Kant: Natural Processes and the Autopoietic Foundations of Biological Individuality', in *Phenomenology and the Cognitive Sciences*, Vol. 1, Issue 2, 2002, pp. 97-125.

Janneke Wesseling, *On Sponge, Stone and the Intertwinement with the Here and Now: a Methodology of Artistic Research*, Amsterdam: Valiz, 2016.

Ludwig Wittgenstein, *Philosophical Investigations*, (Trans.) G.E.M. Anscombe, P.M.S. Hacker and Joachim Schulte, Chichester: John Wiley & Sons, 2009.

Peter Wollen, 'Mappings: Situationist and / or Conceptualists' in Michael Newman and Jon Bird (Eds.), *Rewriting Conceptual Art*, London: Reaktion Books, [1953] 1999, pp. 27-46.

Mary Zamberlin, *Rhizosphere: Gilles Deleuze and the 'Minor' American Writing of William James*, London and New York: Routledge, 2014.

BIOGRAPHIES

KEY RESEARCHERS

EMMA COCKER is a writer-artist and Reader in Fine Art, Nottingham Trent University. Operating under the title *Not Yet There*, her research focuses on the process of artistic endeavour, alongside models of (art) practice and subjectivity that resist the pressure of a single, stable position by remaining wilfully unresolved. Her writing has been published in *Failure*, 2010; *Stillness in a Mobile World*, 2011; *Drawing a Hypothesis: Figures of Thought*, 2011; *Hyperdrawing: Beyond the Lines of Contemporary Art*, 2012; *Liminal Landscapes*, 2012; *Reading/Feeling*, 2013; *On Not Knowing: How Artists Think*, 2013; *Cartographies of Exile: A New Spatial Literacy*, 2016; *Fall Narratives: An Interdisciplinary Perspective*, 2016; *The Alternative Document*, 2018 and as a collection, *The Yes of the No*, 2016. www.not-yet-there.blogspot.co.uk

Key researcher, *Choreo-graphic Figures: Deviations from the Line,* 2014-2017.

NIKOLAUS GANSTERER studied art at the University of Applied Arts in Vienna, Austria and completed his studies at the Jan van Eyck Academie in Maastricht, the Netherlands. He is co-founder of the *Institute for Transacoustic Research* and currently Guest Professor at the *Zentrum Fokus Forschung* at the University of Applied Arts in Vienna. Deeply interested in the links between drawing, thinking and action, his practice is grounded in a trans-medial and trans-disciplinary approach, underpinned by conceptual discourse in the context of performative visualisation and cartographic representations. Gansterer's fascination with the complex character of diagrammatic figures led to his book *Drawing a Hypothesis,* 2011 on the ontology of shapes of visualisations and the development of the diagrammatic perspective and its use in contemporary art and science. Gansterer is internationally active in performances, exhibitions and lecturing. www.gansterer.org

Key researcher, *Choreo-graphic Figures: Deviations from the Line,* 2014-2017.

MARIELLA GREIL works in the fields of dance, choreography and artistic research with a focus on choreographic means in its expansion and somatic practices as compositional tools. She studied at the European Dance Development Centre at the Hogeschool voor de Kunsten Arnhem, at the University of Music and Performing Arts, Vienna, and is currently PhD candidate at Roehampton University, London. Previously, she was Associate Researcher of *Performance Matters* in London and Senior Editor of the e-journal *activate.* She has performed in works by Boris Charmatz, Barbara Kraus, LIGNA, Jan Machachek, Doris Stelzer, Meg Stuart and her own work. Active in the artists' initiative *Sweet&Tender Collaborations* she explores forms of collaboration and the ethics of togetherness. Greil was artistic advisor for the *5th Dance Education Biennale* and lectures internationally. With Vera Sander she co-edited the book *(per)forming feedback,* 2016. www.mariellagreil.net

Key researcher, *Choreo-graphic Figures: Deviations from the Line,* 2014-2017.

WIT(H)NESSES

ALEX ARTEAGA integrates aesthetic and philosophical practices relating to aesthetics, the emergence of sense, meaning and knowledge and the relationships between aurality, architecture and the environment in his research through phenomenological and enactivist approaches. He studied piano, music theory, composition, electroacoustic music, and architecture in Berlin and Barcelona and received a PhD in philosophy from the Humboldt University. He currently heads the *Auditory Architecture Research Unit,* teaches at the MA Sound Studies and Sonic Arts, Berlin University of the Arts, is professor for contemporary philosophy and artistic research at the Research Master in Art and Design, EINA / Universitat Autònoma de Barcelona, and develops his research project *Architecture of Embodiment.* www.architecture-embodiment.org

Sputnik in all Method Labs, 2014-2016.

ARNO BÖHLER teaches philosophy at the University of Vienna, Department of Philosophy and is founder of the philosophy performance festival *Philosophy On Stage.* Currently he heads the PEEK-Project *Artist-Philosophers: Philosophy AS Arts-based-Research* (AR275-G21) at the University of Applied Arts Vienna, sponsored by the Austrian Science Fund (FWF). Fellowships: University of Bangalore, University of Heidelberg, New York University, University of Princeton. Visiting Professor at the University of Applied Arts Vienna, the University of Arts Bremen, the University of Music and Performing Art Vienna and the University of Vienna, Department of Philosophy. Research Interest: Arts-based-Philosophy, Intercultural Philosophy. http://homepage.univie.ac.at/arno.boehler/php/

Critical Wit(h)ness: Summer, Spring and Winter Lab, Tanzquartier, Vienna and AILab, 2015-2016.

CHRISTOPHER DELL works as theoretician and composer. He currently holds a position as Professor for Urban Design Theory at the HafenCity University Hamburg. He held the same position at the Technical University Munich. His teaching in architectural theory includes amongst others the University of Fine Arts Berlin and the Architectural Association London. Dell holds a habilitation in cultural studies and a PhD in Organisation Psychology. Since 2000, Dell is Head of the Institute for Improvisation Technology (ifit), Berlin. His monographs include: *Prinzip Improvisation*, 2002; *Improvisations on Urbanity*, 2009; *Tacit Urbanism*, 2009; *Replaycity*, 2011; *Die improvisierende Organisation*, 2012; *Ware: Wohnen!*, 2013; *Das Urbane*, 2014; *Epistemologie der Stadt*, 2016; *Stadt als offene Partitur*, 2016.

Collaboration with Gerhard Dirmoser for remixed textual-visual contribution.

CHRISTINE DE SMEDT works in the field of choreography, dance and performance. Her work is research-based and develops different methodologies and performance formats, questioning and investigating in long term projects. Over the years she has also engaged in various artistic collaborations with Meg Stuart, Mårten Spångberg, Mette Edvardsen, Philipp Gehmacher, Vladimir Miller, Xavier Le Roy, Mette Ingvartsen, Eszter Salamon, Bojana Cvejic amongst others. She has been curating artistic and residency projects and was pedagogical coordinator for the Brussels based *Performing Arts Research and Training Studio.*

Sputnik in Method Labs, 2015-2016.

CATHERINE DE ZEGHER is the Director of the Museum of Fine Arts, Ghent, Belgium and Member of the Royal Academy of Belgium of Science and the Arts. In 2012-2013, she curated the *18th Biennale of Sydney,* Australia and the *5th Moscow Biennale,* Russia. As Guest Curator in the Department of Drawings at the Museum of Modern Art, New York she organised the large-scale exhibition *On Line: Drawing through the Twentieth Century,* 2010-2011. For many years she was the Director of the Drawing Center, New York. Author and editor of numerous books, her most recent publication is *Women's Work Is Never Done, 2014,* an anthology of her collected essays on the work of contemporary women artists.

Critical Wit(h)ness / Trialogue Conversation, 2016.

GERHARD DIRMOSER lives and works in Linz. He is a systems analyst. Exhibitions and studies (selection): *Architektur & Diagrammatik*, Cologne, 2011; *Ars Electronica Festival*, Linz 2009, 2006, 2005, 2004; *Gerhard Dirmoser, Horst Münch*, Künstlerhaus Palais Thurn und Taxis, Bregenz 2007; *Eine Festausstellung*, Lower Austrian Documentation Centre for Modern Art, St. Pölten, 2006; *Survival and Maintenance of Media Based Art,* Ludwig Boltzmann Institut für Medien.Kunst.Forschung, Linz, 2006; *Lying. Sitting. Standing. Walking. Jumping. Flying. Falling. What people do — and how,* Künstlerforum, Bonn, 2015.

Critical Wit(h)ness: Spring and Winter Lab, Tanzquartier, Vienna and AILab, 2015-2016.

KARIN HARRASSER is Professor for Cultural Theory at the University of Art and Design, Linz. Her research focuses on techniques and media of the body, popular culture and science fiction, gender and agency, genres and methods of Cultural Studies / Kulturwissenschaft. She has realised numerous projects at the intersection of arts, humanities and science communication e.g. with the Mobile Academy Berlin or Tanzquartier Wien. Together with Elisabeth Timm, she is Editor-in-Chief of *Zeitschrift für Kulturwissenschaften.* Recent books include *Prothesen. Figuren einer lädierten Moderne*, Vorwerk 8, Berlin, 2016.

Critical Wit(h)ness: Winter and Summer Lab, Tanzquartier, Vienna and AILab, 2015-2016.

ADRIAN HEATHFIELD writes on, curates and creates performance. He is the author of *Out of Now,* 2009, a monograph on the artist Tehching Hsieh and editor of *Perform, Repeat, Record,* 2012, and *Live: Art and Performance*, 2004. His numerous essays have been translated into eight languages. In 2016 he was a curatorial attaché for the *Sydney Biennale* and, as part of the *freethought* collective, a co-director of the Bergen Assembly. He is curator of Taiwan's exhibition at the *57th Venice Biennale 2017.* Heathfield is Professor of Performance and Visual Culture at the University of Roehampton, London. www.adrianheathfield.net

Critical Wit(h)ness / Trialogue Conversation, 2016.

VICTOR JASCHKE is a photographer, cinematographer and film director. He was co-founder of the film-cooperative *Filmlokomotive,* makes art-documentaries and music videos and has worked with the artist collectives *Geschwister Odradek* and *Gelitin.* He specialises in live documentary and ethnography with a focus on documentaries and video trainings for NGOs in Indonesia. He is known for the *Trilogi Jawa: Jakarta Disorder*, 2013; *Riding My Tiger,* 2014; and *Paradise Later*, 2010, produced in close collaboration with Ascan Breuer.

Video and photographic documentation, 2015-2016.

SIMONA KOCH studied graphic design and fine arts in Nuremberg, Germany. As an artist, she researches on the various aspects of the living being and how they are connected with each other. She has received several awards and grants including the Bavarian Kunstförderpreis for Applied Arts (2012). She also works in the field of book design and collaborated with Nikolaus Gansterer on the book *Drawing a Hypothesis*, 2011. www.en-bloc.de; www.abiotismus.de; www.gestaltgebung.eu

Photographic documentation and development of graphic design and layout, 2014-2017.

KRASSIMIRA KRUSCHKOVA is a theatre, dance and performance theorist and curator. Since 2003 she has been Head of the Theory Centre at the Tanzquartier Wien. She teaches at the University of Applied Arts and the Academy of Fine Arts in Vienna, and was Visiting Professor at the FU Berlin and the University of Vienna, where she did her doctorate and habilitation. Selected publications include *Ob?scene. Zur Präsenz der Absenz im zeitgenössischen Theater, Tanz und Film,* 2005; *It Takes Place When It Doesn't. On Dance and Performance since 1989* (Eds. with M. Hochmuth / G. Schöllhammer), 2006; *Uncalled. Dance and Performance of the Future* (Eds. with S. Gareis), 2009, and *Wissen wir, was ein Körper vermag* (Eds. with A. Böhler / S. Granzer), 2014.

Critical Wit(h)ness: Winter Lab, Tanzquartier, Vienna, 2016.

BRANDON LABELLE is an artist, writer and theorist working with sound culture, voice, and questions of agency. He develops and presents artistic projects and performances within a range of international contexts, often working collaboratively and in public. Recent works include *Oficina de Autonomia*, Ybakatu, Curitiba, 2017; *The Hobo Subject*, Gallery Forum, Zagreb, 2016, and *The Living School*, South London Gallery, 2016. He is the author of *Lexicon of the Mouth: Poetics and Politics of Voice and the Oral Imaginary,* 2014; *Diary of an Imaginary Egyptian*, 2012; *Acoustic Territories: Sound Culture and Everyday Life*, 2010, and *Background Noise: Perspectives on Sound Art*, 2006; 2nd ed. 2015.

Guest in Friday Lecture Series and Critical Wit(h)ness: Summer Lab, AILab, 2016.

ERIN MANNING is Research Chair in Philosophy and Relational Art at Concordia University Montreal and Director of SenseLab. Her artwork moves between textile, movement and collective experimentation and is centred on large-scale participatory installations that facilitate emergent collectivities. Publications include *Always More Than One: Individuation's Dance*, 2013; *Relationscapes: Movement, Art, Philosophy*, 2009; and, with Brian Massumi, *Thought in the Act: Passages in the Ecology of Experience*, 2014, and *The Minor Gesture*, 2016. www.erinmovement.com; www.senselab.ca

Critical Wit(h)ness / Trialogue Conversation, 2016.

DIETER MERSCH is Professor at the University of the Arts Zurich, he studied mathematics and philosophy at the Universities of Cologne and Bochum and made his dissertation on Umberto Eco at the Technical University Darmstadt. He was a Full Professor for Media Theory and Director of the Department for Media and Arts at the University of Potsdam, 2004-13, and since 2013 he is Director of the Institute for Critical Theory at Zurich University of at the University of the Arts Zurich. Main publications include *Was sich zeigt. Materialität, Präsenz, Ereignis*, 2002; *Ereignis und Aura. Untersuchungen zur einer Ästhetik des Performativen*, 2002; *Medientheorien zur Einführung,* 2006; *Posthermeneutik*, 2010; *Epistemologies of Aesthetics*, 2015. www.dieter-mersch.de

Guest in Friday Lecture Series and Critical Wit(h)ness: Summer Lab, AILab, 2016.

LILIA MESTRE is a performing artist and researcher based in Brussels, working mainly in collaboration with other artists. She is interested in art practice as a medial tool between several semiotic domains. Her principal medium is dance and choreography. Mestre works with assemblages, scores and inter-subjective setups as an artist, curator, dramaturge and teacher. She is the Co-Founder and Coordinator of *Bains Connective Art Laboratory*. Since 2008 she works as a Mentor, Workshop Facilitator and Associate Program Curator at a.pass where she has been developing a research practice on scores as pedagogical tools titled *ScoreScapes*. She became a.pass Co-Coordinator together with Kristien Van den Branden in 2017.

Sputnik in all Method Labs, 2014-2016.

WERNER MOEBIUS works in the fields of Sonic Art and Audio Culture in between conceptual art, contemporary music, electronica and weird art-pop. He uses the plasticity of sound to set up dialogues with other media and music methodologies. Generating sounds provides him the basis to develop complex compositions and sound performances, as well as transitive audiovisual intermedia concepts in collaboration with artists of different media. www.wernermoebius.net

Guest Collaborator in all Method Labs, 2014-2016.

ALVA NOË is a writer and philosopher living in Berkeley and New York. He is the author of *Action in Perception*, 2004; *Out of Our Heads: Why You Are Not Your Brain and Other Lessons from the Biology of Consciousness*, 2009; *Varieties of Presence*, 2012; and *Strange Tools: Art and Human Nature*, 2015. He is a Professor of Philosophy at the University of California, Berkeley, where he is also a member of the Center for New Media and the Institute for Cognitive and Brain Sciences. Noë is a 2012 recipient of a Guggenheim Fellowship and a 2018 recipient of the Judd / Hume Prize in Advanced Visual Studies. He is a weekly contributor to National Public Radio's science and culture blog *13.7 Cosmos and Culture.*

Guest in Friday Lecture Series and Critical Wit(h)ness: Summer Lab, AILab, 2016.

JEANETTE PACHER (né Simmons), born into a working / middle-class family in Sunderland in the NE of England, moved at the age of nine to rural Austria. After studying Media Sciences and Art History in Vienna, and thanks to her family's and friends' trust in her, she holds a curator position at the Vienna Secession, an artist run institution for contemporary art (since 2007; and despite her being a single mother to Jonathan, born in 2005). She was part of the editorial team of the radio programme Kunstradio, broadcast on the cultural channel Ö1, assistant curator at Kunsthalle Vienna (1994-99) and has realised a number of freelance projects, both as curator, editor and translator. Rather than opting for a linear career, she has sought to go after her broad-spread interests, and still seeks to combine these, leaving the common boundaries of the 'fine arts' behind in favour of more experimental, open, process-oriented forms of experiencing life.

Critical Wit(h)ness: Summer, Spring and Winter Lab, Tanzquartier, Vienna and AILab, 2015-2016.

JÖRG PIRINGER currently lives in Vienna and is a member of the *Institute for Transacoustic Research* and of the *Vegetable Orchestra.* He has a Master Degree in Computer Science and works as a freelance artist and researcher in the fields of electronic music, radio art, sound and visual electronic poetry, interactive collaborative systems, online communities, live performance, sound installation, computer games and video art. joerg.piringer.net

Guest Collaborator in all Method Labs, 2014-2016.

HELMUT PLOEBST has published in different periodicals as editor and author since 1986, from 1991 focusing on dance / performance. Since 1996 he has been working as a freelance critic (amongst others for Der Standard, Vienna), curator, lecturer and as researcher in different laboratories. Since 2004, he has been teaching Performance Theory, amongst others at Anton Bruckner Private University, Linz. He is founder and editor of the website *CORPUSweb. net — performance .:. philosophy .:. politics.* His selected publications include *VERSEHEN. Tanz in allen Medien* (Eds. with N. Haitzinger) 2011; *NO WIND NO WORD. Choreography in the Society of the Spectacle,* 2001.

Critical Wit(h)ness: Summer and Winter Lab, Tanzquartier, Vienna and AILab, 2015-2016.

P.A. SKANTZE is a director, writer and scholar working in Italy and London, where she is currently Reader in Performance Practices at Roehampton University. Her books *Stillness in Motion in the Seventeenth-Century Theatre,* 2003, and *Itinerant Spectator / Itinerant Spectacle*, 2013, think through early modern theatre as a practice across the weighted worlds of the still and the moving and the craft of spectating as a practice of attention and wandering in Europe in the 21st century. She is Co-Founder of the performance group *Four Second Decay*, which most recently staged 'Orfeo and Eurydice: How to Save Someone You Can't See' at the *No Future Biennale* in Athens, 2016.

Guest in Friday Lecture Series and Critical Wit(h)ness: Summer Lab, AILab, 2016.

ANDREAS SPIEGL studied art history at the University of Vienna. He currently works as Senior Scientist at the Institute for Cultural Studies at the Academy of Fine Arts Vienna where he was also Vice-Rector for Research and Teaching from 2003 to 2011. Since 2015, he is Head of the Institute for Cultural Studies. His research focuses on the intersection of media theories, subject theories and theories of space. He has published numerous texts on contemporary art and art theory.

Critical Wit(h)ness: Summer, Spring and Winter Lab, Tanzquartier, Vienna and AILab, 2015-2016.

IMPRINT

Choreo-graphic Figures: Deviations from the Line
A project by
Nikolaus Gansterer, University of Applied Arts Vienna, Austria
Emma Cocker, Nottingham Trent University, United Kingdom
Mariella Greil, University of Applied Arts Vienna, Austria

www.choreo-graphic-figures.net

Library of Congress Cataloging-in-Publication data
A CIP catalog record for this book has been applied for at the Library of Congress.

Bibliographic information published by the German national library
The German national library lists this publication in the Deutsche nationalbibliografie; detailed bibliographic data are available on the Internet at http:// dnb.dnb.de.

Translations: David Ender; Mariella Greil
Copy editing: Jeanette Pacher
Cover image: Nikolaus Gansterer
Cover design: Simona Koch
Graphic design and book concept: Simona Koch

Photographs by Nikolaus Gansterer, Julian Hughes,
Victor Jaschke, Simona Koch, Tim Tom

Printing: Druckerei Jentzsch, Vienna
Printed on acid-free paper produced from chlorine-free pulp. TCF ∞
Printed in Austria

ISSN 1866-248X
ISBN 978-3-11-054660-6

www.degruyter.com

ACKNOWLEDGEMENTS

We thank our sputniks Alex Arteaga, Christine De Smedt, Lilia Mestre and guest collaborators Werner Moebius, Jörg Piringer for their contributions to our project and publication, alongside those critical wit(h)nesses who have contributed written and conversational responses for the book: Arno Böhler, Catherine de Zegher, Christopher Dell, Gerhard Dirmoser, Karin Harrasser, Adrian Heathfield, Krassimira Kruschkova, Brandon LaBelle, Erin Manning, Dieter Mersch, Alva Noë, Jeanette Pacher, Helmut Ploebst, P.A. Skantze, Andreas Spiegl.

This PEEK project (Programme for Arts-based Research) was made possible by the FWF (The Austrian Science Fund) and has been generously supported by the University of Applied Arts, Vienna: special thanks to Gerald Bast, Rector and Barbara Putz-Plecko, Vice-Rector for Research in Art and Science; Brigitte Kowanz, Head of the Institute for Transmedia Art; Alexander Damianisch, Head of the Department Support Art and Research; Anja Seipenbusch-Hufschmied, Head of the Department of Publications; Alexandra Graupner, Eva Weber, Nico Wind of AILab (Angewandte Innovation Laboratory) and Angelika Zelisko, Wiebke Miljes, Franziska Echtinger for organisational assistance. We thank Walter Heun, Artistic Director of Tanzquartier Wien and his team. Thanks to Karl Regensburger, Director of ImPulsTanz Festival, Rio Rutzinger and his team Ajda Es, Marina Losin, Gabriel Schmidinger, Marques Josanovic for in-kind and organisational support, and to Nottingham Trent University for supporting the project and publication.

Our research has been tested through numerous workshops — we thank supporting institutions and workshop participants at a.pass, Brussels: Elke van Campenhout, Nicolas Galeazzi, Joke Liberge, Michele Meesen for hosting and workshop participants Marcella Carrara, Jim Clayburgh, Robin Creswell, Veronica Cruz, Christophe Dupuis, Ulla Hase, Hector Mamet, Ruth Noyes, Jeremiah Runnels, Mavi Veloso; ttp / WUK, Vienna; Jan Ritsema, Performing Arts Forum, St. Erme; the workshop participants of *visual arts X dance* 'intensives' — Emilie Gallier, Asher O'Gorman, Maite Liébana Vena, Mayson Fung Mei Sheung, Dawn Nilo, Inge Gappmaier, Pedro Henrique dos Santos Risse, Olga Lukyanova, Emily Kessler, Heike Langsdorf, Anna Stamp Møller, Alice Heyward, Ioana-Laura Gheorghiu, Irina Lavrinovic, John Hoobyar, Samira Elagoz, Nami Miwa, Amanda Hohenberg, Liliya Burdinskaya. Thanks to Chris Standfest for moderating our *Friday Lecture Series*. Our thanks extend to critical wit(h)nesses Gabrielle Cram, Susanne Valerie Granzer, Lisa Hinterreithner, Sabina Holzer, Peter Kozek, Anat Stainberg and visiting guests Philipp Gehmacher, Jack Hauser, Martina Hochmuth and Vladimir Miller.

Thanks to Simona Koch for working with us to transform our research into book format. We also thank Julian Hughes, Victor Jaschke and Tim Tom for photographic and video documentation and Daniel Burckhardt for programming our website. We are grateful to Thea Meinharter for her generous support in accountancy. Thanks for technical support specifically to Monika Gruber, Johannes Fürst, Philipp Koestner, André Wagner (Vienna); Jim Boxall, Neil Dixon, Jon Gillie, Mike Kane and Geoff Litherland (Nottingham).

We have developed our artistic research through presentations at conferences and are grateful for the support and feedback of: Alexander Gerner, Irene Mittelberg, Frederik Stjernfelt (*Body Diagrams: On the Epistemic Kinetics of Gesture* conference, Tübingen, 2014); Steen Ledet Christiansen, Jens Lohfert Jørgensen, Frederik Tygstrup (*How to Do Things With Art*, Aalborg, 2015); Andrea Phillips and Simon Critchley (*On Time*, PARSE, Gothenberg, 2015); Krassimira Kruschkova (*Tongues of Artistic Research,* Tanzquartier Wien, 2015*);* Arno Böhler, Susanne Valerie Granzer, Elisabeth Schäfer (*Art as a Medium of Thinking* symposium, AILab, 2016); Yve Laris Cohen, Katarina Kleinschmidt, Gabriele Wittmann (*5th Dance Education Biennale*, Cologne, 2016). We have published previous iterations of our research and thank the editors and peer reviewers for their feedback: Annette Arlander, Markus Kuikka (*RUUKKU*); Scott deLahunta, Kim Vincs, Sarah Whatley (*Performance Research).* We have appreciated the wider critical frame provided by *The Minor Gesture* exhibition, Museum of Fine Arts Ghent; the *AP Talk Series* at AILab; SCORES, Tanzquartier Wien. We are grateful to the editorial team of De Gruyter publishing house, specifically Angela Foessl. Thanks for inspiring conversations with numerous individuals including Ricardo Basbaum, Monika Grzymala, Leandro Nerefuh, Peter Stamer, Vera Sander, Nita Little. We are aware that such a project is always made possible by a great amount of people, thus our thanks also go to those who have not been mentioned in this list.

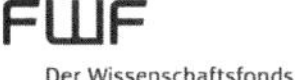

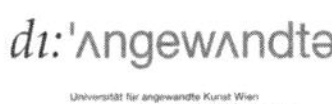

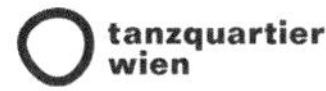

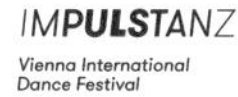

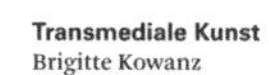

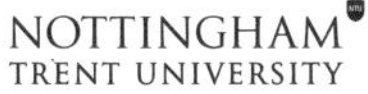

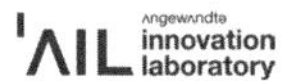

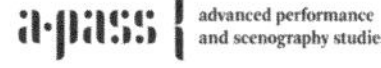